Routledge Handbook of the Olympic and Paralympic Games

This handbook offers an important and timely contribution to the interdisciplinary field of Olympic studies. For the first time a close look into specific issues of the Paralympics is co-hosted in the same volume with the Olympics. It brings together a complete analysis of current and future economic, commercial, socio-political, cultural and governance challenges facing both the Olympic and Paralympic Games, their athletes and institutions.

The book presents new research and broad surveys exploring pressing debates, challenges and possible solutions surrounding the modern Olympic and Paralympic Games, across diverse socioeconomic and political contexts. Featuring chapters written by leading scholars, athletes and administrators from a range of disciplines and backgrounds, the handbook is divided into four main areas: athletes, business, governance, socio-cultural and political issues within the Olympic and Paralympic Games. Examining key themes, theories and new emerging issues within the field, the book offers expert insights into every major topic related to the Olympic and Paralympic Games, including doping, integrity, athletes' rights, culture, nationality, sponsorship, branding, governance, sports policy and law, marketing, social media, technology, e-sports, politics, ethics, international relations, legacy and impact.

The only up-to-date handbook to reflect the true breadth and depth of this international field of research, the *Routledge Handbook of the Olympic and Paralympic Games* is a landmark publication for all students and scholars of sport studies, as well as those working in sport business, media, event management and administration, economics, marketing, management, politics, Olympic studies and cultural studies. It is also an important resource for sport management practitioners and sports officials.

Dikaia Chatziefstathiou is Reader in Olympic Studies and the Social Analysis of Sport, and Director of Research and Knowledge Exchange Environment, School of Psychology and Life Sciences at Canterbury Christ Church University, UK.

Borja García is Senior Lecturer in Sport Management and Policy at Loughborough University, UK. He is a specialist in public sport policy, European Union sport policy and sports governance. He teaches on the Olympic movement's governance at several international universities.

Benoit Séguin is Full Professor in Sport Management at the University of Ottawa, Canada. He specialises in sports marketing, particularly in the areas of sponsorship, ambush marketing and brand.

Routledge Handbook of the Olympic and Paralympic Games

Edited by Dikaia Chatziefstathiou, Editor-in-Chief, and Borja García and Benoit Séguin

Routledge
Taylor & Francis Group
LONDON AND NEW YORK

First published 2021
by Routledge
2 Park Square, Milton Park, Abingdon, Oxon OX14 4RN

and by Routledge
52 Vanderbilt Avenue, New York, NY 10017

Routledge is an imprint of the Taylor & Francis Group, an informa business

British Library Cataloguing-in-Publication Data
A catalogue record for this book is available from the British Library

Library of Congress Cataloging-in-Publication Data
A catalog record for this book has been requested

ISBN: 978-1-138-34117-3 (hbk)
ISBN: 978-0-429-44031-1 (ebk)

Typeset in Bembo
by Apex CoVantage, LLC

Contents

List of figures ix
List of tables x
List of contributors xi
Acknowledgements xvi
Preface xvii

Introduction 1

PART I
Athletes' issues in Olympic and Paralympic Games **7**

1 Dual career: balancing success in sport and life 9
Lucinda Howland, Achilleas Papadimitriou, Vasilis Minoudis and Philip Hurst

2 How a system of judicial precedent may help the rights of athletes before the Court of Arbitration for Sport (CAS) 20
Gregory Ioannidis

3 Disability, classification and the Paralympics: inclusion and exclusion of elite athletes with disabilities 34
Jan Burns

4 Women: rules and classifications in the Olympics and Paralympics 45
Kath Woodward

5 Lesbian, gay, bisexual, transgender and intersex athletes in the Olympic and Paralympic Games: human rights, unfair advantage and exclusion 53
Caroline Symons and Ryan Storr

6 Sport and nationality at the Olympic and Paralympic Games: flags of convenience? 65
Steve Greenfield and Guy Osborn

PART II
Olympic and Paralympic business 73

7 Olympic values: Sponsorship, values and integrity in sport creating a paradigm shift 75
Richard W. Pound

8 Paralympic brand governance: the best of both worlds? 84
Simon Gérard

9 Sponsoring the Paralympic Games and breaking barriers 98
David Legg

10 Olympic broadcast rights 109
Lisa Delpy Neirotti

11 Activation of Olympic and Paralympic sponsorship 120
Stéphan Fuchs and Guillaume Bodet

12 Legal aspects of the Olympics and ambush marketing 130
John Grady

13 The evolving #rule40 of the Olympic Charter: balancing the interest of sponsors vs athletes 139
Gashaw Abeza

14 Towards a shared Olympic responsibility: paradoxes and challenges 149
Aurélien François, Alain Ferrand and Emmanuel Bayle

15 Esports in the Olympic and Paralympic Games: the business case for integration 160
Andy Miah and Alex Fenton

16 Organizing the Olympic Games 171
Milena M. Parent

17 Referendums at Olympic Games 183
Holger Preuß, Anja Scheu and Maike Weitzmann

PART III
The governance of the Olympic and Paralympic Games 201

18 The composition of the IOC: origins and key turning points in the governance of the Olympic movement 203
Jörg Krieger and Stephan Wassong

19 Changing parasport landscape and the evolution of the International Paralympic Committee governance 217
Laura Misener and Landy Di Lu

20 Organisational change campaigns of the Olympic movement: insights from structural and cultural adaptations 229
Eleni Theodoraki

21 Sleeping with an elephant: the relationship between the International Olympic Committee and the International Paralympic Committee 241
P. David Howe

22 The autonomy of the Olympic and sport movement 250
Arnout Geeraert

23 Political autonomy and control of national Olympic committees 265
Henk Erik Meier

24 The changing attitude of the IOC and the IPC towards WADA and the governance of anti-doping 275
Stacie Gray

25 Board renewal and good governance in the Olympic movement 284
Leigh Robinson and Tracy Taylor

26 The relationship between the IOC and international sport federations 294
Jinsu Byun and Becca Leopkey

27 The governance of the Court of Arbitration for Sport 309
Jean-Loup Chappelet

PART IV
Socio-cultural and political issues of the Olympic and Paralympic Games **321**

28 Theory and social science-based research in scholarship around the Paralympic Games 323
Ian Brittain

29 Olympic and Paralympic Games and human rights 334
Bruce Kidd

30 Sport for Development and Peace: convergence and divergence with the Olympic movement 345
Simon C. Darnell and Rob Millington

31 Home advantage in the Olympic and Paralympic Games 355
Girish Ramchandani, Darryl Wilson and Chris Gratton

32 Debating the future of Olympic and Paralympic legacy 365
Vassil Girginov

33 Can health-related legacies through physical activity and sport be delivered by the Olympic and Paralympic Games? 375
Mike Weed

34 Olympic and Paralympic impacts in non-host city regions 385
Shushu Chen and Dongfeng Liu

35 Legacies beyond the Olympic and Paralympic Games: the case of two Youth Olympic Games 398
Ran Zhou, Kyriaki Kaplanidou and Dikaia Chatziefstathiou

36 Arts and culture in the Olympic and Paralympic Games 408
Beatriz García

37 Olympic and Paralympic Games education programmes: education as engagement from a practitioner's view 420
Nick Fuller and Heather Barr

Index *430*

Figures

8.1 The institutional environment of the Paralympic brand 89
10.1 Broadcast revenue from 1964–2018 111
10.2 Broadcasting rights fee 112
10.3 Olympic Games and number of countries/territories broadcasted 112
11.1 The three-level system of sponsorship 122
14.1 The IOC's sustainability strategy and associated objectives for 2020 152
16.1 The lifecycle of an Olympic (Winter) Games and other sports events 171
16.2 The new Olympic process 175
17.1 Revenue and cost overrun of Olympic organizational committees 186
17.2 Criticism of the Olympic Games in Germany 190
17.3 Cost overruns for sports facilities that are predominantly publicly financed 190
17.4 Model for declaration of approval/rejection of Olympic Games 193
19.1 Governance structure of the IPC (1999–2003) 221
19.2 Governance structure of the IPC (2004–2014) 223
20.1 Organisational parts of the Olympic movement (adapted from Theodoraki, 2007) 233
27.1 The five questions associated with Pérez's five levels of governance 311
27.2 Pérez's model applied to the IOC 311
27.3 The five levels of governance within the CAS 313
31.1 Olympic legacy dimensions 356
31.2 Performance in the Summer Olympics (O) and Paralympics (P) by host nation 360
31.3 Performance in the Winter Olympics (O) and Paralympics (P) by host nation 361
34.1 London 2012 Games delivery structure 388
36.1 Visual representation of 'Olympic experience' components 418

Tables

14.1 The road to shared OSR: paradoxes and possible solutions 156
17.1 Referendums at Olympic Games and Olympic Winter Games and their results 187
17.2 Main challenges of the Olympic Games 192
19.1 Standing committees of the IPC (2015–present) 225
20.1 Organisational change drivers, campaigns and structural and cultural adaptations in the Olympic movement 237
22.1 Strategies used by sport governing bodies to maximise their autonomy 257
26.1 Olympic Summer and Winter sports federations 296
28.1 Results for Google Scholar articles (November 2018) 324
31.1 Home advantage conceptual framework comparison 357
31.2 Hosts of the Olympic and Paralympic Games 1992–2018 359
31.3 Average (median) home advantage in the Olympics and Paralympics 363
32.1 Olympic and Paralympic movements' claims and fields of actions 367
32.2 Examples of Olympic movement's main claims and claim parties 368
32.3 Main charges levied at the legacy of the Olympic Games 369
32.4 A four-stage process of Olympic and Paralympic Games legacy creation and knowledge needed 373
35.1 Residents' mean scoresa for 2016 YOG legacies and 2020 YOG impacts 401
36.1 Olympic arts festivals, Summer Games (1952–1988) 410
36.2 Geographical locations for the Cultural Olympiad 416

Contributors

Gashaw Abeza is Assistant Professor at Towson University, Maryland, USA. Abeza published a number of research articles on the topic of social media in sport.

Heather Barr is a recent English language and literature graduate from Lady Margaret Hall, University of Oxford, now working in business development for specialist education agency EdComs.

Emmanuel Bayle is Professor in Sports Management at the Institute of Sport Sciences of the University of Lausanne (ISSUL). He is a specialist of governance, management and performance for Olympic sport organisations and sport national systems and has several experiences in executive education in this area.

Guillaume Bodet is Professor of Sport Marketing and Management at the University of Lyon 1 (Univ. Lyon, France) and a member of the Laboratory of Vulnerabilities and Innovation in Sport. His research interests deal with consumer behaviour in sport and sport branding. He is a board member of the European Association for Sport Management and an associate editor of European Sport Management Quarterly.

Ian Brittain is Assistant Professor in the Centre for Business in Society at Coventry University, UK. He is an internationally recognised expert in the sociological and historical study of disability and Paralympic sport. He is also the Heritage Advisor to the International Wheelchair and Amputee Sports Federation (IWAS).

Jan Burns is Professor of Clinical Psychology at Canterbury Christ Church University, UK, and a board member of the International Federation for Para-Athletes with Intellectual Impairments and also Special Olympics Great Britain.

Jinsu Byun is a doctoral candidate in sport management and policy in the Department of Kinesiology at the University of Georgia, USA.

Jean-Loup Chappelet is Emeritus Professor of Public Management at the Swiss Graduate School of Public Administration of the University of Lausanne in Switzerland.

Shushu Chen is Lecturer in Sport Policy and Management at the University of Birmingham, UK. Her principal research interests include sport policy analysis and evaluation.

Simon C. Darnell is Assistant Professor in the Faculty of Kinesiology and Physical Education at the University of Toronto.

Alex Fenton is an academic researcher and trainer in digital business. He has authored a wide range of academic and practitioner articles relating to digital transformation, digital business and digital marketing including his PhD in social media marketing (2018) and his latest book *Strategic Digital Transformation* (2020).

Alain Ferrand is Professor Emeritus and member of Centre for Business Research (CEREGE – EA 1722) at the University of Poitiers, France, and also a member of the Centre for Sports Law and Economics (CDES) in Limoges, France.

Aurélien François gained a PhD in sports management in 2012 at the University of Burgundy, Dijon, France. He is currently Lecturer at the University of Normandie, Rouen, France. His research topics are focused on CSR in sport, public management specifically for sporting facilities and arenas as well as the professional sports leagues regulations.

Stéphan Fuchs is Associate Professor of Sport Marketing at the University of Lyon 1 (Univ. Lyon, France) and a member of the Laboratory of Vulnerabilities and Innovation in Sport. His research interests deal with sport sponsorship, ambush marketing and sport branding.

Nick Fuller, MBE, is the former head of education for the London Organising Committee of the Olympic and Paralympic Games and is now Chairperson of the International Paralympic Committee's Education Committee.

Beatriz García is Senior Research Fellow in Communication and Media at the University of Liverpool, Culture Advisor to the International Olympic Committee and Director of the Cities of Culture Research Observatory. She is the author of *The Olympic Games and Cultural Policy* (Routledge, 2012).

Arnout Geeraert is Assistant Professor at Utrecht University, Utrecht School of Governance, the Netherlands and a research fellow at KU Leuven, Leuven International and European Studies (LINES), Belgium.

Simon Gérard is a lecturer in sport management in the Faculty of Business and Law at Coventry University (UK) and a research associate in the Olympic Chair Henri de Baillet Latour & Jacques Rogge in Sport Management at UCLouvain (Belgium). His research focuses on organisational change and the governance of sport organisations, with a special interest for the Paralympic movement.

Vassil Girginov is Reader in Sport Management at Brunel University London. He is the author of *Rethinking Olympic Legacy* (Routledge, 2018).

John Grady is a professor at the University of South Carolina in the College of Hospitality, Retail and Sport Management. His research interests focus primarily on the legal aspects of the business of sport.

Chris Gratton was formerly a director of the Sport Industry Research Centre at Sheffield Hallam University, UK and is now an emeritus professor of the same institution.

Stacie Gray is Sport Management Lecturer at Coventry University, England. Stacie's research interests include sport policy and governance, with a particular focus upon the anti-doping regime.

Steve Greenfield is Professor of Law at the Westminster Law School, UK, and Co-Editor of the *Entertainment and Sports Law Journal.*

P. David Howe is a medical anthropologist and holds the Dr. Frank J. Hayden Endowed Chair in Sport and Social Impact in the School of Kinesiology at Western University, Canada with research interests in disability sport and physical activity cultures.

Lucinda Howland is Lecturer in Sport and Exercise Science and Associate Senior Research Fellow at the Centre for Sport, Physical Education and Activity Research (SPEAR) at Canterbury Christ Church University, UK.

Philip Hurst is Senior Lecturer in Sport and Exercise Psychology at Canterbury Christ Church University, UK.

Gregory Ioannidis is a sports lawyer and an anti-doping litigation expert. He is currently the course leader of the master's programme LLM International Sports Law in Practice at Sheffield Hallam University, in the UK.

Kyriaki Kaplanidou is Associate Professor in the Department of Sport Management at the University of Florida.

Bruce Kidd is Professor of Kinesiology and Physical Education at the University of Toronto, Toronto, Canada. A former Olympic athlete, he has written extensively about the history and politics of the Olympic movement and was the founding chair of the Olympic Academy of Canada.

Jörg Krieger is Assistant Professor for Sport and Social Science in the Department of Public Health at Aarhus University, Denmark. He conducts research in the fields of sport history, sport policy and sport sociology. He is the chair of the international research network Sport & Society.

David Legg is Professor in the Department of Health and Physical Education at Mount Royal University and past President of the Canadian Paralympic Committee.

Becca Leopkey is Assistant Professor in Sport Management and Policy in the Department of Kinesiology at the University of Georgia, USA.

Dongfeng Liu is Professor of Sport Management and Co-Dean of the School of International Education at Shanghai University of Sport, China.

Landy Di Lu is Post-Doctoral Research Associate in the School of Kinesiology, Western University, Ontario, Canada. Her expertise lie in the domains of governance, policy enactment and institutional change.

Henk Erik Meier is Professor for the Social Sciences of Sport at the Institute for Sport and Exercise Sciences at Münster University. Among others, he works on global sport governance.

Andy Miah is Co-Chair of the Esports Industry Collaboration programme at the University of Salford, Manchester. He is also Advisory Board member of the British Esports Association and Commission Member of the Global Esports Federation and author of *Sport 2.0: Transforming Sports for a Digital World* (MIT Press, 2017).

Rob Millington is Assistant Professor of Sport and Social Change in the Department of Kinesiology at Brock University, Canada.

Vasilis Minoudis (ex-pro volleyball player) was formerly Head of the Hellenic Professional Volleyball Players Association (HPVPA) and Board Member of the European Elite Athletes Association (EU Athletes). Minoudis is holder of a master's degree in sports management, with a thesis on athletes' dual careers.

Laura Misener is Director and Associate Professor in the School of Kinesiology, Western University, Ontario, Canada. She is a co-author of two books: *Leveraging Parasport Events: Impacts, Promises and Possibilities* and *Global Sport Leadership*.

Lisa Delpy Neirotti is Professor of Sport Management at the George Washington University in the United States and has attended 19 consecutive Olympic Games as a volunteer or researcher.

Guy Osborn is Professor of Law at the Westminster Law School, UK and Director of the Centre for Law, Society and Popular Culture.

Achilleas Papadimitriou was formerly an elite volleyball athlete and member of the Greek volleyball players association. He is holder of a BSc degree in Economics at the University of Crete, Greece and a MSc degree in Environmental Management at the SOAS, University of London. He is co-founder of OPSON company in Nantes, France.

Milena M. Parent is a full professor in sport (event) governance at the University of Ottawa, Canada, and a lecturer and tutor in the Olympic Solidarity-supported Executive Masters in Sport Organization Management (MEMOS) programme.

Richard W. Pound is currently the senior active member of the International Olympic Committee. Commencing in 1983, he was Chair of the IOC's Television Rights Commission and later, Chair of the IOC Marketing Commission. In those capacities he was responsible for television rights negotiations from 1983 until the 2008 Olympic Games and for development of the IOC's international sponsorship programme known as TOP, which began in 1985 and continues to this date.

Holger Preuß is Professor of Sport Economics and Sport Sociology at the Johannes Gutenberg University in Mainz, Germany, and at the Molde University College, Norway. He is also adjunct professor at the University of Ottawa, Canada, and an international scholar at the State University of New York, Cortland.

Girish Ramchandani is Reader in Sport Management at Sheffield Hallam University, UK.

Leigh Robinson is Pro Vice Chancellor and Professor of Sport Management at Cardiff Metropolitan University, UK.

Anja Scheu is a research assistant at the Institute of Sport Science at Johannes Gutenberg-University Mainz, Germany.

Ryan Storr is a lecturer and academic course advisor in Sport Development at Western Sydney University, Sydney, Australia. His research focuses on LGBT+ inclusion in sporting contexts, and diversity and inclusion more broadly within community sport.

Caroline Symons is the pioneering researcher of the LGBTIQ sport experience in Australia and has written extensively on the history and progress of LGBTIQ sports people, best exemplified by her award-winning *The Gay Games: A History*. A former deputy dean of the College of Sport and Exercise Science, Caroline currently serves as an honorary professor with Victoria University.

Tracy Taylor is Dean of Management at RMIT, Melbourne Australia.

Eleni Theodoraki is Associate Professor in Festival and Event Management at the Business School of Edinburgh Napier University.

Stephan Wassong is Professor at the German Sport University Cologne. He is Chair of the Institute of Sport History and Director of the Olympic Studies Centre. Since 2014 he has been a member of the IOC's Olympic Education Commission. He has been elected President of the International Pierre de Coubertin Committee in 2018.

Mike Weed is Professor of Applied Policy Sciences and Pro Vice Chancellor (Research & Enterprise) at Canterbury Christ Church University, UK. He is Editor-in-Chief of the *Journal of Sport & Tourism*, and Co-Editor of the *Routledge Handbook of Physical Activity Policy & Practice*.

Maike Weitzmann is a research assistant at the Institute of Sport Science at Johannes Gutenberg-University Mainz, Germany.

Darryl Wilson is Principal Lecturer on the Sport Business Management programme at Sheffield Hallam University, UK

Kath Woodward is Emeritus Professor of Sociology at the Open University. She has published extensively on feminist theory, embodiment, temporality and social inequalities, especially in the field of sport.

Ran Zhou is a faculty member at Nanjing University of Finance & Economics, China.

Acknowledgements

We would like to thank our publisher for the opportunity to communicate our understandings and experiences on the Olympic and Paralympic Games through this publication. Of course this book would not have materialised without the commitment and expertise of our contributing authors. Thank you all for trusting us with your chapters. Finally, our thanks are extended to our assistant Natalie Edwards who helped us with the laborious task of formatting our manuscript prior to submission.

Preface

The Olympic and Paralympic Games amid COVID-19

Just as we submitted our completed manuscript to the Publisher, the coronavirus pandemic hit the world, and the world of sport inevitably. In our introduction we had concluded that "the 21st century presents us with many new socioeconomic and political realities that are fluid and constantly changing", but COVID-19 was beyond any of our – and in all likelihood anyone else's – forecasts. Undoubtedly, the unprecedented times we are living will have many impacts on the Olympic movement; some are unveiling as this book goes to press, some others we can only guess, and surely there will be consequences we are unable to foresee at this moment. Nobody can predict, while we are writing these lines, when the pandemic will end but also how its consequences will (re)shape the workings of the Olympic movement. This additional preface is the minimum we could do to acknowledge the fluid dynamics and tensions that the Olympic movement, and sport more broadly, is now experiencing.

One thing is for sure: the coronavirus crisis has exposed the fragility of society as a whole, and this of course includes sport, both understood as a social activity and the institutionalised non-governmental network that is best represented in the Olympic movement. When the wider global society started realising the degree to which COVID-19 was spreading around the world, the IOC and its Japanese counterparts appeared reluctant to admit that any changes shall be applied to the scheduled Tokyo 2020 Olympic and Paralympic Games. Their confident statements that the Games will be held as planned fuelled the reactions of athletes and federations who played a catalytic role in the IOC's decision to postpone the Games. Canada, Australia, the US, New Zealand, Britain, Ireland, France and Brazil were among those countries where leading athletes and sporting federations called on the IOC to postpone beyond the July 24th opening ceremony, preferably to 2021, or else they will not be sending their athletes to Tokyo. There have been some speculations that one of the reasons for the delay in deciding the fate of the Tokyo Games was that both parties, the IOC and Tokyo hosts, were hesitant to reach an agreement in the fear of litigation or breach on contracts, thus awaited for the tipping point of countries' withdrawals before proceeding any further. But, certainly, concerns primarily about the health and wellbeing of some 11,000 athletes from 206 NOCs was a key motivating factor for the postponement decision.

It took some time for the IOC and the Tokyo 2020 Local Organising Committee to announce the postponement of the Games, although the decision proved to be unavoidable. Whereas some criticism was levelled at the hesitation of the decision-makers, it is sometimes forgotten what a complex legal, economic and organisational reality the Games are. In these days of immediate consumption and global social networks, it was perhaps necessary some time to tighten all the loose ends. As we clearly demonstrate in this handbook, there are many stakeholders, many interests, many structures involved, which is not the best recipe for quick decision-making.

The postponement of the 2020 Tokyo Olympic and Paralympic Games is perhaps the most visible consequence of coronavirus for the Olympic movement yet, but there might be other important implications. In governance terms, there seem to be two areas in which important changes could be forthcoming as result of the health and economic crisis brought about by coronavirus. These are the relations of the Olympic stakeholders with governments and public authorities, and the networked nature of the movement itself.

This crisis has exposed the limitations of the autonomy of sport. When governments around the world started to take decisions to control the disease, organised mass sport activities were amongst the first casualties, even if federations, clubs or leagues lobbied in some cases, like in Italy for example, for it not to be the case. It was an extreme reminder of the limitations that public and legal regulations impose on the Olympic movement stakeholders. Even as we move away from the peak of the infection, sport can only put together plans to resume activity in the short to medium term under severe control from governments and public health authorities. The cooperation of sport and governmental stakeholders is now even more important, as public health is at stake. Sport organisations and Olympic movement stakeholders have a duty to be loyal and fulfil their societal role, as expressed in the Olympic Charter. These organisations should not put unnecessary pressure on public authorities to take measures that could otherwise be a public health risk. Sport needs to adopt and adapt to this 'new normality', even if there is a need to take some extraordinary social distancing measures to allow the Tokyo Games to go ahead. The effective and loyal cooperation of the Olympic movement with national government is now, perhaps, more important than ever.

On the other hand, such a loyal cooperation could be rewarded, for sport can be one of the 'solutions' to ease the social, mental and physical struggles brought about by coronavirus. Thus, we have seen how physical activity was one of the few reasons the British government allowed the public to go out for during lockdown. Or, similarly, exercise, was one of the first social activities the Spanish government permitted in the first phase of the re-opening after lockdown. The social importance of sport is perhaps at times overstated, as Mike Weed and other colleagues have convincingly argued, but it is nevertheless a reality. Thus, providing opportunities to harness the positive effects of sport post-coronavirus as populations recover from extremely tough times could be a joint effort between the Olympic movement and governments, under the principles of loyal and effective cooperation highlighted in Agenda 2020 and the Basic Universal Principles of Good Governance of the Olympic and Sports Movement.

The consequences of the economic crisis, with forecasts of between five and ten per cent GDP contractions in countries around the world, are likely to increase the dependence of sport governing bodies, National Olympic Committees, elite athletes of less commercialised sports and other stakeholders on public money. This is likely to happen for some time, as the private sector might not be in a position to invest in sport as much as it was doing before coronavirus. The reliance of NOCs and other sport organisations on public funding is not a new phenomenon, but it is quite plausible to see a situation in which this is even stronger. As it is often argued, public money tends to come with some strings attached, if only in terms of financial accountability. In that respect, the different stakeholders will need to be very mindful of their governance obligations, perhaps more than ever before. This is especially true because the recovery effort of this economic crisis is likely to be of colossal dimensions. National governments are already putting in place unprecedented measures tapping into high levels of public debt. Given the need to assist large numbers of the population, sporting organisations might not be the first in the list. It is therefore essential that sport demonstrates it can behave responsibly, with the highest standards of governance, to earn the right to public funding in times of such high social need and demand.

The postponement of the Games also poses huge challenges for Olympic business, in particular for the IOC, Tokyo 2020 organisers and stakeholders such as sponsors, broadcasters and the hundreds of thousands of Olympic fans. In May 2020, the IOC announced that it would devote $800 million to help cover costs for the postponed Games and other expenses stemming from the coronavirus pandemic. However, the exact figure associated with the postponement of the Games is not yet known and could be significantly higher. Consequently, the organisers will look at reducing costs which may impact the Olympic experience. The postponement has also caused headaches for many of the large companies that have paid significant fees to acquire marketing rights (worldwide and domestic) around the Games. Revenue from worldwide TOP sponsors exceed of $1 billion in rights fees while the organisers of Tokyo 2020 have surpassed an unprecedented $3 billion in domestic sponsorship. While these sponsorship contracts will extend to 2021, the marketing and financial impacts of postponing the Games on sponsorship activation programmes are enormous. For example, advertising campaigns, on the ground activities (e.g. hospitality programmes), athlete programmes, digital marketing programmes are usually orchestrated over many months prior to the Games and companies were in final stages of going to market with activation programmes. These companies will be forced to alter plans, decide how 2021 will fit within their marketing programmes and spend additional dollars to adjust.

Broadcasters, which also invest billions in rights fees, are also impacted by the postponement and will have to adjust their plans leading up to 2021. The American broadcaster NBC, which paid $4.4 billion in rights fees for the Games between 2014–2020, was most likely relieved that the rescheduled Games in 2021 will take place during the same timeframe as the ones planed for 2020. As such, the broadcaster, who sold 90% of its advertising inventory for a record $1.25 billion, will not have to compete with other sport properties such as NFL or college football. Broadcasters may also have opportunities to produce new content that documents how the pandemic has impacted the athletes and the way Japan will prepare for 2021. As for Olympic fans who already bought tickets for the Games, the IOC already announced that tickets purchased will be valid for 2021 and those who cannot attend in 2021 will be reimbursed. There is little doubt that coronavirus's impact on Olympic business is enormous. From now on, the Tokyo 2020 Games are inherently connected to the 'COVID-19 brand'. Of course due to the uncertainty of the current times there is a possibility that the Tokyo Games may never take place. Thomas Bach mentioned that if, for whatever reasons, the Games cannot be held in the scheduled dates for 2021, then they will be cancelled. It is certainly wished by billions around the world that Tokyo 2020 Games will actually take place in 2021 and bring the world together in a post-pandemic world. This, we hope, will be a true celebration of humanity and perhaps may reconnect the Olympic movement and its icon brand to the fundamental values of Olympism and contribute to a better world.

This hope has been publicly expressed by the IOC and not only by the President Thomas Bach. One of the most prominent Olympic voices during the coronavirus pandemic, the long-standing and influential IOC member Dick Pound has often talked about it in press. Pound, who served as IOC vice-president from 1987 to 1991, and again from 1996 to 2000, speaking to Associated Press in late February 2020 had prompted athletes to "keep focused on your sport" and that "as far as we all know, you're going to be in Tokyo", while had expressed his doubts that the Games' postponement was a viable solution. He had also estimated that there was a three-month window – perhaps a two-month one – to decide the fate of the Tokyo Olympics, meaning a decision could be delayed until late May 2020. "In and around that time, I'd say folks are going to have to ask: 'Is this under sufficient control that we can be confident about going to Tokyo or not?'" Pound was the first to announce to the press that the IOC had decided to postpone the Games, one day before it was made official on March 24. Later, in an interview with CBC Sports' Scott Russell on 17 April, he said "We really have to hope that we get this act together in time for 2021" but no later than that.

Following the postponement decision of Tokyo 2020 Olympic and Paralympic Games, we asked Dick Pound to comment on the impact of COVID-19 on the Olympic movement. Below is his commentary that we thought would be useful to include in its entirety to our preface.

What will be the Olympic Legacy of the Pandemic?

Richard W. Pound

In 2013, the International Olympic Committee (IOC) selected Tokyo as the host city for the Olympic Games in 2020. The dates settled upon for the Games were 24 July to 9 August. From that moment, a vast international set of plans involving athlete preparations, construction of training and competition venues, construction of an Olympic Village capable of accommodating 11,000 athletes from 206 countries, along with team officials, coaches and medical personnel, was set in motion. In addition, media accommodations and working facilities needed to be secured, hotel arrangements for tens of thousands of incremental visitors confirmed, transportation facilities designed, security of athletes and spectators assured, sponsors contracted and thousands of other matters to be put in place. The Olympic Games are one of the most complex events in the world today.

After a somewhat tentative beginning, in which a ruinously expensive Olympic Stadium was rejected and replaced with another less costly stadium, the Japanese organisers have demonstrated an extremely high degree of competence in their preparations for the 2020 Games. Necessary facilities and all other arrangements were meticulously planned and were in place on schedule. The organisers were on track to deliver splendid Games that would establish new standards in Games organisation and environmental responsibility, and would have been completely carbon-neutral. The type of Olympic paradigm shift that had occurred when the 'new' Japan first organised the 1964 Tokyo Olympics, with a level of sophistication that completely surprised the world was confidently expected again in 2020.

Enter, however, the unexpected: COVID-19. . .

COVID-19 appears to be particularly easily transmitted, a feature exacerbated by the ease of today's travel and the numbers of persons travelling. Identified early in the year, it rapidly escalated into a pandemic that has spread to all five continents. Containment measures have produced severe economic and personal impacts thus far and it is not yet clear when and how recovery will occur. It is clear, however, that the state of preparedness, almost universally, for a pandemic of that nature was woefully short of adequate.

By mid-March, it had become obvious that, as feared, the spread of the virus was beginning to accelerate and that the likelihood of being able to hold the Tokyo Olympics in 2020 as originally planned was increasingly at risk. Many centuries ago, Publilius Syrus observed that it is a bad plan that cannot be changed.

There were three less-than-perfect alternatives: to press on with the original plans in what could only have been a naïve hope that, somehow, the situation would resolve itself; to cancel the Games; or to postpone them. By 23 March, it was evident that the original dates were unfeasible; COVID-19 would not be resolved in the succeeding four months. Cancellation was not an attractive option, either for Japan as the host country, which had invested heavily in the Games, or for the current generation of Olympic athletes who had been preparing for the Games and who, because of the protective measures designed to curb the spread of the pandemic, could no longer train properly. It was, however, within the legal power of the IOC to make a unilateral decision to cancel the Games, on the basis of the health risks for athletes, officials and spectators.

Instead, working closely with the Japanese organisers, the Japanese government, the World Health Organisation (WHO) and after consultations with the Olympic international sport federations, national Olympic Committees and athletes, the IOC agreed with the Japanese suggestion that the Games be postponed to 2021. The proposed new dates were announced almost immediately thereafter – the Games would take place in exactly the same time period as 2020, but in 2021, between 23 July and 8 August. This is a decision not free from either risk or additional cost.

The risk stems from uncertainty regarding sufficient mitigation of the pandemic and the development and widespread availability of a reliable vaccine in the sixteen months between the decision to postpone and the newly scheduled Games. Nor can an impact on the Beijing Winter Games of 2022 be entirely discounted. They are scheduled to be held only six months following the rescheduled Tokyo Games, in close proximity to Japan. If pandemic-related conditions in 2021 were not to permit Tokyo to proceed, the chances of resolving everything in the same area a mere six months later seem improbable.

The additional costs result from, in effect, suspending a finely-tuned and expensive confluence of contractual parties and Organising Committee (and others, such as police and security personnel) that had been preparing for an event that would have been completed, for all intents and purposes, by September 2020. What, too, of the venues that might otherwise have been available for public or private immediately following the Games? And the hotels in which thousands of rooms had been booked? The tickets purchased? The airline reservations made and paid for? The supplier and sponsor expectations? This is a very complex and interwoven tapestry of arrangements that will require extension or redesign for the new schedule, coupled with community, government and private commitment and goodwill to make the best of a complicated world crisis.

For the Olympic movement, given the circumstances of an existential threat to humanity itself, staging successful Games in Japan in the face of these many challenges would provide a splendid example for the youth of the world to be associated with the demonstration of aspirational purposefulness and determination. Many of the qualities required for Japanese success in this venture are common to Olympic athletes: resilience, flexibility, creativity, resourcefulness, courage, confidence, commitment, perseverance and indomitability.

Over the next years, we will have a chance to see how the COVID-19 virus pandemic, which did not cause any of the challenges faced by the Olympic Movement, may nevertheless encourage the Olympic Movement, over and above its responses to the virus as part of its general role in society, to continue improving how it puts sport at the service of the world community.

Introduction

'Olympic Studies' have seen a rapid growth of interdisciplinary approaches into matters related to anything Olympic such as the history of Olympic and Paralympic Games, the social and economic impacts on host cities, the ethical questions arising from doping and corruption scandals, the educational programmes that adopt an Olympic rhetoric. Although a decade ago 'Olympic Studies' was a rather specialised field characterised by a somewhat 'insular' world of the so-called 'Olympic experts', today it has expanded into a large arena of wide scholarship ranging from philosophy, history and sociology to management, policy and organisation studies. Scholars from different disciplines and from different parts of the world write about a range of Olympic-related topics, without labelling themselves 'Olympic' scholars. They are, for example, economists, sociologists or urban geographers who are interested in exploring aspects of the biggest global event in the world today, the Olympic and Paralympic Games. As a result, the area of 'Olympic Studies' is not defined as such anymore.

Similarly, although some ten to fifteen years ago academic undergraduate or postgraduate courses on the Olympic and Paralympic Games were rather sparse and rare – mostly in countries historically linked to the Olympics, e.g. Greece – today we witness the development of such subjects in many programmes around the world (e.g. Poland, Russia, UK, USA) and most importantly the subject of the Olympic and Paralympic Games has been an integral part of several programmes in higher education (sport studies; international relations and diplomacy; management and marketing, economics, etc.).

The *Routledge Handbook of the Olympic and Paralympic Games* contributes to the essential research- and student-focused literature in all those interdisciplinary accounts that deal with the Olympic and Paralympic Games. Featuring chapters written by leading experts from a range of disciplines and backgrounds (e.g. academics, athletes, administrators), the handbook examines key themes, theories and issues within the field. Each chapter offers substantial knowledge on the most important topics related to the Olympic and Paralympic Games, while moving the way forward for understanding this field in a fluid, inter-connected way across disciplines. The editors concur that there are no disciplinary boundaries in understanding the phenomenon of the Games and thus we engage strongly with wider subjects and audiences.

The book is divided into four main parts to establish the thematic coherence of the text. Part I, Athletes' Issues in Olympic and Paralympic Games (edited by Dikaia Chatziefstathiou);

Part II, Olympic and Paralympic Business (edited by Benoit Séguin); Part III, The Governance of the Olympic and Paralympic Games (edited by Borja García); Part IV, Socio-Cultural and Political Issues in the Olympic and Paralympic Games (edited by Dikaia Chatziefstathiou). This categorising facilitates the structure of this handbook and does not mean a compartmentalised treatment of these areas which are rather fluid and interconnected.

The first section of the handbook focuses on athletes' issues. It is often the case that Olympic and Paralympic research does not place athletes at the centre. In this section we address some of the key challenges that athletes are facing and by no means the list of themes covered here is exhaustive. You will notice that many of the issues mentioned here are from a socio-cultural and political perspective (e.g. the sexual and national identity politics). But we opted to include them here, rather than in Part IV, as they relate strongly to athletes' rights, experiences and lives.

The first chapter of this section examines 'dual career'. Few Olympic and Paralympic athletes are paid sufficiently and often face the challenge of combining their sport with an educational or vocational career. Lucinda Howland, Achilleas Papadimitriou, Vasilis Minoudis and Phil Hurst discuss the benefits of this approach to nurturing an athlete's career development. The authors explain in detail the concept of a dual career and, further, they review existing dual career programmes that aim to support athletes competing at the Olympic and Paralympic Games (and elite sport more broadly). Another matter that concerns athletes is the legal resolution of their sporting disputes. Therefore it is very important that the Court of Arbitration for Sport (CAS) operates efficiently, and that sports law, as a separate legal discipline, serves well athletes' interests. Gregory Ioannidis in his chapter discusses the particular and unique elements of practice and procedure before CAS and goes on to demonstrate why CAS is a necessary mechanism for the resolution of sporting disputes and how it can be further improved. (For the governance of CAS see Jean-Loup Chappelet's chapter in Part III.)

The next four chapters deal with some of the most debated issues surrounding Olympic and Paralympic athletes: the eligibility and classification in sport for people with disabilities in the Paralympics; the sexual politics of the Olympics and Paralympics and, in particular, the ways in which women feature in the Games; the human rights of lesbian, gay, bisexual, transgender and intersex (LGBTI+) athletes and their participation in the Olympic and Paralympic Games; the disputes and tensions involved for athletes switching nationalities.

More specifically, Jan Burns's chapter introduces the reader to the concepts behind classification and the challenges of mapping the diversity of real life onto a categorical system. It looks at who currently is, and importantly is not, included in the Paralympic movement, and finally examines the debate around the separation or integration of the Paralympics with the Olympics. Kath Woodward's chapter focuses upon recent developments in understanding the sexual politics of the Olympics and Paralympics, outlining how sex and gender intersect with other axes of power, such as class, disability, race, ethnicity and sexuality. She demonstrates how sport (and Olympic sport more particularly) has been resistant to some of the wider cultural shifts and moves towards crossing rigid traditional gender boundaries and re-workings of sexual identifications. Caroline Symons and Ryan Storr take this discussion further and provide an overview of various human rights risks and challenges faced by LGBTI+ people, particularly athletes, involved with the Olympic and Paralympic Games; the current international legal, policy and political context in relation to human rights and LGBTI+ people; and the existing policy and practices of leading international sports bodies such as the IOC. Finally, Steve Greenfield and Guy Osborn discuss issues of Olympic and Paralympic nationality within the context of sport, nationality and citizenship more generally. To do this, their chapter first examines some key contextual and historical issues, including how the law has responded to such disputes and tensions, before proceeding to examine the Olympic and Paralympic regulations themselves, and concluding with some suggestions as to how this complex issue might be resolved in the future.

Although some athletes may have legitimate reasons to switch nationality, 'imported' athletes may be seeking cash from the Olympic and Paralympic Games contributing further to the growing commercialisation of sports. The collection of chapters in the second part of the handbook covers a variety of aspects related to commercialisation and more broadly to the business of the Olympic and Paralympic Games including brand, sponsorship, broadcasting, legal aspects and brand protection, corporate social responsibility, management of organising the Olympics and the business case for integration of esports. While much attention has been given to the commercial success of the Olympic Games, another important multi-sport event, the Paralympic Games, has made significant strides in the last decade. While competitions for disabled athletes go back to the Stoke Mandeville Games in 1948, the creation of the IPC in 1989 marked a new era for elite sport competition for disabled athletes known as 'para-athletes' (IPC, 2020). The Paralympic Games have been taking part in the same cities and venues as the Olympics since 1988 for the Summer Games and 1992 for the Winter Games. Similar to the IOC, the IPC experienced a rapid growth in the professionalisation and commercialisation of the Paralympic movement. In recent years, the IPC has invested considerable resources in consumer research with the goal of gaining a comprehensive understanding of its brand. Using the Olympic brand governance as a framework, Simon Gérard examines the challenges associated with the Paralympic brand and discusses how decisions around the Paralympic sport programme and the growing partnership with the IOC will not only shape the business of Paralympic Games but also the positioning of its brand within the Paralympic movement, its stakeholders and society as a whole. David Legg argues that the efforts of IPC in building its brand are paying off as major corporations (e.g. Toyota, Bridgestone Tire, Procter & Gamble) are benefiting from partnering with the Paralympic Games and others should consider the opportunities while they still can.

Dick Pound, a long time IOC member and key figure in the commercialisation of the Games, provides a unique 'insider' perspective on important events/factors that led to the commercial success of the Olympic Games and its brand. Pound argues that the future of the Games is directly tied to IOC's ability to safeguard the underlying values of sport. The important role of television broadcast coverage in promoting Olympic values, in experiencing the magic of the Olympic Games and in the funding of the Olympic movement is examined by Lisa Delpy Neirotti. She provides an historical perspective of Olympic broadcasting and considers how the expansion of the broadcast, new technologies and the rise in rights fees define the way the Olympic broadcast has, is and will be seen. The importance of sponsorship to the funding of Olympic movement is second to broadcasting. Stéphan Fuchs and Guillaume Bodet offer a theoretical background of sponsorship and examine sponsors' activation strategies through the analysis of two case studies, long-time Olympic sponsors Visa and Coca-Cola. While sponsorship activation is an important component in the success of sponsorship programmes, the ability of the IOC and IPC in protecting the exclusivity of partners is essential. John Grady offers an in-depth examination of 'brand protection', the legal and marketing strategies used by the Olympic movement to ensure protections and control ambush marketing. Gashaw Abeza delves deeper on the challenges brought by social media in protecting sponsors and the delicate act of the IOC in balancing the interest of sponsors with those of athletes. In this respect, recent changes to Rule 40 and the impact on Olympic athletes are discussed. Aurélien François, Alain Ferrand and Emmanuel Bayle offer a softer side of the Olympic business by focusing the promises implied by the ideal of Olympism, long enshrined in the Olympic Charter as one of the fundamental principles of Olympism. 'Building a better world through sport' suggests great social responsibility, not just on the International Olympic Committee (IOC) itself but on the entire system constituted by the IOC and the Olympic movement. The authors provide an analysis of Olympic Social Responsibility (OSR), defined as the Olympic movement's contribution to sustainable development.

The section ends with three chapters related to the Olympic Games. Andy Miah and Alex Fenton examine the alignment between the worlds of sports and esports. They examine the debate about the relationship between the two and why it is reasonable to conclude that the future of all sports is the integration of esports. The relationships between the Olympic and Paralympic programme and esports are also examined, arguing that the economic environment around these events is aligning to enable a closer relationship, where a number of key strategic interests are met. The possibility of integrating esports in the Olympic and Paralympic Games along other new Olympic sports such as skateboarding, surfing and rock climbing may appeal to younger generations. However, it does bring another layer of complexities in organising the Games. Milena M. Parent provides an excellent overview of the management of organising the Olympic Games taking into account changes made by the IOC in light of recommendations from Agenda 2020, particularly issues about gigantism and debt criticisms. She discusses how the IOC presented a revised planning timeline for how the organising committee-IOC partnership would work, as well as ways to reduce the costs of the Games. However, despite these changes to the bidding process and addressing issues of gigantism and dept, the IOC faces huge challenges as cities showing an interest in hosting the Games are dropping out. Holger Preuß, Anja Scheu and Maike Weitzmann seek to illuminate the current problems and challenges of the Olympic Games as well as previous referendums on the Olympic Games. They aim for a better understanding of the current rejection of the Olympic Games in Western, democratic countries and provide recommendations.

The collection of chapters in the governance section of this handbook has been inspired by the three-fold categorisation of Henry and Lee (2004): systemic governance, political governance and good governance. The former refers to the structures that delineate the relations amongst stakeholders in the sports system. Political governance, in turn, analyses the very particular relations between public authorities and sport non-governmental organisations. Finally, good governance is normative and refers to the structures to secure a transparent, democratic and accountable management of the sport system. Indeed, this section explores aspects of all the systemic, political and good governance of the Olympic and Paralympic movement. This section starts with four chapters that provide an overview of the historical development of the governance structures of both Olympic and Paralympic sport. In our attempt to clearly mainstream the role of the Paralympic Games, one of the contributions this handbook has sought to make, the relations between the IOC and the IPC themselves are also closely explored to discuss the extent to which their mutual co-operation might be beneficial or not. Thus, in this first set of chapters, we have included two analysing the evolution of the IOC with focus on its membership (Krieger and Wassong) and business practices and organisational culture (Theodoraki). Another chapter does similarly examine the historical development of the IPC (Misener and Lu), whereas P. David Howe rounds up the first part of the section with a chapter discussing the relationship between the IOC and the IPC.

Following from that initial discussion of the wider framework of Olympic and Paralympic systemic governance, the chapters by Geeraert and Meier turn to discuss the role of the public authorities, mainly national governments, in the governance of the Olympic and Paralympic Games. In here, we present a critical analysis and discussion of a concept that is paramount for the IOC, that of the autonomy of sport. A critical examination of the autonomy of sport is fundamental, for it has been one of the cornerstones of the IOC's governance vision whilst, at the same time, it has been challenged by many of the involved stakeholders.

Finally, this section presents four further chapters in which the authors explore in detail different structures and stakeholders brought about to provide good normative governance to the Olympic and sporting movement. These chapters provide closer discussion of the contribution to the governance of the Olympic and Paralympic movements by the World Anti-Doping Agency (by Stacie Gray), the Court of Arbitration for Sport (by Jean-Loup Chappelet), International Sport Federations (by Jinsu Byun and Becca Leopkey) and the IOC Executive Committee (by Leigh Robinson and Tracy Taylor).

The chapters included in this section provide actual empirical research, but also a very timely critical discussion of the state of the art of academic research around the governance of the Olympics and Paralympics. The chapters also provide critical assessment of some of the latest reforms introduced by the IOC to improve the governance and legitimacy of the Olympic movement. As a whole, this collection of chapters reflects on what has been done over the last two decades, but also on the gaps that might need to be filled in the not-so-distant future.

The final section of the handbook brings together a series of different topics, which relate to the broader socio-cultural and political layers of the Olympic and Paralympic Games. The introductory chapter of this section talks broadly about social research for the Paralympics, the theories and methods that are most commonly used by scholars. Ian Brittain brings his own experiences and provides a good overview of the developing research on Paralympic Games from a socio-cultural perspective. The following two chapters explore and discuss the international relationships of the Olympic and Paralympic sports movements. Bruce Kidd's chapter sets out the historical relationships of the Olympic and Paralympic sports movements with human rights and places them alongside the articulation and realisation of human rights broadly. Simon C. Darnell and Rob Millington examine various points of convergence and divergence between the conceptualisation and delivery of Sport for Development and Peace (SDP), particularly in so-called 'developing countries', and the organisation and promotion of the Olympic movement, Olympic Games and IOC.

Next follows a cluster of chapters that discuss issues in relation to host nations, audiences and legacies. In particular, Girish Ramchandani, Darryl Wilson and Chris Gratton examine the potential sporting legacy in relation to elite sport from hosting the Games. They consider the extent to which nations that are awarded the right to host the Olympic and Paralympic Games benefit from success in elite sport through a quantifiable home advantage effect. The following four chapters contribute to and expand the debates on legacies. Vassil Girginov submits for debate three questions in the hope that they will challenge the current thinking and help better define this critical issue for the Olympic movement. He questions: "what matters most for the Olympic Movement that is worth striving for?"; "what kind of legacy does the Olympic Movement need?"; and "what is this about legacy we want to know?". Mike Weed focuses on health-related legacies and explores the best evidence for their delivery through physical activity and sport from Olympic and Paralympic Games. He discusses whether it is possible to conclude that the delivery of such health-related legacies in practice is possible.

Shushu Chen and Dongfeng Liu examine the impacts in non-host areas such as Shanghai's and Leicestershire's experiences of being part of the Games when their host nations staged the Olympic and Paralympic Games (Beijing 2008 and London 2012 respectively). Ran Zhou, Kyriaki Kaplanidou and Dikaia Chatziefstathiou provide an overview of the contemporary research with respect to the legacies of Youth Olympic Games (YOG). By using the case studies of Lillehammer 2016 and Lausanne 2020 they empirically investigate residents' perceptions of YOG legacies and their influence on quality of life and event support.

The philosophy of the Olympic Games, Olympism, as stated in the Olympic Charter (2019) blends sport with culture and education in an effort "to create a way of life based on the joy of effort, the educational value of good example, social responsibility and respect for universal fundamental ethical principles" (p. 11). The final two chapters of this section focus on culture and education, key components of Olympism. As has been argued by Velthuis and Baia Curion (2015) art has been 'deterritorialised'. In the Olympic and Paralympic discourses this can be witnessed in the global cultural programmes of the host cities which from one side have a distinctive localism but from the other they are bound to globalism. Beatriz García presents an overview of the Games cultural programme evolution, discusses key trends and challenges and ends by touching on the new thinking emerging in the context of the IOC Agenda 2020 and the growing cultural and artistic aspirations of the Paralympic movement. Finally, Nick Fuller and Heather Barr provide a practitioner's insight into the design and delivery of education programmes for the Olympic and Paralympic Games. They address the links between education and the inception of the modern Olympic Games, before moving into a discussion of how Olympic Education is typically defined and understood though the examples of Sydney 2000, London 2012 and Tokyo 2020.

To conclude, the 21st century presents us with many new socioeconomic and political realities that are fluid and constantly changing. We hope that this handbook will be a useful companion to all those interested in understanding such flows in the most pressing debates facing the Olympic and Paralympic Games on athletes, business, governance and socio-cultural issues.

References

Henry, I. and Lee, P.C. (2004). Governance and ethics in sport. In: S. Chadwick and J. Beech, eds., *The business of sport management*. Harlow: Pearson Education, pp. 25–41.

International Olympic Committee. (2019). *The Olympic Charter*. Lausanne: International Olympic Committee.

IPC. (2020). *History of the Paralympic movement*. Available at: www.paralympic.org/ipc/history [Accessed 22 Jan. 2020].

Velthuis, O. and Baia Curion, S. (2015) (eds.). *Cosmopolitan canvases: The globalisation of markets for contemporary art*. Oxford: Oxford University Press.

Part I

Athletes' issues in Olympic and Paralympic Games

Edited by Dikaia Chatziefstathiou

1

Dual career

Balancing success in sport and life

Lucinda Howland, Achilleas Papadimitriou,
Vasilis Minoudis and Philip Hurst

Introduction

Few Olympic and Paralympic athletes are paid sufficiently and often face the challenge of combining their sport with an educational or vocational career. This is referred to as 'dual career'. Dual career in sport encapsulates the requirement for "athletes to successfully initiate, develop and finalise an elite sporting career as part of a lifelong career, in combination with the pursuit of education and/or work" (European Union, 2012, p. 6). In the last decade, there has been an exponential increase of collaborative dual career research, which has coincided with the emergence of policy, strategy and calls for legislative change at the national and international level, such as the United Kingdom's Duty of Care in Sport Review (Grey-Thompson, 2017) and the International Olympic Committee's (IOC) Athletes' Commission 'All in' Strategy (IOC, 2020).

In consideration of the issues athletes face in their pursuit of competing at the Olympic or Paralympic Games (and at elite sport more broadly), it is essential to understand the principles underlying a dual career. The aims of this chapter are to familiarise the reader with the concept of dual career and the benefits of this approach to nurturing an athlete's career development. Further, this chapter will review existing dual career programmes that aim to support an athlete in their ability to effectively balance their sporting, and educational and/or vocational goals.

What is a dual career?

An athlete's career development is multifaceted, non-linear and dynamic, which includes the social environment, personal factors and sport commitments (Debois et al., 2012; Durand-Bush and Salmela, 2002; MacNamara, Button and Collins, 2010). Acosta et al. (2007) propose a five-stage model to an athletes' sports career: (1) starting of the sport career; (2) sport development; (3) specialisation in sports; (4) career fall; and (5) adaptation to a new life. Athletes typically experience anticipated or 'normative' transitions (e.g. retirement, junior to senior progression) and unanticipated or 'non-normative' transitions (e.g. serious injury, deselection, loss of funding) as they progress through each stage. This can often result in athletes having to choose between education and/or work and their sport.

There is now consensus that transitions in the career development of talented and elite athletes should not be considered in isolation but rather as a holistic approach incorporating the athletic, psychological, psychosocial, academic/vocational and financial domains (Wylleman, Reints and De Knop, 2013). In short, an athlete will have their own pathway to managing their own career (Li and Sum, 2017). Building on this perceptive, Wylleman and Lavallee (2004) introduced the model of transitions faced by athletes. This model combines career development (e.g. transition into post-athletic career) with a holistic perspective (e.g. an athlete's multi-level development), which reflects domain-specific normative transitions in the factors that could influence athletes' psychological, psychosocial and academic/vocational development. In short, this model encourages the consideration and interaction of sport, studies and private life during an athletes' development throughout the lifespan.

To support application of the model, Stambulova et al. (2015) reported the results from a mixed-method study of Swedish student-athletes (N = 10) during their adaption to elite-sport schools. The authors reported that student-athletes would coordinate different layers of their development (e.g. athletic, psychological, educational) to obtain an optimal balance between sport, studies and private life. Importantly, the authors highlighted the demanding lifestyle student-athletes face and that as the year progressed, students' perceptions of their ability to cope with these demands increased. Similarly, in a longitudinal study of personal characteristics of German student-athletes (N = 125), Baron-Thiene and Alfermann (2015) reported that student-athletes were more likely to drop out of sport due to higher physical complaints and lower win motivation and self-optimisation. The authors suggested that to prevent such drop-outs, student-athletes need psychological support to help manage their careers, particularly during key transition periods (e.g. school to Higher Education). Athletes report an appreciation for the support received in the 'personal' domain and being surrounded by a caring agenda (Devaney et al., 2018), with dual career trained support staff including Personal Excellence Advisors and Performance Lifestyle Practitioners also contributing to valuable dual career support services. Further research into applied practice and experiences of such roles in relation to supporting a dual career is required. In a systematic review of qualitative research on dual career athletes, Li and Sum (2017) identified that individual (e.g. psychological condition), interpersonal (e.g. coping strategy) and external factors (e.g. financial support) influence a dual career athlete's development. The authors concluded that these factors all interplay and emphasised the importance of both the individual and the environment in facilitating the development of a dual career athlete.

While the holistic model can provide an understanding of a dual career athlete's development, there is still a lack of research that examines the whole environment. Future research is needed that considers the interaction and relationship of factors (e.g. personal, environmental, psychosocial) influencing an athletes' career development in both sport and elsewhere.

Benefits of a dual career

The simultaneous pursuit of excellence in sport and education/vocation is traditionally argued to be counterproductive (Conzelmann and Nagel, 2003; Douglas and Carless, 2006; Purdy, Eitzen and Hufnagel, 1982). However, several studies report that athletes successfully combine their sporting career with educational and/or vocational aspirations (Henry, 2013; McKenna and Dunstan-Lewis, 2004). The benefits of a dual career are suggested to include, but not limited to, the promotion of a balanced way of life and transferrable skills (Aquilina, 2013; Burlot, Richard and Joncheray, 2018; MacNamara and Collins, 2014), increased socialisation (Knight, Harwood and Sellars, 2018; Stambulova et al., 2015), decreased stress (Sallen, Hemming and Richartz, 2018), development of multiple personal identities that protect an athlete from unilateral identity development (Ryba et al., 2015), improved career planning and termination (Lavallee, 2005; Pink, Saunders and Stynes, 2015) and increased vocational opportunities after a sports career (Barriopedro, de Subijana and Muniesa, 2018).

It is suggested that student-athletes focusing on more than one aspect of life can help relieve tension and the pressure for 'perfect' sport performance. Dual careers can foster the transfer of skills between different sectors (e.g. sports and studies) and effectively prepare an athlete for another career preparation after sports (Aquilina, 2013). In a systematic review analysis of the dual career literature, Aquilina (2013) reported that for some athletes a career in one dedicated area can become all consuming; a sole focus on one career can result in an inability to cope with unanticipated events or transitions. Aquilina (2013) further highlighted that athletes are suggested to be more inclined to have the option of two careers, with the belief that attempting to balance both aspects ensured that they continuously received some form of mental stimulus and heightened their ability to cope with the demands of both careers.

Dual careers and retirement

Dual careers play an important role for those retiring from sport. Sporting retirement is considered challenging, disruptive and stressful (Baillie and Danish, 1992), and if an athlete has undertaken limited or no preparation for this transition away from sport, these challenges and stressors are amplified. With a lack of financial support given to most athletes during their career, smoothly retiring from sport can be difficult. This will be even more difficult for those athletes who cannot rely on their national body or club for psychological and financial support (Stambulova, Stephan and Jäphag, 2007). Collectively, this highlights the need for athletes to develop a dual career or prepare for the termination of their sports career while they are still participating.

There are several research studies investigating the transition of retirement for professional athletes. The French Professional Basketball Players Association (SNB) survey (2014) indicated that 33% of athletes had not chosen a professional career after sports and the Retired and Transitioned Players Report (PFA, 2015) reported that 45% of retired athletes rated the transition to life after sports as 'difficult' or 'too difficult' and preferred their lifestyle as a professional athlete. Reasons cited for this perceived difficulty in transition were related to a lack of mental preparation and communication with their teammates, financial insecurity and unwilling entry into retirement. Research from Europe and America has also indicated that a dual career can reduce the likelihood of reactive coping strategies, including avoidance/denial, venting of emotions and preventing the use of alcohol and substance abuse (Schwenk et al., 2007; Stambulova, Stephan and Jäphag, 2007; Wippert and Fliesser, 2016).

Research commissioned by the United Kingdom Professional Players Federation (Porter and Barnes, 2014) explored the mental, financial and physical wellbeing of more than 1,000 retired professional athletes. Authors indicated that 34% of athletes reported lacking control of their life two years after they ended their career and a quarter of athletes admitted to experiencing ongoing physical, mental, financial issues, in addition to addiction, high stress and a loss of confidence and self-esteem. In a report of retired professional footballers Gouttebarge, Aoki and Kerkhoffs (2016), the authors indicated that mental disorders were highly prevalent amongst athletes (e.g. distress, anxiety/depression, and adverse alcohol, smoking and nutrition behaviour), which was further related to career dissatisfaction. In a qualitative longitudinal study, Torregrosa et al. (2015) examined prospective and retrospective accounts of career development and retirement of Olympic athletes, some of whom pursued dual careers. Most athletes who reported a 'positive transition' experience, where prospective views matched their retrospective views, had adopted a dual career in a convergent or parallel trajectory (Pallarés et al., 2011). The study also found the trajectory followed is highly relevant in athletes' handling of the retirement process and thus the quality of transition. This further emphasises the importance of dual career in facilitating an athletes' ease of transition into retirement from sport.

Finding the right balance in dual career during sport participation can be instrumental in athletes' perception of their adjustment to, and satisfaction with life after sport (Harrison and Lawrence, 2004; Kerr and Dacyshyn, 2000). Dual career athletes appear to anticipate the complexities of retirement better than those who focus solely on one career. The proactive nature of dual career athletes and the conscious planning to 'be ahead of the game' can facilitate an athlete's transition into retirement.

Dual career programmes

Athlete perceptions of combining sport and study/work is juxtaposed. A tension exists for an athlete aiming to compete at the Olympics, for example, while simultaneously planning a career outside of sport for the future. Training and competition schedules can be hampered during high academic workloads or intense work scheduling and vice versa. Thus, to ensure that athletes are in a position to effectively manage their sporting career with education and/or work, dual career programmes can provide athletes with the tools and support to balance both ambitions.

In 2012, after tasking 27 experts within the field of dual career, the European Union published guidelines on how best to support dual career athletes (see Box 1.1). Although this policy outlines what programmes *should* be doing in order to support dual career, the responsibility to ensure implementation, access, inclusion to and progression of a dual career 'System' or 'Strategy' remains with the sporting organisation. For this reason, there are now several dual career programmes that aim to support athletes combining their sporting career with education or work.

Box 1.1 The European Union Guidelines on dual career (2012)

The EU Guidelines on Dual Careers of Athletes (2012) provide three overarching *Guidelines for Actions* to include:

> Talented and elite athletes in amateur and professional sports, including athletes with a disability as well as retired athletes, should be recognised as a specific population group in the relevant policy areas;
>
> Public authorities responsible for policy domains involved in the provision of sport, education, training, social and financial support and employment should consider the establishment of interdepartmental bodies or mechanisms to ensure the coordination, cross-sectoral cooperation, implementation and monitoring of dual career policies for talented and elite athletes including retiring elite athletes;
>
> Authorities responsible for the implementation of dual careers should develop national guidelines for dual careers taking into account the EU Guidelines on Dual Careers and the specificity of the national sport and education system and cultural diversity. They should consider the use of agreements between stakeholders to promote dual careers. Where appropriate, such agreements could involve specific reward mechanisms, such as incentives for educational institutions or employers to recruit dual career athletes.

In 2007, the International Olympic and Paralympic Committee joined with the Adecco Group, a global Human Resources Solution Firm and world leader in professional staffing, to enrich athletes' sporting life with education and adequate life and professional skills. The IOC Athlete Career Programme (ACP) was initially created to help athletes develop an awareness of transferable skills and attributes, discover interests beyond sport and provide internships and experience opportunities. The IOC and International Paralympic Committee (IPC) also created the Athlete 365 Career+ Outreach Programme, which involves in-person group workshops delivered by members of IOC/IPC Athletes' Commission, Olympians and Adecco managers. The workshops aim to educate athletes on several topics such as networking, curriculum vitae/résumé development, interviewing, translating sports to business language, social media, and entrepreneurship, with an overriding goal to create awareness and education about athletes' professional life after sports. Since its creation, the programme has supported more than 30,000 athletes from more than 185 countries and provided over 4,800 adolescent athletes with educational opportunities through outreach activities in four Youth Olympic Games.

Alex Baumann: bridging the '*employability gap*'

Part of the Athlete 365 Career+ Athlete Career Programme (ACP)

Olympic silver medallist (Sochi 2014) in Bobsleigh, Alex Baumann joined the Athlete 365 Career+ ACP Programme through the Swiss Athlete Career Programme. Alex recognised that he lacked the necessary work experience to bridge the gap between his education and prospective employability. Alex was motivated to seek ways to resolve this employability gap and gain experience whilst simultaneously studying for a Masters degree in Food Science. Through the tailor-made solutions and options presented to him as part of the Athlete 365 Career+ ACP programme, Alex located employers willing to support and provide flexibility in his work schedule around his training and academic demands, providing an opportunity to apply his '*athlete qualities*' to the working world and optimise his employment prospects following the termination of his athletic career.

Source: IOC and IPC Athlete Career Programme

Games

In order to help athletes integrate into vocational work during or after their sporting career, the national Collectif Sports Scheme, developed the 'Club Citoyen Collectif Sports' and the 'Sport Compétences' programmes. The Club Citoyen Collective Sports programme aims to promote desired sporting, ethical and moral values, which can be translated in the world of business, and develops relationships with professional clubs, and their partner companies, with athletes. The Sport Compétences, created in 2017, developed by the La Française des Jeux (FDJ) and Collectif Sports, aims to showcase the unique and desirable athlete skill set to the business world and helps support the transition of elite athletes at the end of their careers. Supported by specialist partners in Human Resources and Corporate Social Responsibility policies, former elite athletes and coaches, the programmes focus on professional teams, elite athletes and companies who wish to be enriched with the values of sport.

The Dual Career Accreditation Scheme initiated by the Talented Athlete Scholarship Scheme (TASS) of Sport England recognises an education institution's commitment to dual career support for talented athletes who are in full-time education (TASS National Strategy, 2018–2020).

Gloria Hooper: *"sport and studies are a good distraction in those moments when you might have to stop"*

Part of the TASS Dual Career Accreditation Scheme

Olympian Gloria Hooper relocated to the South East of England to join a small dedicated training team comprised of elite and talented young sprinters. Through her support network, the Italian sprinter, who has competed at London 2012 and Rio 2016, became aware of the TASS Dual Accreditation Scheme and enrolled at a local university offering a desirable course. The scheme provided assurance of the university's commitment to academic flexibility in an environment that is accommodating for dual career athletes. Pursuing a dual career, although challenging, was viewed as a necessary distraction on occasions and in preparation for retirement. Whilst completing a Foundation degree in Human Biology, Gloria has accessed extensions to coursework, personalised catch up sessions with academic staff and support from a Performance Lifestyle Practitioner at times when schedules were conflicting. Her invaluable coaching support network and resources and funding from the university scholarship and dual career scheme have helped to facilitate an unanticipated world class performance at the 2019 Doha World Championships and subsequent qualification for Tokyo 2020 in the women's relay.

Source: Canterbury Christ Church University, with athlete permission

The scheme aims to set minimum standards nationwide for the promotion of academic flexibility within the education sector and accredit academic institutions based on their ability to provide academic support and flexibility to talented athletes. Accredited institutions adopt the framework created by TASS and host dual career educational workshops, which provide athletes with key skills and knowledge in being able to balance their sporting and educational careers. Since its establishment in 2017, 27 Further Education institutions and 11 Higher Education institutions were given accredited status and between July 2017 and July 2019, 166 student-athletes aged 16 to 18 years old competing at regional (32%), national (46%) and international (22%) received dual career support.

Significant programmes have been developed by Athletes Associations such as the UK's Professional Cricketers and Rugby Players Association's (RPA) personal development programme, which was launched in 2004 and supported by the Rugby Football Union (RFU) and Premiership Rugby. Renamed to RPA Gain Line programme, athletes are individually supported regarding their welfare, off-field personal development, education and career transition planning by independent RPA Development Managers. Personal development approaches not only help athletes through encouraging them to pursue a balanced lifestyle and prepare for life after rugby, but also they have been proven to empower their playing performance.

Also, the SNB, the French basketball players association, has developed a network of former players who are now following careers in different fields. This network operates in many levels. It constitutes an advocate team to current athletes, informing them on the different careers available and it supplies a potential mentoring system for athletes focused on certain professional domains. It also provides athletes with working. In football, FIFPro and the University of Nicosia (UNIC) have developed a global initiative that allows over 1,000 professional footballers from all over the world to enrol in a Sports Management and Business Administration online programme. The five-year cooperation provides several benefits to the participants including a Scholars Scheme that gives full scholarships to active professional athletes.

The striking emphasis on dual career programmes is evident globally. Dual career programmes have reached Europe, Oceania, Asia and North America including, but not limited to, Spain (ÈXITS – Excellence and Transitions), Australia (Athlete Career and Education Programme, Elite Athlete Friendly University Programme and Personal Excellence Programme) and Canada (Olympic Athlete Career Centre, Canadian Sports Schools). This show of global unanimity would appear to suggest that dual career is significant and that supporting athletes in their pursuit of balancing in multiple careers is important. While there are guidelines to help develop these programmes (e.g. EU; see Box 1.1), there is incongruence between the delivery of these programmes within and between national and international organisations. The potential problem is a seamless agreement that such programmes are effective in supporting dual career athletes. The breadth of dual career provision is growing, with dual career systems being largely categorised into sport-led, education-led or a combination of sport- and education-led. With continued expansion in the area of dual career provision, definitions of programmes, schemes and initiatives may in time require further validation.

Are dual career programmes effective?

In most countries, athletes have access to dual career support. However, there is significant inconsistency in the structure, content and monitoring of dual career programmes between countries and governing bodies. This inconsistency is further complicated by the fact that educational and/or vocational institutions and stakeholders are often unaware of the dynamic nature of dual careers and have separate expectations and arrangements. Student-athletes have even been reported to be unaware of dual career policies and legislative framework (Condello et al., 2019) and it is not uncommon for athletes to experience a lack of support from their educational and vocational institution. To help overcome this, athletes should first consider that the place of study and/or work adopts a dual career policy. This underscores the importance of ensuring practices and policies are consistent through international standards in the delivery of dual career programmes.

While international standards can help harmonise and ensure consistency between different types of dual career programmes, there are few, if any, systematic evaluations of existing programmes. It is currently unclear what impact, if any, dual career programmes have on an athlete's ability to effectively balance their sporting career with another. Further, there is little evidence monitoring athletes over substantial periods and transition points. We are therefore limited in our understanding of existing programme effectiveness. Given this, there is a need for more systematic evaluations of dual career programmes, to ensure that they are achieving their aim in supporting an athlete balance sporting success in combination with their pursuit of education and/or work. This, in turn, can help shape dual career policy and thus greater consistency in existing programmes.

Tucker Dupree: life beyond athletic victories and stories

Part of the United States Olympic and Paralympic Committee Athlete Career and Education (USOPC ACE) Programme

Four-time Paralympic Medallist Tucker Dupree found employment in corporate America in digital communications for BP with the help of the United States Olympic and Paralympic Committee's ACE Programme, which is supported by career management services sponsor Adecco. Silver and two-time Bronze medallist at the Paralympic Games in London 2012 and Bronze medallist at the Paralympic Games in Rio 2016, Tucker acknowledged he had limited real-world experience and his career had been focused on sport for over a decade. In the lead up to retirement he faced the challenge of what to do next, coming from a world where athletic victories and stories of his sport career were celebrated to experiencing a crisis of identity. The swimmer completed an online degree in communications and marketing towards the end of his sport career. Following retirement on his own terms, the transition from sport to the corporate world was challenging but achievable with assistance in the process viewed as integral to success.

Source: United States Olympic and Paralympic Committee

What to include in a dual career programme?

Although there is limited evidence in effectiveness of existing dual career programmes, there is a growing body of literature indicating that an athlete's career is dynamic, non-linear and distinct.

We recently evaluated TASS's dual career scheme in Further Education institutions (SPEAR, 2019), with the aim to understand why educational institutions are choosing to engage with dual career programmes and explore how the scheme has affected various stakeholders including student-athletes, dual career support staff, academic staff and key stakeholders within education institutions. Collectively, this has allowed a greater understanding of the common issues athletes face during their pursuit of dual careers and the key elements required for existing programmes. We address these in more detail later.

A key finding from the survey indicated that dual career athletes' expectations to support their sport development may unintentionally take priority over their educational and/or vocational career. Dual career athletes appear to have preconceived notions of their own pathway early in their development. This therefore places a greater emphasis for dual career programmes to allow athletes to make a more informed choice about their next step in their career. The most favoured dual career paths appear to be those that integrate education from the start of the sport career. However, athletes have differing aspirations, and programmes will need to ensure a multifaceted approach that addresses the specific needs and circumstances of the target population. Effective programmes should aim to influence multiple determinants of behaviours, lifestyles and competencies, including knowledge, motivations and interpersonal relationships. It should be emphasised that dual career programmes are not exclusive to Olympic/Paralympic and professional athletes. Athletes of a lesser ability who are not sufficiently talented to compete at the Olympic Games, for example, can still have dual career ambitions. Thus, programmes should be flexible to the stage of the sporting career of the athlete, which may in turn contribute to widening opportunities and access to talent development.

Typically, dual career programmes use a combination of didactic and interactive support styles. Formal, non-formal and informal learning in combination with support strategies, including extended education, online programmes, internet-based tools and flexible organisation of exams, assessments and attendance are elements that can be used to address dual career development.

The context of delivery is important when designing the dual career programme. If the goal is to help support athletes balance multiple careers, the programme will only be effective if the content resonates with the target population. The ability to translate dual career programmes between countries and organisations is possible. However, factors such as the culture, type of sport and age of the athlete will need to be considered to ensure programme effectiveness. Given this, we make the following recommendations dual career programmes should address in their development:

1 Tailored to fit the target population (e.g. career stage, career ambitions);
2 Focused on developing core life skills (e.g. communication, decision-making) to allow them to make a more informed choice in their dual career;
3 Monitored and delivered with high degree of consistency, ensuring that the programme is implemented as intended with flexibility to the athlete's current situation;
4 Delivered interactively, emphasising a personal approach, especially through discussions and past athlete experiences;
5 Delivered by well-trained facilitators, who deliver the programme with high fidelity.

Conclusion

While pursuing a lifelong career in sports, alongside education and/or work, can be stressful and demanding, at the same time, it can be exciting and enjoyable. The main challenge for most athletes is having the ability to balance both careers so that they are equally successful. While it has often been viewed as counterproductive for an athlete to prioritise other commitments ahead of their sporting career, a growing body of literature has indicated that dual careers can be highly beneficial.

It is important to note that the dual career is in its infancy, but has generated increased attention over the last decade. We understand more now about an athlete's perception and experience of a dual career and what may facilitate their development and ability to effectively manage multiple careers. Future challenges exist in understanding the effectiveness and appropriateness of dual career programmes. While it is still important to conduct research into identifying the processes underpinning the development of dual career athletes, and the associated benefits, there is a need to generate systematic longitudinal evaluations of existing programmes to ensure they are meeting the needs of those involved.

References

Acosta, J.P., Serganoli, L.G., Parikh, P. and Resch, N. (2007). *Plan B: How to simplify the transition from a sporting career to a new life?* Neuchâtel, Switzerland: The International Centre for Sports Studies (CISE).

Aquilina, D. (2013). A study of the relationship between elite athletes' educational development and sporting performance. *The International Journal of the History of Sport*, 30(4), pp. 374–392.

Baillie, P.H. and Danish, S.J. (1992). Understanding the career transition of athletes. *The Sport Psychologist*, 6(1), pp. 77–98.

Baron-Thiene, A. and Alfermann, D. (2015). Personal characteristics as predictors for dual career dropout versus continuation – A prospective study of adolescent athletes from German elite sport schools. *Psychology of Sport and Exercise*, 21, pp. 42–49.

Barriopedro, M., de Subijana, C.L. and Muniesa, C. (2018). Insights into life after sport for Spanish Olympians: Gender and career path perspectives. *PLoS One*, 13(12), p. e0209433.
Burlot, F., Richard, R. and Joncheray, H. (2018). The life of high-level athletes: The challenge of high performance against the time constraint. *International Review for the Sociology of Sport*, 53(2), pp. 234–249.
Condello, G., Capranica, L., Doupona, M., Varga, K. and Burk, V. (2019). Dual-career through the elite university student-athletes' lenses: The international FISU-EAS survey. *PLoS One*, 14(10).
Conzelmann, A. and Nagel, S. (2003). Professional careers of the German Olympic athletes. *International Review for the Sociology of Sport*, 38(3), pp. 259–280.
Debois, N., Ledon, A., Argiolas, C. and Rosnet, E. (2012). A lifespan perspective on transitions during a top sports career: A case of an elite female fencer. *Psychology of Sport and Exercise*, 13(5), pp. 660–668.
Devaney, D.J., Nesti, M.S., Ronkainen, N.J., Littlewood, M. and Richardson, D. (2018). Athlete lifestyle support of elite youth cricketers: An ethnography of player concerns within a national talent development program. *Journal of Applied Sport Psychology*, 30(3), pp. 300–320.
Douglas, K. and Carless, D. (2006). Performance, discovery, and relational narratives among women professional tournament golfers. *Women in Sport & Physical Activity Journal*, 15(2), p. 14.
Durand-Bush, N. and Salmela, J.H. (2002). The development and maintenance of expert athletic performance: Perceptions of world and Olympic champions. *Journal of Applied Sport Psychology*, 14(3), pp. 154–171.
European Union. (2012). *EU guidelines on dual careers of athletes*. Brussels: European Union.
Gouttebarge, V., Aoki, H. and Kerkhoffs, G.M. (2016). Prevalence and determinants of symptoms related to mental disorders in retired male professional footballers. *Journal of Sports Medicine and Physical Fitness*, 56(5), pp. 648–654.
Grey-Thompson, T. (2017). *Duty of care in sport*. London, UK: UK Sport.
Harrison, K.C. and Lawrence, S.M. (2004). Female and male student athletes' perceptions of career transition in sport and higher education: A visual elicitation and qualitative assessment. *Journal of Vocational Education and Training*, 56(4), pp. 485–506.
Henry, I. (2013). Athlete development, athlete rights and athlete welfare: A European Union perspective. *The International Journal of the History of Sport*, 30(4), pp. 356–373.
Howland, L.J., Hurst, P., Foad, A.J. and Hubbard, K. (2019). *Talented Athlete Scholarship Scheme (TASS) dual career accreditation scheme evaluation report*. The Centre for Sport, Physical Education and Activity Research (SPEAR). Retrieved from https://www.canterbury.ac.uk/social-and-applied-sciences/spear/research-projects/research-projects.aspx
IOC. (2020). *All in*. Lausanne: IOC.
Kerr, G. and Dacyshyn, A. (2000). The retirement experiences of elite female gymnasts. *Journal of Applied Sport Psychology*, 12(2), pp. 115–133.
Knight, C.J., Harwood, C.G. and Sellars, P.A. (2018). Supporting adolescent athletes' dual careers: The role of an athlete's social support network. *Psychology of Sport and Exercise*, 38, pp. 137–147.
Lavallee, D. (2005). The effect of a life development intervention on sports career transition adjustment. *The Sport Psychologist*, 19(2), pp. 193–202.
Li, M. and Sum, R.K.W. (2017). A meta-synthesis of elite athletes' experiences in dual career development. *Asia Pacific Journal of Sport and Social Science*, 6(2), pp. 99–117.
MacNamara, Á., Button, A. and Collins, D. (2010). The role of psychological characteristics in facilitating the pathway to elite performance part 1: Identifying mental skills and behaviors. *The Sport Psychologist*, 24(1), pp. 52–73.
MacNamara, Á. and Collins, D. (2014). Why athletes say no to doping: A qualitative exploration of the reasons underpinning athletes' decision not to dope. *Performance Enhancement & Health*, 3(3–4), pp. 145–152.
McKenna, J. and Dunstan-Lewis, N. (2004). An action research approach to supporting elite student-athletes in higher education. *European Physical Education Review*, 10(2), pp. 179–198.
Pallarés, S., Azócar, F., Torregrosa, M., Selva, C. and Ramis, Y. (2011). Athletic career models in water polo and their involvement in the transition to an alternative career. *CCD: Cultura Ciencia Deporte*, 6(17), pp. 93–103.
PFA. (2015). *Retired and transitioned players report*. Victoria, Australia: Professional Footballers Australia Inc.
Pink, M., Saunders, J. and Stynes, J. (2015). Reconciling the maintenance of on-field success with off-field player development: A case study of a club culture within the Australian Football League. *Psychology of Sport and Exercise*, 21, pp. 98–108.

Porter, A. and Barnes, D. (2014). *Findings from a study of the mental, physical and financial wellbeing of retired professional sportsmen.* London, UK: Professional Players Federation.
Purdy, D.A., Eitzen, D.S. and Hufnagel, R. (1982). Are athletes also students? The educational attainment of college athletes. *Social Problems*, 29(4), pp. 439–448.
Ryba, T.V., Stambulova, N.B., Ronkainen, N.J., Bundgaard, J. and Selänne, H. (2015). Dual career pathways of transnational athletes. *Psychology of Sport and Exercise*, 21, pp. 125–134.
Sallen, J., Hemming, K. and Richartz, A. (2018). Facilitating dual careers by improving resistance to chronic stress: Effects of an intervention programme for elite student athletes. *European Journal of Sport Science*, 18(1), pp. 112–122.
Schwenk, T.L., Gorenflo, D.W., Dopp, R.R. and Hipple, E. (2007). Depression and pain in retired professional football players. *Medicine and Science in Sports and Exercise*, 39(4), pp. 599–605.
Stambulova, N.B., Engström, C., Franck, A., Linnér, L. and Lindahl, K. (2015). Searching for an optimal balance: Dual career experiences of Swedish adolescent athletes. *Psychology of Sport and Exercise*, 21, pp. 4–14.
Stambulova, N.B., Stephan, Y. and Jäphag, U. (2007). Athletic retirement: A cross-national comparison of elite French and Swedish athletes. *Psychology of Sport and Exercise*, 8(1), pp. 101–118.
Torregrosa, M., Ramis, Y., Pallarés, S., Azócar, F. and Selva, C. (2015). Olympic athletes back to retirement: A qualitative longitudinal study. *Psychology of Sport and Exercise*, 21, pp. 50–56.
Wippert, P.M. and Fliesser, M. (2016). National doping prevention guidelines: Intent, efficacy and lessons learned – A 4-year evaluation. *Substance Abuse Treatment, Prevention, and Policy*, 11(1), p. 35.
Wylleman, P. and Lavallee, D. (2004). A developmental perspective on transitions faced by athletes. In: M.R. Weiss, ed., *Developmental sport and exercise psychology: A lifespan perspective*. Fitness Information Technology, pp. 507–527.
Wylleman, P., Reints, A. and De Knop, P. (2013). A developmental and holistic perspective on athletic career development. In: *Managing high performance sport*. Routledge, pp. 191–214.

2

How a system of judicial precedent may help the rights of athletes before the Court of Arbitration for Sport (CAS)[1]

Gregory Ioannidis

Introduction

The author has over twenty years of clinical experience before the Court of Arbitration for Sport (thereafter CAS). Over the years he has witnessed the significant development of this unique court for sport and became witness to a remarkable creation of a separate body of case law and procedure. These unique elements for the practice and procedure of sports law have strengthened not only the argument that sports law deserves to be a separate legal discipline, but they have also created a need for recognition of the importance for protecting the rights of sport participants and other stakeholders, before this supreme court for sport.

Given the significance of CAS in the sport dispute resolution process, it is important for practitioners to identify a framework where clear guidance is given for practice and procedure before such forum. Rules of evidence, rules on examination, as well as a system on decided cases and the force they may have on adjudicating panels, may all be elements that determine the effective and appropriate advice to a client. Consistency and clarity are both important elements in the practice of law and given that clients tend to seek the use of professional advisers and experts for their matters before CAS, it is equally important that a system of judicial precedent is applied and declared before CAS. Although CAS does not apply (at least officially) a system of binding precedent, it is the author's respectful submission that CAS Panels do, silently, operate within the parameters of an undeclared system of judicial precedent.

Although lawyers from civil law systems may find the system of binding precedent anachronistic, nevertheless, the importance of the common law towards the application of a system of binding precedent (and of justice) and its influence on modern legal reasoning and thinking cannot be dismissed at face value. Modern legal thinking is largely based on the application of legal reasoning, which stems from the accumulated experience and wealth of case-analysis and expertise that judicial creativity and ingenuity offer through the system of judicial precedent.

The binding nature of the doctrine underpins the essence of the English legal system and its old-established existence and operation serve to demonstrate its important nature. This, however, is not an anathema, nor is a mechanism which makes the law static. The law develops through the decided cases but the rule of the binding nature of the doctrine is not absolute. The

Practice Direction of 1966[2] recognises that the House of Lords (changed now to the Supreme Court) may treat previous decisions as binding, but may also depart from them when it appears right to do so. In the premises, it is submitted that any perceived limitations of the doctrine of binding precedent that may be apparent to the civil lawyer can be dismissed by the relative freedom of the judiciary, for the determination of the scope and reason of previous decisions and the justification for a departure from a previous decision, when the fresh circumstances of a new case warrant so. This freedom of departure from previous decisions has been reluctantly exercised by the highest court in England over the years.[3] Nevertheless, it remains a freedom, upon which the doctrine operates and exercised for the efficient development of the law.

It is also arguable that this freedom has not stretched the boundaries of judicial creativity. Although one would think that common law remains judge-made law, the critical examination and evaluation of the doctrine of binding precedent suggests that there is a fine balance between case law and statute. Notwithstanding the remarkable elements of stability and certainty the doctrine creates, as practitioners are able to determine, to a great extent, a sound legal advice from the outset, the doctrine walks in tandem with the existence of statute. It is statutory law which forms the genesis of a particular law, but it is case law which interprets such law and explains not only the intention of the legislator, but offers guidance as to its correct and purposeful application. It is submitted, therefore, that judge-made case law is important, as is important the existence of statute.

It is with regret that the author has to submit that the relationship between case law and statute has been remarkably unexplored. It is submitted that such relationship is evident even in civil law systems, where statute plays a primary role in the determination of a legal principle. Although previous decisions do not have a binding effect on judges, in civil law systems reference to such previous decisions is exercised and has a strong persuasive effect.

It is this unexplored relationship that forms the basis for a future international system of judicial decision making, in the sphere of the sports law discipline that the author wishes to promote with the present work. Although the highest court in sport (CAS) does not have a pre-determined application of a specific legal system, the author advocates the importance of common law, in the determination of legal matters before the CAS and its perceived influence in the creation of sports law principles. The common law, it is submitted, plays an important role before the CAS and the doctrine of binding precedent "exemplifies the general balance which the common law strikes between certainty and adaptability. This general balance is a child of common law's methods, and it represents a large part of its genius."[4]

Common law or civil law before CAS?

The main function of the CAS is to resolve sporting disputes between parties. Although such disputes are dealt with via arbitration in practice, a CAS matter takes the form of a full trial, even at the appellate level, as the general applicable rule is that all appeals before the CAS take the form of a *de novo* hearing.[5]

The practice of sports law before the CAS, over the years, has contributed enormously towards the creation of a remarkable body of case law, as well as statutory law. A unique *lex sportiva* is now in place, which highlights the importance of the CAS in the development of sports law principles and its influence on the practice and procedure of sports law. It is the creation of this remarkable body of case law which forms the basis of the present work.

The nature of the proceedings before the CAS is undoubtedly private and it is usually private international law and Swiss law that govern the proceedings, particularly, in the absence of an express agreement between the parties as to the application of a specific law. What is not specifically stated, however, is the choice, if any, of the actual legal system that governs the process before the CAS. Given that there is a mixture of arbitrators (judges) from both common law and civil law jurisdictions, it becomes imperative for the practising lawyer to identify the appropriate medium and, therefore, conduct the proceedings in the appropriate manner.

From the author's experience, it is submitted that proceedings before the CAS (and even during the pre-trial stage) are conducted with the style one meets in a common law jurisdiction. Although the judges, to a certain extent, apply the 'inquisitorial' civil law style of examination, this is limited to questions, during the proceedings, towards the witnesses and sometimes, towards Counsel for either side. Overall, parties are free to submit the evidence of their choice and test it during the proceedings, in the common law style of 'adversarial' examination, that is, through Counsel for either side. Such examination of the evidence may take the form of written statements, witness testimonies and even applications for pre-trial disclosure. Even during the proceedings before the panel of judges, the process is very much influenced by the common law tradition, whereby the process involves opening and closing statements, examination in chief and cross-examination and the right to re-direct.

It is, however, the parties' references to previous decided cases and the continuous use of such decisions by different panels of judges that would allow one to enquire whether there is a system of *stare decisis* before the CAS. One may produce an attempt at dismissing the existence of such system in the proceedings before the CAS and argue that the CAS panels of judges simply take a note of previous cases, for the sake of consistency and clarity. But is it not this contention that forms the basis for the application of a system of judicial precedent?

It is not disputed that there is now a specific system of *lex sportiva* and the sheer volume of decided cases before the CAS serves to demonstrate that different principles of sports law develop through the examination, analysis and, consequently, via the decisions of the CAS. This only can serve as a catalyst towards a persuasive argument that the CAS does have a system of precedent.[6] As the Panel states in the case of *Canadian Olympic Committee & Beckie Scott v International Olympic Committee CAS 2002/O/373*: "CAS jurisprudence has notably refined and developed a number of principles of sports law, such as the concepts of strict liability (in doping cases) and fairness, which might be deemed part of an emerging lex sportiva."

With this in mind, it is worth examining both scholarship and practice, so a determination could be achieved as to whether there is a *de facto* system of *stare decisis* before the CAS. Certain commentators have suggested that the existence of the CAS Awards "demonstrate the existence of a true stare decisis doctrine within the field of sports arbitration,"[7] whereas others have suggested that CAS arbitrators "are not generally obliged to follow earlier decisions but they usually do so in the interests of legal certainty."[8] The author is inclined to accept and follow such interpretation, given that the CAS Panels make constant use of previous decided cases, particularly when they identify the *ratio decidendi* in their Awards. It is common practice and, indeed, usual reference to previous decisions can be identified in almost every single CAS Award. Such is the importance of precedent in the procedure and practice before the CAS, that it is now common practice for Counsel to submit a Bundle of Authorities before the CAS Panel, in support of his/her submissions. This is also true in situations where the composition of the CAS Panel is mixed, with arbitrators from common law and civil law jurisdictions adjudicating together upon a sporting dispute.

There are, however, instances in practice when CAS arbitrators disagree with the earlier interpretation. In the case of *CAS 2008/A/1545*[9] the Panel made reference to the case of *CAS 97/176* (award of 15 January 1998), with regards to the value of judicial precedent, where it was stated:

> In arbitration there is no *stare decisis*. Nevertheless, the Panel feels that CAS rulings form a valuable body of case law and can contribute to strengthen legal predictability in international

> sports law. Therefore, although not binding, previous CAS decisions can, and should, be taken into attentive consideration by subsequent CAS panels, in order to help developing legitimate expectations among sports bodies and athletes.[10]

Similarly, the same Panel also made reference to another CAS Award of *CAS 2004/A/628* (award of 28 June 2004), where it was stated: "In CAS jurisprudence there is no principle of binding precedent, or stare decisis. However, a CAS Panel will obviously try, if the evidence permits, to come to the same conclusion on matters of law as a previous CAS Panel."[11] Having looked at the two aforementioned authorities, the Panel concluded:

> Therefore, although a CAS panel in principle might end up deciding differently from a previous panel, it must accord to previous CAS awards a substantial precedential value and it is up to the party advocating a jurisprudential change to submit persuasive arguments and evidence to that effect.[12]

The earlier analysis suggests that in the CAS procedure there is no *de facto* recognition of the doctrine of binding precedent, at least, not in theory. In practice, however, it is submitted that the constant use of previous decisions and the undisputed reference of different CAS Panels to the elements of consistency, continuity and legal certainty suggest that the doctrine of binding precedent operates before the CAS, albeit, with some minor exceptions. The author submits that, in practice, the CAS operates in a similar manner with regards to the Supreme Court in the UK (previously known as the House of Lords), where judges are allowed to depart from their own previous decisions. The fact that 'persuasive arguments' and 'evidence to that effect' may lead towards a jurisprudential change, demonstrate the argument that if CAS Panels feel 'right to do so,' they may depart or decide not to follow previous decisions. In fact, in such cases the CAS Panels go at length to explain the reasons of their 'departure' from previous cases and they tend to do so by distinguishing relevant authorities on the facts and on the merits.

Binding or persuasive authority?

One issue, which has remained elusive over the years is a clear declaration from the ICAS as to the nature of the Awards pronounced by the CAS. Although the *Anderson*[13] Award explicitly recognises that there is no system of binding precedent before the CAS, nevertheless, such Award also recognises the 'substantial value' of precedent. This situation appears to be self-conflicting and contradictory and to a certain extent, with respect, it does not assist in the procedure and practice before the CAS.

One explanation for the lack of an explicit declaration of the binding (or otherwise) nature of the CAS Awards is possibly the acknowledgement that arbitral awards do not usually contain any form of precedential nature.[14] This may be true, in the sphere of international arbitration; but is the CAS, in practical and pragmatic terms, an arbitral tribunal, or is it a Court, with full power to examine the facts and the law, examine the evidence and the witnesses and produce decisions where future disputes may rely upon for guidance? In pragmatic terms, the CAS procedure and practice resemble practice in a civil or criminal court. The process before the CAS is identical to the process of a civil or criminal court, whereby procedural rules determine the actual practice of Counsel and judges alike and offer guidance as to the rights of litigants. The proceedings are formal, and the primary duty of Counsel remains the same: the duty to the Court. Rules of evidence play an important role in the final determination of the matter in question, whereas language and court-etiquette are observed at all times and those practising advocacy at the highest level are familiar with the appropriate pace, tone of the voice, body posture and eye contact with the judges. These are all issues that play a significant role in the proceedings before the CAS and the formal process applies, without an exception, in the Ordinary and the Appeals Divisions of the CAS.

Moreover, the CAS Awards, in their majority, do not have a confidential nature and, unless the parties agree otherwise, are published on the CAS website and are available and free to everyone. In addition, the CAS website contains a specific 'Jurisprudence' section, where those interested can access recent Awards or even the Archive where older Awards are stored. This creates a useful tool of actual Law Reporting, like the one in the UK. In the author's opinion, this process is substantially relevant and identical to the most important ingredients that form the basis of a common law system.

In the premises, reference needs to be made to statutory interpretation employed by the CAS, which over the years has assumed a significant role in the understanding and appreciation of different relationships in sport. The CAS has assumed a primary role in interpreting rules and regulations of sporting governing bodies. Such regulations, along with the statutes of the said sporting bodies, form the basis of real and actual statutory interpretation and it is, without a doubt, a practice that occurs constantly. One would be hard pressed in discovering one single CAS Award that fails, in one way or another, in its attempt to interpret specific rules and statutes.

The earlier analysis suggests that, in theory, the doctrine of binding precedent does not exist before the CAS. In practice, the author submits, the doctrine of binding precedent is very much exercised, and it occurs more often than not. In the limited amount of CAS Awards that CAS Panels declared the absence of a system of binding precedent, they also took the opportunity to suggest that there must be good reasons as to why a CAS Panel may decide to depart from a previous authority, regardless of the composition of such Panel. In the author's opinion, the CAS is usually reluctant to avoid previous decisions, particularly where facts and *ratio decidendi* of previous and present matters appear to be and, are, as a matter of fact, identical or similar. Although not specifically stated, it is submitted that some form of unique existence of precedent (in the common law understanding) is exercised before the CAS. One may argue that such precedent is not binding, but such is the force of its application on present and future CAS Panels that one would also accept the premise that the persuasive nature and constant reference to such nature of previous decisions constitutes a *de facto* practice of judicial decision making that tends to become binding, in a looser interpretation of the meaning of the word.

The CAS standard of proof as an example of a practising common law tradition

The common law tradition with regards to the rules of evidence has devised two different standards of proof. In civil matters the standard of proof is on the *balance of probabilities* and this is the standard of proof generally required to be met by either party seeking to discharge the burden of proof. On the other hand, the criminal standard of proof is *beyond reasonable doubt.*[15] In the sporting context, sports law jurisprudence has devised a third standard of proof, which is currently identified between the common law civil and criminal standards of proof. Those practising before the CAS recognise and use the *comfortable satisfaction* standard of proof. The CAS jurisprudence suggests that this standard is above the common law civil standard of proof, but below the common law criminal standard of proof.[16] In the case of *IAAF v RFEA & Josephine Onyia*[17] such standard of proof was defined as being "greater than a mere balance of probability but less than proof beyond reasonable doubt."

Although specific CAS Panels have suggested in the past that they are not obliged to follow rules of evidence,[18] it is the author's respectful submission that this is exactly what they do in practice. One would be hard pressed in identifying situations where CAS Panels did not follow the rules of evidence, particularly, during proceedings. As a matter of fact, CAS Panels have consistently used direct and circumstantial evidence and have proceeded with rulings on whether specific pieces of evidence are admissible or not. From the author's experience before the CAS, such instances have been an integral part of the pre-trial stage of a CAS matter and determined the outcome of such matter during the appeal hearing.[19]

It is also worth stating that there is another similarity between the CAS evidential process and the one in the common law tradition. The standard of proof is normally used at the end of the trial, when all the different pieces of evidence have been submitted and examined. It may be also used in the situation where there is a submission of a no case to answer, particularly where one party has failed to adduce evidence.[20]

In terms of the use of evidence, importance must be placed to the procedure at the Ad Hoc divisions of CAS and with reference to the Olympic Games. Given the necessary requirement for a speedy process during the Olympic Games,[21] especially when applications for Provisional & Conservatory Measures are concerned, the examination of material facts and evidence by Panels forms a fascinating blending of common law and civil law attitudes, with the former playing a rather 'heavier' role, where examination in chief and cross-examination are concerned. This is true, especially in anti-doping law matters where the cross-examination of witnesses, in particular, forms the underlying basis for the discovery of the truth and the testing of the evidence's probity. On the other hand, the inquisitorial approach by the Panel may play a subsidiary role, but nevertheless, an important one.[22]

Given the previously mentioned analysis, it is the author's respectful submission that the substantial influence of the common law traditions, with regards to the standard of proof before the CAS, is also evidenced by the use of other considerations, such as the admissibility of evidence, its rebuttal, the use of presumptions and the use of circumstantial evidence. In anti-doping litigation, for example, the use of presumptions is frequent. There is a presumption that the onus of proof is with the sporting governing body (or the anti-doping organisation) to establish the alleged offence, provided that the anti-doping test has been conducted properly and executed correctly. To this effect, the common law influence on the rebuttal of a presumption in anti-doping litigation is evident, as such rebuttal must be made on the balance of probabilities. In other words, if the prosecuting authority is alleging a positive anti-doping test and the presumption is that such test was conducted properly, then the athlete has to show how the substance entered his/her body and in doing so he/she must rebut such presumption on the balance of probabilities.[23]

Similarly, the CAS is not agnostic or unfamiliar with the use of circumstantial evidence (for example, the blood profile of an athlete), particularly in anti-doping litigation. The use of negative inferences is also used before the CAS and Counsel, more often than not, are prepared to make submissions in favour of the Panel drawing negative inferences, in the situation where one or more of the opponent's witnesses are refusing to give oral testimony before the Panel. Oral testimony, or lack of it, carries considerable weight in the final determination of a CAS Panel. As it was stated in the CAS Award of *T v FIG CAS 2002/A/385*,[24]

> The Panel was not afforded the opportunity to form its own impression of the athlete. It is difficult for the Panel to identify further mitigating circumstances if an athlete decides not to appear before the Panel for the hearing of his/her case which may have a very substantial impact on his/her future professional career.[25]

The previously mentioned analysis, with regards to the standard of proof applied by the CAS, suggests that such application is consistent with common law, and given the enormous importance CAS Panels place on the analysis and evaluation of evidence, it is submitted that the influence of traditional common law principles and methods characterises the core of the proceedings before the CAS.[26]

CAS, Olympics and Paralympics: time for review of the sporting justice process

As it was suggested earlier, a speedy resolution of a dispute between an athlete and a governing body must be at the forefront of policy and procedure. Notwithstanding the appreciation of the importance of a Games in the professional career of an athlete, it is submitted that the design and execution of a fast dispute resolution process, before and during the Games, not only would offer redress to situations where justice was denied, but it would also restore public confidence in the system of sporting justice. This is true in a system where judicial precedent could be applied, where certainty, transparency and consistency would add further significant benefits to an even speedier resolution of a sporting dispute.

That said, emphasis must be placed on the important dichotomy between the procedural and jurisdictional requirements of remedial avenues at first instance (where a national and/or international governing body is concerned). Although CAS (at least in theory) has a relatively fast process in relation to its Ad Hoc divisions,[27] such fast process may produce a 'much ado about nothing' result, if procedure at first instance is unnecessarily delayed and/or there are appellate limitations, creating, thereby, a jurisdictional hurdle that cannot be overcome. Where jurisdiction is concerned, CAS's Arbitration Rules applicable to the CAS Ad Hoc division for the Olympic Games create an important appellate limitation, where the claimant/applicant is required to exhaust all internal avenues before an application to the CAS is filed. The second paragraph of Article 1 states:

> In the case of a request for arbitration against a decision pronounced by the IOC, an NOC, an International Federation or an Organising Committee for the Olympic Games, the claimant must, before filing such request, have exhausted all the internal remedies available to her/him pursuant to the statutes or regulations of the sports body concerned, unless the time needed to exhaust the internal remedies would make the appeal to the CAS Ad Hoc Division ineffective.

Although the last sentence of Article 1 leaves a 'window' for bypassing such jurisdictional limitations, in the author's experience, such exception may, sometimes, create a rather high threshold to be met and it requires an examination on a case to case basis, rather than creating a standard and equal approach across the different applications before the CAS. In the premises, it is submitted that such appellate/jurisdictional limitations create an obstacle in the speedy and effective resolution of sporting disputes and, to a certain extent, have the potential of violating established rights afforded to athletes.

In light of these submissions, one may arrive at the conclusion that the current system of sporting justice needs an immediate revision. Such revision would need to strengthen athletes' rights, by incorporating a universal and harmonised system of judicial process, particularly where an immediate examination of a sporting dispute is required and where an athlete's participation at a major event is concerned. There may be instances where the rules of a sporting governing body do not allow for appeals to the CAS, especially where such governing body operates at national level. Although national legislation may exist (towards protecting an athlete's rights), such legislation may not be subject to speedy procedural requirements and it may not offer the athlete the desired effect. This, therefore, creates a jurisdictional limitation where the athlete is unable to appeal to the CAS and seek the appropriate remedies. In this case, international federations have an important role in ensuring that their national members create appeal mechanisms, especially where participation of athletes/players in Olympiads is concerned. This very issue was the subject matter under analysis for the author in one of his recent cases before the CAS.[28]

Similarly to the submissions mentioned earlier, there may be instances where international governing bodies refuse to allow participation of individuals in certain events. In the absence of a compelling justification for refusing an individual his/her participation at an event, especially if reference is made to the Olympic Games, CAS may be the only forum where a speedy resolution may be achieved. This is true where the International Olympic Committee (IOC) is concerned, given that its seat is in Switzerland and, depending on the country where the Olympic Games are organised, CAS (with its Ad Hoc divisions) may be the solution to jurisdictional and other procedural limitations. Notwithstanding the argument that the IOC may not be seen as an organisation above the law and the international legal order, it is important to state that CAS must be seen to act (and act) as the ultimate and supreme arbiter on checks and balances, particularly where an 'abuse of discretion' element is applied against athletes, and/or other fundamental rights afforded to athletes have been violated.

In the premises, it is submitted that the "all internal avenues must be exhausted" instruction in the CAS's procedural rules must be waived, especially during the Olympic Games and/or must, at least, become the exception and not the rule. It is more often than not that sport judicial decisions at the national level and/or appeal decisions before tribunals of international bodies may be characterised as 'hometown' decisions. To ensure that transparency and consistency exist in the decision making of judicial fora, it is the author's respectful submission that the CAS must act as a first instance sporting dispute resolution forum, particularly before and/or during the Olympic Games period, without the need for an athlete to seek redress first at the national/international level. The '*de novo*' doctrine that the CAS applies into its procedure and practice may solve any attempts by national and international bodies to delay the process of an athlete's dispute and/or attempt to limit the available remedies for such athlete days before the Olympic Games or even during the Olympic Games.

The author regrets to submit that the previously mentioned does take place often in the world of sport and it is, without a doubt, an anathema of the worst kind and one that ferociously and revengefully violates established rights afforded to athletes and other general principles of law. The examples are many, but the author would respectfully direct the reader to the case of his client, the Greek sprinter Miss Katerina Thanou, when in 2008 she was refused participation in the Beijing Olympic Games without a compelling justification. The reader may also recall that the refusal of participation of Miss Thanou in the 2008 Games was exclusively and strictly connected to her previous matter before the CAS, which was settled with the IAAF in 2006.[29] The IOC's argument remains, to this date, that Miss Thanou could not have participated in the Beijing Olympics because of her involvement in an anti-doping matter four years previously. The reader may reach appropriate conclusions here, but three years after Miss Thanou's dispute with the IOC, a similar matter was sent to CAS for adjudication, which touched upon a similar issue, that is, the legitimacy of a rule that prohibits a previously banned athlete, to be selected for a national Olympic team and, consequently, prohibits participation in the Olympic Games. In the matter of *CAS 2011/A/2658 British Olympic Association (BOA) v World Anti-Doping Agency (WADA)*, the CAS was asked to rule on the legitimacy and applicability of such rule.[30] This matter referred to an appeal brought forward by the BOA against a decision reached by WADA, to hold BOA's Bye-Law of its Rule 7.4 invalid. Such Bye-Law did not allow for membership or selection of athletes who have, previously, served an anti-doping ban. The Anti-Doping Bye-Law stated:

> Any Person who is found to have committed an Anti-Doping Rule violation will be ineligible for membership or selection to the Great Britain Olympic Team or to receive funding from or to hold any position with the BOA as determined by the Executive Board in accordance with the BOA's Bye-Law on Eligibility for future membership of the Great Britain Olympic Team.

This Bye-Law was ratified by the BOA in 2009 and WADA informed the BOA in November 2011 that such Bye-Law was not in compliance with the WADA Code. In particular, WADA wrote to BOA on 21 November 2011 stating that:

> The British Olympic Association has been determined to be non-compliant with the (WADA) Code because your rule on selection for the Olympic Games is an extra sanction, and non-compliant for the same reason the IOC eligibility rule was deemed non-compliant by the Court of Arbitration for Sport.

This determination constituted the 'decision' against which the BOA appealed to the CAS.

The determination by WADA came as a result of another CAS Award in the case of *US Olympic Committee v International Olympic Committee, CAS 2011/O/2422* (the USOC Award), on 4 October 2011. In this case, the USOC challenged the validity of an IOC rule (IOC Regulation) which stated:

> Any person who has been sanctioned with a suspension of more than six months by any anti-doping organisation for any violation of any anti-doping regulations may not participate . . . in the next edition of the Games of the Olympiad and of the Olympic Winter Games following the date of expiry of such suspension.

The BOA did not share WADA's view and attempted to distinguish the *USOC* Award from its own appeal. In various pieces of correspondence prior to the appeal, the BOA stated that its Bye-Law made reference to a selection policy and it was neither a rule of ineligibility nor a sanction and, consequently, did not violate the WADA Code.

The CAS Panel did not agree with such submission, although it was cautious to acknowledge[31] that "both Parties are strong advocates in the fight against doping" and that "BOA and WADA both recognise that doping is fundamentally contrary to the spirit of sport." The Panel summarised the main issue under consideration at Paragraph 8.2 of its Award and stated:

> The dispute between the Parties here involves one means of pursuing the fight against doping, not the fight itself. The Bye-Law prevents an athlete who has had a doping offence from being selected to represent the British Olympic Team. The core issue to be determined here is whether BOA may pursue that policy on its own or whether that policy must be pursued, if it all, through the world-harmonised WADA Code.

The Panel's reasoning is explicit in terms of the BOA's acceptance of the WADA Code, as the BOA is one of its signatories. The Panel states at Paragraph 8.12 of its Award that the BOA has agreed to limit its autonomy by signing the Code and, therefore, accepting its terms. The

Panel makes the important point that the purpose of WADA's existence is to harmonise different anti-doping rules and sanctions throughout the world.[32] If the BOA was allowed to operate independently and separately from WADA, in terms of sanctions, such harmonisation (and the fight against doping) would assume the risk of being seriously undermined.

The Panel came to the conclusion that the effect of the Bye-Law is to make an athlete 'ineligible' for participation in the Olympics.[33] It is submitted that such interpretation is correct and confirms the argument that the two issues in relation to the application of the BOA's Bye-Law concern the 'eligibility' and 'participation' of athletes in sporting competitions. The Panel, similarly, had no difficulty in finding that the BOA's Bye-Law "renders an athlete ineligible to compete – a sanction like those provided for under the WADA Code" (8.26 and 8.33 of the Award). Accordingly, the Panel concluded that the BOA's Bye-Law has the effect of a disciplinary sanction and it is, therefore, incompatible with the WADA Code.

The discussion serves to illustrate the importance of the CAS as a supreme arbiter of sporting disputes, particularly when reference is made to issues that relate to the Olympic Games that require a speedy resolution. Similarly, an argument must be made for the same process to apply before and during the Paralympic Games. At the moment the CAS does not operate such Ad Hoc division for the Paralympic Games and it may be safe to conclude that this is because the International Paralympic Committee (the IPC) has not asked for one to be created. The IPC may have a good and valid reason for not requesting the introduction of such an important process, but equally one must not dismiss at face value the fact that Paralympic athletes are also elite-level athletes and, on many occasions, they have to compete against adversity (in addition to competing with one another). There may be a compelling justification for the introduction of a similar process before the CAS, for the same reasons already analysed.

Finally, it is respectfully submitted that the arguments may create a more compelling case for the introduction of a system of judicial precedent before the CAS, particularly where the Olympic Games are concerned, along with issues of selection of athletes, participation, classification and so on. It is imperative for stakeholders to communicate effectively with one another and discuss extensively the benefits of such system. A system of judicial precedent would be important during the Olympic and Paralympic Games, because it would offer certainty and consistency and it would contribute further to an even speedier process. This, consequently, would safeguard the rights of individual athletes and it would restore confidence in the judicial function of the CAS.

Conclusion

The analysis in the present work suggests two things: first, the CAS does not consider its decisions to be binding and secondly, the CAS is reluctant to depart from its previous decisions, for reasons of consistency and legal certainty. This, in essence, creates some form of precedent, albeit not binding in the common law meaning. The reader of this work will probably arrive at the same conclusion, which indicates a syndesis between common law and civil law and, at the same time, demonstrates the unique nature of the operation of the CAS. There is a lot to be said from this marriage of common law and civil law traditions and a lot more to be gained.

That said, there is a minority of CAS Panels having declared that the CAS does not consider its previous decisions binding and that there is no operation of the doctrine of *stare decisis*. The present analysis, however, indicates exactly the opposite. Where the facts warrant so (and this is true in the majority of anti-doping litigation), the CAS Panels are reluctant to depart from previous decisions for reasons of consistency and legal certainty. In essence, the CAS operates like another UK Supreme Court, where the judges are not bound by their own previous decisions, but they are vehemently discouraged from departing from them without a compelling justification.

Opponents of the doctrine of binding precedent may argue that this constant reliance on previous decisions and the unparalleled desire for uniformity may lead to oppression and that a bad decision may bind lower courts for years. This may be true in certain situations, but in the author's opinion, such argument cannot dissuade the use of binding precedent, as the CAS is the Supreme Court in sport and, in practice, its decisions are respected and followed worldwide. Its decisions may not be binding over national courts, but they very much form and determine the structure and synthesis of the regulatory framework and overall self-regulation in modern sport.

Despite some of the criticisms of the doctrine of binding precedent, with regards to how oppressive uniformity could be, the author submits that without a system of binding precedent, confusion and uncertainty usually prevail. This is particularly true in anti-doping litigation, where clarity and consistency in the decision making is important and imperative.

It is submitted that the doctrine of binding precedent promotes convenience and predictability. It also promotes consistency and clarity of legal thought. The law moves and develops through judicial decision making and it is evident that judicial precedent is not static, as it promotes flexibility. Above all, it is clear that precedent is a source of law and as such, a compelling justification exists for the CAS to adopt it.

Finally, it has been suggested in this work that there is a fine balance between case law and statute and that this relationship has been unjustifiably unexplored. The time is right for the CAS to adopt a specific method of statutory interpretation, with aids that would stem from the analysis and interpretation of case law. This is true in a situation where statutes and regulations of sporting governing bodies are unclear and confusing. The CAS is not a stranger to rules of sporting governing bodies who cause friction in the relationship between athletes and the governing bodies themselves. It is true that sometimes the rules of sporting governing bodies resemble the architecture of an ancient building.[34] Several parts are missing and several other parts need to be put in the right place so the operation of the building is workable. The same can be said for many of the statutes and regulations of sporting bodies. The CAS judges, therefore, need a clear framework and aids of statutory interpretation, which will assist them during the examination and analysis of case law.

It is this unexplored relationship between case law and statute that needs to be at the forefront of any judicial development before the CAS. As it was suggested at the beginning of this work, the influence of common law to the procedure and practice before the CAS is great and it cannot be dismissed at face value. The analysis in this work suggests that there is a fine relationship and a workable marriage between common law and civil law traditions in the administration and application of justice before the CAS. The author respectfully submits that this is a marriage between equal partners. One needs the other to survive and one cannot function without the other.

In conclusion, it is submitted that the CAS is a necessary mechanism for the resolution of sporting disputes and its operation is important for the development of sports law as a dynamic and separate legal discipline. The CAS procedure and practice, however, can be improved, particularly with an acknowledgement that a system of precedent operates before the CAS and that previous decisions must be binding on sporting governing bodies and their legislative organs. This is true in the case of WADA and the IAAF, where they both tend not only to recognise the judicial superiority of the CAS, but to follow, indiscriminately, its decisions.

In the author's view, therefore, the silent operation of the doctrine of binding precedent confirms to a great extent the remarkable and considerable influence of common law traditions on the procedure and practice before the CAS. Such influence has crawled into the operation of judicial decision making slowly but steadily and has determined, without stretching the boundaries of judicial creativity, the future not only of self-regulation, but also shaped the development of the discipline of sports law as a unique, autonomous and specialised body of law.

Notes

1 A different version of this work, with more emphasis on the system of judicial precedent, is published by the author in the 'Year Book of International Sports Arbitration 2015', Duval & Rigozzi eds, 'The Influence of Common Law Traditions on the Practice and Procedure Before the Court of Arbitration for Sport (CAS).'

2 Practice Direction [1966] 3 All ER 77. See also Duxbury, N. (2008). *The nature and authority of precedent.* Cambridge: Cambridge University Press, pp. 125–149.

3 Some commentators submit the necessity of judicial creativity in stronger terms:

> it is an abdication of judicial responsibility for judges, at least in the law of obligations, to decline to develop the common law on the grounds that legislation is more appropriate. Even if a statutory solution would be better, no-one can predict whether legislation will, or will not, be passed. It is therefore preferable for judges to proceed as they think fit, whether the decision be in favour or against a development, knowing that the Legislature is free to impose a statutory solution if the common law position is thought unsatisfactory or incomplete.

Professor Burrows. (2012). The nature and authority of precedent. *Law Quarterly Review*, 128, pp. 232, 258. Duxbury, N. (2008). *The nature and authority of precedent.* Cambridge: Cambridge University Press, p. 11.

4 Lord Justice Laws, 2012, Our lady of the common law, in: *ICLR lecture*, Mar. 1, p. 3.

5 Pursuant to the CAS Rule 57, which grants CAS Panels the authority to produce a full review of the facts and the law. See also the case of *CAS 2009/A/1880–1881*, where the Panel stated as follows:

> the CAS appeals arbitration allows a full de novo hearing of a case, with all due process guarantees, which can cure any procedural defects or violations of the right to be heard occurred during a federation's (or other sports body's) internal procedure. . . . [I]t is the duty of a CAS panel in an appeals arbitration procedure to make its independent determination of whether the Appellant's and Respondent's contentions are correct on the merits, not limiting itself to assessing the correctness of the previous procedure and decision.
>
> *(paras. 142, 146)*

6 For further discussion see *Canadian Olympic Committee & Beckie Scott v International Olympic Committee CAS 2002/O/373.*

7 *Arbitral Precedent: Dream, Necessity or Excuse?* 23 ARB. International 357, 366 (2007), Gabrielle Kaufmann-Kohler.

8 *Sport, Mediation & Arbitration*, 155 (2009), Ian Blackshaw. Similarly, *Sports Law: Implications for the Development of International, Comparative and National Law and Global Dispute Resolution*, 85 Tul. L. Rev. 269, 29 (2010).

9 *Arbitration CAS 2008/A/1545 Andrea Anderson, LaTasha Colander Clark, Jearl Miles-Clark, Torri Edwards, Chryste Gaines, Monique Hennagan, Passion Richardson v International Olympic Committee (IOC)*, Award of 16 July 2010.

10 At paragraph 40.

11 At paragraph 73.

12 At paragraph 55.

13 Supra 9.

14 *Redfern and Hunter on International Arbitration*, Blackaby et al., 2009.

15 The common law civil standard of proof, obviously, is determined on the balance of probabilities. In *Miller v Minister of Pensions [1947]* Lord Denning explained:

> It must carry a reasonable degree of probability, but not so high as is required in a criminal case. If the evidence is such that the tribunal can say: "we think it more probable than not", the burden of proof is discharged, but if the probabilities are equal it is not.

This suggests that the civil standard of proof requires the party with the burden to prove that the defendant's actions were 'more likely than not.' It has been suggested by Lord Hoffman in the case of *Secretary of State for the Home Department v Rehman [2001]* that the only higher degree of probability required by the law is the criminal standard. This means that the civil standard cannot be broken down into different categories with the aim of producing immediate standards.

16 See the case of *CAS 2010/A/2229*. This standard was first used in sport in the case of *Korneev and Gouliev v IOC, CAS 003–4L (Atlanta)*. Its true origin in the law can be identified in the Australian case of *Briginshaw v Briginshaw [1938] 60 CLR 336*.

17 *CAS 2009/A/1805, CAS 2009/A/1847*.

18 See *D'Arcy v Australian Olympic Committee CAS 2008/A/1574*.

19 See *IAAF v SEGAS, Kenteris & Thanou CAS 2005/A/887* (unreported).

20 *Miller v Cawley [2002] EWCA Civ 1100, The Times 6 September 2002*.

21 See the specific section on CAS and Olympics and Paralympics.

22 This is true where the conduct of the Hearing is concerned. Both the Olympic Chapter (Art. 15.b and d) and the CAS Code (Art. 44.1–44.3) offer to Panels a wide range of powers, particularly on the examination of witnesses and the ordering of evidential proceedings.

23 *IRB v Keyter CAS 2006/A/1067*. It was stated by the Panel: "that the occurrence of a specified circumstance is more probable than its non-occurrence." The athlete may also have the opportunity to demonstrate departures from the International Standards for Testing.

24 At paragraph 57. See also *USADA v Montgomery CAS 2004/O/645, Hamilton v USADA & UCI CAS 2005/A/884, IAAF v SEGAS, Kenteris & Thanou CAS 2005/A/887* (unreported).

25 This much is also supported by the new version of the WADA Code 2015.

26 The common law civil standard of proof, for example, has some flexibility in its application. Such flexibility may be interpreted according to the seriousness of the allegation and suggests that if such allegation exists, then the degree of probability needs to be raised. Although this position has now been rejected, it is submitted that it walks in tandem with the current standard of proof before the CAS. This is true in anti-doping litigation as the WADA Code clearly explains that any anti-doping organisation must establish the alleged anti-doping violation "to the comfortable satisfaction of the hearing body bearing in mind the seriousness of the allegation which is made." This, in essence, means that the more serious the allegation the higher the degree of satisfaction and, consequently, the standard of proof. Further, the earlier submission is well enshrined not only in the CAS jurisprudence but in English and wider common law too, making the argument that the CAS procedure and practice resemble common law, even stronger. For example, the origin of the 'comfortable satisfaction' standard is identified in the Australian case of *Briginshaw v Briginshaw [1938]* where Justice Rich stated:

> In a serious matter like a charge of adultery the satisfaction of a just and prudent mind cannot be produced by slender and exiguous proofs of circumstances pointing with a wavering figure to an affirmative conclusion. The nature of the allegation requires as a matter of common sense and worldly wisdom the careful weighing of testimony, the close examination of facts proved as a basis of inference and a comfortable satisfaction that the tribunal has reached both a correct and just conclusion.

In the English case of *Hornal v Neuberger Products Ltd [1957] 1 QB 247* it was stated:

> The standard of proof depends on the nature of the issue. The more serious the allegation the higher the degree of probability that is required; but it need not, in a civil case, reach the very high standard required by the criminal law.

Similarly, in the CAS Award of *USADA v Montgomery CAS 2004/O/645* it was stated: "the more serious the allegation the less likely it is that the alleged event occurred and, hence, the stronger the evidence required before the occurrence of the event is demonstrated to be more probable than not."

27 This is an important development for the discipline of sports law and in relation to procedure, as CAS has established an Ad Hoc division that sits in the city responsible for organising the Olympic Games. According to Article 1 of the Arbitration Rules applicable to the CAS Ad Hoc division for the Olympic Games:

> The purpose of the present Rules is to provide, in the interests of the athletes and of sport, for the resolution by arbitration of any disputes covered by Rule 61 of the Olympic Charter, insofar as they arise during the Olympic Games or during a period of ten days preceding the Opening Ceremony of the Olympic Games.

Similarly, Article 2 declares:

> For the period fixed in Article 1, the ICAS shall establish an ad hoc Division of the CAS (hereinafter the "ad hoc Division"), the function of which is to provide for the resolution by arbitration of the disputes covered by Article 1 by means of Panels set up in accordance with the present Rules.

28 *CAS 2018/A/5816 Susan Cooke v World Chess Federation (FIDE) and Welsh Chess Union* (unreported).

29 *IAAF v SEGAS, Kenteris & Thanou CAS 2005/A/887* (unreported). Adding insult to injury, the IOC refuses, to the present date, to upgrade Miss Thanou to the first place in the 100m event at the Sydney Olympics in 2000, following the conviction of Marion Jones, and award the gold medal to Miss Thanou. The reader must note that the IAAF has already upgraded Miss Thanou to the first place for that event.

30 A copy of the reasoned decision may be accessed here: www.wada-ama.org/sites/default/files/resources/files/cas-2011-a-2658-boa.pdf. For further discussion see Ioannidis (2012), G. BOA v WADA: Harmonisation v self-regulation, *Denning Law Journal*, 24, pp. 169–176.

31 Paragraph 8.1 of the Award.

32 The Panel states at Para. 8.12:

> However, NOC's like BOA have agreed to limit their autonomy by accepting the WADA Code. In particular, Article 23.2.2 WADA Code, requires that its Signatories, including NOC's do not make any additional provisions in their rules which would change the substantive effect to any enumerated provisions of the WADA Code, including its sanctions for doping. The purpose of Article 23.2.2 WADA Code is indeed the very purpose of the WADA Code: the harmonisation throughout the world of a doping code for the use in the fight against doping. This worldwide harmony is crucial to the success of the fight against doping. The WADA Code is intended to be an all-encompassing code that directs affected organisations and athletes. The WADA Code ensures that, in principle, any athlete in any sport will not be exposed to a lesser or greater sanction than any other athlete; rather, they will be sanctioned equally. By requiring consistency in treatment of athletes who are charged with doping infractions or convicted of it – regardless of the athlete's nationality or sport – fairness and proper enforcement are achieved. Any disharmony between different parties undermines the success of the fight against doping. For these good reasons, NOCs and other Signatories agreed to limit their autonomy to act within their own spheres with respect to activities covered by the WADA Code.

33 Paragraphs 8.24–8.26 of the Award. In particular, the Panel states at Para. 8.24: "disbarment from the Team for life carries with it the direct consequence of never being able to participate in the Olympics and as a consequence to compete in the Games. That is the underlying reality of ineligibility."

34 Michael Beloff QC suggests.

> In my experience, rules of domestic or international federations tend to resemble the architecture of an ancient building: a wing added here, a loft there, a buttress elsewhere, without adequate consideration of whether the additional parts affect adversely the symmetry of the whole.

(2000). Drugs, laws and Verspapaks. *Drugs and Doping in Sport: Socio-Legal Perspectives*. Cavendish, p. 42.

References

Blackaby, N., Partasides, C., Redfern, A. and Hunter, M. (2009). *Redfern and Hunter on International Arbitration* (5th edition). Oxford, UK: Oxford University Press.

Davies, C. (2012). The 'comfortable satisfaction' standard of proof: Applied by the court of arbitration for sport in drug-related cases. *University of Notre Dame Australia Law Review*, 14.

Lord Justice Laws. (2012). Our lady of the common law. In: *International conference on learning representations*, Mar. 1.

3

Disability, classification and the Paralympics

Inclusion and exclusion of elite athletes with disabilities

Jan Burns

Introduction to disability and classification

Inclusion in the Paralympic Games must satisfy three important questions. First, that the athlete has one of the ten impairments recognised by the International Paralympic Committee (IPC); this is called primary eligibility. Second, that the eligible impairment meets the 'minimum disability criteria' of the sport, i.e. that the impairment is sufficient to affect the performance of that specific sport. The third question relates to which class to place the athlete in, such that athletes of a similar activity limitation are grouped together to ensure that they can compete equally (IPC, 2015). The ten impairment groups the IPC recognises are adopted from the World Health Organisation (WHO) International Classification of Functioning, Disability and Health (ICF-WHO, 2001).

The minimum disability criterion is there to ensure that the impairment does have an impact on performance in that sport, and therefore is called 'sport specific'. For example, having some visual acuity problems will not impact on sprinting 100m as much as it would on playing table tennis, hence an athlete may not be eligible for IPC sanctioned 100m events, but would eligible for IPC table tennis competitions.

Classifying athletes into the correct class so that athletes competing together are of a similar limitation and are winning due to training, skill and ability, not due to a lesser impairment, is a complex process. Classification systems have been developed for each IPC recognised sport and are based on a functional not diagnostic approach (Tweedy and Vanlandewijck, 2011). These classification systems are 'owned' by the International Federation (IF) which governs that sport and are required to be based on scientific evidence. However, not all sports have classes for all impairment groups. The number of classes for each impairment group will also differ between national and international competition, with the highest number of classes occurring at international world events and the Paralympic Games. Classes are given a label which depicts which sport, e.g. in athletics it is usually 'T' for track or 'F' for field, and a number which denotes the impairment group and level of impairment. For example, Equestrian includes all impairment types except intellectual impairments, and classifies them into five classes, integrating physical and visual impairments. A higher number usually denotes less impairment.

Despite the governance, codes of conduct and evidence-based requirements, classification remains a highly questioned area, with people's futures, medals, funding, employment and income all being contingent on getting it right and ensuring competition is about fair play and not unfair advantage. There have been, and continues to be, numerous challenges based on conceptual inconsistencies, credibility and robustness of the classification system, negative impact of good training, allegations of cheating, misrepresentation and unfair treatment.

Tweedy, one of the originators of the current model of IPC classification, started from the position of acknowledging the need for a taxonomy which addressed some of the practical problems of a system which needs to transect nations, disability groups, medical and social models of disability, but is robust enough to be accepted globally and be future proof enough to not require constant change (Tweedy, 2002). The ICF-WHO (2001) taxonomy fits this profile and has the added benefit of being 'functional' not 'medical diagnosis' based and was already well established. It was hoped that using this approach would bring a universality to sports classification and ensure that all sports adhere to a consistent framework and terminology. Whilst the use of the ICF as a framework to build sport classification around has been an excellent choice, it has perhaps been underused and the full potential is yet to be realised.

Multiple impairments and classification

One area of tension managed within ICF but not yet adequately dealt with in sports classifications is that of multiple morbidity. Athletes are classified on their primary impairment and if they have more than one they must choose which impairment group to compete within. For example, if an athlete has visual limitations in addition to cerebral palsy, they must choose which to be classified under and no account will be taken of their other impairment even though it may clearly impact upon their performance. For some, where co-morbidity is common, having to be categorised under only one primary impairment group results in an unrepresentative sub-group of athletes rising to the top of elite performance. A clear example of this occurs in the intellectual impairment group, where the most recent and comprehensive survey on the topic suggests that on average a person will have 11 additional health conditions, and 99% of the population will have multiple morbidities (Kinnear et al., 2018). This results in athletes with Down Syndrome very rarely, if ever, being able to compete at an international level in II sport, as alongside their intellectual disability caused by the genetic phenotype, comes physical issues such as short stature, low muscle tone, cardiac problems, etc. which directly impact on sporting performance (Burns, 2018). The athletes that tend to rise to the elite international level for II sport are the minority of those without such common co-morbidity, resulting in an unfair playing field for athletes with the more common multi-disability profile, who are more representative of their population. This has resulted in separate sporting organisations for athletes with Down Syndrome and allegations of discrimination against the IPC. As a way of managing this issue, the International Federation for Para-athletes with Intellectual Impairment (INAS)[1] has developed additional classes for those with more significant overall functional impairments and are developing a classification approach which adheres to a holistic approach to overall functioning (Gilderthorp, Burns and Jones, 2018).

Developing a robust classification system

To be eligible the impairment must be permanent; however performance in the sport might change, for example, due to a change in the impairment, improvement through treatment or rehabilitation innovations, or increased and/or more effective training. In the former two cases, a change in class could be considered reasonable; however for the latter this would be unreasonable. It would be unfair to place an athlete who has improved their performance through training, with no alteration in their original impairment, in a class with those who are less impaired. Therefore, it is imperative that the classification system should not be influenced by training and tightly tied to assessing activity limitation not training (Beckman and Tweedy, 2009).

Developing a classification system that addresses training concerns as well as being built on a conceptually sound framework, and involving robust assessment methods, is a major challenge, requiring funding, research and the collaboration between athletes, IFs and event organisers (Tweedy, Beckman and Connick, 2014). It also requires a potentially unachievable compromise between the inclusivity drive to increase parity in impairment groups and classes, and the pressures of 'selling the product' requiring shorter, faster and more media-appealing events which fuel the economic engine of the Paralympic movement (Howe and Jones, 2006).

The importance and the personal impact of disputes over classification has been well evidenced in the protests raised by some UK athletes and their families which resulted in a Select Committee Inquiry formed by the British Parliamentary Digital, Culture, Media and Sport Committee to examine athlete classification in the context of sport governance (DCMS, 2017). Specific allegations were made about misrepresentation by athletes to manipulate their classification to gain advantage. Within these allegations the UK Sports Federations, the British Paralympic Association and the IPC were accused of poor governance. A robust defence was put up by all parties including the IPC which responded that both the IPC and the Paralympic movement as a whole had to note 'key learning points and action' (IPC, 2017, para. 1.1) and that:

> In our view the Paralympic classification system is fit for purpose. We do, however, acknowledge that improvements have, can and will be made by the IPC to continually make the system more robust for all athletes.
>
> *(para 1.2)*

Following the inquiry Sport England and UK Sport published 'A Code for Sports Governance' (2018) and the British Paralympic Association reviewed its UK classification code. Simultaneously, the Board of United Kingdom Athletics (UKA) initiated a review of classification for UK Para-athletes chaired by the retired Paralympian Ms Anne Wafula-Strike. The conclusion was that:

> There was wide consensus that the current UKA national classification system could be abused, should an athlete or support personnel be sufficiently motivated, have an understanding of the classification process and have an impairment that lends itself to exaggeration. This issue is not exclusive to athletics but reflected across Paralympic sport. Para Athletics is a relatively 'young' sport where records are being broken frequently, sometimes by large margins. This makes it difficult to detect abuse based on performance data only. In addition, classification itself is a developing discipline. There is an ongoing need for vigilance and a regular review, check and challenge of all classification processes to ensure it continues to keep pace with the development of Paralympic sport and to mitigate the risk of exploitation.
>
> *(UKA, 2017, p. 4)*

However, whilst acknowledging that the system could be exploited, the review also concluded "there was no substantive evidence to suggest that this is the case" (p. 4) and set out 16 recommendations to prevent abuse of the system. Interestingly the report went on to benchmark the state of UKA classification against that of World Para Athletics (WPA) and concluded that "the UKA system is robust and mirrors WPA's protocols for classification. Indeed, it was cited as one that is an exemplar of best practise, and one of – if not the – best in the world" (p. 7). Given the acknowledgement of a system open to abuse but the denial of this occurring and it being held up as a gold standard, some would argue that perhaps the governance bar should be raised and the reliance on the spirit of 'fair play' lowered.

Internationally, prior to the Rio Games the IPC initiated a review of 80 individual cases, from 24 countries over a 12-month period. Xavier Gonzalez, the IPC's Chief Executive Officer concluded that:

> The review of the 80 plus cases revealed no instances where the IPC could reasonably allege intentional misrepresentation. In many cases, the information brought forward amounted to nothing more than allegations without substantive grounds.

However, he went on to recognise that some remedial actions were required and that IFs needed to invest in research, classifier training and potentially a revision of some classification systems (IPC, 2016).

Events and reviews such as these serve to demonstrate that classification is still somewhat reliant on the Paralympic sporting spirit, strengthened by research, education and good governance. It is interesting to note that many of the initial classification systems were not based on published, peer-reviewed research, but were an amalgam of experience, medical assessment and existing practice. Ironically, it was the research which went into the development of the II classification system, occurring before the re-inclusion of athletes with intellectual disabilities, which set a higher standard in terms of evidence-based classification. The importance of evidence-based classification has been given further emphasis by the integration into the IPC Athlete Classification Code the mandate to International Sports Federations that they must develop systems based on multidisciplinary scientific research and that athletes must be solicited to assist in the development and improvement of such systems (Section 10.2.1, IPC, 2015).

All of these endeavours together with a burgeoning interest in classification research is leading to stronger classification systems and in the majority of cases provides a showcase of sophisticated research applied to real-life problems, resulting in advanced conceptual understanding and technical solutions. Connick, Beckman and Tweedy (2018) provide an excellent chronological narrative about how this research has evolved and a route map to further research. They point out that classification systems which are invalid, or indeed are seen to be invalid, pose a significant threat to the Paralympic movement and that those involved have a duty to ensure that such systems are based on the best available scientific evidence.

Elite sport for all

Who is, and who is not, included in the Paralympic movement is governed by the classification system described earlier. However, the impairment groups currently included have evolved over time and the current accepted categories are not there by design but through historical events and by no means cover the vast range of impairment groups represented in the disability movement. For example, those with neurological impairments such as dyspraxia, mental health issues and autism are not included. The functional approach to classification (as opposed to a disease or medically based classification) typified by the ICF allows a wider inclusion of causes of impairment under an umbrella of limited functional levels, but the IPC stratification into three impairment groups (physical, visual and intellectual) ignores those who fall outside these groups and also the intersectionality between them.

Autism is a particularly good example of this issue. It is estimated that about 2% of the population of eight-year-olds in the US have autism and this prevalence is increasing (Baio et al., 2018). This is a far greater impairment population than the visually impaired, which compared to a wider age range of 5–17 year olds in the US the prevalence is estimated to be 0.8 (Institute on Disability, 2016). Or if we compare this prevalence to those with achondroplasia, estimated to be less than 0.006% in the US (Waller et al., 2008). Approximately 50–60% of autistic children will also have intellectual disabilities (Baio et al., 2018) so may compete, and many do, under the intellectual impairment group. However, what about the 40–50% who do not qualify in this way? It could be argued that they could compete in the Olympics and again some athletes will. However, there is enough evidence that the cognitive impact of autism can be severe and disabling, resulting in exclusion and the inability to compete on a fair playing field with those without this disability (Duquette et al., 2016). In addition, the classification of having an intellectual disability, or not, is not so clear cut, as many people whilst meeting the criteria in terms of having significant impairments in adaptive behaviour do not meet the INAS accepted IQ criterion of 75 or below. However, we know from both research and the reported experiences of people with autism that competing in mainstream sports can be very difficult and adaptations sometimes need to be made (Webster, 2016). Research evidence is also increasing so that from a very early developmental age differences in gait and fine motor control can be detected, which may become exaggerated in later life (Rinehart and Jest, 2016). Hence, the combination of cognitive and physical differences leads to a consistent range of characteristics termed autism and a significant impairment group currently not catered for within the Paralympics.

Protests about this occur usually from an athlete or family members, but until INAS expanded its remit to include all athletes with autism (those with and without intellectual disabilities) in 2016 there has been no international sports federation attempting to cater for these athletes' needs. The scheduling of the Summer Paralympics is currently saturated, and the competition schedule for qualifying events dense, with pressures to include more sports, wider classes, more events, all of which have economic costs attached. It is not envisaged, given the economic and logistic concerns of the IPC, that they will be looking to expand their inclusion criteria, and such developments remain outside the Paralympics and devolved from its economic and profile advantages.

Another disability group which is absent from the Paralympics, and for very different reasons merits discussion, is Deaf athletes. Nowhere are the issues of the social construction of disability, identity and inclusion/exclusion as clearly played out as in relation to the participation of Deaf athletes. This starts with the use of the words 'Deaf' or 'deaf' (Foster, Fitzgerald and Stride, 2018). Ammons and Eickman (2011) define this distinction:

> 'Deaf' with a capital D is used to signify deaf people who are primarily sign language users, members of the Deaf community, and share Deaf culture and common experiences. By the same token, the authors and others use 'deaf' to indicate the general population of deaf people (people who have hearing loss). This distinction between a sociocultural understanding of Deaf people and a medicalized understanding of the condition of deafness is crucial for any analysis of what it means to be Deaf.
>
> *(p. 1149)*

Central to this distinction is identity, culture and communication which has led to the Deaf community wishing to establish, and maintain, a sporting independence from both the IOC and the IPC and found their own Deaflympics. The application of the category 'disability sport' is contested by the Deaf sporting community, who do not see themselves as having a disability, but being stigmatised and marginalised through a largely invisible difference. This places them in an interesting position between the IOC and the IPC and has led to complex and at times troubled relationships between the International Committee of Sports for the Deaf (ICSD), which governs elite Deaf sport, and the IOC and IPC.

Jerald Jordan (a previous ICSD president) described the position well:

> The Deaf athlete views the disabled athlete as being a hearing person first and disabled second. . . . If Deaf athletes were to compete in the Paralympic Games, then numerous sign language interpreters would be necessary to bridge this communication barrier, otherwise the Deaf athletes would be completely separated from all disabled athletes. The very purpose of the Games – to bring athletes together – would be lost. . . . As a group Deaf people do not fit into either the able-bodied or disabled categories. . . . Our limits are not physical; rather, they are outside of us, in the social realm of communication. Among hearing people, whether able-bodied or disabled, we are almost always excluded, invisible and unserved. Among ourselves however, we have no limits.
>
> *(Jordan, 1996)*

The first Deaflympics was established in 1924 in Paris and has carried on every four years since then, with a break for World War II. It was the second largest international games to be founded after the Olympics and before the Paralympics. The Deaflympics now include 27 different sports and hold the games every four years, usually attracting over 3,000 athletes from over 70 nations. As well as the most common Olympic sports, interestingly the Deaflympics also includes chess. The IOC granted official recognition of the use of name Deaflympics in 2001. A major principle behind the games is that they are entirely organised by the ISDC of whom all the committee members are Deaf. The ISDC holds the same ideals and principles of Olympism and the Deaflympics explicitly sets out to promote these values.

Debates have continued about assimilation into either the Olympics or the Paralympics. In terms of the Olympics, as well as the mutual recognition of events, Deaf athletes commonly compete in both. However, personal accounts depict the 'specialness' of competing in the Deaflympics and Deaf world championships in terms of the rich experience of being able to fully communicate, the universality of sign language and the sense of 'family' and 'belonging' (Ammons and Eickman, 2011; Foster, 2018). In terms of the Paralympics, there is the major obstacle of positioning Deaf sport as part of the community of 'disability sports'. Inclusion also contradicts the classification code as the impairment usually has little impact upon performance, other than in some sports to make technical adjustments to make auditory cues visual, e.g. the starting gun includes a starting light. Indeed, some have pointed to the advantages hearing loss can bring to sport in terms of heightened senses in other modalities, termed 'Deaf gain' (Foster, 2018). To include Deaf athletes in the Paralympic programme, as constrained as it is, would result in a decrease of athlete participation from other impairment groups and to compensate for this a possible reduction in the range of sports included. Such dynamics work against existing para-athletes lobbying for greater inclusion by expanding impairment groups. The cost of sign language interpreters would also be prohibitive and the ISCD is critical of the IOC in terms of the representativeness of impairments within the IOC executive committee. Hence, whilst the Paralympics may have attractions in terms of sponsorship, profile and national funding, the disadvantages are numerous and significant.

A compromise was reached with the IPC and ISCD signing a Memorandum of Understanding in 2004 to agree to collaboration and reach a mutual understanding and promotion of each organisation's roles, responsibilities and ambitions. However, the debate continues to rage and requests for continued and closer dialogue between the ISCD and the IPC endure (Harrison, 2014; Palmer, 2013).

To be distinct, inclusive or integrated

Further debate has raged over whether the Paralympics should be integrated or merged with the Olympics or the order reversed such that the Paralympics would come before the Olympics. The reasons for these suggestions range from the ideological to the practical, with the ideological spanning the continuum from inclusionist to separatist positions, but the majority of the practical issues falling at the separatist position. To unpack this debate, we first have to consider what is meant by the terms inclusion and integration.

A full inclusive position would be to have events for athletes with disabilities fully embedded in the schedule for non-disabled athletes. This is the case with the Commonwealth Games where an agreement was signed between the IPC and the Commonwealth Games Federation (CGF) in 2007 to build on previous exhibition events and the later integration of para-athletes into national teams in the 2002 Manchester Games. The aims of the agreement are to promote the growth of sporting opportunities for Paralympic athletes and to position the IPC as overseeing this co-ordination. In terms of full inclusion for the Commonwealth Games this means no separate tickets or events for para-sports and all medals contributing to the national tally. However, not all sports are included and at a minimum the programme must include Aquatics, Athletics, Lawn Bowls and Powerlifting. Successive games are stretching these boundaries and the 2018 Gold Coast Games included seven para-sports (adding track cycling, table tennis and triathlon) with an increase of 45% more para-athletes and 73% more medals in para-events compared to Glasgow in 2014 (CGF, 2018).

The current situation with the Olympic and Paralympic Games is more that of integration, with a growing closeness, integration in some aspects but maintaining a clear distinction in the delivery of the Games. Misener and Molloy (2018) provide a detailed analysis of this relationship, plotting the collaboration from bid to delivery. Before 2000, the Games were hosted separately with distinct organising committees (OCs), but in 2000 a contract was signed between the IOC and the IPC agreeing that the Paralympics may take place after the Olympics, in the same city, using the same facilities and venues. Also it was agreed that the IPC president be a co-opted member of the IOC and that a funding stream should be established from the IOC to IPC. This contract has been further expanded over the years and the revenue to the IPC significantly increased. A Memorandum of Understanding (MOU) is now in place extending this agreement until 2032 (IOC 2016). As Misener and Molloy (2018) point out, this effectively integrates the bidding, planning and organisation of the Games, but that there remains a commitment to the Games retaining 'distinct identities' and that the IOC and IPC maintain sole responsibility for each event. Whilst this is enshrined in the contract and the Paralympic Handbook, Misener and Molloy (2018) highlight the use of the word 'may' in reference to the current arrangement, suggesting a 'get out clause' should the context shift, as it very nearly did with Rio 2016. They conclude that whilst the OCs are working towards a more integrated model of delivery there is still much work to be done in terms of the balance of focus between the Games and question if currently the Olympics are gaining more than the Paralympics, and indeed if the Paralympics would ultimately suffer from further integration.

David Legg has also contributed much to this debate and has charted the delicate history of the evolving Paralympic movement and IPC in parallel to the established Olympic movement and IOC (Legg, 2018; Legg et al., 2014). He also tackles the contentious issue of disabled athletes competing in the Olympic Games, which, whilst it only so far includes a small number of athletes, does raise questions about the distinctiveness of the two movements. In response to these complex questions, Legg points to a concern that the participation of disabled athletes within the Olympics would devalue the Paralympic Games. He suggests such inclusion would 'denude the Paralympics of some of their most prestigious events', and that the Paralympics would become a less prestigious event for those with more severe disabilities (Legg, 2018). It also might be argued that should this movement occur, those remaining in the Paralympics would just include those athletes for whom prosthetics cannot compensate for their impairment. The rise of the 'cyber athlete', augmented by advanced technology, suggests the IOC/IPC will increasingly be required to manage a situation where the performance of disabled athletes outstrips that of the non-disabled.

Whilst the inclusion of some disabled athletes within the Olympics might be beneficial for a small minority it may not be beneficial for the majority of para-athletes. As it stands now, this issue tends to be managed on a case-by-case basis, but when it does become an issue it is one which attracts wide media attention and raises these complex questions repeatedly. In his analysis Legg (2018) points to the statement made by Elizabeth Dendy, an athlete representative with cerebral palsy, who suggests we must be careful 'not to reinforce the message that the one percent of the elite disabled athletes, who were often the most visible, represented the entire sport movement' (Dendy, 1993, p. 359 cited by Legg, 2018, p. 161).

Where the debate now goes will be interesting, and as Legg points out, national and international laws and treaties such as the UN Convention on Human Rights for Persons with a Disability (UN, 2006) may have an influence on this direction. Contributing to this is the success of Paralympic media to provide a different representation of disability related to empowerment. This has raised questions amongst the general populous about why the Olympics and Paralympics are separate and is this a human rights and inclusion issue? Whilst not being privy to the much more granular and nuanced debates of the actual delivery of the Games, the general public does position this as a rights issue and are more likely to move to an inclusive perspective. One can see why the former IPC President Sir Phillip Craven, possibly as a way of avoiding the conflict, may have shifted his previously oppositional position to adopting the 'possibility' stance focussed on in the press prior to London in 2012.

> The Paralympics and Olympic Games could merge, says the president of the International Paralympic Committee (IPC). Sir Philip Craven said things are developing all the time and nothing is 'set in stone'.
>
> *(BBC, 2012)*

This statement provoked some backlash from athletes concerned about the diminution of the Paralympics and it is notable that no subsequent public statements have been made and the new IPC President Andrew Parsons remains publicly silent on the issue so far.

Whatever the ideological positions, the practical and logistical implications are extremely challenging. To allow complete integration the size of the whole event would increase dramatically. An athlete village which accommodated 11,000 athletes would now need to accommodate 15,000 athletes with a concomitant increase in officials, coaches and other support staff. The transport infrastructure, always a challenging aspect of event delivery, would need to manage a third more extra travellers. The event programme would potentially need to be expanded to five weeks, which could result in 'audience fatigue' and major conflicts about media coverage and timetabling, with those in the Paralympic movement arguing they would be the losers (Heilpern, 2016). In the highly competitive broadcasting space, would the Paralympians get as much coverage as they do now? These are just some of the issues and questions raised by a fully integrated Games, all of which serve to suggest no foreseeable change in the near future and this position has been largely supported by the Paralympic athletes themselves (e.g. Tanni Grey-Thompson, BBC, 2012).

One direction of change which is less often articulated is in the opposite direction, to make the Paralympics more separate. Legg (2018) points out the economic possibilities of this, suggesting that cities unable to accommodate both Games could bid for the Paralympics and gain from what he terms the economic advantages of 'Handicapitalism' (p. 167). This is premised on the belief that hosting the Paralympics without the Olympics would indeed be of economic benefit. Given the economic legacy of both Games which has had winners and losers in the past, this seems a risky strategy. The final permutation to be considered is whether to foreground the Paralympics before the Olympics. Whilst arguments could be presented about 'Disability First' as a way of increasing coverage and representation, the most compelling argument for remaining the same, presented by the IPC Head of Communications and echoed by other stakeholders, is that 'The Olympics is the best test event for the Paralympics' (Springer, 2016). The increasing media and audience impact of the Paralympics would also suggest that a good trajectory is set and so questions the sense of making such a substantial change (Legg and Dottori, 2017). More on the Paralympic governance and the relationship with the Olympics can be read later in the handbook (see for example the chapters by Simon Gérard, David Legg, Laura Misener and Landy Di Lu, P. David Howe).

Conclusion

The Paralympics have come a long way in its relatively short history. It has had a global impact on the representation of people with disability in sport and has forced change in those cities which have hosted the Games and other large Paralympic-sanctioned events. The legacy and generalisation of such gains are disputed and can be criticised for not being sustained or being impactful enough (Brittain, 2018). However, without the Paralympics it is hard to envisage the changes which have occurred happening. The very existence of the Paralympics serves a function at so many levels; from the life-changing experience it offers individuals to the unique natural research opportunities it provides us to understand the impact of impairment. With any large movement spanning ideological, scientific, economic, humanitarian and socio-political domains, it is going to attract controversy and challenge. Because of the very nature of these tensions, it provides an exceptional and unparalleled opportunity for the application of principles which will undoubtedly advance the position of people with disabilities. May the debates continue.

Note

1 INAS is the IPC recognised International Organisations of Sport for Disabled (IOSD) representing athletes with intellectual impairments.

References

Ammons, D. and Eickman, J. (2011). Deaflympics and the Paralympics: Eradicating misconceptions. *Sport in Society*, 14(9), pp. 1149–1164.

Baio, J., Wiggins, L., Christensen, D.L., et al. (2018). Prevalence of autism spectrum disorder among children aged 8 years – Autism and developmental disabilities monitoring network, 11 sites, United States, 2014. *MMWR Surveillance Summaries*, 67(SS-6), pp. 1–23.

BBC News. (2012, 23 May). Paralympics and Olympics merger 'possible after 2020'. *BBC News*. Available at: https://www.bbc.co.uk/news/uk-18174501 [Accessed 2 April 2020].

Beckman, E.M. and Tweedy, S. (2009). Towards evidence-based classification in Paralympic athletics: Evaluating the validity of activity limitation tests for use in classification of Paralympic running events. *British Journal of Sports Medicine*, 43, pp. 1067–1072.

Brittain, I. (2018). Legacy of mega sporting events for people with disabilities. In: I. Brittain, J. Bocarro, T. Byers and K. Swart, eds., *Legacies and mega events: Fact or fairy tales?* London: Routledge, pp. 999–1116.

Burns, J. (2018). Intellectual disability, special Olympics and parasport. In: I. Brittain and A. Beacom eds., *The Palgrave handbook of Paralympic studies*. London: Palgrave Macmillan, pp. 417–437.

CGF. (2018). *Para-Sport*. Commonwealth Games Federation. Available at: https://thecgf.com/our-relevance/para-sports [Accessed 20 Jan. 2019].

Connick, M., Beckman, E. and Tweedy, S. (2018). Evolution and development of best practice in Paralympic classification. In: I. Brittain and A. Beacom eds., *The Palgrave handbook of Paralympic studies*. London: Palgrave Macmillan, pp. 389–416.

DCMS. (2017). *Inquiry into sports governance*. London: DCMS.

Duquette, M.M., Carbonneau, H., Roult, R. and Crevier, L. (2016). Sport and physical activity: Facilitating interventions with young people living with an autism spectrum disorder. *Physical Activity Review*, 4, pp. 40–49.

Foster, R., Fitzgerald, H. and Stride, A. (2018). The socialization and participation of Deaflympians in sport. *Sport in Society*, 22(12), pp. 1904–1918.

Gilderthorp, R., Burns, J. and Jones, F. (2018). Classification and intellectual disabilities: An investigation of the factors that predict the performance of athletes with intellectual disability. *Journal of Clinical Sport Psychology*, 12, pp. 285–301. doi:10.1123/jcsp.2017-0018.

Harrison, S. (2014). *Same spirit – Different team: The politicisation of the deaflympics*. Leicester: Action Deafness.

Heilpern, W. (2016, 17 August). Why the Olympics and Paralympics are still separate events. *Business Insider*. Available at: https://amp.businessinsider.com/why-the-olympics-and-paralympics-are-separate-events-2016-8 [Accessed 2 April 2020].

Howe, P.D. and Jones, C. (2006). Classification of disabled athletes: (Dis)empowering the Paralympic practice community. *Sociology of Sport Journal*, 23(1), pp. 29–46.

Institute on Disability. (2016). *Disability statistics annual report*. Institute of Disability, University of New Hampshire.

IOC. (2016, 4 June). *IOC and IPC long-term agreement supporting the Paralympic movement*. Available at: https://www.olympic.org/news/ioc-and-ipc-sign-long-term-agreement-supporting-the-paralympic-movement [Accessed 2 April 2020].

IPC. (2015). *IPC athlete classification code rules, policies and procedures for athlete classification*. Bonn: International Paralympic Committee.

IPC. (2016). *Update on alleged cases of intentional misrepresentation*. Bonn: International Paralympic Committee.

IPC. (2017). *IPC response to DCMS Select Committee hearing comments and clarifications regarding the first hearing on Paralympic classification*. Bonn: International Paralympic Committee.

Jordan, J. (1996, 2 December). *The world games for the deaf and the Paralympic games*. Position Paper, International Committee of Sports for the Deaf. Available at: http://www.ciss.org/the-world-games-for-the-deaf-and-the-paralympic-games [Accessed 2 April 2020].

Kinnear, D., Morrison, J., Allan, L., Henderson, A., Smiley, E. and Cooper, S.A. (2018). Prevalence of physical conditions and multi-morbidity in a cohort of adults with intellectual disabilities, with and without Down syndrome. Cross-sectional study. *The British Medical Journal Open*, 8(2), p. e018292. doi:10.1136/bmjopen-2017-018292.

Legg, D. (2018). Development of the IPC relations with the IOC and other stakeholders. In: I. Brittain and A. Beacom, eds., *Palgrave handbook of Paralympic studies*. Basingstoke: Palgrave Macmillan.

Legg, D. and Dottori, M. (2017). Marketing and sponsorship at the Paralympic games. In: S. Darcy, S. Frawley and D. Adair, eds., *Managing the Paralympics*. London: Palgrave Macmillan.

Legg, D., Fay, T., Wolff, E. and Hums, M. (2014). The International Olympic Committee – International Paralympic Committee relationship: Past, present, and future. *Journal of Sport and Social Issues*, 39(5), pp. 371–395.

Misener, L. and Molloy, K. (2018). Organising and delivering the modern Paralympic games: Contemporary debates relating to integration and distinction. In: I. Brittain and A. Beacom, eds., *The Palgrave handbook of Paralympic studies*. London: Palgrave Macmillan.

Palmer, A. (2013, 22 August). *The question: Should the Paralympics include deaf sports?* The Limping Chicken [blog post]. Available at: https://limpingchicken.com/2013/08/22/the-question-should-the-paralympics-include-deaf-sports/ [Accessed 2 April 2020].

Rinehart, N. and Jest, S. (2016). Odd gait, clumsiness, and other abnormal motor signs: Clinical insights from the Australian autism spectrum disorder motor research program. *Child and Adolescent Psychiatry*, 55, p. 264.

Sport England and UK Sport. (2018). *A code for sports governance*. Sport England and UK Sport. Available at: https://www.uksport.gov.uk/resources/governance-code [Accessed 2 April 2020].

Springer, S. (2016, 6 September). Paralympics should be held before Olympics, not after. *The Boston Globe*. Available at: https://www.bostonglobe.com/sports/olympics2016/2016/09/06/paralympics-should-held-before-not-after-olympics/Xf40cAnGLNxQmziTLWu5qO/story.html [Accessed 2 April 2020].

Tweedy, S.M. (2002). Taxonomic theory and the ICF: Foundations for a unified disability athletics classification. *Adapted Physical Activity Quarterly*, 19(10), pp. 220–237.

Tweedy, S.M., Beckman, E.M. and Connick, M.J. (2014). Paralympic classification: Conceptual basis, current methods, and research update. *PM & R*, 6, pp. S11–S17.

Tweedy, S.M. and Vanlandewijck, Y.C. (2011). International Paralympic Committee position stand—Background and scientific principles of classification in Paralympic sport. *British Journal of Sports Medicine*, 45(4), pp. 259–269.

UKA. (2017). *A review for the Board of United Kingdom Athletics into the UKA classification of para-athletes*. Birmingham, UK: UKA.

UN. (2006). *Convention on the Rights of Persons with Disabilities (CRPD)*. New York: United Nations.

Waller, D.K., Correa, A., Vo, T.M., Wang, Y., Hobbs, C., Langlois, P.H., Pearson, K., Romitti, P.A., Shaw, G.M. and Hecht, J.T. (2008). The population-based prevalence of achondroplasia and thanatophoric dysplasia in selected regions of the US. *American Journal of Medical Genetics Part A*, 146A(18), pp. 2385–2389.

Webster, A. (2016). *Autism, sport & physical activity. Practical strategies to implement in your delivery of sport and physical activity when working with autistic people*. London: The National Autistic Society.

World Health Organisation. (2001). *International classification of functioning, disability, and health: ICF*. Geneva: World Health Organization.

4

Women

Rules and classifications in the Olympics and Paralympics

Kath Woodward

Introduction

Rules matter in sport, both on and off the pitch. Participants play by the rules and sometimes break them and receive disciplinary sanctions, but all participants are subject to regulatory processes: the rules of the game. There are rules for deciding who can participate in which event and which competition. Such rules often focus upon the gender of the would-be participant, with women being frequently denied the right to join in through the twentieth century and into the start of the twenty-first (Goldblatt, 2016; Hargreaves, 1994; Lenskyj, 2013; Lenskyj and Burstyn, 2000; Woodward, 2009). Rules matter, but rules also change and respond to socio-cultural transformations and to the political activism and campaigning of under-represented and under-privileged groups within the wider society (Maguire, 2005; Dart and Wagg, 2016)

The Paralympics especially have an extensive range of classifications designed to ensure parity among competitors in terms of the nature and specific capacities each participant has (as shown earlier in Jan Burns's chapter). The Paralympic movement offers opportunities for eligible athletes according to their particular activity limitations, subject to medically confirmed diagnoses, but with ten eligible impairments frequently and routinely under review (Paralympic Classification, 2015). The IOC categorises sports, with 28 in the Summer 2016 Olympics and another five to be added for Tokyo 2020. Each sport is subdivided into disciplines, with an ever-expanding range of sports being included.

Sports are divided into groups by age, and some sports like boxing are categorised by body size and mass, but almost all sports are divided into women's and men's competitions, except for a few such as mixed doubles in tennis, figure skating and ice dancing. Tokyo 2020 includes the 4 x 400m relay in athletics and 4 x 100m relay medley in swimming. The binary logic of two sexes, however, which can be determined with some certainty, especially by appealing to the knowledge of 'experts' – for example, in the past, through various processes of gender verification, such as in cases of intersex in the Olympics – has proved much less straightforward than expected. Nonetheless, the division of sports and competitions into women's and men's remains central to the Games and sports federations and regulatory bodies like the International Olympic Committee (IOC) (IOC Rules and Guidance, 2018), and the International Association of Athletics Federations (IAAF) (IAAF Ruling, 2018) continue to occupy a key role in influencing as well as making visible ideas about the authenticity of gender categories and apparent certainties about women and men. Rules change, however, as do the criteria by which decisions are made.

The sexual politics of the Games

This chapter focuses upon recent developments in understanding the sexual politics of the Olympics and Paralympics and, in particular, the ways in which women feature in the Games. Sport has been resistant to some of the wider cultural shifts and moves towards crossing rigid traditional gender boundaries and re-workings of sexual identifications, especially in the global North; not that there has not been reluctance to abandon the constraints of binary logic of sexual difference there too, especially with the rise of reactionary political movements and the failure of neo-liberalism. The women's movement and campaigns such as @EverydaySexism (Bates, 2014) and #MeToo have had considerable impact on the organisation, networks and relationships in sport, not least through changes in the rules and regulations and governance of sport.

Recent developments in explaining sex and gender as part of a changing politics have generated significant shifts and disrupted some of the long-held certainties about how women and men are classified and what rules apply to participation in women's events and men's events. The materialities and embodied specificities of the Olympics as regular, four yearly and very visible mega events have particular resonance for sexual politics, not least because of the inequalities between women and men, some of which are enfleshed and actual as well as being created by particular socio-cultural systems and practices (Woodward, 2009, 2012). The centrality of bodies and body practices in sport has generated a massive range of interventions and ever more sophisticated endeavours to enhance performance and ultimately to beat records as well as to facilitate sporting efforts, so it is not surprising that gendered bodies and how they are made and remade are also a focus of regulatory bodies like the IOC. The regulatory bodies of sport have had to be increasingly attentive to the use of pharmaceutical interventions, in particular. Doping scandals involving the use of performance-enhancing drugs have plagued the Olympics, for example in the case of the infamous East German women's teams of the 1970s and 1980s. Drug testing was brought in by the IOC in 1968 and anabolic steroids were banned in the early 1970s once reliable testing had been introduced, in attempts to prevent what was seen as cheating as well as being dangerous to the athletes themselves. The IOC has focused upon the use of testosterone and steroids especially, but drugs have become ever more sophisticated and difficult to detect. The tradition of the use of testosterone and drugs which lead to the making of hyper-masculine bodies has led those governing sport to concentrate on such interventions and to see gender as classified by testosterone levels alone.

Gender has played a key role in the organisation and regulation of the Olympics and Paralympics as well. For example, women in the history of the modern Games have consistently been marginalised however much they wanted to be involved and compete at the highest levels. The Paralympics were set up to provide athletic competition for ex-servicemen injured in the Second World War, especially for men even if the exclusion of women was not formal. The history of the modern (and the Ancient) Games is one of gender-based exclusion and the limited participation of women (Hargreaves, 1994; Lenskyj, 2013), not least in the case of the modern Olympics, because of de Coubertin's explicit aims to keep women out of competitive sport, which he perceived as inappropriate activity for women. Women were excluded from the 1896 first modern Olympics because the founder's views reflected as well as reinforced those in wide circulation at the time, when it may have seemed to make sense that 'the solemn and periodic exaltation of male athleticism, with internationalism as a base . . . and female applause as a reward' (de Coubertin (2019[1896]; de Frantz, 1997, p. 18) was not only a desirable norm but also expressed high moral standards to which to aspire.

The nineteenth-century rediscovery of Classical culture and ideals, including those embedded in the Ancient Olympics informed the principles of the founder of the modern Games in powerfully patriarchal ways which echoed and reproduced those of Victorian society. Women started participating in 1900, when a Swiss woman, Hélène de Portalès, won a medal in sailing. They were allowed to join in increasing numbers through the twentieth century and into the twenty-first, although the number of women on the IOC itself remains below the modest target of 20% (Women's Sports Foundation, 2017).

Patriarchal views endure in the twenty-first century, albeit in different form, and the battle for gender equality has not been unequivocally won. In the wider arena of sport, women have continued to be paid less and to occupy lesser or supportive, subordinate roles and to be called 'girls' (or sometimes 'ladies') rather than women, for example as 'grid girls' in Formula One or 'walk-on girls' in darts (both of which were not finally stopped until 2018). The contemporary Olympics and Paralympics, however, present a much more equal playing field, with much higher levels of gender equality than the majority of international team games, such as football, rugby and cricket. Things are changing fast, but football, for example, on the global stage is still very much the men's game in terms of media coverage, player remuneration and the wider sports media economics nexus, in spite of the advent of the Super League and greater visibility in increased grass-roots popularity. The Olympics and Paralympics, however, offer a much more level playing field (track, pitch, pool, and boxing ring too, since 2012). More women are present; there are more women's events on a par with men's so that women become part of the narrative, even heroic figures rather than poor relations deemed too weak and feeble to run long distances or sprint over short ones as was suggested in earlier twentieth-century Olympic discourses. The representation of women in the Games varies enormously and is subject to cultural, social and political influences which shape and intersect with sexual politics (Markula, 2009).

Gendered bodies in the Olympics and Paralympics

The Olympics and Paralympics as such high-profile, high-investment mega events highlight many of the big issues about how bodies and gendered selves are defined and classified and the extent to which rules and regulations shape lives as well as provide changes which can facilitate opportunities and new ways of being.

The Games are not only highly visible mega events, which are frequently described as the 'greatest show on earth', they also carry very particular ideological and moral weighting and promote special values. The Olympics are distinctive in their promotion of democratic principles through the Olympic Charter, which has been amended to promote wider and greater social inclusion, alongside the addition of more sports to provide for wider participation. However competitive and elitist the Games may be, they are built upon ideals of amateurism and equality of opportunity (Guttmann, 2002). The Summer Olympics and Paralympics offer sporting sites at which women seem to have reached parity with men. For example, at the 2016 Olympics in Rio 'female athletes accounted for 45% of the participants, an all time high' (Women's Sports Foundation, 2017, p. 1). In 2016, there were 1,670 women athletes out of a total of 4,333 participants, double the number of women from 1996 (Rio 2016).

The Paralympics were developed from political struggles for equal treatment and social inclusion, albeit initially for men injured in war when the Paralympics were established in England in 1948 after the Second World War. The large number of ex-servicemen accounts for the initial, empirical gender imbalance in participation, but synergies between militarism and masculinity also contribute to the patriarchal and heteronormative culture of the games (Woodward, 2012).

Competitive sport is an expensive business and the degree of investment the global North and notably countries like the USA are able to invest in sport far exceeds anything even thinkable in the global South (Goldblatt, 2016). Global sport, even in the Olympics and Paralympics, is not a fair and equal playing field. Not all countries are able to send athletes to the Paralympics, although London 2012 broke all records with 4,250 athletes from 164 countries taking part in 20 sports (IPC, 2019).

There are cultural reasons for the under-representation of women. For example until London 2012, when one woman, Wojdan Shanerkani, competed in Judo, Saudi Arabian women were banned from the Olympics by their own country. Saudi Arabia sent three male athletes to the London Paralympics, but has not sent any women to date.

The Olympics and Paralympics occupy a particularly influential socio-cultural space because of their massive scale and visibility, allied to the meritocratic, democratic principles of their institution and establishment. The visibility of the Games on the world stage makes them an important site for protest and resistance (Woodward, 2012). Nonetheless, patriarchal, hetero-sexist, ethnocentric able-bodied discourses which reflect, refract and create traditional cultural norms persist and continue to shape ways in which sport contributes to, as well as challenges, social divisions and inequalities.

The Olympics and trans and intersex athletes

One of the most disruptive and challenging events in the recent manifestations of the sexual politics of the Games has arisen out of debates about the authenticity of athletes', notably and exclusively female athletes', gender. Female-to-male athletes are not considered problematic because there can be no question of women who transition to or self-identify as men having any advantage in the competitive arena of Olympic or Paralympic sport, or indeed in any sport. The IAAF began testing in 1950 and what was then called sex testing and subsequently gender verification was initiated at the Games in 1968. Controversies about female athletes go back further, notably to the 1936 Summer Olympics in Berlin, the so-called Hitler Games, which is worth mentioning because it contributes to some of the negative thinking which has followed about the idea of men masquerading as women in order to gain unfair advantage; in effect to cheat. It is a fine line between the intentionality of cheating and the need to acknowledge the corporeal and experiential differences between sexed bodies, however complicated they may be, which means that those who have had male bodies and masculine life experience into adulthood are likely to have advantages of strength and speed if not stamina over those who have always competed as women and were assigned that sex at birth. The matter of fair play informs the debate (Woodward, 2009, 2012).

Gender verification initially involved often humiliating and intrusive physical examinations by medical professionals and later chromosome testing, but more recently there has been a significant emphasis upon testosterone (IAAF, 2018) as the key to identifying masculinity and a male body. Testing has been criticised for a number of reasons (Schweinbenz and Cronk, 2010). The very word verification, however, suggests the possibility of truth and certainty and a clarity about the universality of a two-sex norm which lived, enfleshed experience denies and challenges. Nonetheless the regulatory bodies of sport have persisted in trying to find a solution to what has become a pressing and voluble issue. Trans has become a hot topic, which is on the one hand seen as subverting and challenging long-held assumptions about one of the longest standing certainties about social relations and a fundamental feature of all societies, and on the other a marginal esoteric issue affecting relatively small numbers of people. This is not a matter of numbers though because adhering to the two-sex model, although reiterated through heteronormative practices and policies and the insistence that each infant, or even fetus, is either male or female, which begins even before birth, the matter cannot be dismissed. Sport offers an important and necessary site for discussion and for the generation of new democratic, more egalitarian strategies for accommodating diversity. Campaigns and social movements have exerted considerable pressure on the governing bodies of sport with the Olympics occupying a particularly dominant position, along with the IAAF in terms of having to respond to the volume and visibility of dissent and the very public controversies which have surrounded recent cases, where gender verification has proved both inadequate and inept as well as very distressing for athletes. Some of the force of the challenge comes from the radical nature of the challenge to competition and the binary of winners and losers, which is also, of course central to sport. One particularly influential case which has influenced the recent policy shifts by the IOC and IAAF more was that of the South African 800m runner, Caster Semenya.

Caster Semenya won the 800m at the Berlin World Athletics Championship by nearly two and a half seconds. She did not actually set a new record for the distance, but she was significantly faster than her fellow competitors. Rather than being greeted with praise and applause however, the champion was subjected to extremely harsh criticism, largely on grounds of her appearance, which led to accusations that she was a man masquerading as a woman. She was faster than her fellow athletes but also bigger with more muscles in her upper body. Only a few hours after winning gold, her rivals were angrily expressing their views about Semenya's stature and perceived masculine body and comportment. The media joined in (Woodward, 2009, 2012) and the IAAF leaked information about verification tests before the final results were available. The media coverage focused upon visible appearance such as body mass, musculature, height and comportment but also invoked scientific evidence, much of which was based upon the kind of expertise deployed in gender verification testing, including evidence of chromosomal and hormonal variations, as well as psychological factors. Intersex and hyperandrogenism, which are currently recognised conditions, were identified as possibilities but there was little exploration of the complexity of intersex and the extent of lack of conformity to a two-sex norm or the problems of the category of intersex. At this stage, in spite of media hype about visible difference and ways of looking and how one is seen, the discussion concentrated upon scientific discourse and the possibilities of setting boundaries through expert knowledge, with no acknowledgement of lived experience. For example, there was scant attention paid to Semenya's own biography as a black South African girl and then young woman from a poor rural community and her perception of herself as female. Class, race and gender intersect in the making and re-making of this elite athlete, but gender verification and cultural anxieties about subversion of the binary logic of sex and heteronormativity intervene to create a moral panic about cheating and unfair practice.

Recent developments, however, present a radical change with the arrival of self-identification and the idea and political practice of being the sex you feel you are and choose, although having some currency in the wider cultural terrain, especially among the more privileged, came into sport with acknowledgement by the IOC and IAAF.

Change has happened very fast in recent years. The IOC has developed its policies of commitment to gender equality and widening participation for women (IOC Gender Equality, 2018) and reiterates the need to ensure fair play as a priority in dealing with trans women athletes who may be deemed to be at an advantage. The initial IOC views expressed in a document on gender reassignment (Consensus Meeting on Reassignment and Hyperandrogenism, 2015) are resonant of some of the critical thinking which emerged from discussion of intersex after the case of Caster Semenya.

Whilst trans men have no restriction upon their involvement in men's competitions, trans women have been subject to a variety of restrictions, including an insistence on gender realignment surgery to remove male sexual organs. In 2016, however, the IOC ruled that trans male athletes could participate in the Olympics without surgery, but with hormone therapy (Guardian, 2016). In 2018 the IAAF similarly changed its policies to focus almost entirely upon the hormone testosterone, thus rendering sexual difference a matter of hormonal levels only:

> The new regulations require any athlete who has a Difference of Sexual Development (DSD) that means her levels of circulating testosterone (in serum) are five (5) nmol/L or above and who is androgen-sensitive to meet the following criteria to be eligible to compete in Restricted Events in an International Competition (or set a world record in a Restricted Event at competition that is not an International Competition):
>
> (a) she must be recognised at law either as female or as intersex (or equivalent);
> (b) she must reduce her blood testosterone level to below five (5) nmol/L for a continuous period of at least six months (e.g. by use of hormonal contraceptives); and
> (c) thereafter she must maintain her blood testosterone level below five (5) nmol/L continuously (ie: whether she is in competition or out of competition) for so long as she wishes to remain eligible.
>
> *(IAAF, 2018, p. 1)*

This attempt at simplification has not proved entirely successful however, and the IOC has already had to retract on some of its approach in order to secure its commitment to fair play and to promote and defend women participants in the Games (IOC Trans Policy, 2019). The Deaflympics has endorsed IOC trans policies based on an athlete having under 10 nanomoles of testosterone per litre and reiterates the need to ensure 'fair competition' (Deaflympics, 2019), but also recognises some of the problems which have immediately emerged from such a heavy reliance on self-identification, especially as some trans women have started winning competitions rather too easily, putting women competitors at a significant disadvantage. For example Rachel McKinnon a trans female cyclist won the Union Cycliste Internationale (UCI) track championship in 2018. It has, with some support, been suggested that new trans policies will destroy women's involvement in global sport, and counter any IOC policies aimed at promoting greater gender equality. This debate has become particularly contentious and in spite of sharing many of the features of patriarchal oppression and marginalisation, feminist groups and trans activists have not always been able to collaborate, which may partly be a result of the endurance of traditional male dominance within the governance and participation in global elite sport and the speed of some of the changes to policies.

Conclusion

Rules and regulations, often literally, embody social relations and gendered identities. Bodies are not entirely discursively produced but the rules of the game, for example about who can and who cannot participate in the Olympics and Paralympics and in which competitions and events, can generate meanings about sex and gender and set boundaries and restrictions as well as, in changing times, provide opportunities for the re-articulation and reconfiguration of sexual difference. The rules, such as new regulations brought in by the IOC to address challenges to traditional sex gender binary classifications, offer opportunities for change and new ways of thinking and new ways of doing sport, but may also offer further restrictions and constraints, as seemed to be the case in expert interventions manifest in the Caster Semenya case and earlier gender verification.

This chapter has suggested that a number of factors, especially those that are made and implemented by regulatory bodies in sport such as the IOC, contribute to the sexual politics of the Games and sport and social relations more widely. Sex and gender intersect with other axes of power, such as class, disability, race, ethnicity and sexuality. Religious beliefs and faith systems and cultural practices make and remake gendered expectations in sport, as is manifest in the participation rates among women from some countries with strong traditional religious beliefs. Degrees of affluence influence the extent to which some societies are able to engage with fluid categories of gender and explore possibilities of transgression of traditional classificatory systems.

Sport is a particular terrain in which gender identities and classification of sexual identities demands attention to the restrictions and specificities of anatomy and the enfleshed self, which have much less purchase in other areas of social and cultural life. Body mass, strength, musculature and skeletal structures associated with living as a woman or as a man (and training as one or the other) can confer advantages which cannot be eliminated by measuring testosterone levels, as the IOC and IAAF have discovered. Self-identification whether as trans or non-binary can present problems in sport, especially for women competitors who can be disadvantaged by the inclusion of trans women in events, especially if those athletes have previously trained and competed as men. What is instructive about an exploration of sex gender in the Games and the attempts of the IOC to address social and cultural change and growing fluidity and the transgression of previous certainties and claims to authenticity is the deconstructing the elements which make up ideas about gender identity and the ways in which social forces intersect with enfleshed selves. Bodies also fight back and reassert themselves and there is a bottom line in terms of anatomy, flesh, hormones and chromosomes and there are some limitations on how far we can be whoever or whatever we want to be. It is a complex mix of different social, political, cultural and embodied dimensions which generate the picture which emerges from the discussions in this chapter and in the next chapter by Caroline Symons and Ryan Storr.

References

Bates, L. (2014). *Everyday sexism*. London: Simon and Schuster.

Consensus Meeting on Reassignment and Hyperandrogenism. (2015). Available at: https://stillmed.olympic.org/Documents/Commissions_PDFfiles/Medical_commission/2015-11_ioc_consensus_meeting_on_sex_reassignment_and_hyperandrogenism-en.pdf [Accessed 20 May 2020]

Dart, J. and Wagg, S., eds. (2016). *Sport, protest and globalisation: Stopping play*. London: Palgrave Macmillan.

Deaflympics. (2019). *Transgender athlete guidelines*. Deaflympics.

De Coubertin, P. (2019 [1896]). *Olympic studies Olympic Museum*. Lausanne: IOC.

De Frantz, A.L. (1997). The changing role of women in the Olympic Games. *Olympic Review*, 26(15), pp. 18–21.

Goldblatt, D. (2016). *The games: A global history*. New York: W. W. Norton.

The Guardian. (2016). IOC rules transgender athletes can take part in Olympics without surgery. *The Guardian*.

Hargreaves, J. (1994). *Sporting female: Critical issues in the history and sociology of women's sports*. London: Routledge.

IAAF Ruling. (2018). *IAAF introduced new eligibility regulations for female classification*. Monaco: IAAF.

International Paralympic Committee. (2015). *Paralympic classification*. Bonn: International Paralympic Committee.

International Paralympic Committee. (2016). *Rio 2016 in numbers*. Bonn: International Paralympic Committee.

International Paralympic Committee. (2019). *Transforming lives: Barcelona 1992*. Bonn: International Paralympic Committee.

IOC. (2018a). *Gender equality review project*. Lausanne: IOC.

IOC (2018b). Gender Equality Review Project. Lausanne: International Olympic Committee. Available at: https://stillmed.olympic.org/media/Document%20Library/OlympicOrg/News/2018/03/IOC-Gender-Equality-Report-March-2018.pdf [Accessed 20 May 2020]

IOC. (2018b). *Women in sport: Gender equality*. Lausanne: IOC.

IOC Trans Policy. (2019). *In SwimSwam 2019. IOC expected to toughen restrictions on trans athletes*. Lausanne: IOC.

Lenskyj, H.J. (2013). *Gender politics and the Olympic industry*. Basingstoke: Palgrave Pivot.

Lenskyj, H.J. and Burstyn, V. (2000). *Inside the Olympic industry*. New York: SUNY.

Maguire, J. (2005). *Power and global sport: Zones of prestige, emulation and resistance*. London: Routledge.

Markula, P. (2009). *Olympic women and the media: International perspectives*. Basingstoke: Palgrave Macmillan.

Rules and Guidance (2018a). Olympic Charter, International Olympic Committee, Lausanne. Available at: https://stillmed.olympic.org/media/Document%20Library/OlympicOrg/General/EN-Olympic-Charter.pdf [Accessed 20 May 2020].

Schweinbenz, A.N. and Cronk, A. (2010). Femininity control at the Olympic Games: Thirdspace. *A Journal of Feminist Theory and Culture*, 2(9).

Women's Sports Foundation (WSF). (2017). *Women in the Olympic and Paralympic games: An analysis of participation, leadership and media coverage*. June. New York: WSF.

Woodward, K. (2009). *Embodied sporting practices, regulating regulatory bodies*. Basingstoke: Palgrave Macmillan.

Woodward, K. (2012). *Sex power and the games*. Basingstoke: Palgrave Macmillan.

5

Lesbian, gay, bisexual, transgender and intersex athletes in the Olympic and Paralympic Games

Human rights, unfair advantage and exclusion

Caroline Symons and Ryan Storr

Introduction

Lesbian, gay, bisexual, transgender and intersex (LGBTI+) people suffer human rights abuses in many parts of the world, often at the behest of the authorities that are supposed to protect them. Whilst developments in sport have occurred around LGBTI+ rights in sport, some have questioned the extent to which this has happened (Parry, Kavanagh and Storr, 2018). Rigid and dichotomous (either/or) gender binaries grounded in traditional patriarchal expectations about the roles of men and women in society also shape 'naturalised' heterosexist binaries of sex and sexuality. Such rigid gender norms resonate well in mainstream sport, with the most celebrated and rewarded sporting events and heroes exemplifying traditional masculinity and with gender-segregated sports competition tending to reflect traditional binary divisions of male and female.

Males with supposed innate masculine qualities such as strength, aggression/assertiveness, independence and stoicism contrast females with supposed innate feminine qualities such as emotionalism, weakness, nurturance, gentleness and gracefulness (Krane and Symons, 2014). Most modern sports have separate male and female competitions which are based on deeply held views that men are naturally better than women at sport. Furthermore, whilst men's athletic prowess, toughness and physical strength are usually celebrated, such characteristics can be seen as problematic for women unless they can also demonstrate femininity and heterosexuality. Homonegativity/homophobia can come into play when athletes do not fit the gender binary. LGBTI+ athletes can face serious human rights challenges within this sport context.

High-profile cases have accelerated global discussions of LGBTI+ rights including the 2014 Sochi Winter Olympics and Paralympics, in which the host Federation of Russia's legislature had enacted a law in 2014 banning "propaganda of non-traditional sexual relations to children and young people".

> The inconvenient presence of what critics called human rights violations surrounding the 2014 Winter Olympics revitalized the idea that modern sport might serve as a vehicle for

> foreign policy. Specifically, the Sochi Games represented the first mega sporting event that has generated the level of international attention on lesbian, gay, bisexual and transgender (LGBT) rights as human rights in a host country.
>
> *(Van Rheenen, 2014, p. 128)*

The International Olympic Committee (IOC) has taken steps to enable diversity and challenge discrimination, making specific reference to sexual orientation in Principle 6 of the Fundamental Principles of Olympism contained in the IOC's Olympic Charter (added at the 127th IOC Session in Monaco, December 2014). Host bidding contracts for the Olympics and Paralympics from 2022 onwards are also expected to adhere to a binding non-discrimination clause based on Principle 6 (IOC, 2017).

These LGBTI+ human rights initiatives taken by the IOC are only the beginning, as much needs to be done to embed such commitments in the organisation and delivery of a Mega Sports Event (MSE) such as the Olympics and Paralympics, and implementation also relies on many of the affiliated sports organisations, large and small, to firstly recognise LGBTI+ human rights and acknowledge the stigma and discrimination many LGBTI+ people face in sport and society more broadly. This chapter provides an overview of various human rights risks and challenges faced by LGBTI+ people, particularly athletes, involved with the Olympic and Paralympic Games; the current international legal, policy and political context in relation to human rights and LGBTI+ people; and the existing policy and practices of leading international sports bodies such as the IOC. Historical accounts and selected case studies are outlined to illustrate human rights challenges as well as opportunities to further LGBTI+ human rights within the international sports arena.

Defining LGBTI+

Terms such as 'sexual orientation' and 'gender identity' are commonly used to discuss human rights issues for LGBTI+ people within the international context, as they allow for diverse lived expressions and contingent identities based on sexualities (heterosexual, homosexual, pansexual, asexual, etc.) and individuals who are gender or sex-diverse.

In this chapter LGBTI+ is used as an inclusive umbrella term to refer to lesbian, gay, bisexual, transgender and intersex people, as well as those who may define themselves according to other terms in relation to their sexual orientation, sex characteristics and/or gender identity (hence the plus). As such this chapter adopts the term LGBTI+. What follows is a brief definition of each letter of the LGBTI+ acronym:

- Lesbian and gay refers to individuals attracted to people of the same sex as themselves.
- Bisexual refers to people attracted to both sexes to varying degrees.
- Transgender refers to people who live a gender identity that differs from their sex assigned at birth. Transgender people may have any sexual orientation. They may or may not seek surgery or hormonal treatment to bring their sex in line with their core gender identity.
- Intersex refers to a wide range of people with intersex variations – physical and biological sex characteristics (sex anatomy, reproductive organs, hormone patterns, chromosomal patterns), which do not fit typical binary notions or traditional conceptualisations of male and female bodies. These characteristics can be present at birth or emerge later in life.
- + Encompasses people who identify with other terms and lived experiences of sex/gender/sexual orientation than those mentioned earlier, such as non-binary, gender non-conforming, gender fluid, queer and/or questioning.

Whilst LGBTI+ is one of the most common terms used to describe diverse genders and sexualities, especially in Western societies, there is a wide range of different sexual and gendered identities including indigenous societies' third genders and complex variations across sex, sexuality and gender lines. These identities of the Global South differ from the gender binary that predominates in Western societies. For example, there are the *berdache* of the North American Indian, the *kathoey* of Thailand, the Indonesian *waria*, the Moroccan *hasas*, the *manhu* of Tahiti and Hawaii, the Luban *kitesha* in parts of the Congo, the *mati* of Suriname and the *Fa'afafine* of Samoa (Krane and Symons, 2014; Herdt, 1994; Wekker, 1999). Individuals who identify as third gender/indigenous sex/gendering, non-binary, or gender non-conforming are basically absent within discussions of sport and broader human rights, and this is an under-researched area. TI+ as well as third gender/indigenous sex/gendered athletes do not fit well with this binary medically determined sports model.[1]

LGBTI+ and the international human rights and international sports legal and policy landscape

Endemic marginalisation, discrimination, abuse and violence is experienced by many LGBTI+ peoples throughout the world (ILGA, 2017). This treatment has a long history based on religious doctrines, cultural norms and practices, social institutions and national laws framed by *heteronormativity* and conventional sex/gender identity. *Heteronormativity* is based on belief systems that assume heterosexuality is normal, natural and superior when considering other sexual orientations and identities, which are deemed 'other' and/or deviant. In her 2011 landmark speech to the United Nations US Secretary of State Hillary Clinton spoke of LGBT human rights that:

> are denied on too many parts of the world today. . . . They (LGBT) are arrested, beaten, terrorized, even executed. Many are treated with contempt and violence by their fellow citizens while the authorities empowered to protect them look the other way or, too often, even join in the abuse. They are denied opportunities to work and learn, driven from their homes and countries, and forced to suppress or deny who they are to protect themselves from harm.
>
> *(Clinton, 2011)*

There has been considerable discussion, reporting, political pressure and policy/legal deliberation and action over the last decade concerning international LGBTI+ human rights recognition, one of the major landmarks on global action being enshrined in the Yogyakarta Principles of 2007 (Yogyakarta Principles, 2017). These Principles, named after the Indonesian city where they were developed by a distinguished group of human rights experts, outline a broad range of human rights abuses affecting LGBTI+ people as well as specific recommendations to end these abuses. The human rights abuses as identified in the 29 Principles include[2]:

> Sexual assault and rape, extra-judicial killings, torture and other forms of ill-treatment; arbitrary detention; repression of free speech and assembly; invasion of privacy; medical abuses; denial of employment and discrimination at work; denial and unequal access to health, education, housing and justice; discrimination in relation to immigration and refugee status and serious discrimination in terms of the right to participate in public life, leisure and sport.
>
> *(Yogyakarta Principles, 2017)*

In the introduction to these principles it is observed that whilst there have been many advances towards ensuring that LGBTI+ people can "live with the equal dignity and respect to which all persons are entitled", with numerous nations having laws and processes guaranteeing equality and non-discrimination, there are still many States who sanction and violate the human rights of persons because of their actual or perceived sexual orientation or gender identity (United Nations, 2017). In fact there are 74 States that still criminalise consensual same-sex adult relations and several impose the death penalty and imprisonment (The Council of the European Union, 2013). The source of this human rights abuse comes predominantly from the imposition of rigid patriarchal gender and sexuality norms through customs, law and violence and the policing of sexuality also provides the basis of gender-based violence and inequality around the world.

In June 2016, the United Nations Human Rights Council (UNHRC) passed a resolution on the "Protection against violence and discrimination based on sexual orientation and gender identity" (UNHRC, 2016). In this resolution the HRC reaffirmed "that all human beings were entitled to all the rights and freedoms set forth in the Universal Declaration of Human Rights" (UNHRC, 2016). The Council also strongly deplored acts of violence and discrimination based on sexual orientation and gender identity and appointed for a period of three years an Independent Expert with a broad mandate to support the human rights of LGBTI+ people across the globe. In November 2017 the Yogyakarta principles plus 10 (YP+10) were adopted, extending the original 29 Principles based on significant developments in international human rights law and more extensive understandings of human rights violations coming out of research and reporting. These Principles have greatly assisted with advocacy by LGBTI groups as well as contributed positively to progress LGBTI+ rights within the UN human rights system.

Whilst there has been much deliberation within International Human Rights bodies on recognising and progressing human rights for LGBTI+ peoples, there has also been significant backlash. Altman and Symons, in their study of global struggle for sexual and gender minority rights document the fierce opposition to recognising LGBTI+ rights as human rights in many parts of the world (2016). This international polarisation on such rights results from governments and religious leaders using "resistance to 'LGBT rights' to cast themselves as defenders of traditional values against neo-colonial interference and western decadence" (Altman and Symons, 2016, p. 95). For instance, Altman and Symons observed that whilst Clinton's speech reflected US support for international LGBT human rights and the promotion of open societies during the Obama Administration, its Western liberal democratic foundation can also be seen as a form of neo-colonialism by some nations of the Global South, and a source of contention underlying new cold war polemics from States such as the Russian Federation, where President Vladimir Putin continues to pursue anti-LGBT laws to bolster his image as champion of traditional Russian values including patriarchal family and religion. Within this political context LGBTI+ communities and advocacy organisations along with International Human Rights bodies have also increased their efforts to protect human rights abuses as well as work for more open, just and diverse societies (Altman and Symons, 2016).

The IOC supports the human rights of LGBTI+ peoples in Principles 4 and 6 of the Fundamental Principles of Olympism contained in the Olympic Charter as well as in Articles 1.4 and 1.5 of the IOC Code of Ethics (2016) (emphasis added):

> 1.4 Respect of international conventions protecting human rights insofar as they apply to the Olympic Games' activities and which ensure in particular:

- Respect of human dignity;
- Rejection of discrimination of any kind on whatever grounds, be it race, colour, *sex, sexual orientation*, language, religion, political or other opinion, national or social origin, property, birth or other status;
- Rejection of all forms of harassment and abuse, be it physical, professional or *sexual*, and any physical or mental injuries.

1.5 Ensuring the participants' conditions of safety, well-being and medical care favourable to their physical and mental equilibrium.

The principles of Olympism and the IOC Code of Ethics apply to all belonging to the Olympic movement including IOC members and administration, National Olympic Committees (NOCs), Olympic Games participants, International Sports Federation, cities and officials bidding for and staging the Olympics/Organising Committees of the Olympics. Bidding nations for the 2022 Winter Olympic and Paralympic Games were expected by the IOC to include a non-discrimination clause based on Principle 6 of the Charter in the host city contracts from 2022 onwards (IOC Host City Contract Principles, 2017). In early 2017 the IOC announced that as of 2024 new host city contracts will include explicit human rights protection, making specific reference to the United Nations Guiding Principles on Business and Human Rights.

The challenge will be holding the host appropriately accountable throughout the mega-event lifecycle, with effective reporting mechanisms and follow-up processes in place. IOC President Thomas Bach outlined the commitment and progress the IOC had made in relation to human rights and the Olympic movement more broadly at the annual Sporting Chance Forum held in Geneva, Switzerland in 2017, including the work that needed to be done to embed its human rights commitments across the IOC's organisational activities, operations and business relations.[3] It appears that this important work is in the formative stages and there are significant political, cultural and organisational challenges when taking the relatively conservative and traditionally male-dominated international sports movement as well as the contentious international LGBTI+ human rights context into account.

Sex, gender, sexuality and sport as a backdrop to human rights issues for LGBTI+ people within the Olympic Games

Helen Lenskyj (2013) in her critical history and sociology of what she terms the Olympic Industry, outlines the significant power the IOC has had over the past century in shaping global sport practices at the Olympics and through international sports bodies that are an integral part of the Olympic network. Along with other scholars she also documents the history, predominance and power of men with more traditional views of gender, in the leadership of the IOC (Hargreaves, 1994; Wrynn and Smith, 2014). Since the 1980s, sociological research has explored the ways Western sporting practices, including the Olympic Games, conserve, reinforce and at times contest hegemonic masculinities and femininities (Bryson, 1987; Connell, 1987; Messner and Sabo, 1994; Hargreaves, 1994, 2000; Rowe and McKay, 1998, Messner, 2007; Anderson, 2005, 2011, 2015; Brackenridge et al., 2008).

At a time when there are fewer ways for men to display physical strength and prowess, such as in physical toil and/or combat, media-profiled sport, particularly masculine team sport and power/speed/force varieties central to the Olympic programme, provides a proving ground and public displays of hyper-masculinity that are prized and celebrated. Furthermore, a great deal of time and institutional support is given to the masculine sporting pursuits of boys and men due to sports' central role in shaping traditional masculinity in contemporary Western society. Boys and men gain status though sporting achievement, especially in sports demanding strength, endurance and aggression, and this reinforces their heterosexuality.

This also explains why there is a history of men protecting their sport territory from 'female' intruders. According to Lenskyj (2013, p. 26), "The entry of female athletes demystifies and dilutes sport's power to define what it is to be a man". This gendering of sport produces homonegative and discriminatory sporting environments as boys in youth sport and physical education settings who act or appear feminine and or lack sporting skill can be labelled gay and be bullied and girls who appear more masculine, or who excel at sport can be labelled lesbian and may also be bullied by peers. Such homophobic bullying can lead to poor mental health and disengagement in sport (Symons et al., 2014; Brackenridge et al., 2008, Smith et al., 2012, Denison and Kitchner, 2015). Brackenridge et al. concluded in their study of the nature, prevalence and impact of homophobic bullying in sport that this drove down overall participation in sport by boys and girls (2006).

Due to dominant gender stereotypes and expectations for women, participation in sports that are more traditionally masculine coded and celebrated can be discouraged within society and by those responsible for sport, as this is seen as unfeminine. It can also deter heterosexual women from participating in these sports due to fear of the stigma associated with the 'lesbian label' (Griffin, 1998, 2014; CAAWS, 2012; Sartore and Cunningham, 2009, 2010; Denison and Kitchner, 2015). This barrier is most pronounced in conservative societies. Homophobia acts to marginalise women who do not conform to hegemonic femininity. Lesbian women can be made to feel unwelcome in sport because they are perceived as 'problematising' the image of women's sport. Hence, homophobia acts to drive down participation for women more broadly, and homophobic prejudice as well as sexism (being sexually objectified in sport compared to men, discriminated against, treated unequally including receiving less recognition, funding, media coverage, resources) needs to be addressed for the standing of women and girls of all femininities and sexualities in sport to be improved (CAAWS, 2012; Griffin, 2014). It should be noted that there has been a decrease in homophobia within many countries of the Global North over the past decade, and significant social acceptance including marriage equality of same-sex attracted peoples. Along with these social changes has come a more inclusive masculinity (Anderson, 2011, 2015). Women have also made some advances in gender equality including greater opportunities in professional, elite and participatory sport (Cooky and Messner, 2018; Pippos, 2017; IOC, 2018). These changes are uneven, especially when viewed on a global scale.

In societies where LGB discrimination and human rights abuses are significant and/or state sanctioned, their right to privacy over their sexual orientation and dangers to the safety of LGB athletes is of paramount concern. This is illustrated well with two examples: the rape and murder of South African footballer, Eudy Simelane in 2008 (Smith, 2009) and the public outing of LGBTI+ athletes at the 2016 Rio Olympics and Paralympics by reporter Nico Haynes of the online *Daily Beast* (New York Times, 2016).

Simelane was a South African footballer who played for the South African women's Banyana national football team. She also coached football and was training to be a referee. Simelane lived openly as a lesbian in her hometown of KwaThema and was an activist for LGBTI+ rights. In 2009, her partially clothed body was found in a creek in her hometown. Simelane had been abducted, gang raped, beaten and stabbed 25 times. International Non-Government Organisation ActionAid, backed by the South African Human Rights Commission, reported that her murder was a hate crime committed against her because she was a lesbian – attributed to the predominate culture in the country of 'corrective' rape (Martin et al., 2009). Disclosure of sexual identity can have severe repercussions – in this case lethal – within a country in which the human rights of LGBT people is assured within the constitution. Secondly, Journalist Nico

Haynes caused public outrage for going undercover in the Rio Olympics athletes village to identify 'out' or 'closeted' athletes and writing an article in the online *Daily Beast* identifying the sexual identities of various elite athletes. Many of the athletes were from countries where being gay is criminalised or even punishable by the death penalty. Having their right to privacy being violated by being publicly outed at a high-profile event such as the Olympics can seriously jeopardise the athletes' welfare and safety.

Blurring the boundaries: sex testing, gender and testosterone

Lenskyj (2013) observes that the history of sex determination at the Olympic Games demonstrates the commitment of the IOC to privileging certain forms of femininity and masculinity based on sex binaries and conservative gender boundaries. Whilst the IOC's stated aim of sex testing women from 1968–2000 was to ensure that no men posed as women in women's events, the outcome of these practices went against the human rights interests of a number of women with chromosomal, genetic and appearance differences that varied from the accepted conventional standard of 'true' womanhood by significant breaches of privacy, discrimination and resultant harm to their wellbeing.

Recent academic research has covered such topics and controversies around sex testing and testosterone (Schultz, 2011, 2012; Karkazis and Jordan-Young, 2015; Karkazis and Carpenter, 2018; Pielke, 2017), specifically around hyperandrogenism and critiques of using testosterone as a single measure of performance and advantage. Most notable to this area of controversy is the regulation of women's bodies again (Cooky and Dworkin, 2013), and forcing women with Different Sex Development (DSD) or intersex variations to medically alter their body to fit in with the perceived notion of a woman and 'level the playing field' as often cited. Such actions to uphold 'sporting integrity' without proper human rights safeguards are illustrated well by the cases of Dutee Chand and Caster Semenya (for the case of Caster Semenya see also the previous chapter by Kath Woodward).

In 2011, the International Association of Athletics Federations (IAAF) introduced a policy on the intersex condition of hyperandrogenism, which involves greater levels of androgens, in particular testosterone, in the female body than what was deemed natural for the average woman. This policy required women who naturally produced more than the maximum limit of testosterone (seen as advantaged) to undergo surgical or hormonal interventions to reduce their natural testosterone levels to levels deemed 'fair' to other female athletes. The figure the IAAF and IOC agreed upon was anything under 10 nmol/L (Adair, 2017).

Indian sprinter Dutee Chand challenged this new policy in 2015 in the Court of Arbitration of Sport (CAS), after being caught up in the speculative and ambiguous policies surrounding naturally occurring levels of testosterone in women athletes. After becoming a breakout star on winning a series of high-profile sprint races, her home governing body, the Athletics Federation of India, and the IAAF forced her into humiliating and degrading gender verification testing. Subsequent legal battles ensued, and when the IAAF failed to produce any substantial evidence to demonstrate that women athletes with higher naturally occurring testosterone levels had a competitive advantage, Chand was free to run again.

Substantial emotional damage had been experienced by Chand, however, and the human rights regarding this athlete's dignity, identity, privacy, right to fair treatment, and health and wellbeing had been breached. She was not allowed to run until the IAAF could provide evidence, which meant her performance and career were severely jeopardised (Padawer, 2016).

Caster Semenya is a South African middle-distance runner who over the past decade has faced an ongoing battle to be able to complete at the highest level in the 400 and 800 meter running events. Semenya rose to international prominence in 2009 after winning the gold medal in the 800m Athletics World Championships in Berlin. Her win was met with scrutiny, with the revelation a few hours before the final that the IAAF has requested she undergo 'gender testing' to verify her sex and determine if she had an unfair advantage against her competitors (Cooky and Dworkin, 2013). Leaked test results suggested that she was 'hyper-androgenous' (like Chand). Semenya was subjected to a media frenzy and exposure of very personal medical records. It was also revealed that months after the initial tests, Athletics South Africa (ASA) President Leonard Cheune admitted that he had previously lied about the purpose of the tests. He also requested that the ASA team doctor withdraw Semenya from competition due to the 'need' to keep her medical records confidential. Semenya was cleared to compete in 2010, and went on to win the 800m gold medal at the 2012 and 2016 Olympics. Her wins were tainted by media controversy and official criticism with the IAAF moving to return to CAS to try to overturn the 2015 Chand decision on hyperandrogenism. CAS made a determination in June of 2019 that Semenya would have to lower her testosterone levels to 5 nmol/L in order to compete. Savulescu (2019) outlines ten ethical flaws in this decision on intersex women in sport, including that it is based on inadequate science, it confuses sex with gender, it is inconsistent with treatment of other athletes who have biological advantages and are not interrogated and it is inconsistent with the values of sport and human rights. Savulescu (2019) points out that Semenya is essentially being asked to "cobble her natural potential as a female competitor" and take "risky biological intervention to reduce her performance". The UNHRC has stated that this ruling contravenes human rights: "including the right to equality and non-discrimination . . . and full respect for the dignity, bodily integrity and bodily autonomy of the person" (UNHRC, 2019; Gous, 2019).

At the 2015 (Nov) IOC Consensus meeting on Sex Reassignment and Hydrogenism it was emphasised that the overriding sporting objective in determining eligibility for competition is "the guarantee of fair competition. Restrictions on participation are appropriate to the extent that they are necessary and proportionate to the achievement of that objective". Individual sports federations determine the binding regulations for their specific sports and regulations can vary from sport to sport based on the physical demands of the sport, considerations of safety and fairness, whilst also being as inclusive as possible. However, there are detrimental health and rights implications of such determinations of eligibility for female athletes with DSD. This has also been the case for Canadian cyclist Kristen Worley in her ten-year battle with national and international sport bodies over the health implications of transitioned athletes to compete under the rules of hyperandrogenism and sex-testing of XY female athletes.

Testosterone is vital for the health of an athlete and is involved in numerous bodily functions (Harvard Medical School, 2015). After Worsley underwent gender reassignment surgery, she requested a therapeutic use exemption (TUE) to be able to compete whilst taking synthetic testosterone to counteract the lack of naturally occurring testosterone in her body after transitioning. It took nearly ten months to gain this permission and during this time Worley was not able to compete professionally as her body was in a 'severe post-menopausal state'. Worsley also contends that the levels allowed (10 nmol/L) were not enough to support her basic health (cf. Adair, 2017).

Worley took several organisations to formal mediation, including Cycling Canada, Ontario Cycling Association, the Union Cycliste Internationale (UCI) and the Human Rights Tribunal of Ontario arguing for reforms to "the policies, guidelines, rules and processes surrounding XY female athletes, gender verification, and the therapeutic use of required hormones that are captured in the anti-doping regulations" (cf. Adair, 2017). Worley stressed the dangers of such blanket approaches for transgender athletes when having to compete with suppressed testosterone levels that can greatly compromise their health. The UCI accepted Worley's position and is advocating to the IOC and World Anti-Doping Agency for the adoption of policies and guidelines based on objective scientific research and responsive to individual needs of XY females (Union Cycliste Internationale, 2017).

Conclusion

In this chapter we have provided an introduction to issues around LGBTI+ inclusion and human rights within the context of the Olympic and Paralympic Games in particular. We provided an outline of the acronym LGBTI+ and the differences between sexual orientation, gender identity and sex. We then discussed some examples of when LGBTI+ issues intersected with the ideals of the Olympics and the promotion of fairness and equality. The 2014 Sochi Winter Olympics was a key moment for the promotion and discussion of LGBTI+ rights, which attracted much socio-political commentary. We then moved onto discussion of the policing of women's bodies through sex testing and athletes who fall outside traditional social categorisations of a woman, and this related to trans women and women with DSD or intersex variations. The inclusion and rights of women who may fall under the T and I of the acronym have been central in recent discussions around fair play, level playing fields in sport, and 'natural' competitive advantage.

Legal cases surrounding these issues within certain sports, such as athletics and cycling, and developments in polices and selection criteria, means it is hard to predict what will happen in the future and how such complex issues will play out in the international sporting landscape. We can make some general concluding points however, especially in relation to the human rights of women in sport and how their bodies are regulated and policed. Generally, we hear very little if anything about trans men or men with intersex variations. We question why there is not as much scrutiny around trans men within the debates of fair play and natural advantage, and within doping arguments and why trans men are allowed to intentionally dope to bring them up to appropriate levels of testosterone as their male counterparts. We do not question when men are too good or too fast, and assess the differing levels of testosterone in men. Furthermore, athletes with genetic mutations/conditions that give them biological advantages such as an increase in red blood cell mass and significantly enhanced oxygen carry capacity – exemplified by Finnish skier Eero Mantyranta – are not required to lower their biological levels in the name of a 'level playing field'(Cooky and Dworkin, 2013; Savulescu, 2019).

We argue that much more evidence and research is needed on issues related to T and I inclusion, and recognise that it is an area of increasing interest and debate. Alongside a growing portfolio of research around the changing scope of masculinity (Anderson, 2015) and greater opportunities for the advancement of women in sport, the landscape is changing and this presents opportunities for the advancement of LGBTI+ human rights in sport. There are still important challenges for the LGBTI+ communities across the globe when the rights of trans and intersex athletes are put under the spotlight and questioned, and homophobia and heterosexism are still alive in many sporting communities and organisations. One of the most pertinent issues to affect the Olympic and Paralympic Games in years to come will be the inclusion of women who are trans (note women who have transitioned and women who have not fully transitioned) and women with intersex variations or DSD. A concluding remark from Karkazis and Jordan-Young (2015) relating to intersex women in particular, points to the complex nature of the problem and how it is viewed:

> Policy-makers, among others, claim that the problem is that women with naturally high Testosterone have unfair advantage, despite having acknowledged in their Daegu study that "there is no clear scientific evidence proving that a high level of T is a significant

> determinant of performance in female sports". Others see a very different problem: Women who have lived and competed as women their whole lives suddenly find themselves having to undergo medical interventions in order to remain eligible to compete in a category to which everyone agrees they belong.
>
> *(2015, p. 860)*

As a high-profile mega sports event with global mass attention, the Olympic and Paralympic Games are well placed to promote human rights for all during the events' many phases and long lifecycle. The IOC has most recently demonstrated commitment to promoting LGBTI+ human rights and advancing inclusion by changing its laws to be more inclusive towards trans athletes, and even commissioned a series of mini documentaries exploring elite trans athletes which are available on their website. This human rights commitment is also exemplified by the inclusion of a binding non-discrimination clause based on the Olympic Charter as well explicit reference to the UN Guiding Principles on Human Rights (2017) (which are inclusive of LGBTI rights) to host city contracts. The challenge will be embedding such commitments in the organisation and delivery of the Olympics and Paralympics, including all significant sporting, commercial, media and host city/state-based stakeholders.

The Olympic movement is ambitious in its attempts at including all people and all nations within sport, especially LGBTI+ people, when considering the extent of state-sanctioned LGBTI+ human rights abuse in many parts of the world and the backlash from numerous countries led by political and religious leaders' intent on defending traditional values and patriarchal institutions. Considering that several years ago LGBTI+ issues on a global sporting platform were taboo and often ignored, it is quite remarkable that discussions and dialogue on these important issues has taken centre stage.

Notes

1 See Symons (2010, pp. 211–216) for insights into how transgender participants, including a number of indigenous Australian and Pacific Islanders were included in the sports programme of the Sydney 2002 Gay Games.

2 The Principles were first adopted in 2007 and in 2016 a further 10 Principles were added to the original 29. To see the original 2007 Yogyakarta Principles go to Human Rights Watch: hrw.org.

3 See: www.ihrb.org/focus-areas/mega-sporting-events/2017-sporting-chance-forum-meeting-reportfhxftgj

References

Adair, D. (2017, 21 July). Athlete welfare and fair play: Kristen Worley case puts women's sport policy in the dock. *The Conversation*. Available at: theconversation.com [Accessed 4 April 2020].

Altman, D. and Symons, J. (2016). *Queer wars*. Cambridge: Polity Press.

Anderson, E. (2005). *In the games: Gay athletes and the cult of masculinity*. Albany: State University Press of New York Press.

Anderson, E. (2011). Masculinities and sexualities in sport and physical cultures: Three decades of evolving research. *Journal of Homosexuality*, 58(5), pp. 565–578.

Anderson, E. (2015). Assessing the sociology of sport: On changing masculinities and homophobia. *International Review for the Sociology of Sport*, 50(4–5), pp. 363–367.

Brackenridge, C., Alldred, P., Jarvis, A., Maddocks, K. and Rivers, I. (2008). *A review of sexual orientation in sport* (No. 114). South Gyle, Edinburgh: Sportscotland.

Brackenridge, C., Rivers, I., Gough, B. and Llewwllyn, K. (2006). Driving down participation. Homophobic bullying as a deterrent to doing sport. In: C. Atchison, ed., *Sport and gender identities: Masculinities, femininities and sexualities*. London: Routledge, pp. 122–139.

Bryson, L. (1987). Sport and the maintenance of masculine hegemony. *Women's Studies International Forum*, 10, pp. 349–360.
Canadian Association for the Advancement of Women and Sport and Physical Activity (CAAWS). (2012). Seeing the invisible, speaking about the unspoken. In: *A Position Paper on Homophobia in Sport.*
Clinton, H. (2011). *Remarks in recognition of International Human Rights Day.* Geneva: Palaisde Nations.
Connell, R.W. (1987). *Gender and power: Society, the person and sexual politics.* Stanford: Stanford University Press.
Cooky, C. and Dworkin, S.L. (2013). Policing the boundaries of sex: A critical examination of gender verification and the Caster Semenya controversy. *Journal of Sex Research*, 50(2), pp. 103–111.
Cooky, C. and Messner, M.A. (2018). *No slam dunk: Gender, sport and the unevenness of social change.* New Jersey: Rutgers University Press.
Council of the European Union. (2013). *Guidelines to promote and protect the enjoyment of all human rights by LGBTI persons.* Brussels: Council of the European Union.
Denison, E. and Kitchner, K. (2015). *Out on the fields: The first international study on homophobia in sport.* Sydney, Australia: Out on the Fields.
Gous, N. (2019, 19 March). UN backs Caster Semenya in her fight to compete in international athletics. *TimesLive.* Available at: timeslive.com.za [Accessed 4 April 2020].
Griffin, P. (1998). *Strong women, deep closets: Lesbians and homophobia in sport.* Campaign, IL: Human Kinetics.
Griffin, P. (2014). Overcoming sexism and homophobia in women's sport. Two steps forward and one step back. In: J. Hargreaves and E. Anderson, eds., *Routledge handbook of sport, gender and sexuality.* Oxon: Routledge, pp. 265–274.
Hargreaves, J. (1994). *Sporting females: Critical issues in the history and sociology of women's sports.* London: Routledge.
Hargreaves, J. (2000). *Heroines of sport: The politics of difference and identity.* London: Routledge.
Harvard Medical School. (2015). *Testosterone – What it does and doesn't do.* Harvard Health Publishing.
Herdt, G. (1994). *Third sex, third gender: Beyond sexual dimorphism in culture and history.* New York: Zone Books.
ILGA. (2017). *State-sponsored homophobic award survey of sexual orientation laws: Criminalisation, protection and recognition.* 12th ed. Geneva: ILGA.
Institute for Human Right and Business. (2017). *Sporting Chance Forum.* Institute for Human Right and Business.
IOC. (2015). *Consensus meeting on sex reassignment and hyperandrogenism.* Lausanne: IOC.
IOC. (2016). *Code of ethics.* Lausanne: IOC.
IOC. (2017). *Host city contract principles.* Lausanne: IOC.
IOC. (2018). *The IOC takes historic step forward to advance gender equality following Executive Board approval of bold recommendations.* Lausanne: IOC.
Karkazis, K. and Carpenter, M. (2018). Impossible 'choices': The inherent harms of regulating women's testosterone in sport. *Journal of Bioethical Inquiry*, 15(4), pp. 579–587.
Karkazis, K. and Jordan-Young, R. (2015). Debating a testosterone "sex gap". *Science*, 348(6237), pp. 858–860.
Krane, V. and Symons, C. (2014). Gender and sexual orientation. In: A. Papaioanniou and D. Hackfort, eds., *Routledge companion to sport and exercise psychology. Global perspectives and fundamental concepts.* London: Routledge.
Lenskyj, H. (2013). *Gender politics and the Olympic industry.* London: Palgrave Macmillan.
Martin, A., Kelly, A., Turquet, L. and Ross, S. (2009). *Hate crimes: The rise of 'corrective' rape in South Africa.* ActionAid.
Messner, M. (2007). *Out of play: Critical essays on gender and sport.* Albany: State University of New York Press.
Messner, M. and Sabo, D. (1994). *Sex, violence and power in sport.* Freedom, CA: The Crossing Press.
The New York Times. (2016). Daily beast removes article on gay Olympians in Rio. *The New York Times.*
Padawer, R. (2016). The humiliating practice of sex-testing female athletes. *The New York Times Magazine.*
Parry, K.D., Kavanagh, E.J. and Storr, R. (2018). Why sport hasn't made much progress on LGBTI+ rights since the Sochi Olympics. *The Conversation.* Available at: theconversation.com.
Pielke Jr., R. (2017). Sugar, spice and everything nice: How to end "sex testing" in international athletics. *International Journal of Sport Policy and Politics*, pp. 1–18.

Pippos, A. (2017). *Breaking the mould: Taking a hammer to sexism in sport.* South Melbourne, Australia: Affirm Press.
Rowe, D. and McKay, J. (1998). Sport: Still a man's game. *Journal of Interdisciplinary Gender Studies*, 3(2), pp. 113–128.
Sartore, M. and Cunningham, G. (2009). The lesbian stigma in the sport context: Implications for women of every sexual orientation. *Quest*, 61(3), pp. 289–305.
Sartore, M. and Cunningham, G. (2010). The lesbian label as a component of women's stigmatization in sport organizations: An exploration of two health and kinesiology departments. *Journal of Sport Management*, 24(5), pp. 481–501.
Savulescu, J. (2019). Ten ethical flaws in the Caster Semenya decision on intersex in sport. *The Conversation.*
Schultz, J. (2011). Caster Semenya and the "question of too": Sex testing in elite women's sport and the issue of advantage. *Quest*, 63(2), pp. 228–243.
Schultz, J. (2012). Disciplining sex: "Gender verification" policies and women's sport. In: *The Palgrave handbook of Olympic studies.* London: Palgrave Macmillan, pp. 443–460.
Smith, D. (2009). Life for man in rape and killing of Lesbian South African footballer. *The Guardian.*
Smith, M., Cuthbertson, S. and Gale, N. (2012). Out for sport: Tackling homophobia and transphobia in sport. *EqualityNetwork.* Available at: www.equality-network.org.
Smith, M. and Wrynn, A. (2014). History of gender and gender equality in the Olympics and Paralympics. In: J. Hargreaves and E. Anderson, eds., *Routledge handbook of sport, gender and sexuality.* Oxon: Routledge.
Symons, C. (2010). *The gay games: A history.* Oxon: Routledge.
Symons, C. O'Sullivan, G. Borkoles, E. Anderson, M and Polman, R (2014) *Equal Play: The impact of homophobic bullying during sport and Physical education participation on same-sex attracted and gender-diverse young Australian's depression and anxiety levels*, Melbourne, Australia, Beyondblue.
United Nations. (2012). *Guiding principles on business and human rights.* New York: United Nations.
United Nations. (2017). *Fact sheet LGBT rights: Frequently asked questions.* New York: United Nations.
Union Cycliste Internationale. (2017). *Cycling Canada, Ontario Cycling Association, the Union Cyclistes Internationale and Canadian athlete Kristen Worley settle human rights application and promote inclusive sports environments.* Aigle: Union Cycliste Internationale.
United Nations Human Rights Council. (2016). *Resolution on the protection against violence and discrimination based on sexual orientation and gender identity.* Geneva: United Nations Human Rights Council.
United Nations Human Rights Council. (2019). *Elimination of discrimination against women and girls in sport.* Geneva: United Nations Human Rights Council.
United Nations Human Rights Office. (2017). *Tackling discrimination against lesbian, gay, bi, trans, & intersex people: Standards of conduct for business.* Geneva: United Nations Human Rights Council.
Van Rheenen, D. (2014). A skunk at the garden party: The Sochi Olympics, state-sponsored homophobia and prospects for human rights through mega sporting events. *Journal of Sport & Tourism*, 19(2), pp. 127–144.
Wekker, G. (1999). What's identity got to do with it? Rethinking identity in the light of Mati work in Suriname. In: E. Blackwood and S. Weringa, eds., *Female desires: Same-sex relations and transgender practices across culture.* New York: Columbia University Press, pp. 119–138.
Wrynn, A.M. and Smith, M. (2014). History of gender and gender equality in the Olympics and Paralympics. In: J. Hargreaves and E. Anderson, eds., *Routledge handbook of sport, gender and sexuality.* London: Routledge, pp. 77–85.
Yogyakarta Principles. (2017). *Principles on the application of international human rights law in relation to sexual orientation and gender identity.* Available at: Yogyakartaprinciples.org [Accessed 4 April 2020].

6

Sport and nationality at the Olympic and Paralympic Games

Flags of convenience?

Steve Greenfield and Guy Osborn

Introduction

When Aaron Cook was not selected for Team GB before the London 2012 Games, he took radical action. He was world number one in his weight category at taekwondo but was not selected due to a decision he had made to train outside the official Team GB programme in order, he felt, to progress his career. Following this non-selection, Cook first switched his allegiance to the Isle of Man, a non-Olympic nation, which would have potentially allowed him to compete at Rio 2016 as a GB athlete, before switching his allegiance to Moldova for whom he competed at the Rio 2016 Games, and where he was eliminated in the last 16. This switch was funded, in part, by Igor Iuzefovici, President of the Moldovan Taekwondo Federation and a billionaire (Lovatt, 2015). Such is the transnational and fractured nature of Olympic and Paralympic identity in the twenty-first century.

Sport is of course intimately bound up with issues of identity. As Seippel (2017, p. 45) notes, "sports become central symbols in modern societies" nationalism, by producing and, perhaps most importantly, activating the stories about who we are as members of countries'. Global stratification has led to perhaps unsurprising outcomes. Increasingly governments seek to lure talented individuals, the goal for the government being some bolstering of their international stature (Shachar, 2017, p. 790), but these transactions test "our deepest intuitions about the meaning and attributes of the relationship between the individual and the political community to which she belongs" (Shachar, 2017, p. 791). For example, dual nationality is no longer the exception, and this offers the opportunity for what can be seen as anomalous national sporting affiliations (Spiro, 2010). Notions of citizenship have always been contested, but whilst traditionally allegiance was permanent with the four components being membership, rights, duties and participation, more ambiguous notions such as circles of belonging become more blurred.

This chapter places issues of Olympic and Paralympic nationality within the context of sport, nationality and citizenship more generally. To do this, it first examines some key contextual and historical issues, including how the law has responded to such disputes and tensions, before proceeding to examine the Olympic and Paralympic regulations themselves, and concluding with some suggestions as to how this complex issue might be resolved in the future.

At the outset, the distinction between nationality and citizenship must be made clear. Often these concepts coincide but this is not always the case. Nationality denotes the individual's legal bond with a particular state, whilst citizenship implies a number of things including the right of the individual to participate in constitutional life (de Groot, 2006). The issue here is of *sporting nationality*.

Sport and nationality: history, context and *jus talenti*

There are many examples of athletes switching nationalities. Ron Eland, a black South African was forced to compete for Great Britain at the London 1948 Games due to the racist policies in place in his own country, something that Cleophas (2018) has recently examined from a decolonial perspective. Zola Budd is perhaps one of the most (in)famous examples of sporting convenience. During the sporting boycott of South Africa she was persuaded to apply for British citizenship and to compete for Great Britain at the 1984 Los Angeles Games; her participation was met with much disquiet (Nixon, 1992). There are myriad other examples from Bart Veldkamp switching from Holland to Belgium due to strict Dutch qualification criteria (Kostakopoulou and Schrauwen, 2014) to Becky Hammon's notable fast tracking for Russian citizenship to enable competition for Russia in the Beijing 2008 Games (Shachar, 2011). From the Paralympics Stefanie Reid is an interesting example. Born in New Zealand, she grew up in Canada and competed for Canada at the Beijing Games. At London 2012 she represented Great Britain, through parental qualification (Davies, 2012). These examples illustrate the shifting contours of nationality at play in Olympic and Paralympic sport.

Adjaye (2010) illustrates this fluidity for African athletes, pondering whether this represents the advent of transnational societies where attachments are diffused. Adjaye charts the shift from *brain* drain to *brawn* drain and illustrates his argument with a list of notable athletes who have switched citizenship from a variety of African countries, including Christine Ohuruogu who switched from Nigeria to the United Kingdom (Adjaye, 2010, p. 30). More recently the *Kolpak* rule has seen this 'brawn drain' impact on sports such as cricket and rugby (Greenfield, Osborn and Rossouw, 2017). In football Diego Costa took advantage of the Federation Internationale de Football Association (FIFA) Regulations to represent Spain at the 2014 World Cup rather than his native Brazil (Lovatt, 2015). Whilst the Olympic and Paralympic Charter are ostensibly clear (see discussion that follows), some sports federations and organisations have gone beyond the nationality restrictions provided by the Olympic and Paralympic rules. For FIFA, for example, in most cases a player who has participated for one country is permanently barred from competing for another, and ice hockey allows only one, final and irrevocable transfer of allegiance during a player's lifetime (Spiro, 2011, p. 3). Essentially, often a further connection must be indicated, usually something based around residence, parentage or residency. There is in fact little homogeneity between sports as regards the issue: 'Rules concerning the "sporting nationality" are as divergent between the various international sports federations as they are between the different national public laws concerning nationality' (Siekmann, 2006, p. 123). The final element of Olympic nationality may be provided by individual state requirements whereby countries may facilitate naturalisation to allow athletes to compete under their flag, waiving requirements where necessary.

This talent migration challenges notions of nationality and citizenship, and leads to accusations of the marketisation of citizenship (Jansen, Oonk and Engbersen, 2018). Talent migration, especially within the European Union with freedom of movement enshrined within the Treaty, provides an interesting perspective to consider how the law can intersect with sporting rules. Article 165 TFEU provides, *inter alia*, that the specific nature of sport needs to be taken into account and consequently there has been a raft of cases examining the extent that nationality-based restrictions are permissible within sport (Kostakopoulou and Schrauwen, 2014). Sporting nationality cannot be viewed in isolation from broader concepts. Jansen, Oonk and Engbersen (2018) note that citizenship is intrinsically bound to notions of nationality, and that traditionally two key policies for attributing such membership persist. First *jus sanguinis*, the idea that citizenship is acquired through *descent*, and second *jus soli*, where citizenship is acquired through *birth* in the country. They provide Germany as a good example of the former, and the United States as an illustration of the latter. These two concepts are not the only methods of acquiring citizenship which can also occur through *naturalisation*, usually on the basis of *jus domicilii* or *jus matrimonii*. *Jus domicilii* is based on the notion of residence, and may allow immigrants to obtain citizenship once they have resided in their host nation for a period of years. The periods and ancillary conditions that may apply will vary from country to country. *Jus matrimonii* may allow someone to acquire citizenship through marriage, though many countries do not allow citizenship to be acquired solely by this method.

In the broader global economy policies are created and enacted that allow fast track admission for certain highly skilled migrants – usually scientists and doctors and similar high-level professionals (Shachar, 2011). This can evolve into 'cash for citizenship' approaches,

> Shachar and Hirschl have coined 'Olympic citizenship' as a metaphorical and generic term for describing the 'fast-paced race to recruit the world's most creative and brightest' through which countries aim to increase their competitiveness and promote their national projects. The proliferation of these policies points towards the 'marketization of citizenship' – i.e. the reconception of citizenship from 'sacred' bond to marketable 'commodity'.
>
> *(Jansen, Oonk and Engbersen, 2018, pp. 525–526)*

Jansen et al. frame these transactions as *jus talenti*, and here citizenship is granted either through a financial transaction where it becomes a commodity (cash for passports) or where specific skills can be valorised in terms of human or cultural capital. As noted, these sort of transactions have been very visible within the Olympics, and to a lesser extent Paralympics.

Sport and nationality: the Olympics and Paralympics

From its inception, the Olympic Games have always concerned states and nations: 'if we turn our gaze to the past, we see that the Games have been used as a surface for the inscription of narratives of nationhood and a rather noisy arena of citizenship politics' (Kostakopoulou and Schrauwen, 2014, p. 143). Athletes at the Olympic and Paralympic Games are only able to take part after being selected by their respective National Organising Committee (NOC), and competing under its banner.

On a different level, the nationality of athletes has sometimes been used by states as part of a soft power agenda, helping to cement the state's political position and enhancing its prestige on the world stage. Sometimes this has a specific political dimension such as the implementation of Nazi ideology at the Berlin 1936 edition of the Games. National policies have also been the impetus for boycotts and demonstrations, as can be seen by the IOC's stance, admittedly eventual and somewhat late, to apartheid South Africa or the USA boycott of Moscow 1980 on the basis of their ideological opposition to the regime and the invasion of Afghanistan. Indeed, the whole process of bidding for, and successfully hosting the Games can be seen as part of this narrative (Grix and Kramareva, 2017). At the same time, such issues have been used for other political ends.

> Besides the emigration restrictions in former Soviet and Socialist Republics and defections during Olympic Games, the exclusion of apartheid South Africa and Rhodesia from the Games in the 1960s, 1970s and 1980s was a reminder of the global condemnation of institutionalised racialist definitions of sociopolitical and sport memberships. More specifically, South Africa was banned from the 1964 Games in Tokyo over its refusal to condemn racial discrimination and the prohibition of competitions between white and black athletes. And in the 21st Olympic Games in Montreal, twenty-five African countries withdrew in protest over New Zealand's continuing links with South Africa. Kenya's foreign minister James Osogo justified the withdrawal by stating: "The government and the people of Kenya hold the view that principles are more precious than medals." He maintained the view that the decision by the IOC not to ban New Zealand was giving "respectability to the South African racist regime and encouraging it to continue to defy world opinion".
>
> *(Kostakopoulou and Schrauwen, 2014, p. 153)*

For many athletes the Olympic and Paralympic Games are the pinnacle of their career, 'there is just one sporting competition that truly matters' (Duval, 2016, p. 52). Because of this, competition for places at the Games is intense, and some difficult selection decisions have to be made. Unsurprisingly, such decisions have led to dispute, often involving the Court of Arbitration for Sport (CAS) and Duval (2016) provides an excellent overview of the CAS jurisprudence on selection disputes. Interestingly any dispute arising from Olympic Nationality Rules is to be settled by the IOC Executive Board under Rule 44 of the Olympic Charter.

As Kostakopoulou and Schrauwen (2014) argue, issues of Olympic citizenship challenge our notions of community membership, particularly given more fluid understandings and applications of 'belonging'. More broadly, athletes today are no longer solely representatives of the nation state; increasingly they are the faces of global corporations, Twitter celebrities sometimes with millions of followers and influencers in their own right. Spiro (2011, p. 1) refers to a number of examples of stories highlighting "putatively anomalous national affiliations of various competitors" but notes at the same time that perhaps these stances are hypocritical – we don't concern ourselves with athletes that play for teams outside of the city they were born, why should it be different for Olympic athletes? The Olympic nationality matrix is essentially composed of three elements; the Olympic Charter, the rules of the international sporting federation in question, and underlying state citizenship laws. Rule 41 of the Olympic Charter provides as follows:

> Nationality of competitors* 1. Any competitor in the Olympic Games must be a national of the country of the NOC which is entering such competitor. 2. All matters relating to the determination of the country which a competitor may represent in the Olympic Games shall be resolved by the IOC Executive Board.

There is a Bye-law to Rule 41 (1A) which provides that where a competitor is a national of two or more countries at the same time, s/he may represent either one of them. The situation becomes more complicated when a competitor has already represented one country in Olympic, regional or world competition then the ability to represent another country is qualified by the following:

> A competitor who has represented one country in the Olympic Games, in continental or regional games or in world or regional championships recognised by the relevant IF, and who has changed his nationality or acquired a new nationality, may participate in the

> Olympic Games to represent his new country provided that at least three years have passed since the competitor last represented his former country.
>
> *(IOC, 2019, p. 77)*

The Rules further allow that this period may be reduced or cancelled with the agreement of the NOCs, the relevant IF and the IOC executive board. The key classification issue for Paralympians is concerned with the categories and classes in which they are placed and these are covered by a series of rules including the 2015 IPC Athlete Classification code, five international standards and a set of Model Rules (Adams, 2018). Nationality is also an issue however and provisions similar to those in the Olympic Charter are in place:

> Any competitor participating in the Paralympic Games in any Paralympic sport, or in competitions for those sports that are governed by the IPC as International Federation (IF) (referred to as 'IPC Competitions' in this policy), must be a national of the country of the NPC which is entering such competitor. In specific and/or exceptional circumstances this rule may be interpreted or reconsidered by the IPC as outlined in section 3 below.
>
> *(IPC, 2011, p. 1)*

Section 3 provides that where a competitor is a national of two or more countries, s/he may elect to compete for either (3.1.1) but if they had already competed for another country in IPC competitions, or world, regional or continental games, would only be able to compete for a 'new' country where certain conditions contained in 3.1.2 were met:

> Competitors changing or acquiring a new nationality: this section applies to a competitor who has represented one country in the Paralympic Games or in IPC Competitions, in continental or regional games, or in world or regional championships recognised by the relevant IF (being a country for which that competitor is deemed eligible under this policy) and who subsequently changes his/her nationality or acquires a new nationality, or who holds two or more IPC recognised nationalities at the same time and wishes to change the country he/she represents to one of his/her other existing nationalities. In such circumstances the competitor may participate in the Paralympic Games representing his/her new country provided that a waiting period of at least three (3) years has passed since the competitor last represented his/her former country. For participation in IPC competitions (other than the Paralympic Games) the waiting period is one (1) year.

The Rules further provide that these waiting periods may be reduced or eliminated by the IPC, and that such applications to reduce or waive would be judged on their merits and on a case-by-case basis.

What is evident is that globalisation has disrupted nationality and we have entered an era of loose connections and market citizenship (Kostakopoulou and Schrauwen, 2014). This process has occurred in a number of ways, as the Games have become global, commercial interests have increasingly held sway. Increasingly, the role of sponsors and advertisers has become more pronounced, and these relationships and requirements are often reinforced by strict regulatory frameworks, leading to debates as to whether the commercialisation has gone too far (James and Osborn, 2011). In terms of nationality at the Olympics and Paralympics, there have been a number of suggestions as to how this somewhat murky landscape might be dealt with in the future.

Olympic and Paralympic nationality: future trajectories

There is a number of possibilities in terms of how nationality issues for the Olympics and Paralympics might be determined. The first is market driven, where the individual dimension is stressed and market citizenship becomes the norm. Arguably this potentially leads to a 'People's Olympics' where the event is more about the athletes than the overarching states themselves and promotes mobility. This approach does of course devalue the notion of citizenship, and does not take into account the time and effort of states to support and train athletes, making it very much an issue of commodity and exchange. Spiro goes further suggesting the elimination of nationality from eligibility criteria completely. This draws upon that practice of professional sports which are largely based around the concept of teams being geographically affiliated (Bale, 2002) but crucially player eligibility is generally not, although there are some notable exceptions contingent on geographical origin or attachment. The Olympic equivalent is to allow athletes to compete for any nation that is willing to take them. The risk of course is of 'buying success' and removing some of the traditional ideas of sport and nation, although Spiro argues that the integrity of the Games would not be compromised by moving away from nationality-based eligibility, and is in fact a reflection of the fact that citizenship and the state is generally in decline, with hiring out of athletes, and, after Anderson (2016), illustrating imagined notions of national identity.

If such an individualist shift is seen as problematic, an alternative would be to focus on the group dimension. This would most likely necessitate tightening naturalisation requirements, requiring longer-term residence qualification and perhaps successful attainment of civic integration requirements, essentially putting athletes on the same hymn sheet as autochthonous citizens:

> The application of a more communitarian approach to country membership would thus enhance peoples' beliefs in the Olympic spirit of state competition on the global level and their expression of feelings of pride in the achievements of athletes as representatives of bounded units. In this respect, it would be congruent with the traditional association of sporting success and its traditional correlation with the enhancement of national identity.
>
> *(Kostakopoulou and Schrauwen, 2014, p. 156)*

This approach does however discriminate against athletes where currently mobility is the norm. Perhaps the most successful professional sport league, the Football Association Premier League in England, is predicated on the ability to draw players from across the global markets, and notwithstanding impending BREXIT considerations, player movement between European clubs is smoothly facilitated. Kostakapoulou and Schrauwen propose a different way forward based on what they term a 'participatory growth approach'. This would involve a flexible naturalisation process recognising a conscious choice of new place or residence in tandem with participation in civic life, arguably extending any three-year qualification period to include this immersion in socio-economic life and not just residence. A possible problem here however is that this does appear to relegate nationalism to the periphery. That said it does at least offer an attempt to focus on the 'now' rather than the 'then', and tries to imagine an allegiance that does not need to be everlasting or exclusive, as long as 'enmeshed in the present' and tries to ameliorate the worship of often illusory ideas of state or nation. Perhaps this concept, in tandem with Adjaye's (2010, p. 38) idea of transnational citizenship,

> one that allows athletes who have naturalised in other countries continued entry into their birth countries, return home for training, and compete for their mother countries, for they send remittances back and thereby contribute to their home country's economic development,

might foster a more workable and realistic approach to Olympic and Paralympic nationality going forwards, but as the preceding discussion makes clear, the terrain is far from settled.

References

Adams, J. (2018). More than just sport: An inside look at the modern Paralympic classification system. *Law in Sport*. Available at: https://www.lawinsport.com/topics/item/more-than-just-sport-an-inside-look-at-the-modern-paralympic-classification-system.

Adjaye, J. (2010). Reimagining sports: African athletes, defection, and ambiguous citizenship. *Africa Today, Project Muse*, 57(2), pp. 27–40.

Anderson, B. (2016). *Imagined communities*. London: Verso.

Bale, J. (2002). *Sports geography*. London: Routledge.

Cleophas, F. (2018). Narratives about South Africa's Black Athletes need to be reclaimed and retold. *The Conversation*.

Davies, G. (2012). London 2012 Paralympics: Canadian-born British athlete Stefanie Reid tells of near death experience. *The Telegraph*.

De Groot, G-R. (2006). Remarks on the relationship between the general legal nationality of a person and his "sporting nationality". *The International Sports Law Journal*, pp. 1–9.

Duval, A. (2016). Getting to the games: The Olympic selection drama(s) at the court of arbitration for sport. *International Sports Law Journal*, 16, pp. 52–66.

Greenfield, S., Osborn, G. and Rossouw, J.P. (2017). Beyond *Kolpak*: European Union Law's unforeseen contribution to the movement of African cricketers. *International Journal of the History of Sport*, 33(15), pp. 1748–1766.

Grix, J. and Kramareva, N. (2017). The Sochi Winter Olympics and Russia's unique soft power strategy. *Sport in Society*, 20(4), pp. 461–475.

International Olympic Committee. (2019). *Olympic Charter*. Lausanne: International Olympic Committee.

International Paralympic Committee. (2006). *Paralympic handbook*. Bonn: International Paralympic Committee.

International Paralympic Committee. (2011). *Policy on nationality of competitors*. Bonn: International Paralympic Committee.

James, M. and Osborn, G. (2011). London 2012 and the impact of the UK's Olympic and Paralympic legislation: Protecting commerce or preserving culture? *Modern Law Review*, 74(3), pp. 410–429.

Jansen, J., Oonk, G. and Engbersen, G. (2018). Nationality swapping in the Olympic field: Towards the marketization of citizenship? *Citizenship Studies*, 22(5), pp. 523–539.

Kostakopoulou, D. and Schrauwen, A. (2014). Olympic citizenship and the (un)specialness of the national vest: Rethinking the links between sport and citizenship law. *International Journal of Law in Context*, 10(2), pp. 143–162.

Lovatt, A. (2015). The debate over nationality in sport: A comparison of the different rules of governing bodies of sport. *Law in Sport*. Available at: https://www.lawinsport.com/more/blogs/item/the-debate-over-nationality-in-sport-a-comparison-of-the-different-rules-of-governing-bodies-of-sport.

Nixon, R. (1992). Apartheid on the run: The South African sports boycott. *Transition*, 58, pp. 68–88.

Seippel, O. (2017). Sports and nationalism in a globalized world. *International Journal of Sociology*, 47(1), pp. 43–46.

Shachar, A. (2011). Picking winners: Olympic citizenship and the global race for talent. *Yale Law Journal*, 120, pp. 2088–2139.

Shachar, A. (2017). Citizenship for sale? In: A. Shachar, R. Baubock, I. Bloemraad and M. Vink, eds., *The Oxford handbook of citizenship*. [N7] Oxford: Oxford University Press.

Shachar, A. and Hirschil, R. (2013). Recruiting "super talent": The new world of selective migration regimes. *Indiana Journal of Global Legal Studies*, 20(1), pp. 71–106.

Siekmann, R. (2006). Nationality and sport. *The International Sports Law Journal*, pp. 1–2, 122–123.

Spiro, P. (2010). Dual citizenship as human right. *International Journal Constitutional Law*, 8, p. 111.

Spiro, P. (2011). *The end of Olympic nationality in allegiance and identity in a globalised world*. Temple University Legal Studies Research Paper. Kim Rubenstein, ed. Cambridge: Cambridge University Press.

Part II

Olympic and Paralympic business

Edited by Benoit Séguin

7

Olympic values

Sponsorship, values and integrity in sport creating a paradigm shift

Richard W. Pound

Introduction

It is easy to forget, in today's world, that 40 years ago, the Olympic values were solely philosophical and were largely unrecognized outside a small group of International Olympic Committee (IOC) members. The IOC itself was impecunious – members not only personally paid all of their Olympic-related expenses, but also an annual assessment to fund a tiny administrative support staff in Lausanne. Its existence was hand to mouth and its influence within the sport system, aside from selecting Olympic host cities, was minimal.

The IOC's principal intellectual property rights were the five interlocked rings and a claim to ownership of all rights to the Olympic Games, including by then, television rights. Sponsorships were not even on the horizon. The IOC was too timid – not understanding the nature of the rights and fearing risks of financial exposure in an environment that it did not understand – to try to exploit the television rights, leaving the Olympic Organizing Committees (OCOGs) to negotiate them. The IOC contented itself with taking a portion of the negotiated rights fees, much to the displeasure of the OCOGs, who considered, notwithstanding their contractual acknowledgment in their hosting agreements with the IOC that the rights were owned by the IOC, that the television rights fees were rightly theirs, not the IOC's. This model continued through the Games in 1984. Such Olympic sponsorships as existed were generally restricted to the organization of Games, as an event, and were principally domestic, in the sense of being, with very few exceptions, limited to organizations carrying on business in the host country. Those rights were sold by the OCOGs, not by the IOC.

In the early 1980s, under the leadership of a new IOC president, changes began. First, the IOC, somewhat belatedly, recognized the growing importance of the television rights (particularly with the huge increases in rights fees arising from the 1984 Games in Los Angeles) and moved to take control of the negotiation and shaping of them, all this in the face of fierce resistance from the OCOGs. What had become apparent, with television rights fees being negotiated by the OCOGs, was that no individual OCOG had any interest in an Olympic television continuum or what might happen beyond its particular Games. Since the willingness of broadcasters to continue to invest in the Games was essential, it was important for the IOC to develop its own relationships with the broadcasters.

IOC control was acquired in three stages. The first, beginning in 1983, with respect to the Games in 1988, was to have joint negotiations. This meant that both the IOC and the OCOGs were required to agree regarding the timing and manner of negotiations, the selection of broadcasters and the amount of the applicable rights fees. This was awkward, since OCOGs (themselves also having no experience with sports television negotiations) typically had professional advisers who had their own views regarding negotiations, the market value of the rights and other contractual terms and conditions they considered important.

Both sets of 1988 negotiations (Calgary and Seoul) encountered problems as a result of joint negotiations. Calgary wanted to delay the negotiations as long as possible, reflecting the view of its advisers that the longer it waited to award the rights, the more valuable the rights would become. The IOC wanted to negotiate prior to the 1984 Sarajevo Winter Games, since it did not think the US team would do well in those Games and that a poor Games performance, not just in ice hockey, would depress the value of the rights.[1] There was a standoff. The IOC asked Calgary's advisers what they believed would be the outcome. Their answer was $200 million, far in excess of any previous Winter Games. To break the deadlock, the IOC said that if Calgary guaranteed the IOC its share of $200 million, the negotiations could take place whenever Calgary wished. Calgary said it could not take such a risk. The IOC said that Calgary could not have it both ways, so the negotiations took place before Sarajevo and the outcome was an extraordinary $309 million.

In the case of the rights for the 1988 Summer Games in Seoul, the Koreans came to the table with excessive expectations of at least $500 million, based on estimates from the same advisers that had acted for Calgary. It was an unrealistic expectation, considering the location of the Games, the political uncertainties of the day and the prospect of significant boycotts. The negotiations produced an offer of $325 million, which the Koreans refused to accept. That offer was then withdrawn by the bidding network and new negotiations were held a few weeks later, during which the highest (indeed only) offer was $300 million, which was accepted with great reluctance and resentment by the Koreans.

This process evolved to negotiations for the 1992 Games celebrated in Albertville and Barcelona, 1994 in Lillehammer (following the IOC's decision to split the Summer and Winter Games) and 1996 in Atlanta, that were conducted "in consultation with" the OCOGs. The final decision was the IOC's to make but working very closely with the OCOGs, which typically had their own exaggerated views regarding the value of the rights and different economic models of how they should be structured. The IOC assumed full control of the negotiations beginning with the 1998 Winter Games in Nagano.

With the IOC in full control of the negotiations, and in a position to interact directly with broadcasters, the value of the television rights skyrocketed. The IOC understood the broadcasters' reluctance to invest heavily in the promotion of the Games if they were not the ones to benefit from such investment. As such, the IOC was able to take a longer view of maximizing the impact of Olympic television on a worldwide basis.

An early example of this was the IOC's decision to award broadcasting rights for multiple Games.[2] The 2000 Games were in Sydney, Australia, during an awkward season for US television audiences, with major sports events (including Major League Baseball, football and college sports) competing for audience attention at the expense of reduced ratings for Olympic coverage. NBC thought it would lose money on Sydney but believed it could recover and make an overall profit if it could be assured of having the rights for the Winter Games in Salt Lake City in 2002. Consequently, it made an offer for both Games and the IOC was astute enough to accept. The outcome was so successful that very shortly thereafter, another package deal was negotiated with NBC for the rights to the 2004, 2006 and 2008 Games, none of which had even been awarded at the time. The formula was so successful that in 2014, NBC extended its contract until the 2032 Games. It has meant that NBC can, with confidence, invest in and promote its Olympic broadcasts without the concern of providing other broadcasters with a windfall platform that they had done nothing to create.

At the time of writing, nearly 40 years after the IOC first stepped in to play an active, and controlling, role in television negotiations, the Olympic television rights are part of a much more mature (if not declining) market, in which the exponential increases of the past will no longer occur. As a stand-alone phenomenon, with the exception of territories in which the rights had been sold well below market value (as in the case of broadcast unions and emerging economies, including BRIC and others), the value of television rights will not keep pace with inflation, especially where long-term contracts have been signed with major broadcasters. On the other hand, there is growing interest in interactive rights and social media and the delivery of Olympic audio-visual content across an expanding series of platforms. The IOC is actively exploring means of monetizing those platforms, including the Olympic Channel.

As part of the effort to enhance the value of television rights, or at least to maintain those values, the IOC recognized that its desire to move the Games to various countries around the world increased the risk that the Games might be awarded to countries that simply do not have the broadcast infrastructure and experience required to deliver international television signals at the levels now expected by world broadcasters and their audiences. With the twofold objectives of making certain that good coverage would be available to the world and (out of self-interest) to make sure that broadcast partners would be satisfied that they were getting good value for the rights fees they had paid, the IOC established Olympic Broadcast Services (OBS), having as its mission to produce first-class Olympic coverage that could be made available to rights holders. Initial production content was generated at Beijing in 2008, followed by full coverage in Vancouver in 2010 and, thereafter, in all subsequent Games. The OBS production quality has been extremely high, as well as innovative, which has enabled rights holders to reduce significantly their own production risks and costs, thus preserving the value of what they paid for the broadcasting rights and, opportunistically from the Olympic perspective, what they can afford to pay for future rights based on that experience.[3]

It is fair to conclude that, despite its late recognition of the need to control its largest promotional and financial asset, the IOC has managed this aspect of its intellectual property portfolio quite successfully, generating coverage of the Games that is now all but universal, as well as billions of dollars for the benefit of OCOGs and the Olympic movement at large.

Balancing the Olympic revenue model

In the early 1980s, if 95% of the IOC's revenues came from television, some 95% of that amount came from a single source – the United States. But, it was also true that it was the United States that led the 1980 Moscow boycott, in the process of which it was quite prepared to destroy the Olympic movement. As an economic model, it was potentially disastrous. The new IOC leadership recognized that it could not depend for its funds on governments and that, without funds, it was impossible to be functionally independent.

Two developments, at least, were necessary. The first was that all-but-complete financial dependence on the United States had to be reduced. Most other countries were quite content to have the US, with its competitive free enterprise system, pay on the basis of a negotiated market value for the Olympic television rights. Europe had a broadcast union (EBU) as did Eastern Europe (OIRT), Latin America (OTI), Asia (ABU), Africa (URTNA) and other smaller subdivisions, such as the Caribbean and the Arab states. Japan also had a de facto union, in the form of what was called the Japan Pool. All of the unions combined to keep the Olympic rights depressed below any reasonable market price.

The next step was to design and implement an international sponsorship programme, combining the marketing rights of the IOC, the OCOGs and the national Olympic committees (NOCs) in a single bundle of rights available to sponsors, a novel and ambitious undertaking that has been hugely successful.

The IOC's entry into the world of marketing

What appears in retrospect to be almost a natural economic progression into the world of marketing was far from easy to accomplish, since the IOC was not a 'business' that operated in a competitive marketing environment. On the other hand, it had developed relationships with broadcast organizations, in the course of which it had come to understand that, even though it was not itself a business organization, it nevertheless had to act in a business-like manner in the course of engaging in those relationships. That included developing an appreciation of the business concerns and objectives in play and being able to respond to them in a meaningful manner, while still maintaining its own principles. Involvement in marketing would extend both the nature and content of the IOC's business-related communication and conduct.

There were two significant hurdles facing any IOC marketing programme: first, the IOC knew absolutely nothing about marketing and second, the national Olympic committees (NOCs) that effectively controlled the rights to the use of the five-ring Olympic Symbol in their territories (and the OCOGs) were fiercely opposed to the IOC conducting marketing activities in those territories that would compete with their own efforts. The first was the most challenging: what did the IOC have to 'sell' and to whom might it be sold? The second was essentially structural, since the five-ring symbol was the IOC's property and use of it by the NOCs was with the permission of the IOC, which, in the final analysis, could 'legislate' by amending the Olympic Charter if necessary, should the NOCs prove intractable.

Early days

By 1983, the conceptual outlines of a potential international marketing programme had been identified. The idea would be for the NOCs to contribute their marketing rights in a limited number of product or service categories. To these would be added the marketing rights, in the same categories, of the Winter and Summer OCOGs for the particular Olympiad as well as those of the IOC (thus neatly avoiding the existential matter of whether the 'stateless' IOC had any exercisable marketing rights of its own). The direct participation of the IOC in the programme proved to be particularly important, since the IOC was the owner of the key element in the programme, namely the five rings – the NOCs and OCOGs, while important, were only vicarious users of the five rings as part of their composite logos and could not grant enforceable rights to the use of the five rings alone.

Given the IOC's limited expertise in sport marketing, it called upon Swiss-based agency International Sport and Leisure (ISL), the principals of which were well connected with FIFA and the Adidas organization. With extensive contacts within the world sports network, ISL would negotiate the amounts to be paid to the various contributors of marketing rights across the spectrum of categories. The overall programme would be managed by a Marketing Coordination Committee consisting of representatives of the major stakeholders and chaired by the IOC. The initial name of the initiative was the TOP programme, TOP being the abbreviation for The Olympic Programme.

A particularly important element of the programme was that the commercial participants, at least conceptually, could benefit from what was, in effect, one-stop shopping. The outcome of a single negotiation provided access to the marketing rights of both OCOGs, all participating NOC territories and the IOC itself. One of the inhibitors affecting the development of worldwide Olympic marketing had been the complications and expenses involved in gaining territorial access. If a company, such as Coca-Cola, wanted to engage in a broadly based Olympic marketing programme, it had, first, to negotiate with the Winter and Summer OCOGs for permission to use their logos, then go to each NOC where it wished to activate the programme and negotiate individual agreements for use of the rings in its territory. This was, as can be imagined, a time-consuming and expensive undertaking and, because it was one by one, competitors could effectively neutralize efforts simply by signing up nearby territories. What made the TOP programme particularly attractive was that it provided exclusive access to Olympic association, thus precluding disruption by competitors in each category.

As a marketing programme, TOP participants gained access to the markets they considered important from a marketing perspective. The economic value of a particular market had nothing to do with a country's Olympic participation or success on the field of play. In the pre-BRIC days when the programme got started, access to the Belgian market, for example, was more valuable than access to the Chinese or Soviet Union markets. As might be imagined, this often took a great deal of explanation to the sport authorities in countries that were significant on the field of play, but whose commercial markets were undeveloped. At the other extreme, access to the US market was essential: an international marketing programme that did not include the US would have been stillborn. The United States Olympic Committee (USOC) was very much aware of that factor and negotiated accordingly, to the extent that it demanded (and got) from each category an amount equal to the total of all the other NOCs combined.

In principle, marketing revenues (net of commissions and programme administration expenses) generated through the TOP programme were to be split evenly between the OCOGs and the larger family of NOCs and the IOC. The general rule of thumb was that the Summer OCOG would receive two-thirds of the OCOG half and the Winter OCOG one third. The remaining 50% of the revenues were split as to 20% each for the USOC and the remaining NOCs and 10% for the IOC.

The initial categories, seen now from the perspective of a relatively mature programme, were primitive indeed. They were crafted in simple descriptions such as: soft drinks, credit cards, film and package delivery. The categories were intended to be essentially worldwide and, to reduce opposition to the TOP programme from larger NOCs and OCOGs, categories that lent themselves to significant national sponsorships were not included in the international programme, among them, banks, beer, computers and automobiles. As the programme grew more sophisticated, there was considerable category 'creep,' especially as a result of increasing computer-driven technological advances that had application across several formerly stand-alone categories, as well as a commercially driven desire to expand the range of Olympic exclusivity in the marketplace.

Identifying the keys to successful Olympic marketing

Underlying the commercial success has been a growing understanding of Olympic values and the emergence of an Olympic 'brand' that encompasses the aspirational aspects of Olympic sport, youth, peaceful international involvement and fair play. Without the ethical underpinnings of Olympic sport, progress of the magnitude achieved would not have been possible.

The first iterations of the TOP programme were implemented with no fundamental understanding of why the programme could, or should, be attractive either to the general public or to the sponsors themselves. But for the World Wars, there had been a string of reasonably successful Games (after somewhat ambivalent beginnings in 1896, 1900 and 1904), marred only by a few numerically significant boycotts in 1976, 1980 and 1984. The advent of television had enabled the Games to become a genuinely international experience and the technical advances in television coverage produced better and better programming for the benefit of worldwide audiences. Technology enabled coverage to become instantly available as a result of satellite transmission: it no longer mattered where the Games were held. Gone were the days when film from European-based Games had to be flown to New York in order for US audiences to have a next-day view of performances by Olympic athletes. Air transport meant that lengthy travel by sea was no longer necessary for international athletes to participate in the Games.

The IOC did not, however, fully understand what were the elements that made the Games special, nor how people around the world perceived the Games. Was there such a thing as an Olympic 'brand?' If so, of what did it consist? Why were corporations willing to be Olympic sponsors? Did they know what they were buying? How could they measure whether their Olympic investment was providing economic or other benefits?

Satisfying as it was to see the rise in Olympic-related revenues, it became even more important to determine the answers to questions such as those just posed. Following the US efforts to organize the Moscow boycott in 1980, the IOC had quickly recognized the inherent fragility of the Olympic movement when governments were effectively the principal, and often the only, sources of funding for Olympic Games, for national Olympic committees and for national sports federations. The national interests of governments inevitably trumped the interests of sport. If the Olympic movement learned something from the Moscow boycott, so too did governments. Notwithstanding the enormous governmental pressures to postpone, cancel or change the venue of the 1980 Games, the Olympic movement proved resilient enough to ensure that the Games took place as planned, albeit considerably damaged. The boycotting countries did not bring about the desired political changes on the part of the Soviet Union (withdrawal from Afghanistan) and succeeded only in punishing their own athletes. The IOC recognized the importance of increasing the universality of the Olympic movement, strengthening its solidarity and achieving a degree of financial independence.

That had led to the changes in dealing with television rights noted earlier, lessening its all-but-total dependence on the United States and broadening the base of its revenue sources.

For the longer term, this required the IOC to develop a more orderly approach to managing the assets at its disposal. There were, of course, the Games themselves – the greatest sporting event in the world – with a huge worldwide audience. The scarcity was also important – only one of each Games in a four-year period. The upside of that scarcity was that the Games were particularly special and not part of an endless clutter of relatively meaningless sports events. The downside was that, on the traditional model, both Games occurred in the same year, leaving three years with essentially no Olympic content between the Games. From the perspective of commercial interest, especially with respect to television, the value of Olympic rights had a serious impact on other sports events in the year of the Olympics. That conundrum was solved fairly easily, by splitting the Games, so that the Summer and Winter Games were held separately, starting with the Lillehammer Winter Games in 1994. That allowed the rights fees to increase and, for sponsors, enabled them to maintain a much greater presence in the marketplace throughout the full four years of each Olympiad. The expanded Olympic-related promotion enhanced the public interest in the Olympics.

The five rings, already one of the most internationally recognized symbols, remained a significant asset. Careful attention was required to prevent unauthorized usage of the symbol, especially once its commercial value became apparent. The IOC came to understand the value of its historical material, including official films of the Games in the days before complete television coverage, the television footage of past Games, its photographic archive and collections of bid books and official reports of the Games. It began to implement an active programme of obtaining and controlling all such historical materials, which it could use on its own account and which could also be made available to broadcasters and sponsors. Some of the 'softer' aspects of the Games became increasingly valuable, such as the aspirational values of the Games, their universality, their appeal to the youth of the world, the peaceful nature of the Olympics, the concept of fair play and the freedom from discrimination. These had not been immediately apparent when the IOC made its initial foray into the commercial world.

Indeed, it was not until the IOC began to think in terms of a commercially attractive 'brand' that it focused on what the elements of that brand (the 'Olympic' brand) might be. Consequently, the IOC commissioned extensive international research with the goal of identifying those elements. The research included qualitative consumer research with focus groups in ten countries, quantitative consumer research in 11 countries (with some 5,500 respondents), interviews with Olympic family (IOC, IFs, NOCs, OCOGs and athletes) and commercial partner interviews (including TOP partners, other corporations, print media, broadcasters and opinion leaders). This was the largest and most wide-ranging data sample ever gathered in relation to the public perception of the Olympics.

The attributes that consumers (and, as a result of the consumer interest, partners) considered to be the most relevant were highly emotional and aspirational. They included the following: friendship, peaceful, fair competition, global, multi-cultural, striving, honourable, participation, determination, dynamic, festive, being the best and celebration. It was interesting to note that the ethical and social values of the Olympic movement combined well with the intensity of the sport values, such as competitive, striving and celebratory.

It was also important for the IOC to understand the consumers' attitudes and perceptions of its involvement with commercial enterprises. The outcomes of this aspect of the research were quite encouraging, with more than three-quarters of respondents stating: (1) they welcomed commercial associations with the Olympics, if they helped to keep the Olympics going, (2) they would be supportive of Olympic sponsors who made it clear that their commercial spending was helping to fund the Olympic Games, and (3) they agreed Olympic sponsors should link their advertising and promotion with Olympic ideals. Cross-checking consumer-defined aspects with Olympic Charter principles also provided encouraging synergies: exalting and combining in a balanced whole the qualities of body, will and mind (striving, being the best); blending sport with culture and education (multi-cultural, worldly, dignified); placing sport at the service of the harmonious development of man (peaceful, respectful); sport practiced without discrimination in a spirit of friendship, solidarity and fair play (friendship, participation, fair play); and universal and permanent activity covering five continents (unity, global, heritage, tradition).

The conclusions drawn from the research were that Olympic partners could benefit from market execution with a single message that would be appealing across multiple worldwide markets (consumers across 11 countries had rated the same set of equities as highly associative and important) and that there would be broad simultaneous appeal across diverse demographic segments (the Olympic appeal showed little variation by age, gender or income). These were findings that resonated well with large multinational businesses, enabling them to develop an overall theme for their promotions, combined with a degree of tactical flexibility for particular market contexts.

Essential to successful marketing is the association between two brands, with the objective that the whole be greater than the sum of the parts. That will depend on positioning the elements of the Olympic brand such as hope (the Olympics offer hope for a better world and life through sport competition for all without discrimination); dreams and inspirations (the Olympics provide the people of the world with the inspiration to achieve their personal dreams in sport and in life); friendship and fair play (the Olympics demonstrate global friendship and fair play through sport competition for all, without discrimination); and joy in effort (the Olympics celebrate the universal joy in effort through sport competition that is always intense, friendly and fair).

Tailoring of co-branding opportunities provided a broad range of positioning possibilities. Three examples, non-alcoholic beverages, life insurance and annuities, and package delivery, are illustrative of the available flexibility. Beverages: Brand X is about celebrating life's pleasures with friends, wherever you are, around the world (celebration, friendship, multi-cultural). Insurance and annuities: Brand Y has a history of offering a broad range of financial products and services to promote security and stability for your family (tradition and heritage, worldly, trustworthy, honorable). Package delivery: Brand Z provides services you can rely on: fast, dependable, anywhere in the world (trustworthy, global, dynamic, best of the best).

Perhaps the most important change of mental set was that which applied to the IOC. Commercial entities live every day with the pressures and disciplines of the marketplace and are accustomed to competing for market share. They are also accustomed to measuring results, making strategic and tactical adjustments to improve performance, as well as abandoning strategies that are unsatisfactory. The IOC had no such tradition or experience: it had always been highly risk adverse and deeply suspicious of anything smacking of commercialism – perhaps a carryover from its original foundation of amateurism. Having ventured, however, into the waters of commercialism, it soon came to understand that it would need to work for the rewards it sought and that, to get value, it would have to give value. This could not be a one-way street.

The rewards from the interactions with business were significant, not just in terms of enhanced revenues that provided additional stability for the Olympic movement and the Games. There was association with a select group of globally branded partners, extensive exposure and promotion for the Olympic movement as a result of the global marketing activities of the partners, the availability of world-class experience of the partners to help the Olympic movement, and support of the employees, customers and suppliers of the partners. For its part, the IOC made a commitment to help the marketing partners maximize the value of their support. This included leveraging the Olympic brand, with its unique combination of universal appeal, ethical and social issues and sports excellence, use of tangible Olympic assets (some of which have been identified earlier), access to iconic and future Olympic athletes, special opportunities with NOCs and off-season promotions, provision of hospitality opportunities for marketing partners at the Games and creation of associations for the marketing partners with other prestigious global brands – if you were a TOP sponsor, you were seen to be moving in a world-class company.

Conclusions

As other portions of this work demonstrate, the marketplace constantly changes. Industries come and go. Some TOP sponsors never managed to become truly global, despite their regional importance. The television industry has changed enormously since the early days of Olympic television and communications have undergone a paradigm shift that is far from complete. Audiences 'consume' sport quite differently than from almost half a century ago, so much so that many sports have had to re-invent themselves or face a future of irrelevance and vanishing resources. The Olympic programme itself encounters challenges to remain attractive to today's younger generation, whose tastes differ from those of their parents and will certainly differ from those of their own progeny.

Little did the IOC know what changes it would trigger when it took its first cautious steps to step from the sidelines and to begin to manage the Olympic 'assets' that it had allowed others to shape and monetize. Television revenues, before the IOC became directly involved, were low, in part because they were negotiated by the OCOGs, who were stakeholders only in their own Games, having no holistic concept of the Olympics as an ongoing social phenomenon. While the IOC cannot claim credit for the technologies that soon made the Olympics a global phenomenon, to its credit, it recognized the social values inherent in the Olympic movement and acted to maximize the promotion of those values and to use the technologies to make them resonate with global audiences. Only the 'owner' of those rights could promote and enhance the value of them. Only the owner of the other Olympic assets could recognize, manage and maximize the financial and promotional potential of them as well.

Without smacking of hubris, were the IOC to assess the outcomes resulting from its first cautious, and later more confident, involvement in commercial matters, it could justify a conclusion that, all things considered, it has done pretty well. It has grown the universality of the Olympic movement. It has maintained an enviable solidarity. And it has helped to generate significant revenues for the benefit of the Olympic movement and the organization of the Olympic Games. Many IFs are now heavily dependent on revenues generated for them by the IOC, which often exceed what they have been able to raise on their own account.

Who could have imagined, 125 years ago when the IOC was established, how the concept of international sport would develop? The answer, of course, is no one. Going forward from here, there are two aspects to consider. The first is that change will continue, likely at ever-increasing speed. Who knows what sports may emerge, what equipment will be used, how sports will be 'consumed' by audiences and what means of communication will bring the athletes' performances to those audiences? These matters will be what they will be.

More important will be the second aspect: the underlying values of sport. If the values erode or disappear, sport will suffer the same fate. Audiences will have no interest in competitions whose outcomes are decided in advance, whether as a result of cheating, match-fixing, corrupt officiating, doping or other conduct. They will not support competition that is not fair or in which the uncertainty of outcome is compromised. They will not watch. If audiences will not watch, broadcasters (in whatever form they may then take) will not present the competitions and organized sport will cease to exist.

The real future challenge for the IOC is to ensure that the underlying values of sport, indeed the basic integrity of sport, are maintained, promoted and enforced. Those values are the necessary constant theme, the axis around which sport must rotate and without which sport cannot exist. And, as with the actions described earlier that the IOC has taken regarding its sources for revenue, it is actions that will be needed regarding the values of sport, not mere recitation of those values.

Notes

1 For example, in the 1980 Olympic Winter Games in Lake Placid, the United States men's ice hockey team had won an improbable gold medal. ABC, at the time, the usual Olympic rights holder in the United States, was touting Sarajevo as "Miracle on Ice II."

2 The discussion focuses on the US rights, since the US rights were the 'driver' of most advances in Olympic television and were, by far, the largest source of Olympic television revenues.

3 The economic matrix for broadcasters is generally quite simple: advertising revenues, less commission, less production costs = money available for rights fees + profit.

8

Paralympic brand governance

The best of both worlds?

Simon Gérard

Introduction

The International Paralympic Committee (IPC) is the global governing body of the Paralympic movement since its creation in 1989 and aims to promote para-sports at the worldwide level (Brittain, 2010; Legg and Steadward, 2011). The IPC's ultimate aspiration is "to make for a more inclusive society for people with an impairment through para-sports" while its vision is "to enable para-athletes to achieve sporting excellence and inspire and excite the world" (IPC, 2017a). In addition to leading the Paralympic movement, the IPC's purpose is to organize and protect the Summer and Winter Paralympic Games that are seen as a strategic asset to fulfill its objectives. These Games are indeed branded as an elite sport competition that aim to foster social change for all people with an impairment (Howe, 2008; IPC, 2017a). More than 4300 para-athletes from 159 countries competed in 22 sports during the 2016 Summer Paralympic Games in Rio (Brazil) while the Organizing Committee of the 2020 Tokyo Paralympic Games (Japan) envisions to host 4400 para-athletes, making the Paralympic Games the second largest multi-sports events in the world behind the Olympic Games. Compared to the International Olympic Committee (IOC) that does not directly govern any sport, the IPC also acts as the International Federation for ten para-sports for which the IPC supervises World Championships and other competitions (IPC, 2017a).

Like most professional sport organizations (Séguin, Richelieu and O'Reilly, 2008), its brand – building around the core values of courage, determination, inspiration and equality – is a key asset for the IPC. The Paralympic brand has been identified as a strategic priority since 2011 in order to increase its social and commercial values (IPC, 2017a). The IPC Strategic Plan 2015–2018 positions the improvement of the Paralympic brand in terms of recognition and value as one of its three core goals. The IPC further seeks to "develop and implement a long-term brand vision that ensures greater understanding, consistent usage, exposure, recognition and affinity across the world, in particular within key territories" (IPC, 2015).

However, as recently emphasized by Helm and Jones (2010), the management of a company's brand becomes more challenging as fast and continuous changes that characterize contemporary societies can quickly damage or weaken brand equity. In this chapter, brand equity is defined as "a set of assets and liabilities linked to a brand, its name and symbols, that adds or subtracts from the value provided by its product or service to a firm/or to that firm's customers" (Aaker, 1991, p. 12). Helm and Jones (2010) prompted the role of 'brand governance' as a new paradigm in brand management literature that may aid to protect and sustain long-term value of a company's brand. The concept of brand governance was further elaborated and applied to the Olympic brand by Séguin and Abeza (2019). These authors (2019) suggested a shift from strategic brand management – mainly concern with the building, developing and measuring brand equity – to brand governance, defined as "a system of building a brand that is guided by the vision, mission and values of an organization and that systematically nurture a brand value to become and remain a long-term strategic asset" (p. 368).

Building upon this stream of work, this chapter examines key tensions, challenges and paradoxes that intersperse with the development and governance of the Paralympic brand. To this aim, a brief overview of the historical development of the Paralympic movement is first offered to better understand the background on which the Paralympic brand has developed. Second, a theoretical discussion of the concept of brand governance is developed, in particular around the dimensions of brand co-creation (Ferrand, Chappelet and Séguin, 2012; Lucarelli and Giovanardi, 2016) and brand governance in terms of institutional dynamics (Fiss, 2008). Third, the governance of the Paralympic brand is examined, highlighting how the brand operates in a complex institutional system composed of multiple stakeholders with diverging demands that can jeopardize the Paralympic brand's equity. This section also emphasizes how the Paralympic brand is shaped by broader societal discourses and attitudes towards disability and has the potential, thanks to its position at the edge of multiple 'worlds', to support but also potentially to undermine change in society for all people with an impairment.

Historical overview of the Paralympic movement

This section develops a brief overview of the historical development of the Paralympic movement and Paralympic Games. Its aim is to provide the historical context in which the governance of the Paralympic brand will be discussed.

Evidence suggests that physical activities were used since the early 20th century as part of structured rehabilitation programs for people with a disability (Bailey, 2008). However, with the exception of sport for Deaf people that developed by the end of the 19th century, the structuration of sport for people with a physical impairment only begun in the 1940s (Brittain, 2014; DePauw and Gavron, 1995). At the end of WWII, the British government appointed Dr Ludwig Guttmann as director of the newly established National Spinal Unit Centre at Stoke Mandeville Hospital (Aylesbury, UK). Dr Guttmann was convinced of the physical, psychological and social benefits of sport in the rehabilitation process of people with a spinal cord injury (Guttmann, 1975). Sports such as archery, table tennis, darts or athletics were introduced at Stoke Mandeville Hospital (Brittain, 2010) and became soon an integral part of the rehabilitation programs for spinally injured patients. Sport for rehabilitation purpose spread nationally and internationally, notably thanks to Dr Guttmann tirelessly promoting his techniques, medical doctors visiting Stoke Mandeville or former patients structuring sport clubs or groups once they returned to civil life (Brittain, 2010).

Another key mechanism that fostered the development of sport for people with a spinal cord injury was the creation of an annual sport competition, the Stoke Mandeville Games. The 1st Stoke Mandeville Games took place on 29 July 1948 and gathered 16 archers, 14 men and 2 women. While it is unknown whether Dr Guttmann planned this or not, the event coincided with the Opening Ceremony of the 14th Olympic Games in London (UK). The Stoke Mandeville Games became international 4 years later (1952), when a team from the Doorn Military

Rehabilitation Centre (The Netherlands) took part in the event. The Games, held annually, rapidly grew both in terms of sports practiced and para-athletes involved, all of them being spinally injured. As an example, more than 350 athletes from 20 countries competed in 10 sports during the 1958 International Stoke Mandeville Games (Brittain, 2014). The International Stoke Mandeville Games Federation (ISMGF) was created in 1959 with Dr Guttmann as its first president, in order to sustain the growth of the sport movement but also to prepare the 9th International Stoke Mandeville Games in 1960. These were organized in Rome, host city of the 1960 Olympic Games. They took place a few months after the Olympic Games, to stamp these Games with "the Olympic Seal, so consecrating therapeutic roles of sport in paraplegics' rehabilitation".[1] Those Games are today known as the 1st Paralympic Games.

During the 1960s and 1970s, several sports organizations known as International Organizations of Sport for the Disabled (IOSDs) were created to provide sport opportunities to athletes with other 'groups' of impairments (i.e. not only athletes with spinal injuries). The IOSDs were structured according to disability and not sport as usually the case in the Olympic movement (Gérard, Legg and Zintz, 2017). In 1963, the International Sports Organization for the Disabled (ISOD) – not to be confused with IOSD – was founded to develop sport opportunities for people with an amputation, visual impairment and for the category 'Les Autres' that translates from French as 'The Others'. Dr Guttmann became its first president in addition to the ISMGF presidency. The Cerebral-Palsy International Sports and Recreation Association (CP-ISRA) was created in 1978 to oversee sports for people with cerebral palsy. In 1981 the International Blind Sport Federation (IBSA) was established on its own to promote sport for people with a visual impairment. Finally, the International Sports Federation for People with a Mental Handicap (INAS-FID) was set up in 1986. These IOSDs largely contributed to the widening of sport participation for different 'groups' of athletes with an impairment (Howe, 2008).

Each IOSD developed its own sport rules and controlled games and competitions at the medical and technical levels. To preserve fairness among athletes, classifications systems were developed by each IOSD and categorized athletes according to a medical diagnosis of their impairments. According to Tweedy and Vanlandewijck (2011, p. 262), the medical classification systems "reflected the structure of a rehabilitation hospital, with separate classes for people with spinal cord injuries, amputations, brain impairments and those with other neurological and orthopedic conditions".

The International Stoke Mandeville Games continued to be held annually in England and organized every four years, when possible, in the same country or city hosting the Olympic Games during the Olympic year. This quadrennial sport competition progressively became what is known today as the Paralympic Games. Over time, the Paralympic Games were opened to various groups of impairments. As such, athletes with an amputation or a visual impairment competed for the first time during the 1976 Torontolympiad (Toronto, Canada) next to athletes with a spinal cord injury. Athletes with cerebral palsy were added to the sport programme at the 1980 Paralympic Games (Arnhem, The Netherlands). Finally, athletes with an intellectual disability were involved in the 1996 Paralympic Games (Atlanta, USA) for the first time.

In 1982, the International Coordinating Committee (ICC) of World Sports Organizations for the Disabled was created to coordinate the IOSDs and to control multi-IOSD sport competitions. Its creation also reflected the desire of the IOC to only deal with a single organization for sport for people with an impairment. The ICC was composed of representatives of IOSDs, these organizations remaining fully independent under the ICC umbrella. The ICC functioning was rapidly decried by IOSDs membership that denounced the disability-based structuration of the Paralympic movement as well as the medical classification systems that resulted "in too many parallel events and too many classes, as well as too few participants in too many events".[2]

After years of negotiation, the International Paralympic Committee (IPC) was founded in 1989 by the 6 IOSDs (i.e. ISOD, ISMGF, IBSA, CP-ISRA, INAS-FID and the Comité International des Sports des Sourds [CISS] founded in 1924) and 31 nations. The IPC designed its structure to be a sport-based organization and established Sport Assembly Executive Committees (SAECs) to harmonize the governance of para-sports. The SAECs also adapted protocols and sport rules in line with the Olympic sports. Forms of integrated classification were also experienced by grouping athletes not according to disability but according to body functionalities one possessed in a particular sport or discipline (Tweedy and Vanlandewijck, 2011).

The relationships between the Paralympic and Olympic movements progressively strengthened during the 1980s and 1990s. A major step forward occurred in the 2000 when the IOC and the IPC signed a first Cooperation Agreement. This agreement formalized relationships between the two organizations, such as the facts that the IPC president would become an IOC member, more partnerships between commissions would be developed or that the IOC would financially support IPC's operations. A second agreement signed in June 2001 detailed "the conditions which the IOC agreed to assist the IPC in securing and protecting the organization of the Paralympic games, effectively including the obligation to organize the Paralympic Games in the IOC Host City Contract with the OCOGs".[3] This model is known as the "One City Games model" and secured the organization of the Paralympic Games in the same facilities used for the Olympic Games, under identical service standards. Recently the IPC membership voted to renew this model of cooperation until the 2032 Olympic and Paralympic Games.

As a not-for-profit organization based in Bonn (Germany), the IPC has a membership of nearly 200 organizations (with 179 National Paralympic Committees, 5 Regional Paralympic Committees, 15 international Sports Federations and 4 IOSDs) and operated on a budget of nearly EUR 22 million in 2017, mainly coming from marketing and sponsorship activities, broadcasting rights and fundraising (IPC, 2017a). Since 2003, the Paralympic symbol is composed of three Agitos (from the Latin meaning "I move") "encircling a central point symbolize motion, emphasiz[ing] the role of athletes together from all corners of the world to compete" (IPC, 2017b).

The creation of the IPC in the late 1980s signaled a shift from a disability oriented sport movement, underpinned by a strong medical approach to disability sport, to a sport-based organization that soon focused on promoting elite sport competition for para-athletes. It also marked an increasing professionalization and commercialization of the Paralympic movement. Arguably, this rich and complex history is part of the Paralympic brand and influences its governance.

Brand governance

It goes without saying that a strong brand is a key asset for a company that can provide a competitive advantage to the company. The strength or value of a brand is usually understood in terms of brand equity, defined by Aaker (1991, p. 12) as "a set of assets and liabilities linked to a brand, its name and symbols, that adds or subtracts from the value provided by its product or service to a firm/or to that firm's customers". A strong brand equity can trigger customers' loyalty, trust and emotional attachment towards products and/or services offered by a company and, as a consequence, increase the likeliness and repetitiveness of customers' purchase intention.

The importance of adopting a strategic brand management approach to nurture brand equity has been widely recognized in marketing. According to Keller (2003, p. 44) strategic brand management involves "the design and implementation of marketing programmes and activities to build, measure and manage brand equity". Keller (2003, p. 733) also emphasized brand consistency as a cornerstone of brand management programme, to ensure "that diverse brand and marketing mix elements share a common core meaning, perhaps in some cases literally containing or conveying the same information".

However, as put forward by Helm and Jones (2010, p. 547), "although brand equity is increasingly being seen as critical to an organization's future value creation capability, at the same time, it is becoming more fragile". The authors (ibid.) added that "the risks to brand equity of being damaged or dissipated are rising as the potential hazards inherent in managing brands and brand experience multiply". Helm and Jones (2010) identified 6 major threats that can undermine the current and future equity of a brand, whatever the industry in which an organization operates: (1) more uncertain and fiercely competitive industry environments, (2) even more empowered customers, (3) line and brand extension proliferation, (4) a growing number of distribution and communication touchpoints, (5) increased use of strategic partnerships in delivery and finally (6) the risks of using social media. All these threats can scatter customers' experiences of the brand and therefore dilute its consistence and equity.

Due to the complex and fast-paced changing nature of the environment, scholars such as Hatch and Schultz (2010), Helm and Jones (2010) and Ind and Bjerke (2007) among others proposed the concept of brand governance as a new approach for brand management. The role of brand governance is to protect, manage and nurture a brand so it can remain a long-term source of value for a company. Séguin and Abeza (2019) recently brought this idea into sport management literature and further elaborated the concept using the Olympic brand as a case study. They indeed argued that "the preservation of the consistency and coherence of the Olympic brand demands a visionary brand governance approach that transcends strategic brand management" (Séguin and Abeza, 2019, p. 373).

The governance structure of a brand is composed of 3 interconnected systems (see Séguin and Abeza, 2019, p. 374). At the top, brand governance "is a systematic approach for building and nurturing a brand value to become and remain a long-term strategic asset that is built on the vision, mission and values of an organization, developed through long-term policies and governed by processes such as integrity and transparency" (Séguin and Abeza, 2019, p. 374). Stakeholders are also acknowledged as a crucial role in co-creating the brand (Ferrand, Chappelet and Séguin, 2012; Séguin and Abeza, 2019) and can impact on its current and future's equity (Ind and Bjerke, 2007). Overall brand governance long-term policies and processes provide the guiding principles for the strategic management of a brand, that is focused on the development of internal capabilities to develop, manage and measure brand equity. If efficiently integrated, long-term focused brand governance policies and strategic brand management capabilities allow for the consistent delivery of the brand at the operational level, that is mainly "concerned with [its] creative and cosmetic" dimensions (Séguin and Abeza, 2019, p. 375). A feedback loop between systems ensure that decisions and operations undertaken at all three levels contribute to the strengthening of the brand's long-term equity and value.

As highlighted previously, 'participation' is at the core of brand governance as a brand is co-created by a range of internal and external stakeholders (Ind and Bjerke, 2007; Lucarelli and Giovanardi, 2016). Therefore, brand governance is "a negotiated and contested mechanism" (Lucarelli and Giovanardi, 2016, p. 24) that encapsulates political relationships and conflicts between stakeholders. Such an approach echoes with research on organizational governance in which the notions of power, control or regulations lie at the heart of the literature (O'Boyle and Bradbury, 2013; Winand and Anagnostopoulos, 2019).

Aside the political nature of brand governance processes, one should also acknowledge the role of the broader institutional environment, comprised of "cultural-cognitive, normative and regulative elements" that give meaning to social life (Scott, 2014, p. 48). Put differently, a brand does not develop in a 'neutral'" social vacuum exempt of institutional dynamics in the forms of social norms, beliefs, attitudes or stereotypes that can influence how brands are developed and/or perceived. As highlighted by Fiss (2008, p. 390), organizations and, the author argues, their brands are indeed "deeply enmeshed in systems of norms and relations that are both culturally and socio-politically constructed". Governance systems, at the organization or brand levels should therefore be seen "as reflecting underlying cultural narratives or moral orders that define how social relations should be constructed and whose interests has priority" (Fiss, 2008, p. 390).

To sum up, an institutional view of brand governance highlights reciprocal relationships of influence between a brand and its institutional environment. This has at least two implications for this study. First, brands are influenced by larger institutional dynamics that can shape brands' objectives, meanings and narratives as well as their perceptions by stakeholders and the public. Social perceptions and attitudes towards disability and disability sports are therefore likely to impact the Paralympic brand's building, recognition and understanding. In turn, building upon the idea of institutional agency (Giddens, 1984; Lawrence and Suddaby, 2006), it can be argued that a well-governed brand has some hand in the shaping of the institutional environment. Applied to the IPC, it does mean that the Paralympic brand is uniquely positioned to challenge, but also potentially to reinforce, social perceptions, norms and attitudes towards disability and disability sport in society.

The governance of the Paralympic brand

As any other brand, the Paralympic brand evolves in a complex and fast-changing institutional environment that can impact on its equity and consistency. Based on a review of the literature pertaining to disability sports, Figure 8.1 highlights key dimensions that impact the governance of the Paralympic brand. First, the impact of the Paralympic Games and more precisely of the

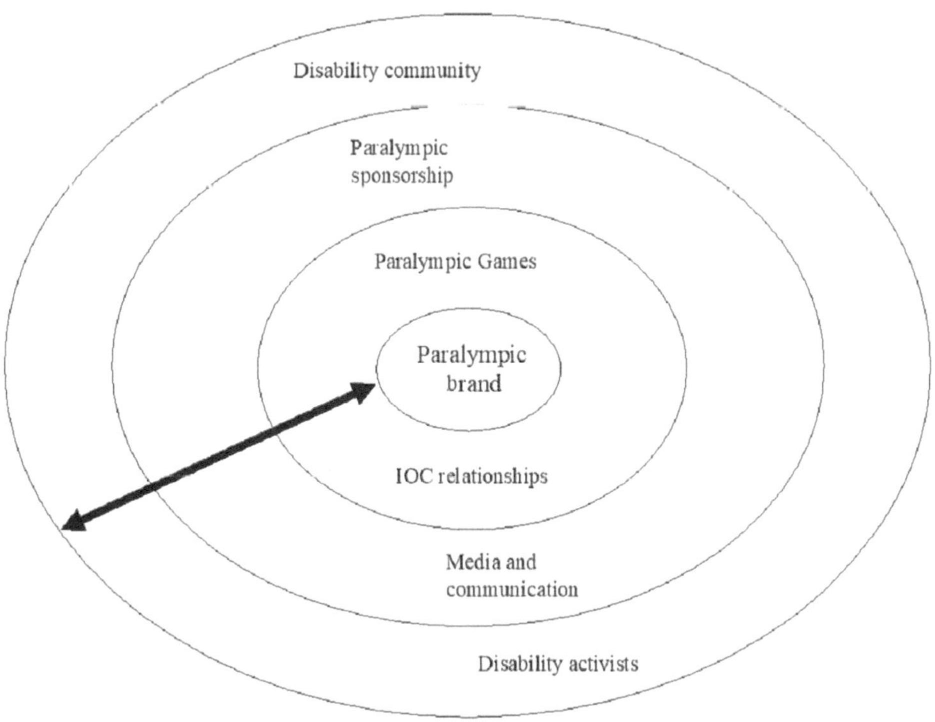

Figure 8.1 The institutional environment of the Paralympic brand

Paralympic Games sports programme on the Paralympic brand is examined. Closely linked to the previous point, the role of the IOC in the shaping of the Paralympic brand is then highlighted. Third, key debates in terms of Paralympic sponsorship are investigated and the role of the media in the building of the Paralympic brand is then described. Finally, the attention is turned to how the Paralympic brand resonates among the disability community and disability advocates, as well as into the larger society.

The Paralympic Games sport programmes and the Paralympic brand

The Paralympic Games are actively promoted by the IPC as an elite sport competition (Cottingham and Petersen-Wagner, 2018; Purdue and Howe, 2012). Nevertheless, a question that is still being discussed within the Paralympic community is whether the Paralympic Games should focus solely on elite athletes or should adopt a more participatory approach, remaining open to a larger range of impairments and athletes, including athletes with more severe impairments (Howe, 2008). This key concern is also reflected in the building process of the Winter and Summer Paralympic Games Sport programme. In a strategic review led by the IPC in 2014, concerns arose about how "strategic objectives such as universality, gender, impairment representation and the combination of different types of sport (individual, teams, endurance, power, combat etc.) with the requirements of professional sport, professional governance, broadcasters, sponsors and spectators"[4] can be reconciled during the construction of the PG sports programme. At the time of writing, the IPC strives to find a balance between the two, a model that is referred as the "best of both worlds". Nevertheless, some IPC members consider that this "in-between" model prevents the IPC from fulfilling its strategic objectives.

The shaping of the Paralympic Games sports programme is therefore a key strategic consideration in terms of brand governance, as it would deeply impact the Paralympic brand's meaning and its perception by the athletes, fans and society at large. An emphasis of elite and spectacular sports is likely to be suitable for sponsors, broadcasters and certain audience streams but could undermine the IPC's capacity to address disability community in all its diversity. On the contrary, a focus on participation is likely to blur the image of the Paralympic Games as a high-performance competition gathering the best athletes in the world.

The role of the IOC in relation to the Paralympic brand governance

As described in the historical overview of the Paralympic movement, a great deal of energy has been spent to develop relationships and partnerships with the IOC, that is, since the advent of the Paralympic movement. As a consequence, the marketing of the Paralympic movement and the governance of its brand cannot be discussed without acknowledging the role of the International Olympic Committee (IOC) (Legg and Dottori, 2017).

The IPC currently explores ways to improve its relationships with the IOC, notably on determining what value the Paralympic movement can contribute to the Olympic movement.[5] At the same time, the IPC questions how to protect the Paralympic movement from the IOC and other stakeholders when necessary. A recent example of this can be identified during the negotiation process of the "Partnership Agreement" signed in 2012. The aim of the agreement was to "extend relationships between the Paralympic and Olympic Movement on the long term and particularly outside the Games context".[6] The negotiation revealed to be complicated, in part because the IOC claimed "ownership rights over the term 'Paralympic' and the IPC's refusal to accept that the IOC was correct on this point".[7] At the end, the IPC protected its rights regarding the Paralympic symbolism and terminology and the agreement ultimately recognized "the mutual benefits of a close cooperation between both organizations to support their vision, mission and strategic objectives".[8] In terms of brand governance, it can be seen as a positive outcome as the IPC safeguards the control of its brand in relation to the word 'Paralympic'.

However, as part of the new IOC's host city contract for 2026, it has been decided that the IOC will jointly negotiate and manage international sponsorship for both the Olympic Games and Paralympic Games from 2021 (Holmes, 2018). It means that the top-tier Olympic Games partners will automatically become sponsors and hold global rights for the Paralympic Games. In addition, the IPC keeps the opportunity to negotiate Paralympic-specific partners in non-competitive categories. This agreement was presented by the IPC President Andrew Parsons as "a healthy boost of revenue" and an increase in stability for the IPC (Holmes, 2018).

Even if it can certainly boost the Paralympic brand in terms of visibility and commercial value, one can argue that this agreement can undermine the IPC's ability to effectively control its brand. As the "exact terms of the agreement are still negotiated" (Morgan, 2018), it remains unclear what exactly will be the role and power of the IPC during the negotiation, implementation and activation of the sponsorship deals. A second potential issue related to this agreement can be explored in terms of congruence between the IPC's objectives and the ones of the top-tier Olympic Games Partners. As reported by Macdougall, Nguyen and Karg (2014), congruence in terms of value and vision between a sponsor and a sponsee is a key feature in disability sports sponsorship. A crucial aspect of the agreement is whether the IPC will have the ability to develop mutually beneficial relationships with all the Olympic sponsors that support the Paralympic Games, in order to fulfill its commercial and social objectives in the long term.

Another aspect of the relationships between the IOC and IPC is related to the One City Games model. The Strategic Review (2014) identified an 'overwhelming' support for the One City Games model within IPC membership which, at the same time, recognized that the dependence to this model is a "major risk" and therefore supported the continued strengthening of the Paralympic Games for the long term.

Such concerns are related to broader discussions in order to avoid the 'Olympification' of the Paralympic movement and its brand, as well as the need for the IPC to take "a more confident approach to development of the Games and being in control of its own destiny, influencing the current IOC relationships where appropriate and shaping the Games to reflect its own vision, purpose, membership, personality and culture".[9] The relationship with the IOC deeply affects the governance of the Paralympic brand, which can be seen at the heart of a contested mechanism of influence between the IOC and the IPC.

Paralympic sponsorship

The ability of disability sports to attract sponsorship for marketing purposes remains a relatively new phenomenon when compared to mainstream sports. In fact, prior to the Salt Lake City Games in 2002, sponsors were concerned of associating their brand with the Paralympic Games as they were concerned of being perceived as 'exploiting' para-athletes (Legg and Dottori, 2017). However, the growth in the professionalization and commercialization of disability sports have reduced such concerns (Macdougall, Nguyen and Karg, 2014). The Paralympic brand is seen as relatively protected and strong (Cottingham and Petersen-Wagner, 2018) and, according to a 2016 Nielsen report, the Paralympic brand echoes with notions around disability and is strongly associated with words such as 'Inspiring', 'Strength', 'Brave', 'Competition' among others (Nielsen Sports, 2016). Moreover disability sports sponsorship landscape remains uncluttered compared to mainstream sports (Legg and Dottori, 2017; Séguin, Richelieu and O'Reilly, 2008). Studies also demonstrated that Paralympic sponsorship had positive effects on corporate image and consumers' purchase intention (Nam and Lee, 2013).

Nevertheless, one could argue that Paralympic sponsorship encompasses unique challenges compared to mainstream sports sponsorship. As mentioned earlier, the narratives developed by the IPC around the Paralympic Games is actively oriented towards elite sport competition (Cottingham and Petersen-Wagner, 2018) in which disability is presented as merely incidental (Silva and Howe, 2012). Similarly, the 2001–2016 IPC President Phil Craven encouraged the media to drop off the word 'disability' in relation to the Paralympic Games, arguing that "This is sport. It is not disability anything" (Gibson, 2012). However it has recently been suggested by Legg and Dottori (2017) that disability could be used as a point of differentiation in a highly saturated media and sponsorship environment. This would also offer a greater reliability and connection with the disabled audience (Silva and Howe, 2012), an argument that is elaborated later in this chapter. This idea is also supported by studies from Cottingham and colleagues (2013, 2015) highlighting that consumers in disability sports are motivated by unique factors such as attachment and involvement in the disability community (e.g. inspiration and a desire to watch athletes to overcome) that differentiate them from mainstream sport consumers' behaviors.

From a sponsor point of view, Macdougall, Nguyen and Karg (2014, p. 86) found that "a strong emphasis [was] placed by sponsors upon value and mission congruence within brand and health objectives focused versus specific sales objectives". Similarly, Cottingham, Gearity and Byon (2013) found that sponsors of disability sports events are more interested in serving the athletes rather than the spectators. They added that sponsors also seemed, implicitly or explicitly, motivated by Corporate Social Responsibility (CSR) initiatives. Even if IPC's strategy and sponsors' needs and objectives seem contradictory, it led Legg and Dottori (2017) to argue that if the IPC manages to find the right balance, the Paralympic movement has the potential to become "a one-stop shop for organizations seeking associations with performance-excellence AND social responsibility" (p. 274).

The role of communication, media and the Paralympic brand

The Paralympic brand, media coverage and communication around the Paralympic movement has evolved over time. If an 'athlete-frame' is now common to portray Paralympians, it was not always the case. For example, Tynedal and Wolbring (2013) found that the coverage of the Paralympic movement by the *New York Times* between 1955 and 2012 was not only minimal compared to the Olympic Games but also stereotypical in different ways. Para-athletes were frequently presented as victims or "suffering entities" as the newspaper used a medical rhetoric to report on para-athletes' performances. This is perhaps not surprising given the birth and development of the Paralympic movement within the medical and rehabilitation sector as explained earlier in this chapter. Similarly, French and Le Clair (2018) found that media portrayal of para-athletes has mainly been paternalistic or that disability was central to the narratives, not the sport achievement. They also acknowledged that new media and in particular social media such as Twitter open the door for more contested or negotiated representation of disability in sport.

A second stereotype frequently reported by the literature is the one of the 'supercrip'. According to Silva and Howe (2012, p. 175) supercrip "implies a stereotypical process that requires an individual 'to fight against his/her impairment' in order to overcome it and achieve improbable 'success'". The source of this narrative is to be found in society's low-level expectations placed upon people with an impairment, resulting in the fact that para-athletes become 'super' or 'heroes' in situations where someone without a disability would be perceived as normal. As a consequence, the supercrip narrative perpetuates the understanding of disability "as a problem" that needs to be overcome (Silva and Howe, 2012).

The supercrip narrative and more broadly stereotypes related to disability impact the ways in which sports organizations, media and sponsors communicate about Paralympic athletes. As an example, para-athletes and disability sport marketers have long discussed if athletes' personal stories should be part of the communication mix. So far, research has been contrasting. Cottingham, Gearity and Byon (2013) studied the perceptions of Paralympic sponsorship from three disability sports administrators. Their results showed that for some individuals, athletes' background is part "of the product" they are selling (p. 95). Others called for more traditional sport marketing strategies and a full focus on athletes' sport achievements and results.

The complexity of this debate becomes apparent when considering the dual role Paralympic athletes have in society, for both the 'able-bodied' audience and the disability community. Following Purdue and Howe (2012), it can be argued that able-bodied spectatorship of disability sports is interested in Paralympic athletes' sporting achievement. On the contrary, a disabled audience is more likely to appreciate Paralympic sport performances and, at the same time, can be "encouraged to identify with the impairment the athletes have" (Purdue and Howe, 2012). This led these authors to theorize the idea of "Paralympic Paradox" that has been described as follows:

> Firstly, there is a fundamental need for the able-bodied audience to be able to identify the Paralympian as having some form of impairment, to ensure the individual is seen as a credible and justified member of a disability sport competition. Secondly, the more an impaired athlete's disability is de-emphasized (the desired reception of able-bodied audience), the more that those viewers with disability may become alienated from their own bodies and disability sport in general. The athlete being viewed at the Paralympic Games may no longer act as a credible role model for individuals with disabilities, as they seemingly distance themselves from particular conditions of disabled people.

In other words, the Paralympic Paradox reflects a tension in terms of identities for an athlete being viewed as an elite athlete as well as a member of the disability community (McNamee, 2017).

The Paralympic paradox can be seen as a key tension within the Paralympic brand, that has the potential to undermine IPC's abilities to foster change in society for all people with an impairment. This aspect is further explored in the next and final section.

Paralympic brand and the disability community

The Paralympic brand blends ideas of sporting excellence and social awareness and change for people with an impairment. As such, a targeted outcome in terms of Paralympic Games' legacy is to challenge attitudes and perceptions of disability in society (IPC, 2015). Even if Paralympic legacy as a field of research is rapidly growing (Misener et al., 2013), there remains a paucity of research investigating the perception of the Paralympic movement from the point of view of the disability activists and disability community (Braye, 2017; Braye, Dixon and Gibbons, 2013; Braye, Gibbons and Dixon, 2013).

Hosting the Games can be a catalyst for cities' urban regeneration, for passing new laws promoting equality, for developing new initiatives towards sport participation and accessibility. Nevertheless Darcy (2003), in the study of the legacy of the 2000 Sydney Paralympic Games, noted a contradiction between the fact that elite disability sport is privileged over the average material position of the disability community. More recently, Weed and Dowse (2009) also argued that a focus on elite sport can prevent the social legacy of the 2012 London Paralympic Games.

In this vein Braye, Dixon and Gibbons (2013) analyzed the views of UK disabled activists regarding the Paralympic Games. Their findings reflected a negative perception of the Games from the activists' point of view as "the Games present an overly optimistic and unrealistic view of living as a disabled person" (p. 5). Braye (2017) also argued that the overly positive narrative the IPC is developing around the Paralympic Games depicts the Games "as a modern day freak show" (p. 225). He further argues that the brand of Disabled People Movement, an international disability advocacy group, is "completely overshadowed by the brand that is the Paralympic Games under the auspice of the IPC" (p. 226). Braye (2017) concluded that there is the potential for the IPC brand 'killing' the DPM brand and therefore undermining the voice of disability activists in society.

With great power comes great responsibility. How the Paralympic brand is perceived by the larger disability community that the IPC intends to serve is determinant on the IPC's ability to break discriminatory barriers for all people with an impairment.

Conclusion

Organizations operate and evolve in a complex and dynamic environment that can alter or damage their brands' equity. In response, scholars emphasized the importance of brand governance as a new approach to protect and sustain brands' long-term equity and value. The governance structure of a brand implies the development of long-term policies, capabilities and guiding principles that are based on the values, mission and vision of the company in order to develop and nurture a brand's equity.

A brand governance approach acknowledges the co-creation of brand by internal and external stakeholders, engaged in power-political relationships and contests. As this chapter highlights, one should also consider the embeddedness of the organization in a larger institutional environment composed of cultural-cognitive, normative and regulative elements (Scott, 2014) that can both shaped, or be altered and transformed by, the core meanings of a brand's company.

The Paralympic brand is at the centre of a complex nexus of inter-related dimensions that influence its short- and long-term governance. Thanks to its growing professionalization and commercialization, the International Paralympic Committee (IPC) is now able to showcase para-athletes' abilities and sporting excellence at the worldwide level. Key partnerships, notably with the International Olympic Committee (IOC) have strengthened IPC's position in the international sport movement. Moreover the Paralympic brand is perceived as strong and well protected while Paralympic sponsorship positively increases sponsors' images. Arguably, the IPC has become the main sounding box for disability sports in society and has the power to challenge social norms, beliefs and stereotypes associated with disability.

However, its relationship with the IOC also presents risks, notably in terms of control of the Paralympic brand and the Olympification of its meaning. Also, by overtly focusing on elite sport, the IPC can potentially alienate a crucial component of its viewership, namely the disability community that increasingly feels disconnected from the Paralympic Games. Moreover, communication about the Paralympic movement and Paralympians offers unique challenges that have the potential to either tackle or reinforce stereotypes associated with disability, such as supercrip.

There are additional brand governance issues that the IPC will have to address in the near future. As sponsors' interest in para-sports is growing, more associations with the Paralympic brand will be developed over time that can undermine IPC's ability to govern it effectively. Moreover para-athletes are increasingly used as activation points by sponsors which, as a consequence, can multiply images, beliefs and narratives associated with Paralympic athletes and therefore undermine the Paralympic brand's consistency. Finally, as sponsors may be willing to invest more and more in the Paralympic brand, they may also want to have a say in the governance of the IPC and its brand. More pressures will therefore be created on the IPC and its board of directors. How the IPC will be able to protect itself and its brand from external stakeholders will be critical for the long-term Paralympic brand's equity.

The Paralympic brand is arguably at the edge of two worlds, aiming to raise social awareness and change for all people with an impairment using elite and high-performance sport as main vehicle. If well governed, the Paralympic brand is in the unique position to take advantage of the best of both worlds and fulfill its strategic objectives in the long term.

Notes

1 Press release by the Fédération Sportive Belge des Handicapés, September 12, 1958.
2 Position paper by the ISOD on the Principles for International Bodies for sports competitions programmes, ICC Seminar, Mar. 13–14, 1987.
3 Quote from a letter from the IPC to the NPC, Aug. 12, 2003.
4 IPC, 2014, Priority Themes "Developing the Paralympic Games Sport Programme", IPC Membership Gathering, Oct. 3–5.
5 IPC, 2014, Priority Themes "Enhancing the Partnership with the Olympic Movement", IPC Membership Gathering, Oct. 3–5.
6 Ibid.
7 Ibid.
8 Ibid.
9 IPC, 2014, Priority Themes "Enhancing the Partnership with the Olympic Movement", IPC Membership Gathering, Oct. 3–5.

References

Aaker, D.A. (1991). *Managing brand equity: Capitalizing on the value of a brand name.* New York: The Free Press.

Bailey, S. (2008). *Athlete first: A history of the Paralympic movement.* Chichester: John Wiley & Sons.

Braye, S. (2017). "You shall not murder": Atos at the Paralympic games. *Journal of Disability & Religion*, 21(2), pp. 215–229.

Braye, S., Dixon, K. and Gibbons, T. (2013). A mockery of equality: An exploratory investigation into disabled activists views of the Paralympic games. *Disability & Society*, 28(7), pp. 984–996.

Braye, S., Gibbons, T. and Dixon, K. (2013). Disability 'rights' or 'wrongs'? The claims of the International Paralympic Committee, the London 2012 Paralympics and disability rights in the UK. *Sociological Research Online*, 18(3), pp. 1–5.

Brittain, I. (2010). *The Paralympic games explained.* London: Routledge.

Brittain, I. (2014). *From Stoke Mandeville to Sotchi: A history of the summer and winter Paralympic games.* Champaign, IL: Common Ground.

Cottingham, M., Gearity, B. and Byon, K. (2013). A qualitative examination of disability sport executives' perceptions of sport promotion and the acquisition of sponsors. *Sport Marketing Quarterly*, 22(2).

Cottingham, M., Pate, J.R. and Gearity, B. (2015). Examining 'inspiration': Perspectives of stakeholders attending a power wheelchair soccer tournament. *Canadian Journal of Disability Studies*, 4(1), pp. 59–88.

Cottingham, M. and Petersen-Wagner, R. (2018). Marketing of Paralympic sports: Attracting spectators and sponsors. In: I. Brittain and A. Beacom, eds., *The Palgrave handbook of Paralympic studies.* London: Palgrave Macmillan, pp. 605–624.

Darcy, S. (2003). The politics of disability and access: The Sydney 2000 games experience. *Disability & Society*, 18(6), pp. 737–757.

DePauw, K.P. and Gavron, S.J. (1995). *Disability and sport.* Champaign: Human Kinetics.

Ferrand, A., Chappelet, J-L. and Séguin, B. (2012). *Olympic marketing.* London: Routledge.

Fiss, P.C. (2008). Institutions and corporate governance. In: R. Greenwood, C. Oliver, K. Sahlin and R. Suddaby, eds., *The Sage handbook of organizational institutionalism.* London: Sage Publications.

French, L. and Le Clair, J.M. (2018). Game changer? Social media, representations of disability and the Paralympic games. In: I. Brittain and A. Beacom, eds., *The Palgrave handbook of Paralympic studies*. Basingstoke: Palgrave Macmillan, pp. 99–121.

Gérard, S., Legg, D. and Zintz, T. (2017). Multi-level analysis of institutional formation and change: The case of the Paralympic movement. *Sport, Business and Management: An International Journal*, 7(5), pp. 515–541.

Gibson, O. (2012). Drop the word 'disabled' from Games coverage, demands Paralympics Committee president. *The Guardian*.

Giddens, A. (1984). *The constitution of society: Outline of the theory of structuration*. Berkeley: University of California Press.

Guttmann, L. (1975). Development of sport for the Spinal Paralysed. *Hexagon Roche*, 3(7), pp. 6–13.

Hatch, M.J. and Schultz, M. (2010). Toward a theory of brand co-creation with implications for brand governance. *The Journal of Brand Management*, 17(8), pp. 590–604.

Helm, C. and Jones, R. (2010). Brand governance: The New Agenda in brand management. *Journal of Brand Management*, 17(8), p. 545.

Holmes, E. (2018). Olympic TOP sponsors to also cover Paralympic games. *SportsPro Media*.

Howe, D. (2008). *The cultural politics of the Paralympic movement: Through an anthropological lens*. London: Routledge.

Ind, N. and Bjerke, R. (2007). *Branding governance: A participatory approach to the brand building process*. John Wiley & Sons.

IPC. (2015). *Strategic plan 2015–2018*. Bonn: IPC.

IPC. (2017a). *Annual Report 2017*. Bonn: IPC.

IPC. (2017b). *International Paralympic Committee brand book*. Bonn: IPC.

Keller, K.L. (2003). *Strategic brand management*. 2nd ed. Upper Saddle River: Prentice-Hall.

Lawrence, T.B. and Suddaby, R. (2006). Institutions and institutional work. In: S. Clegg, C. Hardy, T. Lawrence and W. Nord, eds., *The Sage handbook of organization studies*. London: Sage Publications.

Legg, D. and Dottori, M. (2017). Marketing and sponsorship at the Paralympic games. In: S. Darcy, S. Frawley and D. Adair, eds., *Managing the Paralympics*. Palgrave Macmillan, pp. 263–288.

Legg, D. and Steadward, R. (2011). The Paralympic games and 60 years of change (1948–2008): Unification and restructuring from a disability and medical model to sport-based competition. *Sport in Society*, 14(9), pp. 1099–1115.

Lucarelli, A. and Giovanardi, M. (2016). The political nature of brand governance: A discourse analysis approach to a regional brand building process. *Journal of Public Affairs*, 16(1), pp. 16–27.

Macdougall, H.K., Nguyen, S.N. and Karg, A.J. (2014). "Game, set, match": An exploration of congruence in Australian disability sport sponsorship. *Sport Management Review*, 17(1), pp. 78–89.

McNamee, M.J. (2017). Paralympism, Paralympic values and disability sport: A conceptual and ethical critique. *Disability and Rehabilitation*, 39(2), pp. 201–209.

Misener, L., Darcy, S., Legg, D. and Gilbert, K. (2013). Beyond Olympic legacy: Understanding Paralympic legacy through a thematic analysis. *Journal of Sport Management*, 27(4), pp. 329–341.

Morgan, L. (2018). Top-tier Olympic partners to become sponsors of Paralympics from 2021. *Inside The Games*. Available at https://www.insidethegames.biz/articles/1067457/top-tier-olympic-partners-to-become-sponsors-of-paralympics-from-2021

Nam, S.B. and Lee, K.Y. (2013). The influence of the Paralympic sponsorship on consumers' purchase intention. *Choregia*, 9(1).

Nielsen Sports. (2016). *NPC workshop global position of Paralympic games*. Koln: Nielsen Sports.

O'Boyle, I. and Bradbury, T. (2013). *Sport governance: International case studies*. London: Routledge.

Purdue, D.E.J. and Howe, P.D. (2012). See the sport, not the disability: Exploring the Paralympic paradox. *Qualitative Research in Sport, Exercise and Health*, 4(2), pp. 189–205.

Scott, W.R. (2014). *Institutions and organizations: Ideas, interests, and identities*. Thousand Oaks: Sage Publications.

Séguin, B. and Abeza, G. (2019). Olympic brand governance: Future research directions. In: M. Winand and C. Anagnostopoulos, eds., *Research handbook on sport governance*. Cheltenham, UK: Edward Elgar Publisher.

Séguin, B., Richelieu, A. and O'Reilly, N. (2008). Leveraging the Olympic brand through the reconciliation of corporate and consumers' brand perceptions. *International Journal of Sport Management and Marketing*, 3(1–2), pp. 3–22.

Silva, C.F. and Howe, P.D. (2012). The (in) validity of supercrip representation of Paralympian athletes. *Journal of Sport and Social Issues*, 36(2), pp. 174–194.

Tweedy, S.M. and Vanlandewijck, Y.C. (2011). International Paralympic Committee position stand – Background and scientific principles of classification in Paralympic sport. *British Journal of Sports Medicine*, 45(4), pp. 259–269.

Tynedal, J. and Wolbring, G. (2013). Paralympics and its athletes through the lens of the New York Times. *Sports*, 1(1), pp. 13–36.

Weed, M. and Dowse, S. (2009). A missed opportunity waiting to happen? The social legacy potential of the London 2012 Paralympic games. *Journal of Policy Research in Tourism, Leisure and Events*, 1(2), pp. 170–174.

Winand, M. and Anagnostopoulos, C., eds., (2019). *Research handbook on sport governance*. Cheltenham: Edward Elgar Publishing.

9

Sponsoring the Paralympic Games and breaking barriers

David Legg

Introduction

Calgary hosted a plebiscite in November 2018 asking citizens whether they wanted to pursue a bid to host the 2026 Olympic and Paralympic Games. This would have been the first time that Calgary would have hosted a Paralympic Games as the precedent of hosting both Olympic and Paralympic Games in the same city was not set when Calgary hosted the Winter Olympic Games in 1988. Relevant to this chapter was an issue during the lead up to the plebiscite pertaining to the economics and costs of hosting the 2026 Games. During pre-plebiscite presentations, the operations of the Paralympic Games were presented as requiring additional funds for the operations of the Games which was beyond what sponsors would likely cover. As an interested observer and Paralympic leader, I wondered whether the Calgary 2026 Bidco was underestimating the marketing and sponsorship potential of the Paralympic Games and if these Games were on the cusp of previously unseen growth and support. As it turned out, the plebiscite failed and so, from a Calgary context, my premise will forever remain unknown. Knowing whether the Paralympic Games, athletes, movement and brand are on the cusp of breaking barriers within marketing and sponsorship, however, may happen sooner than some might think.

History of the Paralympic Games

The Paralympic movement has its genesis in rehabilitation centres following World War II. The significant number of war veterans with spinal injuries and the reality that these individuals now had considerably longer life spans due to the invention of penicillin meant an increased focus on rehabilitation. Many medical professionals used sport and recreation as a means of rehabilitation. This practice evolved into small sport events held at hospitals, the most famous of which was Stoke Mandeville in the United Kingdom. Dr. Ludwig Guttmann, the physiatrist there, then created what was called the Stoke Mandeville Games and these grew slowly into what we now know as the Paralympic Games (Legg and Steadward, 2011).

The first Paralympic Games were held in Rome following that city's hosting of the Summer Olympic Games in 1960. Winter Paralympic Games, meanwhile, were not held until 1976. In both cases Paralympic Games were held every quadrennial following the Olympic schedule.

Starting in 1988, due to a precedent being set by the Seoul host organizing committee, every Summer and Winter Paralympic Games have been held in the same city as the Olympic Games. Eventually the IOC and IPC formalized this relationship by signing an agreement in 2001. Beijing 2008 was thus the first Games held under this agreement and it has been renewed several times since then. The agreement now includes marketing and sponsorship.

As the Paralympic Games evolved, it has also grown in every conceivable capacity – including sponsorship and marketing. With this growth, both opportunities and challenges have emerged and with the latest agreement between the IOC and IPC, it will be interesting to see its development, particularly as it relates to marketing and sponsorship.

The purpose of this chapter is to review what is known about the marketing and sponsorship of the Paralympic movement, highlight recent case studies and then postulate about the future of the Paralympic Games and its movement.

To date, few scholars have researched the marketing and sponsorship of the Paralympic movement. The few examples that do exist include the work of Cottingham and his associates including Petersen-Wagner (2018), Byon, Cottingham and Carroll (2010) and Cottingham, Gearity and Byon (2013). Hardin and Hardin (2004) and Hargreaves and Hardin (2009) also focused on disability perception and sport marketing while Park et al. (2011) studied consumer attitudes towards the Paralympic Games along with purchase intentions toward corporate sponsors of the Games. The author of this chapter addressed Paralympic marketing from a variety of perspectives including Legg (2001, 2015, 2016), Legg and Dottori (2017), and Piispanen and Legg (2012). Finally, Purdue and Howe (2012) published a seminal work titled 'See the Sport, Not the Disability: Exploring the Paralympic Paradox.'

This relative dearth of scholarship, however, may be changing with the increasing exposure and interest in Paralympic sport. The reality of sponsorship and marketing of the Paralympic movement changed radically in 2018 with the updated agreement between the IOC and IPC. This agreement now extends from 2021 to 2032. In a presentation to the IPC membership in September 2018 in Madrid, Xavier Gonzalez, the IPC's Chief Executive Officer at that time, reviewed the history of this agreement and its implications. He noted that the original agreement between the IOC and IPC signed in October 2000 was updated a year later to focus on the organization of the Paralympic Games. This was the start of the one bid, two Games system noted earlier where cities would submit bids to the IOC for the right to host both Olympic and Paralympic Games. A series of amendments to the agreement were made in 2003, 2006 and 2012. At the 2014 IPC Membership Gathering, the IPC confirmed a desire to move these agreements further, extending them to 2032. This updated agreement was a commitment to elevate the Paralympic Games' visibility and further develop the Paralympic brand by leveraging the Olympic platform and its global commercial partners (Gonzalez, 2018). The latter is significant for the future sponsorship and marketing opportunities of the Paralympic Games and its movement.

The IOC will manage the commercial aspect of the Paralympic Games including the domestic rights of TOP sponsors. The one exception is Toyota which will not be included as part of the agreement until 2024. National Paralympic Committee (NPC) commercial and institutional rights and obligations will remain as per existing agreements. The IPC retains rights to IPC Sports and World Para Sports as well as institutional non-commercial activities. As for broadcasting, the IPC will be responsible for selling the broadcasting rights on behalf of the Olympic Committee for the Olympic Games (OCOG). Olympic Broadcasting Services (OBS) thus becomes the Paralympic Host Broadcaster for the Paralympic Games, with the Olympic Channel having a prominent role in the coverage of the Paralympic Games and OCOGs being responsible for the broadcasting costs (Gonzalez, 2018).

More specifically, the new IOC–IPC agreement means that

> top-tier Olympic Games partners will receive automatic global rights to the Paralympic Games starting in 2021. The change to the current system, which was published as part of the IOC's new host city contract for 2026, puts an end to separate rights negotiations with the IOC and the International Paralympic Committee (IPC).
>
> *(Holmes, 2018)*

Currently, six of the 13 TOP sponsors (Atos, Panasonic, Samsung, Toyota, Bridgestone and Visa) are also worldwide partners of the IPC, together with Allianz and BP, which have IPC-only deals. The other TOP sponsors, Coca-Cola, Alibaba, Dow, GE, Intel, Omega and P&G, are not currently sponsors of the Paralympic Games (Holmes, 2018).

What is likely to happen at the international level is similar to the situation in the United States, where the USOC already controls and bundles Paralympic rights within its Team USA deals. "I would say from a brand standpoint, the ease of obtaining combined rights should be very welcome," said Dave Mingey, managing director of the advisory group at CSM Sport & Entertainment. "It has been a bit clunky in the past to work through two separate groups for marketing rights and assets that were already so closely linked" (Fischer, 2018). IPC President Andrew Parsons noted that

> It makes more sense for the IOC, for us and for the sponsors, who will get the Paralympics as part of the package. It brings more insurance and stability for us and for the IOC and we think we can generate more revenue with that.
>
> *(Morgan, 2018b)*

This new partnership also builds upon the Paralympic Games success in attracting global interest starting in 2012 at the London Paralympic Games. In 2014, during the Paralympic Games in Sochi, 5.3 million Canadians tuned in to the English language CBC coverage (Bassett, 2014; Powell, 2014). Interest grew again and culminated most recently at the 2018 Paralympic Games in PyeongChang which "broke all international broadcast and online viewing records, attracting more broadcasters and viewers than ever before for a Paralympic Winter Games outside of the host country" (IPC, 2018b). According to Nielsen Sports figures published on behalf of the IPC, the 2018 Games were broadcast in more than 100 territories and attracted a cumulative audience of 2.02 billion people. A further 251.5 million people were reached via Games coverage on the IPC's digital media channels (IPC, 2018b). What the IPC hopes can translate into even greater appeal for the 2020 Games in Tokyo is that for the 2018 Games, "Japanese viewers made up 21 per cent of the overall audience (433 million viewers) with almost half of them consuming the Games through public broadcaster and Paralympic rightsholder NHK" (IPC, 2018b). The number of individuals from China watching the 2018 Games also bodes well for future commercial success of the 2022 Games to be held in Beijing. During the 2018 Games, "TV audiences in China grew to 122.8 million, an increase of 18 per cent on Sochi 2014" (IPC, 2018b). Pascal Schulte, Nielsen Sports Vice President Sales Operations & Account Management, reflecting on this growth suggested that "The positive developments are no coincidence. Para sports play a crucial role in producing the kind of stories which touches media, recipients and sponsors on an emotional level" (IPC, 2018b).

David Lucas, Head of International Federations of Nielsen Sports and Entertainment, noted that the PyeongChang Games reached a new level in terms of broadcast time and the Paralympic Games performed well compared to other major events in terms of media impact. He pointed out that the nine IPC and Paralympic Games partners (including North Face, Samsung, Hyundai, Coca-Cola and Omega) demonstrated significant media value from the first quarter following the 2018 Games. He suggested that compared to other premier events such as Formula 1 and the Tour de France, the Winter Paralympic Games 2018 had a higher share of non-dedicated programs, resulting in an audience being driven by secondary programs such as news, magazines and sports magazines. Moreover, almost half of the event impressions stemmed from non-dedicated coverage (Lucas, 2018).

The Paralympic Games have thus taken a huge step forward in its marketing efforts. What has perhaps helped the Paralympic Games and the movement boost its awareness and coverage is the increased leveraging of the Games by corporate sponsors. Here we will present sponsors that have seen the potential benefit of partnering with the Paralympic movement. They include Bridgestone Tire, British Petroleum, Procter & Gamble and Toyota.

Procter & Gamble

Procter & Gamble (P & G) recently signed as a Gold Partner for the 2020 Tokyo Paralympic Games. P & G has been a member of the TOP programme since 2010 but the move to add the Paralympic Games reflected its commitment to "Promoting diversity and inclusion that aims to respect and leverage individual differences" (Morgan, 2018a). In particular P & G will "contribute to the Paralympic Games Tokyo 2020 and help promote an inclusive society, through the 'Official Sponsor of Mums' campaign" which began years earlier (Morgan, 2018a).

The partnership between the Paralympics and P & G was initially launched through television commercials for the 2012 for the London Paralympics and continued for the 2014 Games in Sochi showcasing the link between mothers and their children with disabilities. The commercial showed "how moms can provide love that encourages you to think beyond your disabilities, so they can produce some really, really tough athletes" (Gianatasio, 2014). Paralympic snowboarder Amy Purdy narrated the 2014 commercial stating,

> You could have protected me. You could have taken every hit. You could have turned the world upside down so that I would never feel pain. But you didn't. You gave me my freedom because you were strong. And now, so am I.

The ad, running both online and on TV, racked up 2.2 million YouTube views at the time of the report by Adweek (Gianatasio, 2014). Four years later in 2018, P & G built upon this campaign with another ad titled "Love Over Bias." Here they imagined what the world could be if we all saw each other through a mom's eyes. Oksana Masters was one of six Paralympic athletes in the commercial. She was a three-time Paralympic medallist who competed in three different Paralympian sports (2012, 2014, 2016).

Toyota

As a new worldwide partner of the IPC, Toyota activated its partnership by launching its first ever global media campaign "Start Your Impossible." This campaign reflects "the Olympic and Paralympic spirit of encouragement, challenge and progress" with the goal being to amplify Toyota's brand messaging as a 'mobility' company. According to Athan Stephanopoulos (2018), the President of NowThis, this campaign resulted in 206 million global impressions, 43.5 million total views, 620k reactions (likes, comments, shares) and 235k hours of content consumed. This campaign allowed Toyota to "support and celebrate the will to move regardless of wealth, impairments, gender, nationality" (Dario Giustini, 2018; Toyota, 2018). "Start Your Impossible marked Toyota's long-term commitment to support the creation of a more inclusive and sustainable society in which everyone can challenge their impossible through stories of determination as well as through Toyota technologies" (Toyota, 2018). This commercial was launched during Super Bowl LII reaching nearly 100 million viewers in the United States.

Bridgestone Tire

Bridgestone, the world's largest tire and rubber manufacturer, became the seventh IPC Worldwide Partner in December, 2018. Like many other IPC partners, Bridgestone, a TOP partner signed through 2024, received global IPC rights in categories that include tires, tire services and selected automotive vehicle services and self-propelled bicycles (Bridgestone, 2018). To start their partnership, the company supported several leading international para-athletes, including eight Bridgestone employees who are training and hoping to compete in the Tokyo 2020 Paralympic Games. Its commitment to support the global Paralympic movement aligned with the company's "Chase Your Dream" message aims at encouraging people to overcome obstacles and persevere in the pursuit of their goals. Bridgestone aims at creating a more inclusive society through para-sport, and seeks to improve the way people move, live, work and play. Bridgestone wanted to amplify the company's core values of service and diversity. Somewhat uniquely, the Bridgestone agreement includes sport-specific support, including the application of its tire and rubber expertise to develop advancements in equipment for para-athletes, such as new rubber soles for prosthetics and rubber grips for gloves.

British Petroleum

Unique among these corporations, British Petroleum (BP) made headlines in 2017 when it substituted its sponsorship of the United States Olympic Committee to six US Paralympic teams (Holmes, 2018). A long-time partner of the Paralympic movement, BP's global brand director was prepared to 'up its game' if more marketers caught on to the growing opportunity. "The Paralympics often lives in the shadows of its Olympic counterpart, but with TV viewership and attendance on the rise it's only a matter of time before more brands start paying attention" (Lyons, 2018).

A spokesperson for BP suggests that the Paralympics are "sport's best kept secret." Speaking at a Sports Industry Breakfast Club in the United Kingdom after the 2012 Paralympic Games, BP representatives acknowledged that in the early days of BP's sponsorship with the Paralympic Games, there were not many commercial partners involved, meaning it was easy for the company to build a presence in that space.

> It's like when you find a really good place to go on holiday, you don't want to tell people where it is because then everybody goes there and it's no longer good anymore. So, the question is: "Do I tell other people?". Because you don't want too many marketers coming in and bidding up the costs.
>
> *(Lyons, 2018)*

When asked whether the Paralympic Games is a hard sell internally, BP spokespersons quickly argued against this notion. BP shares IPC's values such as courage, which employees recognize and appreciate. Accordingly, BP proudly sponsors IPC's annual Courage Award, which celebrates a value shared by both organizations. "You don't have to explain why you're supporting the Paralympic movement. People just get it. It's a good cause and people aren't going to criticize BP for supporting a good cause," he says. "Because the IPC is such a purpose-driven organization, people don't challenge it. People internally get that this is part of BP building its brand but that it's also doing good and they want to be involved in it" (Lyons, 2018).

This sentiment of the Paralympic being a 'diamond in the rough' was further echoed by NBC's chief following the Games of Sochi 2014 (Anderson, 2014).

> We got six sponsors [BMW, BP, Citi, Liberty Mutual Insurance, Procter & Gamble and The Hartford] who were willing and enthusiastic of our coverage, and that gave us the opportunity to broaden it to these 50-plus hours that are now fully streamed on the USOC website.

While acknowledging there was not much to compare with from previous Games, audience figures were up 60 per cent on NBC's cable network and 40 per cent on NBC, adding that "we have found a diamond in the rough with this amazing event that is full of incredible human-interest stories to tell" (Anderson, 2014). For the US, showcasing the abilities of ex-military men and women seems to resonate with the American public with interest peaking when war veterans from Afghanistan and Iraq were profiled (Anderson, 2014).

While the support of companies such as P & G, BP, Toyota and Bridgestone bode well for the future of the Games and movement, challenges remain. For example, in Canada, the small percentage of participation in para-sports was mirrored by the lack of public awareness and brand recognition for Paralympic athletes (Dembe, 2018). While there were "record-smashing international audience numbers for the 2016 Paralympics in Rio, many of Canada's athletes struggled making a significant dent in television ratings and marketability" (Dembe, 2018). Joanne Mortimer, a Canadian-Dutch para swimmer who won four Paralympic medals, including two gold at the 2012 Paralympic Games, echoed this challenge. "Lack of opportunities in Canada have propelled many Paralympians to take charge of their own marketing and promotion." What is hopefully changing is the shift in corporate support as demonstrated by the profiles of Toyota, Bridgestone and Procter & Gamble. Another example is the Canadian Imperial Bank of Canada (CIBC), which began its sponsorship of the Canadian Paralympic Committee in 2013 while not being a sponsor of the Canadian Olympic Committee. Andrew Greenlaw, senior director of sponsorship at CIBC, believes that the Paralympics are a powerful vehicle to shift societal perceptions of disability, stressing that the unique stories are the selling point. "These athletes are great visual representation," said Greenlaw. "From a marketing perspective, storytelling is our greatest asset" (Dembe, 2018).

The future

There are several other companies (e.g. Target and L'Oreal) that are including persons with disability in advertising campaigns and celebrating disability (Smith, 2012). Whether this trend continues or the agreement signed between the IOC and IPC leads to more international/national corporations to support Paralympic athletes is undetermined. Another challenge lies in the way some companies portray athletes with disabilities and whether they do more damage than good for the Paralympic brand.

For example, *Vogue* magazine was criticized for photoshopping disabilities onto able-bodied athletes (Ellen, 2016). In 2013, Guinness Beer launched a commercial that showed a group of men playing wheelchair basketball but at the end of the commercial all but one stood up and walked out of the gymnasium. This ad garnered mixed reviews. Advertisers loved it with the Guinness wheelchair basketball ad spinning "circles around competitors in Q3" (Heine, 2013).

Other headlines included "New Guinness Ad Breaks the Industry Stereotype" (Taube, 2013) and "Guinness Got It Right Where Many Brands Have Fallen Short" (Anselmo, 2013). Others, meanwhile were not as complimentary. This ad was condemned by disability-rights advocates for several reasons. First, they argue that the ad trivializes the difficulties disabled individuals face in purchasing expensive lightweight wheelchairs and learning how to use them well enough to play basketball in them. Second, the comment made to the man in the wheelchair "Next week, buddy" by his friend was seen as patronizing.

> Calling him 'buddy' is an affectionate but infantilizing term and highlights the premise of the ad – that the wheelchair bound must be called out as objects of charity. The portrayal of a disabled man in this ad, according to disability-rights advocates and other critics, only serves to put the other men on a pedestal for being inclusive, when this is a quality that should be normalized – not glorified – in society.
>
> *(The Critical Media Project, 2013)*

Other criticisms were noted by Ladau (2013), Miller (2013) and Ellis (2013) that reaffirmed the previous concerns. The key issue is whether commercials such as these portray persons with disabilities in a dignified way.

The challenge then is for sponsors to not just be partners and tell stories but to tell an authentic one.

> For sponsors who can build an authentic connection to the Movement, the Paralympics offer a potential point of entry for brands that want to be considered among those working towards making a difference – and a chance to leverage this unique position with audiences. However, not every sponsor will be able to tell an authentic story.
>
> *(GMR Marketing, 2018)*

Following the 2016 Rio Paralympic Games,

> some sponsors were questioned for their actual commitment to the Paralympic Games. On the flip side, USOC sponsor BP was applauded for signing more Paralympians than Olympians to its Games' ambassador roster. Toyota, now a global sponsor of the Paralympic Movement, delivered a powerful message toward mobility for all when it aired a Paralympic-focused TV spot during the 2018 Super Bowl.
>
> *(GMR Marketing, 2018)*

Thus, if companies can avoid a focus on pity, it is possible that corporate support for Paralympic sport and athletes can far exceed expectations and change the future of Paralympic sport.

According to a report by GMR Marketing, when the United States hosts the Summer Olympic and Paralympic Games in Los Angeles in 2028, the spoils of US Paralympians will take on a greater importance. But, one of the biggest challenges to the success of Paralympic Games in a host country is the limited awareness enjoyed by the Paralympic movement at home. Thus, it is essential that organizers develop strategies to increase the level of civic and corporate support for the Games. This was successfully accomplished for the 2012 London Games whereas OCOG worked with stakeholders such as local retailer Sainsbury's engagement with TeamGB Paralympic ambassadors and David Beckham or the award-winning promotional campaign from host broadcaster Channel 4. The results were outstanding with record-breaking attendance at venues, increased awareness of TeamGB's athletic achievements and Paralympian athletes recognized for their athletic achievements on par with TeamGB Olympians. Future hosts such as Paris 2024, meanwhile, intend to highlight the Paralympic Games as the pinnacle of a seven-year, sport-led journey towards greater participation and social inclusion of people with disabilities (GMR Marketing, 2018).

The example of London was further highlighted by an announcement on Dec 1, 2018 in recognition of the United Nation's International Day of the Persons with Disabilities. To mark the occasion, the International Paralympic Committee (IPC) and the Office of the UN High Commissioner for Human Rights launched a campaign focusing on the impact of the Paralympic Games in transforming society. On Monday, December 3, the first in a series of videos was released demonstrating how the London 2012 Paralympic Games contributed to greater employment opportunities for persons with disabilities in Great Britain. According to recent figures from the Office of National Statistics, 3.85 million persons with disabilities now have employment in Great Britain, nearly one million more than five years ago (IPC, 2018a).

For those companies that do get it right in supporting and promoting the Paralympic movement, the benefits are significant. As outlined by Jerdee (2018) from Accenture, American companies that embrace best practices for employing and supporting more persons with disabilities in their workforce have outperformed their peers. This was echoed in a Canadian context where better workplace accessibility for Canadians with disabilities was shown to boost economic growth (McQuigge, 2018). This further highlights the potential benefits of 'handicapitalism' through corporate support of the Paralympic movement whereby companies see the benefits of being supportive of persons with disability, and Paralympic sport in particular, not to be inspirational but to profit financially. Examples of this include Xbox (Spencer, 2018) and Microsoft who respectively adapted their gaming controls and controller to make gaming more accessible to people with disabilities (Spencer, 2018; Takahashi, 2018), Tommy Hilfiger who unveiled an innovative clothing line for people with disabilities (Gallucci, 2018) and the NBA, which managed to make its Fifth Avenue store more welcoming to people with autism, PTSD and other sensory disabilities (Segran, 2018). Finally, sporting venues and arenas are being redesigned to make them more accessible for persons with a disability or fans with autism (Anzilotti, 2018). All of these changes and adaptations are likely the results of being more sensitive to diversity but perhaps just as importantly to generate profits!

Dare we say that Paralympics are cool? Almeida (2017) proclaims that disability is the latest fashion industry frontier. The recent cover of *Impact Magazine* profiled Paralympian Brian McKeever as the 'Cool Edition Winter Athlete of the Year' (Welner, 2018). *Strong Fitness Magazine* had Paralympic double amputee snowboarder Amy Purdy on their cover after she almost won Dancing with the Stars (Brown, 2016), and Noah Galloway, an amputee and American military veteran was profiled and sponsored by Kenneth Cole (2014), *Men's Health* magazine and the television show *Ellen* (Moore, 2014).

In an age where diversity is becoming more and more accepted and celebrated, disability, and in particular Paralympic sport, could be seen as a great value investment. But this may not be a secret much longer. The understanding of how many people live with a disability is increasing. In Canada the most recent Canadian Survey of Disability suggests that 22 per cent of Canadians have at least one disability thus representing 6.2 million people (Cloutier, Grondin and Levesque, 2018). This is not an insignificant number, particularly when you consider how many more people are impacted by this percentage as friends, family and colleagues. As was noted at the outset of this chapter, the accuracy of sponsorship and marketing predictions for the 2026 Games was questioned because of rapidly growing interest and acknowledgement of the movement's influence and power. This chapter has presented a number of examples where companies have benefited from partnering with the Paralympic Games and for those that haven't, it might be wise to lock in while they still can.

References

Almeida, A. (2017). *Why disability is the latest fashion industry frontier.* Available at: https://www.bustle.com/p/why-disability-is-the-latest-fashion-industry-frontier-30548 [Accessed 6 December 2018].

Anderson, G. (2014). *Paralympics are "diamond in the rough" claims NBC chief after Sochi 2014 success.* Available at: http://m.insidethegames.biz/paralympics/winter-paralympics/2014/1018969-paralympics-are-diamond-in-the-rough-claims-nbc-chief-after-sochi-2014-success#.UyqOLzr5yGA.twitter [Accessed 6 December 2018].

Anselmo, C. (2013). *Guinness got it right where many brands have fallen short.* Available at: http://www.visiblemeasures.com/2013/10/15/guinness-got-it-right-where-many-brands-have-fallen-short/ [Accessed 6 December 2018].

Anzilotti, E. (2018). *Redesigning sports arenas to make them more accessible to fans with autism.* Available at: https://www.fastcompany.com/40493149/redesigning-sports-arenas-to-make-them-more-accessible-to-fans-with-autism [Accessed 6 December 2018].

Bassett, S. (2014). *5.3 million Canadians tuned in to English TV coverage of the Sochi 2014 Paralympic Winter Games over the first three days.* Available at: http://www.cbc.ca/revenuegroup/mobile/touch/53-million-canadians-tuned-in-to-english-tv-coverage-of-the-sochi-2014-paralympic-winter-games-over.html [Accessed 6 December 2018].

Bridgestone. (2018). Bridgestone becomes worldwide Paralympic partner – World's largest tire and rubber company has global rights to the Paralympic movement through to 2024. *Bridgestone.* Available at: https://www.bridgestone.com/corporate/news/2018101801.html [Accessed 6 December 2018].

Brown, K. (2016). *The unstoppable Amy Purdy.* Available at: https://www.strongfitnessmag.com/motivation/cover-athlete/amypurdy/ [Accessed 6 December 2018].

Byon, K.K., Cottingham, M. and Carroll, M. (2010). Marketing murderball: The influence of spectator motivation factors on sports consumption behaviours of wheelchair rugby spectators. *International Journal of Sports Marketing and Sponsorship*, 12(1), pp. 71–89.

Cloutier, E., Grondin, C. and Levesque, A. (2018). *Canadian survey on disability, 2017: Concepts and methods guide.* Ottawa: Statistics Canada.

Cottingham, M., Gearity, B. and Byon., K. (2013). A qualitative examination of disability sport executives' perceptions of sport promotion and the acquisition of sponsors. *Sport Marketing Quarterly*, 22(2), pp. 92–100.

Cottingham, M. and Petersen-Wagner, R. (2018). Marketing of Paralympic sports: Attracting spectators and sponsors. In: I. Brittain and A. Beacom, eds., *The Palgrave handbook of Paralympic studies.* London: Palgrave Macmillan.

The Critical Media Project. (2013). *Guinness wheelchair ad.* Available at: http://criticalmediaproject.org/guiness-wheelchair-ad/ [Accessed 6 December 2018].

Dembe, J. (2018). Challenges still exist. Struggle with Paralympic exposure in Canada nothing new as Canadian athletes have to fight harder when it comes to marketing themselves. *CBC Sports.* Available at: https://www.cbc.ca/sports/paralympics/struggle-with-paralympic-exposure-in-canada-nothing-new-1.4565864 [Accessed 6 December 2018].

Ellen, B. (2016). *Pretending to be Paralympian is a bizarre insult.* Available at: https://www.theguardian.com/commentisfree/2016/aug/27/vogue-brasil-paralympic-photoshoot-insulting [Accessed 6 December].

Ellis, K. (2013). *Dedication, loyalty, friendship, sort of.* Available at: http://www.abc.net.au/rampup/articles/2013/09/26/3856974.htm [Accessed 6 December 2018].

Fischer, B. (2018). *IOC to take over IPC sponsorship rights in '21.* Available at: https://www.sportsbusinessdaily.com/Global/Issues/2018/07/17/Olympics/IOC-IPC-Sponsorship.aspx [Accessed 6 December 2018].

Gallucci, N. (2018). *Tommy Hilfiger unveils innovative clothing line for people with disabilities.* Available at: https://mashable.com/2018/04/06/tommy-hilfiger-tommy-adaptive-disibility-friendly-clothing/#7C2QXOBErkqm [Accessed 6 December 2018].

Gianatasio, D. (2014). *Meet the superhuman moms in P&G's stirring ad for the 2014 Paralympics – Raising "the world's toughest kids*". Available at: https://www.adweek.com/creativity/meet-superhuman-moms-pgs-stirring-ad-2014-paralympics-155913/ [Accessed 6 December 2018].

Giustini, D. (2018). Start your impossible. In: *Presentation at the IPC marketing & media summit*, Madrid.
GMR Marketing. (2018). Paralympic potential – Brands can lead the charge to increase awareness + engagement. GMR Marketing.
Gonzales, X. (2018). IOC-IPC Agreements. In: Presentation at the IPC Marketing and Media Summit, Madrid.
Hardin, M. and Hardin, B. (2004). The 'supercrip' in sport media: Wheelchair athletes discuss hegemony's disabled hero. *Sociology of Sport Online*, 7(1), pp. 1–16.
Hargreaves, J.A. and Hardin, B. (2009). Women wheelchair athletes: Competing against media stereotypes. *Disability Studies Quarterly*, 29(2).
Heine, C. (2013). *Guinness' wheelchair basketball ad spun circles around competitors in Q3 and Dawn's spot was a slam dunk, too, per Ace Metrix*. Available at: http://www.adweek.com/news/advertising-branding/guinness-wheelchair-basketball-ad-spun-circles-around-competitors-q3-152865 [Accessed 6 December 2018].
Holmes, E. (2018). *Olympic TOP sponsors to also cover Paralympic games – IOC confirms top-tier partners will also support para sport*. Available at: http://www.sportspromedia.com/news/olympic-top-sponsors-paralympic-games [Accessed 6 December 2018].
IPC. (2018a). *IPC joins forces with United Nations Human Rights Office*. Bonn: IPC.
IPC. (2018b). *Record international audiences for PyeongChang 2018*. Bonn: IPC.
Jerdee, C. (2018). *Getting to equal: The disability inclusion advantage*. Available at: https://www.accenture.com/us-en/company-persons-with-disabilities [Accessed 6 December 2018].
Kenneth Cole. (2014). *MANKIND fragrance by Kenneth Cole announces: Noah Galloway revealed as "the ultimate men's health guy"*. Available at: https://www.prnewswire.com/news-releases/mankind-fragrance-by-kenneth-cole-announces-noah-galloway-revealed-as-the-ultimate-mens-health-guy-278381171.html [Accessed 6 December 2018].
Ladau, E. (2013). *Just one of the guys – A critique of the wheelchair basketball Guinness commercial*. Available at: http://wordsiwheelby.com/2013/09/just-one-of-the-guys/ [Accessed 6 December 2018].
Legg, D. (2001). An interview with Dr Robert Steadward, president of the International Paralympic Committee. *International Journal of Sports Marketing and Sponsorship*, 3(3), pp. 5–14.
Legg, D. (2015). Afterword: A personal reflection on how we can communicate about Paralympic athletes. In: D. Jackson, C. Hodges, M. Molesworth and R. Scullion, eds., *Reframing disability? Media, (dis) empowerment, and voice in the 2012 Paralympics*. Routledge.
Legg, D. (2016). Debating disability: Paralympic athletes and the media. In: D. Taras and C. Waddell, eds., *How Canadians communicate about sports*. University of Alberta Press.
Legg, D. and Dottori, M. (2017). Marketing the Paralympic games. In: S. Darcy, D. Adair and M. Frawley, eds., *Managing the Paralympic games*. Palgrave Macmillan, Chapter 12, pp. 263–288.
Legg, D. and Steadward, R. (2011). The Paralympic games and 60 years of change (1948–2008): Unification and restructuring. In: Jill M. Le Clair, ed., *Disability in the global sport arena: A sporting chance*. Special edition of Sport in Society. London: Taylor & Francis.
L'Oreal. (2016). *Meet L'Oréal Paris brand ambassador: Aimee Mullins*. Available at: https://www.youtube.com/watch?v=MGPsP-aF4DM [Accessed 6 December 2018].
Lucas, D. (2018). Pyeongchang 2018 key findings – Media evaluation. In: *Presentation at the IPC marketing & media summit*, Madrid.
Lyons, E. (2018). *BP on why the Paralympics is 'sport's best kept secret' for brands*. Available at: https://www.marketingweek.com/2018/09/21/bp-paralympics-sponsorship/ [Accessed 6 December 2018].
McDowell, J. (2018). *Procter & Gamble launches new thought-provoking Olympic Games film: "Love over bias"*. Available at: https://www.businesswire.com/news/home/20171102005263/en/Procter-Gamble-Launches-New-Thought-Provoking-Olympic-Games [Accessed 6 December 2018].
McQuigge, M. (2018). *Better workplace accessibility for Canadians with disabilities would boost economic growth: Study*. Available at: https://www.theglobeandmail.com/news/national/better-workplace-accessibility-for-canadians-with-disabilities-would-boost-economic-growth-study/article38105222/ [Accessed 6 December 2018].
Miller, C. (2013). *The hidden controversy behind the Guinness wheelchair commercial*. Available at: http://www.transfermaster.com/blog/view-post/The-Hidden-Controversy-Behind-The-Guinness-Wheelchair-Commercial-1 [Accessed 6 December 2018].
Moore, P. (2014). The unstoppable Noah Galloway: From war to one-armed push-ups on 'Ellen'. *Men's Health Magazine*.
Morgan, L. (2018a). *Procter & Gamble (P&G) has signed on as a gold partner of the Tokyo 2020 Paralympic games, it was announced today*. Available at: https://www.insidethegames.biz/articles/1069156/procter-gamble-sign-on-as-gold-partner-of-tokyo-2020-paralympic-games [Accessed 6 December 2018].

Morgan, L. (2018b). *Top-tier Olympic partners to become sponsors of Paralympics from 2021*. Available at: https://www.insidethegames.biz/articles/1067457/top-tier-olympic-partners-to-become-sponsors-of-paralympics-from-2021 [Accessed 6 December 2018].

Park, M., Yoh, T., Choi, Y.S. and Olson, M.W. (2011). Consumer attitudes toward the Paralympic games and purchase intentions toward corporate sponsors of the Paralympic games: Market segmentation strategy. *Journal Venue & Event Management*, 3(2), pp. 2–15.

Piispanen, T. and Legg, D. (2012). Paralympic sponsorship. In: *Presentation at the future of sport marketing seminar*, Vierumäki, Finland.

Powell, C. (2014). *Viewers flock to Paralympic coverage*. Available at: http://www.marketingmag.ca/news/media-news/viewers-flock-to-paralympics-coverage-103558 [Accessed 6 December 2018].

Purdue, D. and Howe, P.D. (2012). See the sport, not the disability: Exploring the Paralympic paradox. *Qualitative Research in Sport, Exercise and Health*, 4(2), pp. 189–205.

Segran, E. (2018). *The NBA's autism-friendly N.Y.C. store is a slam dunk*. Available at: https://www.fastcompany.com/40552184/the-nbas-autism-friendly-nyc-store-is-a-slam-dunk? [Accessed 6 December 2018].

Smith, R. (2012). *Target is 'down' with Down syndrome: 5 things target said by saying nothing at all*. Available at: http://noahsdad.com/target-down-syndrome/ [Accessed 6 December 2018].

Spencer, P. (2018). *Accessible gaming with the Xbox Adaptive Controller*. Available at: https://news.xbox.com/en-us/2018/05/16/xbox-adaptive-controller/ [Accessed 6 December 2018].

Stephanopoulos, A. (2018). *Building the Paralympic brand and communicating its values*. In: *Presentation at the IPC marketing & media summit*, Madrid.

Takahashi, D. (2018). *Microsoft controller makes gaming more accessible to people with disabilities*. Available at: https://venturebeat.com/2018/05/16/microsoft-controller-makes-gaming-more-accessible-to-people-with-disabilities/ [Accessed 6 December 2018].

Taube, A. (2013). *An incredible new Guinness ad breaks the industry stereotype*. Available at: http://www.businessinsider.com/new-guinness-ad-breaks-the-mold-2013-9 [Accessed 6 December 2018].

Toyota. (2018). *Commercials to air during Olympic and Paralympic Winter Games PyeongChang 2018*. Available at: https://newsroom.toyota.co.jp/en/corporate/21064838.html [Accessed 6 December 2018].

Welner, C. (2018). *A true image of Canadian greatness: Canada's 2018 Winter Male Athlete of the Year, Brian McKeever*. Available at: http://impactmagazine.ca/topics/brian-mckeever/ [Accessed 6 December 2018].

10
Olympic broadcast rights

Lisa Delpy Neirotti

Introduction: an overview of the broadcast coverage and the Olympics

The broadcast of the Olympic Games is the main driver for the continued growth of its global popularity and is the main platform through which the Olympic movement can showcase and promote the values of the Olympic Games (IOC, 2019a). The International Olympic Committee (IOC) is the owner of global broadcasting rights for the Olympic Games and is responsible for allocating these rights to media companies throughout the world. This includes broadcasts on television (linear), radio, mobile, and internet platforms (IOC, 2019a). The fundamental IOC broadcast policy as described in the Olympic Charter: "The IOC takes all necessary steps in order to ensure the fullest coverage by the different media and the widest possible audience in the world for the Olympic Games. – Rule 48, Olympic Charter" (IOC, 2020, p. 23).

In 2005, the IOC centralized control over marketing and broadcast rights and created a company called Television and Marketing Services SA (TMS). The preparation and implementation of the IOC's broadcast strategy and future broadcast rights negotiations is the responsibility of TMS along with global sponsorships and brand management.

Broadcast rights are entered into by the IOC and Rights Holding Broadcaster (RHB) (IOC, 2019a). The rights to broadcast the Olympic Games give the broadcaster the right to use the material produced by the host broadcaster, the Olympic Broadcasting System (OBS). Key elements involved in the negotiation of broadcasting rights include territorial exclusivity, linear and digital bundled or unbundled rights packages, duration, and the IOC mandate of free-to-air television (Payne, 2012).

The long-term Olympic broadcast marketing strategy is designed to achieve the following objectives:

1. To establish broadcast partnerships to ensure improved global coverage of the Olympic Games, promote the ideals of Olympism, and raise awareness of the work of the Olympic movement throughout the world;
2. To ensure the long-term financial security of the Olympic movement and the Olympic Games;

3 To ensure that broadcast partners are experienced in providing the highest quality Olympic programming;
4 To allow broadcast partners to develop strong Olympic associations and to strengthen each partner's identity as the Olympic broadcaster within its country or territory;
5 To maximise exposure across all available media platforms and exploit latest media technologies;
6 To strengthen the continuing legacy of broadcasting support from one Olympic Games to the next, allowing future OCOGs to draw on their support, experience and technology.

(IOC, 2020, p. 23)

Broadcast revenues

For more than four decades, broadcast rights fees have been the primary source of revenue for the IOC and the Olympic Games. For the 2017–2020 quadrennium, broadcast rights fees account for 4.5 billion dollars (Inside the games, 2015). The Organizing Committee for the Olympic Games (OCOG) receives forty-nine percent of the broadcast revenues (twenty-nine percent to Summer Games and twenty percent to Winter Games) and represents a significant part of the OCOG's revenue. The remainder is distributed to the National Olympic Committees (NOC) through Olympic Solidarity, International Federations (IFs), and to the IOC.

Olympic Solidarity was created more than 50 years ago to provide financial support to NOCs with the greatest need for sport and athlete development at the national level as a way to increase universality (IOC, 2019b). It is interesting to note that the increasing value of Olympic broadcast partnerships has allowed the IOC to deliver increasing financial support to NOCs, IFs, OCOGs, and Youth Olympic Games (IOC, 2019b).

Historical overview

To understand the role that television plays in funding the Olympic movement and disseminating its spirit and values, it is essential to review the milestones of this symbiotic relationship. The history of Olympic broadcasting begins with the 1936 Berlin Olympic Games. While there was limited radio broadcast for the Amsterdam Games in 1928 and the Los Angeles Games in 1932, the 1936 Games were the first Olympics to be televised and marked the first ever live televised sport event (IOC, 2020). With a total of 138 hours of coverage, 162,000 viewers watched the competition in special viewing booths called "Public Television Offices" located in Berlin and Potsdam (Billings, 2008). However, this broadcast was just an experiment with a new technology and did not become a widespread phenomenon until two decades later. The 1948 London Olympic Games were the first to be shown on home television to an official audience of 500,000 people within the British Isles. The 1956 Cortina d'Ampezzo Olympics were the first Winter Games broadcasted live and were the first to have venues designed specifically with television in mind. The grandstand at the cross-country ski venue (*Lo Stadio della neve*) was built facing south so that the television cameras would not be adversely affected by the rising or setting sun (Comitato Olimpico Nazionale Italiano, 1956).

The first Olympic Games to be viewed on television worldwide was the Rome Olympics in 1960 where a total of 21 countries received live and taped coverage. The 1964 Tokyo Games were the first broadcast in color, including the Opening and Closing ceremonies, a handful of events with competitor times displayed on screen, plus the first to use satellite to broadcast the Games directly to 40 countries. The 1984 Los Angeles Olympic Games became the initial testing ground for high-definition television but it was not until 2008 that the Beijing Games were produced and broadcast entirely in high definition. In 2004, the Athens Games were transmitted to the UK and USA for the first time over the internet as well as conventional television. In 2012 over 230 hours of live 3D broadcast was produced. Rio 2016 paved the way for introducing Virtual Reality (VR) experiences and 8K Super Hi-Vision (SHV) production (IOC, 2016). During the PyeongChang 2018 Games, a wireless onboard point of view (POV) camera was used for the Bobsleigh coverage. This POV camera transmitted using 5G technology, marking the first time such technology was used at an Olympic Games (OBS, 2018). Over time, the sound has also improved with every breath and emotion captured in 5.1 surround sound.

Olympic broadcast rights fees

As can be seen in Figures 10.1–10.3, broadcast rights fees have continually increased, particularly since 1980. The first rights were paid by BBC for the 1948 Olympic Games of US$3,000 (Preuss, 2004). The principle of exclusive broadcast rights fees was added to the Olympic Charter in 1949 and the first broadcast rights negotiations were conducted for the 1952 Helsinki Games (IOC, 2020). For the first and only time in history, European television operators accounted for the majority of the $1.2 million in rights fees for the 1960 Games (Preuss, 2004). Four years later, the 1964 Tokyo Games earned rights fee totalling $1.6 million. The 1968 Games were the first to be broadcast extensively in color which helped garner the first multimillion-person audience of 600 million viewers, and a multimillion dollar increase in rights fees. Rights fees totalled $9.8 million, an increase of $8.2 million over the previous Games (Pena, 2009).

Since 1980, revenues from the sale of broadcast rights have grown steadily. Broadcast rights from the 1984 Los Angeles Games totalled $286.9 million, almost tripling the amount generated by the 1980 Moscow Games. Increasing competition and the advent of new technologies such as the internet has continued to increase rights fees with the 2016 Rio Games earning $2.868 billion and PyeongChang 2018 receiving $1.438 billion (IOC, 2020).

As seen in Figure 10.3, the number of countries that broadcast the Olympic Games continued to grow until the 2000 Sydney Summer Games when the live broadcast was global (IOC,

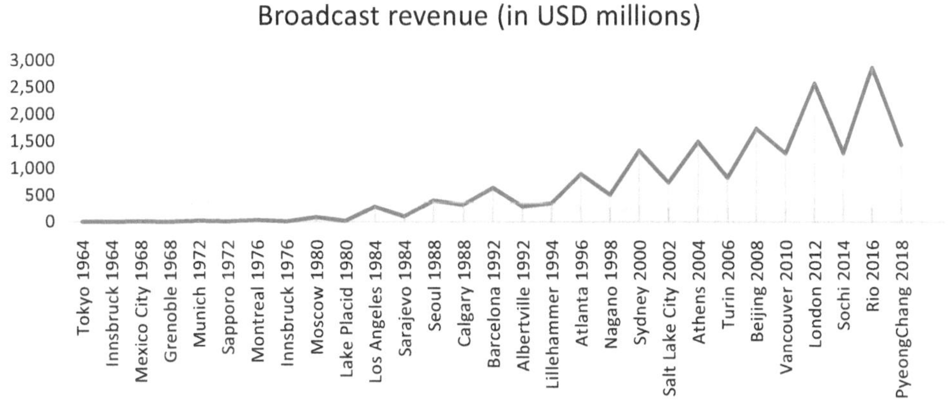

Figure 10.1 Broadcast revenue from 1964–2018

Source: Olympic Broadcast History (2019)

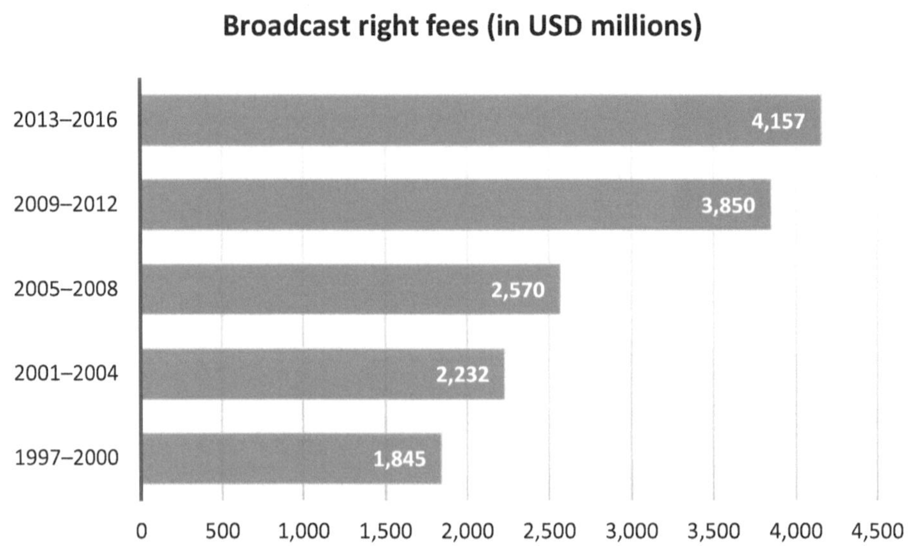

Figure 10.2 Broadcasting rights fee

Source: Olympic Broadcasting History (2019)

Olympic Games: Countries broadcasting

Olympic Games	Number of countries/ territories broadcasting
Berlin 1936	1
London 1948	1
Helsinki 1952	2
Melbourne 1956	1
Rome 1960	21
Tokyo 1964	40
Mexico City 1968	n/a
Munich 1972	98
Montreal 1976	124
Moscow 1980	111
Los Angeles 1984	156
Seoul 1988	160
Barcelona 1992	193
Atlanta 1996	214
Sydney 2000	Global
Athens 2004	Global
Beijing 2008	Global
London 2012	Global
Rio 2016	Global

Olympic Winter Games: Countries broadcasting

Olympic Winter Games	Number of countries/ territories broadcasting
Cortina 1956	22
Squaw Valley 1960	27
Innsbruck 1964	30
Grenoble 1968	32
Sapporo 1972	41
Innsbruck 1976	38
Lake Placid 1980	40
Sarajevo 1984	100
Calgary 1988	64
Albertville 1992	86
Lillehammer 1994	120
Nagano 1998	160
Salt Lake City 2002	160
Turin 2006	Global
Vancouver 2010	Global
Sochi 2014	Global
PyeongChang 2018	Global

Figure 10.3 Olympic Games and number of countries/territories broadcasted

Source: Olympic Broadcasting History (2019)

2020). The first Winter Games broadcasted globally was 2006 Turin. Figure 10.3 shows the number of countries/territories broadcasted from the 1936 Berlin Games.

Prior to the 1968 Olympic Games, broadcast right negotiations were conducted exclusively by the OCOG, with the IOC receiving only one to four percent of the fees. The IOC then decided to establish a broadcast revenue distribution formula for the 1972 Munich Olympic Games. The first million was divided equally between the IOC, IFs, and NOC; the OCOG would receive 1/3 of the second million and IOC the other 2/3, of which 2/9 would be shared with IFs and 2/9 to NOCs; starting with the third million the OCOG would receive 2/3 and IOC 1/3, who would re-distribute as previously described. This formula was to motivate the OCOG to secure the most revenue from broadcasters.

In 1971, the IOC added Article 21 to the Olympic Charter stipulating that only the IOC could negotiate with television operators and that it would be this body that decided on the distribution of broadcast rights (Moragas, Rivenburgh and Larson, 1995). Since this time the IOC has increasingly regulated the rights of media. The high costs of the broadcast centre's infrastructure and maintenance exceeded rights revenues, requiring the IOC to raise the price of its rights fees by ten percent each game until 1980 (Preuss, 2004).

According to IOC member Richard Pound, "The IOC was slow to recognize the importance of television" (Pound, 2010). The year 1980 was a watershed year in the course of Olympic broadcast history. The start of Juan Antonia Samaranch's tenure as IOC president brought new ideas that changed the way that the Olympic Games were marketed. When Samaranch became president, the Olympic movement were on the verge of bankruptcy (Parent and Séguin, 2018). He recognized the potential revenues that broadcast rights offered and using Article 21 as justification, Samaranch convinced the IOC to directly negotiate with television operators (Preuss, 2004). The 1984 Los Angeles Olympic Games was the first time the IOC negotiated the television rights deals (Pound, 2010) and the 1988 Seoul Summer Olympics Games was the first time that they did it without the presence of the host city.

To create revenue stability regardless of where the Olympic Games were to be hosted, Samaranch implemented the philosophy that the IOC should, whenever possible, negotiate long-term contracts prior to the selection of the host city (Payne, 2006). This created a system where the funding of the OCOG is guaranteed no matter which city is chosen to host the Games.

The 1992 Barcelona Games was the first time that a multi-tier television structure was operated. Radio Television Olimpica (RTO '92) sub-licensed coverage of additional events to other cable satellite providers, expanding the total amount of sports coverage (IOC, 2020). The 1992 Games also led to a failed experimentation with Pay per View (PPV) format (Pena, 2009). Using a system called Triple Cast, NBC, the US RHB, signed just 250,000 subscribers instead of the estimated figure of 2.5 million subscribers (Moragas, Rivenburgh and Larson, 1995). This quelled any further experimentation to use paying methods for subsequent Olympic Games.

Development of host broadcasting system

Prior to the 1972 Olympic Games, the domestic Rights Broadcasting Holder (RBH) was responsible for producing both domestic and international feeds. Many international broadcasters, however, complained that this resulted in a bias toward the host national athletes. The host broadcast production system began to take form during the 1972 Olympic Games when for the first time the international signal was created for global distribution and was separate and distinct from the domestic broadcast (IOC, 2020). The domestic broadcasters created a separate team, assisted by international broadcaster mobile units to produce the international signal. The international team's production plan incorporated elements from the domestic international signal mixed with images from its own cameras. The approach is similar to the unilateral signal production method that is used today (IOC, 2019a).

The host broadcast operation as it is recognized today was introduced in 1984. ABC, the US domestic rights holder, served as the host broadcaster. ABC provided the international signal to the 156 nations that were rights holders (IOC, 2020). Unlike previous Games, the broadcaster could supplement the international signal with independently produced unilateral signals. As a result of this, broadcasts became more tailored towards the broadcasters' respective home countries (IOC, 2020).

It was not until the 1992 Olympic Games that an independent entity whose lone responsibility was the production of the host broadcast signal for the Games was instituted. Radio Television Olimpica (RTO '92), formed for the 1992 Barcelona Olympic Games, was the first host broadcaster to be part of the OCOG but not affiliated with any RHB.

OBS and ensuring wide distribution of the Olympic Games

To create a more consistent and organized approach to host broadcasting, the IOC determined that the host broadcaster operations should be performed by a private company funded by and under the direct supervision of the IOC. In May 2001 Olympic Broadcasting Systems (OBS) was created by the IOC and eliminated the need to continually re-staff and rebuild the host broadcast operation for each Games (IOC, 2020).

As the host broadcaster, OBS is responsible for producing and transmitting impartial live radio and television of the Games. The feed is neutral and universally produced so that there is no focus on any one athlete or country. The OBS allows RHBs to add their own commentary and interviews to tailor their coverage for audiences in their home country (IOC, 2020).

The OBS began its work in May 2004 when the Beijing Olympic Broadcasting (BOB) was created as a cooperative joint venture between OBS and the Beijing OCOG (IOC, 2008). Managed by OBS, BOB served as the host broadcasting entity for the 2008 Beijing Olympic Games (IOC, 2008). The 2010 Olympic Winter Games in Vancouver marked the first time that OBS was solely responsible for the Host Broadcasting Organization (IOC, 2020). London 2012 marked the first Summer Games at which OBS acted as the sole broadcaster – OBS was responsible for providing the international television and radio signals from the Games to all RHBs around the world (IOC, 2012).

OBS's efforts have created significant innovations and advancement in the broadcast of the Olympic Games as it is responsible for "improving methods, developing innovative new services and creating efficiencies that benefit Rights Holders" (IOC, 2020).

The expansion of coverage in the 2000s

Olympic Broadcast coverage in the 2000s was defined by drastic increases in the number of broadcast hours. To help defray the escalating costs of rights fees, RHBs expanded coverage to its cable partners. NBC, the highest paying rights holders, exemplifies the changes that were made during the decade.

For the 2000 Sydney Summer Olympic Games, NBC Universal expanded coverage to its cable partners CNBC and MSNBC. Marquee sports events were aired on NBC while its sister cable channels aired other events; the three stations combined broadcast 441 hours of coverage. This was a marked increase from the 171 hours of coverage for the 1996 Atlanta Summer Games (NBC, 2004).

For the 2004 Olympics, NBC Universal paid $820 million for US broadcast rights and expanded coverage to all NBC Universal networks (NBC, CNBC, MSNBC, USA Network, and Telemundo) resulting in over 1,200 hours of coverage during the Games (Greyser and Kogan, 2013). The Games were now on television 24 hours a day. NBC networks presented live coverage throughout the morning and afternoon, while showing marquee events pre-taped in prime time (NBC, 2004).

With the advent of broadband internet and wireless technology, coverage of the Olympics expanded radically beyond traditional television and onto internet accessible devices. The 2004 Games marked the first time that major broadcasters were allowed to stream video coverage of the Olympics over the internet. This occurred with the caveat that service be restricted geographically, geo-blocking, to protect local broadcast rights (Payne, 2012).

NBC subsequently launched its own Olympic website, NBCOlympics.com. Focusing on television coverage of the Games, the site provided video clips, medal standings, and live results. However, the main purpose of the site was to provide a schedule of what sports were on NBC Universal's stations. Comparatively, BBC made their completely live coverage available to UK high speed internet customers for free (Voight, 2008).

NBC paid $900 million for the US broadcast rights to the 2008 Beijing Olympics and were the first to be produced and broadcast entirely in high definition by the host broadcaster (IOC, 2020). This was an expansion from the 2006 Torino coverage where only half of the broadcast was in high definition. The 2008 Olympic Games also saw the first coverage streamed live in the United States (although other countries were streaming in 2004). NBC scheduled 3,400 hours of coverage, 2,200 hours of which was streamed live and for free at NBCOlympics.com (Voight, 2008). The coverage also expanded to nine different television channels, NBC, CNBC, MSNBC, USA, Telemundo, Universal HD, and Oxygen, plus two multiplex digital channels which, on occasions, offered the same programming at different times throughout the day to broadcast (*The New York Times*, 2007).

NBC Universal purchased the broadcasting right to the 2010 and 2012 Olympics for a combined $2.201 billion (Abrahamson, 2003). The $2.201 billion price, including $2.001 billion in television rights, is a forty-six percent jump from NBC's combined $1.508 billion for the 2006–2008 Olympics (Abrahamson, 2003). NBC paid $820 million for the 2010 Winter Games, a thirty-four percent increase from the network's $614 million figure for the 2006 Torino Games (Abrahamson, 2003). NBC paid $1.2 billion for 2012 London Games, $775 million for 2014 Sochi Winter Games, $1.22 billion for 2016 Rio, $963 million for 2018 PyeongChang and $1.41 billion for 2020 Tokyo Games (Greyser and Kogan, 2013). An NBC-signed agreement with IOC from 2021 to 2032 is valued at USD 7.65 billion, plus an additional USD 100 million signing bonus to be used for the promotion of Olympism and the Olympic values between 2015 and 2020 (Zaccardi, 2014).

Olympic broadcasting: why broadcasters still want the Olympics

Television rights for popular sports and sport competitions, such as the Olympics, have become the subject of highly competitive bidding wars between television operators, resulting in unprecedented price increases to the benefit of sports teams, leagues, and federations.

Sport has unique characteristics that increase its broadcast value. First, sport is a temporary product and viewers are mainly interested in watching live broadcasts. Second, substituting the product is difficult. Viewers who want to see a particular event/game/match are unlikely to be satisfied with the coverage of another event (Schaub, 2002). Finally, the bundling of rights by leagues and federations or the sole ownership of rights, such as the IOC's ownership of Olympic Broadcasting rights, reduces the number of rights available. Availability of rights is further reduced by the increasing number of TV rights contracts being concluded on an exclusive basis for a long duration or covering a large number of events (Schaub, 2002).

There is heavy competition to be the exclusive broadcaster of the Olympic Games in a given geographic area because broadcasters want to attract the advertising money that flows from large viewing audiences. In general, the broadcasting of sporting events attracts a large number of viewers with strong purchasing power. This target audience is essential for advertisers because it is a readily identifiable group that is not easily reached through other programming. As a result, the demand to advertise on sports broadcasts has increased, correspondingly increasing the competition between television operators to purchase broadcasting rights. NBC reported earning $1.2 billion in advertising revenue for the 2016 Olympic Games and are on track to surpass this for the 2020 Tokyo Games (Steinberg, 2019).

Historically, international broadcast rights fees were less than US fees as there was less competition and commercial advertising opportunities. Most other countries had only one public television channel free of commercials. As the broadcast industry developed elsewhere so did the rights fees. For example, the fees paid by the European Broadcast Union (EBU), the consortium that previously represented the majority of European countries, rose from $90 million for the 1992 Barcelona Games to $250 million for the 1996 Atlanta Games (Meltz, 1999).

With the largest rights fee of any nation, the United States pays a disproportionate amount of the IOC's broadcast revenue. From 1985 to 2008, US rights fees contributed an average of seventy-one percent of the IOC's overall TV revenue (Mickle, 2009). The IOC has worked to diversify its income and reduce its dependence on the United States by mining the economies of other nations for higher TV rights fees and sponsorship money (Mickle, 2009).

The IOC adopted a new negotiation strategy of moving away from negotiating with broadcasting unions, and directly with national broadcasters (Payne, 2012). This strategy yielded higher rights fees from China and Brazil. During the 2005–2008 quadrennium, the IOC negotiated TV rights with the Asian Broadcasting Union, selling them for $17.5 million. For the 2009–2012 quadrennium, the IOC's decision to negotiate directly with China netted $100 million rights fee from one country. It cut a similar deal in Brazil. For 2005–2008 the IOC received $29.75 million rights fee from negotiating with a regional union. For the 2009–2012 quadrennial, the IOC sold Brazil rights directly for $60 million and $210 million for the 2013–2016 quadrennium, a 250 percent increase.

In 2009 the IOC decided to expand this strategy to Europe as well, discontinuing a 50-year relationship with the European Broadcasting Union (EBU). In Europe, the approach is now a mixed model composed of individual agreements made directly between the IOC and television operators in big European countries such as the United Kingdom, Germany, France, and Spain combined by using an agency to sell the rights in other European countries. The sale of broadcast rights for the 2014 and 2016 Olympics to other European countries was facilitated by Sportfive marketing agency (IOC awards European Broadcast rights to SportFive, 2009). Sportfive purchased a group of broadcasting rights for many territories and then unbundled them by reselling to each territory. This effectively removed the burden from the IOC of having to negotiate numerous separate broadcasting deals (Mickle, 2009). Discovery Eurosport subsequently signed a long-term partnership with the IOC in June 2015, including exclusive multimedia rights in 50 European countries or territories. Infront Sports and Media, a sport marketing company based in Switzerland, has a similar contract for 44 countries or territories in Sub-Saharan Africa through 2024 including both the 2020 and 2022 Youth Olympic Games (IOC, 2019c). The change in IOC strategy has increased revenues while ensuring the game is still widely distributed and available on free-to-air television. All broadcasters are obliged to ensure a minimum of 200 free-to-air hours for the Olympic Summer Games and 150 free-to-air hours for the Olympic Winter Games (Pena, 2009).

New media and the future of Olympic broadcasting

The non-linear convergence of broadcast media and internet technologies is radically changing the media landscape (Miah, Jones and Adi, 2010). This is leading to a new era of network communication in the Olympic movement (Panagiotopoulou and Papa, 2010). The 2004 Olympic Games marked the first time that live coverage was made available on the internet in several territories. This trend continued in 2006 where broadcasters maximized the use of new media technologies, providing viewers with more access and greater choice through the internet as well as mobile phones. The use of digital media continued to expand between 2008 and 2012. The IOC broadcast for the first time live and on-demand coverage of the 2012 London Games on its YouTube Channel (IOC, 2012). By 2014, the amount of digital coverage available exceeded that of traditional broadcast coverage (IOC, 2014). The 2016 Rio Olympics Games was the most consumed Olympic Games ever with half the world's population, taking into consideration both television and digital platforms (IOC, 2016). In 2018, 670 million global online users viewed the PyeongChang Olympic Games, 120 percent more than watched Sochi 2014 (IOC, 2019a). The 2020 Tokyo Olympic Games is expected to continue the growth of digital online coverage.

The future of the Olympic movement's success at utilizing the potential of new media will be determined by how it answers the following three questions. First, is it possible for rights holders to monetize their new media platforms? Second, how can the Olympic movement generate new content around the Olympic experience? Finally, how can the Olympic movement successfully monetize its digital assets?

Olympic Channel

Launched in August 2016, following the recommendations of Agenda 2020, the goal of the Olympic Channel is to provide a new way to engage younger generations, fans, and new audiences with the Olympic movement 24 hours a day, 365 days per year. The Channel provides additional exposure for sports and athletes and serves as a platform to continuously "highlight the relevance of the Olympic Movement ideas to the challenges of today's world" (Olympic Channel Services, 2019). Intended to be inclusive of all Olympic sports and the 206 National Olympic Committees (NOC), programming includes original content, news, live sport events, historical footage from IOC archives, and social media. Subjects range from training, sport sciences and nutrition to sustainability and healthy active lifestyles. The Channel is available via Android and iOS mobile apps, and online at Olympicchannel.com. Linear distribution partnerships have also been established with NBCUniversal and the United States Olympic and Paralympic Committee in the United States, Discovery Communications/Eurosport in Europe, beIN Sports in the Middle East and Northern Africa, and the Japan Consortium.

The Olympic Channel Services is the corporate entity responsible for creating and operating the Olympic Channel. Technical and production units operate out of Madrid while the commercial and distribution departments are located at the IOC headquarters in Lausanne, Switzerland.

Conclusion

Over the years the Olympic Games have served as a platform to introduce and test new technological developments. The expansion of coverage globally, coupled with the increased competition for broadcast content resulting in higher rights fees, helped the International Olympic Committee become financially solvent. The future of Olympic broadcasting and associated rights fees depends on the IOC's ability to continue to attract both television and digital consumers. New programming and new media, similar to Twitch Channel, offer exciting opportunities to create a more interactive Olympic experience. Although host cities have not yet been named for the 2030 or 2032 Olympic Games, and technological advancements are rapidly changing the way people consume content, the IOC has awarded broadcast rights through the 2032 Games. The mutual goal for RHBs and the IOC is to continue to enhance broadcasts through high-definition BS4K/BS8K and the internet so that audiences can enjoy the Olympic Games anywhere and anytime. The IOC also retains non-live rights to use Olympic footage on its own digital platforms.

References

Abrahamson, A. (2003). NBC wins rights to 2010, 2012 Olympics. *Los Angeles Times*. Available at: www.latimes.com/archives/la-xpm-2003-jun-07-fi-oly7-story.html.

Billings, A.C. (2008). *Olympic media: Inside the biggest show on television*. London, England: Routledge.

Comitato Olimpico Nazionale Italiano. (1956). *VII Olympic Winter Games: Official report*. Cortina d'Ampezzo. Available at: https://digital.la84.org/digital/collection/p17103coll8/id/12644/.

de Moragas, M., Rivenburgh, N. and Larson, J.F. (1995). *Television in the Olympics*. London: John Libbey.

Greyser, S. and Kogan, V. (2013). NBC and 2012 London Olympics: Unexpected success. *Harvard Business School*. Available at: www.hbs.edu/faculty/Publication%20Files/14-028_99a0100c-7dcc-4fc4-bf29-6c0bd2f5561d.pdf.

International Olympic Committee. (2008). *IOC marketing media guide: Beijing 2008*. Available at: https://stillmed.olympic.org/media/Document%20Library/OlympicOrg/Games/Summer-Games/Games-Beijing-2008-Olympic-Games/IOC-Marketing-and-Broadcasting-Various-files/IOC-Marketing-Media-Guide-Beijing-2008.pdf#_ga=2.97853855.1820224548.1582284127–1523680289.1582284127.

International Olympic Committee. (2012). *Marketing report: London 2012*. Available at: http://view.digipage.net/go/ioclondon2012/.

International Olympic Committee. (2014). *Marketing report: Sochi, 2014*. Available at: https://stillmed.olympic.org/media/Document%20Library/OlympicOrg/Games/Winter-Games/Games-Sochi-2014-Winter-Olympic-Games/IOC-Marketing-and-Broadcasting-Various-files/IOC-Marketing-Report-Sochi-2014.pdf#_ga=2.61220396.1820224548.1582284127–1523680289.1582284127.

International Olympic Committee. (2016). *Marketing report: Rio 2016*. Available at: http://touchline.digipage.net/iocmarketing/reportrio2016/1-1.

International Olympic Committee. (2019a). *Broadcasters*. Dec. 9. Available at: www.olympic.org/broadcasters.

International Olympic Committee. (2019b). *Funding*. Dec. 17. Available at: www.olympic.org/funding.

International Olympic Committee. (2019c). *IOC awards 2024–2024 broadcast rights in Sub-Saharan Africa*. Dec. 21. Available at: www.olympic.org/news/ioc-awards-2020-2024-broadcast-rights-in-sub-saharan-africa.

International Olympic Committee. (2020). *Olympic marketing fact file: 2020 edition*. Available at: https://stillmed.olympic.org/media/Document%20Library/OlympicOrg/Documents/IOC-Marketing-and-Broadcasting-General-Files/Olympic-Marketing-Fact-File.pdf.

Meltz, M. (1999). Hand it over: Eurovision, exclusive EU sports broadcasting rights, and the article 85(3) exemption. *Boston Law School Student Publications*. Available at: http://lawdigitalcommons.bc.edu/cgi/viewcontent.cgi?article=1202&context=iclr.

Miah, A., Jones, J. and Adi, A. (2010). The Olympic Games and web 3.0: Monetizing the Olympic movement's digital assets. In: *Proceedings of the economics and management of the Olympic Games*, 21–23. Available at: http://cfss.sites.olt.ubc.ca/files/2011/01/symposium-abstracts.pdf.

Mickle, T. (2009). IOC shifts from dependence on US revenues. *Sports Business Journal*. Available at: www.sportsbusinessdaily.com/Journal/Issues/2009/10/12/This-Weeks-News/IOC-Shifts-From-Dependence-On-US-Revenue.aspx.

NBC. (2004). *2004 Olympic Games. Unprecedented 24-hour, around the clock coverage*. Available at: http://www.nbcnews.com/id/5174755/ns/msnbc-about_msnbc_tv/t/olympic-games/#.Xe0RpS3Mzq0.

New York Times. (2007). Will offer Olympics on the internet. *The New York Times*. Available at: http://www.nytimes.com/2007/08/08/sports/othersports/08olympics.html.

New York Times. (2009). IOC awards European broadcast rights to SportFive. *The New York Times*, Nov. 9. Available at: www.nytimes.com/2009/02/18/sports/18iht-olytv18.20285494.html.

OBS. (2018). *Media guide: Olympic Winter Games PyeongChang 2018*. Available at: https://www.obs.tv/assets/media-guides/OBSMediaGuide-PyeongChang2018.pdf.

Olympic Channel Services. (2019). *About the Olympic channel*. Available at: https://olympicchannelservices.com/about/.

Owen, D. (2015). Exclusive: IOC set to generate record $4.5 billion from Pyeongchang 2018 and Tokyo 2020 TV rights. *Inside the Games*. Available at: www.insidethegames.biz/articles/1028704/exclusive-ioc-set-to-generate-record-45-billion-from-pyeongchang-2018-and-tokyo-2020-tv-rights.

Panagiotopoulou, R. and Papa, F. (2010). The Olympic Games and the one media platforms: Business opportunities and constraints in a networked society. In: *Proceedings of the economics and management of the Olympic Games*, 19–21. Available at: http://cfss.sites.olt.ubc.ca/files/2011/01/symposium-abstracts.pdf.

Parent, M. and Séguin, B. (2018). Richard (Dick) W.D. Pound: The architect of Olympic business. In: E. Bayle and P. Clastres, eds., *Global sport leaders*. Palgrave Macmillan, pp. 217–242.

Payne (2006). *Olympic turnaround: How the Olympic Games stepped from the brink of extinction to become the world's best known brand*. London: Praeger.

Payne, M. (2012). *Olympic turnaround*. Infinite Ideas Limited.

Pena, E.F. (2009). *Olympic summer games and broadcast rights. Evolution and challenges in the new media environment*. Unpublished manuscript, Department of Audiovisual Communication and Advertising, Autonomous University of Barcelona, Barcelona, Spain.

Pound, D. (2010). *IOC member*. Proceedings of the Lecture Vancouver 2010 Winter Olympic Games.

Preuss, H. (2004). *Economics of the Olympic Games: Hosting the games 1972–2008*. Gloucestershire: Edward Edgar Publishing.

Schaub, A. (2002). *Sports and competition: Broadcasting rights of sport events*. Available at: https://pdfs.semanticscholar.org/c972/98efc4fcbef40d606a9ff7b37822d6dd1f17.pdf?_ga=2.145042930.770399912.1587499226-1392672022.1587499226.

Steinberg, B. (2019). NBC universal projects more than 1.2 billion in ad sales for 2020 Olympics. *Variety*. Available at: https://variety.com/2019/tv/news/nbcuniversal-2020-tokyo-olympics-advertising-billion-1203277005/.

Voight, K. (2008). *Olympics enter the '2.0' era*. Available at: http://www.cnn.com/2008/TECH/07/09/oly.media/index.html.

Zaccardi, N. (2014). IOC awards Olympic Games broadcast rights to NBC universal through 2032. *NBC Sports*. Available at: https://olympics.nbcsports.com/2014/05/07/olympics-nbc-broadcast-rights-2032/.

11

Activation of Olympic and Paralympic sponsorship

Stéphan Fuchs and Guillaume Bodet

Introduction

Each new edition of the Olympic and the Paralympic Games represents a rare opportunity to experience a unique and global sporting event. Particularly, for athletes it may represent the pinnacle of a sporting career, and participating may not be sufficient to satisfy competitors who seek to be the best in their discipline. Taking part and performing is also the main objective of the sponsors of the Games; even if the focus has shifted over the years. During the eighties, being a sponsor of the Games was almost confounded with performing, as participating meant having beaten their direct competitors to become the sole sponsor in the product category. Nowadays, this participation is not enough and performing seems to be the master word that mainly relies on two series of factors: on one hand the economic, juridical, informational, and societal mutations and their consequences in terms of commercial competition and practices, and on the other hand the consequences of the commercialisation of the Games such as the price to pay to become an official sponsor and the principle of exclusivity per product category applied to partnership levels (The Worldwide Olympic Partners, the Official partners, the Official Suppliers, etc.).

In this context, sponsorship that aims to "create or to directly support an (sporting) event and to be associated with it from a media perspective, to achieve objectives of marketing communication" (Derbaix, Gérard and Lardinoit, 1994) is not sufficient to achieve sponsors' contemporary goals. The badging approach is progressively replaced, or complemented, by another approach that sees sponsors more systematically conducting operations around the Games and its properties. This is known as 'sponsorship leveraging'.

The main methods used to leverage sponsorship investments include thematic publicities and advertising, public relations campaigns, sales promotions, entertainment programmes for clients, and programmes for the sponsors' employees and collaborators (Apostolopoulou Branvold, Pearson and Synowka, 2017). With these additional activities, audiences' participation levels are variable. Some activities aim to increase the message exposure, where the receivers are passive, while others aim to initiate an activity from the receivers, such as acting, reacting, sharing, collaborating, and even engaging; this is sponsorship activation. Immersive activities focusing on customers and spectators' experiences or activities aiming at creating a viral diffusion though the Internet and social networks are examples of this approach.

Nowadays, sponsorship of Olympic and Paralympic Games can take many shapes within a complex, and largely digital, environment. A closer look at the campaigns from the 2018 PyeongChang Games allows us to better describe and analyse sponsors' tactics and strategies and identify the main current challenges and opportunities in relation to activation operations.

This chapter first introduces and characterises the theoretical background of sponsorship activation and sponsorship. It then identifies the specificities of the Olympics and Paralympics in relation with activation. Third, the cases of Visa and Coca-Cola in relation with the 2018 PyeongChang Olympics will be then analysed. From these cases, contemporary trends and challenges in relation with activation will be discussed. As a conclusion, we will offer perspectives regarding the future of activation at the Olympic and Paralympic Games.

Definition and theoretical background

Numerous definitions of sponsorship are available in the academic literature with, sometimes, heterogeneous content. However, a consensus seems to exist regarding key components: the object that is a support to a cause or event; the main objectives that can be corporate or marketing; the counterparts that are the capacity from the sponsor to exploit entities' properties and rights in its commercial activity; and the possibility for both partners to get benefits from it.

Perceived at its origins like a great alternative to advertising, sport sponsorship has now become a true marketing communication technique. It represents a truly integrated platform gathering several practices such as event or cause sponsorship, naming, endorsement, certain forms of ambush marketing, and media sponsorship. It allows sponsors to increase brand equity through awareness, image, perceived quality and customer loyalty, sales, business-to-business relationships, and internal objectives.

Always in transformation, sport sponsorship is now a complete digital tool. Sport sponsorship therefore now follows the rules of digital communication where information is instantaneous, ephemeral, and viral, and where audiences go with groups and communities, sharing and engaging. Beyond the basic diffusion function via the Web, it has become producer of contents, mainly in the form of storytelling, to feed social media in particular. Storytelling represents brands and products' intention and capacity, through telling stories, to allow consumers to achieve proper pleasure through reliving experiences, enact archetypal roles and myths, and make sense of life events (Woodside, Sood and Miller, 2008). Storytelling encompasses a combination of related contents that make receivers feel they actually live these experiences and has a powerful marketing function that activates consumers' linking to brands (e.g. information recall, purchasing intentions) (Laurell and Söderman, 2018). As noted by Laurell and Söderman (2018), the dynamic nature and co-creating dimension of social media has influenced the development of storytelling that is much more co-created between sport organisations and their publics, and even co-created independently from sport organisations. Although this loss of control could appear threatening, this is where its strength resides, explaining why sponsors increasingly engage in these practices as illustrated in the cases of Visa and Coca-Cola at 2018 PyeongChang Olympics, later presented.

Over the years, sport sponsorship success has created inflation in the fees required for the rights to become official sponsor, and more recently in the costs of exploiting such a status. Sponsorship's growth has also created a saturation of media spaces. Ambush marketing, a less expensive and sometimes more clever alternative, is now fully part of the sport sponsorship landscape, and is assumed to reduce advantages official sponsors get from association rights. In

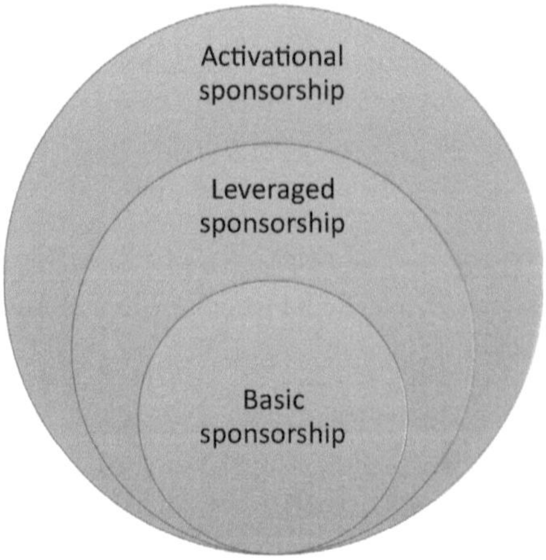

Figure 11.1 The three-level system of sponsorship

this context, the sole promotion of the sponsor-sponsee association via the communication of basic information about the sporting event and or the sponsors, one-directional messages on the Internet, and publicities in link with the events do not seem to be enough to maximise the benefits of the investment. Consequently, raising interest in a sponsorship means that rights holders must further exploit these rights through, for instance, commercial operations in link with the sponsee. Other types of activities rely on the distribution of free samples and discounts, and the launch of new products such as the payment innovations implemented by Visa at the 2018 PyeongChang Games. A sponsorship that uses the rights acquired from the event to implement additional activities, for example promotional activities, is known as sponsorship leveraging.

However, conducting these activities does not necessarily involve the active participation of audiences or real engagement. It requires the implementation of activities that initiate a continuous dialog and generate positive feedbacks and interactions. These opportunities are now possible with Internet 2.0. Thus, activities that are developed to engage audiences within the frame of sport sponsorship are referred to as 'sponsorship activation'. In summary, sport sponsorship can be described as a three-level integrated system (see Figure 11.1) that relies on the promotion of the sponsor-sponsee association, that uses this link to leverage and implement collateral activities, and that aims to activate the link with audiences.

The activation process

Using a time-related perspective, O'Reilly and Horning (2013) described with details the evolution between stages from a sponsor's portfolio of rights to the evaluation of activation operations. The authors identified four stages. First, the activation context is characterised by seven drivers:

> sponsor's sales objectives, sponsor's equity objectives, evidence of past success in sponsorship and activation, sponsor's resources available: financial, human and marketing, agency partner(s) and their capacity, strategic integration ('fit') with other activities, sponsorships and business units, ability of sponsored property versus clutter and/or ambush.
>
> *(O'Reilly and Horning, 2013, p. 435)*

The second stage relies on the decision to activate or not. Four strategic criteria are considered to make this decision: "congruence/fit, priority of sponsorship for the sponsor, integrated marketing communications elements and tactics, capacity to implement activation tactics" (O'Reilly and Horning, 2013, p. 435). The third stage deals with the amount of resources allocated to activation operations. Expressed as a ratio, O'Reilly and Horning (2013) suggest that a ratio from 1.0 to 7.0 (1.0 to 4.0 for media activations) should be considered between the money spent for acquiring the rights and the money spent to exploit them. The fourth and final stage concerns the evaluation of activation operations. The authors proposed six criteria allowing for a simple comparison between the initial and final situation to assess activation efficiency: sales, market share, equity measures, competitive advantage gain, long-term evaluation, comparison to other activations.

The specificities of the Olympics/Paralympics

One element to have in mind is that leveraging and activation strategies are strongly influenced by the context (geographical, regulatory, socio-economic) and by the nature of entities involved that are the sponsee and the sponsor. In that regards, the Olympics and Paralympics Games are special because of the nature of the events as multi-sport events happening every four years, alternating between Summer and Winter Games, with Olympics preceding Paralympics. Olympic and Paralympic Games are awarded to a city (region) and are organised by a single organising committee. The Games' competitions last two weeks and ten days respectively.

These factors obviously have impacts on various audiences including local (athletes from the village, inhabitants of the city and the country) as well as international and global audiences reached and influenced based on geographical distance and time difference.

The second specificity is linked to the event itself, to its branding characteristics and consequently to its properties. In that regard, the Olympics and Paralympics are quite unique with three main global events – Olympic and Paralympic Summer Games, Olympic and Paralympic Winter Games and, since 2010, the Youth Olympic Games. Other properties include the Olympic Hymn, the Olympic Medals, the Olympic Motto "citius, altius, fortius", the Olympic Posters, the Olympic Symbol made of the five interlaced rings, the Olympic Flag, the Olympic Oath, the Olympic Flame, the Olympic Torch Relay, the Olympic Mascots, the Olympic Emblems, the Olympic Pictograms, and Still and Moving Images of the Olympics.

The third specificity relies on the particular nature of the relationship between sponsee and sponsors. In that regard, we mention the category exclusivity offered to Olympic and Paralympic sponsors; the Clean Venue Policy that prevents any commercial advertising at Olympic Games venues and that is unique in the world of sport, and the related brand protection programme comprising, for instance, strong regulatory and legal protections sponsors benefit from ambush marketing (Ellis, Scassa and Séguin, 2011), and the Out-of-Home Advertising policy that "is designed to secure outdoor media properties in and around . . . sites and venues and also major transportation hubs for the official Games partners" (IOC, 2018, p. 126).

The exploitation of property rights by Olympic and Paralympic sponsors is well documented in the academic and professional literatures (e.g. Carrillat, D'Astous and Charrette Couture, 2015; Darcy, Frawley and Adair, 2017). However, it can be noted that the analyses of strategies and activities conducted on digital platforms are still in their infancy (e.g. Weeks, Cornwell and Drennan, 2008; Abeza et al., 2014; Apostolopoulou et al., 2017).

Sponsorship activation is often studied by using a sponsor's marketing communication campaigns in relation to a specific edition of the Games. The perspective is often practitioner-oriented and case studies represent the preferred method. The terms leveraging and activation are often used interchangeably. Two topics are particularly studied. The first one is mainly descriptive and focused on the conceptual field. It aims to identify and categorise the various forms of sponsorship activation. The second is concerned with activation strategies' performance and efficiency, and is mainly descriptive. Within this area, two types of studies are conducted: studies that seek to identify underlying activation processes and mechanisms to better understand their implementation and impacts, and studies that attempt to measure activation's influence and efficiency. For the latter, authors have examined and compared sponsorship with activation versus no activation (i.e. Stipp and Schiavone, 1996; Quester and Thompson, 2001), the link between activation intensity and benefits (Olson and Thjømøe, 2009), and the link between the forms of activation and various sponsorship outcomes (Carrillat, D'Astous and Charrette Couture, 2015; Dees et al., 2018).

The cases of Visa and Coca-Cola at the 2018 PyeongChang Olympics

In the following sections, we will focus on the cases of Visa and Coca-Cola at the 2018 PyeongChang Olympics. After a short presentation of the sponsors, the main activation strategies and operations used are described.

The case of Visa

Visa is the world's leading payment brand, generating more than three trillion US dollars in annual card sales volume; it is accepted in more than 150 countries and has about 21,000 member financial institutions and individual cardholders.[1] The brand started sponsoring the Olympics in 1986 with the primary objective of building brand awareness (Davis, 2012). Over time, their objectives evolved to become more ambitious, extending the benefits of the sponsorship beyond the simple period of the Games and linking it for instance with tourism and destination marketing programmes, to achieve differentiation with the specific industry (Davis, 2012). To achieve these objectives, Visa has mainly used four marketing platforms before, during, and after the Games: advertising to build awareness, promotional to increase usage, corporate relations to build an integrated message, and its products to highlight innovation (Davis, 2012). One of the founders of the TOP programme, Visa is nowadays the exclusive payment technology partner and has extended its partnership with the Olympics until 2032. Visa aims at demonstrating its latest payment innovations and contributions to digital experiences.[2]

For the 2018 PyeongChang Olympic Winter Games, the brand implemented and managed more than 1,000 contactless point-of-sale terminals to facilitate transactions with mobile phones and also wearables they developed for the Games. Especially, the brand developed and implemented payment-enabled gloves and wearable stickers and Olympic pins promoted as innovative and particularly convenient payment solutions under very cold temperatures.[3] These activations correspond to the product and corporate relations marketing platforms as they rely on customer experiences and touchpoints as well as presenting new products.

Visa's other main activation strategy relied on the Team Visa programme that was initiated in 2000. Specifically, it aims to provide athletes with tools, resources, and support to achieve their sporting 'dreams'.[4] The brand emphasises that athletes are chosen based on fit in terms of values (e.g. acceptance, partnership, and inclusion), their personality, and their athletic talent. Team Visa's global roster at the PyeongChang Olympics comprised of 54 Olympics and Paralympics athletes (male and female), hopefuls, and legends participating in 15 sports and representing 21 countries. These include countries that are well-known for their winter sports success (i.e. Norway, Canada, USA, Korea) and other less represented countries such as Philippines, Nigeria, Chile, and Uganda allowing a representation of all continents but Oceania.[5] It should be also noted that the link with American athletes from the Team Visa was reinforced by the fact the Visa sponsored the US Ski Team, US Snowboarding, and US Freeskiing.

The main activation strategy relied on the "Resetting Finish Lines" advertising campaign featuring several athletes in their journey to competing at the Games, and using the latest products and innovations of the brand, and that was first communicated through the athletes' personal social media accounts.

Interestingly, it should be noted that athletes promoted their own personal sponsors. For instance, Mikaela Shiffrin made publicity for Ikon Pass and Oakley, including videos, on her Facebook page.

During the Olympic and Paralympic competitions, Visa posted congratulations and support messages on social media when one of their athletes was involved. However, this activity seemed uneven between social media platforms and countries, which did not have the same amount of athletes involved (e.g. about 18 posts on Twitter by the @Visa account between the 4th February and 18th March 2018 including #TeamVisa). After the Games, the brand occasionally organised contests using athletes from the Team Visa. That was for instance the case with Visa France that set a contest to win a week of skiing, including the opportunity to ski with the French skier Alexis Pinturault.

Similarly to the "Resetting Finish Lines" campaign, both activation tactics were also combined with videos showing Team Visa athletes using the new payment wearables.[6] In these videos, athletes are kind of transformed into demonstrators, and possibly personal sellers, of the product.

The case of Coca-Cola

"The Coca-Cola Company is the world's leading manufacturer, marketer and distributor of non-alcoholic beverage concentrates and syrups used to produce more than 230 brands of products".[7] The company has been a partner of the Olympic movement since 1928 and founding partner of the TOP programme starting in 1986. Since this date, the company has held exclusivity in the non-alcoholic beverage category. The involvement of the company has been motivated by commercial objectives such as increasing sales and market shares, and financial objectives such as increasing its revenues and profits. However, it has also pursued more philanthropic objectives as stated by Davis (2012) for whom "Coca-Cola . . . as an iconic American brand with a well-known global reputation . . . has historically emphasized intangible objectives, including showing they are a responsible corporate citizen and associating the brand with positive, lifestyle values and images".

The PyeongChang Olympic Winter Games represented the opportunity for Coca-Cola to celebrate 90 years of support to the Olympic movement. This exceptional event also represented a great opportunity to feature on the Paralympic competition websites in opposition with Olympics for which this is not authorised.

Using original sponsorship activations targeting athletes and consumers from all around the world, the company aimed to further promote the Olympic spirit and specific associated values that it seeks to support: the search for excellence, a certain vision of fair-play, and the will to build a more peaceful world.

The main theme of the Coca-Cola campaign during the PyeongChang Olympics was "Taste the feeling, Together as One!" and was expressed through the main sponsorship activations in Korea and in the media. These shared moments started several months before the opening of the Olympic Games and went beyond the closing ceremony of the Games.

Specifically, activation operations were conceived and implemented to create a particular brand experience. Three main touchpoints or platforms were used. The first platform was the event itself to benefit from a favourable context: an immersive frame for a memorable moment. The second was the products: the famous soda but also the other drinks "including inspired Coca-Cola Freestyle flavours" to interact with the consumer targets and to constitute the basis for entertaining activities. The third relied on games, and the gamification trend (Terlutter and Capella, 2013).

The company implemented several types of activations around the worldwide event and several examples can be identified to illustrate the diversity of the experiences offered and their originality.

With the torch relay, Coca-Cola provided an immersive and unique experience to about 7,500 individuals,[8] from anonymous to celebrities, and even a robot: receiving, bearing, and transmitting the torch, which is one of the of the most iconic symbols of the Olympic spirit of the modern Games, over few hundreds of meters from the 2018 km overall distance run in the Republic of Korea.

In the main Olympic sites opened to the public, Coca-Cola offered several memorable and entertaining experiences. In the Olympic Park, each visitor could take photos in front of a 15-meter high vending machine or in the Coca-Cola's gallery space. Overall, 250,000 individuals visited the vending machine (IOC, 2018). In the PyeongChang Olympic Plaza, each visitor could assist and take part in funny games to win Coca-Cola gifts and product sampling.

On the Internet and in social networks, Coca-Cola provided participatory and rewarding experiences for consumers of the brand during the Games. Everyday, participants could win instantaneously prizes such as snowboards, duffle bags, Team USA mittens, and airline tickets by scanning with their mobile an icon on Coca-Cola's products or in various locations (in-store signage and cups) after having visited first the dedicated website Coke.com/Olympics, and the section Round-the-Clock Refreshment.[9] Prizes were even greater when they watched the event live. Additional bonuses could be won when participating consumers shared the electronic link with family and friends. Fans were also greatly encouraged to support the athletes of Team USA on social networks and particularly the four ambassadors of the brand: freestyle skier Mac Bohonnon, figure skater Nathan Chen, bobsledder Elana Meyers Taylor, and Paralympic snowboarder Amy Purdy. In return, custom digital content and unique prizes were given to them. The CokePlay platform was used by more than one million target consumers (IOC, 2018).[10]

Trends and challenges

With growing investments in sponsorship deals, attention to returns, and particularly on returns on investments, has increased and consequently emphasised the importance given to activation. This trend has also been supported and accentuated by the growth of social media and their cost. Social media represent an easy and relatively cheap way to conduct activation operations and offer interesting benefits such as a capacity to go global and reach international audiences. In the meantime, given the specificities of social media such as their geographical and socio-demographics segmented nature, it allows sponsor brands to better target their audiences and consumers and to optimise their campaigns. This dimension is well recognised by the IOC and its president Thomas Bach who said in the 2018 IOC Marketing Report (p. 36):

> Through their creative global marketing campaigns, the Worldwide Olympic Partners also helped to bring PyeongChang 2018 to life throughout the world, building excitement

ahead of the Games, promoting the Olympic values and increasing the support for Olympic *athletes through their unprecedented social media activations.*

Furthermore, activations via social media are not restricted by time and can even extend the life expectancy of campaigns due to their viral nature.

The second major trend we can observe is concurrent to the previous one, and characterises a growing role and use of athletes in activation campaigns. This was exemplified in the cases of Visa and Coca-Cola during the PyeongChang Games. Several reasons can justify this trend. First, this is linked to development of celebrity brands (Bouchet, Hillairet and Bodet, 2013) and the fact that athletes are able to increase the strength of their personal branding and are developing skills, particularly media and communication skills, to simultaneously raise their profile and satisfy their sponsors (Dumont, 2016). Second, it allows further extending the reach of activation campaigns using athletes' social media platforms that are followed by many, like a multiplying effect. This also allows enlarging activation periods around events, with for instance a focus on athletes' pre- and post-event periods. Third, focusing and further involving athletes authorises more personalisation, thanks to the strong identification fans and followers can show towards them. 'Athlete materials' appear as a powerful source of storytelling for brands that seek to improve their image and narratives around it. This is especially the case when brands focus on athletes' personal history and life and allow customers and fans to pleasurably relive personal experiences, which is one of the main functions of storytelling (Woodside, Sood and Miller, 2008). Several of these aspects are well illustrated with the P & G's Thank You Mom campaign that started in November 2017 with the "Love Over Bias" film that was viewed more than 300 million times in 18 languages (IOC, 2018).

While the previous trends identified earlier are justified by their physical and temporal disconnections from the events, another trend focuses on the moment of the event and the experiences lived by attendees. This phenomenon is registered within the broader experience economy (Pine and Gilmore, 2011) and experiential marketing approaches that focus on creating highly emotional, memorable, and extraordinary experiences (Chanavat and Bodet, 2014), as exemplified in the Visa and Coca-Cola cases. It is all the more interesting for sponsor brands that it also meets brand events' objectives in creating unforgettable memories while enriching fans and attendees' overall on-site experiences beyond the simple sport contests and stores. Sponsors' pavilions in Olympic villages are not new; however the focus on interacting with consumers and providing them fun and entertaining physical and virtual extraordinary experiences is prevalent nowadays and two quotes taken from the IOC Marketing Report 2018 demonstrate this focus:

> Samsung improved the Olympic Winter Games experience for all[11] by providing real-time updates, athlete information, medal standings and Olympic Games records through the PyeongChang 2018 Olympic Winter Games Mobile Guide.
>
> *(p. 80)*

And:

> Kia Motors also created a 'BEAT-PLAY' showcase in Gangneung to provide visitors with a variety of events, including car displays, a STINGER VR experience, mini-curling games and photo events. The company also ran invitation programmes for customers, giving *them the chance to experience the Games first-hand.*[12]

Conclusion

The interests in Olympic and Paralympic Sponsorship, and consequently the amounts invested in it, have not stopped increasing: from USD 279 million in 1993–1996, the TOP programme has generated USD 1,003 million in 2013–2016.[13] These figures taken from the IOC however underestimate the overall amounts sponsors invest as the cost of activation operations is not taken into consideration. Consistent with the growth of investments, there is an increasing need or focus on return on investments and/or return on objectives from sponsors, which equates further activation of the partnership between brands and the Olympics and Paralympics. The growth of activation activities is welcomed and possibly encouraged by the IOC who sees them as enhancing "the Olympic Games experience for spectators and provides the youth of the world with opportunities to experience the Olympic ideals at global and local levels".[14] The notion of experience highlighted in this quote demonstrates how activation has evolved over time, moving from passive and exposure actions to more experiential activities that encourage participants to become active and engaged with brands' products and services. Beyond the extraordinary experiences they produce, they also aim to increase the symbolic links and meanings about their associations, and heavily rely on digital ways of communicating and on social media in particular to do so. For this reason, and as we could see with the case of Visa, athletes are increasingly used as a focus of activations and storytelling that emphasise this sense-making approach. Although more effective, we can hypothesise that such approaches contribute to the fragmentation of audiences through various supports, platforms, and messages that could possibly challenge the consistency of brands' images and associations, and reinforcing the need for integrated communication marketing. Furthermore, we can also wonder whether the significant growth of activation operations will not create congestion, making it more difficult for sponsors to stand out of the crowds despite having category exclusivity, especially when ambushers get involved in intensive and almost similar types of communications.

Notes

1 www.olympic.org/sponsors/visa accessed 27th October 2018.
2 www.olympic.org/news/ioc-and-visa-extend-partnership-through-to-2032 accessed 27th October 2018.
3 www.olympic.org/news/visa-offers-olympic-fans-and-athletes-innovative-payment-experience accessed 27th October 2018.
4 https://usa.visa.com/about-visa/sponsorships-promotions/olympics-partnership/meet-team-visa.html accessed 27th October 2018.
5 https://usa.visa.com/about-visa/sponsorships-promotions/olympics-partnership/meet-team-visa.html accessed 27th October 2018.
6 https://usa.visa.com/about-visa/sponsorships-promotions/olympics-partnership.html accessed 27th October 2018.
7 www.olympic.org/sponsors/coca-cola accessed 5th November 2018.
8 www.olympic.org/pyeongchang-2018-torch-relay accessed 25th January 2019
9 www.coca-colacompany.com/stories/round-the-clock-refreshment-coke-to-use-sip-scan-technology-to-engage-fans-during-olympic-winter-games-pyeongchang-2018 accessed 8th November 2018.
10 www.instagram.com/p/BfPYdz_BCQc/ accessed 22nd March 2019.
11 Emphasised by the authors.
12 Ibid.
13 https://stillmed.olympic.org/media/Document%20Library/OlympicOrg/Documents/IOC-Marketing-and-Broadcasting-General-Files/Olympic-Marketing-Fact-File-2018.pdf accessed 28th March 2019.
14 https://stillmed.olympic.org/media/Document%20Library/OlympicOrg/Documents/IOC-Marketing-and-Broadcasting-General-Files/Olympic-Marketing-Fact-File-2018.pdf accessed 28th March 2019.

References

Abeza, G., Pegoraro, A., Naraine, M.L., Séguin, B. and O'Reilly, N. (2014). Activating a global sport sponsorship with social media: An analysis of TOP sponsors, Twitter, and the 2014 Olympic Games. *International Journal of Sport Management and Marketing*, 15(3/4), pp. 184–213.

Apostolopoulou, A., Branvold, S., Pearson, J. and Synowka, D. (2017). #ThatsGold: Sponsorship activation in the 2016 Rio Summer Olympics. *Journal of Brand Strategy*, 6(3), pp. 263–280.

Bouchet, P., Hillairet, D. and Bodet, G. (2013). *Sport brands*. London, UK: Routledge.

Carrillat, F., D'Astous, A. and Charrette Couture, M-P. (2015). How corporate sponsors can optimize the impact of their message content: Mastering the message: Improving the processability and effectiveness of sponsorship activation. *Journal of Advertising Research*, 55(3), pp. 255–269.

Chanavat, N. and Bodet, G. (2014). Experiential marketing in sport spectatorship services: A customer perspective. *European Sport Management Quarterly*, 14(4), pp. 323–344.

Darcy, S., Frawley, S. and Adair, D. (2017). *Managing the Paralympics*. Palgrave Macmillan, p. 302.

Davis, J.A. (2012). *The Olympic Games effect-How sports marketing builds strong brands*. Singapore: John Wiley & Sons.

Dees, W., Gay, C., Popp, N. and Jensen, J.A. (2018). Assessing the impact of sponsor asset selection, intangible rights, and activation on sponsorship effectiveness. *Sport Marketing Quarterly*.

Derbaix, C., Gérard, P. and Lardinoit, T. (1994). Essai de conceptualisation d'une activité éminemment pratique: le parrainage. *Recherche et Applications en Marketing*, 9(2), pp. 43–67.

Dumont, G. (2016). Understanding ethnographically athlete's perception and experience of sponsorship: The case of professional rock-climbing. *European Sport Management Quarterly*, 16(4), pp. 525–542.

Ellis, D., Scassa, T. and Séguin, B. (2011). Framing ambush marketing as a legal issue: An Olympic perspective. *Sport Management Review*, 14(3), pp. 297–308.

IOC. (2018). *IOC marketing report 2018*. Lausanne: IOC.

Laurell, C. and Söderman, S. (2018). Sports, storytelling and social media: A review and conceptualisation. *International Journal of Sports Marketing and Sponsorship*, 19(3), pp. 338–349.

Olson, E.L. and Thjømøe, H.M. (2009). Sponsorship effect metric: Assessing the financial value of sponsoring by comparisons to television advertising. *Journal of the Academy of Marketing Science*, 37, p. 504.

O'Reilly, N. and Horning, D.L. (2013). Leveraging sponsorship: The activation ratio. *Sport Management Review*, 16(4), pp. 424–437.

Pine II, J.B. and Gilmore, J.H. (2011). *The experience economy*. Boston: Harvard Business School Publishing.

Quester, P.G. and Thompson, B. (2001). Advertising and promotion leverage on arts sponsorship effectiveness. *Journal of Advertising Research*, 41(1), pp. 33–47.

Stipp, H. and Schiavone, N.P. (1996). The impact of Olympic sponsorship on corporate image. *Journal of Advertising Research*, 36(4), pp. 75–87.

Terlutter, R. and Capella, M.L. (2013). The gamification of advertising: Analysis and research directions of in-game advertising, advergames, and advertising in social networks games. *Journal of Advertising*, 42(2–3), pp. 95–112.

Weeks, C.S., Cornwell, T.B. and Drennan, J.C. (2008). Leveraging sponsorships on the Internet: Activation, congruence and articulation. *Psychology & Marketing*, 25(7), pp. 637–654.

Woodside, A.G., Sood, S. and Miller, K.E. (2008). When consumers and brand talks: Storytelling theory research in psychology and marketing. *Psychology & Marketing*, 25(2), pp. 97–145.

12

Legal aspects of the Olympics and ambush marketing

John Grady

Introduction

While the Olympic Games have become the grandest stage for athletes, it has also become a battleground for corporate marketers to "take gold" in winning over Olympic fans and global consumers (McKelvey and Grady, 2004). At the same time, ambush marketing continues to be an ongoing concern for Olympic organizers and "the protection against ambush marketing is now synonymous with protecting the Olympic brand" (Séguin and Scassa, 2014, p. 507).

While the sophisticated Olympic sponsorship programme known as TOP has been successful in granting an elite handful of brands exclusivity to use the iconic Olympic rings in creating brand associations, there has been an increasing effort to aggressively protect the commercial rights and corporate marketing activities which surround the Games. These efforts invoke the comprehensive intellectual property protection system employed by Olympic movement prior to and during the Games known as brand protection. The brand protection strategy, while heavily grounded in intellectual property laws, is revised for each Olympics to reflect the existing laws of the host country as well as considers additional evolving factors such as technological innovations to close any loopholes which may now exist. It has also spurred creation of an emerging area of law known as "Olympic laws" (James and Osborn, 2015) which focuses on the transnational legal and sponsorship protection issues that surround hosting an Olympic Games.

The evolution of brand protection, detailed later, demonstrates how the Olympic movement has taken full advantage of legal and marketing strategies to ensure maximum protection for their mega event and its sponsors and to curb the practice of ambush marketing. It has also sparked criticism that this approach is often heavy-handed at times and prioritizes commercial interests and corporate goals over the needs of athletes and their sponsors. As suggested by Séguin and O'Reilly (2008), ambush marketing is arguably of less importance to official sponsors than is the strength of the Olympic brand itself. However, the Olympic movement has taken purposeful steps to address changes in marketing and technology which enables ambush marketing to further encroach on the Olympic brand and its elite handful of global sponsors. The steps taken employ a combination of law, policy, and marketing strategy to ensure comprehensive protection for the Olympic Games.

Protecting the 'Rings'

Each Olympic organizing committee (OCOG) has fundamentally relied upon intellectual property laws as the legal basis to protect sponsors' exclusive rights (Grady, 2016a). Specifically, trademark and copyright laws provide the legal basis for protecting the Olympics logos, symbols, and imagery which have become iconic in creating the consumer associations between the Olympics and brands. Seeing these iconic brands appearing together, such as Coca-Cola and the Olympic rings, yields increased brand equity for sponsors and makes controlling use of the Olympic marks the highest priority for event organizers. This is done through a complex patchwork of existing laws, newly enacted event-specific laws that are put in place for the sole benefit of event organizers that often 'sunset' once the event is over, as well as an extensive set of social media rules and advertising regulations about using 'protected' Olympic words and phrases. This list of so-called 'banned' words has expanded with each successive Games to protect every conceivable combination of words that might conjure up an association with the Olympics. For example, a recent iteration for the Rio 2016 Games protected words including Summer, Gold, and Victory when used in an Olympic context (Grady, 2016b). For example, this allowed official sponsor Coca-Cola to theme their 2016 Olympic campaign around "That's Gold" in promotional videos showcasing athletes winning gold in sport.

Beginning with event-specific laws put in place for the Sydney 2000 Games, requiring a host city to enact special legislation to protect Olympic symbols is a routine and expected part of the host city bid process (McKelvey and Grady, 2008). Allusions to event-specific legislation to ensure adequate protection of Olympic marks, symbols, and phrases are now included in every Olympic host city contract and local organizing committees are keenly aware of Olympic expectations in this regard. Yet, these laws have often expanded trademark law theory and practice in ways not previously contemplated within the traditional scope of enforcement (Grady, 2016a). In essence, words and phrases that would not normally be protectable under the host country's trademark laws are given superiority and become registered marks simply because it is associated with the mega event, when it would not otherwise meet the legal requirement to become a registered trademark. By monopolizing use of the term by the Olympics and its partners, this effectively restricts use of the term or mark for the broader society, raising free speech concerns.

While recent iterations of Olympic special legislation have given broad powers to OCOGs (Osborn and James, 2013), these laws have produced uneven results and garnered criticism from advertising industry watchers as well as legal scholars. Despite strict enforcement during the Games, they are not often (if ever) subjected to judicial scrutiny. For example, despite aggressive brand policing in the lead up to the London 2012 Games, "Nike, no stranger to the Olympic ambush game, used its high-profile campaign 'Find your greatness' to showcase ordinary athletes finding greatness in cities (named London) around the world" (Grady and McKelvey, 2012, p. 1). While "Nike's actions initially raised the ire of LOCOG's brand enforcement team," no legal action was taken and the LOCOG promised to monitor the situation (Grady and McKelvey, 2012, p. 1).

At the NOC level, there may be more of a willingness to assert a legal challenge when a non-sponsor allegedly suggests to the public that they have an official sponsor relationship with the Olympics or a NOC when they do not. Such was the case when The Canadian Olympic Committee (COC) threatened to sue The North Face for trademark infringement, claiming that is Villagewear Collection of clothing infringed the COC's trademarks and alleged the name for the collection confused the public into thinking they were an official Olympic sponsor of Team Canada which was not the case (Krashinsky, 2014). The COC claimed the Villagewear Collection was an obvious reference to the Athlete's Village and that some items contained "RU/14" which they claimed was an obvious reference to Russia, host country of the 2014 Sochi Games. In response to the lawsuit, The North Face agreed to change the name of the collection to the International Collection. Despite the name change, the COC claimed the violations still existed and continued pursuing the case for almost two years. The case eventually settled, with The North Face making a monetary donation to the COC (Krashinsky, 2016). The case demonstrates that NOCs may be the ones leading the charge to the courthouse to protect sponsors.

Local organizing committees choosing not to litigate suspected cases of ambush marketing in court, despite the presence of special laws that often criminalize such behavior during the Games period, is often a strategic choice to draw less media attention to ambush incidents when they do occur. Instead, the special laws are utilized as the legal basis in a "cease and desist" request sent to infringing brands. Thus, it can be argued that these event-specific laws have had a deterrent effect on would-be brands wanting to use protected words, phrases, or Olympic imagery in advertising campaigns during the time of an Olympics, and instead causing them to choose more ambiguous sport-themed imagery in their advertising campaigns with less obvious reference to the Olympics. This is also reflective of the overall challenge faced by local organizing committees in balancing brand protection efforts with legal options, as contemporary ambush marketing incidents rarely infringe on the event's protected trademarks, making what ambush marketing activity that does occur often technically not illegal and instead falling within the domain of brand protection teams (Grady and McKelvey, 2012). The intellectual property of the Games includes: logos and symbols; official products; images, videos, designs, and publications; official expressions and designations; historical images; mascots, pictograms, look of the Games; and torch, flames, and medals (Rio 2016 Brand Protection Guidelines Version 2, n.d.).

Ambush marketing

With regard to the Olympic Games, the problem and practice of ambush marketing has been consistently targeted in terms of threatening the overall financial viability of the Olympic movement, devaluing commercial partners' rights, as well as a "possible threat to [Olympic] brand equity" (Séguin and Scassa, 2014, p. 519). Through commercial rights management generally and brand protection efforts specifically, ambush marketing has been on the radar of Olympic organizers since the term was first coined at the 1984 Los Angeles Summer Games (McKelvey, 2014). Kodak's campaign during the 1984 Olympic Games against the backdrop of rival Fuji's official sponsorship is viewed as one of the earliest ambush marketing campaigns (Sandler and Shani, 1989).

Ambush marketing has been defined as "a company's intentional efforts to weaken its competitors 'official sponsorship'" (McKelvey, 1994, p. 20). This is accomplished through various techniques, such as engaging in promotions and advertising which seek to trade off the goodwill of the Games and to confuse consumers about the event's official sponsors (McKelvey, 1994). Ambush marketing tactics have evolved considerably over time as the practice has become an expected presence at each Olympic Games. While many definitions of ambush marketing label the practice in pejorative terms or as unethical behavior, more recent scholarship has raised arguments that modern ambush marketing is now viewed in a more neutral way. For example, Nufer (2009, 2016) suggests ambush marketing as an effective alternative to official sponsorship and describes the practice as innovative marketing. Thus, how ambush marketing is perceived is often influenced by that person's perspective (Ellis, Scassa and Séguin, 2011), as a rival brand, an official sponsor, or as the event organizer seeking to maximize value from the sale of official sponsorship rights.

Legislative efforts, especially those from London 2012 and beyond, have sought to (re) define ambush marketing using the concept of association, essentially deeming it an infringement (and actually a criminal offense in some instances) for non-affiliated brands (i.e. those that are not official sponsors) to create an association with the Olympic Games. For example, in advance of the London 2012 Games, Great Britain passed the London Olympic and Paralympic Marks Act (2006) which created the "London Olympics association right." The law forbade those who were not official sponsors from implying a commercial or contractual connection with the Olympics. At the time of its enactment, the law was considered "an unprecedented approach to protecting Olympic intellectual property that future host cities [were] likely to emulate" (Grady and McKelvey, 2012, p. 1). For Rio 2016, the concept of 'association' also was prominent in the Brazilian special legislation passed to address ambush marketing. Article 8 of Brazilian Law No. 13,284 "prohibit[ed] uses of expressions (outside the lists of protected symbols) that are sufficiently similar (to protected marks and expressions) . . . to invoke an undue association with the Rio Games or Olympic movement" (Lei No. 13.284 de 10 de Maio de 2016). The law, which amended the Brazilian Olympic Act, defined ambush marketing in such a way that marketing brands or products by claiming a direct or indirect association with the Games without permission from event organizers would constitute a crime (Buchanan, 2016). FIFA has also used a similar approach to criminalize ambush marketing using special legislation enacted within each recent host country in order to protect World Cup sponsors.

While the approach of using special legislation with language about unauthorized 'association' with the Olympics has been largely effective in controlling infringement and has had a deterrent effect in dissuading would-be ambushers from pursuing advertising campaigns around an Olympics (Ellis, Scassa and Séguin, 2011), it has garnered significant controversy and criticism. It is further evidence of a "continuing trend towards granting exclusive property rights" around mega sporting events (Erickson and Wei, 2015, p. 10) where the mega sport property's intellectual property becomes over-protected and obtains a level of "super IP" (Osborn and James, 2013). Moreover, by using the concept of association, government leaders define the practice in the broadest way possible (to the benefit of event organizers and their global sponsors), such that almost any marketing campaigns timed to coincide with an Olympic Games would potentially run afoul of the statute. Yet, almost no cases of ambush marketing are ever litigated in court, so there is rarely judicial scrutiny of these newly created laws.

While creating an improper association with the Olympics becomes the targeted behavior, the list of what words and phrases are 'protected' for use by official sponsors keeps increasing, meaning these words and phrases become prohibited from being used by non-sponsors and local businesses attempting to allude to or celebrate hosting the Games. This raises legitimate public policy concerns about whether governments should be enacting laws primarily for the benefit of the Olympics and their global brands as well as alienates local businesses and citizens who will be subject to the law (Grady, McKelvey and Bernthal, 2010). This restrictive approach also stifles advertising messages surrounding an Olympics, raising free speech and individual liberty concerns (Séguin and Scassa, 2014). Creating new intellectual property rights using special legislation gives Olympic organizers unchecked power to decide what words are protected given the subjective nature of the concept of association (Séguin and Scassa, 2014), essentially creating a monopoly over all marketing messages during the Games. However, by primarily framing ambush marketing as a legal issue, it eliminates much of the ethical debate about the propriety of the practice and deems more incidents as infringing when judged against the special event laws in effect. In sum, judging ambush marketing activities against legal concepts of association is an effective approach because it ensnares more ambush incidents, deters other campaigns from ever being attempted, and helps narrow the 'gray' areas of the law where creative ambush campaigns have typically flourished.

Ongoing Olympic brand protection challenges: "social ambush" and Rule 40

In the changing sponsorship climate, Olympic brand protection and enforcement strategies have evolved in two main ways. First, as discussed, the passage of robust legislation by host countries combined with local organizers' efforts in educating stakeholders on "who can tell what story" in relations to the event (i.e. who can associate with the Games and how) (Séguin and Scassa, 2014; Grady, Séguin and O'Reilly, 2015). This has provided local organizing committees with the ability to enforce their rules and regulations on-site and has been primarily accomplished through the use of "clean zones" as well as brand policing and advertising restrictions in each host city to attempt to provide official sponsor brands with contractually promised exclusivity provided in their rights agreements. "Brand policing," typically on-site enforcement by brand protection teams within the host city, as a strategy is also less discussed compared to previous Games, perhaps because so many brands have moved campaigns online. Second, and perhaps more confounding, is that local organizing committees have now focused on social media regulation, including regulating the social media activity of competing athletes, as a 'new' strategy to snuff out ambush marketing in an increasingly digital environment which enables them to enforce these same brand restrictions online (Grady, Séguin and O'Reilly, 2015).

Brand protection teams continue to face challenges in how to regulate athletes and non-affiliated brands on social media who are engaging in what Olympic organizers claim is ambush marketing (although brands and the athletes themselves would likely strongly disagree). This phenomenon, described by Chavanat and Desbordes as "social ambush" (2014, p. 151), currently poses one of the largest threats to official rights holders and local organizing committees and has caused them to have to adapt traditional brand protection strategies in an increasingly digital environment. The evolution in fan engagement tactics toward more social and digital campaigns has had consequent changes in how event organizers respond to ambush. This has resulted in much less on-site visible brand policing compared, for example, to the draconian tactics used for London 2012. It was even reported that two LOCOG lawyers accompanied the torch relay in anticipation ofLondon 2012 on the lookout for infringement and ambush marketing by local businesses along the route (Grady and McKelvey, 2012). Instead, the enforcement that is now conducted against major global brands who are corporate rivals to official Olympic sponsors seems to occur in a much less public way (i.e. not as much high-profile "name and shame" being used by the local organizing committees as in the past). There also appears to be less enforcement targeting celebratory advertising by local businesses after heavy media criticism, notably surrounding London 2012 (Addley, 2012). As more brands that might straddle the line about what is permitted under the rules have moved campaigns online, brand protection responses must evolve. Also, as more brands move toward social media, the risk to run an 'edgy' campaign seems more expected now given the immediacy of social media and its large reach with younger Olympic fans.

At the same time, however, any effort to confuse consumers about who are the official sponsors is increasingly blunted by the sophisticated social media campaigns of official sponsors, reinforcing the long-held belief that better sponsorship activation by official sponsors is still the most effective way to combat ambush marketing. Reaching the Olympic audience now requires a level of creativity which has eclipsed on-site ambushing only and is further evidence that the ambush marketing via social media and regulating athletes who may help non-official brands to spread unauthorized brand messages has become the new focus. Brand protection teams employing anti-ambush strategies in a digital realm must be cognizant, however, that any attempt to over-regulate Olympic messages by athletes could ultimately harm the Olympic brand. For example, at the Sochi Winter Games, Rule 40 enforcement was predicted to be so strict that some first-time younger Olympic athletes admitted to staying off social media all together during the Games to avoid inadvertently breaking the rules. Seeking to control who has access to creating and sharing Olympic moments and content with socially engaged fans is, therefore, a precarious task.

A paradigm shift has occurred in the approach used at four most recent Games (London 2012, Sochi 2014, Rio 2016, and PyeongChang 2018) in that there is now a heavy focus on monitoring and over-regulating the social media of competing athletes. The primary way that Olympic officials have sought to regulate social media activity involving competing athletes during the Games period has been through application and enforcement of Rule 40. Rule 40.3 of the Olympic Charter warns that "no competitor, team official or other team personnel who participates in the Olympic Games may allow his person, name, picture or sports performances to be used for advertising purposes during the Olympic Games" (Butler, 2018). Rule 40 creates the Olympic 'blackout' period, a roughly 3 week period leading up to, during, and shortly after the Games, where Olympic athletes cannot be seen in advertising for brands that are not official sponsors. While Rule 40 has long been on the books, enforcement has mainly been concentrated at Olympics since London 2012.

Criticism against the Rule has been ongoing, especially by American track athletes during London 2012 who used the hashtag #WeDemandChange2012 (Ormond, 2014) to seek reform of a rule they perceived as unfair. Sensing a change was needed for future iterations of Rule 40, Olympic officials relaxed how the Rule was applied and gave some added flexibility to athletes and their personal endorser brands. "For Rio 2016, this flexibility [came] in the form of an amended version of Rule 40 that allowed for athletes to be used in 'generic' advertising during the Games" (Carson, 2018). However, this relaxed approach resulted in more exposure for well-known athletes like Michael Phelps and did not create many new sponsorship opportunities for lesser-known athletes because these athletes still could not make a connection to the Olympics in promoting their personal brands.

As to where Rule 40 fits within the overall brand protection scheme, this has led scholars to question "how Olympic officials have shifted their regulatory efforts toward athletes, such as through a relaxed Rule 40, rather than through traditional [and generally effective] brand-protection efforts," which typically target offending brands (Grady, 2017, p. 1). The risk in this strategy shift is not insignificant. By potentially alienating athletes who feel that they cannot acknowledge their sponsors at the peak of competition when their personal brand is most valuable (even under a relaxed Rule 40), Olympic leaders have seemingly put corporate goals and commercial rights management above the legitimate commercial needs of athletes to share personalized brand messages, which often also includes sharing authentic and spontaneous Olympic moments with fans that ultimately bolsters the Olympic brand.

A brand protection strategy which relies too heavily on Rule 40 also brings additional legal scrutiny and added criticism from athletes and their advocates. For example, in advance of the 2018 PyeongChang Games, the German sporting goods industry, which sponsors several Olympic athletes, challenged the current application of Rule 40 as a violation of German competition laws, analogous in scope and purpose to US anti-trust laws. In late 2017, Germany's Federal Cartel Office, acting on a complaint filed by the German sporting goods industry, took legal action against the German Olympic Sports Confederation (DOSB) and the International Olympic

Committee (IOC). The two main legal claims targeting Rule 40 were that, as applied during Rio 2016, this created an "effective monopolization of marketing rights during the Olympics" and "an abuse of the dominant position of the DOSB and IOC," which resulted in subsequent harm on the earning abilities of athletes.

The challenge was successful in that German athletes were granted added flexibility during the 2018 Games by the IOC to be able to thank sponsors and be congratulated for their accomplishments by brands who were not also official sponsors so long as no Olympic connection was made between the non-affiliated brands and the Olympics, perhaps a distinction without a difference in the views of average social-savvy consumers. Team Germany was the only group of athletes granted this added leniency during the 2018 Games (Associated Press, 2018), which created an odd marketing dynamic, and a prediction that athletes from other European countries with similar competition laws will seek a similar result at future Games, creating a "ripple effect" of legal challenges across Europe (Associated Press, 2018). "The legal challenge [also] shows little hesitation to challenge long-standing Olympic rules where regulators spot potential abuses and see less restrictive means available" and signals that further relaxation of Rule 40 may be necessary (Grady and Moorman, 2018).

Conclusion

In conclusion, the social media regulation of athletes as a 'new' form of brand protection, whether through the use of Rule 40 or through additional regulations about what brands can say about athletes to make an Olympic connection could ultimately backfire in a public relations and fan engagement sense. It is clear that "[t]he OCOG's role in clarifying who can tell the story is now essential from a commercial rights management perspective" (Séguin and Scassa, 2014, p. 510). However, regulating athletes' social media activity too tightly can also have negative consequences and cause competing athletes, especially younger tech-savvy stars, to avoid social media during the Games to avoid breaking the rules, an unfortunate result for building the brand with younger fans. There is also clear risk that, by over-regulating athlete's social media activity in the name of preventing ambush marketing, consumers become disengaged with the Olympics and don't hear the athletes' personal stories. Instead, they see the Games as an overly commercialized enterprise worried more about protecting official rights holders and not about protecting the legitimate needs of athletes with regard to sponsorship. Looking ahead, it will be important for Olympic officials to continue to collaborate with athletes on further reforms of Rule 40, especially as Tokyo 2020 and Beijing 2022 come into view, where there is increased potential for new sponsorship opportunities for athletes and as the global mix of Olympic sponsors continues to diversify.

Concluding thoughts

While the legal issues surrounding staging the Olympic Games continue to evolve, there are still some unresolved issues. Given the current regulatory environment with regard to sponsorship, and within the context of 'relaxed' Rule 40 specifically, it seems athletes will play a larger role in spreading Olympic messages and have wider latitude to include their personal brands in those social conversations in a limited way. This new flexibility by the IOC suggests athletes may now be seen as their allies who can help carry the Olympic message to a new generation of 'social' fans instead of as ambushers themselves as it seems they may have been in the past. Future reforms of Rule 40 at the National Olympic Committee (NOC) level where the Rule 40 guidelines are developed for each country's athletes should chart a new path forward for Rule 40, especially as the Olympics heads to two tech-savvy nations in China and Japan. An open question also exists with regard to the necessity for continued special legislation to give priority to the Olympics and its sponsors (Grady, 2016a). While clearly this legislation provides the legal 'teeth' needed to enforce what would otherwise be marketing and brand regulations, it must be further studied whether host nations can muster support for such one-sided legislation that benefits a private enterprise and global elite brands at the expense of local businesses in some cases. Also, if aggressive enforcement and brand policing is to continue, including now via social media, is this stance potentially doing more harm than good to the Olympic brand and the Olympic movement itself, especially within the host country during the Games period? As ambush marketing becomes more sophisticated with each Games, so too do the strategies to combat it. Thus, legal strategies may ultimately yield to marketing innovation as suggested by Nufer (2016), with more official sponsors joining in on social media to make clear connections with the Olympic brand for their fans in global marketing campaigns that make broad use of Olympic intellectual property.

References

Addley, E. (2012). Olympics 2012: Branding 'police' to protect sponsors' exclusive rights. *The Guardian*, Apr. 13.

Associated Press. (2018). Hold that tweet: Athletes tiptoe around Olympic do's, don'ts. *USA Today*, Feb. 10.

Buchanan, K. (2016). *Laws behind the Rio Olympics. August 3.* Available at: https://blogs.loc.gov/law/2016/08/laws-behind-the-rio-olympics/.

Butler, N. (2018). German panel urge Bach to change Rule 40 and give athletes more money. *Inside the Games*, May 23.

Carson, A. (2018). *#ReadyForRio: How a revised Rule 40 impacted sponsorship at the 2016 Summer Olympics.* May. Honors Thesis. University of South Carolina.

Chanavat, N. and Desbordes, M. (2014). Towards the regulation and restriction of ambush marketing? The first truly social and digital mega sport event: Olympic Games, London 2012. *International Journal of Sports Marketing & Sponsorship*, 15(3), pp. 151–160.

Ellis, D., Scassa, T. and Séguin, B. (2011). Framing ambush marketing as a legal issue: An Olympic perspective. *Sport Management Review*, 14(3), pp. 297–308.

Erickson, K. and Wei, L. (2015). Intellectual property enclosure and economic discourse in the 2012 London Olympic Games. *Media, Culture, & Society*, 37(3), pp. 409–421.

Grady, J. (2016a). Hyper-protection of Olympic marks and the implications for Trademark law. In: *Sport and recreation law association conference*, Las Vegas, NV.

Grady, J. (2016b). Predicting the future for Rio 2016: Legal issues in sponsorship, ambush marketing, and social media. *Entertainment and Sports Law Journal*, 14(2), pp. 1–4.

Grady, J. (2017). Analyzing Rule 40's restrictions on using athletes in Olympic sponsorship at Rio 2016. *Entertainment and Sports Law Journal*, 15(1), pp. 1–5.

Grady, J. and McKelvey, S. (2012). Ambush marketing lessons from the London Olympic Games. *Sports Business Journal.* Available at: https://www.sportsbusinessdaily.com/Journal/Issues/2012/10/22/Opinion/Grady-McKelvey.aspx.

Grady, J., McKelvey, S. and Bernthal, M.J. (2010). From Beijing 2008 to London 2012: Examining event-specific Olympic legislation vis à vis the rights and interests of stakeholders. *Journal of Sponsorship*, 3(2), pp. 144–156.

Grady, J. and Moorman, A. (2018). Rule 40 versus European competition laws: A new challenge to an ongoing sponsorship concern. In: *European Association for Sport Management conference*, Bern, Switzerland.

Grady, J., Séguin, B. and O'Reilly, N. (2015). Olympic ambush marketing: Is social regulation the new way to protect the Olympic brand? In: *European Association for Sport Management conference*, Dublin, Ireland.

James, M. and Osborn, G. (2015). The Olympics, transnational law and legal transplants: International Olympic Committee, ambush marketing and ticket. *Legal Studies*, 36(1), pp. 93–110.

Krashinsky, S. (2014). Canadian Olympic Committee threatens North Face with trademark suit. *The Globe and Mail*, Jan. 21.

Krashinsky, S. (2016). North Face owner settles gear dispute with Canadian Olympic Committee. *The Globe and Mail*, Oct. 19.

Lei No. 13.284 de 10 de Maio de 2016 (Brazil) (2016).

London Olympic Games and Paralympic Games Act 2006 (Great Britain). (2006).

McKelvey, S. (1994). San legal restraint, no stopping brash, creative ambush marketers. *Brandweek*, 35, p. 20.

McKelvey, S. (2014). Memos reveal advent of ambush marketing around '84 games. *Sports Business Journal*, Feb. 17. Available at: https://www.sportsbusinessdaily.com/Journal/Issues/2014/02/17/Opinion/From-the-Field-of-Marketing.aspx.

McKelvey, S. and Grady, J. (2004). An analysis of the ongoing global efforts to combat ambush marketing: Will corporate marketers 'take' the gold in Greece? *Journal of Legal Aspects of Sport*, 14, pp. 191–220.

McKelvey, S. and Grady, J. (2008). Sponsorship program protection strategies for special sport events: Are event organizers outmaneuvering ambush marketers? *Journal of Sport Management*, 22(5), pp. 550–586.

Nufer, G. (2009). Sponsoring the FIFA football world cup: The good, the bad and the surprising. *Journal of Sponsorship*, 2(3), pp. 241–249.

Nufer, G. (2016). Ambush marketing in sports: An attack on sponsorship or innovative marketing? *Sport, Business and Management: An International Journal*, 6(4), pp. 476–495.

Ormond, M. (2014). #WeDemandChange: Amending International Olympic Committee Rule 40 for the modern Olympic Games. *Journal of Law, Technology, and the Internet*, 5, pp. 179–200.

Osborn, G. and James, M. (2013). Guilty by association: Olympic law and the IP effect. *Intellectual Property Quarterly*, 2, pp. 97–113.

Rio 2016. (n.d.). *Brand Protection Guidelines Advertising Market and Advertisers*. Version 2. Rio de Janeiro: Rio 2016.

Sandler, D. and Shani, D. (1989). Olympic sponsorship vs. "ambush marketing": Who gets the gold? *Journal of Advertising Research*, 29(4), pp. 9–14.

Séguin, B. and O'Reilly, N. (2008). The Olympic brand, ambush Marketing and Clutter. *International Journal of Sport Management and Marketing*, 4(1/2), pp. 62–84.

Séguin, B. and Scassa, T. (2014). Ambush marketing legislation to protect Olympic sponsors: A step too far in the name of brand protection? In: B.C. Doagoo, M. Goudreau, T. Scassa and M. Saginur, eds., *Intellectual property for the 21st century*. Irwin Law, pp. 500–520.

13

The evolving #rule40 of the Olympic Charter

Balancing the interest of sponsors vs athletes

Gashaw Abeza

Introduction

The Olympic Charter, a document that dates back to the early days of the modern Olympic Games, guides the Olympic movement. First published in 1908, the year of the fourth Olympiads, the Charter codifies the rules and bye-laws that govern the principles of Olympism, the philosophy of life of the movement. The Olympic Charter also outlines the rights and obligations of multiple organizations, athletes and various other stakeholders that are under the "supreme authority and leadership of the International Olympic Committee" (IOC) (IOC, 2019b, p. 15). Since the first rules' draft by Pierre de Coubertin, credited as the father of the modern Olympics, the IOC has often modified and adapted them when deemed necessary. Arguably, the most notable amendment to the Charter since its inception was in 1984, when professional athletes in tennis, ice hockey and soccer were welcomed as participants for the first time (Thomas, 1985). The same year in 1985, the IOC introduced the Olympic Partner (TOP) programme that attracts sponsors by guaranteeing them exclusive access to the Olympic brand for marketing and advertising purposes. These two developments have precipitated important changes within the Olympic Organization as well as the Charter itself. Some of the most recent modifications concerned Rule 40 which governs participation in the Games and whose stipulation about commercial advertising has, in recent years, been the subject of some debate. First introduced into the Olympic Charter in 1991 (IOC, 1990), Rule 40 prevents non-official Olympic sponsors from associating themselves with the Olympic brand, as well as the Games' commercialization, without authorization (Ormond, 2014). Since the 2012 London Games, for example, Rule 40 has been modified twice: the first time was 16 months before the 2016 Rio Games; the second was in June 2019, a year before the 2020 Tokyo Games. This chapter presents the evolution of the Rule since the 2012 Games and discusses the implications of the 2019 revision.

The IOC works with a range of local, national and global governing bodies, out of which the two most important are the International Sports Federations (IFs) and the National Olympic Committees (NOCs) (Finlay, 2018a). NOCs, like the IOC, "must remain independent of the political pressures of the nations in which they are located" (Spotts, 1994, p. 13), a difficult, if not impossible, ideal to uphold (Chatziefstathiou, 2011). Independence means prioritizing private, rather than public bodies, for financing achieving their mission. In accordance with the Olympic Charter, NOCs are the most significant governing bodies; they are responsible for developing, promoting and preserving the Olympic movement in their respective countries. NOCs monitor and, when needed, sanction athletes who violate the Olympic Charter (IOC, 2019a). Hence, NOCs abide by the Olympic Charter and adapt to any modifications applied to the document. This includes the implemented modifications applied to Rule 40.

The Rule largely came to the public's attention in 2012, during the first Olympics of the social media era, in London, when athletes took to various platforms to communicate their accomplishments and appreciation of companies who helped them make it to the Olympics. At that juncture, it became clear that social media re-defined Rule 40's scope and application (Ormond, 2014). The 2016 Rio Olympics were the first to feel the full effect of the social media era and the controversy surrounding Rule 40 (Hoskins, 2018). Bye-law three of the Rule stated that, "Except as permitted by the IOC Executive Board, no competitor, coach, trainer or official who participates in the Olympic Games may allow his person, name, picture or sports performances to be used for advertising purposes during the Olympic Games" (International Olympic Committee, 2015, p. 79). Despite protests, the rule was still in effect during the 2018 PyeongChang Olympic Winter Games (International Olympic Committee, 2018). Effectively, Rule 40 restrained athletes' promotion of their own sponsors during the blackout period, which runs for the duration of the two weeks of Olympiads and Winter Games competition. In fact, Rule 40 (specifically, the controversial bye-law three) is designed to protect the exclusivity of the IOC's the Olympic Partner 'TOP' programme by prohibiting non-sponsors from reaping the benefits of the goodwill of the Olympics Games, and to protect the reputation and monetary value of being an 'official sponsor' of the Games.

The TOP programme is key to keeping the IOC privately funded and, ideally, independent from any governmental influence. The Rule specifically focuses on athletes featured in advertisements by brands that are not officially affiliated with the Olympics during the Games (the blackout period). Hence, since 2012, modifications to the Rule attempt to represent a balance between protecting the TOP, which ensures funding of the Olympic Games and the Olympic movement, and respecting individual athletes' right to generate income in relation to their sporting career, name and likeness. Indeed, for many athletes, the Olympiad and the Winter Games are the most important time of their professional career; as the IOC does not share its revenue directly with individual athletes/teams, individual sponsorship is the only way that most Olympians are able to secure a viable income.

Role 40 and social media

In the last decade, social media has changed the landscape of marketing and communication around the globe, including within the sport industry (Abeza, O'Reilly and Seguin, 2019). Over the past decade, many have adjusted to the change by gradually modifying their management and marketing approaches (Abeza, O'Reilly and Seguin, 2019). This includes the IOC, whose adjustment can be witnessed through the gradual revisions to Rule 40 in its attempt to ensure that the Olympic Charter's rules and bye-laws remain applicable (Hoskins, 2018). Yet, the attempt was not without challenges. The IOC and NOCs had to determine how to manage what athletes may communicate on social media throughout the Games without infringing on athletes' and official sponsors' rights. While the IOC encourages athletes to use social media during the Games to share their experiences with families and friends (Schlereth and Frederick, 2017), for advertising purposes, the IOC had intervened via Rule 40 to restrict athletes from associating themselves with non-official Olympic sponsors immediately before, during and immediately after the Games (Ormond, 2014).

Social media platforms allow athletes to construct, shape and present their own brand, as well as promote their marketing endeavours, on their own personal platform, directly to their followers, and in their preferred format (Abeza et al., 2017). The Olympic Games also generate worldwide public interest through their ability to deeply engage audiences on social media and other communication platforms. For example, during the 2012 London Summer Olympic Games, over 150 million Olympic-related tweets were shared in 16 (Ormond, 2014) and more than 187 million Olympic events-related tweets were shared during the 2016 Rio Olympics (Hoskins, 2018). Further, during the highest moments of their careers, athletes can use social media to engage in real time and direct one-to-one dialogues with fans who often have a strong association with athletes. One cannot underestimate the level of exposure and the importance of such an opportunity for generating financial rewards. Social media is undoubtedly a powerful modern marketing communication tool for athletes. In some cases, athletes have more social media followers than NOCs.

According to Finlay (2018a), athletes began using social media as early as the 2004 Olympics with blogs. Social media usage was such that the IOC became concerned that athletes might have been overstepping the IOC Charter. This led the Committee to issue its first Blogging Guidelines in 2008 for persons accredited at the Games. Additional guidelines were later introduced to include tweets and various other internet postings and applied to the Games that followed (2014, 2016, 2018, and 2020). While the IOC surveils social media for violations, NOCs are responsible for monitoring their own athletes and enforcing acceptable use rules. Therefore, the guidelines hold NOCs accountable for their own athletes and, by giving the governing bodies the power to implement additional guidelines, the IOC encourages a significant level of policing at the national level (Finlay, 2018a). With the restrictions imposed on athletes' use of social media during the blackout periods of the Games, the IOC and NOCs have the challenging task of balancing the responsibility to protect Olympic sponsors with the obligation to address the needs of athletes and respect athletes' rights. Juggling the interests of the two primary stakeholders of the Olympic Games has engendered successive revisions to Rule 40 over the past few Games, particularly, as noted previously, since the first 'social media Olympics' in 2012. The following sections discuss the evolution of Rule 40 in connection with the 2012 London Games, 2016 Rio Games and the 2020 Tokyo Games.

Rule 40 and the 2012 London Games

During London 2012, Rule 40 restricted athletes from acknowledging their sponsors unless they were official Olympic sponsors (Grady, 2016). With the intention of ensuring that athletes fully grasped the application of Rule 40, the IOC presented Social Media Guidelines to athletes detailing the scope and application of the Rule. During the Games, the IOC encouraged athletes to use social media to share their experiences with families and friends, but prohibited use of the platforms for commercial and/or advertising purposes. The Guidelines stated that athletes could not allow their picture or performance to be used for advertising purposes during the blackout period of the Olympic Games (Ormond, 2014). The exceptions, according to Ormond (2014), were the use of an athlete's personal website; there, athletes could advertise (on their website) for their own sponsors on the condition that those advertisements comply with the set guidelines and that any references to the Games be confined to the biographical details of the athletes' achievements.

Rule 40 drew criticisms from different parties, especially from athletes and their sponsors. For example, during the 2012 Olympics, initiated by the USA Track and Field team and spearheaded by Olympic gold medallist sprinter Sanya Richards-Ross, athletes launched the online #WeDemandChange campaign against Rule 40 of the Olympic Charter. The campaign protested the fact that athletes were unable to blog and/or tweet about their non-Olympic movement sponsors as, athletes argued, it infringed on their ability to generate income or maintain their relationship with sponsors that helped them on their way to the Games (Finlay, 2018b). Olympic athletes were thus severely limited in their ability to promote their sponsors, many of whom are largely responsible for funding the athletes' year-round training.

In light of the fact that the IOC does not (directly) financially compensate Olympians, many argue that Rule 40 prohibits athletes from capitalizing on their success at the Olympic Games – at the peak of their exposure (Ormond, 2014). As Schlereth and Frederick (2017) state, the Olympic qualification process can cost upward of 100,000 USD. This amount is usually covered by contributions from family members, sponsors and/or training stipends or grants. As Finlay notes, a large majority of athletes "primarily subsist on combinations of modest grants from sports organizations, colleges, and, in some cases, governments" (Finlay, 2018b, p. 661). Exceptionally, some Olympians can earn a 'medal bonus' from their NOCs (e.g. the United States Olympic Committee [USOC] provides US$37,500/gold, US$22,500/silver, US$15,000/bronze [Penny, 2016]; Canadian medallists receive C$20,000/gold, C$15,000/silver and C$10,000/bronze [Canadian Olympic Committee, 2019]; and Singapore's receive S$1 million/gold, S$500,000/silver, S$250,000/bronze [Singapore National Olympic Council, 2019]). This, however, is dependent upon each nation's means and, regardless of the amount, these rewards only reach the top of the podium, leaving hundreds of unlucky who cannot expect even the minimum. It might be added that those likely to earn a medal and, thus, a bonus, are top-tier athletes who are likely to already have access to relatively more resources. Hence, athletes rely heavily on sponsors for income, especially if they compete in the various Olympic sports that do not otherwise have lucrative professional circuits (e.g. gymnasts, modern pentathletes or weightlifters' income before sponsorship cannot compare to that of basketball, tennis or hockey players).

The IOC's policy for not paying athletes is anchored in its history and in the principles that govern the Olympic movement. Pierre de Coubertin promoted a philosophy predicated upon the idea that sport (for which the Olympics were to be the purest form) should be practiced for its own sake, not motivated by extrinsic rewards (McFee, 2015). Influenced by a Victorian elitist approach to sport, de Coubertin's writings and leadership in the 20th century continued to support this notion. Like the majority of the ruling class at the turn of the century, de Coubertin believed that amateurism was the best way to ensure and promote sportsmanship, fair play and other such gentlemanly values (Loland, 1995; McFee, 2015). The amateur rule was one of the Olympics' greatest distinguishing feature so, for decades, they operated under the amateur ideology.

It is only relatively recently (since the 1980s) that professional athletes have been able to participate in the Games. At the 1992 Barcelona Games, the highly dominant United States' basketball 'Dream Team' ushered in a marketing frenzy era around celebrity athletes that came to symbolize the professional era of the Olympic Games (Finlay, 2018b; Wenner, 1994). To this day, however, the IOC does not pay athletes for participating, leaving remuneration to external/personal sponsors, IFs and NOCs – although the IOC funds the latter two, it recommends that NOCs "seek sources of revenue of financing in a manner compatible with the fundamental principles of Olympism" (International Olympic Committee, 2019b, p. 65). As noted earlier, private funding is the priority, although this conflicts with the interests of athletes' personal sponsors when it comes to the Games. The IOC insists that any revenues from marketing the Games (TOP sponsors, broadcasting rights, etc.) finance the global promotion of Olympism; the

Committee assumes no responsibility for financing the organization or staging of the Olympic Games, nor for remunerating participant athletes (International Olympic Committee, 2019b).

It is important to note that commercial sponsorship is not easily attainable for low-ranked athletes or for those that compete in less popular sports – that is, the bulk of Olympic athletes. They must look to other venues for sponsorship just to get to the Games. GoFundMe, for example, reported that 140 Olympic athletes started fundraising campaigns to raise money for their 2016 Olympic dreams (Hoskins, 2018). The IOC is not blind to these difficulties; it just draws the line at paying athletes. In fact, ahead of the 2010 Vancouver Winter Games, the IOC began the Olympic Solidarity Scholarship for individual athletes, wherein the Committee helps offset the cost of preparation, training and travel for selected candidates. For Rio 2016, there were 1547 scholarship holders from 185 NOCs, 815 of which participated in the Games (out of 11,238 total participants from 207 nations), in addition to 10 recipients from the Refugee Team – this resulted in 101 medals (33 golds, 26 silvers, 42 bronzes). The IOC indicates that in Rio, 25 NOCs had 50% or more scholarship holders, while six nations sent teams entirely composed of scholarship holders (International Olympic Committee, 2019a). At the PyeongChang 2018 Olympics, 268 scholarship holders (out of 2833 participants) from 60 NOCs (out of 92 total participant countries) participated in the Games; this was out of a total of 435 scholarships and 14 grants allocated to 89 NOCs. The IOC proudly notes that scholarship holders won a total of 13 medals (6 golds, 3 silvers and 4 bronzes respectively) (International Olympic Committee, 2019a). The programme is intended to continue in coming years. To be clear, "PyeongChang scholarships have been designed by Olympic Solidarity to improve the competitiveness of the Olympic Games" (International Olympic Committee, 2019a). On that account, Olympic Solidarity intervenes to support the Olympic ideal by ensuring participation and attendance at the Games, an objective separate from that of remunerating participants for attending the marquee event. Ultimately, Rule 40 protects official sponsors while putting athletes in a precarious position exactly during the rare opportunity they have to be marketable to a bigger market/audience and, perhaps, offset the cost of getting to the Games. This was especially true for the iteration of bye-law three that was in place for the 2012 and 2014 Games. Companies take a risk when investing in young unproven talents, with the hope that their athletes will excel in their sport and, if possible, qualify for the Olympics. Investing in athletes, among others reasons, is done to gain publicity during athletes' victory march and promotional opportunity afterwards. Due to Rule 40, however, an athlete cannot promote their sponsors during the Games on their social media platforms.

Rule 40 and the 2016 Rio Games

In response to criticism following the 2012 Games (Finlay, 2018b), the IOC released a revised and relaxed version of Rule 40 16 months ahead of the 2016 Rio Games, in February 2015 (Grady, 2017). In relaxing the Rule, the IOC stated that it was giving athletes the opportunity to promote their non-official Olympic sponsors on athletes' personal social media platforms, although posts could not refer to the Games (Schwabe, 2018). With this, the IOC intended to let athletes benefit from their individual sponsors, while also continuing to protect the Games from brands that do not have an official association with the Games.

With this relaxed Rule, each NOC (which is responsible for ensuring its athletes' compliance with all rules of the Olympic Charter) was directed to implement a screening process to pre-approve 'generic advertising' and provide appropriate ones with waivers. This ensured Olympians' ads with companies that lack official Olympic sponsor status did not associate themselves with the Olympic Games (Hoskins, 2018). The approved generic ad campaign schedule was expected to be submitted ahead of time with an agreement that the ad would run continuously for at least four months prior to the start of the Games (Hoskins, 2018). The change did not affect bye-law three as it was in 2012, meaning the IOC Executive Board still held the power. Rather, during the blackout period (July 27 to August 24), as listed in the Charter, non-official sponsors of the Games were prohibited from the following:

- Any use of the Olympic properties or any NOC related symbol or design protected under national legislation, trademark or copyright law, or of any symbol, design or terminology or expression creating a risk of confusion with these properties;
- Any express or implied written/visual allusion to the Olympic Games;
- Any use of the image of a Participant, taken during the Olympic Games, in combination with a company or brand;
- Any use of the image of a Participant in a new advertising campaign which was started at such time before the Period of the Olympic Games that the new advertising campaign creates the impression of a commercial connection between the company or brand and the Olympic Games;
- Any reference to a Participant's role in the Olympic Games, or to a Participant's performance during the Olympic Games or during any past editions of the Games of the Olympiad or the Olympic Winter Games;
- Any use of the "Olympic listed terms or expressions" alongside the Participant's name or image;
- Any use of a term or expression alongside the Participant's name or image so closely resembling one of the "Olympic listed terms or expressions" as to be likely mistaken for such term or expression;
- Any use of other "Olympic-related terms" in such a way as to imply an association between, on the one hand, the Participant and, on the other hand, the Olympic Games or any other Games of the Olympiad or the Olympic Winter Games, the IOC, the NOCs or the OCOG.

To illustrate this, Schlereth and Frederick (2017) use multiple-time champion Michael Phelps as example; under the modification to the rule, the swimmer could tweet, "Working hard in the pool tonight – thanks, Under Armour," but was not allowed to tweet, "Training real hard for Rio. Thanks, Under Armour." Kate Grace's experience at the 2016 Games is a case in point: on July 4th, 2016 (during the Olympic Trials and not during the Games), Grace won the 800 meters at the US Olympic Track and Field Trials. Her sponsors, Oiselle, a women's athletic apparel company, posted a picture on its Instagram page with the caption: "She's going to RIO!" The USOC quickly ordered Oiselle to take the post down, citing an alleged violation of the social media guidelines. Following the relaxation, as Grady (2016) pointed put, many of the brands that sought waivers were direct competitors of long-standing official Olympic global partners, such as Coca-Cola and Visa, that worked under the assumption that they had exclusive rights to the Olympic marketing space surrounding Rio 2016.

The issue with the 2016 relaxed Rule 40 is the requirement that athletes submit the plans for their personal sponsors' advertising campaign months in advance. In some cases, the nature, content and strategy of athlete's sponsors' promotional message might be required to be submitted for waiver long before an athlete is selected to a national Olympic team. For example, as Finlay (2018b) stated, the waiver was due in January 2016 when most athletes had yet to be selected to an Olympic team. This makes it difficult for smaller companies to sign agreements and commit themselves to athletes without a guarantee that the athletes would make it to the

Games. A related issue concerns the need to run that advert for a few months (e.g. six months) to the Games. Hence, one can argue that the relaxed rule privileged celebrity athletes and only the non-Olympic sponsors (Finlay, 2018b). As Grady (2016) stated, it is not clear how lesser-known athletes who need Rule 40's relaxation to help them get sponsorship deals are empowered by the amendment. It is also worth noting that, while the IOC allowed athletes to promote sponsors that are not official Olympic partners, athletes were not allowed to promote them in association with the Games. Even those who receive a waiver cannot use any of the Olympics' intellectual property (i.e. including allusions to relevant words and phrases) in their advertisements (Finlay, 2018b). Hence, Rule 40's revision in 2016 did little to curb the original restrictions that bye-law three imposed on athletes.

Rule 40 and the 2020 Tokyo Games

In June 2019, 12 months ahead of the 2020 Tokyo Games, the IOC made a second attempt to relax Rule 40. This time, bye-law three was directly modified to seemingly reinterpret the input of the IOC Executive Board. The newly revised version states that

> Competitors, team officials and other team personnel who participate in the Olympic Games may allow their person, name, picture or sports performances to be used for advertising purposes during the Olympic Games in accordance with the principles determined by the IOC Executive Board.
>
> *(International Olympic Committee, 2019b, p. 76)*

Details on the effect of the changes have yet to emerge and the reason behind the revision to Rule 40 ahead of the 2020 Games has yet to be ascertained. But, for the latter, reports credited the 2019 ruling of the German Federal Cartel Office (Germany's national competition regulator) against the Rule 40. In February 2019, the German Cartel Office stated that the restriction was "too far-reaching" and reportedly qualified it as "abusive conduct" (Cronin, 2019). With that, the Cartel lifted the obligation of German athletes to clear their personal marketing activities with the German Olympic Sports Confederation (DOSB) ahead of the Olympics. In the aftermath of the German ruling (six months after), the IOC released the revised version of Rule 40. With regards to the revision, IOC President Thomas Bach insisted that there is no one size fits all solution, and that NOCs will be responsible for the implementation of the revised Rule in their respective territories (Pavitt, 2019). With the revision, one major concern can be the issue of consistency (in terms of implementation) among the different NOCs.

In July 2019, the Australian Olympic Committee (AOC) was the first to approve changes to its Rule 40 guidelines for its territory. The AOC introduced supplementary guidelines that outline what athletes and their sponsors can do for the duration of the Games, meaning that with less stringent restrictions, Australian athletes were allowed to promote their sponsors. According to Cronin (2019), a statement from the AOC stipulates that athletes' sponsors should be able to continue 'business as usual' regarding advertisement campaigns featuring the sponsored athlete during the Games, as long as the campaign does not use Olympic properties and is not escalated during the Games. According to the AOC, Australian athletes may now thank their personal sponsors for their support during the Games, provided:

- There is no commercial connection made with the Olympic Games and the sponsor;
- The "thank you" doesn't suggest the sponsor was responsible for the athlete's performance;

- The "thank you" can be issued (across multiple social media platforms) once per performance, including any podium ceremony;
- The sponsor cannot congratulate the athlete for their performance.

With the relaxation of Rule 40, companies that were pejoratively labelled ambushers in the past seem to now have the legal backing to execute their strategies in a territory that has historically been exclusively reserved to official sponsors of the Games. Now, the main issue with the Rule is its application, execution, legal ramifications and long-term implications. Particularly, the IOC as well as NOCs will be in a difficult position in trying to balance the interest of two of its main stakeholders: the athletes and sponsors (Schwabe, 2018).

The recent revision of the Rule heightens the challenge of the IOC to ensure that the value of the sponsorships it sells is protected. Rule 40 serves to protect the official Olympic sponsors from ambush marketing that would potentially reap the benefits of the Olympic brand association without any sanctioned investment by the Olympic Organization. At the same time, the athletes who fight hard to make it to the Games and who do not get paid for taking part in the Games cannot promote the brand(s) that fund their way to competition. It is important to remark that the IOC redistributes 90% of its revenues (over 3.4 million/day USD) to support athletes and organizations and ensure the staging of the Games, as well as promote sport globally (International Olympic Committee, 2019c). Without the funds derived from the IOC's commercial strategy (including broadcast rights and sponsors), athletes from several countries would not be in a position to compete (the Olympic Scholarships and grants are a key resource for many). The IOC, therefore, is highly motivated to preserve its TOP programme.

The concern is that official sponsors seem to be waiting to measure the impact of the change in order to determine their next step. For a number of reasons (e.g. six months to be aired, apply way ahead of an athlete's election to the Games), the revisions to Rule 40 have not been damaging to the official sponsors. However, with further relaxation of the Rule, the impact could be alarming to the IOC and could jeopardize close to a billion dollars in income from the Games. The repeated revisions to Rule 40, according to Grady (2016), applies constant pressure on the IOC and on NOCs to continue finding a proper balance between official partners' guarantee of a level of exclusivity (which incentivize them to pay the escalating rights fees) and athletes' right to capitalize on the short window of visibility at the international stage that they have earned. The outcome of the tug of war that opposes the needs and rights of the two key stakeholders to one another is still unknown.

Conclusion

Without sponsors, it is difficult to stage the Games, and there would be no Games without athletes. Past revisions to Rule 40 have not been enough to achieve a stable balance between protecting sponsors and respecting athletes' rights. The effect of the recent revision is still undetermined. Nevertheless, the IOC's task is daunting. It might be argued that there is a tension between the Olympic model such as it was introduced in the early 20th century, and the contemporary operating model. The Olympic Games' most distinguishing feature as a global sport event is that they exist to safeguard and promote an official ideology, i.e. Olympism (Loland, 1995). For decades, it has been increasingly apparent that the IOC's mission conflicts with the interests of modern athletes. As Loland (1995) writes, "In today's commercial and professional world of top-level sport, Olympism appears as an anachronism" (p. 67). This conflict is underscored in the rapidly evolving social media world.

Three pressing questions arise: first is the issue of policing Rule 40. If Rule 40 is violated, it is not clear to athletes and companies how the IOC will respond. While there is a report that athletes may be expelled from the Games or that medals may be stripped from them, no one has witnessed concrete consequences so far. Second, there is little indication that Rule 40 in its current iteration effectively closes all loopholes. Companies with strong marketing teams have learned how to circumvent the Rule and routinely establish indirect connections with the Games, while others have deployed successful ambush marketing strategies. Rule 40 is already not doing enough to protect official sponsors, and that can be alarming when considering the possible long-term investment of these select few brands in the Games. The question is how much is it worth to invest in/purchase rights to be an official sponsor of the Olympic Games? Particularly, with further relaxation of the Rule, companies can invest more money on finding the best and most popular athlete in the Games and in creating 'generic' advertising akin to Under Armour's Rule Yourself campaign. Such a model would be detrimental to the Olympic mission, as fewer athletes would have the opportunity to train, prepare and attend the Games; such a model also has the potential to influence the event's competitiveness and global relevance.

Third, uncertainty seem to have emerged among sponsors following the previously outlined revisions. Some (e.g. Grady, 2017) suggest that brand protections should evolve with each Games and that the IOC should adjust the legal setting within the host country, as well as changes affecting the sponsorship landscape. Grady (2017) argues that the relaxed Rule 40 has the advantage of managing content that will be communicated during Games, as NOCs get a chance to pre-approve the content in the waiver process stage. According to the author, this helps the IOC or NOCs work under proactive measures rather than reactionary mechanisms. As far as Rule 40 is concerned, for the past few Olympic Games, the IOC has demonstrated its ability to adjust itself and manage changes. However, this quality can be considered a threat among official sponsors, leading them to distrust the future and integrity of their signed agreements.

References

Abeza, G., O'Reilly, N. and Seguin, B. (2019). Social media in relationship marketing: The perspective of professional sport managers in the MLB, NBA, NFL, and NHL. *Communication & Sport*, 7(1), pp. 80–109.

Abeza, G., O'Reilly, N., Séguin, B. and Nzindukiyimana, O. (2017). The world's highest-paid athletes, product endorsement, and Twitter. *Sport, Business and Management: An International Journal*, 7(3), pp. 332–355.

Canadian Olympic Committee. (2019). *Canadian Olympic Committee Athlete Excellence Fund (AEF)*. Toronto: Canadian Olympic Committee.

Chatziefstathiou, D. (2011). Paradoxes and contestations of Olympism in the history of the modern Olympic movement. *Sport in Society*, 14(3), pp. 332–344.

Cronin, B. (2019). *Australian Olympic Committee loosens Rule 40 restrictions*. Available at: https://www.sportbusiness.com/news/australian-olympic-committee-loosens-rule-40-restrictions/.

Finlay, C.J. (2018a). National proxy 2.0: Controlling the social media of Olympians through national identification. *Communication & Sport*, 6(2), pp. 131–153.

Finlay, C.J. (2018b). The right to profitable speech: Olympians, sponsorship, and social media discourse. *Communication & Sport*, 6(6), pp. 655–679.

Grady, J. (2016). The Rio 2016 Olympics: Analyzing Rule 40's moment to shine. *Sport Marketing Quarterly*, 25(3), p. 182.

Grady, J. (2017). Analyzing Rule 40's restrictions on using athletes in Olympic sponsorship at Rio 2016. *The Entertainment and Sports Law Journal*, 15, p. 1.

Hoskins, J.R. (2018). Silence is golden: Olympic property protection in the age of social media. *The Capital University Law Review*, 46, p. 125.

International Olympic Committee. (1990). *Olympic Charter '91*. Lausanne: International Olympic Committee.

International Olympic Committee. (2015). *Charter in force as from 2 August 2015.* Lausanne: International Olympic Committee.
International Olympic Committee. (2018). *Rule 40 guidelines, XXIII Olympic Winter Games PyeongChang 2018.* Lausanne: International Olympic Committee.
International Olympic Committee. (2019a). *Athletes: Our priority.* Lausanne: International Olympic Committee.
International Olympic Committee. (2019b). *Charter in force as from 26 June 2019.* Lausanne: International Olympic Committee.
International Olympic Committee. (2019c). *How we do it.* Lausanne: International Olympic Committee.
Loland, S. (1995). Coubertin's ideology of Olympism from the perspective of the history of ideas. *Olympika: The International Journal of Olympic Studies*, IV, pp. 49–78.
McFee, G. (2015). *On sport and the philosophy of sport: A Wittgensteinian approach.* New York: Routledge.
Ormond, M. (2014). #WeDemandChange: Amending International Olympic Committee Rule 40 for the modern Olympic Games. *Case Western Reserve Journal of Law, Technology and the Internet*, 5, pp. 179–200.
Pavitt, M. (2019). *Rule 40 guidelines to be sent to NOCs as IOC claim balance reached between athletes and commercial rights.* Available at: https://www.insidethegames.biz/articles/1081272/rule-40-guidelines-to-be-sent-to-nocs-as-ioc-claim-balance-reached-between-athletes-and-commercial-rights
Penny, B. (2016). *U.S. Olympic Committee significantly increases payments to athletes for Olympic/Paralympic, World medals.* Available at: https://www.teamusa.org/News/2016/December/13/US-Olympic-Committee-Significantly-Increases-Payments-To-Athletes-For-Olympic-World-Medals.
Schlereth, N.G. and Frederick, E. (2017). Going for gold: Social media and the USOC. *Journal of Legal Aspects of Sport*, 27(1), pp. 19–31.
Schwabe, J. (2018). The Pledge to brand loyalty: A gold medal approach to Rule 40. *Harvard Journal of Sports and Entertainment Law*, 9, pp. 55–81.
Singapore National Olympic Council. (2019). Major games award programme.
Spotts, J.D. (1994). Global politics and the Olympic Games: Separating the two oldest games in history. *Dickinson Journal of International Law*, 13(1), pp. 103–122.
Thomas, R. (1985). *Olympics to allow pros in 3 sports.* Available at: https://www.nytimes.com/1985/03/01/sports/olympics-to-allow-pros-in-3-sports.html.
Wenner, L. (1994). The Dream Team, communicative dirt, and the marketing of synergy: USA basketball and cross-merchandising in television commercials. *Journal of Sport & Social Issues*, 18(1), pp. 27–47.

14

Towards a shared Olympic responsibility

Paradoxes and challenges

Aurélien François, Alain Ferrand and Emmanuel Bayle

Introduction: sustainability as a foundation stone for Olympic Social Responsibility

> "The less people believe in the future the more they want to know about the future. This means for us that they want to know more about the sustainability of Olympic Games and all our actions; that they want to know better about our governance and finances; that they want to know how we are living up to our values and our social responsibility."
>
> *Speech given by IOC President Thomas Bach during the opening ceremony for the 127th Session of the IOC in Monaco on 7 December 2014*

When International Olympic Committee (IOC) President Thomas Bach said social responsibility within the Olympic movement was an essential responsibility for Olympism, his words were not chosen idly. In his speech, later printed as the preface to the IOC's Olympic Agenda 2020 (IOC, 2014), Bach referred to the concept of corporate and/or organisational social responsibility, which was first formulated in the early 1950s (Bowen, 1953). According to the ISO 26000 standard, organisations deploy social responsibility in order to "contribute to sustainable development" (International Organization for Standardization, 2014). Although this definition of social responsibility is vague, it is widely accepted and, most importantly, it extends the compass of social responsibility from large corporations to all types of organisations (Bayle et al., 2011). Consequently, it is the definition we have adopted here. Given Olympism's fundamental principles and the IOC's vision, role and position as leader of the international sports movement, the de facto head of world sport must be seen to be socially responsible in the way it addresses the social, economic and environmental impacts of its activities.

Thomas Bach's speech was unusual because the Olympic world rarely employs the term social responsibility, even though it has been a fundamental principle of the Olympic Charter since 2011. According to the Charter, Olympism "seeks to create a way of life based on the joy of effort, the educational value of good example, social responsibility and respect for universal fundamental ethical principles" (IOC, 2017).[1] However, recent usage of the term and its addition to the charter are not at all indicative of the way the Olympic movement initially embraced this concept. In fact, the IOC appears to have practiced, albeit implicitly, a form of Olympic Social Responsibility (OSR) from its earliest days. For example, after reviving the Olympic Games (OG) in 1896, the IOC began addressing matters related to education, societal problems and even peace (Chappelet, 2009, 2011). By 1910, Pierre de Coubertin, the father of the modern OG, was arguing that sport had the power to resolve what he called "the social problem" by integrating the working class into society. Doing so involved addressing some of the scourges of the time, such as illiteracy and alcoholism (Clastres, 2018). This leitmotiv continued over the years, with Olympism's responsibilities expanding as the IOC and the Olympic movement grew. Thus, in 1994, 100 years after the IOC was founded, the environment became the third pillar of Olympism, alongside sport and culture. Following the 1992 Rio Summit, the UN began citing sport and Olympism, via the IOC, as vectors that could help address some of the late 20th-century's greatest societal problems. It was in this context that, in 1999, the IOC drew up its Agenda 21 for the Olympic movement, entitled "Sport for Sustainable Development". One of the key aspects of this strategy was to "encourage members of the Movement to play an active part in the sustainable development of our planet" (IOC, 1999). For the IOC, sustainable development became an umbrella term that covers all of its social responsibility initiatives, and the term "social responsibility" began disappearing from its strategy documents in the mid-2010s (Bayle, 2016). Today, all of the IOC's social initiatives are subsumed within the notion of sustainability, which is both one of the three pillars of Olympic Agenda 2020, alongside credibility and youth (IOC, 2014), and the subject of its Sustainability Strategy (IOC, 2016a). This strategy was greatly influenced by the United Nations' (UN) sustainable development goals, as can be seen by the IOC's promise to contribute to 17 of them, mostly those targeting poverty, climate change and injustice.

In view of the IOC's rhetoric and ambitious promises, the present chapter takes a closer look at Olympic Social Responsibility (OSR), as pursued under the IOC's sustainability strategy. We will do so by analysing the internal documents in which the IOC describes this strategy, which we will then assess in the light of the organisation's objective of sharing its social responsibility. We begin by bringing together the notions of OSR and shared social responsibility (SSR), a conceptual extension of social responsibility that, when combined with Olympism, allowed us to define a form of shared OSR. We then examine the difficulties involved in implementing such a shared OSR and highlight the paradoxes the Olympic movement will have to overcome in order to ensure all its members 'share' its vision of sustainability (IOC, 2016a). This final section not only reiterates the importance of consistency between words and deeds, it also stresses the need for the IOC to have sufficient influence over its stakeholders to ensure they work in concert to help build a better world.

The need for a shared Olympic Social Responsibility: emergence and definition of shared social responsibility

The concept of SSR first emerged at the end of the 2000s in response to questions from European Union governments about the sustainability of Europe's societal models. In 2009, the Council of Europe put together an ad hoc committee of experts to consider possible new solutions to the social, economic and environmental problems facing Europe and the world in general. SSR was a central notion both in defining social cohesion and in the Council of Europe's new social cohesion strategy (2010), which was gradually shaped and refined on the basis of the committee's recommendations. A series of interim publications (Council of Europe, 2011,

2012) culminated in the Council of Europe Charter on shared social responsibilities,[2] which defines social responsibility as:

> the accountability of public and private institutions or individuals for the consequences of their actions or omissions in the context of mutual commitments entered into by consensus, agreeing on reciprocal rights and obligations in the fields of social welfare and the protection of human dignity, the fight against social disparities and discrimination, and the quest for justice, social cohesion and sustainability, showing respect for diversity, with due regard for the applicable legal and social rules or obligations.
>
> *(Council of Europe, 2014)*

The concept of SSR, initially conceived in political circles, is now being examined in academic studies (Galli, Elefanti and Valotti, 2013; Gneezy et al., 2010). Although this work is still at a very early stage, it appears to offer a promising way of extending the concept of CSR, notably via the current trend of considering CSR from a strategic perspective (Lee, 2008; Porter and Kramer, 2006). Moreover, the emergence of concepts such as shared value creation, defined by Porter and Kramer (2011, p. 66) as "policies and operating practices that enhance the competitiveness of a company while simultaneously advancing the economic and social conditions in the communities in which it operates", is also facilitating the adoption of the idea that organisations may have to 'share' their social responsibilities.

The relevance of shared social responsibility to Olympism

The recent strategic changes made by the IOC related to OSR lead us to consider them from the perspective of Shared Social Responsibility. Agenda 2020, which lists sustainability as one of the three pillars of Olympism, alongside credibility and youth (IOC, 2014), contains two detailed recommendations on how sustainability should be incorporated into "all aspects of the Olympic Games" (Recommendation 4) and "the Olympic Movement's daily operations" (Recommendation 5). The IOC subsequently expanded these recommendations into a detailed Sustainability Strategy (IOC, 2016a), structured around "three spheres of responsibility" (as an organisation, as the owner of the OG, as the leader of the Olympic movement) and five "focus areas" (Infrastructure and natural sites, Sourcing and resource management, Mobility, Workforce, Labour). As well as specifying several "strategic intents", the strategy lays down specific objectives with respect to each sphere of responsibility. This structure reflects the IOC's recognition that social responsibility can have a strong impact only if the principles of sustainability are embraced and applied by all stakeholders of the Olympic movement. Hence, the IOC must share its vision of sustainability as a key aspect of Olympism, so it can set guidelines and undertake joint actions, otherwise it risks, at best, failing to follow its principles, or, at worst, contradicting them.

However, the idea of OSR as 'shared' goes much further than the IOC's desire to use sustainability for strategic purposes. In fact, both SSR and OSR have been greatly influenced by supranational organisations, whose debates on how social and environmental transformations impact society have inspired organisational social responsibility since the mid-1980s. Indeed, the very notion of SSR was developed by the Council of Europe, an intergovernmental forum in which European Union Member States can compare views on social issues. In the case of OSR, the IOC has fostered close links with the UN since the 1990s, long before building its vision of social responsibility for the Olympic movement. Consequently, its sustainable development objectives (health/well-being, education, gender equality, etc.) are now largely inspired by the

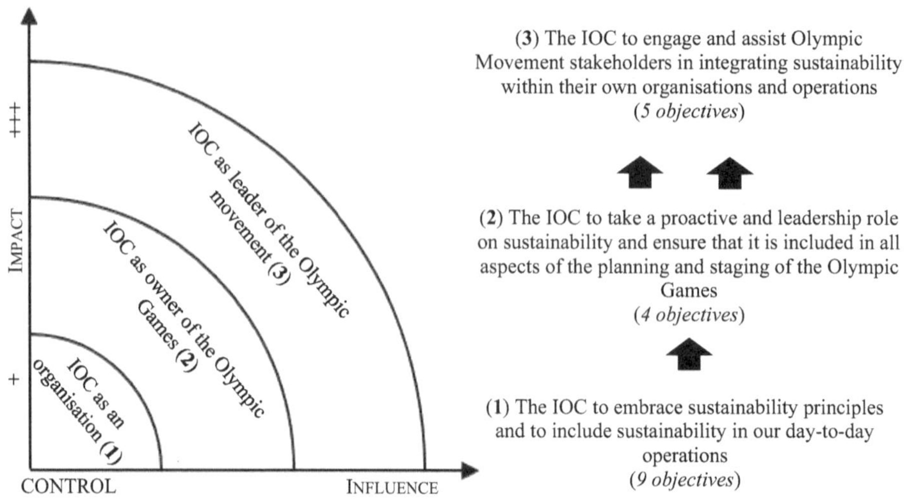

Figure 14.1 The IOC's sustainability strategy and associated objectives for 2020

Source: Figure adapted from the IOC's Sustainability Strategy (2016a)

UN's Agenda 2030. As well as contributing to these objectives itself, the IOC's goal is to ensure the entire Olympic movement follows its path (IOC, 2016a).

Of all the terms used by different bodies in relation to SSR, the most significant may well be interdependence, a term that appears frequently in both the preliminary reports and the final charter produced by the Council of Europe's social commission (Council of Europe, 2011, 2012, 2014).[3] In fact, interdependence between the Olympic movement's stakeholders is so strong that the resulting network is currently referred to as the "total Olympic system" (Ferrand, Chappelet and Seguin, 2012).

As Figure 14.1 shows, the IOC must behave responsibly as an organisation (sphere 1), ensure the OG are organised responsibly (sphere 2) and, as the leader of the Olympic movement, promote responsibility throughout the Olympic System (sphere 3).

This wider view of the IOC's social responsibilities encompasses the particularly dense networks of stakeholders that make up spheres 2 and 3 of the IOC's model, and highlights the need for all its stakeholders to share its vision of social responsibility. As owner of the OG (sphere 2), the IOC selects the host city for each edition of the Games and signs a contract with that city and the host country's National Olympic Committee (NOC). In addition,

> at the discretion of the IOC, other local, regional or national authorities, as well as, if relevant, other NOCs and local, regional or national authorities outside the host country, may also be a party to such agreement. Such agreement, which is commonly referred to as the Host City Contract, is executed by all parties immediately upon the election of the host city.
>
> *(IOC, 2017, p. 72)*

Because Host City Contracts (HCC) provide the IOC with a means of ensuring its contractual stakeholders share and embrace its vision of OSR, recent HCCs have begun including more detailed requirements on social responsibility. For example, provisions related to a positive and durable legacy, which falls within the field of OSR, were included in the HCCs for the 2018 Winter Olympics and 2020 Summer Olympics, but not in the HCC for the 2016 Olympics (Marmayou, 2015). The emergence of these provisions demonstrates the need for the IOC to share a common vision of OSR with their contractual stakeholders or risk not promoting their commitment. Once Organising Committees for the Olympic Games (OCOG) and Olympic cities have accepted the IOC's vision, they must then communicate it to other stakeholders (e.g. local communities, politicians) that may not be contractually bound to the OG but may impact or be impacted by them. If these stakeholders do not share the IOC's/OCOG's vision, they can adversely damage the event's reputation.[4]

The third sphere contains the vast network of stakeholders known as the Olympic movement (Chappelet and Kübler-Mabbott, 2008). Acting under the overall authority and leadership of the IOC, it aims to "contribute to building a peaceful and better world by educating youth through sport practised in accordance with Olympism and its values" (IOC, 2017, p. 15).

Challenges and difficulties associated with implementing a shared OSR: information provided by the IOC on its sustainability strategy

Since adopting its Agenda 2020 and sustainability strategy, the IOC has greatly increased its communication on sustainability, most notably by publishing an annual report. The following paragraphs present the main components of this report, as contained in the 2016 edition (IOC, 2016b). We examine all these components following the three spheres aforementioned.

As an organisation: after creating a Corporate Development, Brand and Sustainability Department in 2015, the IOC recruited a dedicated sustainability manager in 2016. This department title reflects the desire to align the IOC's structure with its strategy (Olympic Agenda 2020 – the strategic roadmap for the future of the Olympic movement) and the three broad pillars: credibility, sustainability and youth. This drives the IOC to integrate sustainability into its day-to-day operations. It also began redeveloping its headquarters in Lausanne, so they could provide a focal point for the Olympic movement. The IOC wanted to minimise the building's environmental impact and use the project as a test bed for several new environmental certifications and thereby gained a place at the table in the debate on environmentally responsible construction in Switzerland. Since then, The IOC claims that its headquarters are "one of the most sustainable building in the world".[5] By using renewable energy provided by solar panels on the roof and pumps taking water from Lake Geneva, it has won numerous international and Swiss awards for sustainability. The IOC's desire to further reduce its environmental impact is shown in several studies carried out since 2014, many of which have led to partnerships aimed at minimising the institution's environmental footprint (e.g. Dow, International Union for Conservation of Nature).

As owner of the OG: In recent years the IOC has endeavoured to raise awareness of societal and environmental issues among OCOGs, NOCs, host cities and other stakeholders. Although some steps were taken prior to the IOC's creation of its sustainability strategy, the importance of these issues has grown substantially. As the owner of the rights to the Olympic Games, the IOC requires an understanding of societal and environmental issues and the implementation of concrete actions by the OCOGs, NOCs, host cities and other stakeholders involved. Hence, in the mid-2000s, the OCOGs for the Turin (Toroc, 2006) and Vancouver (Vanoc, 2010) Winter Olympics produced sustainability reports describing their main initiatives in this area (Chappelet, 2008). Toroc, for example, introduced an environmental management system that enabled the event to obtain both ISO 14001 and Eco-Management and Audit Scheme (EMAS) certification two years before the Games took place. Six years later, the OCOG for London 2012 Summer

Olympics managed its operations in accordance with the precepts of ISO 20121, a new norm for sustainable event management. Consequently, London 2012 became the first OG to be certified as sustainable. The IOC highlighted London's achievement in meeting this standard, hoping to help future events to create positive social and economic legacies and reduce their negative impacts. By pushing OCOGs to incorporate the principles of sustainable development into the organisation of the OG and by providing advice on designing sustainable events, the IOC is promoting this approach. The OCOGs for the Lillehammer 2016 Youth Olympic Games (YOG) and the Rio 2016 Summer Olympics also obtained ISO 20121 certification, with the Lillehammer YOG becoming the first event in Norway to do so. As for Rio 2016, certification was obtained thanks to a partnership with Dow, a sustainability specialist, which enabled the event to reduce its carbon footprint, most notably in the field of spectator transport.

As the leader of the Olympic movement, in line with Recommendation 13 of the Olympic Agenda 2020 to "maximise synergies with Olympic Movement stakeholders", the IOC aims at influencing its stakeholders to follow good practices with respect to sustainability (IOC, 2014). In 2015, the IOC invited several Olympic International Federations (OIFs) to a forum on sustainability in order to compile a series of recommendations on social and environmental practices later shared with other Federations at the 2016 SportAccord forum (IOC, 2016b). The IOC's decision to use the forum's conclusions to help non-Olympic international federations design their own sustainability policies and strategies suggests that it has gone beyond its responsibilities as the leader of the Olympic movement. A memorandum of understanding signed by the IOC and the Global Association of International Sports Federations (GAISF) at the end of 2017 supports this premise, as it allows both organisations to provide extra services to non-Olympic Federations, especially in the fields of good governance, ethics and integrity, protecting clean athletes, development, education and sustainability. The IOC is also targeting NOCs by highlighting the need to consider their activities' social and environmental impacts. As in the case of OIFs, NOCs that received Olympic Solidarity funds to implement sustainability initiatives under the 2013–2016 quadrennial plan were required to report their best practices in the field of sustainability (Olympic Solidarity, 2016). These best practices were then turned into case studies and shared with all the NOCs. This collaborative work helped pave the way for sustainability being made the fifth key theme of the 2017–2020 Olympic Solidarity Plan and highlighted numerous areas of development that need to be addressed and shared among the IOC and its NOCs (Olympic Solidarity, 2017). Finally, in October 2018, the IOC held the "Olympism in Action" forum in Buenos Aires, just before the YOG. This event, centred around building a better world through sport, was designed to find new ideas and identify recent trends in sport, while spreading the Olympic spirit across the world.

Paradoxes associated with shared OSR

The preceding overview of the IOC's three spheres of responsibility brings out a number of difficulties to overcome if it is to succeed in its aim of sharing OSR. First, although CSR/OSR and the wider concept of sustainable development (within which the IOC views its social responsibility) are centred on the ideal of promoting the common good, implementing this ideal in the real world exposes the paradoxes and challenges that organisations, including the IOC, have to face. Consequently, many observers have criticised the concepts of CSR and sustainable development, ever since they first emerged (Friedman, 1970; Baumgartner, 2011; Gond and Moon, 2011). In the case of the IOC, it has to contend with conflicting dynamics between its duties as an organisation and its actions vis-à-vis its other two spheres of responsibility. Thus, it must be exemplary as an organisation, but its overall social responsibility performance is dependent on its influence over its stakeholders, both in its capacity as the owner of the OG and as the leader of the Olympic movement.

Given the Olympic message and values, and the IOC's ambitious sustainability objectives, the institution's first obligation is to be exemplary as an organisation. Unless its internal stakeholders embrace its vision of social responsibility, it will be difficult for the IOC to share this vision with other members of the Olympic movement. The IOC is aware of this challenge and being a "role model in sustainability" is its main objective for the period up to 2030 (IOC, 2016a). However, this task will not be easy, as several recent scandals have deeply stained the Olympic movement and revealed major faults in the governance of the Olympic System. One of the most serious scandals occurred following the attribution of the 2002 Winter Olympics to Salt Lake City. The uncovered corruption resulted in ten IOC members being excluded and a further ten members receiving reprimands. Although the Salt Lake City Olympics were successful, this scandal, together with the numerous cases of doping and violence that emerged in the early 2000s, led to an unprecedented loss of trust in the IOC from the media and governments (Chappelet, 2009).

Another question that arises is the IOC's ability to influence and control the main stakeholders involved in organising and staging Olympic events (e.g. OG and YOG). The IOC hands over the responsibility for organising these events to a small number of stakeholders (host cities, NOCs and OCOGs) with which it signs a contract. Of course, the IOC does have some power over NOCs and over OCOGs, whose executive bodies must include the host country's IOC member(s) (IOC, 2017).[6] However, host cities, especially those in countries whose culture, standards and regulations in the field of sustainability are weak, may not give sustainability the importance the IOC would like. Hence, although some OCOGs (e.g. Turin 2006 and Vancouver 2010) published sustainability reports, others such as Sochi 2014, have not followed suit. Moreover, controversies over issues such as negative environmental impacts (especially the Winter Olympics), and the building white elephants (e.g. Athens 2004, Sochi 2014, Rio 2016), weaken the idea of sustainability as one of the pillars of Olympism. A further risk comes from the recent decline in the number of candidate cities interested to host mega-events, especially the Olympics (Ferrand and Chappelet, 2015). This increases the possibility that the IOC may be 'forced' to attribute the OG to cities and countries that do not share its vision of sustainability. But, the IOC has managed to avoid this risk for forthcoming editions of the Summer Olympics. Even though only two candidates for the 2024 OG – Los Angeles and Paris – continued their bids to the final selection phase, the IOC managed to save face by awarding the 2024 Games to Paris and the 2028 Olympics to Los Angeles, both of which can call upon numerous existing facilities.

Similarly, recent scandals show how difficult it is for the IOC, as the leader of the Olympic movement, to ensure its stakeholders behave responsibly. The World Anti-Doping Agency's (WADA, 2015) revelation of 'institutionalised' doping in Russia, involving several athletes who competed at the London 2012 and Sochi 2014 Olympics, illustrates the size of the obstacles the IOC has to overcome if it is to successfully share its vision of responsibility and sustainability. After a boycott by the United States during the 1980 Moscow Olympics, and a counter-boycott by the USSR at the 1984 Los Angeles Games, Russia once again risked being absent from an Olympic Games. Officially, Russia was excluded from the 2018 PyeongChang Winter Olympics, in South Korea, but 168 Russian athletes were allowed to compete as "Olympic athletes from Russia" and under a neutral flag. This shows that despite the IOC's desire for its model of sustainability to encompass all the stakeholders in the Olympic System, some decisions involve finding a difficult balance between contradictory interests.

Can Olympism really contribute to making a better world?

The IOC's greatest difficulties in ensuring its vision of sustainability arise from the discrepancy between the Olympic movement's objectives and the influence it has over its stakeholders, rather than from any mismatch between words and deeds. The paradoxes noted earlier can, in part, be attenuated by measures aimed at "contributing to a better world" (see Table 14.1).

Given the challenges OSR has to overcome, and despite the possible solutions presented here, doubts remain over Olympism's ability "to place sport at the service of the harmonious development of humankind, with a view to promoting a peaceful society concerned with the preservation of human dignity" (IOC, 2017, p. 11). Moreover, although the IOC's

Table 14.1 The road to shared OSR: paradoxes and possible solutions

	IOC as an organisation	*IOC as owner of the OG*	*IOC as leader of the Olympic movement*
Paradoxes with associated examples	Past scandals (corruption by IOC members in the attribution of some editions of the OG) continue to stain the IOC's reputation, thereby potentially drowning out its sustainability message.	Declining interest from potential host cities may lead to OG being attributed to sites that are questionable from an environmental point of view (e.g. Sochi 2014), thereby increasing the OG's negative environmental impact.	Absence of control over most stakeholders with respect to their efforts in the fields of governance/ responsibility/ sustainability, leading to a lack of results and questioning of the whole system's credibility (cf. FIFAgate and IAAF scandals, etc.)
Notions, key concepts	Exemplarity/Governance	Influence mechanisms/ Legacy	Influence mechanisms/Inter-sector collaboration/ Governance
Possible solutions	1) Ensure transparency and exemplarity within the IOC so it can share its vision, of sustainability/ responsibility, which must be irreproachable internally. 2) Continue efforts to improve governance based on existing initiatives (e.g. Association of Summer Olympic International Federations' (ASOIF) Governance Task Force).	1) Work with host cities and stakeholders to build a shared vision of what a sustainable OG legacy should look like. 2) Systematically produce independently certified sustainable development reports for the OG.	1) Share good practices in terms of governance by continuing to favour bottom-up approaches inspired by existing practices. 2) Re-think international and infra-national governance models around the issue of sharing a model of sustainability.[7]

actions are as far reaching as any multinational's, unlike a multinational it has limited control over its stakeholders and has to contend with the fragility of both the Olympic System and its stakeholders.

For the IOC's approach to succeed it must create a vision of sustainability that is shared inside and outside the Olympic System. Inter-sector collaboration will be a key factor in achieving this as it will generate closer ties with actors such as social entrepreneurs or non-governmental agencies. Consequently, the IOC must define a model of sustainability that is not based solely on the world of sport. Doing so will require introducing innovative management systems based on the network of stakeholders involved in supporting, disseminating, shaping and transforming the model, so they can ensure it considers their interests.

These management systems will enable stakeholders inside and outside the sports sector to build social capital based on confidence, networks and reciprocity (Putnam, 1995). In addition, the strategy must be global and, at the same time, include local mechanisms for developing the capabilities of local communities.[8] However, implementing these principles may not be enough to overcome all the criticisms of a movement whose controversies, especially with respect to the staging of the OG, keep coming back. But their application will undoubtedly increase the credibility of Olympism's model of sustainability and thereby facilitate the inter-sector collaboration needed to build and implement it. The question remains as to whether OSR is truly shared across the Olympic System, which stretches across the globe and which does not always have the culture and or ability to take the actions needed to respond to these societal challenges.

Conclusion

This chapter's goal was to show the paradoxes and challenges involved in sharing the IOC's preferred model of sustainability across all the stakeholders in the Olympic movement. When viewed through the lens of social responsibility, shared OSR does not appear to be that easy to implement, especially when its objective is as ambitious as "contributing to a better world".

Examining the IOC's latest sustainability initiatives shows both the efforts it is making to meet this objective and the road still left to travel. In fact, the growing challenges facing Olympism and the OG could well lead to ethical blowbacks (through poor governance, corruption, cult of money, doping, and the geopolitical and economic instrumentalisation of sport) and pose risks to the reputations of both the IOC and the organisations within the Olympic System. However, neither the IOC nor the OIFs currently have any real power or control over other stakeholders within the Olympic System, although the IOC tries to impose its will as best it can, for example, via HCCs. Thus, according to the IOC's 2016 Annual Report, subtitled "Credibility, Sustainability and Youth", the HCC for the 2024 OG was "modified to reflect the enhanced positioning of sustainability and legacy" (IOC, 2016b, p. 44).[9] It will be interesting to see how these promises of change, made six years before the Paris 2024 Olympics, affect the way the IOC and the stakeholders involved in organising the event co-construct sustainable initiatives and whether they develop a truly shared OSR. Hence, although we are not questioning the IOC's ideal of sustainability, we are not convinced it has the influence required to ensure its stakeholders share the responsibility of working towards this ideal.

Notes

1 Excerpt from the 1st fundamental principle of the Olympic Charter, which came into force on 15 September 2017.

2 Charter adopted by the Committee of Ministers on 22 January 2014 (Council of Europe, 2014).
3 The 'Scope' section of the charter highlights the fact that:

> Shared social responsibilities involve special care for the weakest members of society and expecting their co-operation with policies and institutions striving to improve their economic and social situation; such responsibilities call for a new approach in a context of interdependence.

4 The OG have always been subject to social protests, although contestation has been stronger at some editions than at others. This was the case for the 2016 Rio Olympics, where protest by a minority of Brazilians helped seriously damage the Games' reputation (cf. Soares Gonçalves, Bautès and de Luna Freire, 2016).
5 https://www.aipsmedia.com/index.html?page=artdetail&art=26609&ANOC-General-AssemblyIOC-Thomas-Bach.
6 According to Rule 35 of the Olympic Charter.
7 There are at least two ways in which approaches to sustainable development could be territorialised. The first is to give territories substantial latitude in how they embrace the model of Olympic sustainability, based on their specific characteristics. The second would be to set up an Olympic foundation to promote development through sport in conjunction with UN bodies and local NGOs.
8 According to the Western Australian Department for Community Development (2006), "Community capacity building is about promoting the 'capacity' of local communities to develop, implement and sustain their own solutions to problems in a way that helps them shape and exercise control over their physical, social, economic and cultural environments".
9 According to the HCC, the co-signatories (host city, NOC and OCOG) must "carry out all activities foreseen under the HCC in a manner which embraces sustainable development and contributes to the United Nations' Sustainable Development Goals" (article 15.1). They must also "define, implement and communicate a comprehensive and integrated sustainability programme" (article 15.2).

References

Baumgartner, R.J. (2011). Critical perspectives of sustainable development research and practice. *Journal of Cleaner Production*, 19(8), pp. 783–786.

Bayle, E. (2016). Olympic social responsibility: A challenge for the future. *Sport in Society*, 19(6), pp. 752–766.

Bayle, E., Chappelet, J-L., François, A. and Maltese, L. (2011). *Sport et RSE: vers un management responsable? [Sport and CSR: Towards a responsible management?]* Bruxelles: De Boeck.

Bowen, H.R. (1953). *Social responsibilities of the businessman*. New York: Harper & Row.

Chappelet, J-L. (2008). Olympic environmental concerns as a legacy of the winter games. *The International Journal of the History of Sport*, 25(14), pp. 1884–1902.

Chappelet, J-L. (2009). Corporate social responsibility: A new frontier for the International Olympic Committee. In: P. Rodriguez, S. Késenne and H. Dietl, eds., *Social and sustainability in sports*. Oviedo: Universidad de Oviedo, pp. 17–29.

Chappelet, J-L. (2011). RSE et grandes organisations sportives internationales [CSR and international sporting organisations]. In: E. Bayle, J-L. Chappelet, A. François and L. Maltese, eds., *Sport et RSE: vers un management responsable? [Sport and CSR: Towards a responsible management?]* Bruxelles: De Boeck, pp. 23–54.

Chappelet, J-L. and Kübler-Mabbott, B. (2008). *The International Olympic Committee and the Olympic system: The governance of world sport*. London: Routledge.

Clastres, P. (2018). Pierre de Coubertin: The inventor of the Olympic tradition. In: E. Bayle and P. Clastres, eds., *Global sports leaders: A biographical analysis of international sport management*. Cham, Switzerland: Palgrave Macmillan, pp. 33–60.

Council of Europe. (2010). *New strategy and Council of Europe action plan for social cohesion*. Strasbourg, France: Official Publications of Council of Europe.

Council of Europe. (2011). *Towards a Europe of shared social responsibilities: Challenges and strategies*. Trends in Social Cohesion No. 23. Strasbourg, France: Council of Europe Publishing.

Council of Europe. (2012). *Shared social responsibility: Putting theory into practice*. Trends in Social Cohesion No. 24. Strasbourg, France: Council of Europe Publishing.

Council of Europe. (2014). *Recommendation of the Committee of Ministers to member states on the Council of Europe Charter 'on' shared social responsibilities*. Strasbourg, France: Council of Europe Publishing.

Ferrand, A. and Chappelet, J-L. (2015). Smaller is beautiful: vers de plus petits évènements sportifs? [Smaller is beautiful: Towards new smaller sporting events?] *Reflets et perspectives de la vie économique*, 56(3), pp. 111–125.
Ferrand, A., Chappelet, J-L. and Seguin, B. (2012). *Le marketing olympique. Co-création de valeurs entre acteurs*. Bruxelles: De Boeck.
Friedman, M. (1970). The social responsibility of business is to increase its profits. *New York Times Magazine*, Sept. 13, pp. 122–126.
Galli, D., Elefanti, M. and Valotti, G. (2013). From corporate to shared social responsibility: Community governance and social capital creation through collaboration. In: *APPAM international conference*, Fudan University, Shangaï, May 26–27.
Gneezy, A., Gneezy, U., Nelson, L.D. and Brown, A. (2010). Shared social responsibility: A field experiment in pay-what-you want pricing and charitable giving. *Science*, 329, pp. 325–327.
Gond, J-P. and Moon, J. (2011). Corporate social responsibility in retrospect and prospect: Exploring the life-cycle of an essentially contested concept. In: J-P. Gond and J. Moon, eds., *Major works in corporate social responsibility*. Vol. 1. London: Routledge, pp. 1–28.
International Organization for Standardization. (2014). *ISO 26000. Guidance on social responsibility. Discovering ISO 26000*. Geneva: Official Publications of the International Organization for Standardization.
IOC. (1999). *Olympic movement's agenda 21. Sport for sustainable development*. Lausanne: IOC Official Publications.
IOC. (2014). *Olympic Agenda 2020. 20+20 recommendations*. Lausanne: IOC Official Publications.
IOC. (2016a). *IOC sustainability strategy. Executive summary*. Lausanne: IOC Official Publications.
IOC. (2016b). *IOC Annual Report 2016. Credibility, sustainability and youth*. Lausanne: IOC Official Publications.
IOC. (2017). *Olympic Charter. In force as from 15th September 2017*. Lausanne: IOC Official Publications.
Lee, M-D.P. (2008). A review of the theories of corporate social responsibility: Its evolutionary path and the road ahead. *International Journal of Management Reviews*, 10(1), pp. 53–73.
Marmayou, J-M. (2015). *Le contrat de "ville hôte" pour les Jeux Olympiques [The host city contract for the Olympic Games]*. Droit et Olympisme. Contribution à l'étude juridique d'un phénomène transnational. Aix en Provence: Presses Universitaires d'Aix-Marseille.
Olympic Solidarity. (2016). *2013–2016 quadrennial plan. Final report*. Lausanne: Official Publications of the Olympic Solidarity.
Olympic Solidarity. (2017). *Olympic solidarity plan 2017–2020*. Lausanne: Official Publications of the Olympic Solidarity.
Porter, M.E. and Kramer, M.R. (2006). Strategy and society: The link between competitive advantage and corporate social responsibility. *Harvard Business Review*, 84(12), pp. 78–92.
Porter, M.E. and Kramer, M.R. (2011). Creating shared value. *Harvard Business Review*, 89(1/2), pp. 62–77.
Putnam, R.D. (1995). Bowling alone: America's declining social capital. *Journal of Democracy*, 6(1), pp. 65–78.
Soares Gonçalves, R., Bautès, N. and de Luna Freire, L. (2016). Introduction. Rio de Janeiro 2016 ou les travers de la ville Olympic. [Introduction. Rio de Janeiro as the example of host city shortcomings]. *Problèmes d'Amérique Latine*, 103, pp. 5–15.
Toroc. (2006). *Sustainability report 2006*. Torino: XX Olympic Winter Games.
Vanoc. (2010). *Vancouver 2010 sustainability report 2009–10*. Vancouver: Organizing Committee for the 2010 Olympic and Paralympic Winter Games.
Western Australian Department for Community Development. (2006). *Contemporary literature on capacity building and the strengths perspective and good practice wisdom for the capacity building strategic framework 2005 to 2007*. Perth: Government of Western Australia, Department for Community Development.
World Anti-Doping Agency. (2015). *Final report of the independent commission #1*. Montréal: Official Publications of the World Anti-Doping Agency.

15

Esports in the Olympic and Paralympic Games

The business case for integration

Andy Miah and Alex Fenton

Introduction

Since the Rio 2016 Olympic Games, the public and industry discourses around esports have gone through a series of important and transformative moments. For example, at the Rio 2016 British team pavilion, the International eGames Committee produced a demonstration esports tournament. Also, during the Rio 2016 handover ceremony to Tokyo 2020, the Japanese prime minister appeared dressed as Super Mario, a statement directly referring to Japan's gaming culture and its connection with gaming culture. Super Mario is also the central character in the Olympic movement's official computer game.

Soon after, in 2017, the organisers of the Paris 2024 Olympic Games were widely reported to be interested in discussing the inclusion of esports within their Olympic programme (Massaad, 2017). Subsequently, days ahead of the PyeongChang 2018 Olympic Winter Games, Worldwide Olympic Partner Intel produced its "Intel Esports Masters" event, in what was the first competition to enjoy co-branding with the Olympic emblems. While this event was neither part of the Olympic programme nor a demonstration sport, it reflected the wider awareness among sports federations of esports and the growing alignment of these two worlds. Finally, less than one year before the Tokyo 2020 Olympic Games, the same Intel collaboration that took place ahead of PyeongChang has led to the announcement of a tournament that will begin two days before Tokyo's Opening Ceremony and conclude on the day the Olympic Games opens (Intel, 2019).

A significant part of this trajectory is evidenced by the wider activities of the Olympic and Paralympic financial stakeholders – notably broadcasters and sponsors – and it is worth noting that the historical involvement of some of these organisations goes back to the earliest years of the modern Olympic Games. In this sense, such partners are not merely mechanisms of financial support, but are long-term Olympic Family members, as they are described by the International Olympic Committee (IOC).

In this context, this chapter analyses the involvement of Olympic and Paralympic stakeholders in the production of the relationship between sports and esports. In so doing, it conveys how the financial stakeholders of the Games are aligning with esports and how this is influencing their growing synergy. These connections were most recently apparent at the historic Olympism in Action Forum, which took place in the days preceding the Buenos Aires 2018 Youth Olympic

Games. In the final plenary session of the event, discussion about esports were central to debates about the future of sport, with key players from Olympic partners – notably Intel – indicating further interest in exploring this common ground. The Forum followed a major event at the IOC in Lausanne during the summer of 2018, which brought together members of the General Assembly of International Sports Federations (GAISF) with computer games publishers to discuss the future of their relationship.

By considering these commercial relationships, programmes, and institutional shifts – particularly from Olympic and Paralympic federations – this chapter describes the growing closeness of esports to the Olympic and Paralympic programme. In so doing, it circumvents the often philosophical discussions that take place around the logic of connecting esports with traditional sports, which focus on whether there is enough conceptual overlap between these practices to justify their being within the same programmes. While such discussions remain a critical part of the public dialogue on the subject, these aspects have been analysed elsewhere and, for many within the sports world, are considered inconsequential to the eventual resolution of the matter (see Miah, 2017).

As such, this chapter examines evidence of the aligning worlds of sports and esports, arguing that there are explanations for why the debate about the relationship between the two is taking place and why it is reasonable to conclude that the future of all sports is the integration of esport. More specifically, we examine the relationships between the Olympic and Paralympic programme and esports, to draw attention to the fact that the economic environment around these events is aligning to enable a closer relationship, where a number of key strategic interests are met.

While the conceptual common ground between traditional sports and esports is not our priority in this chapter, it is useful to reflect on the characteristics of this debate. Why is it that the focus of public debate has been on the possibility of esports becoming part of the Olympic programme rather than, say, the Paralympic programme? While there may be a number of practical reasons for this – such as the lack of evidence about gaming titles being sufficiently inclusive to allow people with a wide range of disabilities to take part – there is also something more crucial to this debate that has to do with the symbolic nature of becoming an Olympic sport. Thus, the Olympic programme has an historical gravitas that is rooted in the idea of sports becoming instances of wider cultural importance, such that their inclusion within the Olympic programme becomes a matter of ascribing a special kind of value to them. This interpretation is informed by the wider symbolism of the Olympian as a cultural concept, which dates back to ancient times. Thus, the reason why the alignment of esport with the Olympics is so controversial and so compelling is because it represents a cataclysmic disruption to what we traditionally regard as a sport, of which the IOC is the symbolic guardian in modern times and the public arbiter of such debates. In other words, if the IOC gives esport status by including it within the Olympic programme, then it will do the work of giving legitimacy to esport as a proper sport.

Despite there being compelling reasons for recognising esports as part of the definition of sport, there are far more relevant political and economic factors that are shaping the direction of this conversation and which speak to the need to attend to such matters when thinking about the future of sport. To fully articulate these, this chapter is divided into four sections, each of which speaks to a different dimension of this meta-organisational context that surrounds the discussion. First, we examine how broadcasters are positioning themselves around a series of digital innovations, many of which are exemplified by the emerging media economy of esports. Second, we analyse the activities of traditional Olympic and Paralympic sponsors, drawing attention to their investment into the export programme. Third, we examine how gaming publishers and esport event organisers are becoming closer to sport. Finally, we explore the federations and their integration of esports. Together, these parameters reveal why it is that the future of all sports is esport, as an increasing amount of sports participation becomes located in and driven through digital experiences.

The broadcasters

There are three main indicators of how global sports broadcasters are aligning with the production of esports events. However, perhaps even more crucial to this development is the fact that there is a declining viewership of young people around traditional sports television experience and broadcasters – along with the event proprietors – recognise that there is a need to rethink how to ensure that younger people are not lost to these experiences. As reported from the Rio 2016 Games, the major market in the USA – one of the key Olympic funding territories – has shown a 30% drop in the 18–34 audience viewing figures since London 2012. This reflects a growing awareness that television viewers are getting older, with younger generations turning to YouTube, Instagram, and other social media television experiences. In broadcasting terms, the Olympics has been described by the media as 'old' with its persistently ageing television viewer population (Chang, 2016). The average viewer age of the Beijing 2008 Olympic Games was 47, which rose to 48 for the 2012 London Games (ibid.). Yet, the Rio Paralympics broke all previous viewing records, achieving a global, cumulative TV audience of more than 4.1 billion people in 150 countries (International Paralympic Committee, 2017).

Changing viewing habits, coupled with the rise of esports online audiences, provide the context for this section's consideration of what's happening around the monetisation of the Olympic and Paralympic moving image content. Esports has shown broadcasters that there is a new way to approach the distribution of video content, as more audiences find material through social media platforms, such as video on Facebook or YouTube. In contrast to the Olympics being 'old', esport is young and discussed as "one of the fastest-growing spectator sports in the world and claims to be the second truly global sport after football" (Cooper, 2018).

There is also a need to appreciate how the concept of television has mutated in recent years. A television set is no longer an object that sits alone as a singular platform in a living room, but is accessed in a variety of ways across multiple platforms, simultaneously capable of showing traditional TV schedules or providing on-demand content from the world wide web including social media and YouTube, or dedicated streaming services like Amazon or Netflix.

TV companies are adopting esport streaming principles

A structural analysis of esports event coverage reveals the common ground between the production process and the production of traditional sports. For instance, a typical esports broadcast will consist of live, field-of-play coverage, commentators who are positioned to articulate what's happening in the match second by second. Already, there exists a burgeoning community of esports media professionals who specialise in capturing such events, and new roles have emerged unique to this format, notably the shoutcaster, a term which derives from a software programme called SHOUTcast, which was an early version to allow live streaming of media content over the Internet.

Like a sports commentator, a shoutcaster narrates the match as it happens. The British Esports Association distinguishes between "play-by-play casters (who provide running on-the-fly commentary) and colour casters (who provide supplementary information or comment, usually following a noteworthy moment in a game)". While each role has similarities to sports commentators, there are clear nuances for what each requires. These features of esports coverage reveal how intimately they are connected to the language, grammar, and staging of traditional sports.

Second, major broadcasters around the world are steadily exploring esports as a commercial market, establishing contracts for broadcasting events and regular coverage. For example, in the UK, British Sky and ITV partnered with long-term game competition streamer GINX to create GINX Esports TV, which streams esports 24 hours a day. Alternatively, in the USA, such broadcasters as ESPN and NBC are all producing esports TV coverage and, for many years now, in Asia, the broadcast of esports competitions has been commonplace. In this respect, the number of televised hours is growing quickly, creating a groundswell of excitement about a new era of television audiences.

Esports is innovating with TV

Finally, esports are occupying the televisual broadcast territory by bringing innovation into the broadcast industry. Such platforms as Twitch have created new excitement about the future of television and such things resonate with an industry that is perpetually focused on technological innovation. Indeed, television is a highly technological environment, as evidenced from the many innovations seen in the last 20 years, from the development of flat screens, to 3D and binaural sound. Television industries gravitate to innovation with the moving image and esports have also demonstrated such principles. Twitch, now owned by Amazon, also finds itself amidst a world-leading streaming platform, the delivery products of which span all aspects of human society. Indeed, the Amazon Firestick platform functions not just as a vehicle for the sharing of movie and television content, but has also become a gaming console, with a growing number of apps built into its ecosystem.

Such developments in televisual experiences present challenging circumstances for traditional broadcasters, which may not be in the business of platform innovation, but which have focused their investments around content generation. In one sense, the content generation industry as a standalone component of the sector has steadily diminished and been replaced by content aggregation innovators. These draw creative materials from other spaces to occupy their commercial environment. Consider how Facebook endeavoured to engage newspapers with its Instant Articles proposition, allowing publishers to integrate their content within Facebook and develop deeper insights into viewer experience thereby. While Instant Articles did not work for many publishers as a long-term strategy (Tran, 2018), it speaks to the way in which the distribution of media content is changing around the emergence of new digital platforms and innovation. To function as a commercial entity in the current digital media environment, it is crucial to experiment and iterate with the platforms in which content is situated. Together, these parameters reveal how esports are becoming the reference point for attracting millennials to sports viewing as a televisual experience, as Bernando (2016) describes.

The sponsors

A further indication of the growing alignment of esports with traditional sports businesses is found in the activity of long-term sports sponsors. Recent years have shown that esports represent big business and with huge prizes and audiences, comes sponsorship. There are some notable big-name sponsors that have aligned with esports, such as Mercedes Benz, which has worked with the Electronic Sports League since 2017 and Audi, which has sponsored the Counter Strike GO team Astralis (Ring, 2017). There has also been an increase in sponsors which are affiliated with traditional sports. For example, Adidas has been announcing partnerships with the likes of Danish esports team North which is linked to FC Copenhagen (Collins, 2018). This is the first global esports partnership for this sportswear leviathan. The esports team competes in Adidas merchandise, which again is an interesting comparison to traditional sports players wearing Adidas and other sportswear. As such, the traditional affiliation of sports brands linked with sports clubs is also creating linkages and new sports sponsorships for esports.

Olympic sponsors are also developing esport portfolios or technological propositions for the future of esports. Perhaps the most comprehensive example of this is found in Samsung, a Worldwide Olympic Partner since Nagano 1998 and provider of various forms of technological experience at the Games. For example, Samsung mobile devices are the products athletes receive as gifts when taking part in the Olympic Games, a practice which dates back to London 2012 and which performs the function of generating stories around technological innovation. Among the activities undertaken by Samsung during the Olympic Games, is its promotion of a new mobile device, which may be featured as a showcase technology during the Games. Additionally, Samsung's recent sponsor pavilions have showcased how their mobile devices can be used to create virtual reality experiences, including their use in sports simulators. This alignment with the features of gaming culture are accompanied by the fact that their Samsung Gear VR stores consist of many sports like gaming titles. Samsung also invests into esports more widely, through team sponsorship or wider industry development.

Another major Olympic player to have occupied the esports world is Intel, itself a company sponsoring many kinds of innovation in sports technology. For instance, Intel is also involved with drone racing, a rapidly evolving industry occupying large arenas around the world and integrating computer gaming dynamics. Its drone work and Intel's esport activity at PyeongChang 2018 can be seen as part of its wider strategy to bring innovation into the Olympic programme, across a range of contexts:

> Intel announced a long-term technology partnership to bring the company's leading technology to enhance the Olympic Games through 2024. Intel technology will show viewers the future of the Olympic Games – where greatness is experienced with Intel True VR, esports reaches a world stage, drones take wonder to new heights and 5G powers a connection that's faster and stronger than ever. With Intel technology, fans can do more than just watch the Olympic Games, they can experience them.
>
> *(Intel, 2018)*

It is no coincidence that a number of these Olympic partner headlines around esports innovation are released during the Olympic Games itself, seen by sponsors as a chance to tell their innovation stories to the world. Perhaps the best example of this can be found in Intel's creation of drone choreographies during the Olympic Games Opening Ceremony. This set a world record at the PyeongChang 2018 Olympic Games by creating extraordinary displays in the sky using hundreds of small drones. The appearance of over 1000 drones, lit up in the night sky over PyeongChang, forming the shape of the Olympic rings, was perhaps one of the most historic occasions of how innovation is showcased at the Olympics, akin to the appearance of the flying jetpack "rocket man" at the Los Angeles 1984 Olympic Games Opening Ceremony (Newsman, 2012).

Together, these examples show how traditional sports sponsors are focusing their innovation on developing new audiences through esports gaming, and the growth of such communities is highly attractive in terms of sponsorship and advertising opportunities.

The gaming publishers: technology companies are closing in on sport

A range of media innovation companies are also aligning more with traditional sports events. A significant example of this occurred in 2014 when Coca-Cola began working with the esports industry (Gaudiosi, 2014). Subsequently, it has launched the global EA Sports FIFA tournament called eCOPA Coca-Cola (Anekal, 2016), which is now a global event. Coca-Cola even has its own regular YouTube programme on esports. In addition, Coca-Cola launched the world's first virtual player sponsorship. The virtual FIFA character "Alex Hunter" was created as part of the game and was sponsored by Coca-Cola with a range of media used to publicise this global event. This example of gaming companies aligning with sports events and virtual players further blurs the boundaries between sponsorship deals between video gaming and major sponsors.

Video game publishers such as EA Sport have also been keen to align with traditional sporting events. For example, the FIFA eWorld Cup, which began as the FIFA Interactive World Cup in 2004, and which emerges out of existing FIFA events, has become one of the world's most sustained esports events. Furthermore, there is growing evidence of closely aligning the FIFA World Cup and the FIFA eWorld Cup, reiterating the proposition that esports are often rationalised as additional routes to establishing brand loyalty around traditional sports events, the long tail of a much wider drive towards promoting the principal brand values.

Gaming companies also report a close connection with the sports industry, as Senior Vice President Todd Palowski of Live Experiences at Blizzard reveals:

> When we look at the opportunity that esports is presenting us – relating to how we want to continue to be relevant and connect with our audience – we've taken a lot of learnings from traditional sport. . . . In the way that live experiences have been conducted for so many years, entertaining countless million sports fans around the world; we bought out best practises and brought them into how to run live events for esports. And we're also doing that as it relates to how to broadcast esports.
>
> *(Palowski cited in Elsam, 2018)*

The federations and the organising committees: co-development of game titles between traditional and gaming federations

In recent years, International Sports Federations have developed relationships with esports organisations in a variety of ways. Indeed, the Olympic programme was among the first to signal an interest in this through its collaboration with Games emerging since the 1984 Los Angeles Olympic Games. With the earliest Olympic gaming title called "Hyper Olympic '84" (International Arcade Museum, 2019), we see the beginnings of a long journey in working closely with the games industry through the creation of specific titles alongside each Games. Since then, the Olympic Games has always worked with various gaming companies, mostly recently Ubisoft with a version of its title Steep, "Road to the Olympics", which brought sports content into the portfolio of Games associated with the Olympics. In this case, the game developers worked with Olympic athletes to develop the content (Watters, 2018), but also, rather than create a completely new game, the Olympics benefits from the established player community of the Steep title, which was then developed further with Winter Games content.

Beyond the International Olympic Committee itself, in particular, the IAAF has worked with the International Esport Federation (IESF) to develop a programme of activity designed to nurture the lives of IAAF members. Also, in 2018, the IESF worked with World Taekwondo to release a mobile game inspired by the sport, developed by Swedish gaming company Hello There (World Taekwondo Federation, 2016). In this case, the characters' movements were informed by specific Olympic taekwondo moves and plans to showcase the game alongside WTF events as part of the collaboration. The IESF has also worked with the International Table Tennis Federation to develop an esport title as well (Rowbottom, 2017). The International Cycling Union (ICU) also announced an intention to create an esport World Championships (Cycling News, 2018). A number of other federations have also experimented with gaming titles, such as the International Handball Federation, which worked with Neutron Games to develop "IHF Handball Challenge", in 2011. Finally, and perhaps the most well-known ISF to involve itself in having established the esport industries is FIFA. With its "260 million players" (Elsam, 2019) and an officially licensed title which dates back to 1993, it is indisputably the longest running sports title to enjoy a federation endorsement and is among the largest computer game communities in the world.

There is also evidence of sports federations integrating principles of computer game design and hybrid spectator experience, perhaps the best example of which is found within Formula E racing. Since its inception, Formula E has sought to innovate digitally and includes such things as 'fanboosts', which involves giving fans the opportunity to vote for their favourite driver and award them an extra boost of power during the race. The five drivers with the most FANBOOST votes are awarded a significant burst of power, which they can deploy in a 5 second window during the second half of the race. You can vote to FANBOOST your favourite driver in the 6 days prior to, and leading up to 15 minutes into, each race (Formula E, 2018).

Fans do this via the Formula E mobile app, using Twitter, or by accessing the Formula E website. Such examples are one of many others that Formula E has sought to implement to gamify the viewing experience. In 2018, Formula E announced partnership with Virtually Live, which provides real-time virtual reality ghost racing alongside events. In the 2018–2019 season, Formula E also introduced the 'hyperboost', which would allow a driver to receive a performance boost during the race, by adopting a non-racing line to "catch stars", rather like in Mario racing (Kalinauckas, 2018).

Elsewhere in racing, efforts have been made to develop the professional gamer experience with the professional driver, as described by Nissan's gamer-to-racer programme:

> NISMO PlayStation® GT Academy is an international virtual-to-reality contest by Nissan, PlayStation® and Polyphony Digital since 2008 that allows the best Gran Turismo players to compete for the once-in-a-lifetime opportunity to become a real-life professional racecar driver. . . . Any player who proves his or her skill in the virtual world has a chance to go wheel-to-wheel in a real race car on a real circuit to achieve the grand prize – a spot on the Nissan racing team, and all the training and licensing needed to race in international events.
>
> *(Sony Interactive Entertainment Ltd, n.d.)*

The Olympic movement itself is also critical to these transformations. With its Charter's mission firmly rooted in the ambition to create Games that are for the youth of the world, the IOC's wider activities to include sports within the Olympic programme, which have a younger participation base, is indicative of the wider shift that leads to growing interest in esports. Indeed, the Youth Olympic Games may also be seen as a central component of these aspirations. During Buenos Aires 2018, esports found its way into programming content within the Olympic Channel, which interviewed gamer Jake Lyon, who argued the case for Olympic inclusion (Olympic Channel, 2018).

Indeed, in December 2018, the 7th Olympic Summit held by the IOC (2018) tabled esports specifically, indicating that, not only should it be a strategic interest of the Olympic movement, but that there are formats of esports that should be explored specifically by sports federations, especially those that connect with a federation's principal brand. In this way, the IOC has signalled the desire to support virtual versions of sports, the effects of which we are beginning to see emerge around federations. It states that "The Summit encourages the IFs to explore the potential benefits and applications of the electronic and virtual versions of their sports" (IOC, 2018). Whether such titles will achieve the popularity of major esports titles such as Fortnite, League of Legends, or Dota 2 is unclear, but the weight of the association with sports may develop such communities of players. Yet, it's possible also that sports federations find titles that fit in a variety of ways, either in terms of the values of the sport, or specific types of movements within the game and this looser definition of what constitutes an association may be the more effective way to pursue affiliations. Such titles may be among the most compelling first esports to have medals events within the Olympic programme and there is a direct route towards such outcomes by ensuring that federations have oversight in terms of governance and selection. Moreover, while there has yet to be an Olympic Games to present medals for esports competitions, the 2018 Asian Games included esports as a demonstration event within the programme, a programme which reveals further cooperation between the esports industry and the Olympic movement:

> Esports is a demonstration sport at the 18th Jakarta-Palembang Asian Games 2018 this August. The competition, co-organized by the Olympic Council of Asia (OCA), Asian Electronic Sports Federation (AESF) and the Indonesia Asian Games Organizing Committee (INASGOC), will feature six events.
>
> *(Asian Electronic Sports Federation, 2018)*

Moreover, esports featured as a medal sport in the 2019 Southeast Asian Games, the first occasion for such activity to be sanctioned by the IOC (Ronquillo and Ansis, 2018).

Conclusion: worlds align

The likely first occurrence of esports during the Olympic or Paralympic Games fortnight will take place during Paris 2024, as the World Sailing Federation produces plans for integrating esport elements into its Olympic programme through its game Virtual Regatta. While this is unlikely to be a medal event, it reveals a major shift in the integration of esports content into established sports federation programming time and a clear route forward towards embracing gaming titles that are created in the service of the sports industry more widely, rather than just being a component of the computer games industry.

The growth of esports is central to the alignment of these various financial stakeholders of sports. In recent years, esports prize money and spectators has grown considerably, with tournaments featuring large financial prizes, helping esports to be worth an estimated $1.5 billion by 2020 (Dunn, 2017). This figure does not include esports-related betting, which is also very substantial given the huge audiences tournaments attract both physically, recorded and live streamed through services such as YouTube and Twitch.TV. Prize pools continue to rise, with the International 2018 esports tournament offering a prize pool of $25 million. Other competitions, such as the battle arena game Dota 2 have a £6.7 million prize pool. This compares to the FIFA soccer series (FIFA eWorld Cup) at £193,000 prize money, but this is growing.

In terms of Paralympic players, some disabled players see esports as a great equaliser, enabling them to play on the same level. For example, Mike 'BrolyLegs' Begum learned to play video games without legs or hands and has gone on to enjoy a successful esports career. He said, "places I thought were never possible to go to because of my disability became a reality in competing in fighting games" (Begum, cited in Winkie, 2017). This provides another dimension for players to be able to compete through esports in the Olympics in new ways. Whilst Mike could not enter a traditional Paralympic or Olympic fighting tournament, he can do so through esports with fighting games such as Street Fighter.

Despite the evidence that the worlds of sport and esport are aligning, particularly through the actions of their financial stakeholders, there are further considerations beyond those we outline which provide additional reasons to explore the integration of esport and traditional sports. First, the world of esports is still developing and there are already indicators that its future may look more like traditional sports than traditional computer game playing. Whereas the latter involves mostly sitting in front of a screen playing with a controller or keyboard, the Samsung Pavilion at the Olympic Games included a series of sports simulators which speak to the way in which the future of esport may become a much more physical activity. Indeed, examining the emergence of other gymnasia phenomena such as Les Mills The Trip, which locates a spinning class within a 180 degree virtual world, and even the rise of mobile fitness experiences and Strava virtual runs, reveal just how quickly this environment of gamified experiences is changing. In this respect, one highly compelling dimension of aligning esports and traditional sports has to do with this wider range of stakeholders that exist around the development of simulation technology.

A critical component to this is the emergence of the data-driven economy, which pervades many sectors within society, including sport. Within esport environments, so much more can be predicted about consumer habits and behaviours, compared with physical world sports. Spectators become data points in a cloud, identifiable, trackable, and possible to target with ever more precise advertising and nudge initiatives, designed to promote engagement, purchasing, and further consumption. Similarly, the playing field can be more easily monetised, as computer-generated imagery can easily be manipulated to create more targeted advertising. These aspirations are not new to sports. If one examines even just the Olympic Games over the last 30 years, achieving further precision in how to produce effective advertising has been a crucial determinant of the Olympic industry's economic wealth, if not by direct funding by sponsors, then by the indirect benefit accrued by the sale of advertising space by rights-holders.

Esports therefore represents the ideal environment in which to continue to design effective systems of monetisation, where even conversations between people can be monetised. This is vastly different from traditional sport. For example, if a spectator at a live sport match physically interacts with another spectator, then it is likely that the event owner has no idea that this happened and no opportunity to develop insights from those interactions. Yet, if a virtual spectator is located within an online streaming platform or other virtual reality, interacting with others, then conversations will happen within a data cloud, which can then generate insights into your interests, behaviour, attention capacity, and much more. While the reduction of sports culture to data points in a cloud is not terribly desirable, it is another compelling explanation for why esports has a future in all sports. The economic foundation of sport relies on the capacity to effectively exploit data to generate enough value for rights-holders or sponsors to invest.

The boundaries between esports and traditional sports players are continuing to blur. For example, English football clubs Manchester City and West Ham football clubs have each been experimenting with and embracing esports by signing professional FIFA soccer players to represent them in tournaments. Many of the major European football leagues and MLS in America also have their own esports leagues.

Whilst the English and other European football clubs are entering esports through the EA FIFA Soccer game route, other clubs are taking a more holistic view of esports. Santos FC in

Brazil for example have taken the step of carefully learning about the esports industry through working with partners and then creating tournaments in some of the top esports games including League of Legends, Counter Strike, and Pro Evolution Soccer. This also included employing esports players in these different games to represent their sports brand at tournaments to inspire and engage new and younger fans.

The esports calendar also has its own established industry of live events, driven by such organisations as the Electronic Sports League and individual title owners; just like traditional sports, esports has a huge range of live competitions. Even architects are designing bespoke arenas for esports competition, principles of which are also invigorating wider principles of sports arena design. For instance, the mega-event company Populous opened the world's first dedicated esports arena in Texas in 2018 (Populous, 2018).

In sum, as major financial stakeholders around sports become esport investors, this has an impact on the willingness of federations to seek alliances with esports and these conditions are what provide the most compelling case for why esports are likely to enter the Olympic and Paralympic programme. The alternative is for traditional sports to risk irrelevance as more and more of our past-times become ever more exciting through the integration of digital experiences.

References

Anekal, M. (2016). Coca-Cola eSport is on a Tear. *The Next Level.* Available at: https://medium.com/tnlmedia/coca-cola-esports-is-on-a-tear-92945c4eddbd.

Asian Electronic Sports Federation. (2018). *Road to Asian games.* Hong Kong: Asian Electronic Sports Federation.

Bernando, N. (2016). How can broadcasters use Esports to bring millennials back to TV? *MIP Trends.* Available at: https://mipblog.com/2016/12/how-broadcasters-can-use-esports-to-bring-millennials-back-to-tv/.

Chang, C. (2016). How the Olympics lost millennials. *The New Republic.* Available at: https://newrepublic.com/article/136096/olympics-lost-millennials.

Collins, Y. (2018). Danish eSport team North have announced a partnership with Adidas. *Skysports.* Available at: https://www.skysports.com/more-sports/esports/news/34214/11348168/danish-esport-team-north-have-announced-a-partnership-with-adidas.

Cooper, C. (2018). The rise of eSports. *Broadcast Now.* Available at: https://www.broadcastnow.co.uk/tech/the-rise-of-esports/5128149.article.

Dunn, J. (2017). Competitive video gaming will be a $1.5 billion industry by 2020, researchers say. *Business Insider.*

Elsam, S. (2018). IOC forum: NBC, YouTube, and Blizzard execs on what works and what doesn't in broadcasting esports. *The Esports Observer.*

Elsam, S. (2019). *FIFA's fight to join the "big three" of esports. gamesindustry.biz.* Available at: https://www.gamesindustry.biz/articles/2019-01-08-over-300-people-are-working-on-esports-at-ea-the-rapid-rise-of-fifa-pro-gaming.

Farrand, S. (2018). UCI creates esports rules and world championships. *Cycling News.* Available at: https://www.cyclingnews.com/news/uci-to-create-esports-rules-and-world-championships/.

Gaudiosi, J. (2014). Coca-Cola: Why eSports is important. *AList Daily.*

Intel. (2018). Intel at the Olympic Games. Jan. 29. *Intel Newsroom.* Available at: https://newsroom.intel.com/press-kits/intel-olympic-games/#gs.4luxcw.

Intel. (2019). Intel Technology propels Olympic Games Tokyo 2020 into the future. *Intel Newsroom.* Available at: https://newsroom.intel.com/news-releases/intel-2020-tokyo-olympics/#gs.4lv0gw.

International Arcade Museum. (2019). *Hyper Olympic '84 by Konami.* Available at: https://www.arcade-museum.com/game_detail.php?game_id=8166.

International Olympic Committee. (2018). *Communique of the 7th Olympic Summit.* Available at: https://www.olympic.org/news/communique-of-the-7th-olympic-summit.

International Paralympic Committee. (2017). *Rio 2016 Paralympics smash all TV viewing records.* Mar. 16. Bonn: International Paralympic Committee.

Kalinauckas, A. (2018). Formula E's 'Mario Kart' plan formalised for 2018/19 season by FIA. *Autosport.*
Massaad, J. (2017). Esports to be discussed for 2024 Olympic Games. *The Esports Insider.*
Miah, A. (2017). *Sport 2.0: Transforming sports for a digital world.* Cambridge, MA: MIT Press.
Newsman. (2012). Who was the Rocket Man at the Los Angeles Olympics 1984? *GQ Magazine.*
Olympic Channel. (2018). *2018 Youth Olympic Games.*
Populous. (2018). Esports Stadium Arlington debuts as Esports' largest, most robust venue in America. *Populous.*
Ring, O. (2017). Vorsprung durch Astralis – Audi enters esports. *Esports Insider.*
Ronquillo, R. and Ansis, J.C. (2018). Esports included as official medal sport in SEA Games for first time. *ESPN.*
Rowbottom, M. (2017). ITTF and IeSF sign agreement to create a table tennis esports World Championship. *Inside the Games.*
Sony Interactive Entertainment Ltd. (n.d.) Gran Turismo Academy.
Tran, K. (2018). Publishers turn away from Facebook instant articles. *Business Insider.* Available at: https://www.businessinsider.com/publishers-turn-away-from-facebook-instant-articles-2018-2.
Watters, C. (2018). Olympic athletes lend their expertise to steep road to the Olympics. *XBox Wire.*
Winkie. (2017). For disabled gamers like BrolyLegs, esports is an equalizer. *Vice Sports.*
World Taekwondo Federation. (2016). World Taekwondo Federation announces strategic collaboration with Swedish game developer Hello There, WT.

16

Organizing the Olympic Games

Milena M. Parent

Introduction

Which event is more complex to organize? The month-long, countrywide (and even three countries for the 2026) FIFA World Cup with 32 to 48 teams competing or the 16-day Olympic Games with 206 National Olympic Committees (NOCs) participating in 28 different sports? From a complexity point-of-view, organizing the Olympic Games wins out as (Summer) Olympic Games organizers must deal with not one sport and the international federation (IF), but 28 sports and IFs. This means there are 28 different fields of play, 28 different rules and regulations for the field of play, and 28 different IF needs and desires. And yet, the core process of organizing an Olympic Games is the same as the FIFA World Cup, which is the same as a national or a local sport event. All events follow a basic timeline which moves from bidding to planning, implementation, and wrap-up (cf. Parent, 2008). Figure 16.1 depicts an example of this lifecycle, each section of which we will review in this chapter.

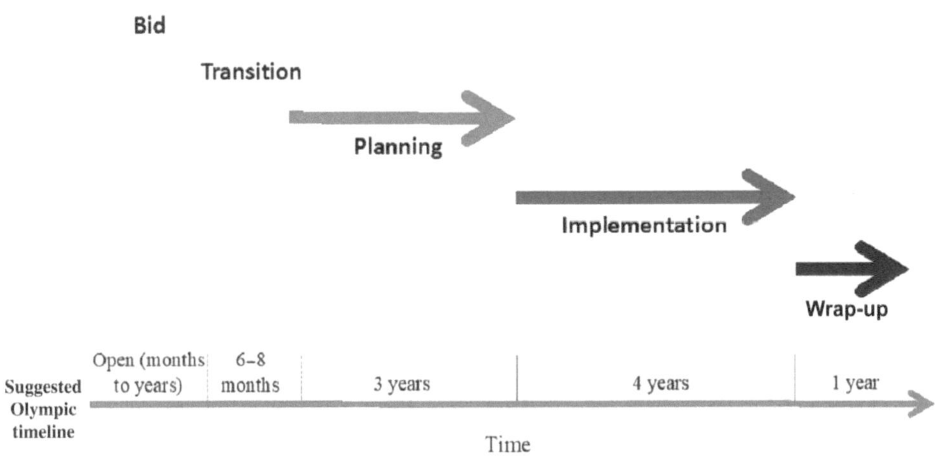

Figure 16.1 The lifecycle of an Olympic (Winter) Games and other sports events

Before doing so, however, two points are worth mentioning. First, the International Olympic Committee's (IOC) Agenda 2020 (IOC, 2014) now affects the organizing of the Olympic (Winter) Games. More precisely, the IOC (2014) suggested 40 (i.e. 20 + 20) recommendations covering the bid process, Games costs, Olympic movement sustainability, inter-Games rights holders cooperation, inter-organizational relationships, gender equality, protecting and supporting clean athletes, promoting values-based sport and education, good governance, sport and culture, and reviewing IOC membership and commissions.

Following Agenda 2020, and associated gigantism and debt criticisms, the IOC presented a revised planning timeline for how the organizing committee-IOC partnership would work, as well as ways to reduce the costs of the Games. The document, called The New Norm (IOC, 2018; Olympic News, 2018), included 118 recommendations to revise the requirements and services for the bidding and hosting of the Games. For example, recommendations dealt with village models, transportation optimization, venue sharing between IFs, and operational systems sharing between Games editions. Whereas Agenda 2020 focused on IOC-led initiatives, The New Norm looked to engage and put responsibility on NOCs, IFs, broadcasters, and The Olympic Partner (TOP) programme sponsors to work with host cities to foster affordability, benefits, and sustainability.

Second, since the 2008 Olympic Games and 2010 Olympic Winter Games, organizing the Paralympic Games has been fully integrated into the Olympic Games organizing committee, which means the same group organizes both the Olympic and Paralympic Games. The New Norm (IOC, 2018) also includes the Paralympic Games in its measures. Nevertheless, as there are some differences in the Paralympic world compared to the Olympic world, in this chapter, we will focus on aspects specific to organizing the Olympic Games.

Bidding

The bid committee is usually composed of a group of business, political, and sport elites within a region (Hautbois, Parent and Séguin, 2012). Past Olympic bids have often been started by businesspersons, usually men with real estate interests (Shaw, 2008). It is important to note that, technically, the bid committee is a distinct organization from the future organizing committee. The bid committee's goal is to obtain the right to host a given edition of the Olympic Games. Whether or not it is successful, it will cease to exist within six to 12 months of finding out which candidate city was successful.

In this section, I review reasons why cities/regions want to bid, as well as current critiques which have led to cities pulling out of the bid race, before presenting the IOC's new bidding process. I end this section by highlighting key success factors for those cities who wish to go all the way.

Bid reasons

According to Emery (2002), the top three reasons cities bid for sports events are (1) to promote sport; (2) economic development; and (3) to increase the host region's profile internationally. Other top reasons include increasing the number of and/or renovating/updating facilities, promoting health and fitness, and stimulating tourism. For example, Beijing (China) hosted the 2008 Olympic Games in part to tell the world China had 'arrived' on the international stage, while the hosting of the 2022 Olympic Winter Games will show the world China has matured. In turn, London hosted the 2012 Olympic Games to reinvigorate its image towards a more youthful and innovative one.

However, research behind these reasons does not necessarily support the idea of using the Olympic Games as a vehicle for garnering some of these benefits. For instance, research has demonstrated the Olympic Games do not increase the number of new sport participants; instead, findings demonstrate existing sport participants may become more deeply engaged in sport (i.e. go to higher/more elite levels of sport) (cf. Taks et al., 2014; Weed et al., 2015). This is not to say that it isn't possible for the Olympic (Winter) Games to promote sport participation; often, the issue is one of limited infrastructure, human resource and financial capacity of the local clubs – they simply cannot accept a large influx of new members (Parent, 2018).

Likewise, researchers continue to find methodological faults with economic impact measurement approaches, rendering bid/organizing committees', event rights holders', and politicians' statements about large positive impacts questionable (cf. Crompton and Lee, 2000; Preuss, 2005; Taks et al., 2011). At best, one needs to divide by 10 (and sometimes up to 100) the number provided by event promoters to get a more realistic picture of the potential economic impact of an event. Having said this, there are potential economic development opportunities that take years to be realized. For example, Barcelona, Spain hosted the 1992 Olympic Games. An unintended and unplanned consequence of this hosting was that Barcelona became the number one destination for international conferences and meetings after the Games, and the number one vacation destination for United Kingdom residents. These unintended and unplanned outcomes boosted tourism and the flow of new money into the local economy. In contrast, Calgary (Canada), which hosted the 1988 Olympic Winter Games, sees higher economic impacts and city awareness from hosting the annual Calgary Stampede than from having hosted the one-off 1988 Games (see Ritchie and Smith, 1991).

Problems associated with bids in today's context

The issues I describe earlier, along with cost overruns, gigantism critiques, and white elephants (empty infrastructure post-Games), have led many potential cities and regions to pull out of Olympic (Winter) Games bid processes. For example, Oslo (Norway) pulled out of the 2022 race, as did Stockholm (Sweden), Krakow (Poland), and Lviv (Ukraine), leaving only Beijing (China) and Almaty (Kazakhstan). For 2024, Boston (USA), Budapest (Hungary), Rome (Italy), and Toronto (Canada) dropped out of the race, leaving only Paris (France) and Los Angeles (USA), which were handed the 2024 and 2028 Games by the IOC in an effort to provide some stability for the coming decade. In turn, Innsbruck (Austria), Sion (Switzerland), Sapporo (Japan), Graz (Austria), and Calgary (Canada) pulled out of the 2026 race, leaving only two candidate cities. Bidding itself also became expensive and labour intensive: the UK spent £30 million to bid for the 2012 London Olympic Games, compared to £12–15 million FIFA World Cup bids (for 2006 and 2018) and £1 million for the Rugby World Cup (Walters, 2008). Some, like Lenskyj (1996), argue the bid losers are the real winners, as they can garner promises of project realization even if the bid is unsuccessful and at the very least, put their name on the proverbial international map.

Many of the cities noted have pulled out because local referenda were negative; residents simply did not believe paying that much to host a big party for 16 days would bring them economic and other benefits. Other cities pulled out due to a lack of government support related to financing the Games and guaranteeing any potential deficits. The trend seems to have started with Denver pulling out of hosting the 1976 Olympic Winter Games in 1972 due to economic and environmental concerns (Sims, 2017). Individuals leading anti-Olympic movements, such as Chris Shaw for the 2010 Vancouver Games (unsuccessful campaign) or Chris Dempsey (see www.nobostonolympics.org/) for the 2024 Olympic Games (successful campaign) cite valid reasons, such as these events benefiting the rich in the city (e.g. through increased property values benefiting land owners). Thus, bid committees and the IOC need to address these issues head on if they hope to be successful in the bid process. In fact, the IOC decided in June 2019 to ask future bid cities to hold referenda *before* submitting their bids (Morgan, 2019b).

A key issue is that the IOC has been slow to react to criticism. It has been reactive instead of proactive. It only started talking about taking a partnership approach to bidding – as opposed to a wait and see, bidders do all the work, incur significant expenses, and compete in an auction or race approach – in 2018 with its New Norm and the site visit to Calgary (see also Strashin, 2017). It is critical for the IOC as well as bid committees that they clearly, explicitly, and succinctly state what the planned benefits of hosting this event will be. Stating the event will bring economic and social benefits is not enough. What will these supposed economic and social benefits be exactly? What is the plan to realize them? And how will economic risks and potential cost overruns be mitigated? What will the Games bring to the host city/region and what will the host city/region bring to the Games? Simple, consistent communication and messaging is critical.

IOC bid process

Based on the failed referenda and ongoing criticisms as noted, the IOC adjusted the bidding process and timeline for the Olympic Games following Agenda 2020, The New Norm, and additional changes in June 2019. The revised approach was first implemented for the 2024/2028 Olympic Games and 2026 Olympic Winter Games host city selection processes (IOC, 2017a). The process now includes an ongoing and permanent Continuous Dialogue Stage followed by a Targeted Dialogue Stage (Bogner, 2019; IOC, 2019, n.d.; Morgan, 2019c). While host city elections used to be held seven years before the Games, now, election timing is flexible so the IOC can react more quickly to opportunities or take more time if issues arise. Figure 16.2 provides an overview of the new Olympic bidding process.

The ongoing, permanent, and non-committal "Continuous Dialogue Stage" sees a shift in the IOC's approach, whereby the IOC's experts now work with interested parties, be they cities or regions, to develop a potential bid plan that works for the city and aligns with Olympic Agenda 2020 (Bogner, 2019). After the IOC's Future Hosts (Summer or Winter) Commission provides its feasibility assessment of the interested cities, and together with an assessment of public support, the IOC's Executive Board will instruct the Future Hosts Commission on which interested parties are allowed to enter into an edition-specific targeted dialogue (Bogner, 2019; IOC, 2019, n.d.). For instance and though not formally named as such at the time, for the 2026 Olympic Winter Games bids, Erzurum (Turkey) was dropped on October 8th 2018, while Calgary (Canada), Milan-Cortina d'Ampezzo (Italy), and Stockholm (Sweden) were put forward as preferred hosts.

During the "Targeted Dialogue Stage," the IOC's experts continue to work with the preferred host(s) to help align the proposed Games plan with the cities'/regions' long-term plans. Over an estimated 6–12 months, preferred hosts will answer a shortened candidate questionnaire and provide the host guarantees, and the Future Hosts Commission may visit the preferred host(s) if it is deemed necessary (Bogner, 2019). The Future Hosts Commission will prepare and submit a report to the IOC Executive Board. At this time, the IOC Executive Board will either put forward one or more preferred hosts for an edition of the Games for consideration (election) by the IOC Session or will reject the preferred host(s) and return them to the Continuous Dialogue Stage (Bogner, 2019; IOC, n.d.). As such, the IOC Session may vote for a host much earlier than the traditional seven years – such as in the case of the 2028 Los Angeles Olympic Games – or it could be less than seven years – such as in the case of the 2022 and 2024 (Winter) Youth Olympic Games.

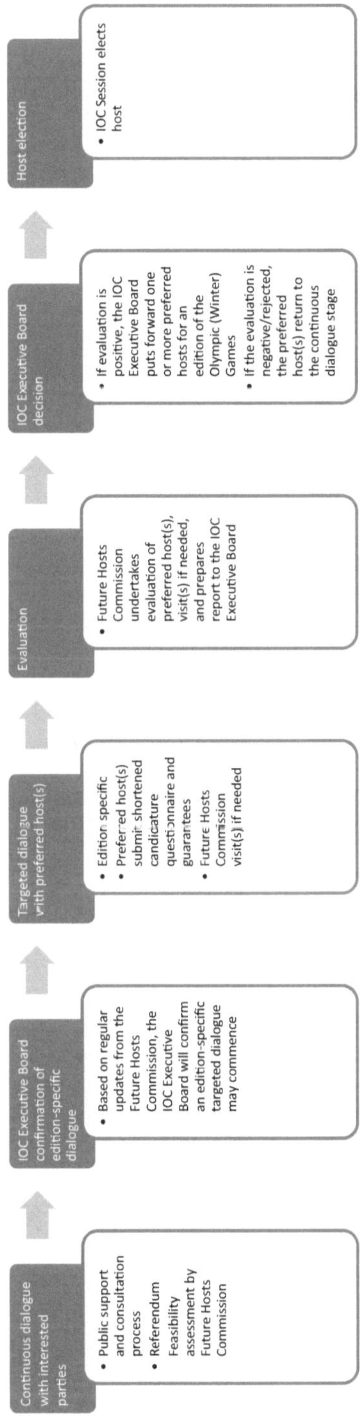

Figure 16.2 The new Olympic process

Source: Bogner (2019); IOC (2019, n.d.); Morgan (2019c)

Key success factors

So what does a bid committee need in order to be successful? At a minimum, the city/region and bid committee have to do their homework. They must complete a feasibility study, which includes reviewing and assessing the city's costs and potential economic impacts, infrastructure and fit-out requirements, hosting capabilities (accommodation for athletes, hotels, food preparation and distribution, volunteer requirements, VIP requirements, etc.), transportation capabilities, community support, and sport expertise (Masterman, 2004). They also need to really look at positioning the Games within their event portfolio (Ziakas, 2013) to understand how the Games can be leveraged to garner potential, sustainable legacies. Beyond this, there are internal, process, and external factors to consider in order to be successful (Parent and Smith-Swan, 2013):

- *Internal factors*: maximizing bid team composition (i.e. the experts around the table whom the IOC and IFs know and trust), showing the team and city are capable of hosting the event, and demonstrating real interest in bidding through past bid attempts;
- *Process factors*: understanding the bidding requirements as well as the formal and informal decision-making processes, not assuming IOC members are experts or use rational criteria when voting, customizing (in)tangible products/services to the Olympic movement, and exceeding expectations;
- *External factors*: knowing the bid's strengths and weaknesses relative to other bids (i.e. demonstrating your strengths to highlight [indirectly] weaknesses in the other bids), figuring out the agendas and power/influence of different stakeholders and IOC members, and understanding local, regional, and/or national policies.

Planning

As Figure 16.1 illustrates, the planning mode lasts about half the organizing committee's life. The IOC calls this mode the "Think and Design" phase (IOC, 2018). Before starting this mode, the successful bid committee must actually dissolve and the Organizing Committee for the Olympic Games (OCOG) will be created, usually as an independent non-profit organization or association. The OCOG will have a board of directors with representatives from the host governments (local, regional/state/provincial, and national/federal), national Olympic and Paralympic committees, IOC and IPC, and other key Games partners. However, in some cases, the OCOG may be a semi-public entity under the national government's leadership.

The OCOG is constituted and its board of directors as well as its key leader (i.e. the Chief Executive Officer or CEO) are appointed during the transition phase. Ideally, this phase lasts six to eight months. When it lasts longer (e.g. Athens 2004, Rio 2016), there often seems to be planning and delivery issues that linger throughout the OCOG's life. A good transition phase is pre-planned in the bid, often with some kind of agreement or memorandum of understanding between Games partners in the eventuality that the bid is successful. This was the case with the Vancouver 2010 Olympic Winter Games: the agreement signed between the key partners during the bid process set out the transition process, the composition of the board, the respective responsibilities of each partner, and conflict resolution procedures (Government of Canada et al., 2002; Parent, Rouillard and Leopkey, 2011; Parent, Rouillard and Naraine, 2017).

The planning mode includes developing the business plan, operational plan and divisional plans or work packages (for more information, see Parent, 2008; Parent and Smith-Swan, 2013). As planning an Olympic (Winter) Games can take a whole book (e.g. Parent and Smith-Swan, 2013), in this section, I provide a brief overview of key leadership, organizing committee structure, project management, financial management, human resource management (HRM), and stakeholder management aspects.

Leadership

Being the leader of an Olympic (Winter) Games is a tough job. Until the 2010 Olympic Winter Games, no leader had managed to go from running the bid committee all the way to the closing of the Games. Usually, the bid leader and OCOG leader were different and, often, leaders changed during the OCOG's planning and/or implementation modes. But John Furlong (2010 Olympic Winter Games) and then Lord Sebastian Coe (2012 Olympic Games) managed to lead successful bid committees and last throughout the planning and hosting of their respective Games.

The OCOG leader should be charismatic, transformational (focused on helping OCOG staff and volunteers), authentic, flexible, and adaptive (cf. Parent, Olver and Séguin, 2009; Parent and Smith-Swan, 2013). To be a successful OCOG leader, you need a variety of skills including networking (relationship building and maintenance), access to various resources (especially financial and human), HRM skills, credibility as a leader of an international multi-sport event, communication/public relations skills, organizational skills, financial skills, and legacy planning and management skills (Parent, Beaupré and Séguin, 2009). Which skills are used will depend on the OCOG's mode, but networking and HRM skills are consistently needed (Parent, Beaupré and Séguin, 2009). And within the network aspect, we find political, business, and sport/event networks at play (Parent, Beaupré and Séguin, 2009).

Organizing committee structure

Along with developing the business plan, the leader's first task will be to set up the OCOG's organizational structure. Usually, the OCOG will start small with only the board, leader (CEO), and his/her senior executive team. But as the Games approach, the workforce (the human resources) will grow exponentially, especially within the last few months. The number of divisions and functional areas (FAs) or departments (e.g. accreditation, anti-doping, ceremonies, transportation, sport, legal, workforce, food and beverage, and event services) will also grow. Vancouver 2010, for example, had 53 FAs at its peak.

During the planning mode, the OCOG is headquarter-centred, meaning it has a relatively flat but growing structure, it is focused on strategy, and formed mainly of executives (Parent and Séguin, 2010). By the time the Games start, the OCOG has transformed into a venue-centred structure, where venue teams called Vteams run each venue like mini OCOGs. These Vteams are operationally focused and composed mainly of lower-level paid staff and volunteers (Parent and Séguin, 2010). Once the closing ceremonies are over, the OCOG returns to a headquarter-centred structure. But this time, it is operationally focused on transferring legacies and closing the books (see the wrap-up mode section).

Project management

Planning and hosting an Olympic (Winter) Games is about project management. Like other projects (e.g. construction and movies), Olympic (Winter) Games include technical, resource, and organizational complexity. Time, quality, and cost must be managed. Hence, project management procedures apply, such as creating a work breakdown structure (WBS) and determining milestones as well as the critical path (for more information, see Parent and Smith-Swan, 2013).

London 2012, for instance, had a project management division. This allowed Lord Coe and his executives to ensure all divisions are coordinated and working towards the same goal.

Financial management

OCOGs have two types of budgets, which are plans in themselves, just plans in the form of numbers. The *operational budget* covers all activities associated with putting on the Games themselves. In contrast, the *capital budget* covers the infrastructure needed to put on the Games.

OCOGs have different sources of revenues available to them. The IOC will actually share a percentage of its sponsorship and broadcasting revenues to the OCOG from its TOP sponsors and broadcasting deals. These amounts are usually known by the bid committee and typically constitute the largest part of the OCOG's operational budget. Next, OCOGs can obtain national sponsors in categories not covered by TOP sponsors, as well as government grants/funding. Government grants often form the majority of the capital budget, as the infrastructure will remain post-Games and likely be owned by the respective government. Olympic tickets are also a source of revenue, as are merchandise and food and beverage sales.

Human resource management

Contrary to popular belief, most hires occur within the last year before the opening ceremonies. In addition, there are different types of human resources found in OCOGs: paid staff, volunteers, secondees (employees loaned by another organization), contractors, and consultants (Parent and Smith-Swan, 2013). Together, these human resources form the workforce that will plan and implement the Games. Regardless of the type of human resource, they all go through an HRM process, from needs assessment analyses through to recruitment, training, evaluating, and recognizing the individuals (Parent and Smith-Swan, 2013).

Stakeholder management

Also contrary to popular belief, the OCOG does not do all the work to plan and host the Games by itself. The OCOG is actually at the centre of a network of stakeholders, which it coordinates. The various stakeholders include:

- Internal stakeholders: the *workforce* noted previously is considered a stakeholder as it must be managed by the board and leader;
- External stakeholders:
  - The *host governments*: local, regional/provincial/state, and national/federal;
  - The *community*: local residents and businesses, tourism commissions, community groups, schools and activists;
  - The *sport organizations*: local, regional, national, continental, and international sport clubs/organizations/federations, as well as the IOC and IPC;
  - The *media*: television broadcasters, the written press, radio, and internet/digital media;
  - The *delegations*: athletes, their entourage, and the mission staff; and
  - *Other stakeholders* such as the World Anti-Doping Agency, Court of Arbitration for Sport, United Nations, and various experts and consultants.

Having good relationships with these stakeholders is critical for the success of the Games. But, managing the stakeholder network and building these good relationships is not easy. As Parent and colleagues (2011) found, there are various issues associated with coordinating efforts for an Olympic Games, including contextual issues (funding, geography, political situation, time, and other resources) and other types of issues: accountability/authority, activation/leveraging, knowledge management, legal, operational, planning, power, relationships, social issues, structure, and turnover. The OCOG and its stakeholders can use various strategies to mitigate and/or resolve these issues, such as facilitating communication processes, using decision-making frames, fostering engagement, having a flexible approach, establishing formalized agreements, implementing human resource management procedures/principles, integrating strategic planning, and creating a structural framework (Parent, Rouillard and Leopkey, 2011).

A good strategy is to have individuals within the OCOG identified as liaisons for each stakeholder group or client. This facilitates the communication channels between the OCOG and stakeholder, allows for a relationship to develop, and helps decrease potential misunderstandings and mixed messages as one person is the proverbial file-holder.

Implementation

As Figure 16.1 illustrates, the implementation mode lasts about four years. The IOC calls this mode the "Plan, Train and Act" phase (IOC, 2018). In the implementation mode, OCOGs will transform the plans they created during the planning mode into specific venue plans. In other words, they 'venuize' the plans to be able to answer the question: what does a day in the life of _____ (insert a specific client, such as athlete, dignitary, volunteer, paid staff, or media, here) look like on this particular site? Following this venuization of plans, the actual Games take place. The implementation mode ends when the closing ceremonies conclude.

A key aspect of the implementation mode is the venues. OCOGs have to manage competition venues (the venues where the actual sport competitions occur) and non-competition venues (e.g. athletes' village, airport, training venues, and dignitary hotels). Within the venue portfolio of activities, we find site planning, operations, and logistics as key activities and FAs. Site planning refers to the look and function of the venue (Parent and Smith-Swan, 2013), the plans for which are started as far back as the bid phase. The New Norm recommends that multiple sports and federations should share a given venue (IOC, 2018), which increases the need for site planning as early as possible. Venue site plans are created using CADs (computer-assisted designs). CADs are critical for the proper coordination of all FAs' work during Games time.

Next, the Operations FA brings together the venue's individuals/stakeholders, procedures, and systems within a set of spatial and temporal constraints to offer different services to different client groups (Parent and Smith-Swan, 2013). These can include, for example, the technology operations centre and transportation systems. In turn, the Logistics FA is in charge of the timely coordination of people and other resources (mainly materials) for a given venue, in terms of delivery/commissioning and in terms of decommissioning. Logistics will consider the movement of people in and out of the venue, registration, ticketing and admission, money flows, procurement and supply-chain management, permits, and traffic management.

Come Games-time, a number of FAs kick their activities into high gear. While space limits the ability to go through the 50+ FAs, here are key ones to know (Parent and Smith-Swan, 2013):

- *Accommodations* is in charge of the accommodations reservation/booking and services for the Games' main clients (e.g. delegations and the Olympic Family);
- *Accreditation* is in charge of determining who can access each part of the Games and its venues. Having an accreditation means you are security cleared, and your accreditation card will indicate the venues and spaces in the venues you can access to perform your duties;

- *Ceremonies* is in charge of organizing and/or coordinating the various types of ceremonies found at the Games, such as the delegation welcome ceremony at the village, the opening and closing ceremonies, the victory ceremonies, and the flag raising ceremonies;
- *Event services* is the face of the Games with all its volunteers. It deals with crowd management (directing people in the right places and checking accreditations);
- *Food and beverage* provides the food and beverage services for all groups (e.g. athletes, dignitaries, and spectators) at all Games venues. It also deals with food contractors and sponsors;
- *Sport* deals with the technical side of the sport competitions, everything that occurs around and on the field-of-play;
- *Sport production* deals with the spectator experience during the sport competitions (e.g. the entertainers and the announcers);
- *Ticketing* deals with the distribution and selling of tickets;
- *Transportation* deals with all modes of Games-specific transportation (e.g. athletes, media, and dignitary transportation) as well as coordinating with public transportation authorities; and
- *Venue management* integrates the various FAs' plans during the planning mode and coordinates the FAs in a given venue during Games-time.

Wrap-up

After the closing ceremonies have ended, the wrap-up mode begins and it lasts about one year. During this time, the OCOG will (Parent and Smith-Swan, 2013):

- Decommission the venues and transform them into their post-Games uses;
- Debrief with the IOC and the next host of the Games as part of the Olympic Games Knowledge Management process;
- Write the final reports to the IOC and to Games partners (e.g. governments); and
- Transfer the resources left to create the legacies, which will need to be managed by another entity as the OCOG will cease to exist (see, for example, the 2010 Games legacy video by the IOC [2017b]). The potential legacies need to be planned from the bid phase, if not before (Leopkey and Parent, 2012, 2015, 2017).

Conclusion

As noted earlier, the IOC has typically been slow to respond to issues surrounding its Olympic Games. However, it has started taking steps and opening itself to alternative ways of doing, so to speak, where its Games are concerned. For instance, at its June 2019 Session, the IOC approved the changes noted earlier to the bidding process, the idea of multiple regions as one Games host, and the idea that athletes should be housed near their competition venues, which could mean a dispersion of the athletes, though the athletes would have the option of staying in the main Athletes' Village when not competing (Livingston, 2019).

Although such changes demonstrate a willingness to change on the IOC's part, such measures may (1) increase logistical and coordination challenges if multiple regions or countries are involved – just think of the potential transportation and immigration/visa issues between countries; and (2) dilute a key part of the Olympic Games, which is the atmosphere created in the Athletes' Village when all the countries' athletes are together for an extended period of time. Finally, the increasingly rapid technological changes and the ageing Olympic consumer demographic (or the need to capture the youth market) add a level of complexity that the Olympic movement decision-makers, generally older white males, must grapple with. That the IOC hosted an Olympism in Action Forum before the 2018 Youth Olympic Games in Buenos Aires, Argentina, to open the discussion on some of these issues is a step in the right direction. How well the IOC can accept criticism (i.e. not dismiss it), co-opt dissenting views from external individuals/groups/organizations, and act rapidly and proactively to change its ways of doing and stay with (or, better yet, get ahead of) the proverbial times will determine its continued relevance and ultimately its survival.

References

Bogner, M. (2019). New approach to future host elections [Webinar]. In the Olympic Studies Centre's *On the line with an expert*. Dec. 12.

Crompton, J.L. and Lee, S. (2000). The economic impact of 30 sports tournaments, festivals, and spectator events in seven U.S. cities. *Journal of Park & Recreation Administration*, 18(2), pp. 107–126.

Emery, P.R. (2002). Bidding to host a major sports event: The local organising committee perspective. *The International Journal of Public Sector Management*, 15(4), pp. 316–335.

Government of Canada, Government of British Columbia, City of Vancouver, Resort Municipality of Whistler, Canadian Olympic Committee, Canadian Paralympic Committee, et al. (2002). *Multiparty agreement for the 2010 Winter Olympic and Paralympic games*. Vancouver, Canada: Author.

Hautbois, C., Parent, M.M. and Séguin, B. (2012). How to win a bid for major sporting events? A stakeholder analysis of the 2018 Olympic Winter Games French bid. *Sport Management Review*, 15(3), pp. 263–275.

IOC. (2014). *Olympic Agenda 2020: 20 + 20 recommendations*. Lausanne, Switzerland: IOC.

IOC. (2017a). *Candidature process 2026 evolution*. Lausanne: IOC. Available at: https://www.olympic.org/videos/candidature-process-2026-evolution/.

IOC. (2017b). *Vancouver legacy: The games lives live here*. Lausanne: IOC. Available at: https://www.olympic.org/videos/vancouver-legacy.

IOC. (2018). *Infographic – New norm*. Lausanne: IOC.

IOC. (2019). *Future hosts commissions: Terms of reference*. Oct. 3. Lausanne: IOC.

IOC. (n.d.). *The evolution of future Olympic host elections: Six years of constant improvement*. Lausanne: IOC. Available at: https://www.olympic.org/future-host-election.

Lenskyj, H.J. (1996). When winners are losers: Toronto and Sydney bids for the summer Olympics. *Journal of Sport & Social Issues*, 20(4), pp. 392–410.

Leopkey, B. and Parent, M.M. (2012). The (neo) institutionalization of legacy and its sustainable governance within the Olympic movement. *European Sport Management Quarterly*, 12(5), pp. 437–455.

Leopkey, B. and Parent, M.M. (2015). Vancouver 2010 Olympic Winter Games: Modes of legacy network governance. In: R. Holt and D. Ruta, eds., *The Routledge handbook of sport and legacy: Meeting the challenge of major sports events*. London: Routledge, pp. 82–96.

Leopkey, B. and Parent, M.M. (2017). The governance of Olympic legacy: Process, actors and mechanisms. *Leisure Studies*, 36(3), pp. 438–451.

Livingston, R. (2019). *IOC Session approves significant changes to the Olympic bid process*. June 26. Available at: https://gamesbids.com/eng/summer-olympic-bids/future-summer-bids/ioc-session-approves-significant-changes-to-the-olympic-bid-process/.

Masterman, G. (2004). *Strategic sports event management: An international approach*. Oxford, UK: Elsevier.

Morgan, L. (2019a). *Bach suggests IOC could recommend a single city to host Olympic Games but dismisses claims it will end bidding contests*. June 14. Available at: https://www.insidethegames.biz/articles/1080633/bach-suggests-ioc-could-recommend-a-single-city-to-host-olympic-games-but-dismisses-claims-it-will-end-bidding-contests.

Morgan, L. (2019b). *IOC to ask cities to hold referendum before submitting Olympic bid under. changes to candidature process*. June 20. Available at: https://www.insidethegames.biz/articles/1080952/ioc-to-ask-cities-to-hold-referendum-before-submitting-olympic-bid-under-changes-to-candidature-process.

Morgan, L. (2019c). *Significant changes to Olympic bid process approved by IOC Session*. June 26. Available at: https://www.insidethegames.biz/articles/1081246/significant-changes-to-olympic-bid-process-approved-by-ioc-session.

Olympic News. (2018). *The new norm: It's a game changer [Press release]*. Feb. 6. Available at: https://www.olympic.org/news/the-new-norm-it-s-a-games-changer.

Parent, M.M. (2008). Evolution and issue patterns for major-sport-event organizing committees and their stakeholders. *Journal of Sport Management*, 22(2), pp. 135–164.

Parent, M.M. (2018). Les grands événements sportifs dans les villes nord-américaines: mythes et réalités. In: J. Fuchs, T. Michot and C. Parmantier, eds., *La ville et le sport*. Brest, France: Université de Bretagne Occidentale, pp. 147–156.

Parent, M.M., Beaupré, R. and Séguin, B. (2009). Key leadership qualities for major sporting events: The case of the world aquatics championships. *International Journal of Sport Management and Marketing*, 6(4), pp. 367–388.

Parent, M.M., Olver, D. and Séguin, B. (2009). Understanding leadership in major sporting events: The case of the 2005 World Aquatics Championships. *Sport Management Review*, 12(3), pp. 167–184.

Parent, M.M., Rouillard, C. and Leopkey, B. (2011). Issues and strategies pertaining to the Canadian governments' coordination efforts in relation to the 2010 Olympic Games. *European Sport Management Quarterly*, 11(4), pp. 337–369.

Parent, M.M., Rouillard, C. and Naraine, M.L. (2017). Network governance of a multi-level, multi-sectoral sport event: Differences in coordinating ties and actors. *Sport Management Review*, 20(5), pp. 497–509.

Parent, M.M. and Séguin, B. (2010). Change as routine? Understanding organizational change in Canadian major sporting events. In: *Paper presented at the International Federation of Scholarly Associations of Management*, Paris, France, July.

Parent, M.M. and Smith-Swan, S. (2013). *Managing major sports events: Theory and practice*. London: Routledge.

Preuss, H. (2005). The economic impact of visitors at major multi-sport events. *European Sport Management Quarterly*, 5(3), pp. 281–301.

Ritchie, J.R.B. and Smith, B.H. (1991). The impact of a mega-event on host region awareness: A longitudinal study. *Journal of Travel Research*, 30(1), pp. 3–10.

Shaw, C.A. (2008). *Five ring circus: Myths and realities of the Olympic Games*. Gabriola Island, Canada: New Society Publishers.

Sims, S. (2017). *How Bostonians defeated the Olympics*. Available at: https://www.citylab.com/equity/2017/06/how-bostonians-defeated-the-olympics/529155/.

Strashin, J. (2017). The Olympics have a host-city problem. *CBC Sports*. Available at: https://www.cbc.ca/sports/olympics/olympics-host-city-problem-1.4414207.

Taks, M., Green, B.C., Misener, L. and Chalip, L. (2014). Evaluating sport development outcomes: The case of a medium-sized international sport event. *European Sport Management Quarterly*, 14(3), pp. 213–237.

Taks, M., Kesenne, S., Chalip, L., Green, B.C. and Martyn, S. (2011). Economic impact analysis versus cost benefit analysis: The case of a medium-sized sport event. *International Journal of Sport Finance*, 6(3), pp. 187–203.

Walters, G. (2008). Bidding for major sports events: Key issues and challenges faced by sports governing bodies in the UK. *Birkbeck Sport Business Centre Research Paper Series*, 1(1).

Weed, M., Coren, E., Fiore, J., Wellard, I., Chatziefstathiou, D., Mansfield, L., et al. (2015). The Olympic Games and raising sport participation: A systematic review of evidence and an interrogation of policy for a demonstration effect. *European Sport Management Quarterly*, 15(2).

Ziakas, V. (2013). Planning and leveraging event portfolios: Towards a holistic theory. *Journal of Hospitality Marketing & Management*, 23(3), pp. 327–356.

17

Referendums at Olympic Games

Holger Preuß, Anja Scheu and Maike Weitzmann

Introduction

With 206 participating nations, the Olympic Games are the world's largest sporting event alongside the FIFA World Cup (Young and Abrahams, 2019). In the past two decades globalization, commercialization and professionalization have grown the event enormously and had a lasting impact on it. However, in the course of their transformation the Olympic Games have increasingly been confronted with problems that can be attributed primarily to gigantism (Chappelet, 2014). This started discussions in Western, democratic countries about the costs and benefits of the Olympic Games for the society (Schäper, 2017). As a result, politicians started referendums to better understand whether or not citizens agree to bid for the Olympic Games. The discussions about bidding focus on an uncertain cost estimation and presumed high cost overruns (in particular driven by questionable studies by Flyvbjerg, Stewart and Budzier, 2016 and the media), whereby high costs are often accompanied by unclear benefits. It is extremely difficult to compare the costs and benefits of the Olympic Games. While most costs can be quantified in monetary terms, many benefits are intangible and context-specific and therefore very difficult to measure and present. Thus, the costs cannot be directly compared with the benefits obvious to the consumer.

Agenda 2020, which International Olympic Committee (IOC) President Bach initiated in 2013 and which is now partly being implemented in concrete terms with the so called "New Norm", comes at the right time. The gigantism of the Games, their commercialization and the revelations of self-enrichment by individual officials repeatedly published via the media have led to a critical position against the organization of the Olympic Games in recent years. Additionally, there have been numerous aborted application processes, which have either been decided by politicians (e.g. Oslo 2022, Budapest 2024, Rome 2024) or failed due to the majority will of the population, determined by referendums (e.g. Hamburg 2024, Innsbruck 2026, Sion 2026, Calgary 2026, Vienna 2028). The number of cities applying to host the Olympic Games has fallen sharply in recent years (Könecke and de Nooij, 2017). Nevertheless, even in these Western, democratic countries, there are currently efforts to bid for the Olympic Games. The motives for this are manifold, whereby "national prestige", "image gain and position improvement in the global competition between metropolises", but also "personal profiling and power ambitions of individual politicians" (Güldenpfennig, 2017, p. 207) seem often to be in the foreground. Furthermore, in the past the organization of Olympic Games often served to accelerate the implementation of (controversial) urban development measures (Häußermann and Siebel, 1993; Matheson and Baade, 2004). These motives are particularly targeted by politicians, while the general population is for whatever reason skeptical about them. The power of the population when a city wants to bid for the Olympic Games should not be underestimated, since it is given decision-making power in the event of a referendum. For this reason, it is of great importance to deal decisively with this group of stakeholders.

Therefore, we want to scientifically illuminate the current problems and challenges of the Olympic Games as well as their referendums. The aim is to better understand the currently frequent rejections of the Olympic Games in the population of Western, democratic countries.

The next part will therefore deal with the citizens' referendums against Olympic Games. To this end, direct-democratic procedures and their influence variables will first be discussed in general, before the state of research on referendums and the Olympic Games will be outlined.

Influences on direct-democratic procedures and their significance for the Olympic Games

The number of referendums has increased in Western, democratic countries (Casella and Gelman, 2008). A "trend towards an increase in direct-democratic procedures" has been observed (Mittendorf, 2008, p. 82).

Democracy theorists attribute the advantage to direct-democratic procedures that, in contrast to representative democracy, the will of the citizen comes to bear abruptly and unadulteratedly (Barber, 2003). Schiller (2007) also considers referendums to be a suitable instrument for controlling elected representatives. Referendums also promote dialogue between government and people (Freitag and Wagschal, 2007). Ultimately, the use of direct-democratic procedures also contributes to the legitimacy of political decisions (Geißel, 2012). Nevertheless, they are usually perceived as an ungainly and unsatisfactory instrument. They also make no contribution to political democracy that they are supposed to make (Smith, 1975). Referendums are often supported by those who are dissatisfied with the political system or an upcoming project. They feel that they have no say in the political decision. Referendums therefore often reflect disappointment about democracy in sections of society (Bowler and Donovan, 2019). This problem is evident in the numerous referendums held in the past on independence from territories or countries, such as in Quebec (Canada) in 1980 and 1995, Scotland (Great Britain) in 2014 and Catalonia (Spain) in 2014 and 2017. Both referendums in Quebec and Scotland were negative, whereas both referendums in Catalonia were declared unconstitutional, although Catalan citizens voted for Catalonia's independence. The referendum on the withdrawal from the European Union of Great Britain in 2016, which was approved by the population, showed a similar result. As of 2019, the resignation has not yet taken place, as a large part of the population is dissatisfied with the election result. Just recently another referendum on legislative decisions was used. In May 2019 in Romania, 89% of the population voted against arbitrary justice when it comes to corruption suspects.

Overall referendums have a lower participation than in parliamentary elections. This causes a problem because a low participation rate can severely influence the result of a referendum. (Hajnal and Trounstine, 2005; Lutz, 2007). This can be illustrated by a simple example. It is assumed that with a population of 1,000, 60% are in favor of a project and 40% against. Since it is generally known among the population that the majority is in favor of the project, only 50% of the people who vote for the project go to the polls (n=300). The opponents of the project also know that they are in the minority, but 80% of the 400 opponents go to the polls (n=320) to set an example. Under these premises, 52% ultimately vote against and 48% in favor. The election result representing the population was thus turned around. The project is rejected, although the majority of the population would be for it. While the turnout for the Hamburg referendum for/against the 2024 Olympic bid was relatively high at 50.2% (Statistisches Amt für Hamburg und Schleswig-Holstein, 2015), it was only 28.9% (Focus, 2015) two years earlier in Munich for/against a 2022 Olympic bid. It could be demonstrated that the extent of political participation essentially depends on socio-economic or structural characteristics such as education, income or gender (e.g. Bödeker, 2012; Marg et al., 2013; Schäfer, 2010). With increased use of direct-democratic procedures, the differences in participation between social strata that already exist in representative procedures would thus be even greater (Schäfer and Schön, 2012). Participation researchers therefore criticize the representativeness of such surveys, as the results may be distorted. In turn, these problems can lead to a lower acceptance of the referendum results (Leininger and Heyne, 2017; Streicher, Schmidt and Schreyer, 2018). Leininger and Heyne (2017) conclude that a higher turnout would not necessarily radically change the outcome. Nevertheless, there are suggestions for improving the representativeness of referendums. Referendums usually prioritize votes because they are at the end of a process. A consultative model involving residents in all steps of the political process would emphasize the importance of voices (LeDuc, 2015). In addition, Kellison and Mondello (2012) propose linking effective organizational perception management to a referendum. This could be incorporated into the decision-making processes of 'no' voters and ultimately lead to a review of their own judgment. Another possible measure to increase voter turnout in such a referendum is to link voting to election dates. An overview of referendums based on referendums in Germany shows that the average turnout for referendums linked to election dates was 61.8%, compared to 34.1% for votes not linked to election dates (Rehmet, 2018).

Two other important factors that can influence the outcome of a referendum (e.g. referendum for/against a bid for the Olympics in Hamburg 2024) are timing and eligibility.

In the case of Olympic Games and the NIMBY (Not in my backyard)[1] effect (described later), it is worth questioning whether citizens of a bidding city should be the only ones to vote when a referendum for/against is taking place. This is especially pertinent given that Olympic Games are financed by all level of governments (e.g. municipal, federal, state) although not constitutionally provided for (BPB, n.d.) and as such taxpayers' money of an entire nation are used.

The timing of the Hamburg referendum for/against Olympic Games 2024 was subsequently criticized by supporters, as the financing of the Games was not clear at the time. This lack of clarity was for many a major reason for not supporting the Games (Nielsen, 2015). We argue that a referendum should only be held when the costs of the Games are clearly presented. However, according to the latest studies by Preuss, Andreff and Weitzmann (2019), this would mean that the referendum could only be held approximately four years before the Games, i.e. after the bid had been accepted. As such, the "sunk costs" incurred in the event of a negative referendum would be immensely high, i.e. the non-reversible costs that have already arisen as a result of the bidding process and the first years of preparation for the Games (Schaub, 1997).

The voters' size of territory, time of vote and mobilization of voter minorities have a decisive influence on the outcome of a referendum and distort the actual mood of the population. As demonstrated by Freitag, Vatter and Müller (2003), the direct-democratic procedures are more of a "brake than an accelerator" for an increase in government spending. Wagschal and Obinger (2000, p. 493) also found a "restraining effect on the level of government spending". Furthermore, the study by Moser and Obinger (2007) found that referendums tend to confirm the status quo rather than advocate government spending. These studies show the difficulty of legitimizing

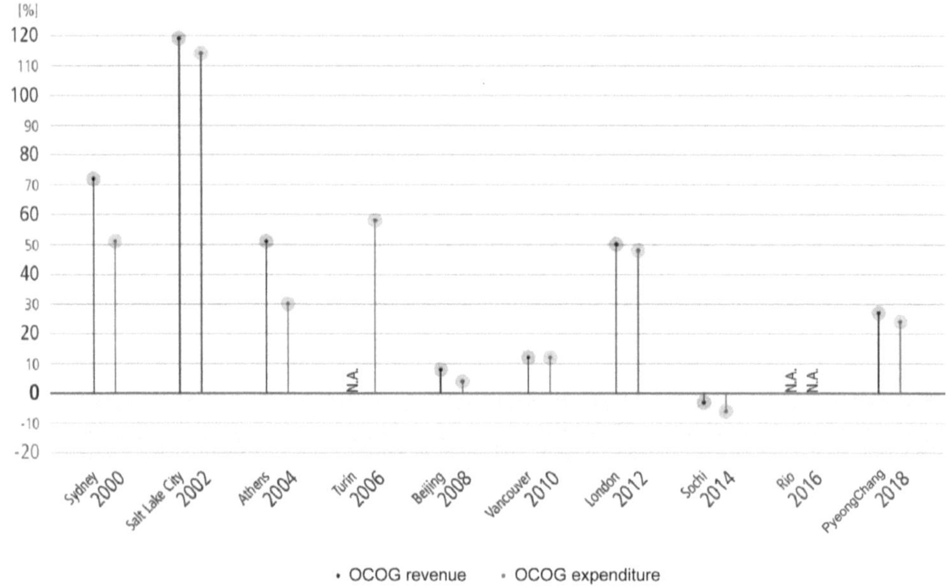

Figure 17.1 Revenue and cost overrun of Olympic organizational committees

Source: Preuss, Andreff and Weitzmann (2019, p. 115)

the Olympic Games by means of a referendum, provided that high infrastructure investments can be raised through tax revenues.

However, Preuss, Andreff and Weitzmann (2019, p. 115) argue that the organization of the Games is in itself associated with real cost overruns, but that the revenue overruns compensate for these. The revenues are generated mainly from private sources. As such, educating citizens is key for successful outcome.

The figure shows that revenue overruns were more likely to occur. Since the budgets of the organizing committees were all balanced at the beginning of a bid, a consistently slight profit can be demonstrated.

As explained in the introduction, the importance of regional direct-democratic procedures is increasing in Western, democratic countries, so that future applications for the Olympic Games will presumably continue to be linked to a referendum. The question therefore arises as to how the chances of a positive outcome to such a referendum can be increased.

Referendums at Olympic Games

The trend to use more direct-democratic procedures for decisions at the state and local levels has spread to the Olympic Games. One of the first statewide referendums for/against the hosting of the Olympic Games took place in 1972 for the 1976 Games. While the Games were already awarded to Denver in 1970, they were moved to Innsbruck following the referendum results in Denver (Coates and Wicker, 2015). Table 17.1 lists all the referendums that took place with regard to the Olympic Games. There is a trend towards negative outcomes of referendums with regard to bidding for the Olympic Games.

Table 17.1 Referendums at Olympic Games and Olympic Winter Games and their results

Positive/ negative decision	*City*	*Olympic Games/ Olympic Winter Games*	*Date of referendum*	*Result of referendum*	*Turnout*
-	Vienna (A)	Olympic Games 2028	2013-03-12	Yes: 28.06% No: 71.94%	31.54%
-	Calgary (CAN)	Olympic Winter Games 2026			
-	Sion (CH)	Olympic Winter Games 2026			
-	Innsbruck (A)	Olympic Winter Games 2026			
-	Graubünden (CH)	Olympic Winter Games 2026	2017-02-12	Yes: 39.9% No: 60.1%	51%
-	Hamburg (GER)	Olympic Games 2024	2015-11-28	Yes: 48.8% No: 51.6%	50.2%
-	Krakow (POL)	Olympic Winter Games 2022	2014-05-25	Yes: 30.3% No: 69.7%	36%
-	Munich (GER)	Olympic Winter Games 2022		Munich Yes: 47.8%/No: 52.1% Garmisch Yes: 48.88%/No: 51.56% Traunstein Yes: 40.33%/No: 59.67% Berchtesgadener Land Yes: 45.9%/No: 54.1%	
-	St. Moritz/Davos/ Graubünden (CH)	Olympic Winter Games 2022	2013-03-03	Yes: 47.3% No: 52.7%	59.14%
+	Oslo (NOR)	Olympic Winter Games 2022	2013-09-10	Yes: 53.6% No: 46.4%	66%
+	Munich (GER)	Olympic Winter Games 2018	2011-05-08	Yes: 58.07% No: 41.93%	59.64%
-	Bern (CH)	Olympic Winter Games 2010	2002-09-22	Yes: 21.2% No: 78.8%	
+	Vancouver (CAN)	Olympic Winter Games 2010	2003-02-22	Yes: 64% No: 36%	46%
-	Innsbruck (A)	Olympic Winter Games 2006	1997-03-09	Yes: 47.3% No: 52.7%	35.7%
+	Sion (CH)	Olympic Winter Games 2006	1997-06-08	Yes: 67% No: 33%	
-	Innsbruck (A)	Olympic Winter Games 2002	1993-10-17	Yes: 26.6% No: 73.4%	45.2%
+	Salt Lake City (USA)	Olympic Winter Games 1998 & 2002	1989-11-09	Yes: 57% No: 43%	

(*Continued*)

Table 17.1 (Continued)

Positive/ negative decision	*City*	*Olympic Games/ Olympic Winter Games*	*Date of referendum*	*Result of referendum*	*Turnout*
-	Aosta Valley (I)	Olympic Winter Games 1999	1992-06-19	Yes: 15.3% No: 84.7%	60.7%
-	Lausanne (CH)	Olympic Winter Games 1994	1988-06-26	Yes: 38% No: 62%	45.8%
-	Chur/Graubünden (CH)	Olympic Winter Games 1988	1980-03-02	Yes: 23% No: 77%	
-	Denver (USA)	Olympic Winter Games 1976	1972-11-07	Yes: 40.56% No: 59.44%	
+	St. Moritz/ Graubünden (CH)	Olympic Winter Games 1976	1969-11-09	Yes: 70.1% No: 29.9%	54%
-	Zürich (CH)	Olympic Winter Games 1976	1969-11-02	Yes: 22% No: 78%	
-	Interlaken (CH)	Olympic Winter Games 1976	1969-10-26	Yes: 48.4% No: 51.6%	
+	Sion (CH)	Olympic Winter Games 1976	1969-07-13	Yes: 68.7% No: 31.3%	41.8%
-	Sion/Wallis (CH)	Olympic Winter Games 1968	1963-12-08	Yes: 49.4% No: 50.6%	

Source: Könecke and de Nooij (2017); Maennig (2019); Schnitzer and Haizinger (2019)

Of note, studies on referendums and the Olympic Games are rarely examined (Könecke, Schubert and Preuß, 2016). In the following, the existing studies dealing with referendums on the Olympic Games and their main results are presented.

One of the first studies took place in connection with the referendum on the application for/against the Olympic Winter Games in Munich 2022 by Könecke, Schubert and Preuß (2016). The authors systematically examined the outcome of the referendum ('no' vote) from three selected German daily newspapers by content analysis. The results revealed concerns around legacy, 'damaged' image of the international sports organizations (see also Nielsen, 2015) and their events (i.e. World Cups and World Championships).

Similarly, Seippel et al. (2016) analyzed media coverage in the run-up to the Oslo referendum for the 2022 Winter Olympics. The findings indicate that 45% of the articles related to Oslo's bid were neutral, 31.7% positive and 22.7% were negative. It seems that media reporting did influence public opinion as the outcome of the referendum was 53.6% in favor of bidding for the Games.

Coates and Wicker (2015) conducted another study on Munich 2022. On the basis of secondary data, they identified factors that influenced voting behavior. They examined which characteristics influenced the referendum results in all 52 municipalities entitled to vote. They found that municipalities with higher unemployment rates were more inclined to approve of a bid while municipalities with a higher proportion of Green and Left Party voters, as well as those with a high number of hotel beds per capita, were less inclined to approve of a bid.

A data set of Nielsen (2015) deals with the referendum on Hamburg 2024. In August 2015, a representative telephone survey (ADM master sample for telephone studies) was conducted among the population aged 16 and older. The sample comprised more than 1,000 Hamburg citizens. Accordingly, more than 70% of those who rejected and supported the bidding believed that the costs (and follow-up costs) of the Games would be far higher than planned. Overall, over 50% assumed a positive development of the economy and the image of Hamburg, the infrastructure, as well as the creation of new jobs. The strongest supporters for participation in the referendum can be found in the city clusters 1 (i.e. Blankenese) with 71% and 2 (i.e. Rotherbaum) with 68% where rich people live. Support for the Hamburg Olympic bid in city cluster 5 (i.e. Bahrenfeld) is comparatively low at 57% as here live lower stratifications.

Wicker and Coates (2018) also conducted a survey shortly before the election. In contrast to Nielsen (2015), 41.2% of the respondents intended to vote 'yes' in the referendum (52% for Nielsen in November 2015). Using contingent valuation measurement only 30.1% were "willing to pay" for the event whereas that figure was 23% in the Nielsen study 2015.

Wewer (2017) examined the NIMBY phenomenon (explained in more detail later) in connection with the Hamburg referendum. They found that the distance from one's home to the potential venues had a significant influence on voting behavior. He also demonstrated that the benefits of hosting the Games for the entire city play a minor role in the voting compared to the personal advantages and disadvantages of hosting. He recommends that the fears/disadvantages of the citizens be taken seriously and tackled strategically.

As mentioned previously, voter turnout can have a major impact on the outcome of a referendum. Streicher, Schmidt and Schreyer (2018) therefore examined factors that affect voter turnout in referendums for/against Olympic Games. For this purpose, they conducted a representative online survey in 12 democratic countries. Their study shows that voter turnout is highest among people who strongly support or reject the event, while people that are indifferent participate less in the election. As a consequence, advocates should try to confuse the opponents by providing strong arguments for the Olympics, and persuade the other advocates to vote in favor. Furthermore, it is known that voter turnout increases with age, which tends to lead to a rejection of the Games, as support for the Olympics is stronger amongst the younger age groups (Streicher et al., 2017).

Key criticisms of the Olympic Games

The analysis of the main points of criticism is based on an extensive literature search on the failure of the last two Olympic bids due to referendums in Germany (Munich 2022 and Hamburg 2024). The five areas of criticism of the Olympic Games can be summarized under costs, legacy, image, lack of governance and NIMBY ("Not in my backyard").

Criticism is often directed at the expected costs and cost overruns of organizing the Olympic Games (Figure 17.2; Könecke, Schubert and Preuß, 2016; Scheu and Preuss, 2018). Since the 2000 Olympic Games in Sydney, the respective OCOGs have spent more than originally planned, but have also generated at least as much money. In fact, most of the organizing committees reported a positive balance. Meanwhile, cost overruns in the area of traditional cost overruns for major projects were found for specific Olympic investments (Figure 17.3) (Preuss, Andreff and Weitzmann, 2019).

In view of the need for investment, many argue that more should be invested in popular sport and less in high-performance sport (Könecke, Schubert and Preuß, 2016). Wicker and Coates (2018) found that expected costs have a greater impact on voting behavior than expected benefits. This is also confirmed by a survey conducted by Nielsen for the Hamburg 2015 bid reporting that the three most frequently cited reasons for rejecting the Olympic Games are "Costs/financing/economy", "Costs/financing/too expensive/economic reasons/

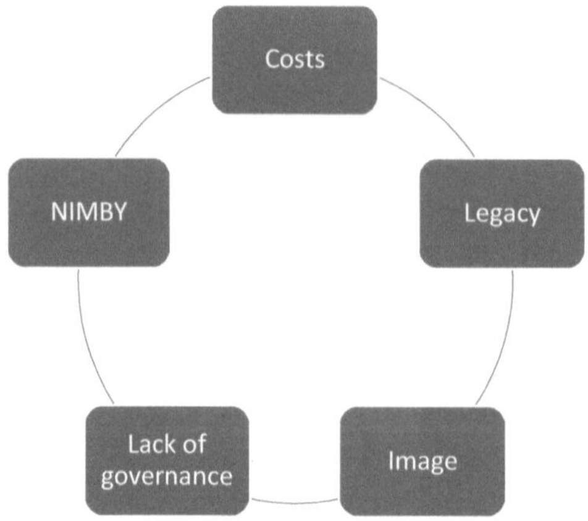

Figure 17.2 Criticism of the Olympic Games in Germany

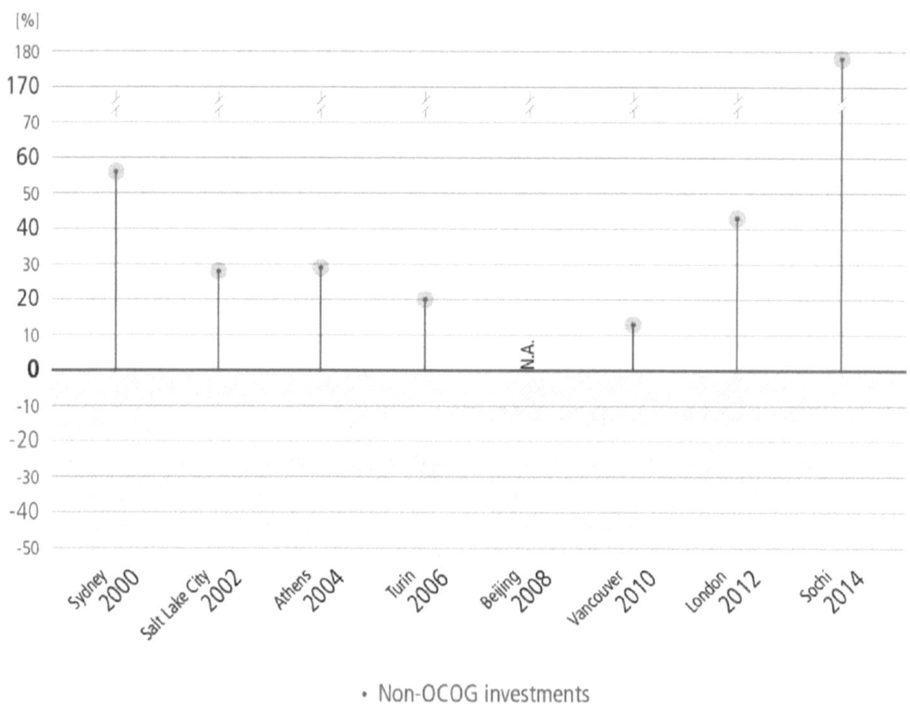

Figure 17.3 Cost overruns for sports facilities that are predominantly publicly financed

Source: Preuss, Andreff and Weitzmann (2019, p. 116)

non-transparent/non-foreseeable expenditure" and "Infrastructure/construction measures/sustainability" (Nielsen, 2015).

The next criticism is linked to the expected legacy of an event as well as the attitude towards the event (e.g. Gursoy and Kendall, 2006; Kim, Choi and Kaplanidou, 2015; Vetitnev and

Bobina, 2017). Schnitzer and Haizinger (2019) also point to these fields of research and write: "Thus, understanding this opposition to the OG and the attitude towards such events as well as analyzing the possible heritage they leave for hosting sites is more important than ever" (ibid., 2019, p. 1). For Germany it could be argued that "citizens see no individual benefit" in the Games (Scheu and Preuss, 2018) and that citizens fear a negative legacy, e.g. environmental damage (Könecke, Schubert and Preuß, 2016; Scheu and Preuss, 2018).

The next area of criticism concerns the image of the Games and the federations behind them. The population seems to be driven by "mistrust of federations, officials and politics" (Könecke, Schubert and Preuß, 2016). This was also reported by Wicker and Coates (2018). Further, Könecke, Schubert and Preuß (2016) state that respondents see a "loss of Olympic ideas in modern Olympic Games" and reject the IOC's "gag contracts and gigantism" (Könecke, Schubert and Preuß, 2016).

The fourth criticism is about international federations themselves. Greed for profit, corruption and lack of transparency (Könecke, Schubert and Preuß, 2016) are often mentioned. In other words, the lack of good governance by the federations is perceived as a real problem by the public. In recent years, cases of corruption in the awarding of mega sports events have repeatedly been discussed in the media (Kempe, 2018, Sueddeutsche, 2010). These are closely related to private bribery, which in turn reflects the greed for profit of individual officials.

The last area of criticism of the Olympic Games is related to the NIMBY effect. Ahlfeldt and Maennig (2012) examined the attitudes of the residents of Munich for the construction project of a football stadium. On the city level, the construction was supported by many people, whereas the inhabitants of the corresponding district were strongly opposed to it. Similar results were found for the Olympic Games in Rio de Janeiro, Brazil (Weimar and Rocha, 2019; Wewer, 2017). The surveys clearly show that respondents like the Olympic Games but don't want them in their city. 'NIMBYs' strategy is to communicate these disadvantages to other members of society by making themselves heard through various platforms (e.g. traditional media, social media, etc.).

The study by Scheu and Preuss (2018) provides an overview of public perception regarding legacy and impact linked to the possible hosting of the 2024 Olympic Games by Hamburg (GER). Key findings include respondents' belief that high costs are linked to hosting the Games in Hamburg while very little benefits are possible. It was apparent throughout the questionnaire that respondents feared financial burdens in hosting the Games. The accumulated Likert scale results of all individual expectations of legacies showed that 55% of the respondents assume that the negative legacies will outweigh the positive ones. A negative legacy for the city is therefore ultimately expected in the long term. Nevertheless, 65% of the respondents intended to vote in favor of Hamburg's candidacy, which clearly demonstrate that this was not simply a rational decision. Social Exchange Theory (Emerson, 1976) was chosen for explanation (see also Karadakis and Kaplanidou, 2012; Waitt, 2003). A detailed examination of the decision-making behavior of the 1,000 Hamburg citizens surveyed showed that 77% of the respondents voted in accordance with the social exchange theory, while the remaining 23% did not.

The subsequent multinomial logistic regression analysis in Hamburg shows that the perception of the positive legacies had the strongest influence on the decision-making behavior. That means the stronger the perception linked to positive legacies, the higher the probability that a bid for the Olympic Games will be supported. Another important factor for a successful outcome is the "perceived joy about the Olympic Games". This result shows that the decision for or against the Olympic Games is not purely rational, but also emotional.

Important implications can be derived from these results. The fact that the interviewees expect mostly positive legacies but do not perceive improvement in their personal quality of life is controversial. Therefore, it may be strategically wise to clearly communicate the relationship between positive legacy and individual quality of life for future applications. This could certainly provide a counter argument to the media's often biased focus regarding the costs of hosting the Games. However, the connection between positive Olympic legacy and individual quality of life has not received much attention from researchers to date.

In the next section, the challenges and problems linked to hosting the Olympic Games are discussed. A cause-effect model demonstrates the factors that influence the public when voting for the right to bid for the Games or not.

Current challenges and problems in the organization of Olympic Games

Over the past decades, both the size and the complexity of the Olympic Games have increased immensely (Liao and Pitts, 2006; Malfas, Theodoraki and Houlihan, 2004), leading to various problems. Few scholars have examined the challenges of organizing the Olympic Games and their implications for future host cities. Chappelet (2018) describes the main challenges in a working paper. Since these contain redundancies, the overarching challenges were named in a further column of Table 17.2.

Digel (2010) suggests eleven challenges concerning the organization of Olympic Games, whereby many of them (e.g. sports programme, IOC membership, Olympic education or doping) are only indirectly related to the organization of Olympic Games. Only the challenges of 'sustainability' and 'commercialization' are reported by both authors.

Of note, both publications are subjective assessments by scholars that have studied the Olympic Games for many years. Neither of them examined the cause-effect relationships. On the basis of the study results presented earlier, the state of research and the assessments of Chappelet

Table 17.2 Main challenges of the Olympic Games

Chappelet (2018)	*Overarching topics*
Total cost of the Games	Cost
Cost of bidding	
Keeping within budget	
Opportunity cost	
Debt	
Legacy	Legacy and sustainability
Sustainability	
Impact assessments (especially economic impact)	
White elephants	
Economic impact	Short-term effects (impacts)
Impact on employment	
Social impacts	
Environmental impact	
Gigantism	Developments
Displacement and gentrification	
Commodification	

Source: Chappelet (2018)

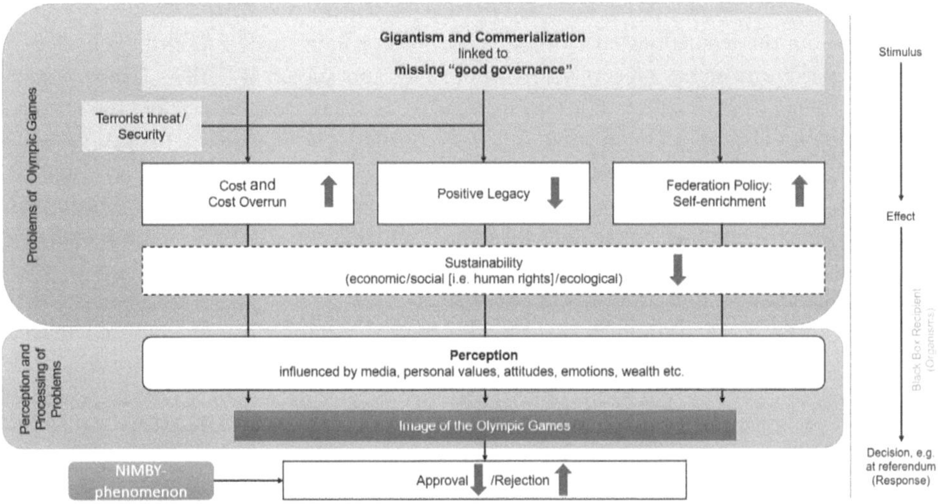

Figure 17.4 Model for declaration of approval/rejection of Olympic Games

(2018) and Digel (2010), we have developed a model that represents the most important challenges of organizing the Olympic Games.

Figure 17.4 shows two areas: the upper part illustrates the problems of today's Olympic Games and the main influencing factors (stimulus and effect). The lower part illustrates how problems are perceived and individually processed by the recipient, resulting in a subjective picture of the Olympic Games. Ultimately, these play a key factor in deciding whether the Games are approved or rejected. The individual areas of the model are explained later.

In the past three decades, mainly due to IOC President J.A. Samaranch, the Olympic Games have been characterized by increasing 'gigantism' and strong 'commercialization' (Chappelet, 2014). Commercialization in the general sense means a process "in which an area of human life that does not primarily contain an economic orientation is discovered as an area for economic interests and exploited in this sense" (Kutsch, 1972, p. 121). Commercialization in sport means "that goods produced in and with sport are sold via the market, i.e. according to the principle of performance and consideration" (Heinemann, 1992, p. 239). Commercialization and gigantism in themselves are not necessarily negative. However, weak governance structures of the federations have led to an explosion of costs. Further, not everything that is built is meaningful for the public while individuals linked to the federations enrich themselves.

Governance is a system by which the elements of an organization are managed, controlled and regulated (Hoye and Cuskelly, 2007). For example, the German Olympic Sports Confederation (DOSB) peruses with its good governance regulations the goal of aligning the pursuit of the federation's goals, the federation's control and the federation's actions with ethical standards. For this purpose, four principles of good governance are pursued: integrity, accountability, transparency and participation and inclusion (DOSB, 2018). Non-compliance with these principles usually leads to ethical misconduct. This can also be observed at the Olympic Games. For example, the gigantism observed in Sochi, Beijing or Rio de Janeiro was the result of a lack of regulation that led to the construction of oversized sports facilities with high costs on the one hand and invisible costs on the other, which led to strong media criticism (e.g. Freestone and Gunasekara, 2017; Giulianotti, 2015; Kasimati, 2015). Moreover, there is a link between negative legacy and weak governance (Girginov, 2012; Leopkey and Parent, 2016). As a result, weak governance structures within the federations enables the federations or individuals within these to enrich themselves (self-enrichment), especially since more and more money is in the Olympic system due to the strong commercialization (Simeoni, 2016). For example, shortly before the referendum for/against a Hamburg Olympic bid, there were reports in the media that FIFA sponsors were demanding the resignation of the FIFA president (2 October 2015). A few days later the FIFA president, FIFA secretary general and UEFA president were suspended for 90 days (dpa, 8 October 2015). While not directly linked to the Hamburg's bid (i.e. FIFA and IOC are two separate organizations), these events impact public perception in relations to these mega events, in this case Hamburg's bid to host the Olympic Games.

As argued, gigantism and commercialization should not be a problem in themselves, provided that good governance structures do not lead to any misuse of resources.

In addition to gigantism and commercialization, the threat of terrorism, which is frequently discussed in the media, can also be an influential factor. It leads to an important rise in the costs of hosting the Games (although not a direct cost of OCOGs) as well as on its legacy. For example, the attacks of September 11, 2001 led to an increase in the level of security at the subsequent Games in Athens in 2004 (Preuss, Andreff and Weitzmann, 2019). These and other terrorist attacks lead to increased general insecurity among the population. Shortly before the referendum for/against a bid by Hamburg in 2024, a bomb attack was carried out at the Stade de France in Paris on 13 November 2015. A few days later, an international football match featuring the German national team in Hanover (GER) was cancelled due to a bomb threat. This led to an increased discussion regarding security at major sporting events. Given the challenges in securing the Olympic Games, which cover an entire city, high security costs are to be expected. For London 2012, the organizing committee spent 18 million Euros (Preuss, Andreff and Weitzmann, 2019), while the government raised a further 148 million Euros (House of Commons, 2012). However, these costs are offset by a relatively low long-term benefit, as this is purely a temporary security cost for the event.

The developments described earlier, resulting in high costs, lack of perceived legacy and enrichment of the federations, have a negative impact on the sustainability of the Olympic Games. This should be understood as

> a form of ecological and economic action that is intended to secure comparable or better living conditions for present and future generations by carefully applying the necessary element and protecting it accordingly. Sustainability focuses on the environment, economic and social aspects.
>
> *(N.N., 2015)*

Due to high costs and relatively common cost overruns in large-scale projects, economic sustainability is difficult to be recognized by the public. In addition, the developments mentioned (gigantism, commercialization) and the resulting problems often lead to a lack of ecological sustainability. In PyeongChang, between 60,000 and 100,000 trees were cleared for the 2018 Winter Olympics (Erdmann, 2017). The Olympic Games in Rio de Janeiro and Sochi also caused irreversible environmental damage (Kassens-Noor et al., 2016; Müller, 2015). With regard to social sustainability, the effects on visitors to the Games and the local population are considered (see Gans, Horn and Zemann, 2003). One example of negative social sustainability is the 2014 Winter Games in Sochi, where citizens were not involved in decision-making processes, contrary to what was announced. In addition, foreign workers were given preference, so that hardly any additional employment was created locally (Müller, 2015).

This upper part of the model includes facts that are observable. The way these are received and evaluated by the recipient (i.e. public) is determined by one's perception as illustrated in the lower part (perception and processing of the problems) of the model. Perception, in turn, is a psychologically cognitive function that enables the individual to receive and process information from the outside world (Arnold, Eysenck and Meili, 1996). This is not observable.

It is the stories in the media that are communicated, received and evaluated by the consumer that ultimately may influence one's opinion. The reports meet an individually different value system, i.e. different personal attitudes, in a certain emotional context. Finally, the prosperity of the person, i.e. the economic situation in which one finds itself, is also important in assessing an Olympic problem area. In other words, the information disseminated via the mass and social media is highly context specific and individually interpreted. The media therefore have a special role to play as opinion formers (Könecke, 2018), since they can filter information and position it in a certain manner. Negative messages have higher news value (Kepplinger, 1998) and are picked up more frequently. Koenigstorfer and Preuss (2019) have found that Brazilians, for example, reject the Games in their own country more if they consider self-centred values (e.g. personal best, striving for excellence) to be important among the Olympic values. Among other things, this can also lead to an increased perception of reports of a corrupt IOC. The study shows that people perceive media reports differently on the basis of their attitudes and values and that this then leads to approval or rejection of Games in their own country.

The perception (lower part of the model) of the problems linked to the Olympic Games has high influence on the attitude towards voting for or against the Olympic Games in a referendum. In other words, it contains all the federations (e.g. FIFA example previously mentioned) that an individual connects (rightly or wrongly) to the Olympic Games (Trommsdorff, 2009), and thus one's image. This image and the contextual situation in which one finds itself ultimately decides whether someone approves or rejects the bidding for Olympic Games. Since the last component of the model ('approval' or 'rejection') is behavior, this can be measured in a citizen's decision. The model simplifies the current problems and challenges identified in the literature for the Olympic Games including their causes and creates a first understanding for the current rejection of the Games in Munich and Hamburg as well as in many other Western, democratic countries.

Concluding remarks

The financial success of the 1984 Olympic Games in Los Angeles and the positive urban legacy of the 1992 Olympic Games in Barcelona were followed by a high number of bidders seeking to host the Olympic Games. Not only the number of bidders increased, but also the revenue from sponsorship and broadcasting rights. More and more urban planning projects (the driving force behind gigantism) and the financial desires of world federations, NOCs and host cities (the driving force behind commercialization) followed. The IOC saw little need for action to adapt to the changes even in the frenzy of success. The Olympic Games, for example, became bigger and bigger in the perception of the population due to the connection of urban development projects. The desire for international prestige of host cities increased and with it the construction of extravagant and oversized sports facilities. The number of candidate cities led into the rationality trap, i.e. the candidates outbid each other in the size and unusualness of the Games in order to receive votes from the IOC and please international federations (of which 15 are also IOC members). This was maintained for many years and led to increasing problems. The enthusiasm that once prevailed for hosting the Olympic Games has clearly diminished in recent years. Media reports about the IOC and international federations regarding weak governance structures and self-enrichment (real or perceived), as well as high costs and reported cost overruns, support general skepticism about the Games. Although high costs or cost overruns are often observed in the area of urban development projects that are not directly tied to Olympic sports venue construction, they are one and the same in the public's mind. In addition, there is a lack of perceived individual benefit and a lack of observable positive legacy, so that the event in one's own city does not seem desirable.

In order to ultimately change this perception, which would consequently lead to higher approval for hosting the Olympic Games, the problems associated with the Games must be solved. IOC President Bach has long recognized the need for action and adopted Agenda 2020 with its 40 recommendations as early as 2014. Today it has resulted in numerous implementations. In 2018, the New Norm was implemented, with 118 concrete measures in the three areas of bidding process, legacy and event implementation (IOC, 2018). Thus, the bidding process for awarding the Games changed for the 2026 election of Milan/Cortina while the costs for Tokyo 2020, Beijing 2022 and Paris 2024 were already greatly reduced. These measures can be seen as positive, but their implementation is a prolonged process, which means the results will not be visible for nearly a decade. It will most likely take until 2028 for the population to understand and recognize these changes. At present, it can be seen that many changes and improvements to the IOC are not reaching the population, especially as long as the media report on a different, current reality. For example, just one year after the 2018 Olympic Winter Games in PyeongChang, it was reported in the media that the legacy of many sports facilities is problematic and as such many will not be used again (Deutsche Welle, 2019). According to media reports, the 2020 Olympic Games are primarily associated with cost overruns (Neidhart, 2019; Spiegel, 2018), while the Winter Games two years later, in Beijing 2022, are expected to lead to "considerable environmental destruction" (Strittmatter, 2018). Under these circumstances, it is difficult to change the current rather negative image of the Olympic Games, despite the fact that the IOC has already implemented change processes.

Bids for the Olympic Games from Western, democratic countries should nevertheless be sought. The changes made by Agenda 2020 encourage this, as many reasons against the Games are becoming obsolete. Nevertheless, the prospect of a positive referendum may be less than desirable. Therefore, a high turnout should be sought, the population should be well educated and smart concepts developed, costs should be kept low and individual benefits increased through positive legacy. A bid should focus on the needs of the citizens.

Early action must be taken to increase the chances of success of a referendum and bid. This can be achieved by the participants intensively dealing with a referendum and its influence variables. Innovative procedures must also be considered. Loos (2016) proposes, for example, a "combination of chance and plebiscite" in order to obtain a reliable result in a referendum. For this purpose, a representative group of citizens will be drawn by lot, which will be divided into small groups capable of discussion. In these small groups, the project to be voted on is discussed from all perspectives, so that all participants have a profound basis for decision-making. After the conclusion of the discussion phases, a referendum is held within this group (ibid.). Such a procedure could be carried out in the event of a new bid for the Olympic Games and made public through the media. This could prevent a petition for a referendum after a referendum or broaden the arguments in the media of relatively one-sided negative reporting. This procedure could also help politicians, since a combination of chance and plebiscite with a large number of selected citizens could legitimize public support as representative as possible.

Note

1 NIMBY stands for "Not in my backyard" and means the political position that individuals do not want to endure problems in their immediate environment. The term refers in particular to an attitude of mind of people who take advantage of the Olympic Games but do not want to accept any disadvantages (e.g. construction noise, price increases) in their own environment.

References

Ahlfeldt, G. and Maennig, W. (2012). Voting on a NIMBY facility: Proximity cost of an 'iconic' stadium. *Urban Affairs Review*, 48(2), pp. 205–237. doi:10.1177/1078087411423644.

Arnold, W., Eysenck, H.J. and Meili, R. (1996). *Lexikon der Psychologie*. Augsburg: Bechtermünz.

Barber, B.R. (2003). *Strong democracy. Participatory politics for a new age*. Berkeley: University of California Press.

Bödeker, S. (2012). *Soziale Ungleichheit und politische Partizipation in Deutschland. Grenzen politischer Gleichheit in der Bürgergesellschaft*. Zugriff unter: www.otto-brenner-stiftung.de/fileadmin/user_data/stiftung/02_Wissenschaftsportal/03_Publikationen/AP01_SozialeUngleichheit_Boedeker_2012_02_07.pdf [zuletzt geprüft am 7 May 2019].

Bowler, S. and Donovan, T. (2019). Perceptions of referendums and democracy: The referendum disappointment gap. *Politics and Governance*, 7(2), pp. 227–241.

Bundeszentrale für politische Bildung (BPB) (o.J.). (n.d.). *Volksabstimmung*. Zugriff unter: www.bpb.de/nachschlagen/lexika/recht-a-z/23190/volksabstimmung [zuletzt geprüft am 1 May 2019].

Casella, A. and Gelman, A. (2008). A simple scheme to improve the efficiency of referenda. *Journal of Public Economics*, 92, pp. 2240–2261.

Chappelet, J-L. (2014). Managing the size of the Olympic Games. *Sport in Society*, 17(5), pp. 581–592.

Chappelet, J-L. (2018). *Challenges and opportunities for past and future Olympic cities*. IDHEAP Working Paper No. 6/2018. Zugriff unter: https://serval.unil.ch/resource/serval: BIB_29F28F9E5192.P001/REF [zuletzt geprüft am 1 May 2019].

Coates, D. and Wicker, P. (2015). Why were voters against the 2022 Munich Winter Olympics in a referendum? *International Journal of Sport Finance*, 10, pp. 160–174.

Deutsche Welle. (2019). *Ein Jahr danach: Tristesse in Pyeongchang*. Zugriff unter: www.dw.com/de/pyeongchang-olympia-winterspiele-s%C3%BCdkorea/av-47441241 [zuletzt geprüft am 5 May 2019].

Deutscher Olympischer Sportbund (DOSB). (2018). *Good Governance Regularien*. Zugriff unter: https://cdn.dosb.de/alter_Datenbestand/fm-dosb/downloads/dosb/Good-Governance-Regularien_29.11.2018.pdf [zuletzt geprüft am 7 May 2019].

Digel, H. (2010). Olympic challenges. *The International Journal of the History of Sport*, 27(16–18), pp. 2665–2676.

Dpa. (2015). Chronologie der FFA Affäre. Ein fünf Jahre währender Skandal. *Frankfurter Allgemeine*, Oct. 8.

Emerson, R.M. (1976). Social exchange theory. *Annual Review of Sociology*, 2, pp. 335–362.

Erdmann, K. (2017). *60.000 Bäume für eine Sprungschanze*. Zugriff unter: www.deutschlandfunk.de/olympia-2018-60-000-baeume-fuer-eine-sprungschanze.890.de.html?dram:article_id=394041 [zuletzt geprüft am 5 May 2017].

Flyvbjerg, B., Stewart, A. and Budzier, A. (2016). *The Oxford Olympics study 2016: Cost and cost overrun at the games (RP 2016–20)*. Said Business School.

Focus. (2015). *Beim Hamburger Olympia-Referendum zeichnet sich eine rege Wahlbeteiligung ab*. Zugriff unter: www.focus.de/sport/olympia-2016/olympia-referendum-rege-wahlbeteiligung-in-hamburg_id_5120042.html [zuletzt geprüft am 1 May 2019].

Freestone, R. and Gunasekara, S. (2017). Sydney 2000. In: J.R. Gold and M.M. Gold, eds., *Planning, history and environment series. Olympic cities. City agendas, planning, and the world's games, 1896–2020*. London and New York: Routledge Taylor & Francis Group, pp. 317–332.

Freitag, M., Vatter, A. and Müller, C. (2003). Bremse oder Gaspedal? Eine empirische Untersuchung zur Wirkung der direkten Demokratie auf den Steuerstaat. *Politische Vierteljahresschrift*, 44(3), pp. 348–369.

Freitag, M. and Wagschal, U. (2007). *Direkte Demokratie. Bestandsaufnahmen und Wirkungen im internationalen Vergleich*. Berlin: LIT Verlag.

Gans, P., Horn, M. and Zemann, C. (2003). *Sportgroßveranstaltungen – ökonomische, ökologische und soziale Wirkungen: Ein Bewertungsverfahren zur Entscheidungsvorbereitung und Erfolgskontrolle. Schriftenreihe des Bundesinstituts für Sportwissenschaft 112.* Schorndorf: Hofmann.

Geißel, B. (2012). Politische (Un-) Gleichheit und die Versprechen der Demokratie. *Aus Politik und Zeitgeschichte*, 62(38–39), pp. 32–37.

Girginov, V. (2012). Governance of the London 2012 Olympic Games legacy. *International Review for the Sociology of Sport*, 47(5), pp. 543–558.

Giulianotti, R. (2015). The Beijing 2008 Olympics: Examining the interrelations of China, globalization, and soft power. *European Review*, 23(2), pp. 286–296.

Güldenpfennig, S. (2017). Bewerbung um Sport-Großveranstaltungen als Faktor der Stadtpolitik. In: J. Förster, A. Hebbel-Seeger, T. Horky and H-J. Schulke, Hrsg., *Talk, meet, innovate. Sport und Stadtentwicklung: 16. Hamburger Kongress für Sport, Ökonomie und Medien.* Aachen: Meyer & Meyer Verlag, pp. 202–239.

Gursoy, D. and Kendall, K.W. (2006). Hosting mega events: Modeling local's support. *Annals of Tourism Research*, 33(3), pp. 603–623.

Hajnal, Z. and Trounstine, J. (2005). Where turnout matters: The consequences of uneven turnout in city politics. *Journal of Politics*, 67, pp. 515–535.

Häußermann, H. and Siebel, W., Hrsg. (1993). *Festivalisierung der Stadtpolitik. Stadtentwicklung durch große Projekte.* Opladen: Westdeutscher Verlag.

Heinemann, K. (1992). Kommerzialisierung. In: P. Röthig, Hrsg., *Sportwissenschaftliches Lexikon.* 6th Auflage. Schorndorf: Hofmann.

House of Commons. (2012). *Olympics security.* Zugriff unter: https://publications.parliament.uk/pa/cm201213/cmselect/cmhaff/531/531.pdf [zuletzt geprüft am 7 May 2019].

Hoye, R. and Cuskelly, G. (2007). *Sport governance.* Sport Management Series. London: Routledge.

International Olympic Committee (IOC) (2018). *The new norm: It's a games changer.* Zugriff unter: www.olympic.org/news/the-new-norm-it-s-a-games-changer [zuletzt geprüft am 7 May 2019].

Karadakis, K. and Kaplanidou, K. (2012). Legacy perceptions among host and non-host Olympic Games residents: A longitudinal study of the 2010 Vancouver Olympic Games. *European Sport Management Quarterly*, 12(3), pp. 243–264.

Kasimati, E. (2015). Post-Olympic use of the Olympic venues: The case of Greece. *Athens Journal of Sports*, 2, pp. 167–184.

Kassens-Noor, E., Gaffney, C., Messina, J. and Phillips, E. (2016). Olympic transport legacies. *Journal of Planning Education and Research*, 6(1). doi:10.1177/0739456X1668322.

Kellison, T.B. and Mondello, M.J. (2012). Organisational perception management in sport: The Use of corporate pro-environmental behaviour for desired facility referenda outcomes. *Sport Management Review*, 15, pp. 500–512.

Kempe, R. (2018). *Fußball WM 2018 in Katar. Korruption und Menschenrechtsverletzungen.* Zugriff unter: www.deutschlandfunk.de/fussball-wm-2022-in-katar-korruption-und.890.de.html?dram:article_id=430814 [zuletzt geprüft am 27 July 2019].

Kepplinger, H.M. (1998). Der Nachrichtenwert der Nachrichtenfaktoren. In: C. Holtz-Bacha, H. Scherer and N. Waldmann, Hrsg., *Wie die Medien die Welt erschaffen und wie wir darin leben.* Opladen: Westdeutscher Verlag, pp. 19–38.

Kim, A., Choi, M. and Kaplanidou, K. (2015). The role of media in enhancing people's perception of hosting a mega sport event: The case of Pyeongchang's Winter Olympics bids. *International Journal of Sport Communication*, 8(1), pp. 68–86.

Koenigstorfer, J. and Preuss, H. (2019). Olympic Games-related values and host country residents' pre-event evaluations in the run-up to the 2016 Olympic Games. *Global Sports Management*, 3(81), upcoming.

Könecke, T. (2018). *Das Modell der personenbezogenen Kommunikation und Rezeption.* Wiesbaden: Springer Fachmedien Wiesbaden.

Könecke, T. and de Nooij, M. (2017). The IOC and Olympic bids from democracies and authoritarian regimes – A socioeconomic analysis and strategic insights. *Current Issues in Sport Science*, 2(9).

Könecke, T., Schubert, M. and Preuß, H. (2016). (N)Olympia in Germany? An analysis of the referendum against Munich 2022. *Sportwissenschaft*, 46, pp. 15–24.

Kutsch, T. (1972). Kommerzialisierung. In: P. Röthig, Hrsg., *Sportwissenschaftliches Lexikon.* Schorndorf: Hofmann.

LeDuc, L. (2015). Referendums and deliberative democracy. *Electoral Studies*, 38, pp. 139–148.

Leininger, A. and Heyne, L. (2017). How representative are referendums? Evidence from 20 years Swiss referendums. *Electoral Studies*, 48, pp. 84–97.
Leopkey, B. and Parent, M.M. (2016). The governance of Olympic legacy: Process, actors and mechanisms. *Leisure Studies*, 22, pp. 1–14.
Liao, H. and Pitts, A. (2006). A brief historical review of Olympic urbanization. *The International Journal of the History of Sport*, 23(7), pp. 1232–1252.
Loos, A. (2016). *Sind 52 Prozent eine Mehrheit?* Zugriff unter: www.zeit.de/politik/2016-06/eu-referendum-grossbritannien-brexit-mathematik-messfehler [zuletzt geprüft am 1 May 2019].
Lutz, G. (2007). Low turnout in direct democracy. *Electoral Studies*, 26, pp. 624–632.
Maennig, W. (2019). Olympic Games: Public referenda, public opinion and willingness to pay. In: P. Downward, B. Frick, B.R. Humphreys, T. Pawlowski, J.E. Ruseski and B.P. Soebbing, eds., *The Sage handbook of sports economics*. London: Sage Publications Ltd, pp. 367–376.
Malfas, M., Theodoraki, E. and Houlihan, B. (2004). Impacts of the Olympic Games as mega-events. *Municipal Engineer*, 157(3), pp. 209–220.
Marg, S., Geiges, L., Butzlaff, F. and Walter, F. (2013). *Die neue Macht der Bürger. Was motiviert die Protestbewegungen?* Reinbek bei Hamburg: Rowohlt.
Matheson, V.A. and Baade, R.A. (2004). Mega-sporting events in developing nations. Playing the way to prosperity? *South African Journal of Economics*, 72(5), pp. 1085–1096.
Mittendorf, V. (2008). Europa im Ausverkauf. Liberalisierung und Privatisierung öffentlicher Dienstleistungen und ihre Folgen für die Tarifpolitik. In: T. Brandt, T. Schulten, G. Sterkel and G. Wiedemuth, Hrsg., *Bürgerbegehren und Volksentscheide gegen Privatisierungen und die Rolle der Gewerkschaften*. Hamburg: VSA-Verlag, pp. 310–329.
Moser, J. and Obinger, H. (2007). Schlaraffenland auf Erden? Auswirkungen von Volksentscheiden auf die Sozialpolitik. In: M. Freitag and U. Wagschal, Hrsg., *Direkte Demokratie. Bestandsaufnahmen und Wirkungen im internationalen Vergleich*. Berlin: LIT Verlag, pp. 331–362.
Müller, M. (2015). (Im-)Mobile policies: Why sustainability went wrong in the 2014 Olympics in Sochi. *European Urban and Regional Studies*, 22(2), pp. 191–209.
Neidhart, C. (2019). *Wie Japan die Probleme vor Olympia wegwischt*. Zugriff unter: www.sueddeutsche.de/sport/tokio-2020-olympia-1.4536514 [zuletzt geprüft am 24 July 2019].
Nielsen. (2015). *Bevölkerungsrepräsentative Befragung zur Akzeptanz der Bewerbung Hamburgs für die Ausrichtung der Olympischen und Paralympischen Spiele 2024*. Berichtsband Fieberkurven, Hamburg Olympiabewerbung, Nov. 15. Typoskript.
N.N. (2015). *Nachhaltigkeit Definition*. Zugriff unter: www.nachhaltigkeit.info/artikel/definitionen 1382.htm [zuletzt geprüft am 15 May 2019].
Preuss, H., Andreff, W. and Weitzmann, M. (2019). *Cost and revenue overruns of the Olympic Games 2000–2018*. Wiesbaden: Springer Fachmedien Wiesbaden.
Rehmet, F. (2018). *Volksentscheide aufgrund von Volksbegehren in Deutschland*. Zugriff unter: www.mehr-demokratie.de/fileadmin/pdf/Uebersicht-Volksentscheide-BL.pdf [zuletzt geprüft am 1 May 2019].
Schäfer, A. (2010). Die Folgen sozialer Ungleichheit für die Demokratie in Westeuropa. *Zeitschrift für Vergleichende Politikwissenschaft*, 4(1), pp. 131–156.
Schäfer, A. and Schön, H. (2012). Mehr Demokratie, aber nur für wenige? Der Zielkonflikt zwischen mehr Beteiligung und politischer Gleichheit. *Leviathan*, 41(1), pp. 94–120.
Schäper, S. (2017). The number of bids for the Olympic Games since 1984. "Agenda 2020" as a potential new turning point? In: J. Förster, A. Hebbel-Seeger, T. Horky and H-J. Schulke, Hrsg., *Talk, meet, innovate. Sport und Stadtentwicklung: 16. Hamburger Kongress für Sport, Ökonomie und Medien*. Aachen: Meyer & Meyer Verlag, pp. 34–65.
Schaub, H. (1997). *Sunk Costs, Rationalität und ökonomische Theorie*. Stuttgart: Schäffer Poeschel.
Scheu, A. and Preuss, H. (2018). Residents' perceptions of mega sport event legacies and impacts. *German Journal of Exercise and Sport Research*, 48(3), pp. 376–386.
Schiller, T. (2007). Direkte Demokratie auf Bundesländer- und Kommunalebene. In: M. Freitag and U. Wagschal, Hrsg., *Direkte Demokratie. Bestandsaufnahmen und Wirkungen im internationalen Vergleich*. Berlin: LIT Verlag, pp. 115–150.
Schnitzer, M. and Haizinger, L. (2019). Does the Olympic Agenda 2020 have the power to create a new Olympic heritage? An analysis for the 2026 Winter Olympic Games bid. *Sustainability*, 11(2), p. 442.
Seippel, Ø., Broch, T.B., Kristiansen, E., Skille, E., Wilhelmsen, T., Strandbu, Å. and Thorjussen, I.M. (2016). Political framing of sports: The mediated politicization of Oslo's interest in bidding for the 2022

Winter Olympics. *International Journal of Sport Policy and Politics*, 8(3), pp. 439–453. doi:10.1080/19406940.2016.1182047.
Simeoni, E. (2016). *Die rasante Talfahrt des IOC.* Zugriff unter: www.faz.net/aktuell/sport/olympia/sportpolitik/schwere-zeiten-fuer-ioc-olympia-nach-skandal-um-patrick-hickey-14394995.html [zuletzt geprüft am 14 May 2019].
Smith, G. (1975). The referendum and political change. *Government and Opposition*, 10(3), pp. 294–305.
Spiegel. (2018). *Olympia in Tokio könnte 22 Milliarden Euro kosten.* Zugriff unter: www.spiegel.de/sport/sonst/sommerspiele-2020-olympia-in-tokio-koennte-22-milliarden-euro-kosten-a-1232344.html [zuletzt geprüft am 5 May 2019].
Statistisches Amt für Hamburg und Schleswig-Holstein. (2015). *Olympia-Referendum am 29. November 2015 in Hamburg. Endgültiges Ergebnis.* Zugriff unter: www.statistik-nord.de/fileadmin/Dokumente/Wahlen/Hamburg/Volksentscheide/2015/endg%C3%BCltig/Olympia-Referendum_am_29.November_2015_in%20_Hamburg_%28Landesergebnis%29.pdf [zuletzt geprüft am 1 May 2019].
Streicher, T., Schmidt, S.L. and Schreyer, D. (2018). Referenda on hosting the Olympics: What drives voter turnout? *Journal of Sports Economics*, 5, pp. 627–653.
Streicher, T., Schmidt, S.L., Schreyer, D. and Torgler, B. (2017). Is it the economy, stupid? The role of social versus economic factors in people's support for hosting the Olympic Games: Evidence from 12 democratic countries. *Applied Economics Letters*, 24, pp. 170–174.
Strittmatter, K. (2018). *Skifahren im Wüstenklima.* Zugriff unter: www.sueddeutsche.de/sport/olympia-peking-kritik-umweltschutz-1.3883868 [zuletzt geprüft am 5 May 2019].
Sueddeutsche. (2010). *Korruption bei der FiFA?* Zugriff unter: www.sueddeutsche.de/sport/fussball-weltverband-fifa-prueft-bestechungsvorwuerfe-1.1012879 [zuletzt geprüft am 27 July 2019].
Trommsdorff, V. (2009). *Konsumentenverhalten.* Stuttgart: Kohlhammer.
Vetitnev, A.M. and Bobina, N. (2017). Residents' perceptions of the 2014 Sochi Olympic Games. *Leisure Studies*, 36(1), pp. 108–118.
Wagschal, U. and Obinger, H. (2000). Der Einfluss der Direktdemokratie auf die Sozialpolitik. *Politische Vierteljahresschrift*, 41(3), pp. 466–497.
Waitt, G. (2003). Social impacts of the Sydney Olympics. *Annals of Tourism Research*, 30(1), pp. 194–215.
Weimar, D. and Rocha, C.M. (2019). Does distance matter? Geographical distance and domestic support for mega sports events. *Journal of Sports Economics*, 20(2), pp. 286–313. doi:10.1177/1527002517724505.
Wewer, T. (2017). NIMBY & (N)Olympia – An analysis of the Olympic Referendum in Hamburg 2015. In: J. Förster, A. Hebbel-Seeger, T. Horky and H-J. Schulke, Hrsg., *Talk, meet, innovate. Sport und Stadtentwicklung: 16. Hamburger Kongress für Sport, Ökonomie und Medien.* Aachen: Meyer & Meyer Verlag, pp. 110–131.
Wicker, P. and Coates, D. (2018). Flame goes out: Determinants of individual support at the 2024 Hamburg games referendum. *Contemporary Economic Policy*, 36, pp. 302–317.
Young, D.C. and Abrahams, H.M. (2019). *Olympic Games.* Zugriff unter: www.britannica.com/sports/Olympic-Games [zuletzt geprüft am 4 Apr. 2019].

Part III

The governance of the Olympic and Paralympic Games

Edited by Borja García

18

The composition of the IOC

Origins and key turning points in the governance of the Olympic movement

Jörg Krieger and Stephan Wassong

Introduction

Studies on the governance of international sport organisations have increased exponentially in recent years. Therein, researchers focus mainly on the analysis of good governance principles in the world's leading governing bodies of sport (Geeraert, 2016; Lee and Hardin, 2015) and the link of ethics and governance (Vanden Auweele, Cook and Parry, 2016). Significantly, the role of the members of the International Olympic Committee (IOC) as umbrella organisation of the international sport system has been little discussed so far in previous research. This is despite the fact that IOC members' influence in the decision-making processes of almost all spheres of the Olympic movement has been widely acknowledged (Chappelet, 2016; Ferrand, Chappelet and Séguin, 2012). Hence, this chapter focuses on the roles and responsibilities of IOC members as defined within the Olympic Charter and presents different phases in the historical development of IOC membership. The central argument of the chapter is that the change in tasks and set-up of the IOC membership in each phase is linked to overall transformation processes in the Olympic movement. These developments are signified through reforms in the IOC. The historical approach taken in this chapter aims at developing a broad and in-depth knowledge about the genesis of IOC's governance structures. Such insights contribute to a better understanding of the IOC's institutionalised strategies to govern the international sport system in general and to organise the Olympic Games in particular.

The IOC's self-recruiting nature (1894–1921)

The IOC was founded on 23 June 1894 on initiative of French Baron Pierre de Coubertin during the *Congrès International De Paris Pour Le Rétablissement Des Jeux Olympiques* at the Sorbonne in Paris (Müller, 2000). The establishment of the IOC was preceded by years of discussion and networking through Coubertin with US-American scholars, British sport officials and representatives of the international peace movement (Quanz, 1993; Wassong, 2002). Hence, it is not surprising that the inaugural IOC was mainly composed of individuals who had supported Coubertin's idea in the years prior to the establishment of the modern Olympic movement. In total, sixteen people from thirteen different nations constituted the original IOC; its first president became the Greek business man and writer Dimítros Vikelas (Morbach, 1998).

The international composition reflected Coubertin's universal ambitions with the Olympic movement. He foresaw that the IOC maintained an exclusive group of individuals that self-recruited new members who could contribute to the global development of the Olympic movement. According to Coubertin, the IOC members needed to be politically independent, could afford their own travel expenses to IOC meetings and had a respected social status within their countries (Gutmann, 2002). As a consequence, IOC membership mainly consisted of individuals with a European, aristocratic background during the first two decades of its existence. There were a few exceptions: Leonard Cuff from New Zealand was amongst the first IOC members in 1894 and represented Australasia (Jobling and Letters, 1996), in 1909 Japanese educator Kano Jigoro became the first IOC member from Asia (Watson, 2012) and in 1910 the Greek Angelo Bolanaki, who also had an Egyptian passport, became the first African IOC member (Lyberg, 1989). The self-understanding of the sport officials was that of themselves being an 'elite', much like the amateurs that should be the only ones participating in Olympic sport (Llewellyn and Gleaves, 2016). However, this was a very pragmatic approach that proved functional and secured the survival of the Olympic movement in its early years (MacAloon, 2006). Hence, rather than the representative and decision-making roles we attribute to the IOC members today, the early IOC members occupied strategic managerial roles within the IOC.

The first regulations on the recruitment of IOC members appear in the first Olympic Charter, published in 1908. Therein, the self-recruiting process is determined and the independence of each member is emphasised. The first Olympic Charter regulated that IOC members who do not actively participate in meetings or voting procedures may be excluded from the IOC (IOC, 1908). Therewith Coubertin maintained a degree of control over the members. Nevertheless, it is difficult to make any concrete statements regarding the influence of the IOC membership on IOC governance prior to the First World War. Coubertin essentially ran the organisation by himself in collaboration with the respective Organising Committees of the Olympic Games. In 1915, Coubertin undertook an important pioneering administrative step and moved his own residence and the bureaucratic organisation of the IOC to Lausanne, Switzerland, in an attempt to protect the neutrality of the Olympic movement in the War (Chappelet and Bayle, 2016). This did not have any direct consequences on the decision-making processes in the IOC, however.

The establishment and the continuity of the Olympic Games in the first decade of the 20th century caused the genesis of stakeholders that would influence the IOC membership and the governance of the Olympic movement decisively. National Olympic Committees (NOCs) were created in many countries to coordinate the teams for the Olympic Games. By the time of the 1912 Stockholm Olympic Games, 22 NOCs had been founded in Argentina, Austria, Belgium, Bohemia, Canada, Chile, Denmark, Finland, France, Germany, Great Britain, Greece, Hungary, Italy, Luxembourg, Norway, Russia, Switzerland, Serbia, South Africa, The Netherlands and the United States (IOC, 1996). This development accelerated with the increasing global reach of the Olympic movement (Chappelet and Kübler-Mabbot, 2008). The International Sport Federations (IFs) are the other type of organisations that emerged. Before the First World War, thirteen of these international governing bodies of individual sports had been founded: gymnastics (founded in 1881), rowing (1892), ice hockey (1892), ice skating (1892), cycling (1900), football (1904), shooting (1907), sailing (1907) and swimming (1908), athletics (1913), wrestling (1913) and fencing (1913).

The foundation of the International Amateur Athletics Federation (IAAF) serves as an example of early synergies in international sports governance and the core responsibility lying with a few individuals who became IOC members. Coubertin had initially vigorously dismissed any attempts to establish an international athletics federation because he considered the IOC to be the sole governing body of athletics (Molzberger, 2012). It was only the need for the international harmonisation of technical rules and diplomatic skills by the Head of the Organising Committee of the 1912 Stockholm Olympic Games, Sigfrid Edström, which eventually led to the foundation of the IAAF (Krieger, 2016). In particular, Edström's integration of Coubertin in inaugural meetings and his assurances that the Federation would closely cooperate with the IOC convinced Coubertin about the advantages of an international athletics federation. In subsequent years, Edström became an important contributor to the development of the Olympic movement and joined the IOC in 1920 (Yttergren, 2008). His inclusion marks the start of a new phase in the IOC membership in which individual IOC members represented the interests of various organisations.

Emerging stakeholders (1921–1973)

After the First World War, the IOC members held their first post-War meeting at the IOC Session in April 1919 in Lausanne. Until this time, the IOC had elected 87 different men to become IOC members (Scherer, 1974). The future of the Olympic movement was still unclear at this point and therefore the members focused on the staging of the 1920 Antwerp Olympic Games (Müller, 1981). However, an Olympic Congress was planned in 1921 in Lausanne to address the increasing demands of the IFs, voiced during the Antwerp Olympic Games (Grosset and Attali, 2009). The Congress was held in conjunction with the annual IOC Session at which Coubertin initiated a reform of the governance processes in the IOC with the introduction of an Executive Board. Coubertin wanted to have a decision-making body in place for times when he was personally not available. However, the development of this new process took time. For example, in 1925 the British IOC member Robert Kentish threatened to step down from his duties on the Executive Board and the IOC, accusing Coubertin of non-transparent and inefficient decision-making (Wassong, 2003). The inclusion of IAAF President Edström on the Executive Board was a strategic move as the Swede could act as an intermediary between the IFs and the IOC in the Executive Board. Hence, from now on certain individuals like Edström occupied double functions in the IOC. The first half of the 1920s also saw an increasing internationalisation of the IOC membership. In total 43 new IOC members from 29 different countries were co-opted between 1919 and 1925. Such geographical diversity made communication and coordination much more challenging (Scherer, 1974).

Subsequent Olympic Congresses in 1925 and in 1930 were further landmarks in the history of IOC governance as more reforms were initiated. The IF's had met prior to the Berlin Congress and requested that representatives of all IOC-recognised IFs would get IOC membership (Müller, 1981). There was little support from the NOCs for such a proposal because they were represented well in the IOC. Hence, the IOC members rejected that suggestion because they feared conflicts of interest and, of course, a consequential watering down of their own decision-making power. In subsequent years, the Executive Board negotiated between the IOC and the IFs (Müller, 1981). This was also a consequence of Coubertin's retirement in 1925 and the election of Belgian aristocrat Henri de Baillet-Latour as IOC president (Carpentier, 2004). Eventually, the IFs stopped their demands of IOC memberships during the Olympic Congress in 1930 in Berlin when a Consultative Council of the IFs was installed. This body occupied an influential advisory role for specific legislative and technical issues such as the amateur question (Llewellyn and Gleaves, 2016). Hence, whilst the IFs were not successful in gaining IOC memberships or initiating constitutional changes in the IOC, the IFs' demands reformed mechanisms in the governance of the Olympic movement permanently – without affecting the IOC's composition. From the Olympic Congress in 1930 onwards, the IOC had to deal with the IFs on a regular basis (Müller, 1981) but the governance remained in the hands of the self-selected IOC members.

After the Second World War, the Olympic movement grew in size and global appeal, but IOC governance did not change much for a few decades. Under the conservative IOC President Avery Brundage (USA), who followed Edström as IOC president in 1952, the IOC tightly controlled challenging issues such as increasing secret professionalism, commercialisation and doping. This was opposed to significant developments in the Olympic movement that remained unaddressed. In particular, the rapid decolonialisation in Asia and Africa led to a significant increase in the number of NOCs in the 1950s and the 1960s. Before the Second World War, the IOC had only recognised six NOCs from Asia and Africa. This number increased to 48 NOCs in the 1970s. This internationalisation was only little reflected in IOC membership, though, as the IOC remained an elite, upper-class, male, European patrimony. The IOC had only co-opted nine African IOC members by 1972 (Lyberg, 1989).

A significant discussion on IOC membership evolved in 1948, when IOC member Sir Arthur Porritt (New Zealand) raised for the first time a possible introduction of age limits for IOC members (IOC, 1948). The debates in the IOC Session reflect the awareness of the IOC about the old average age of the members but hesitancy towards the introduction of a limit is recorded. Many IOC members argued that the IOC must retain Coubertin's traditions and should not bow to external criticism (ibid.). The IOC eventually appointed a working group under the leadership of Pieter W. Scharroo (The Netherlands) to investigate this issue. The working group proposed an age limit of 70 with retiring IOC members automatically becoming Honorary Members. However, the IOC Session in 1949 rejected the age-limit proposal (IOC, 1949) but the status of Honorary Members was introduced. Hence, the IOC members successfully protected their privileged status in order to maintain control over the Olympic movement. Ricardo Camillo Aldao (Argentina) became the first Honorary Member at the age of 86 in 1949 (Lyberg, 1989). A consequence of the rejection of the age limit was the lack of turnover within the IOC membership. The majority of the IOC members remained largely of aristocratic background and lacked an understanding for the realities of Olympic sport.

Whilst the IOC changed the status of the NOCs so that they had to be autonomous from governmental control (Henry and Al-Tauqi, 2008, see also the contribution by Henk Erik Meier in this volume), it effectively failed to deal with the political influence some states achieved through their selections of IOC memberships. The global expansion of the Olympic movement meant that IOC members from communist states could clearly not be independent from the control of their governments (Girginov, 1998). As a result, the discussions in the IOC became increasingly political, especially against the backdrop of the Cold War. In this context of increased politicisation, the IOC introduced the Committee of International Olympic Aid (CIOA) to support the development of sport in the newly independent states. The USSR heavily supported this decision because it aimed to extend its influence in Africa because it regarded the new states as an exploitable target to spread communism. The British IOC member Lord Luke warned the IOC that the USSR saw the IOC only as a means to an end (Henry and Al-Tauqi, 2008).

A new membership type of sport administrators entered the IOC after the Second World War, largely pushed by the socialist countries that rejected a pure aristocratic membership (Scherer, 1974). It were often those members with a sporting background that pushed for changes in the IOC's organisational structures and a broader IOC membership. The first Black African IOC member, Nigerian Ade Ademola, entered the IOC in 1963 (Lyberg, 1989). By the mid-1960s, it became obvious that the IOC in its traditional organisational structure could not maintain control over the governance processes in the Olympic movement. It was also then that the IOC eventually introduced an age limit for new members that had to retire at the age of 72 (IOC,

1966). Retiring members were usually replaced with new members from the same country. An obvious consequence was the increase of honorary members that the IOC appointed individually. The honorary members did not receive any voting rights but occasionally were awarded a special permission to make interventions during the IOC Sessions when they were experts on a topic.

The increasing complexity of the Olympic Games led the IOC Session to introduce statutory and thematic commissions in 1968. For example, an IOC Finance Commission, an IOC Commission for Press and Public Relations, an IOC Commission on Amateurism, an IOC Medical Commission and an IOC Commission for the Protection of Emblems were founded. The commissions were composed of IOC members and in some cases external experts (such as for example the IOC Medical Commission) and deal with individual topics in detail (Chappelet, 2012). Members of the various IOC commissions were appointed by the IOC president.

Again, it was pressure from the NOCs and the IFs that enforced bigger action from the IOC. In 1959, the IOC had still been able to reject the demand of the NOCs and IFs to have a permanent member in the IOC (Müller, 1981). But in 1966, the NOCs established the Permanent General Assembly of National Olympic Committees (ANOC) and in 1967, the IFs formed the Global Association of International Sports Federations (GAISF) (Müller, 1981). Therewith both set of stakeholders had created forums to join forces in their demands to shape the future policies of the Olympic movement. As a consequence, Brundage opted to stage the first Olympic Congress after the Second World War in order to address – amongst others – governance issues in the IOC. This Congress was held in Varna, Bulgaria, in 1973 and marks yet another reform of the IOC's governance processes with regards to its membership.

Addressing challenges and initiating changes: from Varna to Baden-Baden (1973–1981)

The IOC Executive Board delegated the organisation of the Olympic Congress to a new Commission (Wassong, 2018). Moreover, the IOC membership structure was one of the Commission's main concerns. However, the Commission mainly dealt with the geographical spread of the IOC members' origins (IOC, 1969). It recommended that the IOC maintains its basic structures but envisages an improvement and progressive balancing out of its direct representation on the different continents (ibid.). As the Commission foresaw an increasing workload in the preparation of the Olympic Congress, it proposed the formation of a new commission consisting of representatives of the IOC, IFs and the NOC. In 1971, this new Tripartite Commission was officially installed (Wassong, 2018), consisting of three representatives of the NOCs, three representatives of the IFs and three IOC vice-presidents. The eventual presentations at the Olympic Congress in Varna focused on the improvement of working processes between the IOC and the NOCs/IFs. However, in contrast to the IOC's fears, the stakeholders were loyal towards the IOC's governance and satisfied with the outcome of the Congress to include IF and NOC representatives in IOC commissions and future Congresses. On this basis, the new IOC President Lord Killanin (Ireland) eventually rejected structural changes in the IOC in his concluding remarks amidst the lack of alternatives (Müller, 1981). Rather, in an attempt to strengthen the relationship between the three main stakeholders in Olympic governance, it was recommended that the Tripartite Commission remained in existence. Its main task remained the organisation of the Olympic Congress with the next edition to be staged in 1981 (IOC, 1973c).

The involvement of athletes' representatives in the IOC also has its origins in the Olympic Congress in Varna in 1973 and in the discussions on the Tripartite Commission. It was mainly the representatives of the NOCs and the IFs who advocated for an inclusion of athletes in decision-making processes. However, IOC President Killanin was very cautious in his approach towards the institutionalisation of athletes and the IOC only granted athletes observer status at the Olympic Congress in 1973. It appears that the IOC members were anxious about unpredictable consequences if athletes were given influence in decision-making processes (ibid.). Nevertheless, their role constantly appears on the agenda of the Tripartite Commission in the time period leading to the next Congress in Baden-Baden in 1981.

Whilst the role of athletes' representatives was discussed but not institutionalised, another revolutionary recommendation of the Olympic Congress in Varna influenced IOC membership in the future. This was the recommendation that the IOC, the IFs and the NOCs should consider the inclusion of women in their membership and commissions (IOC, 1973a). The IOC Session discussed this proposal in its meeting directly after the Congress. Whilst the IOC members decided that women's names could be recommended for IOC membership, hesitancy remained. The IFs and the NOCs ought to have more women on their boards as a first step before the IOC could follow (IOC, 1973b). Hence, the IOC members delegated the responsibility to other stakeholders. In the following years, the IOC Session discussed the election of women on various occasions and undertook individual attempts to approach potential female IOC members (IOC, 1976a, 1977) but the IOC did not co-opt female IOC members until the beginning of the 1980s. That said, the 1970s saw the emergence of long-lasting female influence in the IOC through the appointment of Monique Berlioux as IOC Director in 1971 (Davenport, 1996b). Berlioux effectively ran the IOC business in Lausanne until 1985. Whilst her role is not directly linked to the IOC membership, her influence certainly affected the IOC's organisational structures and the strengthening of the IOC administration in the long term.

Even though the Olympic Congress in Varna did not have any immediate effects on the IOC membership, the discussion on the IOC's composition continued throughout the 1970s. In particular, the issue of the membership size was debated at various IOC Sessions. The IOC had an unwritten rule that there should be no more than 80 members but the IOC Session delegated the task to find the 'ideal' size of membership to the IOC Executive Board in 1976 (IOC, 1976b). In 1978, the Executive Board and the IOC Session discussed extensively the size of membership and geographical spread of IOC members. Whilst there was general agreement that the IOC should aim for continental balance, the majority of the IOC members and Monique Berlioux from an administrative point of view also saw a need for a limitation of memberships for organisational reasons (IOC, 1978b). It also becomes obvious in the discussions that IOC President Killanin and the Executive Board anticipated that the IOC Session accepted its nominations of new members (IOC, 1978a). Such expectations point towards the continuing strong role of the Executive Board in the 1970s.

The time period between the Olympic Congress in Varna in 1973 and the preparation of the Olympic Congress in Baden-Baden in 1981 can be defined as a transition phase in Olympic governance. Many prospective changes such as the inclusion of women in the IOC membership and the involvement of athletes' representatives were initiated. However, it is significant that the IOC members continued to protect their status in this phase and did not implement decisive changes, yet.

Implementing reforms: the effects of Baden-Baden (1981–1999)

Without question, the election of Juan Antonio Samaranch to IOC president in 1980 and the debates at the 1981 Olympic Congress in Baden-Baden were substantial for the development of the Olympic movement that we know today. Samaranch advocated for the abandonment of the amateur regulation and was successful (and powerful enough) to lead the IOC into the commercial age. By the time of the 1988 Olympic Games, all athletes were eligible for competing at the Olympic Games with the exception of professional boxers, basketball players of the National Basketball Association (NBA) and football players older than 23 years (Gutmann, 2002). These exceptions had been introduced by the respective IFs, though. The representatives of the Eastern bloc strongly opposed the "open games" but were outvoted by the majority of the IOC members that saw commercial benefits for the Olympic movement. Against such developments, the financial negotiations of the IOC Finance Commission became increasingly influential in the governance of the Olympic movement. The commercialisation was further accelerated through the introduction of the global sponsorship scheme The Olympic Programme (TOP) administered by Swiss marketing firm International Sport and Leisure (ISL) (Chappelet and Kübler-Mabbot, 2008). The increase in television and sponsorship money allowed the IOC to pay the expenses of the IOC members from the 1980s onwards (Girginov, 1998).

The reform surrounding the events in Baden-Baden also influenced the IOC membership. In 1981, the IOC Session voted in Pirjo Haggman (Finland) and Flor Isava-Fonseca (Venezuela) the first women onto the IOC (Davenport, 1996a). This revolutionary step was followed by other women's elections: Mary Alison Glen-Haig (Great Britain) in 1982, Princess Nora of Liechtenstein in 1984, Anita DeFrantz (USA) in 1985; H.R.H. Princess Anne (Great Britain) in 1988; Carol Anne Letheren (Canada) in 1990. Six of these women were Olympic athletes and all of them had been involved in the leadership of various sport organisations. In 1992, DeFrantz became the first woman on the IOC Executive Board and in 1997 she was elected the first female IOC vice-president (Davenport, 1996a; IOC, 1997).

After the Congress in Baden-Baden at which athletes were again given the stage to present their opinions, the IOC under Samaranch's leadership changed its strategy towards athletes' representation. In light of the opening for professional athletes, the IOC members became wary about an active inclusion of athletes in order to avoid a public confrontation through a potential foundation of an independent athletes' union (Wassong, 2018). Samaranch was aware that he needed the athletes on his side in order to execute his envisioned Olympic reform. Hence, the IOC created the IOC Athletes' Commission at the Executive Board meeting in Sarajevo in 1981 (IOC, 1981). The IOC president appointed the Commission's members and therewith the IOC still maintain a large degree of control over the Commission. The role of the Athletes' Commission remained consultative for two decades as the IOC did not award IOC membership to the commission members. The Commission's chair Peter Talberg (Finland) was already an IOC member.

The installation of the Court of Arbitration of Sport (CAS) at the IOC Session in 1983 saw the emergence of regulators within Olympic governance (Chappelet and Kübler-Mabbot, 2008). The IOC established the CAS mainly "to find an ultimate, authoritative and neutral solution to judicial disputes among athletes, international and national sports federations, national Olympic committees and Olympic and other games organizers" (McLaren, 2001). With the installation of the CAS, the IOC was able to protect the authority of sport, attempting to solve legal disputes within its own spheres. However, there was no unanimous agreement for the introduction of CAS as some IOC members regarded a regulating body as irrelevant. Even some major IFs like the IAAF objected to recognising the legal authority of the CAS (ibid.).

With regards to the inclusion of the NOCs and the IFs in the governance processes, the Tripartite Commission remained in place following the Baden-Baden Congress but was renamed as the Olympic Movement Commission. The IOC also redefined the Commission's task as it did not deal with the organisation of an Olympic Congress but rather current issues of the Olympic Games (Wassong, 2018). The Commission was also expanded to the IOC president, the members of the Executive Board, nine representatives each of NOCs and IFs and the Chair of the IOC Athletes' Commission. This high-profile composition points towards the significance of the Commission. Nevertheless, discussions on an even closer cooperation between the IOC, the NOCs and the IFs remained on the agenda. At the 1984 IOC Session it was suggested that the presidents of the Summer and Winter IFs as well as the president of ANOC should be co-opted as ex-officio members without voting rights (IOC, 1984a). Significantly, this discussion was made against the background of the television rights negotiations for the 1988 Seoul Olympic Games as the IOC continued to receive increasing financial benefits (Barney, Wenn and Martyn, 2004). The Executive Board seemed aware of a potential vote against the inclusion of IF and NOC representatives, which would clearly result in bad relations with the other stakeholders that had to agree to the ongoing television negotiations (IOC, 1984b). Eventually, the IOC decided to include a paragraph that allowed the IOC Session to especially invite representatives of IFs and NOCs on relevant matters (IOC, 1985).

The lack of an institutional inclusion of IFs and NOCs representatives did not stop Samaranch from establishing close links to the most influential individuals from other stakeholders such as FIFA President João Havelange (Brazil), IAAF President Primo Nebiolo (Italy), ANOC President Mario Vázquez Raña (Mexico) and ASOIF President Kim Un-Young (Republic of Korea). Sport historian Allen Guttmann refers to this circle as "The Club" (Gutmann, 2002). Allegedly, these men supported Samaranch in his attempt to overturn the age of mandatory retirement at the IOC Session in Budapest in 1995 (ibid.). The then existing age limit of 75 would have meant that Samaranch could not stand for re-election in 1997. In the second attempt, the IOC members voted for Samaranch's motion, much to the anger of individual critical IOC members such as Richard Pound (Canada) (ibid.).

Without a doubt, the composition of the IOC also reflects broader developments in world politics. The fall of the Berlin Wall in 1989 that ended 40 years of division between the capitalist Western and the communist Eastern blocs serves as an example for this. The IOC had a high interest in integrating the new Eastern European countries' leaderships into the Olympic movement and met twice with political representatives to discuss a potential involvement in the 1992 Olympic Games (Girginov, 1998). Against the background of the political developments and the rapid emergence of numerous NOCs in Eastern Europe, the IOC Session in Albertville in 1992 took the unprecedented step to delegate full powers to the IOC president and four vice-presidents to take all decisions relating to the recognition of the NOCs of republics which were part of the former Union of Soviet Socialist Republics (USSR) (IOC, 1992). Hence, politics shaped decision-making processes in the IOC decisively in this regard. Nevertheless, it took until September 1994 until Valeriy Borzov (Ukraine) became the first IOC co-opted member from an independent country that had been a Soviet territory (IOC, 1994). This was followed by further inclusion of members from outside Europe to reach a better geographical balance in the 1990s that eventually led to an increasing internationalisation of IOC membership.

Crisis causes change: the Salt Lake City scandal and its consequences (1999–2013)

In November 1998, publications of accusations that the Bidding Committee for the 2002 Salt Lake City Winter Olympic Games had bribed several IOC members shook the world of sport (Mallon, 2000; Mason, Thibault and Misener, 2006). IOC member Marc Hodler (Switzerland) confirmed publicly that this problem was not a sole incident. Such tension is a consequence of the IOC's membership composition when individuals also serve governments or NOCs (Mason, Thibault and Misener, 2006). Eventually, the IOC sanctioned sixteen members, changed the election system for the 2006 Winter Olympic Games, established an IOC Ethics Commission and founded the IOC 2000 Commission (also known as IOC Reform Commission) (MacAloon, 2011). In October 1999, the IOC 2000 Commission recommended a total of 50 measures that addressed governance issues in general and IOC membership in particular. The IOC Session accepted all recommendations in December 1999 (IOC, 1999).

The consequences of the reform for IOC governance were drastic, even though the IOC membership on the Samaranch's leadership remained in control over the processes (MacAloon, 2011). A few experts were consulted but in essence the IOC members had to work their way through the crisis together – a process that contributed to the transformation into the post-Samaranch era following the election of Jacques Rogge as IOC president in 2001 (MacAloon, 2011). Especially as the reform enhanced the characteristic that the IOC president has considerable less powers than the IOC Executive Board (Chappelet, 2012). Due to the strong involvement of the existing co-opted IOC members, the one country/one voting representative was never considered during the reform process, mainly to maintain IOC members' independence. Nevertheless, changes to the IOC membership and the nomination of new IOC members were made. Since 2000, new members can be proposed by the IOC, the IFs, the NOCs and the IOC Athletes' Commission with a new IOC Nominations Committee screening the applications (IOC, 1999).

The reform also saw a change in the overall IOC membership as the IOC now targets for a total of 115 members, amongst them fifteen athletes' representatives, fifteen IF representatives and fifteen NOC representatives (Chappelet, 2012). Whilst this distribution of IOC members leads to a better balance and more expertise in sport on the IOC, the regulation also introduced a conflict of interest into the IOC governance (MacAloon, 2011, p. 299). The IFs representatives must now act in the best interest of the IOC whilst they might have alternative strategies in their respective IF roles. An additional change concerned the member age limit for new IOC members. Whereas the age limit for members co-opted between 1966 and 1999 remained 80 years, the age limit for new members is 70 years (IOC, 2016). An enlargement of the IOC Executive Board from eleven to fifteen members and a term limit for the IOC president – an eight-year mandate, renewable for a further four years – was also agreed (IOC, 1999).

It is noteworthy that within the context of the Salt Lake City scandal, the term 'governance' first appeared in international sport (Chappelet, 2016). However, whilst the reform process tackled some of the issues that were later attributed to governance principles, it was only in 2004 that the word 'governance' appeared in the Olympic Charter for the first time. Since 2011, the promotion of ethics and good governance is included in the mission and role of the IOC (ibid.). The inclusion of the term is not mere lip service. In 2012, the IOC Session excluded the International Federation of Associated Wrestling Styles (FILA) provisionally because it did not follow good governance principles (Kaya, 2015).

The IOC 2000 Reform also affected the role of the IOC Athletes' Commission as twelve of its members – eight summer sport and four winter sport active or recently retired athletes – are now elected by Olympic athletes for eight-year terms at the Olympic Games (Wensing, 2004). The IOC president appoints the other seven IOC Athletes' Commission members with the aim to ensure gender, sports and geographical balance. Most significantly, the voted athletes' representatives have full voting rights whereas only three of the appointed members have voting rights (unless they are already IOC members). Moreover, the Chair of the Athletes' Commission is now a member of the Executive Board.

The changes in the IOC membership affected governance processes but the inclusion of additional stakeholders also influenced the governance processes in the Olympic movement. The then President of the International Paralympic Committee (IPC), Robert Steadward (Canada), was part of a Working Group contributing to the IOC reform process and he engaged in the formulation of Recommendation 15 related to the Paralympic Games (Bailey, 2008). As a consequence, the IOC and the IPC signed an agreement in October 2000 that also included the recommendation that the Paralympic movement, through a member of the IPC and Paralympic athletes, could be represented in the IOC. This led to Steadward's election as an IOC member at the same IOC Session (IOC, 2000). Moreover, non-profit organisations became increasingly influential, contributing with consultancy functions to the IOC members' work in the IOC commissions. For the 2000 Sydney Olympic Games, the IOC invited Greenpeace to monitor the environmental practices at the Olympic Games (Leopkey and Parent, 2012). Other NGOs have followed but it is continuously claimed that a closer cooperation with organisations such as Amnesty International or Human Rights Watch is necessary to strengthen the IOC's moral authority (Kidd, 2010).

Despite the installation of good governance principles in the IOC and the attempt to act as an international forerunner in reform processes, the Olympic movement continued to be hit by corruption scandals in recent years (Chappelet, 2018). In 2015 and 2016, FIFA and the IAAF have faced allegations of corruption and manipulation on all levels (Krieger, 2018). Significantly, the corruption scandals involving other sport federations also influenced the IOC and had wider consequences for the Olympic movement. For example, former FIFA President Joseph Blatter (Switzerland) and former IAAF President Lamine Diack (Senegal) were both IOC members at the time of the accusations (Tomlinson, 2017; Krieger, 2018). As a consequence, the perception of the Olympic Games is significantly impacted by the IOC's image (Giesen and Hallmann, 2018), and the negative perception of IOC members had led to numerous cases of residents' rejections of staging the Olympic Games in recent years. Thus, the need for another reform became apparent to the IOC membership.

The latest reform: the Olympic Agenda 2020

Against the background of the threat of fewer and fewer cities bidding to host the Olympic Games, the IOC under the new leadership of IOC President Thomas Bach (Germany) introduced the Olympic Agenda 2020 in 2014. The core areas of the reform package are the intensification of the international anti-doping fight, the modernisation of the competition programme, the overhaul of the bid process for the Olympic Games, the sustainability of the Olympic Games and dual career programmes for Olympic athletes (IOC, 2014).

A part of the Olympic Agenda 2020 recommendations is directed at the IOC itself. Some recommendations such as the revision of the Code of Ethics, a review of the commission structures and compliance with good governance principles are considered to have little effect on the public image of the IOC (MacAloon, 2016). With regards to the IOC membership, the decision to target new IOC members with IOC relevant competencies requires special attention. The IOC Nominations Commission is in charge of this targeted recruitment process. The composition of the Nominations Commission is evidence for the progressive change in the IOC member co-optation strategy as it includes at least one representative of the IOC Ethics Commission and one representative of the IOC Athletes' Commission (IOC, 2016). This body examines all candidates and hands its evaluation to the IOC Executive Board, which then proposes new members to the IOC Session. The IOC Nominations Commission focuses on the following four criteria: (1) the IOC's needs in terms of skills and knowledge, (2) geographic balance, (3) gender balance, (4) the existence of an athletes' commission within the organisation for representatives of IFs/NOCs (IOC, 2014). As we have demonstrated in this chapter, these four themes are reoccurring constantly in the discussion on the IOC membership, significantly impacting governance processes in the Olympic movement. The focus on skills reflects a modern governance approach.

As a result of the new policy, the IOC puts more emphasis on the sporting background of its members. Currently, the IOC has 99 members and 36 of the members have competed in the Olympic Games. Twenty-nine IOC members have won Olympic medals (IOC, 2016). With this strategy, the IOC membership aims to demonstrate its proximity to the realities of the sporting world. However, as former IOC member Johann Olav Koss (Norway) has argued, the athletes' representatives on the IOC do not necessarily represent the best interests of the Olympic participants (Koss, 2011).

Individual incidents that have occurred after the implementation of the Olympic Agenda 2020 recommendations confirm concerns that some issues remain unaddressed. For example, IOC member Patrick Hickey (Ireland) was arrested during the 2016 Rio Olympic Games over alleged ticket touting. In 2017, the IOC suspended its member Frankie Fredericks (Namibia) after he had been charged with money laundering and corruption (IOC, 2017). Clearly, the many-times-reformed membership structure still lacks targeting obvious conflicts of interest. As a result, the absence of public confidence in the IOC membership remains a key issue. The continuing voting against staging the Olympic Games in several referenda over the past few years is a consequence. This could be witnessed, for example, in June 2018 when the population of the Swiss Canton of Valais voted against staging the 2026 Winter Olympic Games in the region.

Conclusion

We highlighted in this chapter, through a historical review, that the IOC's membership influence the governance of the Olympic movement. Changes to the composition of the IOC are linked to significant IOC reforms. Six different phases were identified. First, the IOC's founder Pierre de Coubertin shaped the governing body's self-recruiting nature with his vision that IOC members must adopt representative as well as managerial roles. Second, Coubertin's installation of the IOC Executive Board in 1921 demanded more responsibility for a selected group of IOC members and the emergence of significant stakeholders such as the NOCs and the IFs changed the decision-making processes in the IOC decisively. Third, growing tensions within the Olympic movement led to intensive debates at the Olympic Congress in Varna in 1973 that led to the IOC to address challenges and initiate changes in its composition. Fourth, in the aftermath of the Olympic Congress in Baden-Baden in 1981, many of the changes such as the inclusion of female IOC members and the establishment of an IOC Athletes' Commission were implemented. Fifth, the IOC 2000 Commission brought about the most decisive changes in IOC membership on the back of the Salt Lake City scandal with an increased involvement of representatives from sport organisations and (former) athletes. And sixth, the Olympic Agenda 2020 called for a targeted recruitment process in the IOC that has consequences for the profiles of future IOC members.

References

Bailey, S. (2008). *Athlete first: A history of the Paralympic movement.* West Sussex: John Wiley & Sons.

Barney, R.K., Wenn, S.R. and Martyn, S.G. (2004). *Selling the five rings: The IOC and the rise of the Olympic commercialism.* Salt Lake City: University of Utah Press.

Carpentier, F. (2004). *Le Comité international olympique en crises: la présidence de Henri de Baillet-Latour, 1925–1940.* Paris: L'Harmattan.

Chappelet, J-L. (2012). From daily management to high politics: The governance of the International Olympic Committee. In: L. Robinson, P. Chelladurai, G. Bodet and P. Downward, eds., *Routledge handbook of sport management*. Oxon: Routledge, pp. 7–25.

Chappelet, J-L. (2016). Autonomy and governance: Necessary bedfellows in the fight against corruption in sport. In: Transparency International, ed., *Global corruption report: Sport*. Oxon: Routledge, pp. 16–28.

Chappelet, J-L. (2018). Beyond governance: The need to improve the regulation of international sport. *Sport in Society*, 21(5), pp. 724–734.

Chappelet, J-L. and Bayle, E. (2016). From Olympic administration to Olympic governance: Challenges for our century. *Sport in Society*, 19(6), pp. 737–738.

Chappelet, J-L. and Kübler-Mabbot, B. (2008). *The International Olympic Committee and the Olympic system: The governance of world sport*. London: Routledge.

Davenport, J. (1996a). Breaking into the rings: Women on the IOC. *Journal of Physical Education, Recreation and Dance*, 67(5), pp. 26–30.

Davenport, J. (1996b). Monique Berlioux: Her association with three IOC presidents. *Journal of Olympic History*, 4(3), pp. 10–18.

Ferrand, A., Chappelet, J-L. and Séguin, B. (2012). *Olympic marketing*. Oxon: Routledge.

Geeraert, A. (2016). Indicators and benchmarking tools for good governance. In: Transparency International, ed., *Global corruption report: Sport*. Oxon: Routledge, pp. 56–61.

Giesen, N. and Hallmann, K. (2018). The impact of the perceived image and trust in the International Olympic Committee on perceptions of the Olympic Games in Germany. *International Journal of Sport Policy and Politics*, 10(3), pp. 509–523.

Girginov, V. (1998). Capitalist philosophy and communist practice: The transformation of Eastern European sport and the International Olympic Committee. *Culture, Sport Society*, 1(1), pp. 118–148.

Grosset, Y. and Attali, M. (2009). The French initiative towards the creation of an international sports movement 1908–1925: An alternative to the IOC. *Journal of Sport History*, 36(2), pp. 120–142.

Gutmann, A. (2002). *The Olympics: A history of the modern games*. Urbana: University of Illinois Press.

Henry, I. and Al-Tauqi, M. (2008). The development of Olympic solidarity: West and non-west (core and periphery) relations in the Olympic world. *The International Journal of the History of Sport*, 25(3), pp. 355–369.

IOC. (1908). *Comité International Olympique 1908 – Annuaire*. Paris: IOC.

IOC. (1948). *Minutes of the 43th IOC Session, held in London* [Minutes]. Lausanne: Archive of the IOC's OSC.

IOC. (1949). *Minutes of the 44th IOC Session, held in Rome* [Minutes]. Lausanne: Archive of the IOC's OSC.

IOC. (1966). *Minutes of the 65th IOC Session, held in Rome* [Minutes]. Lausanne: Archive of the IOC's OSC.

IOC. (1969). *Minutes of the IOC Executive Board Meeting, held in Lausanne, 22nd and 23rd March 1969* [Minutes]. Lausanne: Archive of the IOC's OSC.

IOC. (1973a). *10th Olympic Congress. The Olympic movement and its future. Sport for a world of peace*. Lausanne: IOC.

IOC. (1973b). *Minutes of the 74th IOC Session, held in Varna* [Minutes]. Lausanne: Archive of the IOC's OSC.

IOC. (1973c). *Olympic rules and regulations*. Lausanne: IOC.

IOC. (1976a). *Minutes of the 77th IOC Session, held in Innsbruck* [Minutes]. Lausanne: Archive of the IOC's OSC.

IOC. (1976b). *Minutes of the 78th IOC Session, held in Montreal* [Minutes]. Lausanne: Archive of the IOC's OSC.

IOC. (1977). *Minutes of the IOC Executive Board Meeting, held in Prague, 13th and 14th June 1977* [Minutes]. Lausanne: Archive of the IOC's OSC.

IOC. (1978a). *Minutes of the 80th IOC Session, held in Athens* [Minutes]. Lausanne: Archive of the IOC's OSC.

IOC. (1978b). *Minutes of the IOC Executive Board Meeting, held in Athens, 13th to 18th May 1978* [Minutes]. Lausanne: Archive of the IOC's OSC.

IOC. (1981). *Minutes of the IOC Executive Board Meeting, held in Sarajevo, 2nd to 4th December 1981* [Minutes]. Lausanne: Archive of the IOC's OSC.

IOC. (1984a). *Minutes of the 88th IOC Session, held in Los Angeles* [Minutes]. Lausanne: Archive of the IOC's OSC.

IOC. (1984b). *Minutes of the IOC Executive Board Meeting, held in Los Angeles, 21st July to 13th August 1984* [Minutes]. Lausanne: Archive of the IOC's OSC.

IOC. (1985). *Minutes of the IOC Executive Board Meeting, held in Calgary, 25th to 28th February 1985* [Minutes]. Lausanne: Archive of the IOC's OSC.
IOC. (1992). *Minutes of the 98th IOC Session, held in Courchevel* [Minutes]. Lausanne: Archive of the IOC's OSC.
IOC. (1994). *Minutes of the 103rd IOC Session, held in Paris* [Minutes]. Lausanne: Archive of the IOC's OSC.
IOC. (1996). *The International Olympic Committee one hundred years [3]: The idea, the presidents, the achievements*. Lausanne: IOC.
IOC. (1997). *Minutes of the 106th IOC Session, held in Lausanne* [Minutes]. Lausanne: Archive of the IOC's OSC.
IOC. (1999). *Minutes of the 110th IOC Session, held in Lausanne* [Minutes]. Lausanne: Archive of the IOC's OSC.
IOC. (2000). *Minutes of the 111th IOC Session, held in Sydney* [Minutes]. Lausanne: Archive of the IOC's OSC.
IOC. (2014). *Olympic Agenda 2020. 20 + 20 recommendations*. Lausanne: IOC.
IOC. (2016). *Factsheet IOC members* [Online]. Available at: https://stillmed.olympic.org/media/Document%20Library/OlympicOrg/Factsheets-Reference-Documents/Olympic-Movement/IOC-Members/Factsheet-IOC-Members-April-2016.pdf (Accessed 12 April 2020).
IOC. (2017). *IOC statement on IOC member Mr. Frank Fredericks* [Online]. Available at: https://www.olympic.org/news/ioc-statement-on-ioc-member-mr-frank-fredericks-1 (Accessed 12 April 2020).
Jobling, I. and Letters, M. (1996). Forgotten links: Leonard Cuff and the Olympic movement in Australasia, 1894–1905. *Olympika: The International Journal of Olympic Studies*, 5(1), pp. 91–110.
Kaya, A. (2015). Survival of the International Federation of Associated Wrestling Styles: A personal retrospective. *International Journal of Wrestling Science*, 5(1), pp. 63–65.
Kidd, B. (2010). Human rights and the Olympic movement after Beijing. *Sport in Society*, 13(5), pp. 901–910.
Koss, J.O. (2011). Athletes' rights and Olympic reform: A discussion with Johann Koss, Ann Peel and Alexandra Orlando. *Sport in Society*, 14(3), pp. 309–318.
Krieger, J. (2016). "Born on the wings of commerce": The world championships of the International Association of Athletics Federations. *The International Journal of the History of Sport*, 33(4), pp. 418–433.
Krieger, J. (2018). Manipulation in athletics: Historical and contemporary ties between on- and off-field corruption in the International Association of Athletics Federations (IAAF). *The International Journal of the History of Sport*, 35(2–3), pp. 231–246.
Lee, J. and Hardin, R. (2015). *Policy and governance in sport: Issues, organizations, and practical application*. Durham: Carolina Academic Press.
Leopkey, B. and Parent, M.M. (2012). The (neo) institutionalization of legacy and its sustainable governance within the Olympic movement. *European Sport Management Quarterly*, 12(5), pp. 437–455.
Llewellyn, M.P. and Gleaves, J. (2016). *The rise and fall of Olympic amateurism*. Champaign: University of Illinois Press.
Lyberg, W. (1989). *The IOC Sessions I and the IOC Sessions II: 1894–1955 and 1956–1988*. Lausanne: IOC.
MacAloon, J.J. (2006). The mighty working of a symbol: From idea to organization. *The International Journal of the History of Sport*, 23(3), pp. 528–570.
MacAloon, J.J. (2011). Scandal and governance: inside and outside the IOC 2000 Commission. *Sport in Society*, 14(3), pp. 292–308.
MacAloon, J.J. (2016). Agenda 2020 and the Olympic movement. *Sport in Society*, 19(6), pp. 767–785.
Mallon, B. (2000). The Olympic bribery scandal. *Journal of Olympic History*, 8(2), pp. 11–27.
Mason, D.S., Thibault, L. and Misener, L. (2006). An agency theory perspective on corruption in sport: The case of the International Olympic Committee. *Journal of Sport Management*, 20(1), pp. 52–72.
McLaren, R.H. (2001). Introducing the court of arbitration for sport: The ad hoc division at the Olympic Games. *Marquee Sports Law Review*, 12(1), pp. 515–542.
Molzberger, A. (2012). *Die Olympischen Spiele 1912 in Stockholm. Zwischen Patriotismus und Internationalität*. St. Augustin: Academia Verlag.
Morbach, A. (1998). *Dimítrios Vikélas. Patriotischer Literat und Kosmopolit: Leben und Wirken des ersten Präsidenten des Internationalen Olympischen Komitees*. Baden-Baden: Ergon-Verlag.
Müller, N. (1981). *Von Paris bis Baden-Baden. Die Olympischen Kongresse 1894–1981*. Niedernhausen: Schors-Verlag.
Müller, N., ed. (2000). *Pierre de Coubertin 1863–1937. Olympism: Selected writings*. Lausanne: IOC.

Quanz, D. (1993). Die Gründung des IOC im Horizont von bürgerlichem Pazifismus und sportlichem Internationalismus. In: G. Gebauer, ed., *Die Aktualität der Sportphilosophie*. Sankt Augustin: Academia, pp. 191–216.

Scherer, K.A. (1974). *Der Männerorden. Die Geschichte des Internationalen Olympischen Komitees*. Frankfurt: Limpert.

Tomlinson, A. (2017). FIFA: "For the game. For the world"? The world governing body's escalating crisis of credibility. In: A. Bairner, J. Kelly and J.W. Lee, eds., *Routledge handbook of sport and politics*. London: Routledge, pp. 151–265.

Vanden Auweele, Y., Cook, E. and Parry, J. (2016). *Ethics and governance in sport*. Abington: Routledge.

Wassong, S. (2002). *Pierre de Coubertins US-amerikanische Studien und ihre Bedeutung für die Analyse seiner frühen Erziehungskampagne*. Würzburg: Ergon.

Wassong, S. (2003). The playing fields sub-commission of the International Olympic Committee (1926–1930). *Stadion International Journal of the History of Sport*, 29, pp. 167–181.

Wassong, S. (2018). The International Olympic Committee's Tripartite Commission and its influence on the foundation of the Athletes' Commission. *International Journal for the History of Sport*, 35(9), pp. 836–857.

Watson, B.N. (2012). *The father of judo: A biography of Jigoro Kano*. New York: Kodansha Amer.

Wensing, E.H. (2004). The IOC and the Athletes' Commission. In: K.B. Wamsley, S.G. Scott and R.K. Barney, eds., *Cultural relations old and new: The transitory Olympic ethos*. London, ON: University of Western Ontario, pp. 93–103.

Yttergren, L. (2008). Patriarch and a charismatic leader? Some reflections on IOC president J. Sigfrid Edström's leadership style based on Max Weber's concept of charisma. In: R.K. Barney, M.K. Heine, K.B. Wamsley and G.H. MacDonald, eds., *Pathways: Critiques and discourse in Olympic research*. Ninth International Symposium for Olympic Research. London, ON: University of Western Ontario, pp. 296–301.

19

Changing parasport landscape and the evolution of the International Paralympic Committee governance

Laura Misener and Landy Di Lu

Introduction

International sport governing bodies that regulate world sports claim a variety of governance structures, mechanisms and functions. These sport organisations, through appropriate structures, rules and regulations, and ethical decision-making and processes, are responsible for governing sports in a transparent manner (Geeraert, Alm and Groll, 2014). Some of these organisations make public their missions, visions, objectives and functional statements for public consumption (Forster, 2006). Typically, their functions comprise some subset of activities such as developing the laws, policies and rules of a sport and its competitions; organising international/global sporting events and tournaments, facilitating and advancing the global development of a sport at all levels; providing guidance and caring for the welfare of athletes within a sport (Chelladurai and Zintz, 2015; Forster, 2006). Further, these organisations also serve as the main sites for the 'arbitration and/or resolution of disputes within a sport' (Forster, 2006, p. 72) and foster and maintain relationships with a list of external stakeholders, including national sport associations, governments, regulatory authorities and business entities (e.g. commercial sponsors; Forster, 2006). How international sport governing bodies achieve this varies somewhat and is often reflective of the overall context in which the sporting environment is conceived and evolving (Edwards, Mason and Washington, 2009; Kikulis, 2000).

Within existing research on the governance of international sport governing bodies, much attention has been paid to examining the organisation and structure of the International Olympic Committee (IOC) (e.g. Chappelet, 2008; Geeraert, Alm and Groll, 2014; Leopkey and Parent, 2012; Mason, Thibault and Misener, 2006). Relatively little is known about the governance and management of the International Paralympic Committee (IPC). The IPC, as the global governing body of the Paralympic movement, is responsible for convening both the Summer and Winter Paralympic Games. The IPC also serves as the international federation for a number of sports (e.g. para swimming, para ice hockey – discussed later) and helps stage and organise associated world championships and competitions for people with disabilities (IPC Annual Report, 2007). From the beginning the IPC has had a dual purpose of serving 'Paralympic athletes to achieve sporting excellence' (ibid., p. 14), while also providing and improving sporting opportunities for all para-athletes from the grassroots to the elite level (IPC Annual Report, 2007). Further, the IPC aims to promote the Paralympic values, which include 'courage, determination, inspiration and equality' (IPC Strategic Plan, 2015b, p. 9). In the case of the IPC, the governance structure has evolved over time to reflect the changing landscape of disability sport (parasport hereafter) globally. Further, their relationship with other organisations such as the IOC has evolved and influenced the governance structure.

In this chapter, we examine the evolution of this governance structure of the IPC, focusing on organisational structure and design to demonstrate how the changing environment of governance has influenced and is influenced by the evolving parasport field. While the IPC has attempted to remain a distinct global sport organisation, we noted the tendency of the IPC to imitate the IOC's governance and management structures throughout its history. We reflect on four distinct phases of governance for the IPC: (1) initial formation; (2) professionalisation; (3) separation of management and governance; and (4) streamlining. Our aim is to reflect how governance has evolved overtime to meet the needs of a changing global sport organisation and the landscape of parasport governance.

Stage 1: Initial formation (1989–1998)

The initiation of the Paralympic Games preceded the formation of the IPC. As has been chronicled by other scholars (e.g. Gold and Gold, 2007; Howe, 2008; Legg and Steadward, 2013), there is much contested history about the formation of the Paralympic Games. But the accepted initial stages stemmed from rehabilitation practices at Stoke Mandeville Hospital in the United Kingdom (Brittain, 2012). The early Paralympic Games were organised for military veterans returning from war with spinal cord injury (Brittain, Ramshaw and Gammon, 2013). As sport for persons with disabilities grew in popularity, a number of organisations were formed to support the movement focusing on different impairment groups. Each federation had a structured sporting calendar for specific impairment groups, from the grassroots to the international level. In the early 1960s, the International Stoke Mandeville Wheelchair Sports Federation (ISMWSF, formed in 1960) and the International Sports Organization for the Disabled (ISOD, formed in 1964) were established to sanction international competitions and provide sporting opportunities for people with locomotor disabilities (Depauw, 2012). In the following years, more organisations/associations such as the Cerebral Palsy International Sports and Recreation Association (CPISRA, founded in 1968) and the International Blind Sports Association (IBSA, founded in 1981) were formed and became integral to creating opportunities for people with disabilities and using sports as a vehicle for empowerment. The International Stoke Mandeville Games Federation (ISMGF) and ISOD, alongside the aforementioned organisations, were the precursors to the formation of the IPC (Bailey, 2008; Depauw, 2012; Gérard and Zintz, 2017). These organisations were involved in the planning and organisation of the Paralympic Games between the 1960s and the 1980s. However, during that time the IOC was becoming concerned about managing these growing Games and the special requests from each group. In 1982, a group called the International Coordinating Commission (ICC) of World Sports Organizations for the Disabled was developed to liaise with the IOC and help coordinate the Paralympic Games (Depauw, 2012). The ICC was originally composed of the four presidents of CPISRA, IBSA, ISMGF and ISOD, the general secretaries and one additional member (in the beginning it was the vice-president, and later on the technical officer). The International Committee of Sport for the Deaf (ICSD) and International Sports

Federations for Persons with an Intellectual Disability (INAS-FID) joined in 1986, but the ICSD still maintained their own organisation. With no country representatives, the ICC suffered from lack of national influence and support (Gérard and Zintz, 2017). Member nations required more national representation in the organisation. Lack of formalisation of this group and the rotating presidents also presented a challenge for the ongoing and sustainable communication with the IOC. The complication of coordinating such a diverse group of organisations raised another challenge for the ICC to achieve effective stakeholder management. There were clearly too many divergent agendas and beliefs around how the goals of the ICC should be realised.

In 1983, Dr. Robert Steadward and Anne Merklinger, President and Executive Director of the Federation of Sport Organizations for the Disabled (precursor to the Canadian Paralympic Committee), wrote a position paper outlining a potential new direction for the ICC (Bailey, 2008). They indicated 'sport for the disabled has developed to a level of excellence where the long-term competitive needs of our international athletes are dependent on one voice that can provide a coordinating authority for disabled sport development' (Bailey, 2008, p. 49). It took several years for these ideas to solidify and much work on behalf of the ICC and Dr. Steadward to bring together nations to discuss these challenges and the formation of one governing body (for further discussion on this history, see Bailey, 2008). On 14 March 1987, representatives from 39 countries and six international federations met at the Arnhem Seminar in the Netherlands and reached an agreement that a new international sports governing body should be developed to 'have national representation from every nation with a disability sport program' (Depauw, 2009, p. 21) and to be governed by a council of nations. In Seoul, Republic of Korea (site of the 1988 Paralympic Games), a task force was elected, which eventually evolved into the IPC in 1989 after several meetings. The IPC became the new and central governing body of the Paralympic movement and was in charge of organising the Paralympic Games and multi-disabled world and regional Games. Dr. Steadward served as the first president of the IPC from 1989 to 2001.

During this initial stage, the governance structure of the IPC followed a relatively loose organisational arrangement with a hierarchical design modelled off the IOC structure. The focus of this time was about building relationships with international federations, various countries, sport groups, all of which had their own constituencies with ideas on how the IPC should be structured. There was also a lot of work being done on moving from a disability structure to a sports structure with a primary purpose of integration (Bailey, 2008). Accordingly, the IPC founded the Sport Assembly Executive Committees targeted at centralising governance and developing rules of multi-disability sports (Gérard and Zintz, 2017).

Stage 2: Professionalisation (1999–2003)

As the Paralympic Games gained momentum and the relationship between the IOC became more solidified with the formation of one organising committee for the Sydney Olympic and Paralympic Games, the structure of the IPC continued to evolve. In the late 1990s, in order to handle the increasing growth and complexity of its operations, the IPC underwent a process of professionalisation. According to Suarez (2010, p. 311), professionalisation refers 'to the increasing presence of specialized expertise in an organization and to shifts from volunteer labor to paid staff'. One of the IPC's first attempts at professionalisation was to choose a permanent home for the administrative offices. In 1999, the IPC selected the city of Bonn, Germany, as the site for the IPC headquarters. This enabled the organisation to begin setting up a formal management structure run by a team of professional staff. The federal government of Germany and the city of Bonn provided necessary funding and resources for the construction and renovation of the IPC headquarters (Depauw, 2009). The first professional staff were later employed at the IPC headquarters, moving the management from a kitchen table organisation to a formal management structure.

At the 2001 Strategic Planning Congress in Malaysia, a number of items regarding the governance structure were brought to the fore. Namely, the membership wanted to see a move where the IPC would be solely responsible for the Paralympic Games; ISODs would continue to focus on sport development; sports were encouraged to move towards independence through close integration with international sports federations; greater synergies between partners were embraced; regional representation would continue to be emphasised; and the IPC would support the relationships with the National Paralympic Committees (NPCs) and National Olympic Committees (NOCs). A working group at that session put forth some clear recommendations for the IPC to solidify its position and continue to work towards a more professional governance structure. A lengthy set of recommendations for the future of the IPC resulted from the Strategic Planning Congress. Later that same year, there was a changing of the guard with the transition of Bob Steadward out of the role as president after 13 years, and the election of Sir Philip Craven, a five-time Paralympic athlete and then President of the International Wheelchair Basketball Federation.

Further attempts at greater professionalisation involved the creation of internal regulations to support the evolving approaches to good governance. This structure involved the development and formalisation of the General Assembly (GA). The GA becomes the supreme governing body of the IPC, composed of NPCs, International Federations, Regional Associations and IOSDs. The GA is responsible for defining the vision and general direction of the IPC, assuming the responsibility of governance-related mechanisms, including electing the president and Executive Committee members, and reviewing and approving the IPC's budget, funding and financial reports ('IPC operational structure,' n.d.). A formalisation of the membership of the Executive Committee (EC) was also an important step that occurred during this time. The EC which had been in place since 1990 was made up of 22 members from the GA, eight of whom came from the Management Committee (IPC Annual Report, 2004). In addition to the Executive and Management Committees, one Sports Council, ten standing committees (e.g. Medical Committee, Ethics Committee, Development Committee) and two Commissions (i.e. Commission for Women in Sport, Commission for Athletes with a Severe Disability) provided counselling and advice to the governance and running of the IPC (IPC Annual Report, 2004). It is worth noting that many of these committees mirror those of the IOC, demonstrative of the mimetic isomorphic approach to organisational design (Haveman, 1993) of the IPC during this time of professionalisation. Figure 19.1 illustrates the governance structure of the IPC during this stage. At this point in time the structure mimicked how other international sports federations were structured with the formalisation of one Council and a number of Committees and Commissions.

Further, there was also important work being done on building relationship with the IOC president and IOC members. An important structural element that was put in place at that this time was to have an IPC representative sit on the IOC Bid Review team and other joint coordinating committees (International Olympic Committee, 2012; Legg et al., 2015). This ensured a voice on matters related to the Games and consideration for many of the overlapping issues that needed to be addressed. Ultimately many of the governance and organisational management changes occurred during this time because of the need for growth and greater levels of professionalisation in the movement.

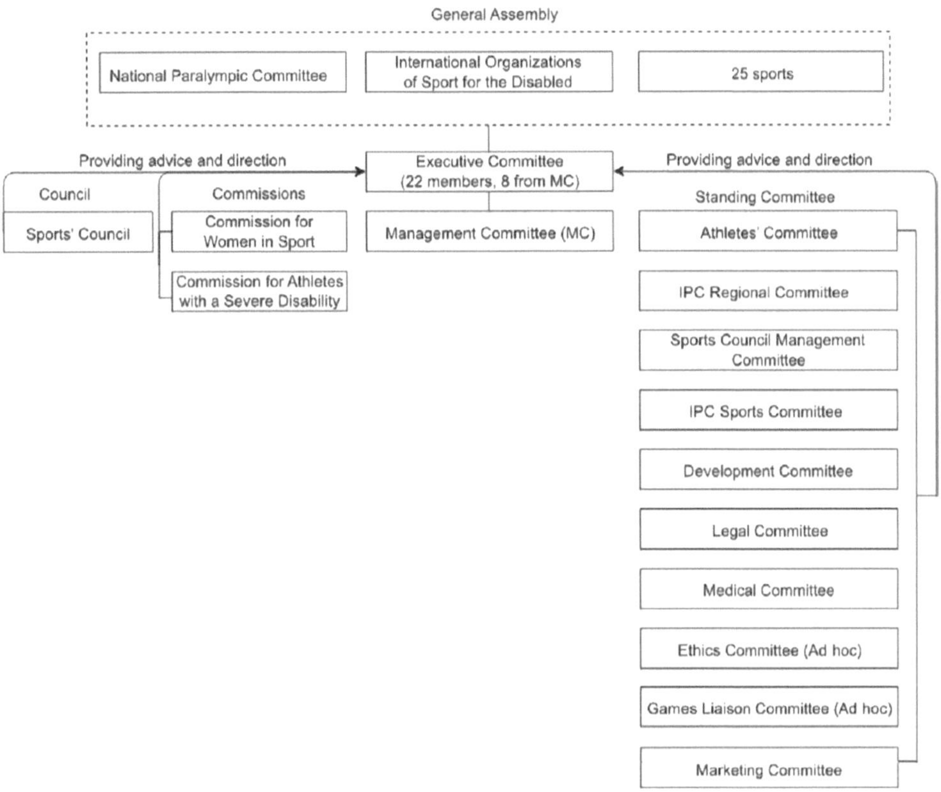

Figure 19.1 Governance structure of the IPC (1999–2003)

Source: Data from IPC Annual Report (2004)

Stage 3: Separating governance from management (2004–2014)

As the Paralympic movement continued to grow throughout the 1990s into the 2000s there was an increased need to consider how the IPC governed Paralympic sports. With the success of the Sydney 2000 Paralympic Games, the IPC was growing into more than an organiser of major games, as it also helped support opportunities for the development of Paralympic sport in countries around the world. During this time, a number of governance mechanisms were put in place to help advance both the development agenda and the high performance aims of the organisation. This development agenda alongside the high-performance agenda of the Games was critical to the spread of what the movement was about. The 2002 Salt Lake City Winter Olympic Games bribery scandal also prompted international sport governing bodies to deal with the growing concern of agency problems (Mason et al., 2006). The fundamental element here was a clear separation of management and governance, and mechanisms put in place to mitigate the self-governing and self-regulating activities of large-scale organisations.

In the wake of changes made to the IOC's governance structure, on 25 November 2004, a special session of the IPC General Assembly was held to overhaul the organisation's governance approach. As noted by Sir Philip Craven, IPC President at the time, 'the IPC Extraordinary

General Assembly held in Cairo, Egypt, in November was a turning point for the reorganization of our membership and organizational structure' (IPC Annual Report, 2004, p. 1). One of the most important changes to the governance during this stage was the separation of the governance and management. The EC was replaced with the Governing Board, which becomes the key representative of the GA and assumes the responsibility of overseeing the implementation of policies set by the Assembly. As part of this restructuring, a new IPC Constitution was adopted which involved new nomination and election procedures for the Governing Board. This involved the election of 14 members, 12 of whom are elected directly by the GA, the other two being an athletes' representative and the Chief Executive Officer (CEO) with non-voting membership (IPC Annual Report, 2004). The Management Committee was also replaced with the Management Team overseen by the CEO, which is a formal paid position within the IPC and is used as a way to ensure internal controls of management separate from governing structures. Compared to the prior Management Committee, the Management Team took on a greater level of prominence to oversee the operational role of the Games, sports delivery, administration and finance. With the authority delegated by the Governing Board, the CEO became the liaison between the governance and management responsibilities within the organisation (IPC Handbook, 2006b). This follows a more traditional governance and management structure where the CEO became a non-voting member of the Board and was responsible for leading the organisation to achieve its short- and long- term goal. Xavier González was appointed as the first CEO of the IPC. The IPC, therefore, operates under a structure that '"separates governance" (p. 4), referring to the role of the IPC Governing Board, "from management", which is the responsibility of the Management Team under the leadership of the CEO' (IPC Handbook, 2015a, p. 4). Separating governance from management constitutes a system of checks and balances and facilitates the implementation of internal control (Enjolras, 2009; Geeraert, Alm and Groll, 2014). This structure also mimics the IOC and other International Sport Federations in many ways. This beginning phase of the separation of the governance and management is critical to ensure oversight of the organisation and help reduce the potential of agency-related problems that have been apparent in the IOC (see e.g. Mason et al., 2006).

Apart from the development of the Governing Board and the Management Team, International Sport Federations (IFs) and Regional Organizations (ROs) were also made eligible to become full members of the IPC, enabling a greater level of oversight and involvement from the sport community in the activities of the IPC (IPC Annual Report, 2005). In addition to these changes, a number of regional changes took place that influenced the governance procedures of the IPC. One change in particular was influential in the governance structure. In 2005, the IPC Middle East Region merged into the IPC Asia Region, altering the regional structure of the IPC from six regions to five (IPC Annual Report, 2005). This impacted the overall structure of the GA and helped solidify the IPC as serving both a high-performance agenda in the Paralympic Games and a development agenda through the organisation of the Agitos Foundation.

During this stage, the organisational structure of the IPC changed to a more unit-based approach where the GA took over the role of governance through the NPCs, IOSDs, IFs and Regional Organizations (see Figure 19.2). The Governing Board reports directly to the GA. In addition to the existing Sports Council, three new Councils – the Athletes' Council, the IOSD Council and the Regions Council – were created to serve an important governance role. A particularly important council is the establishment of the Athletes' Council, composed of Paralympic athlete representatives. The creation of the Athletes' Council contributes to advocating for rights and needs of athletes within the Paralympic movement and to ensuring the voices of athletes were part of the decision-making processes (IPC Annual Report, 2006a). Active and

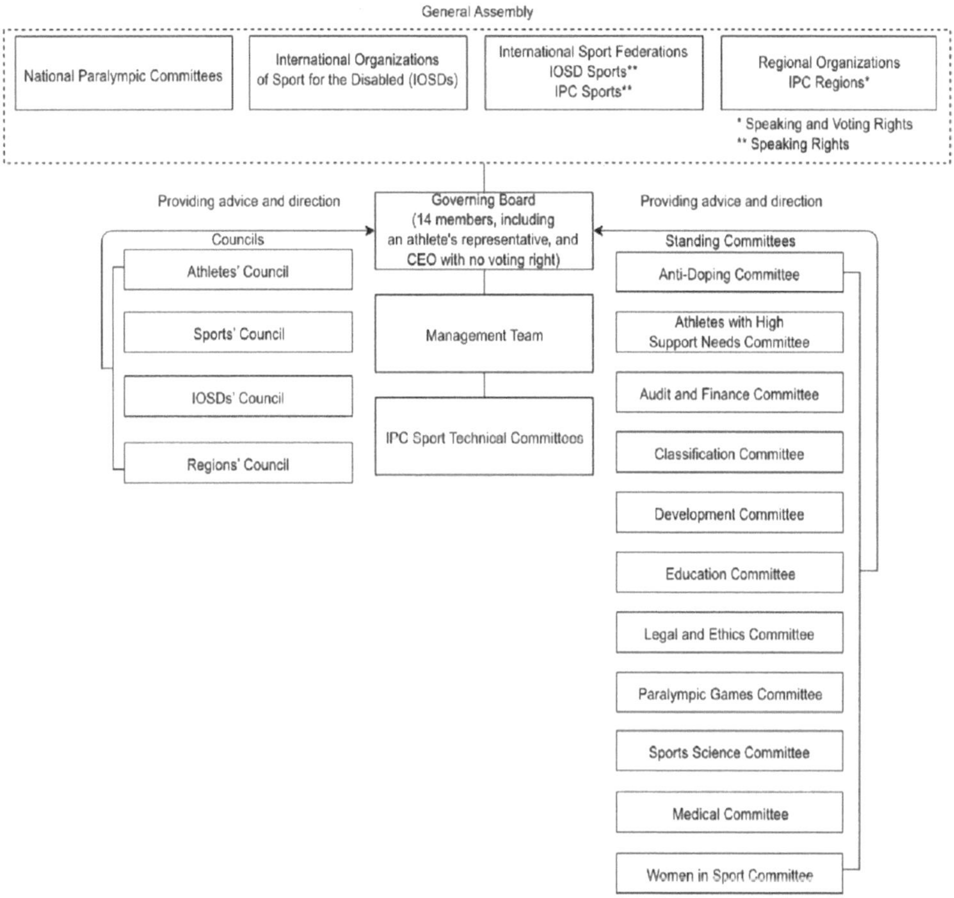

Figure 19.2 Governance structure of the IPC (2004–2014)

Source: Adapted from the IPC Annual Report (2012, p. 8)

equal participation of Paralympic athletes in the governance process also helps provide valuable input to Board-level decisions. The Athletes' Council also works across the organisational structure to ensure athlete representation at all levels of the organisation. In additional to the Councils, there are 11 standing committees. These Councils and Committees provide counselling, advice and direction and report directly to the Governing Board. See Figure 19.2 (adapted from the IPC Annual Report, 2006a, p. 8) for an updated list of standing committees and their role in the organisation.

Another layer to the governance structure that was put in place during these transition years were the sport technical committees (see Figure 19.2), which play an important consultative role from a governance perspective in terms of issues of classification, sport development and delivery and Games structure. These committees are also intimately involved in the management structure with the delivery and advisory roles reporting directly to the Management Team on issues related to individual sport delivery and operational issues.

During this time, there was also a change in structure regarding the role that IPC played in governing specific sports (IPC Technical Manager personal communication, May 14, 2019).

The IPC began to work more closely with international able-bodied counterparts for para swimming, para-athletics and boccia. The objective of this agenda was to ensure distinctiveness and sustainability of the sports over the long term. It also offered the IPC the opportunity to become financially viable and less reliant on the IOC for funds by hosting stronger competitive pools and tapping into the marketing and advertising of other international federations. World Championships for each of the sports were run now through the IPC, allowing them to reap the benefits of the event hosting structure in terms of sponsorship, media rights and exclusive marketing opportunities.

In addition to the already mentioned structural changes in the governing mechanisms, the IPC also undertook a substantial strategic planning process in 2004 to help the Management Team develop clear and concise strategic direction. The main strategic aims of the Management Team were identified as 'achieving global recognition, the success of the Paralympic Games, to be a leading sport organization and to enable membership autonomy' (IPC Annual Report, 2004, p. 9). The review specifically considered the Mission of the IPC and how this could be achieved through the ongoing work and efforts of the Management Team. A key element in this strategic direction was the formalisation of a working relationship with the IPC Standing Committees. Several new Committees (e.g. Anti-Doping Committee, Classification Committee, Audit and Finance Committee) had been formed during this period to provide advice and direction to the IPC. Each of the committees noted earlier serves (or served) an important governance function in terms of advising the IPC Governing Board and Management Team on matters of importance for Paralympic sport. This is important for ensuring the continuity, sustainability, viability and functional direction of the organisation. Further, it helps to ensure there are multiple layers of oversight to help reduce the risk of problems of corruption and power struggles within the IPC, as have been apparent in the IOC (see e.g. Mason et al., 2006). The structure had become highly complex at this point in time and was creating problems of alignment and stakeholder engagement. This complexity led to a number of concerns about the use of resources and discussions about the need to simplify the overall approach that would be more efficient and streamlined.

Stage 4: Streamlining organisational structure (2015–2019)

In recent years, the focus on governance and management of the IPC has been about efficiency and maximising of resources. As a result, there have been a number of structural changes which have brought the governance and management approaches closer together. The potential concern with this approach is the conceivable lack of oversight regarding agency-related challenges. One of the key changes that came about after the 2015 GA was the reduction in the number of standing committees. The aim here was to reduce the redundancy of some of the committees and create more focus on the core mission of the IPC. Currently, there are eight standing committees with the roles noted in Table 19.1 (IPC Standing Committees, 2019a). Further, the roles of the IOSDs Council, Regions Council and Sports Council were dissolved at the 2015 IPC GA, but many of the organisations still remain important members of the GA. An Independent Council of IOSDs and Association of Paralympic Sports Organizations (APSO) will be established in the near future with new communication mechanisms set in place to maintain clear interactions between the IPC and the Regional Associations. Effectively, this move allowed the IPC to adopt a more focused business model aimed at revenue generation and reach of the Paralympic Games, leaving the associations to focus more on the sport development agenda. In this way, the Agitos Foundation (philanthropic arm of the IPC) works more closely with the Regional Associations

Table 19.1 Standing committees of the IPC (2015–present)

Standing committee	*Role/responsibility*
Anti-Doping Committee	Provide consultation to the IPC on issues on how to monitor and fight against doping in parasports
Audit and Finance Committee	Provide consultation to the IPC on finance-related issues
Classification Committee	Provide consultation to the IPC on issues related to classification of athletes with disabilities
Education Committee	Provide consultation to the IPC on issues related to education in the Paralympic movement
Legal and Ethics Committee	Provide consultation to the IPC on legal and ethics-related issues (e.g. membership confirmation)
Medical Committee	Provide consultation to the IPC on how to provide better medical care for Paralympic athletes
Paralympic Games Committee	Provide consultation to the IPC on issues related to the Paralympic Games and programmes
Women in Sport Committee	Provide consultation to the IPC on issues of gender equity

Source: Data from IPC Handbook (2019)

through strategic infrastructure and development grants to promote Paralympism and sport development in the regions.

The overall structure of governance and management also changed in recent years to emphasise a more traditional top-heavy organisational structure that directly mimicked the IOC's structure. This hierarchical approach means that the GA, made up of NPCs, representation from the Independent IOSD's council, IFs and Regional Associations remains the primary mechanism of governance, internal regulation and control. The Governing Board serves as the governance mechanism that liaises with the Management Team. Thus, in essence the IPC remains a self-governing organisation with very little structural oversight from outside organisations.

A key issue that remains a challenge for the IPC today is the clear representation of the voices of persons with disabilities in all elements of the governance and management structure. In no place in the IPC Constitution does it suggest that members from any of the governing organisations or members need to have experience with impairment and/or disability. While we can imagine that member organisations might have that level of accountability in their own roles, this remains an area of contention. Only the Athletes' Commission which is made up of current and former Paralympic Athletes has any assurance that disability rights and issues are front and centre in the governing agenda. This becomes further complicated in the hosting of the Games as the Organizing Committee is the same for both Games as a result of the cooperative agreements which have been in place since 2000 (see Chapter 21 for further discussion on this relationship). As noted by IPC President Andrew Parson, the relationship between the IOC and IPC is helping drive the mechanisms of governance but also to help reach the potential of the IPC as an international organisation. The challenge for the IPC is to remain a strong distinctive organisation. Yet, in many respects, the IPC continues to mimic the workings of the IOC. It's likely the continued attempts as a closer relationship that drives these isomorphic tendencies, but this of course can be a risky approach to ensuring distinctiveness. As Andrew Parsons has stated:

> But we have to keep our own distinctive elements. We don't want a smaller version of the Olympic Games or the IOC. It's not what we want and it's not what they want. We want exactly what we bring to the table because I'd say it enriches the whole sport movement and the whole experience of the Olympic and Paralympic host city.
>
> *(Connolly, 2018, para. 21)*

As part of working towards this new agenda, in April 2018, the IPC announced that they would undergo an extensive governance review. The results of that review have culminated in the new 2019–2022 IPC Strategic Plan. This document sets forth a new agenda that is highly focused on international prominence, acquisition of resources, further professionalisation of the IPC (in particular the classification system). Further with the recent doping challenges facing all of international sport, the IPC must continue to determine its most appropriate course of action to work with the relevant stakeholders to manage these challenges. In the new Strategic Plan, the key approaches put forth to make a transformational impact include:

- Implement a global engagement strategy that communicates the values of the Paralympic brand and showcases activities within the Paralympic movement;
- Safeguard and further develop the Paralympic brand, its statement, attributes and graphical representation throughout the year;
- Enhance the Paralympic brand through greater activation and collaboration with IPC members, the IOC, broadcasters, commercial and strategic partners.

(IPC Strategic Plan 2019–2022, 2019b, p. 19)

The implications of this broad sweeping agenda will impact both the governance and management aspects of the movement. It is a highly ambitious agenda that helps enable a wide range of activities emanating from the IPC. However, there are questions about the feasibility of such a broad agenda and the role of an international sport governing body in making such global social change.

Conclusion

In this chapter we examine the evolution of governance and organisational structure of the IPC from 1989 to 2019 and correlate those changes with the evolving landscape of parasport governance. In the first stage (1989–1998) the increasing demand to build a parasport governing body with good national and sport representation and capability to maintain sustainable communication with the IOC led to the formation of the IPC. Following attempts of the IPC focused on building relationships with various countries and international and national sport entities. In the second stage (1999–2003), attention shifted toward professionalisation as the Paralympic Games became more popular and prominent globally along with the growing need to handle the complexity of running the Games. Specific efforts at professionalisation included a selection of a permanent site for the IPC headquarters, recruitment of full-time and professional staff, creation and implementation of internal regulations, formalisation of the GA and the EC, and strengthening the relationship with the IOC. In the third stage (2004–2014), attention shifted yet again to include growing concern for potential agency problems, leading to a series of attempts to separate governance from management and enhance the IPC oversight capabilities: the Governing Board was formed to replace the EC and excluded members of the Management Team to have voting rights on the Board; the IFs and ROs were invited on the Board to strengthen oversight from broader sport communities; the sport technical committees and a series of new councils and standing committees were founded to provide consultation and advice to the Board and the Management Team on the governance of the IPC, providing additional layers of oversight to reduce potential risks of corruption and power struggles within the IPC. In the fourth stage (2015–2019), the IPC spent more efforts at streamlining its governance and management structures to avoid redundancy, improve resource efficiency and highlight the core mission of the IPC. Important structural changes included reducing a number of standing committees and councils and strengthening a more traditional hierarchical organisational structure.

An overall review of its governance structure reveals several challenges for the IPC in the near future. First, the IPC still suffers from a lack of structural oversight from external and independent organisations. One area for the IPC to consider going forward is to include outside oversight; and have external stakeholders sit on the Governing Board where there are corruption risks. This outside oversight group should maintain its independence from the IPC and include members from a variety of sectors, such as the international sport organisations/governing bodies, private sectors, and civil communities and societies. A creation of such group helps reduce opportunities of any misconduct and distrust within the IPC. The IPC should also consider empowering the Ethics Committee, which should have the power and independence to initiate investigation on its own initiative (Geeraert, Alm and Groll, 2014). Second, despite the IPC's intention to maintain its distinctive identity and avoid being 'a smaller version of the IOC' (Connolly, 2018, 'Paralympic movement,' para. 21), many of its current structures and management approaches still mimic and mirror those of the IOC. As the IPC is currently undergoing an extensive governance review, the IPC should also think about how to upgrade its organisational structure to keep its distinctiveness and unique identity from the IOC. Last, the current IPC governance and management structure also lacks representation of people with disabilities. Future efforts should be made to intentionally include persons with disabilities in the policy and decision-making processes that are decisive to creating regulations and rules that govern their activities and benefit.

References

Bailey, S. (2008). *Athlete first: A history of the Paralympic movement.* Hoboken, NY: John Wiley & Sons.

Brittain, I. (2012). *From Stoke Mandeville to Stratford: A history of the summer Paralympic games.* Champaign, IL: Common Ground Publishing.

Brittain, I., Ramshaw, G. and Gammon, S. (2013). The marginalisation of Paralympic heritage. *International Journal of Heritage Studies*, 19(2), pp. 171–185.

Chappelet, J.L. (2008). *The International Olympic Committee and the Olympic system: The governance of world sport.* London, UK: Routledge.

Chelladurai, P. and Zintz, T. (2015). Functions of national sport governing bodies: A network perspective. *Public Policy and Administration*, 14(4), pp. 529–544.

Connolly, E. (2018). IPC president Andrew Parsons on what lies ahead for the Paralympic movement. *SportsPro.* Available at: https://www.sportspromedia.com/from-the-magazine/ipc-president-andrew-parsons-on-what-lies-ahead-for-the-paralympic-movement.

DePauw, K.P. (2009). Disability sport: Historical context. In: H. Fitzgerald, ed., *Disability and youth sport.* London, UK: Routledge, pp. 23–35.

DePauw, K.P. (2012). A historical perspective of the Paralympic games. *Journal of Physical Education, Recreation & Dance*, 83(3), pp. 21–31.

Edwards, J.R., Mason, D.S. and Washington, M. (2009). Institutional pressures, government funding and provincial sport organisations. *International Journal of Sport Management and Marketing*, 6(2), pp. 128–149.

Enjolras, B. (2009). A governance-structure approach to voluntary organizations. *Nonprofit and Voluntary Sector Quarterly*, 38(5), pp. 761–783.

Forster, J. (2006). Global sports organisations and their governance. *Corporate Governance: The International Journal of Business in Society*, 6(1), pp. 72–83.

Geeraert, A., Alm, J. and Groll, M. (2014). Good governance in international sport organizations: An analysis of the 35 Olympic sport governing bodies. *International Journal of Sport Policy and Politics*, 6(3), pp. 281–306.

Gérard, S. and Zintz, T. (2017). The IPC as a change-maker? Insights from the institutional theory. *Diagoras: International Academic Journal on Olympic Studies*, 1, pp. 95–116.

Gold, J.R. and Gold, M.M. (2007). Access for all: The rise of the Paralympic games. *Journal of the Royal Society for the Promotion of Health*, 127(3), pp. 133–141.

Haveman, H.A. (1993). Follow the leader: Mimetic isomorphism and entry into new markets. *Administrative Science Quarterly*, 38(4), pp. 593–627.

Howe, D. (2008). *The cultural politics of the Paralympic movement: Through an anthropological lens*. London, UK: Routledge.

International Olympic Committee. (2012). *IOC/IPC renew agreement through to 2020*. Lausanne: International Olympic Committee.

International Paralympic Committee. (2004). *International Paralympic Committee Annual Report*. Bonn: International Paralympic Committee.

International Paralympic Committee. (2005). *International Paralympic Committee Annual Report*. Bonn: International Paralympic Committee.

International Paralympic Committee. (2006a). *International Paralympic Committee Annual Report*. Bonn: International Paralympic Committee.

International Paralympic Committee. (2006b). *International Paralympic Committee handbook*. Bonn: International Paralympic Committee.

International Paralympic Committee. (2007). *International Paralympic Committee Annual Report*. Bonn: International Paralympic Committee.

International Paralympic Committee. (2012). *International Paralympic Committee Annual Report*. Bonn: International Paralympic Committee.

International Paralympic Committee. (2015a). *International Paralympic Committee handbook*. Bonn: International Paralympic Committee.

International Paralympic Committee. (2015b). *International Paralympic Committee strategic plan 2015–2018*. Bonn: International Paralympic Committee.

International Paralympic Committee. (2019a). *International Paralympic Committee standing committees*. Bonn: International Paralympic Committee.

International Paralympic Committee. (2019b). *International Paralympic Committee strategic plan 2019–2022*. Bonn: International Paralympic Committee.

International Paralympic Committee. (n.d.). *International Paralympic Committee operational structure*. Bonn: International Paralympic Committee.

Kikulis, L.M. (2000). Continuity and change in governance and decision making in national sport organizations: Institutional explanations. *Journal of Sport Management*, 14(4), pp. 293–320.

Legg, D., Fay, T., Wolff, E. and Hums, M. (2015). The International Olympic Committee – International Paralympic Committee relationship: Past, present, and future. *Journal of Sport and Social Issues*, 39(5), pp. 371–395.

Legg, D. and Steadward, R. (2013). The Paralympic games and 60 years of change (1948–2008): Unification and restructuring from a disability and medical model to sport-based competition. In: J.M. Le Clair, ed., *Disability in the global sport arena*. London, UK: Routledge, pp. 41–57.

Leopkey, B. and Parent, M.M. (2012). Olympic Games legacy: From general benefits to sustainable long-term legacy. *The International Journal of the History of Sport*, 29(6), pp. 924–943.

Mason, D.S., Thibault, L. and Misener, L. (2006). An agency theory perspective on corruption in sport: The case of the International Olympic Committee. *Journal of Sport Management*, 20(1), pp. 52–73.

Suárez, D.F. (2010). Collaboration and professionalization: The contours of public sector funding for non-profit organizations. *Journal of Public Administration Research and Theory*, 21(2), pp. 307–326.

20

Organisational change campaigns of the Olympic movement

Insights from structural and cultural adaptations

Eleni Theodoraki

Introduction

This chapter deals with how the International Olympic Committee (IOC) changed to adapt in the last twenty years. Acting as the official spokesperson, and de facto leader of the Olympic movement, the IOC spearheaded numerous internal reviews and external consultations and engagements in order to improve, adapt and communicate its intended evolution to stakeholders across the movement. Starting in 1998 with the crisis of trust stemming from the Salt Lake City Olympic Games (OGs) scandal, the IOC sought to reform with the work of the IOC 2000 Commission. After a series of OGs where costs to hosts skyrocketed and legacy promises vanished, there was reputational damage to the Olympic brand. In many cases negative impacts outweighed the numerous positive impacts in public opinion (Glynn, 2008). The loss of previous levels of connection to younger audiences was another significant issue that led the IOC to action. To address challenges the IOC introduced further structural and cultural change measures in the Agenda 2020 campaign: 'We want to be the leaders of change, not the object of change' (IOC, 2014b, p. 2). In 2018, the IOC went one step further with structural modifications to propose new ways of working in the so-called *New Norm campaign*.

The aim of this chapter is to introduce the IOC's major organisational change campaigns since 1998 and to draw on organisational theory literature in order to discuss the implications of structural and cultural adaptations. As discussed in the literature (Kidd and Dichter, 2011), '[t]he Olympic world, the broader political, economic, social and demographic contexts, and the organizations within the Olympic movement themselves are continually changing, requiring a constant reassessment of purpose and progress'.

In the following sections, the chapter addresses these four questions:

- What are the main governance-related challenges that the Olympic movement faced in the last twenty years?
- What are the component parts of the change campaigns that were launched as the IOC sought to respond to those challenges?

- How can structural and cultural changes that ensued from the campaigns be commented upon utilising conceptual lenses from organisation theory literature?
- Finally, how do the changes relate to effectiveness of governance in the Olympic movement?

The following sections of the chapter consider in turn the notion of change in the Olympic movement as a collection of organisations working together, how the IOC discussed that change, and in which changes one can observe the ensuing adaptations.

Conceptualising change in the Olympic movement and the 'change or be changed' logic

The conceptual framework of configuration (Mintzberg, 1979) allows viewing the organisations that make up the Olympic movement as a whole within their particular context. Literature on the structuring of organisations allows researchers to understand the main parts of organisations that constitute them (strategic, managing, supporting, operating, etc.), how work is coordinated through design parameters of systems and groupings and what is the role of contingency factors such as age, size, technical system, environment and power. This framework has been employed in the study of the Olympic movement (Theodoraki, 2007) and Organising Committees for the Olympic Games (OCOGs) (Malfas, 2003).

When convergences appear among these elements, clusters or types of configurations are observed ranging from a variety of simple structures to more bureaucratic or divisionalised or ad hoc structures. Configurations are in flux as circumstances change and the whole edifice is rejigged and realigned into new structural configurations as required. Configuration theory helps analysts observe parts of the organisation in the Olympic family, how work is coordinated between members, and the parameters of design selected over the years in the pursuit of Olympism as an ideology and to sustain and grow the Olympic Games as showpiece events. Changes in the age, size, power and the environment help researchers explore why and when the family adapted its behaviour and structures to reconfigure and adapt to the new conditions.

In a similar fashion to the way in which structural configuration theory considers the changing contingency factors as some of the determinants of structural change, institutionalism (DiMaggio and Powell, 1983) enables analysts to understand organisational contexts as origins of pressures for conformity. Institutionalism explains how organisational fields become established in OGs host cities (Glynn, 2008) and explains pressures in the organisational field made up of a number of organisations. It also highlights processes that shape organisations in the way they are structured, their culture and how they are run. Through mimesis, norm sharing, and regulation, researchers can observe processes of isomorphic change, processes that lead to organisations sharing a field becoming more similar in their behaviour and structure. Such similarity fosters clarity in the external image and facilitates internal/inter-organisational dialogue. However, it can also restrain free thought and inhibit dramatic structural and cultural transformation. Institutionalism also gives rise to logics that permeate organisations via a process of diffusion of ideas (Hinings, 2012). When the IOC president declared the 'change or be changed' (Bach, 2014; IOC, 2014a) mantra at the IOC session where he launched the Agenda 2020 campaign, he was in effect endorsing a particular institutional (Meyer et al., 2014) logic.

New managerialist thinking (Clarke et al., 2000) and the notion of corporatisation (Landoni, 2018) as embraced by state and not-for-profit organisations (Nelson and Nikolakis, 2012) can help explain the recent decision of the IOC and allied organisations to take more responsibility for delivering the OGs event with the host government relinquishing some of its previously held control. New managerialism as a conceptual framework equips researchers with the tools to see changes in the way management professionals in the Olympic movement gained control over sport professionals and elected volunteers. It can be used to illuminate behaviours, processes and instances – like the movement's leadership embrace of private sector principles of financial efficiency, competition among bidding cities and use of host city contracts, performance measurement of member organisations, and an enterprising ideology. More recently, following the decline in number of cities interested in hosting the OGs, new managerialist ideology and practice manifests itself in the way the IOC introduced greater management control as well as corporatisation to improve performance and limit costs to hosts and overall reputational risk that relates to legacy (Schnitzer and Haizinger, 2019).

The theoretical lenses mentioned earlier allow vignettes of adaptations over the last twenty years in the organisations that make up the Olympic movement. These perspectives enable the construction of respective narratives on how the overall group navigated and evolved. In conclusion, the chapter reflects upon the utility of the three theories: (1) for understanding configuration and diagnosis of any design misfit; (2) to explore the emergence of logics in organisational fields as well as the exploration of causality between norms, rules, dominant trends and organisational adaptation; (3) to reflect upon the implications of the new managerialist ideology and the ensuing transnational corporatisation in the Olympic movement. Notwithstanding the utility of the previously menioned, in seeking to conceptualise any organisational change campaigns it is pertinent to consider the limitations of using change campaign-related communication efforts of the IOC and text from campaign documents. These may be presented as factual strategic level blueprints, but they are also part of the IOC's brand making and public relations effort. Selectivity in the communication of organisational messages has also been evidenced in the case of OCOGs who embark on communication campaigns to present impacts of the OGs before, during and after the event (Theodoraki, 2009b).

The Olympic movement as a family and a transnational corporation

The Olympic movement involves a number of organisations. These vary in size and significance and are geographically spread around the world.

> The Olympic Movement is the concerted, organised, universal and permanent action, carried out under the supreme authority of the IOC, of all individuals and entities who are inspired by the values of Olympism.
>
> *(IOC, 2019c, para. 1)*

To a larger or smaller extent, the organisations within the Olympic movement are shaped by the underpinning philosophical and value frameworks of Olympism. Ideals originate in Coubertin's system of thought that 'endorses Hellenistic perfectionism and striving [as] a driving force for mankind' (Cléret and McNamee, 2012, p. 193).

Organisations that make up the movement comprise the IOC, National Olympic Committees (NOCs) in recognised countries, OCOGs for the Summer and Winter OGs and Youth Olympic Games (YOGs), International Sport Federations (IFs) in the OGs programme and a number of other related organisations (IOC, 2019c). The IOC runs what can be described as a chain of NOCs across nations in all continents and IFs have authority over National Federations (NFs). The IOC and IFs have year-round operations while OCOGs are created and dissolved as limited companies that are set up for the purposes of preparing for the Games, and acting as a conduit between the IOC and the host government.

The *raison d'être* of the movement is to celebrate the Olympic values as exemplified and epitomised in the celebration of the OGs. These OGs bring together the NOCs who come to the OGs with the national teams. IFs are responsible for the conduct of the competition in the field of play of the various sports. OCOGs have led on host-related preparations and cooperated with central and local government departments in the build-up period. Even though they are not listed as part of the movement, the Olympic Partners are described as indispensable collaborators:

> Support from the business community is crucial to the staging of the Games and the operations of every organisation within the Olympic Movement, including funding, technical services, and products. The Olympic Partners (TOP) programme is the highest level of Olympic sponsorship, granting category-exclusive marketing rights to the Summer, Winter and Youth Olympic Games to a select group of global partners.
>
> *(IOC, 2019d, para. 1)*

Current Olympic partners include Coca-Cola, Alibaba Group, Atos, Bridgestone, Dow, General Electric, Intel, Omega, Panasonic, Procter & Gamble, Samsung, Toyota and Visa. In return, partners offer financial resources, products, services, technology, expertise, staff deployment, direct support for training of athletes, global marketing campaigns, activations to enhance Olympic Games experiences for spectators, and essential services for athletes participating at the Games (IOC, 2019d). Since the birth of the IOC in 1894 (IOC, 2019e), the movement has evolved with sustained growth:

> [T]he IOC s acts as a catalyst for collaboration between all parties of the Olympic family, from the NOCs, the IFs, the athletes and the OCOGs to the Worldwide Olympic Partners, broadcast partners and United Nations (UN) agencies, and shepherds success through a wide range of programmes and projects.
>
> *(IOC, 2019e, para. 7)*

The IOC celebrates OGs, promotes Olympism in society, leads the Olympic movement, supports and protects clean athletes (IOC, 2019e). It runs the movement, the chain of NOCs and the various Summer and Winter OGs and YOGs editions in what can be described as a global value chain of a 'quasi-transnational corporation' (Donnely and Kidd, unknown).

Figure 20.1 presents a snapshot of the current main component parts of the Olympic movement's structure using terminology from configuration theory (Mintzberg, 1979) and Theodoraki's (2007) previous work to name the parts of the movement to name the parts of the movement. Some member organisations may straddle more than one of the five parts of the overall Olympic movement organisation but they are visually positioned in this manner because of their primary role. For example, Olympic Solidarity plays a support and technology transfer role. Likewise, Olympic Education (notably via the work of the Olympic Studies Centre, the MEMOS programme and the work of the International Olympic Academy) supports the movement but also plays a technology role in knowledge capture and dissemination. It is also important to note that the organisational structure of the IOC is in flux, it has evolved over time and is constantly being reshaped by external drivers as well as internal responses, actions and processes.

Understandably, the Olympic movement is affected by wider socio-cultural, environmental, political, economic and technological changes. These changes alter the operating environment for the structures of agents and organisations involved in the movement. They also shape the actions of numerous agents involved in the Games hosting processes. The following section dis-

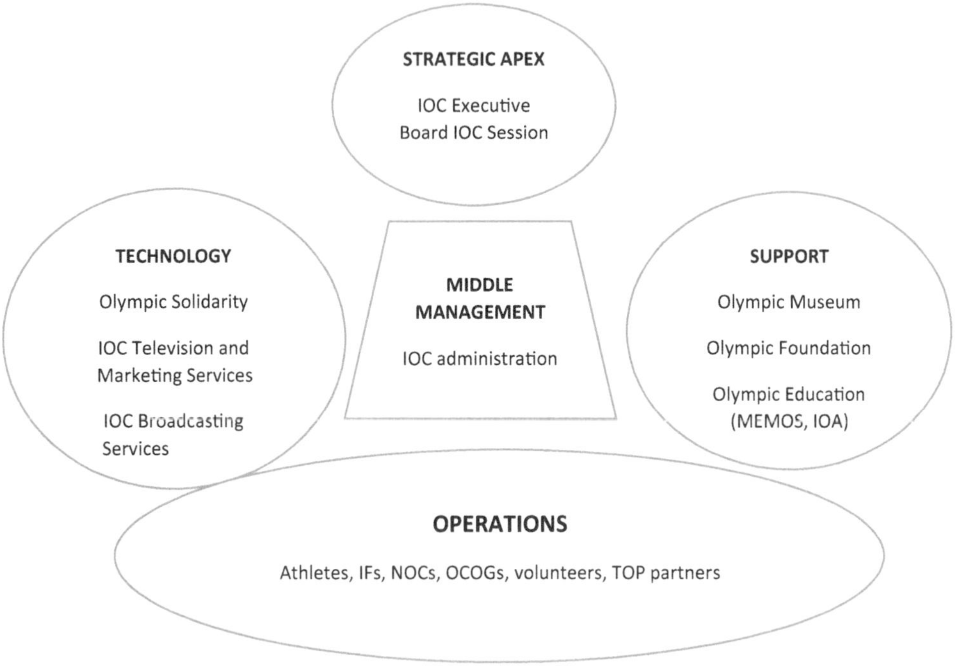

Figure 20.1 Organisational parts of the Olympic movement (adapted from Theodoraki, 2007)

cusses the challenges that arose in the last twenty years that in turn led to organisational change campaigns being launched in the Olympic movement.

Change campaigns

The Salt Lake City 2002 OGs corruption scandal created considerable pressure on the IOC membership for changes in policy and practices. There were accusations over the behaviour of some IOC members who were subsequently removed from office or given warnings (Zappelli, 2016). A special committee was set up by the IOC to investigate, an ethics commission was established and a code of ethics adopted. The necessary changes identified by the committee were intended to 'lead to a more contemporary and transparent IOC' (IOC, 1999, para. 1). Key IOC governance-related recommendations were as follows:

> The invitation of 15 active Olympic athletes elected by their peers to become full IOC members; the lowering of the age limit for membership to 70 years; the application of eight-year, renewable terms of service; the setting of the eventual composition of the IOC membership to a maximum of 115, 15 of which to be chosen from active Olympic athletes, 15 from NOC presidents, 15 from IF presidents, and 70 as individuals; the creation of a nomination and screening process that would recommend candidates for membership to the IOC; the enlarging of the IOC Executive Board to allow for a better representation of the new composition of the IOC membership; the application of term limits to the IOC presidency.
>
> *(IOC, 1999, para. 4)*

As regards operations of the Olympic movement in the build-up to the OGs, key recommendations were to:

> Require all NOCs to participate in the Summer Olympic Games; publish additional financial reports that clearly illustrate the flow of the sources and uses of IOC revenues in order to enhance its financial transparency; require that every entity that receives funds from the IOC provide the IOC an accounting of the use of those funds, again, to enhance financial transparency; limit both the number of events and athletes at the Summer Games in order to control the growing size of the Games and the resulting managerial challenges; work with the World Anti-Doping Agency to distribute 'passports' containing all necessary information to carry out efficient doping controls and to monitor the athletes' health; refuse participation to sports that do not apply the Olympic Movement's Anti-Doping Code or perform out of competition testing.
>
> *(IOC, 1999, para. 9)*

Fifteen years after the reforms in response to the Salt Lake City scandal, the Olympic movement acknowledged another set of challenges related not to the administration, but mostly to the OGs themselves this time. As widely acknowledged, the modern Summer and Winter OGs have numerous impacts (Malfas, Theodoraki and Houlihan, 2004). The scope of these events, the complexity of the global supply chain of goods and services and the multiple stakeholders involved and affected by the OGs lead to the difficulty of measuring these impacts (Theodoraki, 2016). Although there are many and multifaceted positive impacts, the scale is such that there are winners and losers (Theodoraki, 2009a). White elephants, cost overruns, abuse of civil liberties, environmental damage from Games preparations, unjustifiably high carbon emissions embodied in products and via travel to and from the OGs, legitimisation of political regimes otherwise deemed dangerous are some of the many negative issues that present a major challenge to the sustainability credentials of the Olympic movement. In his preface to the Olympic Agenda 2020 blueprint, the IOC President Thomas Bach explained the issues faced by the Olympic movement. Referring to the challenge of sustainability, in particular, he wrote:

> The less people believe in the future the more they want to know about the future. This means for us that they want to know more about the sustainability of Olympic Games and all our actions; that they want to know better about our governance and finances; that they want to know how we are living up to our values and our social responsibility. This modern world demands more transparency, more participation, higher standards of integrity. This modern world takes less for granted, has no place for complacency, questions even those with the highest reputation. This world takes much less on faith.
>
> *(Bach, 2014, p. 3)*

In addition to the obvious concern for negative impacts of the OGs, the Olympic movement also faced a drop in its popularity among younger generations. As a result, the IOC embarked on the ambitious path of market and service development, adding the Summer and Winter YOGs to the list of Olympic events and launching the Olympic Channel. Another measure involved adding sports to the OGs that are popular with younger people and removing some sports from the Olympic programme (Thorpe and Wheaton, 2011, 2019). This process started with the introduction of snowboarding at the Nagano 1998 Winter Olympic Games and more sports were added in the Tokyo 2020 Summer OGs programme. As (Thorpe and Wheaton, 2011, p. 830) explain:

> [A]ction sports are shifting, and are likely to continue to shift, the representation and consumption of the Olympic Games. Thus, in revealing some of the unique cultural politics involved in action sports incorporation into the Olympic programme, our article also illustrates the complex power relations involved in modernizing the Olympic Games in the early 21st century.

Agenda 2020 was approved by the IOC session and the proposed 40 recommendations were enacted under the overarching themes of sustainability, credibility and youth. The agenda focussed on the holistic concept of respect for the environment, feasibility and of development, to leave a lasting legacy. The Olympic movement vowed to 'strengthen our good governance, transparency and ethics' and to introduce an 'Olympic Channel to give athletes exposure, give attention to values, give the youth better access' (IOC, 2014a, pp. 4–5). The following were the recommendations with the first six listed focusing on aspects of the organisation of the Olympic Games:

> Shape the bidding process as an invitation; Evaluate bid cities by assessing key opportunities and risks; Reduce the cost of bidding; Include sustainability in all aspects of the Olympic Games; Reduce the cost and reinforce the flexibility of Olympic Games management; Maximise synergies with Olympic Movement stakeholders; Include sustainability within the Olympic Movement's daily operations; Cooperate closely with other sports event organisers; Strengthen relationships with organisations managing sport for people with different abilities; Forge relationships with professional leagues; Set a framework for the Olympic programme; Move from a sport-based to an event-based programme; Foster gender equality; Strengthen the 6th Fundamental Principle of Olympism; Change the philosophy to protecting clean athletes; Leverage the IOC $20 million fund to protect clean athletes; Honour clean athletes; Strengthen support to athletes; Launch an Olympic Channel; Enter into strategic partnerships; Strengthen IOC advocacy capacity; Spread Olympic values-based education; Engage with communities; Evaluate the Sport for Hope programme; Review Youth Olympic Games positioning; Further blend sport and culture; Comply with basic principles of good governance; Support autonomy; Increase transparency; Strengthen the IOC Ethics Commission independence; Ensure compliance; Strengthen ethics; Further involve sponsors in "Olympism in Action" programmes; Develop a global licensing programme; Foster TOP sponsors' engagement with NOCs; Extend access to the Olympic brand for non-commercial use; Address IOC membership age limit; Implement a targeted recruitment process; Foster dialogue with society and within the Olympic Movement; Review scope and composition of IOC commissions.
>
> *(IOC, 2014a, pp. 7–8)*

Although Olympic Agenda 2020 continued some of the themes introduced by the IOC 2000 Commission (such as ethics, transparency and good governance) it appeared to focus on sustainability-related measures. A more recent challenge to the Olympic movement was the lack of cities interested in bidding for Summer and Winter OGs due to the reputational damage of the Olympic brand from previous unsustainable practices (Bull, 2018; Schnitzer and Haizinger, 2019). Following Agenda 2020 in 2014, the IOC announced in 2018 six additional recommendations and 118 measures to 'reimagine, redesign, rethink, reshape every aspect of the games and save 100 of millions of dollars' (IOC, 2018a). This New Norm proposed a seven-year process for the OGs hosting, more expertise from the IOC and the International Paralympic Committee (IPC), IFs, NOCs TOP Partners and Rights Holding Broadcasters (RHBs). It proclaimed a fundamental structural and ideological change as the Games adapt to the city; the city does not adapt to the Games.

Following the six recommendations from Agenda 2020 on Games organisation (IOC, 2018a), this New Norm spearheaded a review of how the Games are organised. The outcomes of the review led to a toolkit of 100 measures, relating to both the OGs and the Paralympic Games (PGs) and were categorised within three streams of activity: (1) OGs governance, (2) OGs requirements and (3) support to organisers (IOC, 2018b). The IOC argues that although measures 'are specific and detailed in their descriptions, they aim to give more flexibility to designing Games that meet the long-term development plans of different future host cities' (IOC, 2018a, p. 19). The New Norm's main proposition is to mitigate the negatives for hosts of cost, complexity, risk and waste with value from the Olympic movement through flexibility, efficiency, sustainability and partnership. Under these proposals the IOC and the Olympic movement will 'play a greater part in the overall governance of the Olympic Games' (IOC, 2018b, p. 7) and help with 'identifying specialist companies to deliver complex services over a longer period than just one Games edition' (IOC, 2018b, p. 9). For OG and PGs organisation there is reference to the 3 + 4 year together model that involves 'transferring parts delivery from OCOGs to IFs and NOCs, [so that] technical expertise is better leveraged, OCOG workforce is reduced, organisational efficiency is enhanced' (IOC, 2018b, p. 43).

The New Norm toolkit includes 'Turnkey solutions for OCOGs ranging from an entire planning methodology for the procurement processes of services and commodities to an end-to-end service designed to deliver a product or service more easily' (IOC, 2018b, p. 44). Examples of turnkey solutions cited in the campaign include 'helping organisers to design sports venues, transport or security systems or launch tenders to procure the right products in the right quantity at the right price' (IOC, 2018b, p. 9). As for the new role for OCOGs, they are described as being 'tasked with finding the most efficient way to deliver each discipline and event on the programme, using the capabilities of IFs, NFs, operators of existing venues, local event organisers or, as in the past, built in-house capabilities' (IOC, 2018b, p. 22). OCOGs will also be invited to 'assess the strategic capabilities in their market during the Candidature Process' and will be expected to 'follow through and deliver on TOP Partners' supply rights' (IOC, 2018b, p. 22).

The *foci* of the latest New Norm campaigns are on credibility, sustainability and efficiency. These are echoed in the three main themes of credibility, sustainability and youth cited in the 2019 IOC's annual report (IOC, 2019b) and build upon the foundations laid in the Agenda 2020. The manifestation of the change campaigns in the form of structural and cultural adaptations (in policies, practices and processes) are listed in Table 20.1.

Conclusion

The aim of this chapter was to explore the drivers for organisational change campaigns in the Olympic movement in the last twenty years, to understand their main identity and examine the implications they create for the structures and cultures of the overall body of organisations that make up the Olympic family. The three analytical frameworks of configuration (Mintzberg, 1979), institutionalism (DiMaggio and Powell, 1983) and new managerialism (Clarke et al., 2000) were mentioned briefly at the start. These help to discuss and signpost the trajectory of change in the movement since 1998. From the Salt Lake City vote scandal, through the years of sustainability concerns, to diversification with the youth OGs and the most recent 'new norm'

Table 20.1 Organisational change drivers, campaigns and structural and cultural adaptations in the Olympic movement

Drivers	*Campaigns*	*Structural and cultural adaptations*
Credibility	IOC 2000 Commission	Renewed IOC membership criteria and control mechanisms; Statement of ethical standards and transparency-led reporting.
Sustainability	Agenda 2020	Renewed coordination mechanisms; Structural expansion (YOGs, Olympic Channel services); Globalisation of value production chain.
Efficiency	New Norm	Outsourcing; Horizontal centralisation of power; Vertical decentralisation of OGs roles; Host city seen as legacy service recipient; Corporatisation of some state role of OGs preparation and delivery.

era where the IOC takes more control of governance in the host city (IOC, 2019a). The Olympic movement's structural configuration shows a divisionalised structure made up of a central administration, a chain of NOCs and IFs in the Olympic programme and a set of temporary franchisee companies for the Summer and Winter OGs and YOGs. At an additional, parallel, level, the Olympic movement offers broadcasting services, an Olympic Channel and runs an international development programme though the work of Olympic Solidarity that distributes funds and runs staff training. The description of the New Norm is indicative of processes of structural redesign and service relaunch. In structural configuration terms, such designing means 'turning knobs that influence the division of labour and the coordinating mechanisms, thereby affecting how the organisation functions – how materials, authority, information, and decision processes flow through it' (Mintzberg, 1979, p. 65). The references to strategic partnerships with other organisations in the campaign texts echo corporatisation ideas in the globalised value chains used in modern city operations.

As regards the Olympic movement's organisational field, this is populated by organisations in Figure 20.1 but also by the OGs and YOGs host country organisational landscapes, and the businesses and governments around the world where members of the chain and franchisees operate. The concept of the field helps explore 'how sets of ideas and practices arise, are developed, adopted, and changed over time. Of importance here is the movement of these ideas from the field level to organizations within the field' (Hinings, 2012, p. 100). The organisational field of the Olympic movement creates pressures for isomorphic change that can be felt around the Olympic family and traced in the spirit and the letter of organisational change campaigns.

New managerialist thought is evident in the transnationalisation of operations, the emphasis on efficiency and the corporatisation of delivery where 'corporatization leads to enhanced commercial performance through improving clarity around business decisions and increasing the autonomy of managers' (Nelson and Nikolakis, 2012, p. 2). The modernisation process is still underway as regards IOC membership criteria, gender balance in governance and competition programmes, transparency, accountability and ethical conduct of officials. This is in line with prevalent global bureaucratic and market logics that also propose the use of intermediaries as instruments during corporatisation processes (Landoni, 2018). Market development has occurred with the YOGs and the adaptation of the programme of events to ensure its relevance to younger generations of audiences. Finally, changes occurred in the centralisation of power and control over OGs and YOGs processes. These involve power being taken away from host organisers and more roles being offered to established collaborators of the IOC or other long-standing key organisations that make up the Olympic movement. This is in line with current corporatisation dogmas: 'with a growing share of product value being provided by the supply chain, firms that genuinely collaborate can secure preferred customer status and benefit from new product ideas or process efficiencies bubbling up from suppliers' (McKinsey Global Institute, 2019, p. 18).

The emphasis on adapting the OGs and the YOGs to the needs of the city shows leadership from the IOC and acknowledges the mistakes of the past where Games inflation ruined legacy visions for hosts. Nevertheless, in the proposed standardisation of processes, the focus on repeat service suppliers and the reduced ownership of the host city there is a risk of legacy-related policy solutions and development advice being followed that is not fit for purpose or did not involve local community engagement (Snell, 2016). The structure of the movement has been tweaked with new commissions set up, the new Summer and Winter YOGs and new physical headquarters in Lausanne for the IOC. The Olympic movement as a transnational corporation, with the IOC at the helm, clearly comprises of a global value production chain of partners and sponsors and now makes a renewed value proposition to cities as future hosts. A proposition along the lines: You do not need to tell us what you can do for the Games; let us discuss together what the Games can do for your city and country.

At the same time, the IOC is adamant that the Olympic spirit will remain intact:

> But while we work together to reimagine, redesign, rethink, and reshape the games, one think will remain the same. The unique magic of the OGs where the athlete experience is still its beating heart. What truly defines the games are sporting endeavours and iconic images, helping to bring the world together and connecting and uniting us in the true Olympic spirit and that will never change.
>
> *(IOC, 2018a)*

These organisational changes have affected perceptions about the value of the Summer and Winter OG and YOGs. The opinions of the different actors within the Olympic movement on the effectiveness and governance of the Games has been affected, at times negatively. The changes initiated by the IOC indicate a willingness to align with mainstream ideals for progress, ideals of credibility, sustainability and efficiency. They also portray a confident expansionist IOC as leader of the movement who is proposing to hold the reigns whilst producing legacy for host cities. With delegation of work to trusted partners, suppliers and collaborators, the business model allows confidence in more predictable outcomes. The vulnerability of such a direction can be envisaged in the soft area of living the Olympic values and ensuring these are still relevant to humanity. If the Olympic movement can put its values first in guiding all decisions, the world can truly be a better place. Such idealism is what Olympism is made of. And senior staff in the Olympic movement need to safeguard these values from the influences and effects of insatiable corporate greed. The partnership proposed in the New Norm model can bear fruit for all and all eyes are on the leaders to lead the Olympic movement through its values.

References

Bach, T. (2014). *Speech by IOC President Thomas Bach on the occasion of the opening ceremony, 127th IOC Session*, Monaco, Dec. 7.

Bull, A. (2018). *Nobody can afford to host the Olympics but at the IOC the largesse never stops. The Guardian.* Available at: https://www.theguardian.com/sport/2018/oct/23/olympic-games-host-ioc-money.

Clarke, J., Gewirtz, S., McLaughlin, E. and Open, U. (2000). *New managerialism, new welfare?* London: SAGE.
Cléret, L. and McNamee, M. (2012). Olympism, the values of sport, and the will to power: De Coubertin and Nietzsche meet Eugenio Monti. *Sport, Ethics and Philosophy*, 6(2), pp. 183–194.
DiMaggio, P.J. and Powell, W. (1983). "The iron cage revisited" institutional isomorphism and collective rationality in organizational fields. *American Sociological Review*, 48, p. 147.
Donnely, P. and Kidd, B. (unknown). *Olympic reform: Current status and future steps.*
Glynn, M. (2008). Configuring the field of play: How hosting the Olympic Games impacts civic community. *The Journal of Management Studies*, 45(6), p. 1117.
Hinings, B. (2012). Connections between institutional logics and organizational culture. *Journal of Management Inquiry*, 21(1), pp. 98–101.
IOC. (1999). *Recommendations for IOC reform finalized* [Press release].
IOC. (2014a). *Olympic Agenda 2020 20 + 20 recommendations.* Lausanne: IOC.
IOC. (2014b). *Olympic Agenda 2020: Context and background.* Lausanne: IOC.
IOC. (2019a). *The International Olympic Committee at 125.* Available at: https://www.olympic.org/news/the-ioc-at-125.
IOC. (2019b). *IOC Annual Report 2018: credibility, sustainability, youth.* Available at: https://stillmed.olympic.org/media/Document%20Library/OlympicOrg/Documents/IOC-Annual-Report/IOC-ANNUAL-REPORT-2018.pdf#_ga=2.4663924.696208025.1562412191-455125231.1562412191.
IOC. (2019c). *Leading the Olympic Movement.* Available at: https://www.olympic.org/the-ioc/leading-the-olympic-movement.
IOC. (2019d). *The Olympic Partner Programme.* Available at: https://www.olympic.org/partners.
IOC. (2019e). *Who we are.* Available at: https://www.olympic.org/about-ioc-olympic-movement.
IOC (Producer). (2018a). *Learn about Olympic Agenda 2020.* The New Nork. Available at: https://www.youtube.com/watch?v=DW8ApF-7qXg.
IOC (Producer). (2018b). *Olympic Agenda 2020. Olympic Games: the New Norm.* Available at: https://stillmed.olympic.org/media/Document%20Library/OlympicOrg/News/2018/02/2018-02-06-Olympic-Games-the-New-Norm-Report.pdf#_ga=2.69913817.894524996.1562931607-1421324646.1562931607.
Kidd, B. and Dichter, H. (2011). Introduction. *Sport in Society*, 14(3), pp. 289–291. doi:10.1080/17430437.2011.557264.
Landoni, M. (2018). Corporatization and internationalization of state-owned enterprises. *International Journal of Public Sector Management*, 31(2), pp. 221–240. doi:10.1108/IJPSM-03-2017-0076.
Malfas, M. (2003). *An analysis of the organisational configurations over the life cycle of the Sydney organising committee for the Olympic Games.* PhD Thesis, University of Loughborough, Loughborough.
Malfas, M., Theodoraki, E. and Houlihan, B. (2004). Impacts of the Olympic Games as mega-events. *Proceedings of the ICE – Municipal Engineer*, 157(3), pp. 209–220. doi:10.1680/muen.157.3.209.49461.
Mangan, J.A. (2008). Prologue: Guarantees of global goodwill: Post-Olympic legacies – Too many limping white elephants? *The International Journal of the History of Sport*, 25(14), pp. 1869–1883. doi:10.1080/09523360802496148.
McKinsey Global Institute. (2019). *Globalisation in transition: The future of trade and value chains.* Available at: https://www.mckinsey.com/~/media/mckinsey/featured%20insights/innovation/globalization%20in%20transition%20the%20future%20of%20trade%20and%20value%20chains/mgi-globalization%20in%20transition-the-future-of-trade-and-value-chains-full-report.ashx.
Meyer, R.E., Egger-Peitler, I., Höllerer, M.A. and Hammerschmid, G. (2014). Of bureaucrats and passionate public managers: Institutional logics, executive identities and public service motivation. *Public Administration*, 92(4), pp. 861–885. doi:10.1111/j.1467-9299.2012.02105.x.
Mintzberg, H. (1979). *The structuring of organizations: A synthesis of the research.* London: Prentice-Hall.
Nelson, H. and Nikolakis, W. (2012). How does corporatization improve the performance of government agencies? Lessons from the restructuring of state-owned forest agencies in Australia. *International Public Management Journal*, 15(3), pp. 364–391. doi:10.1080/10967494.2012.725323.
Schnitzer, M. and Haizinger, L. (2019). Does the Olympic Agenda 2020 have the power to create a new Olympic heritage? An analysis for the 2026 winter Olympic Games bid. *Sustainability*, 11(2), p. 442. doi:10.3390/su11020442.
Snell, S. (2016). *Citizen participation within mega event planning: The case of the London 2012 Olympic Games.* PhD Thesis, Edinburgh Napier University, Edinburgh.
Theodoraki, E. (2007). *Olympic event organisation.* London: Elsevier.

Theodoraki, E. (2009a). The modern Olympic Games: Governance and ownership of risk. *Monitor*, 8(3), pp. 7–9.
Theodoraki, E. (2009b). Organisational communication on the impacts of the Athens 2004 Olympic Games. *Journal of Policy Research in Tourism, Leisure and Events*, 1(2), pp. 141–155. doi:10.1080/19407960902992191.
Theodoraki, E. (2016). The problem with sporting mega-event impact assessment. In: Transparency International (ed.) *Global corruption report: Sport*. London: Routledge, pp. 143–151.
Thorpe, H. and Wheaton, B. (2011). 'Generation X Games', action sports and the Olympic movement: Understanding the cultural politics of incorporation. *Sociology*, 45(5), pp. 830–847. doi:10.1177/0038038511413427.
Thorpe, H. and Wheaton, B. (2019). The Olympic Games, Agenda 2020 and action sports: The promise, politics and performance of organisational change. *International Journal of Sport Policy and Politics*, pp. 1–19. doi:10.1080/19406940.2019.1569548.
Zappelli, P. G. (2016). The International Olympic Committee's actions to protect the integrity of sport. In: Transparency International (ed.) *Global corruption report: Sport*. London: Routledge, pp. 309–312.

21

Sleeping with an elephant

The relationship between the International Olympic Committee and the International Paralympic Committee

P. David Howe

Introduction

In the contemporary world of sporting politics there are many unbalanced relationships – international organisations that are very large and more influential than others. This is not new but in the case of the International Olympic Committee (IOC) and the International Paralympic Committee (IPC) cooperation, it is reminiscent of a speech by former Canadian Prime Minister Pierre Trudeau, who travelled to Washington to meet with US President Richard Nixon in 1969 and stated:

> Living next to you is in some ways like sleeping with an elephant. No matter how friendly and even-tempered is the beast, if I can call it that, one is affected by every twitch and grunt.[1]

In other words, changes in policy by the IOC have often unintended consequences in the organisation and structure of the IPC because one organisation has lots of money and influence and the other is dependent on its more influential partner. As it currently stands the IOC and the IPC are currently 'in bed together' until 2032 (IPC, 2016). The IPC has been throughout its history the 'little brother' to the IOC, which is one of the most powerful organisations in international sport. Almost since the beginning of the IPC some 70 years ago when it was known as the International Stoke Mandeville Games Federation (ISMGF) established to help injured ex-servicemen rehabilitate following spinal cord injury, there has been a desire for a closer working relationship with the IOC (Guttmann, 1976; see more details on this in the chapter by Misener and Lu in this volume).

In a short chapter such as this, there is limited space to do justice to the colourful history of the IPC (Bailey, 2008; Brittain, 2012). But, in a nutshell, early ISMGF events that were designed to rehabilitate servicemen through the use of sport at least in part so that they could actively seek employment (Anderson, 2003; see also Misener and Lu in this volume) have become what we know now as the Paralympic Games. Since that time, the IPC has developed into an increasingly professional and commercially driven organisation where rehabilitation, participation and high-performance components of sport are involved (see Howe, 2008). While high-performance sporting spectacles are the hallmark of the contemporary IPC, the first games were a small festival of archery organised by a neurosurgeon, Dr Ludwig Guttman (Guttman, 1976), held in Stoke Mandeville (UK) on 28th July 1948, the same day as the opening of the London Olympic Games. As a result, there has been a close link between the fledgling IPC and the Olympic movement since its very beginning. While the first formal agreement between the IOC and IPC was not established until 2000, there has being an ongoing interaction between the organisations since just after the Second World War (Guttman, 1976). This chapter outlines early relations between the IOC and the IPC before going on to analyse their 21st-century formalised relationship. The significance of the latter is that some believe that the partnership could lead to a merger of the Olympic and Paralympic Games in the future (BBC, 2012; Rose, 2012). Currently the agreement between the IOC and the IPC runs until the 2032 Games (IPC, 2016) and there has been no discussion of a closer relationship between the two organisations. This renewed partnership was a long time in the making.

The structure of this chapter is broadly divided along two distinct time periods. First, the chapter starts by exploring the early interactions between the IPC predecessors and the IOC in the period 1948–1999. Following this important historical section that documents celebration as well as tension between the IOC and the IPC, the chapter turns to the 'marriage' between the two organisations that occurred at the dawn of the new millennium. That section is followed by a discussion and a brief conclusion.

The early relationship (1948–1999)

The fledgling relationship between the IOC and IPC has received limited attention (Bailey, 2008; Brittain, 2008, 2012; Howe, 2008; Purdue, 2011). Sir Ludwig Guttmann, founding father of the Paralympic movement, in the *Textbook of Sport for the Disabled* (1976) celebrates the early connections the ISMGF had with the IOC. From the outset, those involved in the Paralympic movement had aspirations for the involvement of the IOC, (Guttmann, 1976; Scruton, 1998). Scruton, the personal assistant to Guttmann, documents that in 1949, on the forecourt of Stoke Mandeville Hospital, Sir Ludwig spoke of his vision that 'one day the Stoke Mandeville Games would achieve world fame as the disabled men and women's equivalent of the Olympic Games' (Scruton, 1998, p. xii). Further, during the Melbourne Olympic Games of 1956 the IOC 'awarded the Fearnley Cup to the International Stoke Mandeville Games (ISMG), the antecedent of the Paralympic Games for "outstanding achievement in the service of the Olympic ideals"' (Goodman, 1986, p. 157). In 1957 at the opening ceremonies of the ISMG Guttmann stated,

> I hope this is only the beginning of a closer connection between the Stoke Mandeville Games and the Olympic Games. In the past few years I have always emphasised that the Stoke Mandeville Games have become the equivalent of the Olympic Games.
>
> *(Bucks Herald, 2 August, cited in Brittain, 2008, p. 22)*

In spite of this celebration of the fledgling IPC, the IOC were inflexible when it came to the use of the word Olympic. One of the greatest hurdles over which IOC and IPC have still not fully cleared relates to the use of the term 'Olympics' in regard to Paralympic sport (Bailey, 2008; Guttmann, 1976; IPC, 2008; Scruton, 1998). Back in 1965 the IOC 'raised the strongest objections to the use of the word Paralympics' (Brittain, 2008, p. 25). This term had been used by the organisers of the 2nd Paralympic Games in Tokyo in 1964 and it is the term 'celebrated' by the IOC today. In 1976 there was explicit internal resistance to the term Paralympic, because of its close association with the term paraplegic. The Games in Toronto, Canada in 1976 were coined *Torontolympiad* since it was the first Paralympic Games where athletes with spinal cord injuries there were with those with visually impairments and amputations (Legg, 2003).

While this more inclusive term was broadly supported by the increasingly diverse athlete community, it did not win favour with the IOC. Guttmann was contacted by the President of the IOC, Lord Killanin, who in private correspondence expressed his displeasure at the use of the term *Torontolympiad* as only the IOC had the authority to use the term 'Olympics'. Following meetings and further correspondence, the IOC president wrote to Guttmann in March 1976 to confirm that the IOC Executive Board had agreed to recognise the ISMGF 'in principle', providing this body refrained from the use of Olympic terminology after Toronto (Brittain, 2008, p. 29).

When Guttmann passed away in March 1980, there was not official recognition of the Paralympic movement by the IOC and the relationship further soured, in part because the 1980 Arnhem (The Netherlands) Games were called *Olympics for the Disabled* which forced the IOC to threaten legal action (Brittain, 2008, p. 30). During the second World Championships in Winter Sport for the Disabled, held in Switzerland on 11th March 1982, four international organisations of sport for the disabled (IOSDs), namely, International Stoke Mandeville Games Federation (ISMGF), International Sports Organization for the Disabled (ISOD), International Blind Sports Federation (IBSA) and Cerebral Palsy – International Sports and Recreation Association (CP-ISRA) came to an agreement and formed the International Coordinating Committee of World Sport Organizations for the Disabled (ICC) (Bailey, 2008 p. 46). The move to establish an organised platform for the Paralympic movement according to Scruton was supported by the IOC:

> Mr Samaranch [IOC President 1980–2001] made it clear that IOC wished to deal with one organization which represented all disability groups. In return for acceptance into the Olympic Family, bringing with it the benefits of IOC financial aid and patronage, ICC agreed to refrain from using the words "Olympic Games". However, Mr. Samaranch expressed approval of the term 'Paralympics'.
>
> *(Scruton, 1998 p. 300)*

In spite of the establishment of the ICC in the early 1980s, the Paralympic movement was cut adrift by the IOC since negotiations to have harmonised games had to be conducted through the local organising committee. Negotiations with the United States Olympic Committee were short lived as they claimed to lack the financial backing to host the Paralympic Games as part of the 1984 Los Angeles Summer Olympics (Bailey, 2008 p. 52). As a result, the 1984 Paralympic Games were quickly arranged and hosted at different venues on different continents with ISMGF athletes competing in Stoke Mandeville, England, and ISOD, CP-ISRA, and IBSA athletes competing at Long Island, NY, United States (Steadward, 1996). The 1984 Los Angeles Olympic Games did provide the opportunity for ISMGF athletes to be involved in demonstration track events (1500m men and 800m women) and a couple of events were also offered at the Paralympic Winter Games (Bailey, 2008; Legg et al., 2009). This gave an opportunity to the ICC to highlight the abilities of various impairment groups on the world's largest sporting stage.

Building upon the momentum established by having demonstration events included within the Olympic Games, the ICC in March of 1985 agreed to use the term 'Paralympic Games' for their games that were held in the same year as that of the IOC's Olympic Games (Scruton, 1998 p. 290). The first Games to adopt this format was the 1988 Seoul Paralympic Games, which were hosted at the same venues that had staged the Summer Olympic Games in the South Korean capital. This was seen as a hugely positive step taken by the host nation. However, the Seoul Paralympic Organizing Committee (SPOC) got themselves and ICC into conflict with the IOC because of the Paralympic logo they had developed to celebrate the Games. The logo was composed of five *Tae-Geuks* (or 'teardrops') in the colours of the Olympic rings and a 'W' configuration (Scruton, 1998, p. 343). This logo was so well received by the athletes and officials at the Games it was officially adopted as the ICC's official symbol after the Games and the following year 1989 it became the symbol for the newly formed IPC (IPC, 2011). The celebration of this new brand was short lived because in 1990 'IOC had requested that the logo created by SPOC of the five "tear drops" not be used, as it was considered to be too close to the IOC five ring emblem' (Scruton, 1998, p. 296). In order to placate the IOC a new Paralympic logo was developed using three *Tae-Geuks* and noticeably different hews of the same colours and was officially launched in 1994 (IPC, 2011). While the ICC/IPC was dealing with issues related to the legality of how they could be represented in the eyes of the IOC, Special Olympics International was receiving IOC support. Special Olympics International was invited to sign a Protocol Agreement with the IOC on 15th February 1988 over the use of the word Olympic and what it meant to both organisations going forward. This double standard may have existed for two reasons: unlike the IPC, the Special Olympics was not a high-performance-based sports organisation and this organisation was founded and led by Eunice Kennedy Shiver. Kennedy Shiver was the sister of the late John F. Kennedy, and their family still exhibited international political influence.

Tying the knot: a marriage made in heaven?

By the turn of the millennium it became mutually beneficial for the IOC and the IPC to establish a formal agreement that ultimately would lead to host nations supporting both Games (IOC, 2000, 2003, 2006; International Paralympic Committee [IPC], 2001, 2010; Mason, 2002). Without question these agreements have been in the interest of both parties. The IPC has received much needed financial investment that has helped with the professionalisation of their organisation, with the IOC fresh from the scandal surrounding the Salt Lake City Winter Olympic Games where the reputation of the Olympic movement was tarnished. Helping the 'less fortunate' IPC was a good way to save a tarnished brand. The Paralympic movement was becoming more professionalised and this could continue with the IOC's financial support. A commentator prior to the signing of the agreement stated, 'In some quarters the Paralympics may be seen as a necessary evil, an inferior sports event that has to be tolerated because they are part of the Olympic package' (Hughes, 1999 p. 171). This statement was made over 20 years ago but while never publicly articulated in this fashion I believe it is salient today. In the lead up to the London 2012 Olympic and Paralympic Games in early 2011, the BBC (2011a) reported, quite interestingly, about budgetary debates between the British Olympic Association (BOA) and London Organizing Committee of the Olympic Games (LOCOG): 'The BOA claims that the Paralympics will make a substantial loss. The BOA is entitled to 20% of any surplus from London 2012 and wants its share to be paid before the Paralympics are taken into account'. Incidences such as this highlight that the relationship between the Olympic and Paralympic movements is not an equal one and potentially debates over financial gain from hosting the Games will be a contentious issue for years to come.

In the early 2000s IOC and IPC signed several contractual agreements. The October 2000 IOC–IPC Agreement stated that:

> The IPC President will be co-opted as a member of the IOC. An annual financial contribution for the IPC administration of US$300,000 (three hundred thousand US dollars) from 2001 to 2004, with the possibility of a new assessment in 2002. . . . An annual subsidy of US$100,000 (one hundred thousand US dollars) for development projects.
>
> *(IOC, 2000)*

The next year this agreement was expanded:

> The agreement reaffirms that the Paralympic Games always take place shortly after the Olympic Games, using the same sporting venues and facilities. There will be only one joint organizing committee for both Olympic and Paralympic Games. . . . It was agreed that the sports programme for the Paralympic Games shall contain no more than 22 sports/disciplines for the Summer Games and 8 sports/disciplines for the Winter Games.
>
> *(IPC, 2001)*

Focusing on these first two formal agreements, Mason (2002) suggested that, 'the close association with the IOC affirms the power of the IPC over international disability sport, which remains somewhat fragmented, and thus represents a consolidation of power for the IPC' (p. 117). While this may have been seen as a positive step, the 2003 amendment to the agreement reaffirmed the position of the IPC as taking a handout from the local organising committees. The Organising Committees for the Olympic Games (OCOGs) were required to pay the following amounts to the IPC: Nine million US dollars for the Games of the XXIX Olympiad in 2008, and 14 million dollars for the XXI Olympic Winter Games in 2010 and the Games of the XXX Olympiad in 2012. This was for the broadcasting and marketing rights for these Paralympic Games (IOC, 2003).

This lucrative but controlling financial agreement was extended in 2006 to include the 2014 and 2016 Games (IOC, 2006). The 2006 IOC–IPC Agreement also led to 'an increase in funding for the IPC of 25 per cent for 2014 and of 20 per cent for 2016' (IOC, 2006). With the current agreement running until 2032 (IPC, 2016) there is a clear sign that this cooperation is beneficial to the IOC. These agreements regulate the relationship between the IOC and the IPC but do place the latter in a relationship of servitude. At the time of writing this chapter, the IOC is going through a crisis where nations and their large metropolitan areas no longer wish to bid for the Games in large numbers (Vomiero, 2018). The securing of the relationship between the IOC and IPC may help the movement weather the storm but more and more high-performance sport drawn along nationalistic lines is increasingly becoming irrelevant to individuals born in the millennium.

Discussion

In this chapter I have attempted to map out the relationship between the IPC and the IOC since the founding of the former in 1948. Since the turn of the new millennium the relationship has been documented through commercial agreements between the two institutions that have placed the IOC in a position of power over the IPC. The financial obligations of the IOC to fund the Paralympic movement can be seen as a laudable result of such an agreement. But what has the International Paralympic movement lost in regard to autonomy because of the contracts it has signed? There have been critiques of the Paralympic movement's desire for professionalism and commercialisation (Howe, 2008) and to some extent this critique is still valid, although perhaps somewhat outdated. In this discussion I will try to look at the cultural political meaning of the IOC–IPC relationship.

The rhetoric surrounding the IPC and the importance that the organisation places upon being athlete-centred is significant to discuss the relationship with the IOC. As the organisation has developed a more professional and commercially viable existence, greater pressure has been placed on a crucial debate: who is an eligible Paralympian? In the 1988 Seoul (Korea) Games the diversity of impairments on display was far greater than it is today (Howe, 2008; Howe and Silva, 2017a), and as such the IPC has fallen short of one of its professed goals to increase inclusion and sport. This mandate has often been critiqued, however, because performance sport such as that practised by the IPC needs to be exclusionary (Howe and Silva, 2017b). In essence, then, it is not the fault of the IPC that the practice of sport by its very nature is exclusionary. The Olympic moto, 'higher, faster and stronger' needs on one hand to be celebrated within the Paralympic movement, but on the other hand there needs to be a realisation that the lofty goals set forward in the ethos of Paralympism are unattainable (Howe and Silva, 2018; Silva and Howe, 2018). However, the need to tie the IPC to the IOC in part can be seen as required because of the 'trouble' the IPC had been to the IOC in the past (Bailey, 2008).

The use of the state-of-the-art facilities (primarily built for the Olympic Games) have allowed performances for Paralympians to improve greatly; and advances in technology are commonplace in a performance-enhancing environment where technologies develop with every Paralympiad. The use of these large stadia where tickets can be sold and revenue gained is no doubt useful as this economic capital from the IOC allows for the further professionalisation of the IPC. However, the wording of the IOC–IPC agreement to some may seem like a form of charity, with all the negative connotations (Howe, 2008). As a result, the economic capital is not effectively turned into symbolic capital because the Paralympic field has effectively accepted a 'handout' from the IOC (Purdue, 2011; Purdue and Howe, 2015). More importantly perhaps, is that the agreements require the IPC to hand over control of both branding and marketing of the Games to the IOC. The IOC effectively controls how the Paralympic Games are perceived by the public. While the argument would be that if the Olympic and Paralympic Games are to be understood as a single sporting festival then marketing them should be controlled with a single message: it detracts from what some feel is the importance of the celebration of difference within IPC sport (Silva and Howe, 2018).

The rules and regulations in place between the IPC and the IOC are creating a barrier which controls what the Paralympic movement can say about itself – at least in relation to its flagship event. There is also a trickle-down effect at national levels. Many National Paralympic Committees (NPCs) rely upon the IPC for financial support, and therefore the NPCs will toe the line with the policies of the international organisation. There is a need to be mindful of the protectionism regarding images and symbols that the IOC is diligent to police. Why, for example, was the IPC not afforded the same consideration as Special Olympics International? It may have been the fact that the sporting model used by Special Olympics International was about participatory competition rather than narrowly focused high-performance sport that was considered acceptable by the IOC. But a more detailed exploration of this topic would need more space than is available here.

Because the unwritten mandate of the IPC has been to replicate the IOC in the world of disability sport, there might always be a tension between the two organisations. The IOC looks good to the outside world because of the perceived charity that it is shown to an organisation that historically has had trouble financially. Hosting of the Paralympic Games has increasingly become popular to organising committees because it shows the municipality in a good light. Often, hosting the Paralympics Games requires more investment in accessible transport which is beneficial to whole communities and not just the athletes. In other words, there are some concrete physical legacies that can be associated with running a Paralympic Games. The credit for this is not given to the IPC; because it is under the umbrella of the Olympic and Paralympic Games, the image of which is controlled by the IOC, people within these communities have been traditionally predisposed to celebrate the Olympic movement for these advances in accessibility (Kerr and Howe, 2016). Issues of legacy aside, access to Paralympic sporting provision is by no mean universal for two reasons in terms of equality. First, the nature of high-performance sport is such that some people will always be excluded due to a lack of ability (Jones and Howe, 2005) and second, the vast number of impaired athletes are excluded from the Paralympic provision (Howe and Silva, 2018). Unfortunately, because of the IPC's association with the IOC and the recent high profile marketing campaigns, all too often the public and policy makers alike assume Paralympic sport is disability sport, but it is not and, in fact, IPC sport only is available to a small section of the world's disabled population. Of course, the marketing of the IPC outside the major games it shares with the IOC has done little to illuminate that parasport is not accessible to all members of the international disabled community (Purdue and Howe, 2012a; Purdue and Howe, 2012b).

The exclusion of many disabled athletes with high-support needs from sporting opportunities that they may have enjoyed and excelled at because it does not make media-friendly television (Howe, 2008; Purdue, 2011) has been a problem for the IPC. The IPC might say that the athletes have not shown an interest in certain sports, but with the practice of removing events from a Paralympic programme well in advance, it is hard not to make the vicious circle a self-fulfilling prophesy. But the real agenda may be simply the fact that athletes with high-support needs might make it difficult for the IOC to sell advertising. It is rather harsh, but it is one of the unintended consequences of the IPC's decision to be professional that they may have to sacrifice some of their core values. Perhaps there is a need for the IPC to rethink the manner in which it celebrates sporting excellence (Purdue and Howe, 2013).

As the IPC pursues the rewards that the IOC has had for some time now there are increasing demands being placed on NPCs and most importantly the athletes they have under their care. No longer is it simply about equitable and fair competition for athletes with difference, whether they be physical or sensory; but it is about lending the IOC their cyborgs – i.e. the high-performance sporting bodies that are part human, part advanced technology. Wheelchair and prosthetic limb-wearing athletes fit this bill nicely. The *cyborgification* of the Paralympic Games (Howe and Silva, 2017b) can be harnessed by the IOC to attract new viewers, but with the potential to further marginalise the athletes who have impairments but are unable to make use of advanced technologies in such an explicit manner (Howe and Silva, 2017a, 2018).

Conclusion

It is argued here that an opportunity for activism in favour of disability sport and integration might be missed currently because of the agreements with the IOC, and perhaps because of the desire of many within the IPC to not bite the hand that feeds it. Forget the trapping of the commercially successful Paralympic Games and go back to what matters by celebrating the differences between Olympians and Paralympians but also between the later. There are an increasing number of people with disabilities involved in the Paralympic movement. Sir Philip Craven, the second president of the IPC was a wheelchair basketball player before he sought to get involved in the infrastructure of Paralympic sport initially with ISMGF. Xavier Gonzalez, until 2019 the Chief

Executive Officer, also had an impairment, but the vast majority of people who work within the Paralympic movement have limited personal experience with disability. Of course, even people with the best intentions for an organisation can be influenced by attentions of historically reverent organisation in sport.

The changing fortunes of the IOC with an increased public apathy for the Olympic Games (Vomiero, 2018) means that it should begin to pay more attention to the distinctiveness of the Paralympic brand and how it can enhance the IOC's tarnished imagine. If this is the case, then the IPC should flex its muscle to allow it to more overtly celebrate the ethos of Paralympism that could be central to the improved quality of life of all people who experience disabilities. We need to recognise that all athletes – Olympians and Paralympians – as well as those that cannot achieve these lofty statuses need to be celebrated.

> Recognition that elite sportsmen and women possess a range of bodies and hence sporting excellence is relative to a specific sport may lead to reaffirmation of a sporting consumer more receptive to a range of sporting performers including, in this instance, elite athletes with a disability.
>
> *(Purdue and Howe, 2013, p. 39)*

In other words, in order for the IOC–IPC agreement to be fruitful to both parties, they have to be more nuanced because to the outsider the inclusion of Paralympic Games within the matrix of the Olympic festival may be seen as a statement of a progressive world view in tune with the need for adherence to diversity and ultimately human rights. However, this critical examination highlights that completely integrating the IOC and the IPC would be hugely problematic. Because the Paralympic Games since the turn of the century have been in league with the IOC to secure funding, they have streamlined the Games programme, at the expense of high-performance sporting opportunities for those with the highest support needs. As a result, the division between the able and the disabled has grown within the IPC as well as society more generally. The IPC, while still reliant on IOC 'handouts', now may be in a position to push back since increasingly the IOC position as the foremost international sport institution is under threat. It is hoped that over the next decade and a half the IPC's relationship with the IOC will be less like sleeping with an elephant and more like a harmonious couple.

Note

1 Please see this link to the Canadian Broadcasting Corporation archive www.cbc.ca/player/play/1797537698

References

Anderson, J. (2003). 'Turned into taxpayers': Paraplegia, rehabilitation and sport at stoke Mandeville, 1944–56. *Journal of Contemporary History*, 38(3), pp. 461–475.

Bailey, S. (2008). *Athlete-first: A history of the Paralympic movement*. Chichester, UK: John Wiley.

BBC. (2011a). London 2012 board suspends Lord Moynihan and Andy Hunt. *BBC*.

BBC. (2011b). BOA and Locog agree deal in 2012 games finance dispute. *BBC*.

BBC. (2012). London 2012: World 'split' over Olympic Games merger. *BBC*.

Brittain, I. (2008). The evolution of the Paralympic games. In: R. Cashman and S. Darcy, eds., *Benchmark games: The Sydney 2000 Paralympic games*. Sydney, Australia: Walla Walla, pp. 19–34.

Brittain, I. (2012). *From stoke Mandeville to Stratford – A history of the Summer Paralympic games*. Champagne, IL: Common Ground.

Goodman, S. (1986). *Spirit of stoke Mandeville: The story of Ludwig Guttmann*. London: Collins.

Guttmann, L. (1976). Textbook of sport for the disabled. Aylesbury, UK: HM & M.

Howe, P.D. (2008). *The cultural politics of the Paralympic movement: Through an anthropological lens.* London, UK: Routledge.
Howe, P.D. and Silva, C.F. (2017a). Challenging 'Normalcy': Possibilities and pitfalls of Paralympic bodies. *South African Journal for Research in Sport, Physical Education and Recreation,* 39(1–2), pp. 191–204.
Howe, P.D. and Silva, C.F. (2017b). The cyborgification of Paralympic sport. *Movement & Sport Sciences,* 97, pp. 17–25.
Howe, P.D. and Silva, C.F. (2018). The fiddle of using the Paralympic games as a vehicle for expanding [dis]ability sport participation. *Sport and Society: Culture, Commerce, Media, Politics,* 21(1), pp. 125–136.
Hughes, A. (1999). The Paralympics. In: R. Cashman and A. Hughes, eds., *Staging the Olympics: The event and its impact.* Sydney, Australia: UNSW Press, pp. 170–180.
International Olympic Committee. (2000). *IOC and IPC sign cooperation agreement.* IOC Press Releases. Oct. 20.
International Olympic Committee. (2003, August 25). *IOC and IPC sign amendment to 2001 agreement.* IOC Press Releases. Aug. 25.
International Olympic Committee. (2006). *IOC and IPC sign agreement extension for 2014 and 2016.* IOC Press Releases. June 22.
International Paralympic Committee. (2001). *IPC and IOC enter second phase of cooperation.* Paralympian, 3. Bonn: IPC.
International Paralympic Committee. (2008). *History and use of the term "Paralympic."* Bonn: IPC.
International Paralympic Committee. (2010). *IPC-IOC co-operation.* Bonn: IPC.
International Paralympic Committee. (2011). *Paralympic symbol and motto.* Bonn: IPC.
International Paralympic Committee. (2016). *IOC and IPC agree principles for new agreement through to 2032.* Bonn: IPC.
Jones, C. and Howe, P.D. (2005). The conceptual boundaries of sport for the disabled: Classification and athletic performance. *Journal of Philosophy of Sport,* 32, pp. 133–146.
Kerr, S. and Howe, P.D. (2016). What do we mean by Paralympic legacy? In G. Poynter, V. Viehoff and Y. Li, eds., *The London Olympics and urban development.* London: Taylor & Francis, pp. 193–204.
Legg, D. (2003). The role of Canadian organisations in the development of adapted physical activity: Case studies of the active living alliance for Canadians with a disability and the Canadian Paralympic Committee. In R. Steadward, G. Wheeler and E. Watkinson, eds., *Adapted physical activity.* Edmonton, Alberta, Canada: University of Alberta Press, pp. 115–129.
Legg, D., Fay, T., Hums, M. and Wolff, E. (2009). Examining the inclusion of wheelchair exhibition events within the Olympic Games 1984–2004. *European Sport Management Quarterly,* 9, pp. 243–258.
Mason, F. (2002). Creating image and gaining control: The development of the cooperation agreements between the International Olympic Committee and the International Paralympic Committee. In: K.B. Wamsley, R.K. Barney and S.G. Martyn, eds., *The Global nexus engaged: Past, present, future interdisciplinary Olympic studies: Sixth international symposium for Olympic research.* London, Ontario, Canada: ICOS, University of Western Ontario, pp. 113–122.
Purdue, D.E.J. (2011). *Conflict and consensus within the Paralympic field: A sociological investigation of an elite disability sport competition.* Unpublished PhD thesis. Loughborough University.
Purdue, D.E.J. and Howe, P.D. (2012a). See the sport, not the disability? – Exploring the Paralympic paradox. *Qualitative Research in Sport, Exercise and Health,* 4(2), pp. 189–205.
Purdue, D.E.J. and Howe, P.D. (2012b). Empower, inspire, achieve: (dis)empowerment and the Paralympic games. *Disability & Society,* 27(7), pp. 903–916.
Purdue, D.E.J. and Howe, P.D. (2013). Who's in and who is out? Legitimate bodies within the Paralympic Games. *Sociology of Sport Journal,* 30(1), pp. 24–40.
Purdue, D.E.J. and Howe, P.D. (2015). Plotting a Paralympic field: An elite disability sport competition viewed through Bourdieu's sociological lens. *International Review for the Sociology of Sport,* 50(1), pp. 83–97.Rose, D. (2012). *Paralympics and Olympics merger "possible after 2020".*
Scruton, J. (1998). *Stoke Mandeville: Road to the Paralympics.* Aylesbury, UK: Peterhouse Press.
Silva, C.F. and Howe, P.D. (2018). The social empowerment of difference: The potential influence of parasport. *Physical Medicine and Rehabilitation Clinics of North America,* 29(2), pp. 397–408.
Steadward, R. (1996). Integration and sport in the Paralympic movement. *Sport Science Review,* 5(1), pp. 26–41.
Vomiero, J. (2018). *Hosting the Olympics has become the contest no one wants to win, and the IOC is worried,* Global News Canada, retrieved from '*Global News,* Canada https://globalnews.ca/news/4029340/hosting-olympics-ioc-worried-expensive/'.

22

The autonomy of the Olympic and sport movement

Arnout Geeraert

Introduction

When the then newly elected International Olympic Committee (IOC) President Thomas Bach addressed the United Nations General Assembly in November 2013, he stressed that 'sport has to enjoy responsible autonomy' and that '[p]olitics must respect this sporting autonomy' (Bach, 2013, p. 3). This dual statement is indicative of two central realities that define the complex and often conflicted relationship between the private Olympic and sport movement, on the one hand, and political actors on the other. First, Bach's postulation that politics must respect sporting autonomy echoes the public-private tensions that emerge when politicians aim to instrumentalise sport for political reasons or when public authorities aim to hold sport organisations accountable to legal, ethical, and performance standards (Geeraert and Drieskens, 2015, 2020; Meier and García, 2015; Weinreich, 2014). Second, Bach's notion of 'responsible autonomy' is indicative of the realisation and acknowledgement that sporting autonomy is not unconditional. Sport organisations that do not adhere to applicable laws or ethical norms have indeed had their autonomy curtailed on numerous occasions (Chappelet, 2018; Geeraert and Drieskens, 2015; Nelson and Cottrell, 2016; Weatherill, 2017).

Thomas Bach's statement should not come as a surprise. The autonomy of sport is a fundamental principle for the Olympic and sport movement (IOC, 2018, rule 2.5). It is also a guiding principle with regard to public policies in sport, particularly at the international level (Chappelet, 2010, 2018). More specifically, the notion is used as an axiom to prescribe, justify, and conceptualise the relationships between sport organisations and different types of stakeholders. One could argue, in fact, that it has been referred to so frequently that it has become devoid of meaning. Tellingly, the United Nations Educational, Scientific and Cultural Organization (UNESCO) did not include a reference to the autonomy of sport in its revised International Charter of Physical Education and Sport in 2015 because 'the term was deemed insufficiently clear' (CIGEPS, 2015, p. 9; see also Chappelet, 2018, p. 163).

Why is the autonomy of sport such an essential notion and what can it tell us about the relationship between sport organisations and their environment? A growing body of relevant scholarly literature offers partial responses. It shows that sporting autonomy is closely interlinked with notions of self-regulation, specificity and idiosyncrasy, (private) authority, independence, freedom of association, and accountability (e.g. Chappelet, 2010, 2018; Geeraert, 2016, 2019; Geeraert, Mrkonjic and Chappelet, 2015; Parrish and Miettinen, 2008; Pielke, 2013; Smith and Stewart, 2010). It represents a fragmentation in sporting autonomy research which is a testament to the complexity and conceptual ambiguity of an abstract notion. Most importantly, it underscores the need for conceptual clarity and systematic discussion.

This chapter aims to shed light on what accounts for the enduring appeal and utility of sporting autonomy as well as how the notion can be meaningfully employed to understand dynamic interplays in sport governance. The first section discusses the conceptual history and ideological background of sporting autonomy. The following section looks into existing definitions and subsequently presents a neutral definition that moves beyond existing normative and descriptive conceptualisations of the autonomy of sport. The subsequent sections employ that definition in order to systematically take stock of existing research, discussing the threats to sporting autonomy as well as how they are mitigated. The following section explores the link between autonomy and good governance. The final section summarises the discussion and explores the way forward. The present chapter focuses mainly on sport governing bodies (SGBs) which are for the present purpose defined as international and continental sport federations and the IOC. It refers to sport organisations more broadly when the arguments presented are relevant for different types of Olympic and sport movement organisations.

Conceptual history and ideological foundations

One cannot appreciate the relevance and idiosyncratic character of autonomy within the context of sport without taking a closer look at the history and ideological basis of this notion. Indeed, the mere fact that the sport world cherishes its autonomy is not special or surprising in itself. Scholars generally assume that private entities value their autonomy and thus seek to maximise it. What distinguishes sporting autonomy from general conceptions of decision-making autonomy, however, is the way in which the underlying ideology has shaped the Olympic and sport movement's identity, beliefs, and discourse and contributed to the latter's effectiveness.

Classic liberalism and the freedom of association

The seminal works of both Jean-Loup Chappelet (2010, also 2018) and Stefan Szymanski (2006) provide the historical and ideological context that is necessary to shed light on the idiosyncrasies of sporting autonomy. Szymanski (2006) argues convincingly that the construction that is modern sport is, in essence, rooted in classic liberalism, namely in the concept of freedom of association. In the most rudimentary terms, freedom of association can be defined as people's freedom to engage in 'any kind of formalized, non-governmental, human interaction' (Tamir, 1998, p. 216). More specifically, Szymanski (2006) describes how organised sport emerged in England in a political, social, and intellectual context that was conductive to voluntary association. Indeed, the normative justification for people's right to associate freely has its intellectual roots in the works of Enlightenment philosophers like John Locke, whose classic liberal ideas had a profound impact on particularly British and American politics (Bresler, 2004; Claeys, 2008).

Because people were considered, by nature, free, equal, and independent, their freedom to associate was self-evident for liberal thinkers. The political and practical consequences of the freedom of association, however, were most famously articulated by the French civil servant and scholar Alexis de Tocqueville (Maletz, 2001). In his classic 19th-century work *Democracy in America*, de Tocqueville highlighted the intrinsic values of associations. Associative freedom, he argued, is necessary to ensure innovation and vitality by teaching people the habits of self-reliance and responsibility (de Tocqueville, 2003). Because it is conductive, even necessary, for the formulation and expression of ideas, freedom of association also prevents the tyranny of the state, which has a tendency to regulate and impose its own ideas (Bresler, 2004; Maletz, 2001).

These liberal views are strongly reflected in the writings and actions of the founder of the modern Olympic Games, Pierre de Coubertin. Both a student and a strong sympathiser of the writings of liberal thinkers like de Tocqueville, de Coubertin showed 'a profound aversion for any state intrusion in people's private lives' (Clastres, 2018, p. 38). Tellingly, he stressed that 'the goodwill of all the members of any autonomous sport grouping begins to disintegrate as soon as the huge, blurred face of that dangerous creature known as the state makes an appearance' (de Coubertin, cited in Chappelet, 2010, p. 14). According to Chappelet, the IOC still echoes these words when holding that 'only an autonomous movement, namely one that is self-regulated and self-managed without any interference, can guarantee a philosophy of life, exalting and combining in a balanced whole the qualities of body, will and mind' (ibid.).

Freedom of association is recognised as an important, even constitutional principle in liberal democracies, albeit to varying degrees (Bresler, 2004). It is, however, a primary target for repression in non-democratic societies. It is therefore not surprising that the IOC first enshrined the principle of autonomy in the Olympic Charter in 1949, at a time when it feared that the independence and autonomy of the National Olympic Committees in Soviet countries could not be ensured (Chappelet, 2010, p. 11). Today, the IOC still considers autonomy an essential principle for the Olympic and sport movement. The Olympic Charter thus establishes that one of the IOC's missions is 'to take action to strengthen the unity of the Olympic Movement, to protect its independence, to maintain and promote its political neutrality and to preserve the autonomy of sport' (IOC, 2018, rule 2.5).

The IOC's autonomy discourse thus follows naturally from the liberal notion of freedom of association. Autonomy is, in fact, the *sine qua non* of freedom of association (Lomasky, 2008, p. 185). On one hand, free association can only exist when voluntary associations have the right to establish themselves and to create their own rules and regulations to establish some form of order (Szymanski, 2006, p. 9). On the other hand, associations can only ensure innovation and vitality when 'conceptions of the good are not . . . imposed from above' (Lomasky, 2008, p. 185). In liberal democracies, associations have therefore been allowed to operate independently from the state and also to deal with matters of public interest including sport (Maletz, 2001; Szymanski, 2006, p. 10). This is why these states, in Chappelet's words, 'allowed sports organisations to develop as bodies fully independent of the public authorities' (Chappelet, 2010, p. 7).

Restraining freedom of association

Liberal ideology never intended voluntary associations' autonomy from the state to be absolute. Locke and de Tocqueville, for instance, recognised that freedom of association needs restraints (Claeys, 2008; Maletz, 2001). Indeed, unchecked associations risk creating an autonomous private sphere wherein rules and norms are detached from the moral and political consensus. Public authorities must therefore defend the common good by ensuring that associations cannot use their freedom to violate public laws or the freedom of others (Bresler, 2004, p. 22; Claeys, 2008, p. 39) or to engage in 'unchecked pursuit of material interests' (Maletz, 2001, p. 463). In other words, unchecked associations risk producing the very tyranny, inertia, and moral abuse that freedom of association is supposed to provide an antidote for.

While there is thus a consensus among liberal scholars that freedom of association needs restraints, there is an endless philosophical and ideological debate on where exactly the line should be drawn (Bresler, 2004; Claeys, 2008; Lomasky, 2008). A similar ideological discord is reflected in the strong variation on the extent to which public authorities intervene in the affairs of sport organisations at the national level (Vocasport, 2004; Chappelet, 2018). In other words, there is no public consensus on the *degree* of autonomy that should be granted to sport organisations.

The lack of a clear ideological basis for determining a suitable degree of autonomy for sport organisations is also apparent at the international level. The notion of sporting autonomy naturally finds resonance with the interests, identities, and discourse of liberal-democratic international institutions (Geeraert and Drieskens, 2017). It is therefore no surprise that the European Union (EU), the Council of Europe, and the United Nations General Assembly have responded positively to Olympic and sport movement lobbying. Since the 1990s, they have repeatedly expressed their respect for the autonomy of sport (Chappelet, 2010, 2018; United National General Assembly, 2014, para. 8). While effective public oversight of private transnational actors is difficult to achieve in any case, the strong support for sporting autonomy further hampers international public intervention in sport. At the same time, however, this support is neither absolute, nor unconditional. UNESCO, as noted in the introduction of this chapter, deliberately opted not to include a reference to the autonomy of sport in its revised International Charter of Physical Education and Sport in 2015 (CIGEPS, 2015, p. 9, also Chappelet, 2018, p. 163). Moreover, international organisations such as the Council of Europe increasingly assert themselves as actors in international sports governance and EU laws and policies have had a significant impact on SGBs' functioning (Council of Europe, 2018; Geeraert, 2016).

In recent years, international institutions have changed their discourse, making the conditional nature of sporting autonomy more explicit. It is a consequence of governance failures that have led to debates about the accountability of SGBs, including that of the IOC (Geeraert, 2019; Henry and Lee, 2004; Nelson and Cottrell, 2016; Pielke, 2013). As public interventions in sport became more common and gained legitimacy, the discourse on sporting autonomy has shifted away from acknowledging autonomy per se. In practice, this means that SGBs are increasingly expected and called upon to implement good governance. The European Commission has formulated this most forcefully by stressing succinctly that 'good governance is a condition for the autonomy and self-regulation of sport organisations' (European Commission, 2011, p. 10).

The IOC has partly embraced this discourse, acknowledging that good governance is 'the fundamental basis to secure the autonomy of Olympic and sports organisations' (IOC, 2008a, resolution 5). Yet while the European Commission's discourse on autonomy emphasises good governance as a *necessary* condition for sporting autonomy (i.e. to achieve autonomy, at least good governance has to be implemented), the Olympic movement appears to regard it as a *sufficient* condition (i.e. to achieve autonomy, implementing good governance is enough). IOC President Thomas Bach's doctrine of 'responsible autonomy' indeed implies, quite literally, that, when sport organisations 'respect national laws which are not targeted against sport and its organisations alone' and act 'in accordance with the rules of good governance', '[p]olitics *must* respect . . . sporting autonomy' (Bach, 2013, p. 3, emphasis added).

Bach's doctrine is thus clear: when sport organisations respect (general) laws and implement good governance, their autonomy should not be restrained by public authorities. This doctrine is debatable from a liberal ideological point of view, as there is a need to hold sport organisations accountable in order to defend the common good beyond implementing good governance. Moreover, the doctrine leaves a number of important practical issues pertaining to sporting autonomy unresolved. Regarding compliance with legal norms, for instance, the Olympic and sport movement has often had an idiosyncratic interpretation of the extent to which national and European laws are applicable to sport and which laws target only sport and its organisations

(Parrish and Miettinen, 2008; Meier and García 2015; Weatherill, 2017). Furthermore, while good governance is an abstract concept for which there exists no single definition, the principles of good governance advanced by the Olympic and sport movement are too vague to serve as a clear minimum standard (Geeraert, 2019). This leads to questions and debates about what principles should be implemented by sport organisations and how (Geeraert, 2018). Finally, acknowledging responsibility does not necessarily mean taking responsibility. An important and contentious issue is the result: to what extent and by what means must public actors and other stakeholders see to it that sport organisations implement good governance and, more generally, act in the public interest (Geeraert, 2019; Geeraert and Drieskens, 2017; García and Meier, 2017)?

Defining the autonomy of sport

Since 2011, the Olympic Charter has clarified that the autonomy of the Olympic and sport movement includes (but is not limited to) 'freely establishing and controlling the rules of sport, determining the structure and governance of [sport] organisations, enjoying the right of elections free from any outside influence and the responsibility for ensuring that principles of good governance be applied' (IOC, 2018, p. 11). This phrasing more or less incorporates the first three points of Chappelet's definition of sporting autonomy:

The autonomy of sport is, within the framework of national and international law, the possibility for non-governmental non-profit-making sports organisations to:

1. Establish, amend and interpret rules appropriate to their sport freely, without undue political or economic influence;
2. Choose their leaders democratically, without interference by states or third parties;
3. Obtain adequate funds from public or other sources, without disproportionate obligations;
4. Use these funds to achieve objectives and carry on activities chosen without severe external constraints;
5. In consultation with the public authorities, contribute to the drafting of legitimate standards proportionate to the fulfilment of these objectives.

(Chappelet, 2010, p. 83)

To achieve these aspects, Chappelet argues for 'negotiated autonomy', a type of negotiated cooperation between sport organisations and governments which comes down to 'finding a halfway point between liberalism and interventionism' (Chappelet, 2010, p. 52). While Chappelet's and the IOC's definitions establish a useful normative standard for the practical implementation of sporting autonomy, other conceptualisations focus on the nature of SGBs' autonomy. Weatherill (2017) advances the notion of 'conditional autonomy' to conceptualise the relation between SGBs and EU law. He clarifies that 'autonomy granted to sport by EU law is conditional on meeting the expectations located in the tests of justification recognized by EU internal market law' (Weatherill, 2017, p. 92). A related notion, 'supervised autonomy', has been introduced by Foster (2000) within the context of the EU as well. Finally, Geeraert, Mrkonjic, and Chappelet (2015) refer to 'pragmatic autonomy' to emphasise SGBs' rational use of strategies to maximise different dimensions of their autonomy (i.e. political, legal, financial, and pyramidal).

Moving beyond normative and descriptive definitions and conceptualisations, this chapter introduces a neutral definition to aid analysis of the autonomy of sport organisations. Drawing on Hawkins et al. (2006, p. 8), the autonomy of a sport organisation can be defined as the range of potential independent action available to the sport organisation after other entities have employed mechanisms that constrain its behaviour. This definition employs an institutional perspective that puts the analytical focus on the external actors that constrain sport organisations' autonomy as well as the mechanisms they employ to this end. The definition also allows taking into account the strategies sport organisations employ to influence the behaviour of (potential) autonomy challengers in order to reclaim and protect their autonomy. These mechanisms, actions, and strategies can be operationalised and analysed through rational and/or constructivist epistemologies (Geeraert and Drieskens, 2017). The definition highlights that the degree of autonomy enjoyed by a sport organisation is determined by a dynamic interplay between the organisation and those actors that challenge its autonomy (Geeraert and Drieskens, 2015). The subsequent sections focus on how different groups challenge SGBs' autonomy and how SGBs mitigate these challenges by means of different strategies.

Internal and external challenges to the autonomy of sport governing bodies

When we take the earlier definition into account, it is fair to say that the autonomy of sport has never been absolute. Sport organisations' autonomy has always been restrained by public actors and stakeholders' expectations and demands. At the same time, however, it is not plausible to maintain that sport organisations' autonomy is what it once was. This section elaborates on this reality by focusing mostly on SGBs, though similar claims could be made about other types of sport organisations. In brief, while SGBs have been able to accumulate more authority, their autonomy to wield that authority has increasingly been challenged by different groups (Geeraert, 2016).

As the world of sport grew more complex due to commercialisation and globalisation, SGBs increasingly adopted more and more diverse tasks on behalf of a larger and more diverse group of actors. Actors affected by and cognisant of the augmented powers of SGBs have responded to the organisations' increasing reach. They have increasingly tried to align the actions of SGBs with their respective interests and beliefs, consequently decreasing the organisations' leeway to administer and regulate sport. In this regard, two types of SGBs' autonomy have been under threat: internal and external autonomy (cf. Pauly and Grande, 2005, p. 11). Regarding internal autonomy, SGBs are subject to bottom-up, systemic pressures from increasingly empowered and organised internal stakeholders such as athletes, clubs, and/or subordinate sport organisations. In some cases, internal stakeholders have even acquired formal decision-making power or de facto veto power (Holt, 2006; García, 2007; Thibault, Kihl and Babiak, 2010). The IOC's autonomy to regulate the Olympic movement, for instance, has been particularly challenged by the demands imposed by powerful international federations like the Fédération Internationale de Football Association (FIFA) and the International Association of Athletics Federations (IAAF) (Chappelet and Kübler-Mabbott, 2008; Wagner, 2011).

With regard to external autonomy, different external groups have been able to control SGBs' behaviour. Three are particularly noteworthy. First, market actors have been successful in exerting pressure on SGBs in order to have their own interests met (Chappelet, 2018; Tomlinson, 2005). For example, since it professionalised the sale of marketing and media rights in the 1980s, the IOC has been coping with increasing pressure from its corporate sponsors to expand the commodification of the Olympic Games (Tomlinson, 2005). Second, public authorities at different levels have pressured SGBs to alter their policies in a number of areas, including doping, dispute-settlement, match-fixing, corruption, the allocation of major events, and good governance (Chappelet, 2010; Geeraert, 2019; Geeraert and Drieskens, 2020; Henry and Lee, 2004). However, the EU has had the most profound impact on SGBs' autonomy owing to its internal market competences (García and Meier, 2017; Geeraert and Drieskens, 2017; Weatherill, 2017). Third, SGBs have delegated authority to both the World Anti-Doping Agency (WADA) and the Court of

Arbitration for Sport (CAS) with the aim of keeping anti-doping policy and dispute settlement within the sport system. Though the IOC played a key role in the establishment of both WADA and CAS, public interventions barred it from formally controlling these organisations (Geeraert and Drieskens, 2020; Ravjani, 2009; Casini, 2012).

These trends imply a shift in the institutional set-up, power relations, and policies that define international sports governance. Unable to chart their own course at any time, SGBs must take into account the interests of those who impede their autonomy (Henry and Lee, 2004). This implies a shift from the traditional hierarchical mode of governing toward horizontal forms of governance that include negotiating and joint decision-making. In other words, policy making and implementation increasingly occur through governance networks, that is, 'a web of interrelationships' between SGBs and their public and private stakeholders (Klijn, 2008, p. 511). Nonetheless, different actors have had varying success in limiting SGBs' autonomy. This reality implies a deepening in the complexity of autonomy, which has become a multi-dimensional phenomenon, as SGBs have varying degrees of autonomy in relation to different types of autonomy challengers (Chappelet, 2010; Geeraert, 2016; Geeraert, Mrkonjic and Chappelet, 2015).

Protecting the autonomy of sport

Faced with increased challenges to their autonomy, SGBs have proven to be purposive and proactive. Using different strategies, they have managed to mitigate and minimise threats to their internal and external autonomy by influencing the behaviour of autonomy challengers (Geeraert and Drieskens, 2015; Geeraert, Mrkonjic and Chappelet, 2015; Meier and García 2015). The strategies can be grouped in two categories according to the differential theoretical-epistemological approaches to behavioural change that explain the causal mechanisms at work (see Table 22.1). The first group entails strategies that can be explained with a rationalist approach, the second one groups together strategies that are best explained using a constructivist approach.

The rationalist approach to protecting autonomy

The rationalist approach to behavioural change assumes that actors engage in instrumental decision-making based on a rational cost-benefit analysis of the consequences of different courses of action in terms of power and/or welfare gains (March and Olsen, 1989). Actors' behaviour thus changes when the expected costs or benefits of a particular course of action increase. Accordingly, SGBs engage in punishing or rewarding the behaviour of (potential) autonomy challengers. By imposing costs or granting benefits, they alter the incentive structure of internal stakeholders away from controlling SGBs in at least three distinct ways. First, SGBs make cooperation more beneficial than confrontation by granting internal stakeholders the benefit of having a (limited) degree of ad hoc or institutionalised decision-making influence (García, 2008, pp. 228–229; Holt, 2006, p. 116). For example, the IOC to some extent involves athletes in its policy-making via its Athletes' Commission, established in 1981, and it constantly consults with the international federations in what has been characterised as 'a constant attempt to seek consensus' (Chappelet and Kübler-Mabbott, 2008, p. 65; Thibault, Kihl and Babiak, 2010). Second, SGBs have mitigated threats of litigation against their rules and decisions by settling cases out of public courts. Litigants have been awarded with monetary and non-monetary benefits (García, 2008, p. 228; Van den Bogaert, 2005, p. 106) and sport arbitration, a system that offers faster and less costly redress for dispute settlements outside the (public) judicial system, has been expanded (Geeraert and Drieskens, 2015; Duval, 2015; Weatherill, 2017). The IOC played a

Table 22.1 Strategies used by sport governing bodies to maximise their autonomy

Approaches to behavioural change	*Mechanisms for influencing behaviour*		*Strategies employed in relation to internal stakeholders*	*Strategies employed in relation to public actors*
Rationalist: cost-benefit driven	Altering actors' incentive structure	Imposing costs	Establishing disciplinary sanctions for seeking recourse before public courts Establishing disciplinary sanctions for participating in sporting competitions organised outside the traditional sport movement	Engaging in public shaming Blocking national teams and clubs from participating in international competitions Withdrawing the opportunity of hosting major sport events
		Providing benefits	Granting internal stakeholders (institutionalised) decision-making influence Providing monetary benefits Providing fast and relatively cheap private dispute resolution	Granting access to decision-making power in sport Providing technical expertise and legitimacy Providing soft power via the hosting of major sport events Contributing to popularity with voters
Constructivist: norm and belief-driven	Redefining actors' beliefs	Discursive action	Promoting the autonomy of sport through discourse Promoting the specificity of sport through discourse	
		Self-legitimising action	Pursuing partnerships with (international) political actors Implementing internal procedures and bureaucratic practices associated with 'good governance'	

key role in the expansion of sport arbitration in 1983 via the establishment of the CAS, a global arbitral institution created to resolve disputes directly or indirectly related to sport (Casini, 2012). Third, adopting a model implemented by major SGBs like the IOC and FIFA, a growing number of international federations increase the costs of litigation by requiring internal stakeholders to 'contract into' the system of sport arbitration (Weatherill, 2017, p. 8). This entails that they enshrine a clause in their statutes stipulating that any disputes shall be resolved *exclusively* through arbitration. Similarly, a number of international federations have adopted statutory 'loyalty clauses' that forbid athletes from participating in non-sanctioned events (Van Rompuy, 2015, p. 198). They are intended to protect the traditional sport system by limiting athletes' 'freedom to dissociate' from international federations (Lomasky, 2008, p. 182).

Regarding external autonomy, the international federations and the IOC have displayed considerable unity and coherence when faced with challenges to their autonomy from governments. To retain their autonomy to a maximum, they may provide a number of benefits to public authorities and individual politicians, including access to decision-making power in sport (Weinreich, 2014), soft power via the hosting of major sport events (Cornelissen, 2010; Nye, 2008), popularity with voters (García 2007; Niemann and Brand, 2008), as well as legitimacy and technical expertise (Geeraert, 2016). Regarding the latter, for instance, the European Olympic Committees EU office, acting on behalf of the IOC and the Olympic movement in general, has been able to influence the content and direction of EU initiatives by giving significant input to the preparation of (multi-annual) sport policies. SGBs can also impose costs on public actors that challenge their autonomy. Relying on their good relations with (sport) journalists, they can publicly shame politicians (Geeraert, 2016, p. 151). More significantly, however, they can employ their private regulatory authority to block national teams and clubs from participating in international competitions or withdraw the opportunity to host major sport events (García and Weatherill, 2012, p. 249; Meier and García, 2015). For example, upon winning the bid for the 2012 Olympic Games, the UK government was required to implement tax breaks for the IOC's commercial partners before formally obtaining the hosting rights (Tetlak 2013). Finally, with a view to limiting regulatory interference from their host countries, SGBs can threaten to relocate to another country, since they operate on a global playing field. In 1995, for instance, the IOC and other international federations threatened to relocate when the Swiss Federal Administration of Finance rejected their request to be exempted from a new VAT law (Geeraert, Mrkonjic and Chappelet, 2015, p. 475).

Apart from public authorities, as mentioned, commercial partners have also challenged SGBs' external autonomy. SGBs' threats to engage in partnerships with alternative commercial parties has however decreased these challenges somewhat. For example, the professionally organised sale of marketing and media rights by the IOC through the Olympic Partner (TOP) programme has made these rights extremely desirable (Chappelet and Kübler-Mabbott, 2008). The competition among firms for limited marketing and media contracts limits influence of private companies and to some extent rebalances the relationship between commercial partners and the IOC.

The constructivist approach to protecting autonomy

The second category of strategies SGBs use to protect their autonomy comprises strategies that can be explained through the constructivist approach to behavioural change. This approach rests on the premise that interactions occur on the basis of internalised norms and beliefs of appropriate behaviour without or even in spite of rational calculations of costs and benefits (March and Olsen, 1989). Accordingly, SGBs must redefine the beliefs of autonomy challengers to minimise threats to their autonomy.to minimise threats to their autonomy. Three strategies are noteworthy in this regard. The first pertains to the discursive promotion of the autonomy of sport. By stressing the importance of the autonomy of sport in public discourse and by lobbying for the inclusion of the notion in public policy documents, SGBs promote a principled belief about the 'proper' relationship between public authorities and private sport authorities (see Blyth, 2002). As noted, sporting autonomy, through its interconnectedness with freedom of association and liberal ideology, has a positive appeal to liberal-democratic institutions, particularly international ones. Furthermore, the sports world appears to recognise that the concept of sporting autonomy is best kept vague, so as to appeal to a broad range of actors that hold heterogeneous preferences (see Béland and Cox, 2016). In a document submitted to the EU by the IOC on behalf of the Olympic and sports movement, for example, autonomy is said to mean 'preserving the values of sport and the existing structures through which it has developed in Europe and in the world'. Regarding justification, the text stresses rather ambiguously that 'the autonomy with which [sport] regulates itself, [has] led to its credibility and legitimacy' (IOC, 2008b, p. 1).

The second constructivist strategy SGBs deploy concerns the discursive promotion of the belief that sport constitutes a sector with specific characteristics and holds important sociocultural benefits. A tailored application of public laws is thus justified. For instance, at a recent meeting of the EU ministers of sport, IOC President Thomas Bach expressed his concern about 'certain interpretations of the European treaty and EU competition law with regard to sports'. He continued, 'If everything in Europe is looked at only from a business perspective, the social value of sport is lost. Sport is about so much more than business' (Bach in IOC, 2017). In fact, the successful promotion of the belief that sport constitutes a special sector has impacted sport policy and the application of (EU) laws to SGBs (García 2007; Parrish and Miettinen, 2008). Yet, while legal provisions need to be tailored to sport's specific characteristics such as the mutual interdependence between sport clubs, the special features of sport are often 'overstated' (Smith and Stewart, 2010, p. 10). As Weatherill puts it succinctly, '[s]porting activity is not completely without analogy to normal industry and it is certainly not as special as those engaged in sports governance commonly claim' (Weatherill, 2017, p. 3).

The final strategy in the constructivist category pertains to increasing external legitimacy. Legitimacy is defined as 'a social status' that is 'recognised as good, proper, or commendable by a group of others' (Coleman, 2007, p. 20). When SGBs and their behaviour is regarded as legitimate, those that are impacted by their actions more easily accept or tolerate these actions, even when these have damaging effects on their interests (Easton, 1965, p. 273). In other words, SGBs' autonomy is less likely to be challenged. An established strategy to solidify legitimacy credentials for SGBs has been to pursue 'partnerships' with (international) public actors such as the UN and the EU (García, 2007). Significantly, since 2009, the IOC has been enjoying observer status in the United Nations General Assembly and in April 2014, a Memorandum of Understanding was signed between UN Secretary-General Ban Ki-moon and the IOC (IOC, 2014). In addition, SGBs have openly engaged in processes intended to implement internal procedures and bureaucratic practices associated with 'good governance'. They do this in order to signal their commitment to governance improvements and to minimise both public interventions and reputation costs imposed by civil society actors (Geeraert, 2019). A case in point are the governance reforms undertaken by the IOC following the Salt Lake City scandal in 1999. John MacAloon (2011) notes that these reforms were extremely successful in alleviating pressure from governments and sponsors. The final section elaborates on governance reforms and what they mean for the autonomy of sport.

The autonomy of sport and good governance

To come full circle, the chapter ends where it started by focusing on the topical and often-assumed link between implementing good governance and achieving autonomy. Good governance is a fuzzy concept. Within the context of SGBs, it generally refers to a normative framework that both prescribes and allows for judging bureaucratic practices, rules, and procedures (Geeraert, 2018). There are two particular ways in which implementing good governance can increase SGBs' autonomy. First, by implementing commonly accepted bureaucratic practices, rules, and procedures, SGBs establish external legitimacy by generating perceptions of fairness and responding to public demands and societal pressures (DiMaggio and Powell, 1983; Tyler, 2001). Second, implementing bureaucratic practices, rules, and procedures that contribute to transparency, democracy, and internal accountability positively affects internal organisational dynamics (Geeraert, 2018). More specifically, implementing these three dimensions of good governance decreases the likelihood of corruption and increases the likelihood of effective policies (e.g. Bovens, 2007; De Graaf, 2007; Elster, 1998; McCubbins and Schwartz, 1984).

When SGBs command external legitimacy, implement effective policies, and behave in an ethical manner, external actors are less likely to curb their autonomy. Conversely, SGBs that are ineffective, unethical, and illegitimate risk having their autonomy challenged. In this regard, good governance can be perceived as a *conditio sine qua non* for the autonomy of sport as a lack thereof will almost certainly lead to a loss of autonomy in the long run. However, implementing good governance does not *automatically* lead to autonomy. There are two important caveats. First, SGBs often do not actually need to implement high standards of transparency, democracy, and internal accountability and control in order to enhance their legitimacy in the short run. The mere perception of good governance often suffices to ward off external interference. At the same time, organisations are often rather resilient to change (Pierson, 2004). There is therefore a real risk that governance reforms are symbolic rather than substantial, particularly when compliance with well-defined standards of good governance is not monitored and enforced (Geeraert, 2019). Second, even when SGBs do implement a high standard of good governance, it increases the likelihood of effectiveness and ethical behaviour, but it does not guarantee it. Moreover, SGBs that implement good governance still have opportunity to pursue their own privately held interests at the expense of the public interest, when they are not held to account in an appropriate manner (Geeraert and Drieskens, 2020).

Even when SGBs do implement good governance, there is thus a liberal ideological rationale for holding them to account: protecting the common good. In this regard, the prevailing discourse on conditional and responsible autonomy, which connects achieving autonomy with implementing good governance and respecting the law, is rather narrow.

Conclusion

This chapter aims to explain why the autonomy of sport is such an essential notion for the Olympic and sport movement and how it can usefully be employed to analyse dynamic interplays between sport organisations and their environment. The notion's ideological roots in classical liberalism and freedom of association concepts underscore that autonomy is essential for guaranteeing the innovation and vitality of sport organisations and for keeping them free from state oppression and instrumentalisation. At the same time, however, liberal thought acknowledges that an essential task of public authorities is to defend the common good by ensuring that freedom of association cannot be abused to act against the common interest. While it is therefore clear that autonomy needs to be checked, there is no ideological agreement on where public authorities should draw the line between ensuring free association and protecting the common good.

Though freedom of association and sporting autonomy are inextricably linked, autonomy also goes beyond freedom of association, which takes the state as the point of reference. This chapter introduces a neutral definition of sporting autonomy that takes into account how different institutional actors constrain sport organisations' behaviour. It shows that shifts in the power relations and actor constellations in sports governance have led to a deeper complexity of the concept of autonomy. Sporting autonomy proves a multi-dimensional and dynamic phenomenon as SGBs have varying degrees of autonomy in relation to different types of actors and constantly deploy different strategies to maximise their autonomy in relation to (potential) autonomy challengers. This neutral analytical perspective strips sporting autonomy of its ideological veil and underscores that SGBs, like all private actors, seek to maximise their autonomy. From this point of view, the Olympic and sport movement's discourse on sporting autonomy can be viewed as the discursive promotion of a principled belief about the proper relationship between public authorities and private sport authorities. The successful promotion of this belief in international fora can be explained by the ideational vagueness of sporting autonomy and its interconnectedness with freedom of association and liberal ideology.

The proposed neutral definition deliberately avoids making normative claims about desired degrees of autonomy. The prevailing (international) discourse on conditional and responsible autonomy makes sporting autonomy contingent upon implementing good governance and respecting the law. It is true that by implementing good governance SGBs are more likely to gain external legitimacy, implement effective policies, and behave in an ethical manner. Consequently, external actors are less likely to curb their autonomy. Yet, implementing good governance by no means guarantees that SGBs will act in the public interest. From the point of view of classical liberalism, public actors should therefore hold SGBs to account, even when they implement bureaucratic practices, rules, and procedures associated with good governance. 'Conditional' or 'responsible' autonomy would then imply that SGBs can only enjoy autonomy when they act in the interest of the common good. The common good obviously includes but also goes beyond implementing good governance. In other words, implementing good governance is a necessary condition but cannot be a sufficient condition for the autonomy of sport.

Liberal ideology legitimises the Olympic and sport movement's claim for autonomy. However, under the same ideology, freedom of association cannot imply freedom of accountability. Public authorities have a responsibility to ensure that SGBs act in the interest of the common good. Particularly at the international level, public attempts to hold SGBs to account have been modest at best. This has rendered international sports governance an autonomous private sphere that has become overly detached from the liberal ideology upon which it was initially founded. For sure, accountability is difficult to achieve at the global level. It becomes all the more difficult, however, when the idea of sporting autonomy restricts any public intervention in sport a priori. That is against the ideology in which the autonomy of sport is fundamentally rooted.

References

Bach, T. (2013). *Statement on the occasion of the adoption of the resolution 'Building a peaceful and better world through sport and the Olympic ideal'*. 68th Session of the UN General Assembly, New York, 6 November. New York: United Nations.

Béland, D. and Cox, R.H. (2016). Ideas as coalition magnets: Coalition building, policy entrepreneurs, and power relations. *Journal of European Public Policy*, 23(3), pp. 428–445.

Blyth, M. (2002). *Great transformations: Economic ideas and institutional change in the twentieth century*. Cambridge: Cambridge University Press.

Bovens, M. (2007). Analysing and assessing accountability: A conceptual framework. *European Law Journal*, 13(4), pp. 447–468.

Bresler, R.J. (2004). *Freedom of association. Rights and liberties under the law*. Santa Barbara: ABC-CLIO.

Casini, L. (2012). The making of a lex sportiva by the court of arbitration for sport'. In: R. Siekmann and J. Soek, eds., *Lex sportiva: What is sports law?* The Hague: T.M.C. Asser Press, pp. 149–172.

Chappelet, J.L. (2010). *The autonomy of sport in Europe*. Strasbourg: Council of Europe.

Chappelet, J.L. (2018). The autonomy of sport and the EU. In: J. Anderson, R. Parrish and B. García, eds., *Research handbook on EU sports law and policy*. Cheltenham: Edward Elgar, pp. 157–172.

Chappelet, J-L. and Kübler-Mabbott, B. (2008). *The International Olympic Committee and the Olympic system: The governance of world sport*. London: Routledge.

CIGEPS. (2015). *The intergovernmental committee for physical education and sport. Extraordinary session*. CIGEPS/2015/INF.REV. UNESCO: Paris.

Claeys, E.R. (2008). The private society and the liberal public good in John Locke's thought. *Social Philosophy and Policy*, 25(2), pp. 201–234.

Clastres, P. (2018). Pierre de Coubertin: The inventor of the Olympic tradition. In: E. Bayle and P. Clastres, eds., *Global sport leaders. A biographical analysis of international sport management*. New York: Palgrave MacMillan, pp. 33–60.

Coleman, K.P. (2007). *International organizations and peace enforcement*. Cambridge: Cambridge University Press.

Cornelissen, S. (2010). The geopolitics of global aspiration: Sport mega-events and emerging powers. *The International Journal of the History of Sport*, 27(16–18), pp. 3008–3025.
Council of Europe. (2018). *International partnership against corruption in sport (IPACS)*. Strasbourg: Council of Europe.
De Graaf, G. (2007). Causes of corruption: Towards a contextual theory of corruption. *Public Administration Quarterly*, 31(1), pp. 39–86.
de Tocqueville, A. (2003). *Democracy in America. And two essays on America*. London: Penguin Publishing.
DiMaggio, P.J. and Powell, W.W. (1983). The Iron Cage revisited: Institutional isomorphism and collective rationality in organizational fields. *American Sociological Review*, 48(2), pp. 147–160.
Duval, A. (2015). The court of arbitration for sport and EU law: Chronicle of an encounter. *Maastricht Journal of European and Comparative Law*, 22(2), pp. 224–255
Easton, D. (1965). *A systems analysis of political life*. New York: Wiley.
Elster, J. (1998). *Deliberative democracy*. Cambridge: Cambridge University Press.
European Commission. (2011). *Developing the European dimension in sport*. COM (2011) 12 final. Brussels: European Commission.
Foster, K. (2000). Can sport be regulated by Europe? an analysis of alternative models. In: A. Caiger and S. Gardiner, eds., *Professional sport in the European Union: Regulation and re-regulation*. The Hague: TMC Asser Press, pp. 43–64.
García, B. (2007). UEFA and the European Union: From confrontation to co-operation? *Journal of Contemporary European Research*, 3(3), pp. 202–223.
García, B. (2008). *The European Union and the governance of football: A game of levels and agendas*. PhD thesis, Loughborough University.
García, B. and Meier, H.E. (2017). Global sport power Europe? The efficacy of the European Union in global sport regulation. *Journal of Common Market Studies*, 55(4), pp. 850–870.
García, B. and Weatherill, S. (2012). Engaging with the EU in order to minimize its impact: Sport and the negotiation of the treaty of Lisbon. *Journal of European Public Policy*, 19(2), pp. 238–256.
Geeraert, A. (2016). *The EU in international sports governance. A principal-agent perspective on EU control of FIFA and UEFA*. Basingstoke and New York: Palgrave Macmillan.
Geeraert, A. (2018). *Sports governance observer 2018. An assessment of good governance in five international sports federations*. Aarhus: Play the Game/Danish Institute for Sports Studies.
Geeraert, A. (2019). The limits and opportunities of self-regulation: Achieving international sport federations' compliance with good governance standards. *European Sport Management Quarterly*, 19(4), pp. 520–538.
Geeraert, A. and Drieskens, E. (2015). The EU controls FIFA and UEFA: A principal-agent perspective. *Journal of European Public Policy*, 22(10), pp. 1448–1466.
Geeraert, A. and Drieskens, E. (2017). Normative market Europe: The EU as a force for good in international sports governance? *Journal of European Integration*, 39(1), pp. 79–94.
Geeraert, A. and Drieskens, E. (2020). The dynamics of de-delegation: a principal-agent explanation of the reversal of private authority in international sport governance. *Public Administration* (forthcoming), doi: 10.1111/padm.12668.
Geeraert, A., Mrkonjic, M. and Chappelet, J-L. (2015). A rationalist perspective on the autonomy of international sport governing bodies: Towards a pragmatic autonomy in the steering of sports. *International Journal of Sport Policy and Politics*, 7(4), pp. 473–488.
Hawkins, D.G., Lake, D.A., Nielson, D.L. and Tierney, M.J. eds. (2006). *Delegation and agency in international organizations*. Cambridge: Cambridge University Press.
Henry, I. and Lee, P.C. (2004). Governance and ethics in sport. In: S. Chadwick and J. Beech, eds., *The business of sport management*. Harlow: Pearson Education, pp. 25–42.
Holt, M. (2006). *UEFA, governance and the control of club competition in European football*. London: Birbeck Sport Business Centre.
IOC. (2008a). *Resolutions of the second seminar on the autonomy of the Olympic and Sports Movement*. Lausanne: IOC [online]. Available at: https://stillmed.olympic.org/AssetsDocs/ importednews/documents/en_report_1294.pdf [Accessed 1 Dec. 2018].
IOC. (2008b). *Position of the Olympic and sports movement on the specificity and autonomy of sport*. Lausanne: IOC.
IOC. (2014). *IOC and UN Secretariat agree historic deal to work together to use sport to build a better world* [online]. Lausanne: IOC. Available at: https://www.olympic.org/news/ioc-and-un-secretariat-agree-historic-deal-to-work-together-to-use-sport-to-build-a-better-world [Accessed 1 Dec. 2018].

IOC. (2017). *IOC President at the Council of the European Union for meeting on 'sport in the 21st century'*. Lausanne: IOC. Available at: https://www.olympic.org/news/ioc-president-at-the-council-of-the-european-union-for-meeting-on-sport-in-the-21st-century [Accessed 1 Dec. 2018].
IOC. (2018). *Olympic charter*. Lausanne: IOC.
Klijn, E.-H. (2008). Governance and governance networks in Europe. An assessment of ten years of research on the theme. *Public Management Review*, 10, pp. 505–525.
Lomasky, L.E. (2008). The paradox of association. *Social Philosophy & Policy Foundation*, 26(2), pp. 182–200.
Maletz, D.J. (2001). Tocqueville on the society of liberties. *The Review of Politics*, 63(3), pp. 461–483.
MacAloon, J. (2011). Scandal and governance: Inside and outside the IOC 2000 commission. *Sport in Society*, 14(3), pp. 292–308.
March, J.G. and Olsen, J.P. (1989). *Rediscovering institutions: The organizational basis of politics*. New York: Free Press.
McCubbins, M.D. and Schwartz, T. (1984). Congressional oversight overlooked: Police patrols versus fire alarms. *American Journal of Political Science*, 28, pp. 165–179.
Meier, H.E. and García, B. (2015). Protecting private transnational authority against public intervention: FIFA's power over national governments. *Public Administration*, 93(4), pp. 890–906.
Nelson, T. and Cottrell, M.P. (2016). Sport without referees? The power of the International Olympic Committee and the social politics of accountability. *European Journal of International Relations*, 22(2), pp. 437–458.
Niemann, A. and Brand, A. (2008). The impact of European integration on domestic sport: The case of German football. *Sport in Society*, 11(1), pp. 90–106.
Nye, J. (2008). *Soft power and the Beijing Olympics*. Belfer Center for Science and International Affairs.
Parrish, R. and Miettinen, S. (2008). *The sporting exception in European Union law*. The Hague: T.M.C. Asser Press.
Pauly, E. and Grande, L.W. (2005). *Complex sovereignty: Reconstituting political authority in the twenty-first century*. Toronto: University of Toronto Press.
Pielke, R. (2013). How can FIFA be held accountable? *Sport Management Review*, 16(3), pp. 255–267.
Pierson, P. (2004). *Politics in time: History, institutions, and social analysis*. Princeton, NJ: Princeton University Press.
Ravjani, A. (2009). The court of arbitration for sport: A subtle form of inter- national delegation. *Journal of International Media & Entertainment Law*, 2(2), pp. 241–284.
Smith, A.C. and Stewart, B. (2010). The special features of sport: A critical revisit. *Sport Management Review*, 13(1), pp. 1–13.
Szymanski, S. (2006). *A theory on the evolution of modern sport*. International association of sports economists Working Paper Series, No. 06–30 [online]. Available at: http://college.holycross.edu/RePEc/spe/Szymanski_Evolution.pdf [Accessed 1 Dec. 2018].
Tamir, Y. (1998). Revisiting the civic sphere. In: A. Guttman, ed., *Freedom of association*. Princeton, NJ: Princeton University Press, pp. 214–238.
Tetlak, K. (2013). The taxpayer as the unofficial sponsor of the London 2012 Olympic Games. *International Sports Law Journal*, 13(1), pp. 97–103.
Thibault, L., Kihl, L. and Babiak, K. (2010). Democratization and governance in international sport: Addressing issues with athlete involvement in organizational policy. *International Journal of Sport Policy and Politics*, 2(3), pp. 275–302.
Tomlinson, A. (2005). The commercialization of the Olympics: Cities, corporations and the Olympic commodity. In: K. Young and K. Wamsley, eds., *The global Olympics: Historical and sociological studies of the modern games*. London: JAI Press, pp. 179–200.
Tyler, T. (2001). A psychological perspective on the legitimacy of institutions and authorities. In: J.T. Jost and B. Major, eds., *The psychology of legitimacy: Emerging perspectives on ideology, justice, and intergroup relations*. Cambridge: Cambridge University Press, pp. 416–436.
United Nations General Assembly. (2014). *Sport as a means to promote education, health, development*. Resolution 69/6 adopted by the General Assembly on 31 October. New York: United Nations.
Van den Bogaert, S. (2005). *Practical regulation of the mobility of sportsmen in the EU post Bosman*. The Hague: Kluwer Law International.
Van Rompuy, B. (2015). The role of EU competition law in tackling abuse of regulatory power by sports associations. *Maastricht Journal of European and Comparative Law*, 22(2), pp. 174–204.
Vocasport. (2004). *La formation dans le domaine du sport en Europe*. Lyon: European Observatoire of Sport and Employment.

Wagner, U. (2011). Towards the construction of the World Anti-Doping Agency: Analyzing the approaches of FIFA and the IAAF to doping in sport. *European Sport Management Quarterly*, 11(5), pp. 445–470.
Weatherill, S. (2017). *Principles and practice in EU sports law.* Oxford: Oxford University Press.
Weinreich, J. (2014). *Macht, Moneten, Marionetten: Ein Wegweiser durch die Olympische Parallelgesellschaft. IOC, FIFA, Bach, Putin, Blatter, Scheichs und Oligarchen.* Berlin: Krautreporter.

23

Political autonomy and control of national Olympic committees

Henk Erik Meier

Introduction

In December 2012, the International Olympic Committee (IOC) suspended the National Olympic Committee (NOC) of India, the Indian Olympic Association (IOA), for its failure to comply with the Olympic statutes on good governance. Therefore, the three Indian athletes participating in the Sochi 2014 Winter Olympic Games competed as so-called 'Independent Olympic Participants' under the Olympic flag. The suspension was provoked by attempts of the Indian government to control the composition of the IOA. The minister for sport had proposed a new bill imposing a maximum age of 70 and a limited number of terms in office. In case the bill would have been adopted, it would have resulted in the sacking of several long-term IOA members (Chappelet, 2014). Only after the Indian government made concessions, the IOC Executive Board lifted the suspension and the Indian flag was raised in the Olympic Village of the Sochi Games.

The suspension of the Indian NOC illustrates the IOC's intensified efforts to enforce the political autonomy of NOCs. However, the pivotal role occupied by NOCs within the Olympic system creates substantial incentives for national governments to assume control of NOCs. Therefore, this chapter aims to shed some light on the conflicts about political independence and control of the NOCs. Unfortunately, little systematic research on the NOCs and their political ties is available. By far the most comprehensive account is provided by Chappelet and Kübler-Mabbot (2008) who present a number of general claims but not very detailed data. Given the lack of research, a general caveat concerning the validity of generalizations applies.

The chapter proceeds as follows: first, the specific position of the NOCs in the Olympic movement is depicted. Then, the political role of NOCs for national governments. Then, several cases of political interference and the IOC remedies are examined.

The position of NOCs within the Olympic movement

NOCs occupy a pivotal position between the IOC and national governments within the Olympic system. The Olympic Charter stipulates very clearly that NOCs act as the national representatives of the IOC within the respective country. Article 27 states that the 'mission of the

NOCs is to develop, promote and protect the Olympic Movement in their respective countries, in accordance with the Olympic Charter'.

The Olympic Charter assigns the NOCs a number of key tasks, which come with implications for national sport policies. Thus, the NOCs supervise the organization of Olympic sports in each country and choose the athletes that will represent their respective countries in the Olympic and other regional games. The NOCs have to promote Olympism mostly in the national educational system and to deploy all Olympic policies. Moreover, the NOCs make the final decision on whether or not the national teams will participate in the Games. In addition, the NOCs are instrumental in choosing host cities and states. Any application to host Olympic Games must be submitted to the IOC by the responsible public authorities with the approval of the NOC of the respective country (Olympic Charter, 2013, Bye-law to Rule 33.1.2).

Whereas the Charter recognizes that, in order to fulfill their mission, 'the NOCs may cooperate with governmental bodies, with which they shall achieve harmonious relations' but demands:

> The NOCs must preserve their autonomy and resist all pressures of any kind, including but not limited to political, legal, religious or economic pressures which may prevent them from complying with the Olympic Charter.
>
> *(Olympic Charter, 2013, Art. 27.6)*

The Olympic Charter includes regulations on the composition and procedures of the NOCs. It states in particular that governments and other public authorities shall not designate any members of an NOC. Yet, the Charter allows NOC to decide, at its discretion, to elect as members representatives of such authorities.

The Charter authorizes the IOC Executive Board to protect the Olympic movement by suspending or withdrawing the recognition of a NOC 'if the constitution, law or other regulations in force in the country concerned, or any act by any governmental or other body causes the activity of the NOC or the making or expression of its will to be hampered' (Olympic Charter, 2013, Art. 27.9). A suspension represents a less drastic sanction than a complete withdrawal of recognition. Nevertheless, the – rarely implemented – suspension represents a highly visible sanction as athletes of the suspended NOC are not allowed to participate in the Olympics under their country's flag.

The political role of the NOCs

Although the Olympic Charter defines the NOCs clearly as institutions of the IOC, the NOCs occupy a key role for national sport policies. The political interest of national governments in the NOCs results from the well-known 'Olympic paradox' (Mandell, 1976, p. 80). Although the Olympics claim to endorse internationalism, the very organization of the Olympic Games is based on the principle of national representation, which invokes a nationalistic worldview that structures the world in nations; thus, national belonging is central (Holt, 1990; Hargreaves, 1992; Billig, 1995). The reinforcement of a nationalistic worldview is one of the reasons why participating in the Olympics is often seen as full-fledged national sovereignty (Sugden and Tomlinson, 1998; Balbier, 2005; Darby, 2005).

Former versions of the Olympic Charter nurtured such nationalistic sentiments. The Olympic Charter of 1950 simply assumed that NOCs naturally represent countries. The 1962 version explained in a footnote that

> Since the Olympic Movement is non-political the words 'country' or 'nation' are in these rules intended to apply also to a geographical area, district or territory within the limits

of which an Olympic Committee recognized by the International Olympic Committee functions or operates.

(Olympic Charter, 1962, p. 10)

The 1966 version qualifies – again in a footnote – that recognition does not imply political recognition and is dependent on the area having had a stable government for a reasonable period of time (Olympic Charter, 1966, p. 12). In the 1975 version, these qualifications had been made part of the rules for recognition (Olympic Charter, 1975, Art. 8).

Thus, former versions of the Olympic Charter suggested that recognizing a NOC indicated the existence of a viable political unit. As O'Neill (1988, pp. 408–409) has put it: 'Recognition by the IOC, therefore, implies or results in the recognition of that state's jurisdiction within its territory, and its stability as a government.' The current version does not include such stipulations. According to Chappelet and Kübler-Mabbot (2008), the IOC accepts today only independent states as recognized by the international community.

Nevertheless, recognizing a NOC inevitably implies some form of national representation. The athletes will wear the official colors of their respective states and the national anthem of the winning athlete or team is played following a victory. However, the Olympic Games are not only a stage for national representation but also for political protest. Accordingly, some governments might fear that the Olympic stage might be exploited by 'dissident' athletes. Moreover, communist countries faced the problem that their athletes defected during the Games compromising the claim that living under communism was desirable. Thus, whereas governments have a symbolic interest in the recognition of a NOC, they might also have substantial incentives to control nomination decisions by the NOCs or in disciplining the athletes.

Furthermore, the NOCs are of further political interest for national governments as they can influence national and – to some extent – international sport policies. Concerning domestic sport policies, many NOCs perform a number of functions related to the national sport sector, all the more as most NOCs serve also as national Sports Confederation or Sports Council. In that case, the NOCs work not only as lobby organization for the entire sport sector but act also often as agents of their respective national governments, which delegate responsibilities for policy development and implementation. Thus, NOCs allocate resources, organize events and competitions and implement anti-doping policies (Chappelet and Kübler-Mabbot, 2008, p. 53). It should be noted that in a number of countries, such as Germany, the Netherlands and South Korea, formerly separated NOCs have merged with the national Sports Confederation or Sport Council.

Concerning international sport politics, the NOCs have acquired some political role of their own within the Olympic movement. This development has been partially provoked by the autocratic rule of Avery Brundage who served as IOC president from 1952 to 1972. Since the 1960s, the NOCs demanded a bigger say in policy making as well as a greater share of the Games' revenues (Senn, 1999, p. 13; Guttmann, 2002, chap. 8). Therefore, the NOCs formed their own interest representation, the Association of National Olympic Committees (ANOC). As Chappelet and Kübler-Mabbot (2008) put it mildly, the IOC was first suspicious of ANOC. The IOC saw itself as exclusive representative of the entire Olympic movement and was clearly outnumbered in terms of membership numbers by ANOC. Moreover, ANOC was founded on the principle of 'one country/NOC = one vote', which actually seemed to define NOCs as national representatives. In 1979, after much reluctance of the IOC, ANOC was formally made part of the Olympic bureaucracy. However, it is important to note that notwithstanding tensions between the IOC and NOCs, the ANOC has never acted as counter-power to the IOC (Chappelet and Kübler-Mabbot, 2008, p. 54).

Yet, when the successful commercialization of the Olympics created an unprecedented influx of TV money, the NOCs as well as the International Federations asserted their claims in participating in the IOC's revenue. With regard to the participation in IOC's revenue streams, ANOC (and its continental branches) have grown in importance since 2001. The commission supervising the Olympic Solidarity programme, which has been officially created in 1971, is since then chaired by the president of ANOC. This initiative of then IOC President Jacques Rogge has strengthened the position of the NOCs within the Olympic movement (Chappelet and Kübler-Mabbott, 2008). Thus, the NOCs are important because of their access to revenue streams. Moreover, the subsidies from the Olympic Solidarity programme can turn NOCs in poor countries into relatively wealthy sport organizations creating incentives for political control of these resources. In any case, the Olympic Solidarity programme has facilitated the expansion of the Olympic movement in the non-Western context (Zammit and Henry, 2014).

The autonomy of the NOCs

The Olympic Charter demands the NOCs to preserve their autonomy without specifying what such autonomy really means. Following the most encompassing definition of Jean-Loup Chappelet (2010), the autonomy of sport can be understood as the possibility of the sport organizations to:

1. Establish, amend and interpret rules appropriate to their sport freely, without undue political or economic influence;
2. Choose their leaders democratically, without interference by states or third parties;
3. Obtain adequate funds from public or other sources, without disproportionate obligations;
4. Use these funds to achieve objectives and carry on activities chosen without severe external constraints;
5. Draw up, in consultation with the public authorities, legitimate standards proportionate to the fulfilment of these objectives.

Here is important to note that autonomy of sport is in essence a Western concept, where sport has been framed as part of the leisure activities of free citizens who have to right to form their own associations and to adopt the rules they wish (Chappelet, 2016). However, even some Western countries prefer a more active role of the state in sport policy-making (Henry and Ko, 2009). Moreover, it seems useful to follow Geeraert, Mrkonjic and Chappelet (2015) who have distinguished between four different subdimensions of sports autonomy: political autonomy (absence of political interference), legal autonomy (private autonomy of sport organizations), financial autonomy and pyramidal (hierarchical) autonomy. Even in Western contexts, sport autonomy has come under pressure in all of these subdimensions due to a mix of attempts of political instrumentalization, diverse failures of autonomous governance, self-commercialization and abuse of monopoly positions, competence creeping by supranational institutions, increased financial dependency and intensified conflicts within the sport sector.

Outside a Western context, in particular in less liberal cultures with a weak civil society, it seems even less persuasive for governments to rely on autonomous societal organizations for sport policy-making (Chappelet, 2016). Accordingly, the realities of many NOCs do not adhere to the doctrine of the autonomy of sport. First of all, a number of resource dependencies exist, which create opportunities for political control. Thus, many NOCs are subsidized by their governments or by state lotteries. In a number of Western countries, a laissez faire approach to sport policy-making has been replaced by some supervised autonomy where the provision of subsidies and organizational autonomy is only granted when performance targets are met (Green and Houlihan, 2006). In addition, the NOCs have to cooperate with national educational institutions in order fulfill their task to promote Olympism. The need for cooperation between the sport sector and the states increases also due to the complexities of regulating commercialized sports. In case a country hosts the Olympics, cooperation between NOCs and governments has inevitably to intensify due to the need to heavily invest in sport facilities and transport, to amend national legislation and to provide security. Finally, NOCs can be controlled via personal interlocks, that is, by staffing the NOC with government or party representatives.

Thus, according to Chappelet and Kübler-Mabbot (2008), the situation of NOCs varies substantially across the world. Without providing detailed data, they propose the following classification of NOC's autonomy *vis-à-vis* national governments:

- Politically independent NOCs with substantial financial resources;
- Politically independent NOCs without substantial financial resources;
- NOCs controlled by government on both a financial and political level;
- So-called 'fantasy' NOCs, which are created for a symbolic participation in the Olympics.

Chappelet and Kübler-Mabbot (2008) claim that the majority of NOCs, in particular in non-Western countries, belong to the third category of government-controlled NOCs. In these arrangements, the NOC represents an annex to the national sport ministry and the sport minster acts as president of the NOC. Yet, since 2000 the IOC has adopted a policy trying to enforce the autonomy of the NOCs. In the following section, several cases of governmental control of NOCs will be shortly discussed.

Cases of government control of NOCs

Government control of NOCs was in particular prevalent during the cold war era, which put the IOC in a difficult position to enforce its stipulation on autonomy, in particular since political interference was practiced in communist *and* capitalist countries. However, the means to exercise government control differed substantially in both political blocs.

The history of the 'querelle d'allemand', that is, the struggle about the recognition of two distinct German NOCs after the Second World War has been told several times. For the communist government of the East German Democratic Republic (GDR) participating in the Olympic Games was a tool to gain the very diplomatic recognition the West Germans worked hard to prevent (Blasius, 2001; Balbier, 2005). Thus, East German athletes were supposed to serve as 'diplomats in training suits' and political control of the GDR NOC was of strategic importance. The German divide in sports materialized when a West German NOC was founded in 1949 and the East Germans responded in April 1951 by creating their own NOC.

From the beginning, the GDR NOC was constructed as element of a state sport system. Thus, the election of the NOC followed the 'democratic' practices typical for communist countries. After intense preparation by the communist party an open *en bloc* vote was held (Spitzer, 1999). The problem of political control of the NOC was solved by turning party members into 'multi-functionaries'. Thus, Manfred Ewald who became president of the GDR NOC in 1973 served as head of the East German Sports Confederation (Deutscher Turn- und Sportbund – DTSB) and was a member of the Central Committee of the East German communist party since 1963. As such, Ewald was a regular participant in the sessions of the power centre of the communist party, the so-called Politburo. Therefore, the sport diplomacy of the GDR NOC was instructed and supervised by the communist party (Teichler, 2002). Ewald was further head of the Central Commission for High Performance Sport (Zentrale Leistungssportkommission – LSK), which designed the East German state doping system. After reunification, Ewald was sentenced on probation for his involvement in these illegal practices (Latzel, 2009).

Whereas the NOCs in the communist block were integral part of a state sport system, Western governments also managed to influence key decisions of their NOCs. The boycott of the 1980 Olympic Games in Moscow allows to demonstrate how political interference in the West worked.

After the Soviet invasion of Afghanistan in December 1979, US President James Carter started a campaign to orchestrate a global boycott against the Moscow Olympics. On 20 January, 1980, Carter addressed the chairman of the American Olympic Committee (USOC) and insisted that the Committee suggest to the IOC to transfer, postpone or cancel the Games unless all Soviet troops had been withdrawn from Afghanistan within a month. Otherwise, the US would not send a team to Moscow. Within a week, the presidential request to USOC received support in resolutions of the US House of Representatives and the Senate. Whereas the Carter administration failed to pressurize the IOC to postpone or relocate the Games, it succeeded in 'convincing' the USOC by resorting to a mix of 'threats and intimidation' (Guttmann, 2002, p. 151).

More precisely, the Carter administration threatened the USOC with a withdrawal of public subsidies, waive of tax exemptions, a trade embargo or refusal of exit permits for athletes. Facing immense pressure from the president, the legislature as well as public opinion, the USOC gave in and voted in April 1980 for a boycott (for details see: Sarantakes, 2011). Despite skepticism about the efficacy of a boycott, the West German government supported the US initiative because Chancellor Helmut Schmidt was afraid of further alienating the US. The federal parliament voted with an overwhelming majority in favor of a boycott. According to the president of the West German NOC, the political volition ultimately convinced the NOC to support the boycott (Braun, 2015). Thus, dependence on public funding as well as clear and highly visible political demands from governments and legislatures served to convince NOCs to submit to political pressure. It should be mentioned, however, that the British Olympic Association (BOA) resisted the pressure of Prime Minister Thatcher and insisted on the autonomy of sport. Even the threat to withdraw public funding could not change this stance, as the BOA was able to secure alternative funding (Jefferys, 2012).

Thus, the autonomy of many Eastern bloc NOCs was more than questionable and the enforcement of the 1980 boycott by the Carter administration could have been considered to represent a violation of the Olympic Charter. However, the fate of the Olympic movement during the cold war was far too precarious to allow drastic sanction and retaliations. Thus, facing a 'civil war for control of the Olympic movement' ignoring the Charter might have been the most reasonable response by the IOC (Sarantakes, 2011, p. 264).

Nevertheless, IOC President Lord Killanin announced in January 1978 plans to form a council of the IOC to control political interference (Nafziger and Strenk, 1978). However, a deliberate policy to use monitoring of NOCs and (threats) of suspensions as enforcement mechanism of NOC autonomy evolved only slowly. By now, 'political interference' represents the most common reason for the suspension of a NOC. Before, the IOC used suspension primarily to sanction the violation of fundamental principles of the Olympic movement such as racial non-discrimination (Chappelet and Kübler-Mabbot, 2008).

Thus, the IOC Session held in October 1963 prepared the suspension of the South African Olympic Committee to sanction its Apartheid policy. In 1964, South Africa was actually suspended and forbidden to participate in any subsequent Olympic Games (IOC Session, 1989). Yet, the IOC used the instrument also to mitigate threats to its authority and event monopoly.

Thus, the IOC of Indonesia was suspended after the Indonesian government announced to 'reorganize' international sports and organized the Games of the New Emerging Forces (GANEFO) as a rival to the Olympic Games. The IOC considered GANEFO to represent an example for blatant political use of sport (IOC Session, 1964) and since then regularly resorted to threats of suspension in order to enforce political autonomy (IOC Session, 1973).

In 1974, the IOC started monitoring the statutes of the NOCs and technically suspended all NOCs, which had not submitted their statutes (IOC Session, 1974). In 1975, the IOC president suggested to amend the IOC Charter in order to expand the opportunities for using suspension as a less harsh enforcement mechanism than a full-fledged withdrawal of NOC recognition (IOC Session, 1975, 1976). The era of politically motivated boycotts provoked a discussion within the IOC about suspending non-participating NOCs (IOC Session, 1983, 1984). However, IOC President Juan Antonio Samaranch stressed that participating was a moral but not a legal obligation. Thus, the only sanction against non-participating NOCs was denying them TV revenues from the Games (IOC Session, 1988).

Enforcing NOC autonomy today

Since the end of the cold war, the IOC started enforcing autonomy of the NOCs in a more determined manner. In 1985, the IOC created a department for NOC relations and started monitoring the NOCs more systematically. At the same time, the IOC, which since the 1980s has enjoyed more financial resources, expanded the Olympic Solidarity programme in order to provide assistance to particularly poor NOCs.

At first glance, the policy developed by the IOC seems to resemble the ones practiced by the international governing body for football, the Fédération Internationale de Football Association (FIFA), which does not hesitate to impose its power on national governments (Meier and García, 2015). However, in contrast to FIFA, the IOC does resort much more rarely to suspensions. Moreover, responding to the political pressure by the European Union (EU), the IOC has emphasized that 'good governance' is fundamental to preserving the autonomy of sport and protecting it from governmental interference (Around the Rings, 2008). Thus, the 2009 Olympic Congress in Copenhagen adopted 'Basic Universal Principles of Good Governance'. The IOC recommend that the NOCs included these principles in their statutes (Chappelet, 2016). Among others, the IOC (2008, p. 5) suggested that 'Precise, clear and transparent regulations should be established and applied, and effective controlling systems and checks and balances should be put in place.'

In order to illustrate why and how the IOC mitigates currently political interference, a few cases are shortly depicted:

Afghanistan. After the Taliban had taken over power in Afghanistan, they deprived the incumbent NOC of its power and organized elections for a new NOC. The Taliban regime pursued extreme religious fundamentalism also with regard to sport. Among others, the Taliban insisted on a strict Islamic dress code – including beards and long trousers – and the exclusion of women (Reuters, 2008). As the Taliban's ideas about sport were incompatible with Olympism, the IOC suspended the old Afghan NOC and refused to recognize the new Taliban NOC (IOC Session, 2000). After the fall of the Taliban regime in 2001, the IOC helped to rebuild a new NOC and finally lifted the ban in 2003 (BBC, 2003).

Iraq. In May 2008, the Iraqi sports minister assumed control of the NOC and replaced the incumbent staff with government appointees. The Iraqi government justified its move by claiming to have solid evidence of blatant corruption, lack of legitimate transparent electoral processes and accountability as well as absence of ratified legislation. The government deemed the NOC to be illegitimate because it lacked a legal quorum. However, the minister failed to mention that four members of the NOC had been kidnapped two years ago and that their fates were unknown. In addition, the sacking of the NOC apparently reflected the ongoing feud between Shiites and Sunnis in post-Saddam Hussein Iraq (CBS, 2008). In July 2008, the IOC suspended the Iraqi NOC and barred five qualified athletes from participating in the Beijing Games. The suspension was lifted after the Iraqi government agreed to hold NOC elections before the end of November. In the meantime, the Iraqi NOC was run by an interim Committee approved by the IOC.

Kuwait. The Kuwait NOC was for the first time suspended in January 2010. Accordingly, Kuwaiti athletes competed under the Olympic flag at the 2010 Summer Youth Olympics. In July 2012 the suspension was lifted and Kuwaiti athletes were allowed to participate in the 2012 Summer Olympics under their own flag after the Kuwait government included provisions in the national sports law, which recognized sports arbitration and the authority of the Court of Arbitration for Sport (CAS) as well as the Anti-Doping Code of the World Anti-Doping Agency (WADA). Yet, new sports legislation of 2015 overturned these provisions and permitted the government the dissolution of national federations and the NOC. Thus, the NOC was suspended for a second time (Sport Digest, 2016). However, the Kuwait government was not willing to give easily in. It seized the offices of the NOC claiming financial irregularities and installed a new NOC, which the IOC did not recognize. Several other national sport federations were also dissolved. Moreover, Kuwait sued the IOC in 2016 before a Swiss civil court for 1 billion dollars as compensation for the suspension. Not only was the case denied (Zeit, 2016), fifteen Kuwaiti sport bodies were suspended by international sport federations, including the national football association. Given the determination of IOC, FIFA and other sport bodies, in July 2017 the Kuwaiti government amended its national sport legislation and contacted the IOC to discuss the matter (Reuters, 2017).

Conclusion

This chapter has demonstrated that the political independence of NOCs is at stake due to their political significance for national representation and sport policies. Whereas the Olympic Charter demanded the autonomy of the NOCs since the end of the 1940s (Chappelet, 2016), the political reality of a substantial number of NOCs has looked quite different. During the era of block confrontation, the NOCs in communist regimes were integral part of state sport systems and Western NOCs faced immense political pressure to submit to the logics of cold war politics.

The end of block confrontation and the increase of the IOC's commercial powers improved the opportunities to enforce NOC autonomy. The IOC developed a deliberate policy to monitor NOCs and to enforce NOC autonomy. Yet, in contrast to FIFA, the IOC makes substantially less often use of its sanctioning powers, which invites speculations that the IOC lacks comparable power as FIFA because it does not control an entire sport industry. Nevertheless, the cases shortly referred support the idea that NOC suspensions represent an effective mechanism to enforce NOC autonomy. However, it is important to realize that the IOC has suspended so far only NOCs of limited athletic and economic relevance. Furthermore, the rare empirical evidence on the NOCs makes it difficult to provide general claims concerning their political independence and control. Thus, there is a lot of unexplored territory for researchers.

References

Around the Rings. (2008). *IOC takes action to protect autonomy of sport*. Lausanne: IOC.

Balbier, U.A. (2005). *Kalter Krieg auf der Aschenbahn*. Paderborn: Schöningh.

BBC. (2003). Afghanistan back in Olympics. *BBC*.

Billig, M. (1995). *Banal nationalism*. London: Sage.

Blasius, T. (2001). *Olympische Bewegung, Kalter Krieg und Deutschlandpolitik 1949–1972*. Frankfurt am Main: Lang.

Braun, J. (2015). Wettkampf zwischen Ost und West. Sport und Gesellschaft. In: F. Bösch, Hrsg., ed., *Geteilte Geschichte: Ost- und Westdeutschland 1970–2000*. Göttingen: Vandenhoeck& Ruprecht, pp. 411–448.

CBS. (2008). *Iraqi teams banned from Beijing Olympics. CBS News*.

Chappelet, J-L. (2010). *Autonomy of sport in Europe*. Strasbourg: Council of Europe.

Chappelet, J-L. (2014). The global governance of sport: An overview. In: I. Henry and L-M. Ko, eds., *Routledge handbook of sport policy*. New York: Routledge, pp. 63–74.

Chappelet, J.L. (2016). Autonomy and governance: Necessary bedfellows in the fight against Corruption in sport. In: Transparency International, ed., *Global corruption report 2015: Sport*. New York: Routledge, pp. 45–60.

Chappelet, J.L. and Kübler-Mabbott, B. (2008). *The International Olympic Committee and the Olympic system: The governance of world sport*. New York: Routledge.

Darby, P. (2005). Africa and the 'World' Cup: FIFA politics, eurocentrism and resistance. *International Journal of the History of Sport*, 22(5), pp. 883–905.

Geeraert, A., Mrkonjic, M. and Chappelet, J-L. (2015). A rationalist perspective on the autonomy of international sport governing bodies: Towards a pragmatic autonomy in the steering of sports. *International Journal of Sport Policy and Politics*, 7(4), pp. 473–488.

Green, M. and Houlihan, B. (2006). Governmentality, modernization, and the 'disciplining' of national sporting organizations: Athletics in Australia and the United Kingdom. *Sociology of Sport Journal*, 23(1), pp. 47–71.

Guttmann, A. (2002). *The Olympics: A history of the modern games*. 2nd ed. Urbana and Chicago: University of Illinois Press.

Hargreaves, J. (1992). Olympism and nationalism: Some preliminary consideration. *International Review for the Sociology of Sport*, 27(2), pp. 119–135.

Henry, I. and Ko, L-M. (2009). European models of sport: Governance, organisational change and sports policy in the EU. In: W. Tokarski and K. Petry, eds., *Handbuch Sportpolitik*. Schondorf: Hofmann, pp. 25–47.

Holt, R. (1990). *Sport and the British: A modern history*. Oxford University Press.

International Olympic Committee (IOC). (2008). *Basic universal principles of good governance of the Olympic and sports movement*. Lausanne: IOC.

IOC Session. (1964). *Minutes of 61st session of the International Olympic Committee: Innsbruck/Landeshaus, January 26th, 27th and 28th 1964*. Lausanne. IOC.

IOC Session. (1973). *74th Session of the International Olympic Committee, 5th, 6th and 7th October 1973, Varna*. Lausanne: IOC.

IOC Session. (1974). *75th Session of the International Olympic Committee, Vienna, 21st to 24th October 1974*. Lausanne: IOC.

IOC Session. (1975). *76th Session of the International Olympic Committee, Lausanne, 21st to 23rd May 1975*. Lausanne: IOC.

IOC Session. (1976). *77th Session of the International Olympic Committee, Innsbruck, 2nd to 3rd February 1976*. Lausanne: IOC.

IOC Session. (1983). *86th Session of the International Olympic Committee, New Delhi, from 26th to 28th March 1983*. Lausanne: IOC.

IOC Session. (1984). *Minutes of the 89th IOC Session: Distributed to the Members of the IOC, Lausanne, 1st and 2nd December 1984*. Lausanne: IOC.

IOC Session. (1988). *Minutes of the 93rd IOC Session: Distributed to the Members of the IOC, Calgary, 9th to 11th February 1988*. Lausanne: IOC.

IOC Session. (1989). *Minutes of the 95th IOC Session: Distributed to the Members of the IOC, Puerto Rico, 30th August to 1st September 1989*. Lausanne: IOC.

IOC Session. (2000). *Minutes of the 111th IOC Session: Distributed to the Members of the IOC, Sydney, 11, 12, 13 and 30 September 2000*. Lausanne: IOC.

Jefferys, K. (2012). Britain and the Boycott of the 1980 Moscow Olympics. *Sport in History*, 32(2), pp. 279–301.
Latzel, K. (2009). *Staatsdoping: der VEB Jenapharm im Sportsystem der DDR*. Köln and Weimar: Böhlau Verlag.
Mandell, R.D. (1976). *The first modern Olympics*. Berkeley: University of California Press.
Meier, H.E. and García, B. (2015). Protecting private transnational authority against public intervention: FIFA's power over national governments. *Public Administration*, 93(4), pp. 890–906.
Nafziger, J.A. and Strenk, A. (1978). The political uses and abuses of sports. *Connecticut Law Review*, 10(2), pp. 259–289.
O'Neill, B.A. (1988). International sports: Have states succeeded athletes as the players? *Penn State International Law Review*, 6(3), pp. 403–436.
Olympic Charter. (1962). *The Olympic Games: Fundamental principles, rules and regulations, general information*. Lausanne: IOC.
Olympic Charter. (1966). *The Olympic Games: Fundamental principles, rules and regulations, rules of eligibility, general information*. Lausanne: IOC.
Olympic Charter. (1975). *Olympic rules: Bye-laws and instructions*. Lausanne: IOC.
Olympic Charter. (2013). *Olympic Charter*. Lausanne: IOC.
Reuters. (2008). *Taleban hope to get ban revoked*.
Reuters. (2017). *Olympics: Suspended Kuwait ready to talk with IOC, Kenya drags feet*.
Sarantakes, N.E. (2011). *Dropping the torch: Jimmy Carter, the Olympic boycott, and the Cold War*. Cambridge: Cambridge University Press.
Senn, A.E. (1999). *Power, politics, and the Olympic Games: A history of the power brokers, events, and controversies that shaped the games*. Champaign, IL: Human Kinetics.
Spitzer, G. (1999). Zwischen 1945 und 1952: Drei NOKs in Deutschland. In: Nationales Olympisches Komitee für Deutschland, Hrsg., *Deutschland in der Olympischen Bewegung: Eine Zwischenbilanz*. Frankfurt am Main: NOK, pp. 177–204.
Sport Digest. (2016). *Kuwait ponders dissolution of sports federations and Olympic committee*.
Sugden, J. and Tomlinson, A. (1998). Power and resistance in the governance of world football: Theorizing FIFA's transnational impact. *Journal of Sport and Social Issues*, 22(3), pp. 299–316.
Teichler, H.J. (2002). Die SED und der Sport. In: H.J. Teichler, ed., *Die Sportbeschlüsse des Politbüros: Eine Studie zum Verhältnis von SED und Sport mit einem Gesamtverzeichnis und einer Dokumentation ausgewählter Beschlüsse*. Köln: Sport und Buch Strauß, pp. 13–66.
Zammit, M.T. and Henry, I. (2014). Evaluating Olympic solidarity 1982–2012. In: I. Henry and L-M. Ko, eds., *Routledge handbook of sport policy*. New York: Routledge, pp. 93–105.
Zeit. (2016). *Kuwait verliert Rechtsstreit mit*. https://www.zeit.de/news/2016-08/02/olympia-kuwait-verliert-rechtsstreit-mit-ioc-02221605.

24

The changing attitude of the IOC and the IPC towards WADA and the governance of anti-doping

Stacie Gray

Introduction

Prior to 1999, the IOC was the primary actor within the anti-doping regime. Despite the IOC's position as the core organisation responsible for coordinating the fight against doping, during the 1980s and 1990s, the IOC expressed indifference towards doping developments and scandals. Notable examples of the IOC's passivity include the IOC's slow response to doping revelations regarding the former East Germany doping policies and the IOC's lack of attention to the Chinese doping scandal at the 1994 World Aquatics Championships (Hoberman, 2006). The ineffectiveness of the IOC's anti-doping efforts was emphasised through the 1998 Ben Johnson and the 1998 Tour de France scandals. Additionally, allegations of corruption during the bidding process for the 2002 Salt Lake City Winter Olympics severely undermined the IOC's moral authority and legitimacy as the core anti-doping governing body. Together, the incidents led to governmental mistrust of the IOC and contributed towards the IOC's eventual loss of formal leadership within the anti-doping regime (Ritchie and Jackson, 2014).

The increasing involvement of governments following the 1998 Tour de France scandal threatened the IOC's authority as a leading organisation within the anti-doping regime. In an attempt to affirm their authority and restore their integrity within the world of anti-doping, the IOC leadership convened and carefully planned the agenda of the 1999 World Conference on Doping in Sport (the Lausanne Conference). However, despite the IOC's reactionary efforts, the IOC was unable to control all outcomes of the Conference (Houlihan, 2002). The Lausanne Conference provided a forum for powerful North American, Australasian and European governments to unite and collectively challenge the leadership of the IOC. In particular, influential actor Barry McCaffrey, Director of the White House Office of National Drug Policy, spearheaded governmental mistrust of the IOC. Consequently, contrary to the IOC's proposal to create an anti-doping agency solely funded by the IOC, in November 1999, the World Anti-Doping Agency (WADA) was established as an independent agency (Hanstad, Smith and Waddington, 2008). The IOC's decision to relinquish control and support WADA as an independent agency demonstrates the ability of powerful governments to challenge the transnational status of the Olympic movement and International Federations (IFs) (Houlihan, 2007). However, it is important to recognise that this represents one of the few cases in which governments have managed to obtain reforms from sport bodies. Other notable examples include the European Union forcing reforms on the Fédération Internationale de Football Association's transfer system (Parrish, 2018) and the more recent reform of the International Skating Union's participation rules following a decision of the European Commission in an anti-trust case.

The governance of WADA

WADA aims to bring global consistency to regulations and anti-doping policies within governments and sport organisations. Since 2002, the Olympic movement and governments have provided equal funding for WADA and have equal representation on WADA's Foundation Board (the supreme decision-making body) and Executive Committee (the policy-making body). Additionally, to ensure equal partnership between WADA's funders, the WADA presidency is alternated between the Olympic movement and governments. The organisational structure of WADA has raised numerous concerns regarding the governance of anti-doping (Chappelet and Luijk, 2018). First, the independence of WADA's Foundation Board has been criticised due to an overlap of personnel on the thirty-eight member Foundation Board and the twelve member Executive Committee; in 2018, nine members held positions on both boards (WADA, 2018a). For the Foundation Board to effectively fulfil its oversight role, personnel overlaps between the Foundation Board and Executive Committee should be eliminated (Ordway, 2016).

Second, many of the Olympic movement representatives on WADA's Foundation Board simultaneously hold presidential or administrative positions within the Olympic movement; in 2018, WADA's Foundation Board included active IOC and IPC members, in addition to presidents of the International Weightlifting Federation, World Archery, United World Wrestling, the International Skating Union and the World Rowing Federation (WADA, 2018a). However, there is a conflict of interest between elite sport development and anti-doping; rigorous anti-doping efforts that expose elite athletes have the potential to threaten relationships with commercial entities, alienate corporate sponsors and damage the image of the IOC, IPC, IFs, the Olympic and the Paralympic Games. Consequently, IOC, IPC and IF members on the Foundation Board have a clear conflict of interest with WADA; they must protect their sports and income whilst simultaneously controlling doping. Such conflict has the potential to undermine the commitment of Foundation Board members to anti-doping policy (Sugden and Tomlinson, 2012). Travis Tygart, Chief Executive Officer at the United States Anti-Doping Agency (USADA), has frequently expressed his concern regarding the inherent conflicts of interest and has urged actors within the anti-doping regime to be 'cognisant and honest about the tension between promoting and policing your sport' (The Guardian, 2016).

The potential for conflicts of interest also exists at the presidential level. WADA's inaugural President, Richard Pound, was also vice president of the IOC. As a respected figure with an international profile, Pound enhanced the credibility of WADA (Wenn and Martyn, 2006). Furthermore, Pound strengthened the accord between WADA and the IOC. During WADA's early years, the close relationship between WADA and the Olympic movement played a crucial role in generating IF support for the World Anti-Doping Code. Adopted in 2003, the Code represents the core document that globally harmonises anti-doping regulations and policies across all sporting organisations and countries (Houlihan, 2012). Similar to Pound, WADA's current President, Craig Reedie, simultaneously held the position of IOC vice president. The IOC's desire to maintain a strong relationship with the WADA president has been evident during the course of the WADA presidential elections; traditionally, the IOC has lobbied to ensure that the Foundation Board select a candidate acceptable to the Olympic movement. However, such efforts may be perceived as an attempt by the IOC to manipulate the leadership of WADA and assert influence over the governance of anti-doping (Selliaas, 2018). Furthermore, Pound's position as the IOC vice president, combined with his responsibility for marketing the Olympic Games, conflicted with the goals of anti-doping. The conflicts of interest incurred by WADA's organisational structure has been emphasised by Travis Tygart, Chief Executive Officer at USADA who likened Pound's election to 'putting the fox at the top of guarding the henhouse' (Tygart, 2018). Additional stakeholders within the anti-doping regime have expressed similar concerns. For example, the independent foundation FairSport conducted a survey with over 2100 athletes (85% of which competed at the international level), to determine athlete's opinions on their currents rights and the environment of cheating within sport. The results revealed that 54% of respondents felt that their leadership was subject to conflicts of interest (Bokel, 2018). Such findings indicate the need to restore stakeholder trust and confidence in anti-doping organisations and the governance of anti-doping.

Third, WADA's lack of geopolitical representation has been critiqued; the governance of WADA is largely influenced by Anglo-Saxon, Scandinavian and North American representatives. Currently, WADA's Foundation Board, Executive Committee and four of its five standing committees are chaired by European or North American members. Combined, the standing committees comprise fifty-seven members and five chairs, of which almost two-thirds are from English-speaking or European countries (WADA, 2018a). However, the centre of gravity in global sport is gradually shifting; Far East countries, including emerging superpowers, are hosting an increasing number of major international sporting events (Cornelissen, 2010). Examples include the Beijing 2008 Summer Olympic Games, PyeongChang 2018 Winter Olympic Games, 2019 Rugby World Cup held in Japan and the Tokyo 2020 Summer Olympic Games. As a result, WADA faces the challenge of achieving greater geopolitical representation than is currently reflected in its governance structures. In recognition of the governance challenges within the anti-doping regime, in 2016, WADA announced the establishment of a working group to investigate strategies to enhance the governance structure of WADA. The findings are expected to be reported to the Foundation Board in November 2018 (WADA, 2018a).

Increasing tension between WADA and the IOC: the Russian scandal

In 2014, WADA initiated an independent investigation to explore allegations regarding a sophisticated system of state-sponsored doping in Russia. The Independent Person Report (henceforth the McLaren report), found that a sample-swapping methodology, which aimed to protect athletes who doped, was in operation at the Moscow laboratory. The report concluded that a widespread and 'deeply rooted culture of cheating' existed within Russia and confirmed the systematic and regular use of PEDs by many Russian athletes (McLaren Report, 2015, p. 10). Despite the severity of the findings, WADA does not possess the authority to impose sanctions upon signatories that are non-compliant with the Code. Instead, WADA is dependent upon a network of actors, including the IOC, IPC and IFs, to impose appropriate sanctions. As a result, the IOC and IPC play a crucial role in Code implementation (Chappelet and Luijk, 2018). Informed by the McLaren report, WADA's Executive Committee put forward a clear recommendation to the IOC and IPC: Russian athletes should be prohibited from competing at the Rio 2016 Olympic and Paralympic Games. However, WADA's recommendation created a dilemma for the IOC and IPC. As one of the largest delegations to compete at the Olympic and Paralympic Games, Russia's participation contributes towards the competitive nature of the Games. The IOC also generates a significant amount of sponsorship and broadcasting revenue from the Olympic Games. For a long time, the USA and USSR sporting rivalry has been a significant ingredient in broadcaster's marketing of the Olympic Games, particularly in the USA. Consequently, to enhance the relevance and competitiveness of the Games, it is desirable for the IOC to have all member nations competing (Ordway, 2016). To further complicate the issue, McLaren's accusation regarding a state-dictated failsafe system conflicted with the IOC's position against the articulation of a corrupt government discourse (Wagner and Pedersen, 2014). WADA's recommendation therefore highlighted the tension associated with the dual responsibility of promoting and policing sport.

Following the evaluation of evidence, which included an opportunity for the Russian Paralympic Committee to put forward its case, the IPC Governing Board unanimously decided to suspend Russia from the Rio 2016 Paralympic Games. Although sympathy was expressed for the Russian athletes, former IPC President Philip Craven stated that Russia's corrupt system struck at the 'very heart of the spirit of Paralympic Sport' and emphasised that the IPC's decision was driven by the need for accountability (IPC, 2016). The IPC's response signified harmony between WADA and the IPC and conveyed a message of zero tolerance towards institutionalised doping. Throughout the IOC's decision-making process, numerous anti-doping stakeholders placed pressure upon the IOC to suspend the Russian Olympic Committee. Fourteen National Anti-Doping Agencies (NADOs) sent a letter to the IOC President, Thomas Bach, urging the IOC to exclude Russia from the Rio 2016 Summer Olympic Games (Inside the Games, 2016). Additionally, Claudia Bokel, Chair of the IOC Athletes' Commission, asked athlete commissions around the world their opinions on whether the Russian delegation should be banned from the Games. After the overwhelming majority expressed support for a blanket ban, Bokel presented her findings to the IOC (Bokel, 2018). Nevertheless, in contrast to the IPC, the IOC did not ban Russia from participating at the Rio 2016 Summer Olympic Games; at the IOC session in Rio de Janeiro, only Great Britain voted in support of the motion. Instead, the IOC delegated the decision to individual IFs. The International Association of Athletics Federations and the International Weightlifting Federation were the only IFs to ban all Russian athletes (Chappelet and Luijk, 2018). The IOC's decision has been criticised for conveying the message that 'Olympic goals, including supporting one of the IOC's strongest members, are prioritised over the aims of WADA' (Ordway, 2016, p. 1). Additionally, the IOC's failure to implement WADA's recommendation has placed strain on the relationship between WADA and the IOC. WADA openly expressed its disappointment in the IOC and stated that the decision signified a lack of harmonisation within the anti-doping regime and undermined anti-doping efforts. In particular, the fragmented responses of WADA, the IOC and the IPC raise questions as to whether the organisations responsible for the global governance of anti-doping are able to adopt a unified approach towards the doping threat (Girginov and Parry, 2018).

Although the IOC did not implement WADA's recommendation, the IOC responded to the McLaren report with the establishment of two disciplinary commissions. First, the Oswald Commission investigated allegations of doping amongst Russian athletes at the Sochi 2014 Winter Olympic Games; all available samples from Russian athletes who participated in Sochi were re-analysed. Forty-three athletes received lifetime bans from the Olympic Games and were retrospectively disqualified from the Sochi 2014 Winter Olympics (Oswald Commission, 2017). However, of those athletes, forty-two filed cases to the Court of Arbitration for Sport (CAS). In twenty-eight of the cases, the appeals were upheld due to insufficient evidence; the sanctions were declared invalid and the results of the individual athletes at Sochi were reinstated (CAS, 2018). Driven by their dismay regarding the decision, the IOC (with the support of WADA) is considering an appeal to the Swiss Federal Tribunal. The rift between the CAS and the IOC/WADA, combined with CAS's ruling, has elevated the levels of confusion and frustration amongst athletes. Second, the Schmid Commission concentrated upon the institutionalised doping in Russia, with a specific focus upon the Sochi Games. The Schmid Commission confirmed numerous findings contained within the McLaren report, including the manipulation of the anti-doping system and sample tampering. However, in contrast to McLaren, Schmid did not find evidence to confirm state involvement in the system (Schmid, 2017). Informed by the commission's conclusions, the IOC changed its position; in contrast to the Rio 2016 Summer Olympic Games, the IOC suspended the Russian Olympic Committee from the PyeongChang 2018 Winter Olympics. However, the IOC invited individual Russian athletes to compete under the name 'Olympic Athlete from Russia' and stated that the suspension may be lifted in full or part from the commencement of the closing ceremony (IOC, 2017a). The IOC's desire to verify the findings contained within the McLaren report, combined with their unwillingness to impose a blanket ban based upon McLaren's findings, indicates a lack of trust in WADA and undermines the credibility of the anti-doping regime.

With regard to the reinstatement of the Russian Anti-Doping Agency (RUSADA), WADA has adopted an unequivocal stance; Russia must meet all criteria detailed in the Roadmap to Code Compliance. To date, there are two outstanding criteria. One, to publicly accept the outcomes of the McLaren report. Two, to provide access to the Moscow laboratory and provide the necessary data to investigate outstanding cases. The IPC has expressed its support for the Roadmap to Code Compliance, and, similar to WADA, the IPC has refused to reinstate Russia until the final two criteria are met (Inside the Games, 2018a). In contrast, IOC President Thomas Bach has expressed his desire to 'draw a line under this damaging episode' (IOC, 2017a). Although sanctioned for the duration of the PyeongChang 2018 Winter Olympic Games, the Russian NOC was reinstated by the IOC three days after the Winter Olympics ended (Inside the Games, 2018b). The IOC and IPC's conflicting stances have the potential to create tension between the two organisations. On the one hand, the IOC and IPC's recent long-term agreement, which established a partnership between the IOC and IPC until at least 2032, has strengthened the existing relationship between the two organisations. On the other hand, as part of the agreement, the IOC will provide financial stability to the IPC. The IPC's financial dependency upon the IOC has raised speculation as to whether the IOC will pressure the IPC to reinstate Russia. During a media briefing in PyeongChang, such speculation was addressed by Craig Spence, the IPC Media and Communications Director. Spence reiterated the IPC's support for WADA's Roadmap to Code Compliance and stated that the IOC/IPC cooperation agreement 'does not mean we [the IPC] will change our stance on Russia' (Inside the Games, 2018a).

Organisational restructuring in the anti-doping regime

Recent doping scandals and revelations have significantly reduced public and athlete confidence in the organisations responsible for compliance with the Code (Wagner and Pedersen, 2014). In particular, the Independent Observer (IO) report for the Rio 2016 Summer Olympic Games raised concerns regarding the ability of major actors, specifically WADA, the IOC and IFs, to ensure that an effective anti-doping programme is delivered. Of the 11,470 confirmed entrants, 4,125 (1,913 of which were from high-risk sports) had no record of testing during 2016. Furthermore, the IO Report concluded:

> It was only due to the enormous resourcefulness and goodwill of some key doping control personnel working at the Games that the process did not break down entirely.
>
> *(IO Report, 2016, p. 7)*

Described by WADA as one of the most 'destabilising incidents for sports in recent memory' (WADA Annual Report, 2016, p. 5), the Russian doping scandal has further undermined the legitimacy and credibility of the anti-doping regime. The damaging effect of the Russian scandal was evident at the PyeongChang 2018 Winter Olympic Games; the IO report found that suspicion regarding the integrity of the anti-doping programme was prevalent during the Games (IO Report, 2018).

Throughout the history of the anti-doping regime, exogenous events, specifically doping scandals, have instigated anti-doping inquests, policy reappraisals and policy changes which aim to improve the effectiveness of the anti-doping regime. Prompted by the revelation of institutionalised doping in Russia, a number of organisational changes have occurred within the anti-doping regime. In 2015, WADA established the Compliance Review Committee (CRC), an independent body that comprises compliance experts from non-sporting sectors, in addition to athlete, government and sport representatives. The primary role of the CRC is to provide advice and recommendations to WADA's Foundation Board on issues relating to signatory compliance. Where compliance problems are discovered, a taskforce is created to investigate and recommend corrective actions to the given Code signatory. Unresolved problems are forwarded to the CRC, which recommends that the signatory be declared non-compliant, or be placed on a watch list with a specific timeframe for resolution (Chappelet and Luijk, 2018). The independent nature of the CRC signifies WADA's attempt to alleviate concerns regarding conflicts of interest within WADA's Foundation Board. Simultaneously, the CRC contributes towards restoring WADA's credibility and trust in the anti-doping regime (Efverström et al., 2016). However, although WADA has endorsed the CRC's recommendations, harmonisation within the anti-doping regime is dependent upon the willingness of anti-doping actors to align their actions with the CRC and WADA's recommendations. This problem was emphasised through the fragmented responses to the Russian scandal. At the same time, the Russian scandal exposed WADA's weaknesses, particularly its reliance upon other anti-doping organisations and its inability to impose sanctions (Müller, 2017).

Despite repeated calls to enhance the independence of WADA, arguably, the IOC has been reluctant to weaken its influence within the anti-doping regime (iNADO, 2017). The IOC's continued position as a primary actor within the anti-doping regime and the power of the Olympic movement is enhanced through WADA's constitution and funding structure, both of which are largely influenced by the Olympic movement (Müller, 2017). As a consequence of WADA's composition, Travis Tygert, Chief Executive Officer at USADA, has argued that WADA is 'controlled by sport' (Tygart, 2018). The balance of power has also been discussed by Linda Helleland, WADA's Vice President, who stated 'it [WADA] needs a more equal partnership. Right now, the perception is that the Olympic Movement is the strongest partner' (BBC, 2018). Recently, the IOC indicated a change in attitude towards the governance of anti-doping. At the 5th Olympic Summit, the IOC recognised the need to enhance the independence of the anti-doping system and improve WADA's governance structure. In recognition of the inherent conflicts of interest, the IOC stated that the WADA president and vice president must be neutral with no function in any sports or governmental organisation. However, at the same time, the IOC maintained that, as founding partners, the Olympic movement and governments must maintain equal representation on the Foundation Board and Executive Committee (IOC, 2017b). Whilst the IOC refuses to relinquish its operational influence and involvement in WADA, the extent to which WADA can be empowered and made truly independent is questionable. The IOC also proposed the establishment of a new independent testing authority. Despite the IOC's emphasis upon institutional independence, the International Testing Authority (ITA) is funded by the IOC and three of its five Foundation Board members are representatives from the Olympic movement. As a result, the ITA has been dismissed as an attempt by the IOC to drive the construction of the new system and regain greater control of international anti-doping efforts (iNADO, 2017).

The future direction of WADA

The scale of the current compliance problem has placed WADA at a crossroads in the fight against doping. As Craig Reedie's presidential era comes to an end in November 2019, the upcoming WADA president will play an important role in shaping the future direction of WADA and the anti-doping regime. To date, Linda Helleland (WADA's current Vice President and Norwegian Minister of Children and Equality) and Witold Banka (Polish Sports Minister) have announced their candidacy for WADA president. Throughout her candidacy, Helleland has clearly expressed her vision for WADA, stating that the organisation 'needs more independence, more transparency and more democracy' (BBC, 2018). Currently, the IOC represents WADA's largest financial contributor; the IOC matches the financial input of governments. However, in an attempt to alleviate resource constraints within the anti-doping regime, WADA recently announced its efforts to pursue additional funding strategies that target private donor, corporation and foundation contributions (WADA, 2018b). Helleland's desire to increase WADA's independence from the Olympic movement, combined with WADA's potential to secure alternative funding sources, threatens the IOC's leadership and influence within the anti-doping regime.

Tension between Helleland and the IOC has also developed during her current position as WADA vice president. Helleland has been highly critical of the IOC, particularly the IOC's failure to ban Russia from the Rio 2016 Olympic Games and the IOC's 'confusing' response to the PyeongChang 2018 Winter Olympic Games (Inside the Games, 2018b). Alluding to the IOC's decision to reinstate Russia, Helleland reiterated the need to continue with the Roadmap to Code Compliance, even if 'some are intending to undermine its legitimacy' (BBC, 2018). The ongoing Russian scandal has also played a focal point in Banka's election campaigns. However, in contrast to Helleland, Banka has conveyed his desire to adopt a softer approach towards Russia. Similar to the IOC, Banka perceives the two remaining Roadmap to Code Compliance criteria as unrealistic and has argued that new reinstatement criteria are necessary. Banka's position aligns closely with the IOC's desire to resolve the Russian case. Consequently, compared to Helleland, Banka is widely perceived as the preferred candidate by the Olympic movement. Nevertheless, if Helleland is successful in her bid for the WADA presidency, the governance of WADA and the relationship between WADA and the Olympic movement could undergo significant changes (Selliaas, 2018).

Conclusion

In contrast to the IPC, the IOC has a long and well-established history as a primary actor within the anti-doping regime. However, the IOC's inconsistency towards the fight against doping, in addition to unresolved tensions between the IOC and WADA, has undermined the effectiveness of anti-doping efforts. Furthermore, the scale of the recent Russian scandal has significantly weakened the credibility and legitimacy of WADA and its major partners. In particular, the fragmented responses of WADA, the IOC, the IPC and IFs has created doubt regarding their ability to adopt a unified approach towards the doping threat. With the anti-doping regime currently at a crossroads, significant efforts to reform the governance of anti-doping are essential to restore faith and trust in the anti-doping regime and the organisations responsible for the global governance of anti-doping. Key governing challenges include increasing the independence of WADA, removing the conflicts of interest from WADA's Foundation Board and Executive Committee and achieving greater geopolitical representation than is currently reflected in WADA's governing structures.

References

BBC. (2018). Linda Helleland: The woman seeking to clean up the world of anti-doping. *BBC.*

Bokel, C. (2018). The willingness for reforms to protect clean athletes. In: *Presented at the anti-doping in sports conference*, Oslo.

CAS. (2018). *Anti-doping – Sochi 2014.* CAS.

Chappelet, J.L. and Luijk, N. (2018). The institutional governance of global hybrid bodies: The case of the world anti-doping agency. In: A.B. Savignon, L. Gnan, A. Hinna and F. Monteduro, eds., *Hybridity in the governance and delivery of public services.* Bingley: Emerald Group Publishing, pp. 167–191.

Cornelissen, S. (2010). The geopolitics of global aspirations: Sport mega-events and emerging powers. *The International Journal of the History of Sport,* 27(16–18), pp. 3008–3025.

Efverström, A., Bäckström, A., Ahmadi, N. and Hoff, D. (2016). Context and conditions for a level playing field: Elite athletes' perspectives on anti-doping in practice. *Performance Enhancement and Health*, 5(2), pp. 77–85.

Girginov, J. and Parry, J. (2018). Protecting or undermining the integrity of sport? The science and politics of the McLaren report. *International Journal of Sport Policy and Politics,* 10(2), pp. 393–407.

Hanstad, D., Smith, A. and Waddington, I. (2008). The establishment of the world anti-doping agency: A study of the management of organisational change and unplanned outcomes. *International Review for the Sociology of Sport*, 43(3), pp. 227–249.

Hoberman, J. (2006). *Testosterone dreams: Rejuvenation, aphrodisia, doping.* Berkeley: University of California Press.

Houlihan, B. (2002). *Sport policy and politics: A comparative analysis.* London: Routledge.

Houlihan, B. (2007). *Sport and society: A student introduction.* London: Sage.

Houlihan, B. (2012). Doping and the Olympics. In: J. Sugden and A. Tomlinson, eds., *Watching the Olympics: Politics, power and representation.* London: Routledge, pp. 97–107.

iNADO. (2017). *Institute of National Anti-Doping Organisations Board of Directors' response to International Olympic Committee (IOC) Declaration.* iNADO.

Inside the Games. (2016). *Fourteen national anti-doping agencies urge blanket ban on Russia in letter to IOC.* Inside the Games.

Inside the Games. (2018a). IPC claim there will be no pressure to reinstate Russia. *Inside the Games.*

Inside the Games. (2018b). *WADA Vice-President criticises IOC handling of Russian doping crisis in hard-hitting address.* Inside the Games.

IO Report. (2016). *Report of the Independent Observers.* Montreal, Canada: WADA.

IO Report. (2018). *Report of the Independent Observers.* Montreal, Canada: WADA.

IOC. (2017a). *Olympic highlights: IOC activities.* Lausanne: IOC.

IOC. (2017b). *Declaration of the IOC executive board.* Lausanne: IOC.

IPC. (2016). *The IPC suspends the Russian Paralympic committee with immediate effect.* Bonn: IPC.

McLaren, R. (2015). *Independent person report.* Montreal, Canada: WADA.

Müller, D. (2017). How to protect the clean athletes? *German Journal of Exercise and Sport Research,* pp. 1–11.

Ordway, C. (2016). *Cleaning up sport: Conflicts of interest at the top.* Transparency International.

Oswald Commission. (2017). *IOC sanctions 11 Russian athletes as part of Oswald commission findings.* Lausanne: IOC.

Parrish, R. (2018). Sources and origins of EU sports policy. In: J. Anderson, R. Parrish and B. García, eds., *Research handbook on EU sports law and policy.* UK: Edward Elgar Publishing, pp. 24–48.

Ritchie, I. and Jackson, G. (2014). Politics and shock: Reactionary anti-doping policy objectives in Canadian and international sport. *International Journal of Sport Policy and Politics*, 6(2), pp. 195–212.

Schmid, S. (2017). *IOC disciplinary commission's report to the IOC Executive Board.* Lausanne: IOC.

Selliaas, A. (2018). *Norwegian WADA Vice President Linda Helleland steps up fight for top job in WADA.* Play the Game.

Sugden, J. and Tomlinson, A. (2012). *Watching the Olympics: Politics, power and representation.* London: Routledge.

The Guardian. (2016). IOC has behaved like keystone cops in anti-doping fight, say US Chief. *The Guardian.*

Tygart, T. (2018). Fox in the Henhouse. In: *Presented at the anti-doping in sports conference*. Oslo, June 25.
WADA. (2016). *Annual Report 2016*. Montreal, Canada: WADA.
WADA. (2018a). *Governance*. Montreal, Canada: WADA.
WADA. (2018b). *14th annual WADA symposium*. Montreal, Canada: WADA.
Wagner, U. and Pedersen, K. (2014). The IOC and the doping issue – An institutional discursive approach to organisational identity construction. *Sport Management Review*, 17(2), pp. 160–173.
Wenn, S. and Martyn, S. (2006). Tough love: Richard Pound, David D'Alessandro, and the Salt Lake City Olympics bid scandal. *Sport in History*, 26(1), pp. 64–90.

25

Board renewal and good governance in the Olympic movement

Leigh Robinson and Tracy Taylor

Introduction

Governance is a topic of much current debate and discussion in the sport world, mainly with respect to a number of high-profile examples of poor governance and associated integrity and corruption issues. While many of these cases are from outside the Olympic movement (e.g. FIFA, International Cricket Council), there have also been examples from within the Olympic family of organisations. The International Olympic Committee, the parasport movement, International Federations, and the Association of National Olympic Committees all promote good governance principles, as it relates to the broad scope of system of rules, practices, and processes by which the sport organisation is directed and controlled. This chapter covers one specific critical aspect of governance, namely board renewal.

Principles of good governance would suggest that 'forced' board renewal is a desirable practice, as it provides the opportunity for greater organisational accountability. By developing and implementing structures associated with board renewal, organisations in the Olympic movement have the opportunity to ensure that the human resources (paid and unpaid) of the organisation have the right roles and skills to be able to deliver on organisational objectives. In particular, renewal of board personnel, however facilitated (e.g. through term limits), not only provides an opportunity for the infusion of new skills and abilities, but it also brings in different ideas from new people and allows the board to address diversity considerations at the strategic level of the organisation. Research shows that organisations that strategically plan for and manage board renewal, particularly turnover, outperform their peers, and below-standard organisations tend to be those with no turnover, or with excessive turnover (Anderson and Chun, 2014).

However, in practice many organisations within the Olympic movement, such as international or national federations have few or no mechanisms for board renewal. There is limited board training or development and board members often remain in place for many years and in some instances, many decades. This lack of renewal has many consequences, including having a negative impact on the development of human capital, limiting the capacity of the sport organisation, and more recently it has been associated with corrupt practices and integrity breaches. In particular, long tenures have allowed board members to create networks that have benefitted them personally, hidden poor practice, particularly financial irregularities, and had a detrimental impact on election practices. As a consequence of these breakdowns in governance, it appears reasonable to argue that governance in the Olympic movement would benefit from a greater focus on board renewal. This chapter elaborates on this argument and considers the impact of board renewal on good governance and suggests some ways that board renewal can be approached. The chapter starts with a consideration of the context surrounding board renewal, setting out the arguments for renewal, particularly within the Olympic movement. It goes on to focus on the use of limited terms as a method of encouraging board renewal and concludes with a discussion of other renewal techniques.

Board renewal: context and rationale

In recent years there has been a global movement, primarily by public funding bodies, to improve the governance practices of national and international sporting organisations (Walters and Tacon, 2018). The impetus to improve governance has been triggered by corruption scandals and challenges about legitimacy (Hoye, 2017), concerns about board members' business/commercial acumen and skills (Taylor and O'Sullivan, 2009), and attention drawn to the lack of gender diversity of board members (Adriaanse, 2016). The gender-diversity issue is highlighted in data showing that a large proportion of sport organisations across the globe continue to have under-representation of women, even though research has demonstrated that the ratio of women directors is positively related to board effectiveness and good governance (Adriaanse and Schofield, 2014).

Despite pressure from stakeholders, governments, and the general public to reform governance structures in sport, resistance to changing the status quo is quite widespread, and most clearly evidenced in board member longevity and lack of turnover. For example, ten IOC members have been members for over 30 years, 22 have been members for more than 20 years and ten have been members for more than ten years. The International Federations have also been slow to address board turnover. For example, in 2017 Hungary's Tamas Aján was re-elected for the fifth time as president of the International Weightlifting Federation (IWF) having first assumed the post in 2000. Mexico's Olegario Vazquez Raña is serving a ninth term and 40th year as International Shooting Sport Federation head after first assuming the position in 1980, and Klaus Schormann has already served 24 years as president of the International Modern Pentathlon Union (UIPM) after being re-elected for a seventh time in 2016.

Concerns about board stagnation and associated performance issues has resulted in governments and associated bodies developing an array of good governance principles, which in some cases are also used to determine a sport body's funding and/or performance. For example, in the UK, National Federations that seek public funding for sport and physical activity must meet new so-called gold standards of governance established by UK Sport. Chappelet (2018) estimates governmental and intergovernmental agencies, national and international sport governing bodies have put forward more than 30 sets of good governance guidelines/principles in recent years, including the Basic Universal Principles of Good Governance from the International Olympic Committee. The justification and rationale for introducing these policies and guidelines is strikingly similar around issues of accountability and performance, although there is variability in the ways in which they are implemented, the relative emphasis on specific elements, evaluation methods used, and there are a variety of consequences related to non-adherence or poor performance.

Good governance seeks to establish appropriate standards and behaviours that add value to an organisation (Walters, Tacon and Trenberth, 2011). Governance guidelines and policies may cover: democratic structures/democracy, accountability, transparency, professionalisation, control/supervisory mechanisms, fairness, solidarity/social responsibility, equality, elected presidents, board skills (instead of representation) and term limits, separation of board chair and CEO roles, codes of ethics and conflicts of interest, athlete involvement/representation, stakeholder participation/representation, anti-bribery/corruption codes, equity, respect, autonomy/independence, evaluation, effectiveness, efficiency, planning standards, structure standards, and access and timely disclosure of information (Chappelet and Mrkonjic, 2013; Parent and Hoye, 2018).

The board members of sport organisations have a central role in the process of good governance and organisational performance. The board is responsible for setting the organisation's strategic direction and leadership, responding to and facilitating change, organisational performance and other related functions that are critical for the organisation's long-term success and sustainability. Over time the operating environment, skills, networks, knowledge, and experience required to be an effective board member can change and, in consequence, board composition may need to shift accordingly. Planning for board renewal provides a basis for the sport organisation to have board members that align with future requirements.

Alongside the value of board renewal in terms of organisational success and sustainability, as mentioned previously, there is an increasing awareness of the opportunities that long board tenures provide for the manipulation of power and corruption. In their discussion of success and good governance in sport organisations, Taylor and Robinson (2019) highlight how the unethical and arguably corrupt practices of a number of senior sport administrators (e.g. Sepp Blatter, Patrick Hickey, and Lamine Diack) were facilitated by tenures of over 30 years. This allowed the development of alliances that led to potential corrupt practice and the creation of power bases that meant they had control over nearly all aspects of international sport bodies.

Reference to this was made by United States Attorney General, Loretta Lynch, who, in a news conference alleged that '[FIFA executives] used their positions to solicit bribes. They did this over and over. Year after Year. Tournament after tournament' (The United States Department of Justice, 2015). This issue was also considered by Geeraert (2015) in a review of International Federations, where he noted that the longer an individual has been on a board, the more likely they are to be re-elected, leading to the development of an increasingly substantial power base, which then can be used to stay in office through patronage or covert activity. He also noted that incumbents are 'more likely to target voters who benefit most from their policies' (Geeraert, 2015, p. 34), with the potential to lead to practices that benefit particular groups, rather than the organisation as a whole. He argued for the introduction of board renewal mechanisms in order to reduce the impact of lengthy tenures on good governance.

Governance within the Olympic movement

In 2017 a review of the IOC governance structures and processes was carried out by the International Institute for Management Development (IMD). IMD made 22 recommendations to improve structures and processes for governance, and 11 recommendations for longer-term transformation of governance practices, noting that these would support the IOC on its path to continued governance improvement. In addition, seven dilemmas that the IOC will need to face in the next ten years were identified; these were seen as measures to ensure its governance practices keep pace with its evolving role and increasing societal expectation (IMD, 2017). Within the primary recommendations there was a call for a 'professionally managed succession process', including a need to articulate targets for gender and age diversity at the Executive Board level. One of the dilemmas listed was a review of the member nomination process (for a detailed analysis of the IOC members' nomination and election processes, see the contribution of Krieger and Wassong in this volume). In July 2018 the IOC reiterated their commitment to the implementation of recommendation 27 of the Olympic Agenda 2020, related to the basic principles of good governance across the Olympic movement and to the implementation of the People Management 2020 programme, which is intended to improve gender equity and succession planning.[1]

Although board renewal is an increasingly discussed concept within the Olympic movement, there is limited evidence of it in practice, particularly through formally required board turnover. In an initial review of the governance practices of national federations in eight countries, Geeraert (2017) established that only 44% of the federations surveyed had term limits, which are a means of encouraging turnover. There was a mixed picture across the nations involved in the research with 100% of the federations in the Netherlands and Poland employing term limits, while no federation in Denmark and Montenegro did so. At the international level, only 20 of the 206 National Olympic Committees had renewal mechanisms enshrined in their constitutions, eight out of 35 International Federations had term limits and only six had rules set out for age limits for board members (Geeraert, Alm and Groll, 2014). The International Paralympic Committee has a term limit of four years, but no limit to the number of terms a person can serve on their Sport Technical Committees. In a study of United Kingdom National Governing Bodies (NGB), Walters, Tacon, and Trenberth (2011) found that only 27% of survey respondents had a strategy for board renewal, including initiatives for succession planning. Their study also found that only about half of the NGBs surveyed had specific limits on the total number of and/or consecutive terms for board members and, namely, for board chairs. By 2017, a follow up survey of sport boards found that 41% of boards reported that they still did not have a succession plan in place (Birkbeck, 2018). A lack of succession planning in sport organisations has also been identified in Australia, Canada, and New Zealand (Taylor, Doherty and McGraw, 2015).

Board renewal via the use of limited terms

Concerns around board renewal and tenure have, in the Olympic World, coalesced around the concept of 'limited terms', where an individual's time on the board is restricted to a maximum number of years (e.g. Council of Europe, 2012; Geeraert, 2015). For example, the Governing Council of the International Paralympic Council (IPC) is elected every four years and members can serve a maximum of three terms. The IOC has a mixture of practices in relation to term limits. In illustration, IOC members are elected for a period of eight years but their mandate can be renewed. The IOC has also chosen to manage board renewal by establishing an age limit of 70 years of age, except for members co-opted between 1966 and 1999, for whom the age limit is 80 years. The Session may, on the proposal of the IOC Executive Board, extend the age limit for any IOC member for a period of a four year maximum. In recent years some world governing bodies, including the International Association of Athletics Federations, International Cycling Union (UCI), and football, i.e. FIFA, have all introduced maximum limits of three terms of four years. The International Volleyball Federation also has a 12-year limit, but with a first term of eight years and a second term of four years. The International Swimming Federation, however, relaxed their limits from two to three terms alongside a deletion of age limit rules in 2015 in order to allow the current President Julio Maglione, from Uruguay, to stand for another term in office. Many other Olympic-related organisations, including National Olympic Committees and Continental Associations, have no such limits.

Benefits of fixed terms and board renewal

Board refreshment, board leadership succession planning, and board change can also drive strategic change in a board's composition and its diversity. These issues can be of critical importance if the board is 'aging', lacks gender and/or cultural diversity, or is not representative of its current membership. While long-term board members may have accumulated intensive knowledge of their sport and years of dedicated service, their longevity as board members does not always serve the best interests of the membership, especially if the latter has undergone significant change (e.g. declining numbers, changing socio-demographic composition, changing expectations, etc.).

Wertheim et al. (2016) suggest there are two distinct sides of the debate on the length of tenure and effectiveness. On the one hand there is the contention that board members become more successful as their understanding of how the organisation works develops, and on the other side is the view that board members can become complacent and torpid if they remain on the board for too long. They argue the benefit of long-term board tenure is beneficial only up to a certain time, and beyond that point tenure does not have a significant effect on corporate governance. There are compelling arguments both for and against term limits in both the not-for-profit and business/corporate worlds. Some of these are discussed next.

The benefits of term limits include a guaranteed board renewal period and forced change of board members. This is especially salient where an incumbent may hold an advantage over other potential board members merely due to 'seniority' or become entrenched and not as responsive to the membership due to complacency. The length of tenure is of particular importance in certain cultural contexts where respect and difference are given for years in a role. An extended tenure may lead to a power imbalance and the development of close relationships among long-standing board members, stakeholder groups, and management. As noted by Geeraert (2015), long-serving board members may establish a power base through accumulated dominance, networks, acumen, and standing and thus be in a position to exert pressure and influence on board decisions, which may not always be in the organisation's best interests. In complement, Huang and Hilary (2017) examined the relationship between board tenure and firm value and found that organisations with a high proportion of board members that had served 15 years or more, showed a measurably decreased organisational value. It was proposed that nine years is the empirically proven optimal tenure. Within the business community many countries have introduced regulations (e.g. UK, Australia, India, Hong Kong, Singapore), that impose term limits on independent directors of nine–ten years. The justification of these term limits is that board member change can provide impetus for new ideas, solutions, and guard against a concentration of power.

A recent study (Jia, 2017) found that long-serving directors are less effective in advising management on innovation activities. It has also been suggested that, typically, longer-tenured board members are older and therefore may be out of touch with current trends, developments, changing economic, business, and technological environments and thus less likely to be able to contribute new ideas or recognise the need for change (Canavan et al., 2004; Terjesen, Aguilera and Lorenz, 2015). Extended board service might also create an unhealthy symbiotic relationship in management, particularly in cases where the secretary general/highest level senior executive also has held the position for many years.

Term limits also give boards the chance to exit board members whose attendance or participation is poor. While this may seem to be a performance issue that should be addressed regardless of term length, in practice board members are volunteers and/or elected by the membership, often without defined roles and/or performance criteria. In consequence, exiting non-performing board members is not a straightforward task, especially if there is no board evaluation process or threshold performance criteria. Establishing term limits and staggering terms assures the entry of new board members. This is a protocol that acts to preserve the balance between old and new directors. This mixture of the 'old and new' makes it easier for new board members to have their voices heard. Best practice for boards that incorporate term limits is having staggered terms so that the entire board is not up for re-election or re-appointment at the same time. The Australian Sport Commission offered specific guidance about this, stating:

> Each [NF] should have a staggered rotation system for Board members with a maximum term in office of no more than 10 years to encourage Board renewal while retaining corporate memory. As a guideline, good corporate practice is for around one third of the Board to retire each year, noting that retiring Directors are able to seek re-election within term limits.

The IOC and the IPC differ in their practices in this aspect. The IOC elects new members on an annual basis, which ensures that member turnover is staggered. As stated earlier, the IPC elects its Governing Council every four years, with a maximum of three terms. Although there is some board renewal during the 12-year period, the majority of the Council starts and leaves the Council at the same time, which may cause challenges in terms of ensuring adequate institutional knowledge.

Why organisations might not have limit terms

Arguments against term limits include the contention that long career board members can develop knowledge, experience, networks, relationships, and skills that the organisation would benefit from retaining. For example, Dou, Sahgal, and Zhang (2015) argued that long director tenure is associated with tighter control and fewer agency problems. In many situations the potential board member talent pool might be limited, and specific skill sets and experience may be difficult to replace. Such arguments may provide a rationale for the IOC practice of allowing members of the IOC Executive Board to be elected back to the Executive Board after a two-year stand-down period. It is a tenuous rationale, however, because when the significant number of long-serving members within the IOC is considered, it is clear that there should be ample candidates for the Executive Board with substantive experience of the organisation. There is also a view that longer-serving members are more likely to take a long-term strategic view versus a shorter-term perspective based on the limited time they are able to serve on the board. Longer-serving board members may also be more open-minded to short-term failure, an important factor in facilitating innovation. It has also been suggested that having term limits may reduce the value of holding a board position (Bos et al., 2013) and therefore not attract the best talent potentially available.

There are also specific reasons for not limiting terms that are directly related to the Olympic movement and these promulgate resistance to change. The electoral structure of international sport often requires an individual to hold a particular position in an organisation before they can be considered for election to a position in an organisation with more influence. Individuals are often required to be a member of a national federation in order to be elected to the respective sport's international federation. For example, in order to be a board member of the International Basketball Federation (FIBA), an individual needs to be a member of their nation's basketball federation. This has an 'escalating effect' in that individuals join their national federation and after some time have developed relationships and networks outside their country and thus are well positioned to be elected to the International Federation. If elected they are also required to hold their position on the National Federation for as long as they are on the International Federation. This reduces the opportunities for board renewal within the national federation. To change this would require International Federations to amend their constitutions to allow board members to relinquish their place on their National Federation board and still belong to the board of the International Federation.

Board renewal strategies

Term limits mean that there is a requirement for continual board renewal. In these instances planning for succession should be clearly identified as a required organisational activity. Pre-determined time-bound decisions need to be made about replacements, facilitating discussion and decisions about the prerequisite criteria for new board members, and the development of human resource management strategies for recruitment. If well managed, the planned turnover has the potential to bring in new people, with innovative ideas, new and expanded networks and relationships, and associated sources of revenue (Yeh and Taylor, 2008). Renewal and succession planning can be used to ensure that board has members with the optimal mix of skills and experience for their respective organisation's goals and aspirations.

The consideration of designating appropriate limits on board service to ensure timely renewal of board members is one way to address the concerns outlined in the previous section, but there are also other methods that can be used to achieve positive outcomes. For example, as mentioned earlier, many Olympic sport organisations face particular challenges with respect to board composition as many sports board members are elected in line with federated model requirements or representative structures, or, in some cases, to recognise length of service. In order to address this, it is becoming increasingly common in National Federations to be able to directly appoint (versus elect) directors to the Board in order to address skill gaps. The Australian Sport Commission provides this advice:

> An NSO board, through its nominations committee, should have a clear process to determine the skills mix of directors required to carry out the board's governance role at any point in time. NSO boards need to have the ability to appoint directors to address gaps, and board-appointed directors should have the same terms as elected directors.

The IOC has a Members Election Commission, comprising of at least one representative of the IOC Ethics Commission and one representative of the IOC Athletes' Commission. This Commission examines each candidature file and forwards these in the form of a report to the IOC Executive Board. The IOC Executive Board proposes candidates to the IOC members who then elect these by secret ballot. In the past, the criteria for what constitutes a suitable candidate has not been discussed, nor have the criteria been made public. However, as a consequence of Olympic Agenda 2020 recommendation 38, the IOC Members Election Commission will take a more proactive role in identifying the right candidates to fill vacancies in order to best fulfil the mission of the IOC. The Commission will identify the fields where there are or will be a lack of expertise in the Membership to then conduct a recruitment process, including interviews if required, to fill the identified gaps.

The IPC elects its Governing Council from its members and this is done by secret ballot. There are no criteria to guide who may be nominated or criteria for the members to use to differentiate candidates.

Another approach to facilitating effective board renewal is through having a programme of systematic board member development, which includes providing training for board members in aspects of governance and strategy. For example, in 2018, the Executive Board of the IOC decided to conduct self-assessments and regular information sessions for each of its members, aimed at optimising their skills and expertise to effectively face current and future societal, political, and technological governance challenges. The activities undertaken included:

- Education about the updated staff regulations, which strengthen existing formalities and include a robust code of conduct, based on the IOC Code of Ethics;
- An e-learning module on ethics for all staff;
- An awareness programme (including real-life scenarios, as well as past experiences) on all ethical matters, including conflicts of interest, delivered to all the IOC Members, IOC staff, and directors;
- Information about the dedicated 'Alert Transmission Mechanism', which IOC staff must use in the event of concerns about possible unethical conduct to alert the Ethics and Compliance Office;
- Customised ethics training for IOC Members; and
- Wide dissemination of the Code of Ethics across various stakeholder groups.

If this type of activity is supported with a performance appraisal and evaluation process, an organisation can ensure that board members are up to date with the sporting context, the issues facing the organisation and their role in dealing with these. A board review process should be undertaken annually and provide an opportunity for the board to reassess not only the contributions of departing board members, but also assess the skills, experience, and knowledge represented on the board, and to plan board development accordingly. When boards evaluate their qualifications and performance, they should consider the specific skills required for the board, its committees, and individual directors to carry out their responsibilities effectively. In their assessment, boards need to determine the extent to which those skills exist and whether they have been properly exercised or if there is a need for any skills improvement. Then the board, or a subset of the board, can craft a plan to address the board's talent needs. For example, new directors with specific identified experience and expertise might be recruited to succeed board members whose terms are coming to an end.

Conclusion

In conclusion, all sport organisations, including those within the Olympic movement, should engage with good management and governance practices and ensure regular board assessment and renewal. As outlined at the outset of this chapter, contemporary sport governance is a topic of much attention due to a continuous stream of governance failures, as evidenced in the many integrity breaches and corruption scandals in sport. Cases of poor organisational performance outcomes including insolvency, cronyism in board member selection, and membership alienation and decline have all contributed to the current calls for sport organisations to better adhere to principles of good governance. The lack of forced board member turnover, through term limits, has also meant that the IOC, the IFs, and many NOCs and NFs are yet to reach the gender-diversity targets set by the IOC.

While the IOC promotes good governance principles, when it comes to board renewal within the Olympic movement, constitutional board membership requirements and perceived advantages associated with retaining the status quo have meant that many Olympic organisations have not fully capitalised on the evidence-based benefits of strategic board renewal approaches. However, led by the IOC and IPC, there is a growing move towards the use of term limits within global sport organisations, which alongside increasing pressure from many governments and their associated national sport policies is beginning to create an environment where board renewal will be expected.

Note

1 For more details, see the IOC website at www.olympic.org/news/ioc-executive-board-reviews-progress-of-governance-reforms-decides-on-further-action

References

Adriaanse, J. (2016). Gender diversity in the governance of sport associations: The Sydney scoreboard global index of participation. *Journal of Business Ethics*, 137(1), pp. 149–160.

Adriaanse, J. and Schofield, T. (2014). The impact of gender quotas on gender equality in sport governance. *Journal of Sport Management*, 28(5), pp. 485–497.

Anderson, G.M. and Chun, D. (2014). How much board turnover is best? *Harvard Business Review Idea Watch*. (April 2014 issue).

Bos, A., van Eekeren, F., Houlihan, B. and Policy, S. (2013). Implementation and compliance of good governance in international sports organisations. In: J. Alm, ed., *Action for good governance in international sports organisations*. Final report. Copenhagen: Play the Game/Danish Institute for Sports Studies.

Canavan, J., Jones, B. and Potter, M.J. (2004). Board tenure: How long is too long? *Boards and Directors*, 28, pp. 39–42.

Chappelet, J-L. (2018). Beyond governance: The need to improve the regulation of international sport. *Sport in Society*, 21(5), pp. 724–734.

Chappelet, J-L. and Mrkonjic, M. (2013). Existing governance principles in sport: A review of published literature. In: J. Alm, ed., *Action for good governance in international sports organisations*. Final report. Copenhagen: Play the Game/Danish Institute for Sports Studies.

Council of Europe. (2012). *Good governance and ethics in sport. Parliamentary debate*. Brussels, Belgium. 25 April, 2012. Available at: https://assembly.coe.int/nw/xml/XRef/Xref-XML2HTML-en.asp?fileid=18258&lang=en (Accessed April 12 2020).

Dou, Y., Sahgal, S. and Zhang, E. (2015). Should independent directors have term limits? The role of experience in corporate governance. *Financial Management*, 44, pp. 583–621.

Geeraert, A. (2015). *Sports governance observer 2015: The legitimacy crisis in international sports governance*. Report. Copenhagen: Play the Game/Danish Institute for Sports Studies.

Geeraert, A. (2017). *National sport governance observer: Indicators of good governance in national federations*. Preliminary report. Copenhagen: Play the Game/Danish Institute for Sports Studies.

Geeraert, A., Alm, J. and Groll, M. (2014). Good governance in international sport organizations: An analysis of the 35 Olympic sport governing bodies. *International Journal of Sport Policy and Politics*, 6(3), pp. 281–306.

Hoye, R. (2017). Sport governance. In: R. Hoye and M.M. Parent, eds., *Handbook of sport management*. London: SAGE, pp. 9–23.

Huang, S. and Hilary, G. (2017). *Zombie board: Board tenure and firm performance*, pp. 1–78. Research Collection School of Accountancy. Singapore Management University.

IMD. (2017). *Governance review at a glance: Good governance at the International Olympic Committee Summary of recommendations*. Lausanne: IMD.

Jia, N. (2017). Should directors have term limits? – Evidence from corporate innovation. *European Accounting Review*, 26(4), pp. 755–785.

Parent, M.M. and Hoye, R. (2018). The impact of governance principles on sport organisations' governance practices and performance: A systematic review. *Cogent Social Sciences*, 4, p. 1. doi: 10.1080/23311886.2018.1503578.

Taylor, M. and O'Sullivan, N. (2009). How should national governing bodies of sport be governed in the UK? An exploratory study of board structure. *Corporate Governance: An International Review*, 17(6), pp. 681–693.

Taylor, T., Doherty, A. and McGraw, P. (2015). *Managing people in sport organisations: A strategic human resource management perspective*. Routledge: Oxford.

Taylor, T. and Robinson, L. (2019). Succession planning and good governance. In: M. Winand and C. Anagnostopoulos, eds., *Research handbook on sports governance*. London: Routledge.
Terjesen, S., Aguilera, R.V. and Lorenz, R. (2015). Legislating a woman's seat on the board: Institutional factors driving gender quotas for boards of directors. *Journal of Business Ethics*, 128(2), pp. 233–251.
The United States Department of Justice. (2015). *Nine FIFA officials and five corporate executives indicted for racketeering conspiracy and corruption*. New York, United States. 27 May 2015. Available at: https://www.justice.gov/opa/speech/attorney-general-loretta-e-lynch-delivers-remarks-press-conference-announcing-charges (Accessed 17 March 2017).
Walters, G. and Tacon, R. (2018). The 'codification' of governance in the non-profit sport sector in the UK. *European Sport Management Quarterly*, pp. 1–19.
Walters, G., Tacon, R. and Trenberth, L. (2011). *The role of the board in national governing bodies of sport*. Working Paper. University of London, Birkbeck.
Wertheim, P., Neill, J., John, D. and Curtis, E. (2016). Director tenure and leadership effectiveness over internal controls. *Journal of Leadership, Accountability and Ethics*, 13(2), pp. 61–75.
Yeh, C.M. and Taylor, T. (2008). Issues of governance in sport organisations: A question of board size, structure and roles. *World Leisure Journal*, 50(1), pp. 33–45.

26

The relationship between the IOC and international sport federations

Jinsu Byun and Becca Leopkey

Introduction

The continued growth and popularity of the Olympic Games has resulted in the need to recognize an ever-increasing number of event stakeholders in the Olympic movement to ensure the proper management and sustainability of the event. Thus, the last several years have seen a heightened focus on the governance of the Games and the broader movement (e.g. Leopkey and Parent, 2017). Governance can be understood as the process of interaction among various stakeholders towards achieving collective goal(s) (Girginov, 2011; Lange et al., 2013). Existing literature on the topic (e.g. Chappelet, 2016) has demonstrated how diverse actors, such as the International Olympic Committee (IOC), the International Sport Federations (IFs), and the National Olympic Committees (NOCs) facilitate the work of the Olympic movement (e.g. the regular celebration of the Olympic Games and the promotion of education through Olympism and its values) while at the same time maintain their symbiotic independent relationship with each other (Chappelet, 2008).

Within the field, the IOC serves as the central actor whose job is to promote the Olympic movement and its values, as well as to recognize and coordinate the large number of stakeholders (e.g. NOCs and sponsors) involved in its governance system (Chappelet, 2008). International Sport Federations (IFs) are also key to its functioning because of their role in managing individual sports at the global level. That is, while the IOC owns the rights for the Olympic Games, the IFs govern the sports that are contested at the event. Therefore, understanding the relationship between the IOC and the IFs is imperative for developing a more holistic understanding of the governance system of the Olympic movement. Thus, the focus of this chapter is on breaking down the relationship between the IOC and the IFs. More specifically, we present the current status and the historical development of the relationship between the organizations. Furthermore, existing research on the topic will be reviewed in addition to the provision of potential future research directions that seek to better understand the dynamics of the relationship between the two key actors. By doing so, this chapter aims to provide a broad picture of the past history, current environment, and future development of the relationship between the IOC and the IFs.

The current environment

In this section, a brief outline of the current status of the relationship between the IOC and the IFs is provided in order to illustrate how the two actors collaborate. According to the Olympic Charter (IOC, 2019a), IFs are one of three key constituents that comprise the Olympic movement along with the IOC and NOCs. The IOC has an authoritative role in terms of recognizing IFs, as well as other actors in the movement, and determining which sports are included on the Olympic programmes (Theodoraki, 2007). In order to promote and develop the Olympic movement, the IOC sanctions one IF per sport. In some cases, an IF may control multiple sports that fall under the same umbrella such as in the case of Fédération Internationale de Natation (FINA), the international swimming federation, who administers international competitions for a number of aquatic disciplines including water polo, diving, and synchronized swimming to name a few (Chappelet, 2008). All specific details related to the recognition procedures are under the purview of the IOC Executive Board. Full recognition or withdrawal of IFs, however, is determined by the Session, that is to say, the supreme organ of the IOC at an annual general meeting of IOC members. Depending on their status (i.e. recognition by the IOC), IFs can be categorized into three types of international sport organization groupings: Olympic Summer federations, Olympic Winter federations, and IOC-recognized IFs (non-Olympic federations). This section briefly illustrates how IFs are acknowledged by the IOC and are selected to be part of the Olympic programme.

In order to achieve IOC recognition, interested federations must meet a number of criteria including compliance with IOC policies, a detailed history of the sport (e.g. date of international competitions first organized by the IF), universality in the sense that the sport has a degree of global participation, and popularity as demonstrated by spectator attendance and television coverage (IOC, 2013). For instance, IFs must comply with the rules and bylaws of the IOC, the World Anti-Doping Code of the World Anti-Doping Agency (WADA), and the Olympic Movement Code on the Prevention of Manipulation of Competitions of the IOC; however each IF also has its autonomy and independence to control various actors within its sport(s)' governance system such as athletes, officials, fans, and National Federations (NFs) (IOC, 2019a). Specifically, the IOC (2019a, p. 56) noted the role and mission of an IF in the Olympic movement as follows:

> – to establish and enforce, in accordance with the Olympic spirit, the rules concerning the practice of their respective sports and to ensure their application;
> – to ensure the development of their sports throughout the world;
> – to contribute to the achievement of the goals set out in the Olympic Charter, in particular by way of the spread of Olympism and Olympic education;
> – to support the IOC in the review of candidatures for organising the Olympic Games for their respective sports;
> – to assume the responsibility for the control and direction of their sports at the Olympic Games;
> – for other international multisport competitions held under the patronage of the IOC, IFs can assume or delegate responsibility for the control and direction of their sports;
> – to provide technical assistance in the practical implementation of the Olympic Solidarity programmes;
> – to encourage and support measures relating to the medical care and health of athletes.

In addition, the IOC allocates a portion of IOC membership to the IFs, which allows the sports to promote their interests in the Olympic movement (IOC, 2019a). According to the Olympic Charter, the total number of IOC members may not exceed 115 and includes representatives from diverse organizations and groups in the Olympic movement (e.g. NOCs, IFs, and active athletes). Specifically, 15 spots are reserved for individuals holding executive or senior leadership positions within IFs, the associations of IFs, or other organizations recognized by the IOC (e.g. World Olympians Association, International Olympic Truce Centre, World Union of Olympic Cities). By being a part of the Olympic movement, an IF can have an opportunity to increase its power in the international sport terrain by having IOC members promote their interests to the IOC Session. Status as a recognized international federation does not guarantee a spot on the Olympic programme. Once acknowledged by the IOC, a recognized international federation that wishes to be considered must meet a number of criteria set by the IOC (e.g. business model, value added to the Olympic Games, and popularity). Given the importance of the event, the Olympic programme is reviewed by the Olympic Programme Commission after each edition of the Games.

As of Fall 2019, a total of 33 Summer IFs including the five new IFs related to the sports were added for the Tokyo Games (World Baseball Softball Confederation, International Federation of Sport Climbing, World Karate Federation, World Skate, International Surfing Association) and seven Winter IFs are accepted by the IOC as Olympic IFs (see Table 26.1), a recognition that comes with a number of benefits.

Table 26.1 Olympic Summer and Winter sports federations

Olympic Summer sport federations	*Olympic Winter sport federations*
1 International Association of Athletics Federations	1 International Biathlon Union
2 World Rowing	2 International Bobsleigh and Skeleton Federation
3 Badminton World Federation	3 World Curling Federation
4 International Basketball Federation	4 International Ice Hockey Federation
5 International Boxing Association	5 International Luge Federation
6 International Canoe Federation	6 International Skating Union
7 Union Cycliste Internationale	7 International Ski Federation
8 International Equestrian Federation	
9 International Fencing Federation	
10 International Association Football Federation	
11 FIFA International Golf Federation	
12 International Gymnastics Federation	
13 International Weightlifting Federation	
14 International Handball Federation	
15 International Hockey Federation	
16 International Judo Federation	
17 United World Wrestling	
18 International Swimming Federation	
19 International Modern Pentathlon Union	
20 World Rugby	
21 World Taekwondo	
22 International Tennis Federation	
23 International Table Tennis Federation	
24 International Shooting Sport Federation	
25 World Archery Federation	

Olympic Summer sport federations	Olympic Winter sport federations
26 International Triathlon Union	
27 World Sailing	
28 International Volleyball Federation	
29 World Baseball Softball Confederation (Tokyo 2020)	
30 International Federation of Sport Climbing (Tokyo 2020)	
31 World Karate Federation (Tokyo 2020)	
32 World Skate (Tokyo 2020)	
33 International Surfing Association (Tokyo 2020)	

For example, following the conclusion of the Rio 2016 Olympics, Summer Olympic IFs were awarded $540 million from the IOC, $20 million more than after London 2012 Games ($520 million) (IOC, 2019b). The IOC distributed $215 million to the Winter Olympic IFs following the PyeongChang 2018 event, an increase of 8% ($199 million) over the Sochi 2014 Winter Olympics distribution (Morgan, 2019). The revenues secured from the selling of Olympic broadcasting rights is crucial for most Olympic IFs because they redistribute the proceeds to their respective NFs in order to aid the global development of the sport with funds supporting the training of athletes, judges, and coaches as well as the construction of sport facilities (Chappelet, 2008).

Given their central roles in the Olympic movement, the IOC and the IFs have collaborated in order to promote the Olympic movement around the world; however this has not occurred without tension (Chappelet, 2008). In the following section, a brief historical review of the development of the relationship between the IOC and the IFs is provided.

Historical development of the relationship between the IOC and IFs

There have been a number of contentious issues that have affected the governance of the Olympic movement over the last several decades, including but not limited to professionalization (i.e. eligibility of professional athletes), commercialization (e.g. selling of rights for association with the Games), and the need to ensure the long-term sustainability of the Olympic Games. It has been within this context that the IOC and the IFs have developed their relationship through confrontation, negotiation, and collaboration surrounding these issues. In doing so, the IOC has tried to maintain its power as the central leader of the movement, while at the same time the IFs have attempted to protect their interests.

1960s–1980s: the commercialization and professionalization of the Olympic Games

In 2018, broadcasting rights (73%) and sponsorship (18%) accounted for over 90% of the IOC's revenue (IOC, 2018a). The 1960s–1980s saw the globalization of television and multinational corporations. Stakeholders within the Olympic movement saw these advancements as an opportunity to increase their revenue by selling broadcasting and sponsorship rights to commercial and broadcast organizations (Stokvis, 2000). The IFs attempted to gain additional revenue by making their sports and events more attractive to television viewers. As early as the 1970s, some IFs created their own world championships or international event series (e.g. the volleyball Grand Prix and Ski World Cup) to help capitalize on these opportunities (Chappelet, 2008). While some exceptions exist, relatively few IF have highly lucrative world championships like the Fédération Internationale de Football Association (FIFA) World Cup and as such the majority of IFs have remained highly dependent on the IOC for their sport's promotion via the regular hosting of the Olympic Games and access to financial resources for sport development (Stokvis, 2000). Given this dependence, the IFs began to ask the IOC for a larger share of the revenues, and as a result the distribution of profit from Olympic television rights became a key antagonist in their existing relationship.

During the tenure of IOC President Avery Brundage (1952–1972), tensions reached a climax between the IOC and IFs because of ongoing issues with the interpretation of amateurism, as well as the commercialization of the Games. As television revenue increased in the 1960s, IFs placed additional pressures on the IOC to disseminate a larger portion of these resources (Wenn, 2012). At the time, amateurism was a key ideological tenet of the Olympic movement which senior IOC officials tried to maintain (Stokvis, 2000). According to the eligibility rules of the IOC published in 1964, an amateur is someone who 'participate[s] and always has participated in sport as an avocation without material gain of any kind' and thus are eligible to participate in the Olympic Games (IOC, 1964).

President Brundage was a strong defender of amateurism and its connection to the Olympic Games and thus was against the commercialization of the event, as indicated in the following quotation:

> We can only rely on the support of those who believe in the principles of fair play and sportsmanship embodied in the amateur code in our efforts to prevent the Games from being used by individuals, organizations or nations for ulterior motives.
>
> *(Greene, 2012)*

As such, he did not show a favourable attitude toward the IF's request for sharing the television broadcasting revenue and loosening the amateur eligibility restrictions.

As a result, associations of IFs began to form. While there had been a permanent bureau of IFs that was created to promote their interests and objectives in the Olympic movement under the leadership of Paul Rousseau, Secretary General of the Union Cycliste Internationale in 1921 (IOC, 2019c) the organization lacked influence. As such, it was necessary for the IFs to create their own associations in order to use their collective power to protect their rights and interests against the IOC (Chappelet, 2008). Thus, the General Assembly of International Federations (GAIF) was formed in 1967, and renamed the General Assembly of International Sport Federations (GAISF) in 1976.

Following the Presidency of Avery Brundage, the word 'amateur' was removed from the Olympic Charter by incoming IOC President Lord Killanin at the 1973 Olympic Congress in Varna, Bulgaria (Wagg, 2012). This action represents a major shift in the direction of the movement because it demonstrated the IOC's willingness to relax eligibility criteria for athletes to compete in the Olympic Games (Wagg, 2012). More transformations came during Juan Antonio Samaranch's presidency (1980–2001). Samaranch, a former IOC Vice-President from 1974 to 1978, had an even more responsive position on the issue of amateurism and as such tried to secure economic prosperity for the Olympic movement through the commercialization of the Games (Llewellyn and Lake, 2017). Under his leadership, in order to gain a more stable and diversified revenue stream, the IOC established 'The Olympic Programme' (TOP), now 'The

Olympic Partners' programme in 1985. This programme provided an opportunity for a limited number of multinational corporations to obtain worldwide service and product category exclusivity and protection including the use of Olympic trademarks (e.g. Olympic rings) and marketing rights not only prior to but also during the Games (Stotlar, 2005). Through the creation of the sponsorship programme, the IOC has achieved huge revenue increases from 1985 to 2016 (Ferrand, Chappelet and Séguin, 2012).

In line with this approach, the IOC has since allowed professional athletes to compete in the Olympic Games. By 1986, the IOC had modified its amateur rules to allow the participation of professional athletes to compete at the Games; however they left athlete selection to the discretion of individual IFs to determine which athletes would be considered eligible for Olympic competition (Teetzel, 2011). Consequently, professional tennis players took the court as early as the 1988 Olympic Games in Seoul, South Korea, while boxing, for example, did not allow professional athletes to compete until the Rio 2016 edition of the event. Furthermore, in 1991 all passages related to amateurism were removed from Olympic Charter. This precipitated the appearance of the United States men's basketball national team, also known as the 'Dream Team', which included professional players from the NBA in the 1992 Barcelona Olympics (Llewellyn and Lake, 2017). Through the process of slackening eligibility rules, the IOC allowed IFs to pursue the inclusion of professional athletes at major international events.

At the same time, it was important to maintain the unity of the existing system of the Olympic movement (Chappelet, 2008, 2018). In order to do so President Samaranch saw that it was necessary to weaken the power of GAISF, a gathering of IFs led by Thomas Keller. To this end, Samaranch established the Association of the International Olympic Winter Sport Federations (AIOWF) and the Association of Summer Olympic International Federations (ASOIF) in 1982, two organizations that were designed to divide the GAISF and weaken Keller's position (Chappelet, 2016). Furthermore, Kim Un-yong, the successor of Keller, and then President of the World Taekwondo Association (notably not an Olympic sport at that time) exuded a more cooperative attitude to the IOC than his predecessor, which provided the impetus for the creation of the Association of Recognised International Sports Federations (ARISF) in order to represent non-Olympic programme sports' interests and rights at the Olympic level (Chappelet, 2008).

While conflict continued to emerge between the IOC and the IFs the two actors were ultimately effectively able to manage the existing tensions. More recently, GAISF launched the SportAccord International Convention in 2003 in order to provide IFs with opportunities to share their knowledge and broaden their network. The association was subsequently rebranded as SportAccord in 2009 (SportAccord, 2019).

Recent changes: fostering the sustainability of the Olympic movement

In the past two decades, increasing criticisms regarding the potential negative environmental, social, and economic impacts of the Olympic Games have emerged as a result of the event's growing scope and complexity (Chappelet, 2014; MacAloon, 2016). The most recent withdrawal of bid contenders for the 2026 Winter Olympic Games suggests a potential crisis for the future sustainability of the event in its current form (MacAloon, 2016). In response to these issues, the IOC proposed 'Olympic Agenda 2020', a strategic roadmap for the future of the Olympic movement, including a number of proposals to improve the longevity of the event for future generations. Suggested modifications included amendments to the bidding process and reducing the overall costs associated with hosting the premiere event (IOC, 2014b). More recently, the IOC released the 'New Norm', a plan to make the event even more affordable, sustainable, and beneficial through a number of collaborative approaches for delivering the Olympics (e.g. acceptance of joint bids) (IOC, 2018b).

Improving the sustainability of the Olympic Games is important for the IFs as well as the IOC, and tensions again have been augmented. In particular, a clash between the IOC and the IFs occurred in 2015 during the opening remarks of the SportAccord General Assembly in Sochi. Marius Vizer, then President of SportAccord (now renamed as GAISF; read on for details), criticized the IOC and its President Thomas Bach for the exclusion of IFs from many of the key decisions made affecting the future of the Olympic movement (e.g. the Games' host selection process) (GamesBids, 2015c). In the same speech, he was also critical of Agenda 2020: 'the IOC system is expired, outdated, wrong, unfair and not at all transparent. The Olympic Games belong to all of us and we need real reforms' (GamesBids, 2015b). In doing so, Vizer argued that the Olympic Charter does not guarantee enough positions directly associated with sport and that more representatives directly related to sport should have the majority of votes in order to protect the interests of sport within the Olympic movement (GamesBids, 2015a). Following the incident, some IFs (e.g. World Rowing and the International Shooting Sport Federation) withdrew from the association in protest in order to show their disagreement with this message (Morgan, 2017).

Following the resignation of Vizer in 2015, the heightened tension between the IOC and the IFs mollified as the presidents of the two entities, Thomas Bach and Patrick Bauman, signed a Memorandum of Understanding (MOU) in 2017. The intention of this agreement was designed to facilitate cooperation between the two organizations leading to strengthened unity in the Olympic movement (IOC, 2017b). In referencing the MOU, GAISF President Bauman noted:

> I would like to thank IOC President Thomas Bach and the IOC for the trust that they offer GAISF and its members through this MoU, which articulates and cements our relationship, makes clear that we are all members of the Olympic Movement and will see us working even more closely together, to ensure that the values of the Olympic Movement remain paramount in an ever-changing sports landscape.
>
> *(GAISF, 2017)*

In a further attempt to build a collaborative relationship with the IOC, President Bauman also attempted to rebrand the organization from a political group to a service provider for its members. In doing so, GAISF attempts to assist its members by helping them to address and manage important issues in the movement, as well as within their specific sport environment (e.g. anti-doping, corruption, and match fixing) (Butler, 2017; Chappelet, 2015). In order to do so and as a sign of reform, the organization changed their logo and name from SportAccord to the Global Association of International Sports Federations (GAISF) (Morgan, 2017). Moreover, President Bauman also modified the leadership system of the organization by setting up a two-year rotation alternating the presidential role between the four founding member groups: (1) ASOIF (i.e. Summer Olympic sports); (2) AIOWF (i.e. Winter Olympic sports); (3) ARISF, formed by the IFs that are recognized by the IOC but not on the Olympic programme (e.g. International Wushu Federation, International Cricket Council); and (4) the Alliance of Independent recognized Members of Sport (AIMS) established for sports within GAISF that are not in any of the three previous groupings (e.g. Ju-Jitsu International Federation, International Soft Tennis Federation).

Baumann's term as president of GAISF was due to conclude in 2020. However, on 13th October 2018 he died at the age of 51 following a heart attack while attending the Youth

Olympic Games in Buenos Aires. Following the passing of President Baumann, the presidential rotation of GAISF was brought forward by a year, and Raffaele Chiulli who had served as ARISF president since 2013 was unanimously elected in May 2019. After Chiulli's tenure ends in 2021, he will be succeeded by a representative from AIOWF from 2021 to 2023, and a member from AIMS will lead the organization from 2023 to 2025 completing the full rotation cycle.

In this section, the historical evolution of the relationship between the IOC and IFs was reviewed. Notably, for decades, the Olympic movement has had to appropriately respond to various societal issues (e.g. the commercialization, professionalization, and sustainability of the Olympics). In doing so, the IOC and IFs have negotiated ways for each of the organizations to protect their individual interests and rights from one another while at the same time continuing to collaborate on improving the sustainability of the Olympic movement. In the following section, potential issues associated with relationship dynamics between the IOC and IFs are outlined, along with the presentation of potential future research directions in this area.

Relationship dynamics and future research directions

While there has been increasing attention on the governance of the Olympic movement as well as global sport issues such as doping, match fixing, and corruption (Chappelet, 2019; Chappelet and Mrkonjic, 2013; Geeraert, Alm and Groll, 2014; Miller, 2011), relatively little research focus has been placed on the relationship between IFs, the IOC, and the broader Olympic movement. As such, in this section, the relevant studies on the topic will be reviewed and future research directions are provided. In order to do so, the discussion of this chapter is based on two organization theories (institutional theory and resource dependence theory). The application of an organization theory perspective can be useful to help explain how organizations operate in relationship to their organizational field (Cunliffe, 2008) and as such it can facilitate our understanding of how organizations should be designed and managed in order to operate more efficiently and effectively in their respective environments. Thus, this chapter aims to offer insights for practitioners as well as researchers in terms of the relationship between two of the key actors in the movement.

Institutional theory and new sports in the Olympic movement

As the globe's premier international sport event, the Olympic Games are in a constant state of flux to ensure its relevance to both its audience and supporters. In order to accomplish this, the Games have seen many changes to its Olympic programme over the years from the inclusion of professional athletes to the debut of new more alternative sports. Given these occurrences, it is important to understand how the IOC manages relationships with emergent IFs and how they work to embrace the culture of the newer alternative sports. Chappelet (2008) identified three major waves in the creation of IFs. The first having begun prior to World War I, when the federations of most traditional sports (e.g. athletics, gymnastics, swimming, football, skating, etc.) were established. The second phase of creation occurred from 1920 to 1950 when the remaining sports formed IFs (e.g. hockey, ski, badminton, etc.). The current phase which began in 1970 reflects the formation of IFs for relatively new sports, many of which are not on the Olympic sport programme but are GAISF members (e.g. World Karate Federation, World Association of Kickboxing Organizations).

The three waves emphasize how the scope of the Olympic programme has expanded and evolved over time. Today, a review of the Olympic programme is conducted after each edition of the Games by the Olympic Programme Commission which includes members from the IOC as well as representatives from NOCs, IFs, outside experts, and athletes. Following conclusions made by the committee, the Commission provides advice to the IOC Executive Board who then reports to the IOC Session (IOC, 2017a). In response to these recommendations, the IOC has included several new sports in the Games in order to help promote new values (e.g. innovation, flexibility, and youth) and to ensure the sustainability of the Olympic movement.

In addition to the regular Olympic programme review process, following the creation of Olympic Agenda 2020, the IOC has also allowed Organising Committees of the Olympic Games (OCOGs) to propose additional events not included in the Olympic programme but popular in the host country for the specific edition of the Games (IOC, 2016). On August 2016, it was announced that five new/returning sports (i.e. baseball/softball, karate, skateboard, sports climbing, and surfing) will be part of the Olympic programme at the Tokyo 2020 Olympic Games, a decision that was made at the 129th IOC session in Rio De Janeiro (IOC, 2017a).

Despite the potential benefits of adding new sports to the Olympic programme, integrating their unique culture and governance structures into the highly institutionalized international sport system may be a difficult task for the IOC. Several studies (e.g. Batuev and Robinson, 2019a; Strittmatter et al., 2019; Thorpe and Wheaton, 2011) have discussed potential issues related to managing the new sports (e.g. action sports like snowboarding, bicycle motocross [BMX]) in the Olympic movement.

Thorpe and Wheaton (2011) identified a complex set of intra- and inter-politics among stakeholders (e.g. the IOC, related sporting bodies, the action sport industries and cultures, and media conglomerates) who negotiated with each other during the selection process. They also pointed out the problem of incorporating the action sports under existing IFs that have little knowledge of their unique culture (e.g. snowboarding was included as a discipline of skiing). This has created some anxiety for some of the sport's participants because they are afraid of losing their autonomy if included in the Games. Recently, the World Skateboarding Federation was created rather than including skateboarding under the umbrella of a recognized sport organization, suggesting a growing flexibility by the IOC about exercising its power over new sports (Batuev and Robinson, 2017). Examining various issues (power relations and values/culture difference) between the IOC and the IFs governing new sports and how they are handled by the actors in the Olympic movement will be an important future research topic in order to expand our understanding of the governance dynamics in this context.

In that regard, researchers may investigate how new sports and their IFs are included into the Olympic governance system by framing the investigation with institutional theory. This perspective can help both researchers and practitioners understand how norms, practices, or rules are developed, adopted, and diffused within specific organizational fields (DiMaggio and Powell, 1983; Meyer and Rowan, 1977; Washington and Patterson, 2011). For instance, previous studies (e.g. Batuev and Robinson, 2017, 2018, 2019a; Batuev and Robinson, 2019b; Strittmatter et al., 2019) have examined how action sports such as skateboarding, snowboarding, and sport climbing have been institutionalized within the Olympic movement and how their IFs have evolved within their organizational environments. More specifically, recognition of the respective sports by the IOC was considered a form of legitimation (i.e. gaining legitimacy from key actors in an organizational field) from the institutional theory perspective, and the diverse forces that influenced the legitimation of the new sports and their IFs (e.g. commercialization, media pressure, professionalization, and bureaucratization including the IOC's criteria on the structure of a sports and its IF) have been investigated (Batuev and Robinson, 2017, 2018).

Furthermore, additional research has explored the impact of institutional pressures and resultant responses of the new sports to help highlight emergent relationship issues between the IOC and the IFs. Batuev and Robinson (2017) discussed problems caused by structural and cultural differences between the IOC and the skateboarding community. That is, the IOC usually requires a sport to be governed by a single organization, but skateboarding has traditionally been developed and managed through a network of the sport community involving various organizations. This difference illustrates the gap between the two actors which has the potential to create tension regarding autonomy. Additionally, cultural gaps between the traditional values of alternative sport and the competitive values of traditional sport were demonstrated. Therefore, an interesting avenue of future examination could delve into how tensions between not only the IOC and the IFs but also other stakeholders (recreational participants, athletes, administrators, event organizers, and media) are managed.

Moreover, as an impact of the inclusion of new sports on the Olympic programmes, the evolution of the action sport organizations has been noted. Batuev and Robinson (2019b) suggested that the organizational evolution of sport climbing was impacted by Olympic inclusion, as it acted as a catalyst for the International Federation of Sport Climbing to further develop the sport and expand their relationship with the IOC. In a similar vein, Strittmatter et al. (2019) discussed how the incorporation of snowboarding into the Olympic Games resulted in the emergence of dual governance structures (i.e. the industry-based and nation-based governance model).

As eSports gains traction globally, it has been argued that it is time to consider embracing eSports into the field of sport and its related industries (Heere, 2018). However, debates surrounding eSports and whether it should be considered a sport remain with much of the negative criticisms relating to its lack of physicality (e.g. required physical skills for better performance) (Funk, Pizzo and Baker, 2018; Heere, 2018). However, it is evident that change is occurring and that eSport should be viewed as a new player in the field. The Olympic Council of Asia (OCA) has included eSports on the official sport programme of the 2022 Asian Games, the continent's biggest multi-sport games after the Olympics (OCA, 2017). Furthermore, in 2017, President of the IOC, Thomas Bach, reflected on some of the obstacles to incorporating eSports into the Olympic movement, noting the lack of consensus regarding the status of eSports, as well as the absence of national and international formalized organizational structures (Hallmann and Giel, 2018). However, the organization and establishment of eSports in the broader sports industry has continued to grow, especially in relation to the development of professional leagues (e.g. the NBA 2K League that started in 2018 and is the first official eSports league managed by a USA professional sports league [National Basketball Association]), the foundation of amateur and professional teams (e.g. 23 teams participated in the NBA 2K League in 2019), and the accumulation of a large fan base. Specifically, it is estimated that the eSports market will generate $1.8 billion in 2022 (Newzoo, 2019). Moreover, there have also been attempts to conceptualize eSports as a sport by arguing that the activity requires at least certain extent of physical skills (Funk, Pizzo and Baker, 2018).

Therefore, in the near future, eSports may have an opportunity to be officially recognized as a sport and ultimately incorporated into the Olympic programme if it will conform to some degree by establishing formalized national and international organizational structures to ensure the promotion of the values of the Olympic movement (Hallmann and Giel, 2018). As such, it would be important to investigate the dynamic relationship between the IOC and eSports organizations in the process of institutionalization of the activity in the Olympic movement. Given that institutional theory has been utilized by previous researchers to examine newer action sports (e.g. snowboarding and sport climbing), the perspective could be beneficial in providing theoretical and practical implications to broaden our knowledge of the evolution of eSports and the dynamic relationship among actors involved in the process.

To summarize, future research drawing on institutional theory could be beneficial for exploring the institutionalization of new sports and their IFs within the Olympic movement, which may also offer insights on the dynamic relationship that exists between the IOC and IFs. In particular, given that each sport and IF has a unique culture and structure, the influence of and responses to each of these organizations being adopted into the movement may vary. Thus, researchers need to investigate similarities and differences of these experiences in the Olympic context. Finally, the impact of these changes will need to be examined at multiple levels: micro (individuals like officials and athletes), meso (internal organizational structures and interorganizational relationship), and macro (the impact of the changes on the field of sport) in order to fully understand the phenomenon.

Resource dependence theory and the relationship between the IOC and the IFs

As discussed earlier, historically, there has been a strain on the relationship between the IOC and IFs regarding resource distribution. Given that there are power relationships among organizations in terms of resource sharing in the sport field (Dittmore et al., 2009), these dependencies need to be further investigated. In that regard Resource Dependence Theory (RDT) can be employed to explore this phenomenon. RDT contends that no organization possess all the critical resources required for it to achieve its goals and objectives and as such it is reliant on other organizations in its environment for securement of these resources (Pfeffer and Salancik, 1978). Key tenets of RDT include social context issues, organizational strategies, and power (Davis and Cobb, 2010). Among these three principles, power is the most significant concept of the theory because organizations try to increase their own power over other organizations while at the same time aim to decrease others' power over them. Employing a RDT lens can help researchers investigate how power relationships and resource dependence between the IOC and the IFs are formed. Moreover, it could help us better understand the strategies they use to manage this dependence, as well as the use of power in their organizational environment (Ulrich and Barney, 1984).

Several studies have examined power relationships and related resource dependence by focusing on various types of sport organizations, such as community sport organizations (e.g. Bingham and Walters, 2013; Patterson and Parent, 2017; Sotiriadou and Wicker, 2013) and disability sport organizations (e.g. Brown and Pappous, 2018; Walker and Hayton, 2017).

With the exception of some unique cases (e.g. FIFA), most IFs are dependent on financial support from the IOC's media revenue. In that vein, Batuev and Robinson (2019b) suggested that the International Federation of Sport Climbing (IFSC) could gain funding for developing the sports across nations through its direct connection to the IOC by being a Recognized Olympic IF because many countries tend to only fund the Olympic sports federations. Even though the federation traded in its autonomy to some degree in the process, they saw an opportunity to develop sport climbing worldwide in a more efficient and effective manner. Batuev and Robinson (2017) also illustrated how the International Skateboarding Federation (ISF) strategy is different from the IFSC's approach as alluded to earlier. More specifically, they highlighted how the ISF kept its autonomy by establishing interorganizational relationships with commercial actors such as board producers, skateboarding facilities, and media companies, which helped the federation reduce its resource dependence on the IOC.

As such it can be argued that IFs may choose from a variety of organizational strategies in order to best achieve their desired goals and objectives. Some IFs may focus on forming partnerships (e.g. Jones et al., 2017; Misener and Doherty, 2013) which can be effective for sport organizations to increase their autonomy by decreasing resource dependence on funding providers in their organizational field (e.g. federal government for national sport organizations). Others may choose to compromise their autonomy in order to gain more resources for their sport development programmes from the IOC. Therefore, further research should be undertaken to explore how IFs manage the resource/power dependence with the IOC by employing various organizational strategies (e.g. forming partnerships).

More recently, the IOC has focused on limiting the size of the Olympic Games in order to help facilitate the traditional one city host format. This issue was reflected in the IOC Agenda 2020 and according to Recommendation 9, limitations to accreditations of athletes, coaches, other support personnel, and events for the Summer and Winter Olympics should be considered (IOC, 2014a). The recent addition of five new sports for the 2020 Tokyo Olympics was considered a decision that went against Recommendation 9. This decision was made with the permission of the IOC (IOC, 2017a) since these suggestions were considered independent from the regular Olympic IFs programme review process. That is, additional events and athletes in the new sports are not considered as the part of the quota illustrated by the Olympic Charter because the addition of new sports could also help ensure the future sustainability of the event.

However, with the acceptance of this strategy a decrease in the number of athletes allocated to some traditional sports is a potential, thus ill will among IFs within the Olympic movement may develop. Already, there have been ongoing debates regarding the inclusion of new sports to the Games to the detriment and exclusion of traditional sports (e.g. wrestling) (ESPN, 2013), resulting in strife among actors within the international sport system. Specifically, adding new sports to the Olympic programme may decrease the amount of resources generally available for the established sports. Therefore, future research will also need to explore how the IOC can handle the potential conflict among IFs regarding resource distribution.

In sum, future research employing resource dependence theory will facilitate our understanding of the power relationship between the IOC and the IFs within the Olympic movement. Investigating these issues will enable a deeper understanding of these problems and result in the provision of theoretical and practical implications for the field.

Conclusion

This chapter outlined the current status, historical development, and future research opportunities of the relationship between the IOC and IFs. For decades, two of the key actors of the Olympic movement have developed their relationship through negotiation, confrontation, and collaboration in relation to various issues, such as professionalization, commercialization, and sustainability. It would be interesting to see how the IOC and IFs interact with each other and further build their relationships when responding to environmental changes in the future. Given the importance of their role in the Olympic movement and global sport field, understanding the relationship between them is crucial for both researchers and practitioners. Hopefully, this chapter will serve to inspire researchers, students, and practitioners by providing them with a basis for understanding and exploring the topic.

References

Batuev, M. and Robinson, L. (2017). How skateboarding made it to the Olympics: An institutional perspective. *International Journal of Sport Management and Marketing*, 17(4/5/6), pp. 381–402.

Batuev, M. and Robinson, L. (2018). What influences organisational evolution of modern sport: The case of skateboarding. *Sport, Business and Management: An International Journal*, 8(5), pp. 492–510.

Batuev, M. and Robinson, L. (2019a). International governance of action sports: An organisational legitimacy perspective. In: M. Winand and C. Anagnostopoulos, eds., *Research handbook on sport governance*. The Lypiatts: Edward Elgar Publishing, pp. 168–184.

Batuev, M. and Robinson, L. (2019b). Organizational evolution and the Olympic Games: The case of sport climbing. *Sport in Society*, 22(10), pp. 1674–1690.
Bingham, T. and Walters, G. (2013). Financial sustainability within UK charities: Community sport trusts and corporate social responsibility partnerships. *VOLUNTAS: International Journal of Voluntary and Nonprofit Organizations*, 24(3), pp. 606–629.
Brown, C. and Pappous, A. (2018). The organisational performance of national disability sport organisations during a time of austerity: A resource dependence theory perspective. *International Journal of Sport Policy and Politics*, 10(1), pp. 63–78.
Butler, N. (2017). *New logo launched by GAISF to symbolise break with past.* Lausanne: GAISF.
Chappelet, J-L. (2008). *The international Olympic committee and the Olympic system: The governance of world sport.* Oxford: Routledge.
Chappelet, J-L. (2014). Managing the size of the Olympic Games. *Sport in Society*, 17(5), pp. 581–592.
Chappelet, J-L. (2015). The Olympic fight against match-fixing. *Sport in Society*, 18(10), pp. 1260–1272.
Chappelet, J-L. (2016). From Olympic administration to Olympic governance. *Sport in Society*, 19(6), pp. 739–751.
Chappelet, J-L. (2018). Juan Antonio Samaranch: From Barcelona Elite to the Olympic world. In: E. Bayle and P. Clastres, eds., *Global sport leaders.* New York: Springer, pp. 191–215.
Chappelet, J-L. (2019). Towards a global framework to fight the dark side of sport. In: J. Krieger and S. Wassong, eds., *Darks sides of sport.* Champaign, IL: Common Ground Research Networks, pp. 5–16.
Chappelet, J-L. and Mrkonjic, M. (2013). *Basic indicators for better governance in international sport (BIBGIS): An assessment tool for international sport governing bodies.* Working paper de l'IDHEAP, IDHEAP, (1/2013), p. 54.
Cunliffe, A.L. (2008). *Organization theory.* Thousand Oaks, CA: Sage.
Davis, G.F. and Cobb, A.J. (2010). Resource dependence theory: Past and future. In: C.B. Schoonhoven and F. Dobbin, eds., *Stanford's organization theory renaissance, 1970–2000.* Bingley, UK: Emerald Group Publishing Limited, pp. 21–42.
DiMaggio, P. and Powell, W.W. (1983). The iron cage revisited: Collective rationality and institutional isomorphism in organizational fields. *American Sociological Review*, 48(2), pp. 147–160.
Dittmore, S., Mahony, D., Andrew, D.P. and Hums, M.A. (2009). Examining fairness perceptions of financial resource allocations in US Olympic sport. *Journal of Sport Management*, 23(4), pp. 429–456.
ESPN. (2013). Wrestling reinstated for 2020 games. *ESPN.*
Ferrand, A., Chappelet, J-L. and Séguin, B. (2012). *Olympic marketing.* London: Routledge.
Funk, D.C., Pizzo, A.D. and Baker, B.J. (2018). eSport management: Embracing eSport education and research opportunities. *Sport Management Review*, 21(1), pp. 7–13.
GAISF. (2017). *IOC and GAISF signal new era of co-operation and alignment with the memorandum of understanding.*
GamesBids. (2015a). *Federations' Chief Vizer blasts bach over agenda 2020, host city selection and his dysfunctional.* Lausanne: IOC.
GamesBids. (2015b). *Full text of the opening address of SportAccord President Marius L. Vizer at the SportAccord convention.*
GamesBids. (2015c). *SportAccord counts its losses after chief's attack on Olympics backfires.*
Geeraert, A., Alm, J. and Groll, M. (2014). Good governance in international sport organizations: An analysis of the 35 Olympic sport governing bodies. *International Journal of Sport Policy and Politics*, 6(3), pp. 281–306.
Girginov, V. (2011). Governance of the London 2012 Olympic Games legacy. *International Review for the Sociology of Sport*, 47(5), pp. 543–558.
Greene, B. (2012). What changed the Olympics forever. *CNN.*
Hallmann, K. and Giel, T. (2018). eSports – Competitive sports or recreational activity? *Sport Management Review*, 21(1), pp. 14–20.
Heere, B. (2018). Embracing the sportification of society: Defining e-sports through a polymorphic view on sport. *Sport Management Review*, 21(1), pp. 21–24.
IOC. (1964). *Eligibility rules of the International Olympic Committee.* Lausanne: IOC.
IOC. (2013). *Recognition procedure.* Lausanne: IOC.
IOC. (2014a). *Olympic Agenda 2020.* Lausanne: IOC.
IOC. (2014b). *Olympic Agenda 2020 127th IOC session.* Lausanne: IOC.

IOC. (2016). *Olympic Games Tokyo 2020. Tokyo 2020 OCOG proposal on new sports*. Lausanne: IOC.
IOC. (2017a). *Factsheet – The programme of the games of the Olympiad*. Lausanne: IOC.
IOC. (2017b). *IOC and Global association of international sports federations (GAISF) sign ground-breaking MOU*. Lausanne: IOC.
IOC. (2018a). *IOC Annual Report 2018*. Lausanne: IOC.
IOC. (2018b). *The new norm: It's a games changer*. Lausanne: IOC.
IOC. (2019a). *Olympic charter*. Lausanne: IOC.
IOC. (2019b). *Olympic marketing fact file 2019 edition*. Lausanne: IOC.
IOC. (2019c). *VII Olympic Congress – Lausanne 1921*. Lausanne: IOC.
Jones, G.J., Edwards, M., Bocarro, J.N., Bunds, K.S. and Smith, J.W. (2017). Collaborative advantages: The role of interorganizational partnerships for youth sport nonprofit organizations. *Journal of Sport Management*, 31(2), pp. 148–160.
Lange, P., Driessen, P.P., Sauer, A., Bornemann, B. and Burger, P. (2013). Governing towards sustainability – Conceptualizing modes of governance. *Journal of Environmental Policy & Planning*, 15(3), pp. 403–425.
Leopkey, B. and Parent, M.M. (2017). The governance of Olympic legacy: Process, actors and mechanisms. *Leisure Studies*, 36(3), pp. 438–451.
Llewellyn, M.P. and Lake, R.J. (2017). 'The old days of amateurism are over': The Samaranch revolution and the return of Olympic tennis. *Sport in History*, 37(4), pp. 423–447.
MacAloon, J.J. (2016). Agenda 2020 and the Olympic movement. *Sport in Society*, 19(6), pp. 767–785.
Meyer, J.W. and Rowan, B. (1977). Institutionalized organizations: Formal structure as myth and ceremony. *American Journal of Sociology*, 83(2), pp. 340–363.
Miller, S. (2011). Good governance and anti-doping policy: An international federation view. *International Journal of Sport Policy and Politics*, 3(2), pp. 279–288.
Misener, K. and Doherty, A. (2013). Understanding capacity through the processes and outcomes of interorganizational relationships in nonprofit community sport organizations. *Sport Management Review*, 16(2), pp. 135–147.
Morgan, L. (2017). *SportAccord changes name to Global Association of International Sports Federations*. Lausanne: GAISF.
Morgan, L. (2019). *IOC to distribute $430 million to International Federations and NOCs following Pyeongchang 2018*.
Newzoo. (2019). *Newzoo global esports market report 2019 Version*. Lausanne: GAISF.
OCA. (2020, 8 April).*Asian Summer Games*. Olympic Council of Asia. Available at: https://www.ocasia.org/Game/GameDetailsByGameID?q=BrMykyrnI530p/vsnX+Z8vJNguoh97VGtnRABxESGMU–
Patterson, D. and Parent, M.M. (2017). The (un) importance of existing: Community sport organizations' environmental negotiation. *Sport in Society*, 20(1), pp. 84–106.
Pfeffer, J. and Salancik, G.R. (1978). *The external control of organizations: A resource dependence approach*. New York: Harper and Row Publishers.
Sotiriadou, P. and Wicker, P. (2013). Community sports clubs' responses to institutional and resource dependence pressures for government grants. *Annals of Leisure Research*, 16(4), pp. 297–314.
SportAccord. (2020, 8 April). *Who we are*. SportAccord. Available at: https://www.sportaccord.sport/who-we-are.
Stokvis, R. (2000). Globalization, commercialization and individualization: Conflicts and changes in elite athletics. *Culture, Sport Society*, 3(1), pp. 22–34.
Stotlar, D.K. (2005). *Developing successful sport sponsorship plans*. 2nd ed. Morgantown, WV: Fitness Information Technology.
Strittmatter, A-M., Kilvinger, B., Bodemar, A., Skille, E.Å. and Kurscheidt, M. (2019). Dual governance structures in action sports: Institutionalization processes of professional snowboarding revisited. *Sport in Society*, 22(10), pp. 1655–1673.
Teetzel, S. (2011). Rules and reform: Eligibility, gender differences, and the Olympic Games. *Sport in Society*, 14(3), pp. 386–398.
Theodoraki, E. (2007). *Olympic event organization*. London: Butterworth-Heinemann.
Thorpe, H. and Wheaton, B. (2011). 'Generation X Games', action sports and the Olympic movement: Understanding the cultural politics of incorporation. *Sociology*, 45(5), pp. 830–847.
Ulrich, D. and Barney, J.B. (1984). Perspectives in organizations: Resource dependence, efficiency, and population. *Academy of Management Review*, 9(3), pp. 471–481.
Wagg, S. (2012). Tilting at windmills? Olympic politics and the spectre of amateurism. In: *The Palgrave handbook of Olympic studies*. New York: Springer, pp. 321–336.

Walker, C.M. and Hayton, J.W. (2017). Navigating austerity: Balancing 'desirability with viability' in a third sector disability sports organisation. *European Sport Management Quarterly*, 17(1), pp. 98–116.
Washington, M. and Patterson, K.D. (2011). Hostile takeover or joint venture: Connections between institutional theory and sport management research. *Sport Management Review*, 14(1), pp. 1–12.
Wenn, S. (2012). Rivals and revolutionaries: Avery Brundage, the marquess of Exeter and Olympic television revenue. *Sport in History*, 32(2), pp. 257–278.

27

The governance of the Court of Arbitration for Sport

Jean-Loup Chappelet

Introduction

The idea for setting up a Court of Arbitration for Sport (CAS) was first put forward in the early 1980s by Keba Mbaye, then the IOC member for Senegal and a judge at the International Court of Justice at The Hague (the UN's main judicial organ). Mbaye's proposal was made in response to International Olympic Committee (IOC) President Juan Antonio Samaranch's desire to create a way of settling sporting disputes that would be quicker and cheaper than going through national civil courts. As well as being considered slow, expensive, and unfamiliar with the particularities of sport, the transnational nature of sport meant that national courts were often inappropriate places for resolving sporting disputes as parties would typically belong to different jurisdictions. Mbaye's solution was to set up a system of arbitration, an internationally recognized technique that was already being used in other transnational domains, most notably international trade, to adjudicate disputes between parties belonging to different jurisdictions. Acting on Mbaye's proposal, the IOC agreed on the statutes for CAS in 1983, allowing the court to begin operations in 1984 with Mbaye as its first president. In fact, the creation of CAS could not have been more timely for the Olympic and Sports movement, which was becoming alarmed by the increasing tendency for dissatisfied parties (particularly athletes) to challenge the legality of its rules and decisions. For example, the years preceding the creation of the CAS had seen rulings by two sport federations (football, Dona-Mantero case in 1976; cycling, Walrave and Koch case in 1974) overturned by the European Court of Justice (formerly the Court of Justice of the European Communities and now known as the Court of Justice of the European Union) and a Taiwanese IOC member had filed a lawsuit against the IOC in a Lausanne court (location of the IOC's headquarters) in 1979.

In the three-and-a-half decades since its foundation, the CAS has become a key institution for ensuring the integrity and regulation of the world's sport organizations and the Olympic movement (Chappelet, 2016, p. 54). It has been recognized as a true arbitration tribunal by the supreme courts of both Switzerland and Germany (see later), and has been designated the highest body of appeal by most international sport federations (IFs), including the IFs for all Olympic and many aspiring Olympic sports, the IOC, the International Paralympic Committee (IPC), the World Anti-Doping Agency (WADA, since 2003), the Fédération Internationale de Football Association (FIFA, since 2002), the International Association of Athletics Federations (IAAF, since 2001), and the Union of European Football Associations (UEFA). Most importantly, it has created a body of jurisprudence for sports disputes and contributed to the harmonization and evolution of sport organizations' sporting rules so they comply with basic principles of justice, such as the right to be heard and the proportionality of punishment. This has led to the formation of what is generally known as the *lex sportiva*, a compendium of transnational sporting rules for IFs and arbitrational jurisprudence arising from decisions (known as 'awards') made by the CAS over the years. Many sports disputes end up in front of the CAS, whose decisions are generally accepted as final by the parties involved, especially in cases concerning the integrity of sports administrators (e.g. the CAS reduced from six years to four years the suspension imposed on UEFA's former president, Michel Platini, in the wake of the "FIFA scandal" in 2015–2016).

Despite being rooted in the Olympic and world sport system, the CAS and the way it operates have not always been well understood. In order to help remedy this situation, this chapter provides an overview of the CAS's governance and suggests possible ways of improving it. The concept of governance was constructed in the 1990s by scholars investigating the operating modes that sectors combining public and private actions were adopting in order to avoid intrusive regulation by public entities, the state, or the courts (e.g. Kooiman, 1993; Leftwich, 1994; Rhodes, 1996) – what Rosenau and Czempiel (1992) referred to as "Governance without government".

This chapter is structured as follows. First, we describe a practical, hierarchical model of governance that goes beyond the internal day-to-day management of organizations. Systematically applying this model to the CAS provides a clear overview of the court governance (which is done in the third section) and reveals a number of issues that could be explored in order to improve this governance. The fourth section describes these issues, which are put forward for discussion within the CAS and beyond. The conclusion highlights the importance of continually improving the CAS's governance and thereby ensuring the continued legitimacy of "sports justice" in the eyes of all its stakeholders.

A practical model of governance

In a famous paper published in 1996, Rhodes argued that the word governance had too many meanings (he listed six) to be useful. Nevertheless, the term, if not all its possible meanings, has flourished to such an extent that it is now part of the everyday lexicon. Governance first became an important issue in the world of sport in 1999, when the so-called Salt Lake City scandal (Wenn, Barney and Martyn, 2011) forced the IOC to reform its structure and introduce major changes to the Olympic Charter. These reforms included measures to improve the organization's governance, such as setting an age limit for IOC members (70 years old), restricting presidential terms of office to a maximum of 12 years, introducing a Code of Ethics to be overseen by an Ethics Commission, and setting up a nominations commission (now known as the Members Election Commission). In 2009 the IOC adopted its "Basic Universal Principles of Good Governance of the Olympic and Sports Movement" (IOC, 2008), generally referred to as the BUPs, and used its Code of Ethics to make them obligatory within the Olympic movement. In 2015, following scandals within the IFs for football (FIFA) and athletics (IAAF), the IOC issued a declaration on "good governance in sport and the protection of clean athletes". It also welcomed the decision by the Association of Summer Olympic International Federations (ASOIF) to set up a working group on the governance of sport in order to evaluate the governance of its members and help them improve it (IOC, 2015).

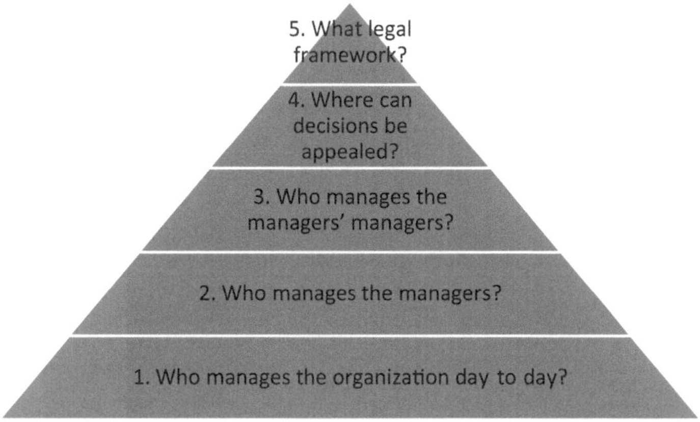

Figure 27.1 The five questions associated with Pérez's five levels of governance

Source: Author adapted from Pérez (2003)

Figure 27.2 Pérez's model applied to the IOC

Source: Author

Beyond Rhodes's and other authors' theoretical approaches, a practical approach to analyzing governance is provided by Pérez's hierarchical model, which divides governance into five levels, from day-to-day management to the legal framework within which an organization operates (Pérez, 2003). Although this model was conceived in relation to the corporate world, it provides an excellent template for examining the structural governance of sport and its organizations. Pérez drew up his model to answer five fundamental questions about an organization's operating mode and structures (Figure 27.1).

Figure 27.2 shows the answers to these questions in relation to the IOC, following the reforms introduced in 1999 in the wake of the Salt Lake City scandal (for more details, see Chappelet, 2012). Under the Olympic Charter (rule 61), appeals against decisions made by the

IOC and its Executive Board can be taken to the CAS, but only in "certain cases" (not specified). However, the IOC explicitly designates the CAS as the sole body of appeal in the case of disputes between the IOC and an Olympic host city or its National Olympic Committee (NOC) (article 51.2 HCC, 2016). What is more, Olympic Games entry forms and the byelaws to rule 44 of the Olympic Charter stipulate that athletes and officials participating in the Olympic Games must submit "Olympic disputes" to the CAS. All the IFs that recognize the CAS have included a similar obligation for their competitions, notably in the case of disciplinary sanctions. Nevertheless, the CAS has overturned or modified numerous decisions made by sport's governing bodies. For example, the CAS found against the IOC in a case brought by Canadian snowboarder Ross Rebagliati in 1998, and it suspended the IAAF's rules on hyperandrogenism (athletes recognized as female but who have naturally high testosterone levels) following the Dutee Chand case in 2015, an issue not yet resolved in 2020. Another example is the CAS 2018 award cancelling the IOC's doping bans on 28 Russian athletes while upholding the bans against 11 other Russian athletes a few days before the start of the PyeongChang Olympic Winter Games 2018 (Perez-Peña and Panja, 2018).

In the case of the IOC, levels 1 to 3 of Pérez's model are comprised almost entirely of structures and rules put in place by the IOC itself through its statutes, whereas levels 4 and 5 involve external structures and require state intervention in the form of national and sometimes international laws. The IOC, like many other international sport organizations, most of which are associations set up under articles 60–79 of the Swiss Civil Code, is subject to Swiss law. In contrast, the CAS was set up as an arbitration tribunal under chapter 12 of Switzerland's Federal Act on Private International Law (LDIP in the French acronym: Loi fédérale sur le droit international public). Olympic sport organizations welcome such cooperation with governments (and their laws) and accept the need to practice "good governance" (see, for example, point 7 of the BUPs) in exchange for maintaining their autonomy: they call this attitude "responsible autonomy" or, in other words, a sport organization deserves autonomy if it does "good governance".

International law applicable to sport is still in its infancy. To date, it covers just four areas, each of which is the subject of an international treaty:

- Spectator violence and misbehavior (Council of Europe, 1985, 2016);
- Corruption (not only in sport) (UN, 2003);
- Doping in Sport (UNESCO, 2005);
- Manipulation of sports competitions (Council of Europe, 2014).

The Council of Europe's 2014 Convention on the Manipulation of Sports Competitions and 2016 Convention on an Integrated Safety, Security and Service Approach at Football Matches and Other Sports Events, which builds on the 1985 Convention on Spectator Violence and Misbehavior, have now (in 2020) been ratified. The 2005 UNESCO Convention on Doping in Sport and the 2003 UN Convention Against Corruption have also been ratified by many countries and therefore incorporated into their national legislation. Countries which ratify the Convention Against Corruption (public and private, passive or active) are required to criminalize corrupt practices, such as bribery, influence peddling, fraud, and money laundering, if these practices are not already criminal offenses under existing national laws. Other conventions against corruption, such as those drawn up by the Council of Europe and the Organization for Economic Cooperation and Development (OECD), may also apply to sport cases.

Moreover, judicial authorities are increasingly using national laws to sanction misconduct in sport. As noted previously, many sport organizations are subject to Swiss law, with the result that some have felt the attentions of Switzerland's civil and criminal prosecutors (FIFA affairs, see Chappelet, 2010). However, such actions are not restricted to Switzerland. For example, in 2016 France's Financial Prosecutor's Office opened an inquiry into a former IAAF President, and Brazilian prosecutors carried out investigations into allegations of ticket-touting by an IOC member and corruption by the president and director general of the Rio 2006 organizing committee (who all deny the accusations). Some countries, notably Germany, Austria, France, Italy, and Kenya, have made doping by athletes a criminal offense (trafficking in performance-enhancing drugs is a criminal offense in most countries).

However, the most notable development has been the United States justice system's increased willingness to police international sport. High-profile examples of this include the US Attorney General asking the Swiss authorities in 2016 to arrest 12 FIFA members of its executice committee for extradition to the United States, and an investigation by a New York district prosecutor into doping at the 2014 Winter Olympics in Sochi, Russia. Such actions are made possible by US laws such as the Racketeer Influenced and Corrupt Organization (RICO) Act and the Foreign Corrupt Practices Act (FCPA), which extend US jurisdiction beyond the United States' geographical borders (Henning, 2016; Lipschutz, 2009). The Rodchenkov Act discussed in the US Congress in 2020 would criminalize doping and give American prosecutors unprecedented authority over global sport.

Pérez's model applied to the CAS

Applying Pérez's model to the CAS (see Figure 27.3) provides a systematic overview of how the tribunal functions (by level); it identifies its weak points and highlights the role of the International Council of Arbitration for Sport (ICAS). It helps us understand how the CAS complex regime, mixing public and private law, functions.

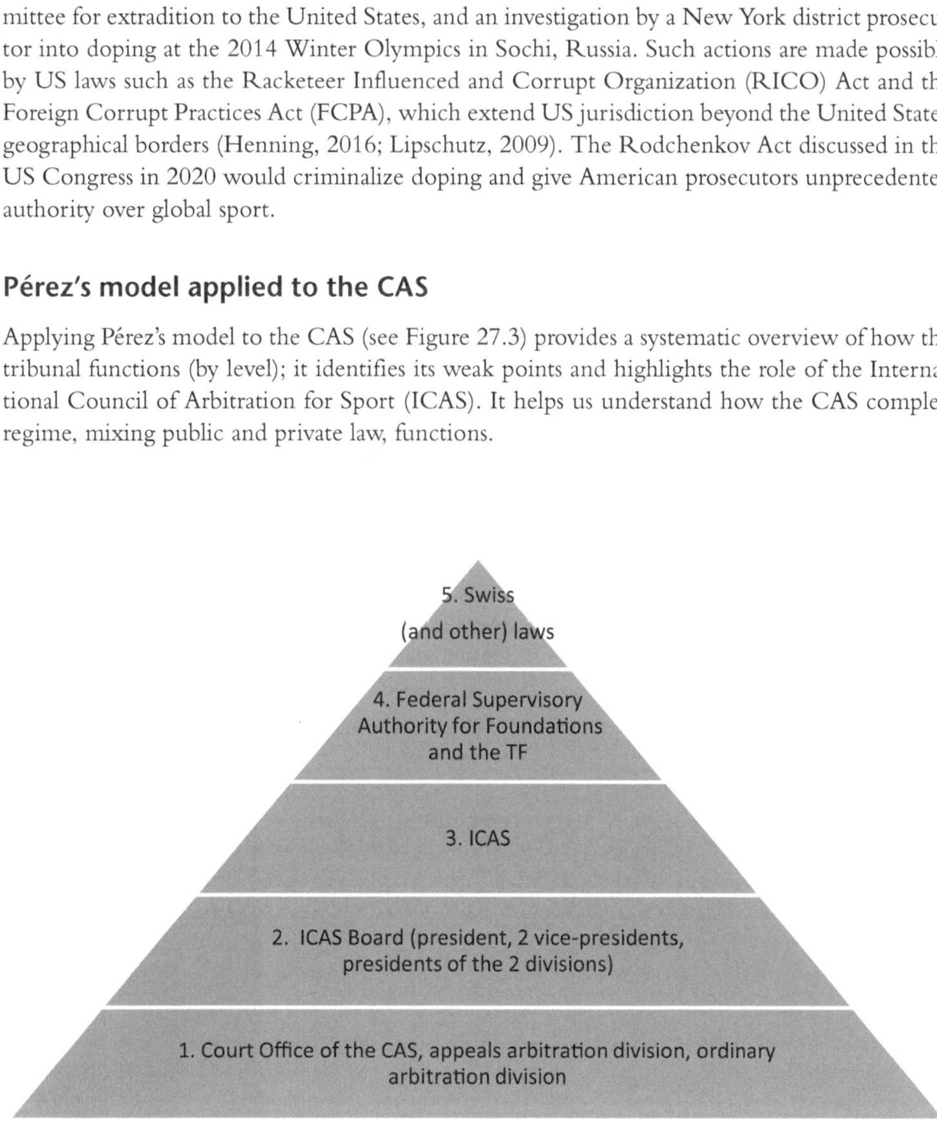

Figure 27.3 The five levels of governance within the CAS

Source: Author

The analysis of each level will provide us with suggestions (in the next section) on how to improve CAS or further develop its structure and organization.

Pérez's first level (Who manages the organization day-to-day?) is composed of the CAS's Court Office, which, following a current trend in justice-system management research, can be considered the CAS's 'management' (Lienhard, Kettinger and Emery, 2016). It consists of a permanent secretary general, a deputy secretary general, a financial director, 11 councilors (all legal experts), and secretaries. The councilors can be considered 'managers' because they are responsible for the day-to-day organization of the numerous procedures submitted to the CAS. They are supervised by the secretary general, who is a sort of chief executive officer (CEO). In addition, the CAS has three divisions to which the different types of dispute it is asked to arbitrate are assigned. As its name suggests, the Appeals Arbitration Division deals with appeals against disciplinary sanctions handed down by sport organizations (once the organization's internal appeals procedures have been exhausted). The Ordinary Arbitration Division hears all the other cases accepted by the CAS, except doping disputes. An Anti-Doping Division was added in 2019.

Neither division has permanent, salaried arbitrators. Instead, they call upon arbitrators from pre-established lists (see later discussion), as and when required. These arbitrators receive a fee of CHF300 to 500 (in 2020) for each hour they work. There are four types of dispute-resolution procedure: appeal, ordinary, mediation, and ad hoc. (Ad hoc divisions are set up on site during major events, such as the Olympic Games, so any disputes that arise can be resolved quickly. A separate ad hoc division to adjudicate cases of doping was set up for the first time at the 2016 Rio Olympics.) Disputes brought before the CAS are processed according to a set of Procedural Rules. Mediation cases are governed by a separate set of rules. The CAS registered almost 600 procedures in 2016, and has processed more than 5,000 procedures since its foundation (CAS, 2017). Most procedures are appeals (458 appeals procedures in 2016) and are related to cases of doping. This is likely to continue given the IOC's desire to make the CAS the primary adjudicator in all doping cases (through new Anti-Doping Division which started operations in 2019). The CAS's non-binding mediation service is rarely used, undoubtedly because it is not obligatory to first go through a mediation process (in contrast to the arbitration procedure introduced by France's NOC, in which cases must first go to mediation). Ordinary procedures, of which there were 100 in 2016, concern contractual and commercial relationships. The ad hoc divisions at the 2016 Rio Olympics heard 41 cases (CAS, 2017). More recent statistics are not publicly available.

As well as its headquarters in Lausanne, the CAS has decentralized offices in New York and Sydney, and alternative hearing centres in Abu Dhabi, Kuala Lumpur, Cairo, and Shanghai. As noted, temporary offices, including a specific division for processing doping cases (since Rio 2016), are set up for major competitions, most notably the Olympic Games (since Atlanta 1996). The CAS's website provides a schedule of arbitration costs, which consist of a fixed Court Office fee (currently CHF1,000), an administration fee that varies according to the size of the disputed sum (from CHF100 to CHF25,000), and the arbitrators' costs and fees. Under certain circumstances, and on request from the parties, the ICAS may provide financial aid to cover part of the parties' costs.

The second level of Pérez's model (Who manages the managers?) consists of the ICAS Board, whereas the third level (Who manages the managers' managers?) consists of the full ICAS (International Council of Arbitration for Sport). The ICAS was founded in Paris as a Swiss foundation in 1994, the IOC's centenary year, by the IOC, the Association of National Olympic Committees (ANOC), and the umbrella associations for the IFs of Summer and Winter Olympic sports (ASOIF and AIOWF). Together, these organizations provide about two-thirds of the ICAS's (and, therefore, of the CAS's) funding. In 2016, the IOC, ANOC, and ASOIF/AIOWF each provided 21% of the ICAS/CAS's funding (Sternheimer, 2016); however, it should be remembered that the ANOC, ASOIF, and AIOWF are mostly funded by the IOC. The ICAS obtains the remaining third of its budget from the fees paid by the parties whose cases are heard by the CAS.

The ICAS was created in 1994, in response to remarks about the CAS's independence by Switzerland's supreme court, the Tribunal Fédéral, in its judgment on a case brought before it by horse rider Elmar Gundel. Gundel had challenged CAS's decision concerning his appeal against a doping sanction imposed by the International Equestrian Federation (FEI), claiming that the CAS was not independent from sport's governing bodies. Although the Tribunal Fédéral rejected Gundel's appeal, ruling that the CAS was independent from the FEI, the judges noted that the IOC's close links with the CAS might have prevented them reaching a fair decision if the case had involved the IOC directly (Tribunal Fédéral 1993). In fact, at that time the IOC not only financed the CAS, it also provided its premises and appointed its arbitrators. The Tribunal Fédéral's remark led the CAS's founders to create the ICAS, approving its statutes in what became known as the "Paris Agreement". These statutes, which also cover the CAS, are known as the "Code of Sports-Related Arbitration" and have been updated regularly since they first came into force, in 1994. A set of Procedural Rules, approved by the ICAS, supplements the Code.

The ICAS Board is a subset of the ICAS, consisting of five of its 20 members: ICAS's president and two vice-presidents, plus the president of the Ordinary Arbitration Division, and the president of the Appeals Arbitration Division. The CAS's secretary general is also the Board's secretary, but is not a voting member of the Board. ICAS's president, who is also the president of the CAS, oversees the application of the Code. The CAS provides the infrastructure needed to resolve, by arbitration, the sporting disputes submitted to it. Hence, the president fulfills the role of chairman (of the board), distinct from the CEO (secretary general), quite rightly from a governance point of view.

All 20 members of the ICAS are appointed for renewable periods of four years as follows: the IOC appoints four members, the Olympic IFs appoint four members (three for the ASOIF and one for the AIOWF), the ANOC appoints four members; these first 12 members appoint a further four members, as a way of "safeguarding the interests of the athletes" (article S4 of the Code), and the first 16 members appoint the remaining four members from among personalities independent of the IOC, ANOC, ASOIF, and AIOWF.

The ICAS has numerous attributions (article S6 of the Code), but many of these attributions can be (and often are) delegated to the Board. Attributions that cannot be delegated include revising the Code (any revisions to the Code must be approved by at least two-thirds of the ICAS's members), electing ICAS's president and vice-presidents, and the presidents of the CAS's divisions, and approving the CAS's budget and accounts, which are prepared by the Court Office and submitted to the Board. The ICAS meets at least once a year.

One of the ICAS's main responsibilities is to appoint general or football-specific arbitrators and mediators. Potential arbitrators are nominated by the Board and are appointed for terms of four years, renewable without limit. The ICAS can also remove arbitrators from the CAS's lists. In 2020, the CAS's lists (published on its website) included 393 general arbitrators from more than 95 countries, 104 football arbitrators, and 58 mediators. For each procedure, three arbitrators are chosen from these lists by the parties involved: one party chooses the first arbitrator, the other party chooses a second arbitrator, and the first two arbitrators choose the president of the panel by mutual agreement. If mutual agreement is not reached within a set time limit, the president of the relevant division appoints the president of the panel. The president of the panel can be recused by the ICAS or must recuse himself/herself if legitimate doubts could be raised about his/her independence (article S21 of the Code). The choice of arbirtrators by the parties is crucial. Following their appointment, arbitrators and mediators must sign a declaration of impartiality and independence. As a further measure to avoid accusations of conflicts of interest, a new rule added to the Code excludes any person who is acting as counsel for a party before the CAS from serving as an arbitrator (article S18 of the Code). Similarly, members of the ICAS cannot be arbitrators (article S5). On the other hand, some arbitrators are selected much more frequently than others and therefore have much more information than other arbitrators or potential parties. A system of financial aid and pro bono legal advice has been recently introduced. The appeals procedure is free, with the exception of a set fee of CHF1,000; however, the parties often incur substantial legal costs. (WADA complained that the appeal by the cyclist Floyd Landis in 2007–2008 cost it more than €840,000.) Sometimes, upon its division president, the CAS appoints a one-member only panel (instead of three).

The 1994 Paris Agreement (Reeb, 2004, p. 680 and subsequent) created the ICAS as a foundation established under Swiss law (articles 80–89a of the Swiss Civil Code). All important foundations registered in Switzerland are monitored by the Federal Supervisory Authority for Foundations, a public body within the Federal Department (ministry) of Home Affairs, which checks that a foundation's assets are used for their declared purpose and that any modifications to its statutes (here the Code) comply with Swiss law. Hence, the Federal Supervisory Authority, together with the Tribunal Fédéral, constitutes the fourth level in Pérez's model (Where can decisions be appealed?). This legal arrangement is subject to the Federal Act on International Private Law (LDIP), which governs arbitration in Switzerland. More specifically, cases heard by the CAS are subject to "Chapter 12 International Arbitration" (articles 176 to 194) of the LDIP, unless both parties are domiciled in Switzerland (such cases fall within the jurisdiction of Switzerland's civil courts). The CAS's awards can be appealed to the Tribunal Fédéral, but only in certain circumstances set down in the LDIP, most notably irregularities in the designation of the arbitration panel, failure to respect procedures, or an award that is "incompatible with Swiss public policy". The CAS's decisions are applicable in every country that has ratified the 1958 New York Convention on the Recognition and Enforcement of Foreign Arbitral Awards (over 125 countries in 2017, with the exception of certain African countries) and every sport/IF which has recognized CAS in its statutes.

Some of the CAS's awards have been appealed to the Tribunal Fédéral by one of the parties. The Gundel case led to the creation of the ICAS and major reforms to the CAS's statutes. In 2010, German speed skater Claudia Pechstein filed an appeal with the Tribunal Fédéral in which she contested the CAS's independence from the concerned IF. The Tribunal Fédéral rejected her appeal, and she took her case to the German courts over abuse of dominant position by the IF, where her arguments were eventually rejected by Germany's Federal court despite an initial ruling in her favor by a Bavarian court. If Germany's highest civil court had found in Pechstein's favor, this decision would have called into question the entire edifice patiently constructed by the CAS and the ICAS. A further appeal by the athlete to the European Court of Human Rights in Strasbourg was dimissed in 2019 but recommends public hearings. In 2019, another appeal to the German Constitutional Court is pending (Reinholz, 2019).

Level 5 of Pérez's model (What legal frameworks?) comprises all Swiss legislation relating to what Pérez calls 'metagovernance', including the previously mentioned 1987 Federal Act on Private International Law (LDIP) and some international legislation such as the 1958 New York Convention (ratified by Switzerland). However, the parties in a dispute may, by common accord, choose to have their case heard under a law other than Swiss law, which is the default law for CAS arbitration procedures. Similarly, the parties may agree to the case being heard in a language other than one of the CAS's two default languages, English and French. Furthermore, if there is no contractual clause obliging the parties to accept arbitration by the CAS, they may submit their dispute to the civil courts in their country of residence or to any other arbitrational authority (including the CAS by later agreement). However, all international sport federations currently oblige their athletes to accept arbitration by CAS when they sign their entry form for a competition.

In 2019, the LDIP has been revised in order to maintain Switzerland as a major, attractive centre for arbitration. Several countries, including Germany, Canada, France, New Zealand, and the United Kingdom, have national courts of arbitration for sport that are not affiliated to the CAS. (The CAS can also accept cases in which both parties are Swiss if they are not resident of the same canton.) The obligation for athletes to submit disputes to the CAS, imposed by many IFs and sports competitions, has been judged to be legally acceptable and not to be an abuse of their dominant position in the market (judgment in the Pechstein case).

All criminal cases are heard in the relevant national courts (as CAS only deals with civil cases). For example, FIFA's former president Sepp Blatter will face criminal proceedings in Switzerland over allegations of mismanagement and misappropriation of funds (articles 138 and 158 of Switzerland's criminal code). Revelations of corruption within FIFA had already led to Blatter being banned by FIFA from all footballing activities for eight years, later reduced to six years (sporting sanction). Blatter's appeal to the CAS was rejected but he decided not to take his case to the Tribunal Fédéral.

Issues to explore in order to improve the CAS governance

A striking feature of the first level of governance is the small size of the CAS's day-to-day management team, as the Court Office employs just 15 people, plus secretaries, to deal with more than 600 procedures a year (in 2016). Of course, arbitrators, once appointed, run their procedures themselves, but the Court Office still has to supervise these procedures (most of which take around six to 12 months), organize hearings (which are held in Lausanne, unless the parties agree otherwise), slightly copyedit and publish certain awards, etc. Nevertheless, the Court Office has increased in size over the years, as when the CAS was founded it had just one, part-time, secretary general. The Court Office currently occupies an entire mansion in Lausanne (known as the "Château de Béthusy"), but it is due to move into larger premises in the Palais de Beaulieu (Lausanne's conference centre). Because the Court Office constitutes the entire first level of Pérez's model (2003), its modest size could affect CAS's award delays and quality as the Court Office is clearly overburdened. Statistics on how long procedures take are needed in order to determine to what extent this is the case.

The biggest hurdle to expanding the Court Office would probably be cost, but data on the CAS's finances is difficult to obtain because the CAS does not publish an annual report, which is clearly not a good example of transparency: a basic feature of organizational governance. According to the IOC Annual Report of 2015, the IOC allocated US$7,931,000 to the ICAS/CAS in 2015 and US$8,275,000 in 2014 (IOC, 2015, p. 170). Given that this sum is supposed to cover 21% of the CAS's budget (Sternheimer, 2016), its total budget for 2016 can be estimated to have been approximately US$38 million. All the CAS's awards since 1986, except confidential awards (mostly arising from ordinary procedures), have been added to a database consultable via the CAS website. Publishing these awards has greatly increased the court's transparency, which is one of the pillars of organizational governance (see, for example, the fourth pillar of the BUPs – Basic Universal Principles of Good Governance in the Olympic and Sport Movement).

The CAS also publishes useful commentaries on cases and digests of awards (see, for example, Mavromati and Reeb, 2015).

ICAS's five-member Board plays a fundamental role at level 2 because its five members draw up draft decisions, which are then presented to the full ICAS for approval (level 3). The president of the Appeals Arbitration Division has a particularly heavy workload, as this division processes many of the CAS's procedures (this might change with the new Anti-Doping Division). It is the division president who chooses the president of each arbitration panel (under article R54 of the Procedural Rules, each of the parties chooses one of the other arbitrators from the CAS's list of arbitrators). Consequently, the division president can influence decisions through his/her choice of arbitrators. In 2020, the president of the Appeals Arbitration Division is Mrs. Corinne Schmidhauser, an attorney and former ski racer, and the president of Antidoping Switzerland, who took over from Thomas Bach in 2013, when he was elected president of the IOC. None of the ICAS's members, including the members of the Board, receive a salary from the CAS, but they probably receive some sort of remuneration and, of course, the CAS covers their expenses. The CAS's remuneration policy is not made public, which questions its transparency and accountability.

Level 3 consists of the 20 members of the ICAS, nine of whom are women in 2020 (a rare example of near gender parity). Two members of the ICAS are also members of the IOC, including its current president, Mr. John Coates from Australia, who was a vice-president of the IOC (2013–2017). Although ICAS membership has been recently reviewed, its members are still often closely associated with organizations within the Olympic movement, and we do not know which founding organization proposed each ICAS member. In addition to approving any modifications to the Code (two-thirds majority required), the ICAS's main roles are to appoint the CAS's arbitrators, the members of its Board, and its secretary general. The ICAS can also recuse arbitrators when required. All appointments are for four years, which is short compared with the usual rules about the immovability of judges. However, in contrast to many other sport organizations, including the IOC, there are no limits on how often terms can be renewed or on the age of appointees. Also unlike the IOC and FIFA, the CAS does not have an ethics commission or rules about conflicts of interest which are now common in many sport-related organizations.

Although the biographies of arbitrators on the CAS's website are very succinct, it can be seen that most arbitrators have close links with the world of sport, especially the IFs and NOCs. In fact, until 2010 these organizations nominated all the CAS's arbitrators. Of course, it is natural, if not essential, for the CAS's arbitrators to be familiar with the specificities of sport. However, the way in which arbitrators are appointed frequently raises questions about their independence from sport organizations (Vaitiekunas, 2014; Duval, 2015), even though this independence has been recognized by the supreme courts of both Switzerland and Germany (Gundel, Lazutina, and Pechstein cases). The ICAS can take steps to minimize this type of criticism by recusing an arbitrator from a procedure (or even removing him/her from the CAS list) if that arbitrator's independence is questioned, for example, by one of the parties in a dispute. Another issue relating to the choice of arbitrators is that many athletes feel they are underrepresented among the arbitrators. However, it is difficult to conceive of a system that would allow athletes to nominate arbitrators with a thorough knowledge of both sport and (sports) law. Organized representation for athletes through 'unions' such as UNI World Athletes, EU Athletes, and FIFPRO, many of which are mono-sport, is yet to receive widespread recognition, especially from sport organizations. The CAS recently began taking steps to increase the number of athletes and women on its lists of arbitrators by organizing free training seminars for, for example, former athletes with legal training.

More generally, greater representation for stakeholders (athletes, sponsors, broadcasters, sports event organizers, governments, etc.) other than traditional sport organizations could help improve the CAS's governance. It would be useful to have more detailed information about the arbitrators available, especially a list of the cases each arbitrator has adjudicated (in order to assess their experience). In fact, many arbitrators never sit on an arbitration panel and are listed merely to demonstrate the CAS's geographical diversity.

Under certain circumstances described in the LDIP, appeals against decisions made by the CAS can be submitted to Switzerland's supreme court, the Tribunal Fédéral (Pérez's level 4). As the guarantor of the country's legal system, it is funded by Swiss tax payers. It is based in Lausanne, which facilitates exchanges with the CAS if necessary. All the Tribunal Fédéral's rulings, including appeals concerning the CAS, are published (www.bger.ch/fr/jurisdiction-recht). A private website run by lawyers provides English translations of opinions issued by the Tribunal Fédéral in the field of international arbitration (www.swissarbitrationdecisions.com). Although the Tribunal Fédéral rejects the vast majority (93%) of appeals against CAS awards (Sternheimer, 2016), it has canceled several awards for a procedural reasons (see Mavromati and Reeb, 2015, pp. 562–600). The most recent award canceled by the Tribunal Fédéral because it was "contrary to public policy" followed an appeal by a Brazilian professional footballer called Matuzalem who had been banned from playing/working for a Spanish club because he was unable/unwilling to pay his former employer the €12 million in compensation set by FIFA (Tribunal Fédéral, 2012). Matuzalem had taken his case to the Tribunal Fédéral after his initial appeal to the CAS had been rejected.

The legal framework governing the CAS's operations is set by Swiss law (level 5 of Pérez's model). Some parties (mostly athletes) have filed appeals with state jurisdictions (German courts, European Court of Human Rights, Court of Justice of the European Union), following unsuccessful arbitration procedures. In addition, some countries have set up national courts of arbitration for sport (Germany, Canada, France, New Zealand, and United Kingdom), thereby creating the risk that the jurisprudence emanating from these courts will differ from the jurisprudence produced by the CAS. Such an eventuality would imperil the harmonization of the jurisprudence developed by the CAS over the years.

Conclusion

This chapter provides a brief overview of the CAS's governance and suggests a number of ways of improving it, taking into account the main precepts of modern governance, especially transparency, independence, and the representation of stakeholders. Stakeholder representation, in terms of the choice of arbitrators, is an especially important issue for the CAS.

Given the current spotlight on organizational governance – the period 2000–2013 saw the publication of more than 30 sets of principles of good governance in sport (Chappelet and Mrkonjic, 2013) – the CAS must ensure its governance is irreproachable and set its sights on achieving ever better governance, rather than just "good governance". Addressing the issues set out in this chapter as soon as possible would help the CAS achieve this and thereby maintain its legitimacy in the eyes of all its stakeholders.

References

CAS. (2017). *Statistiques – Statistics*. Available at: www.tas-cas.org/fileadmin/user_upload/CAS_statistics_2016_.pdf.

Chappelet, J-L. (2010). *L'autonomie du sport en Europe*. Strasbourg: Council of Europe.

Chappelet, J-L. (2012). From daily management to high politics: The governance of the International Olympic Committee. In: L. Robinson et al., eds., *The handbook of international sport management*. London: Routledge, pp. 7–25.
Chappelet, J-L. (2016). *Jeux Olympiques: raviver la flamme*. Lausanne: PPUR, chapter 3.
Chappelet, J-L. and Mrkonjic, M. (2013). *The basic indicators for better governance in international sport (BIBGIS)*. Lausanne: IDHEAP Working Papers.
Council of Europe. (1985). *European convention on spectator violence and misbehaviour at sports events and in particular at football matches*, Aug. Strasbourg: Council of Europe.
Council of Europe. (2014). *Convention on the manipulation of sports competitions*, Sept. Macolin: Council of Europe.
Council of Europe. (2016). *European convention on integrated safety, security and service approach at football matches and other sports events, 218, July*. Saint-Denis, France: Council of Europe.
Duval, A. (2015). *The court of arbitration for sport after Pechstein: Reform or revolution?* Asser International Sports Law Blog.
Federal Court. (1993). Judgment of the Federal Court of 15 Mas. *Official Collection of Federal Court Judgments*, 119 II 271.
HCC. (2016). *Host city contract, principles, games of the XXXIII Olympiad – Candidature process 2024*.
Henning, P.J. (2016). Road map for pursuit of soccer charges. *International New York Times*, p. 14.
IOC. (2008). *Basic universal principles of good governance of the Olympic and sports movement*. Lausanne: IOC.
IOC. (2015). *OC Executive Board adopts declaration on good governance in sport and the protection of clean athletes*. Lausanne: IOC. Press release, Dec. 10.
Kooiman, J., ed. (1993). *Modern governance: New government – Society interactions*. London: Sage.
Leftwich, A. (1994). Governance, the state and the politics of development. *Development and Change*, 25(2).
Lienhard, A., Kettinger, D. and Emery, Y. (2016). What management methods for justice? *Le Temps*.
Lipschutz, R.D. (2009). *The constitution of imperium*. London: Paradigm.
Mavromati, D. and Reeb, M. (2015). *The code of the court of arbitration for sport: Commentary, cases and materials*. The Hague: Kluwer Law International.
Pérez-Peña, R. (2003). *Corporate governance*. Paris: Discovery.
Perez-Peña, R. and Panja, T. (2018). 28 Russian athletes win appeals of doping bans. *The New York Times*.
Reeb, M., ed. (2004). *Digest of CAS awards III 2001–2003*. The Hague: Kluwer Law International.
Reinholz, F. (2019). Latest developments in the Pechstein case. 15 March. *ISLA website*. Available at: www.islasportlawyer.com/latest-developments-pechstein-case-ruling-european-court-human-rights/.
Rhodes, R.A.W. (1996). The new governance: Governing without government. *Political Studies*, 44(4).
Rosenau, J.N. and Czempiel, E-O., eds. (1992). *Governance without government: Order and change in world politics*. Cambridge: Cambridge University Press.
Sternheimer, W. (2016). *Introduction to the Court of Arbitration for Sport (CAS) and its procedures*, presentation in Geneva.
Tribunal Fédéral. (2012). *Francelino da Silva Matuzalem/FIFA: Statutory punishment contrary to public order*.
UN. (2003). *Convention against corruption*, Oct. New York: United Nations Organization.
UNESCO. (2005). *International convention against doping in sport*, Oct. Paris: United Nations Education, Science and Culture Organization.
Vaitiekunas, A. (2014). *The court of arbitration for sport: Law-making and the question of independence*. Bern: Stämpfli.
Wenn, S., Barney, R. and Martyn, S. (2011). *Tarnished rings: The International Olympic Committee and the Salt Lake City bid scandal*. Syracuse: Syracuse University Press.

Part IV

Socio-cultural and political issues of the Olympic and Paralympic Games

Edited by Dikaia Chatziefstathiou

28

Theory and social science-based research in scholarship around the Paralympic Games

Ian Brittain

Introduction

As I enter my twenty-first year of researching and writing about the Paralympic Games and movement it gives me the benefit of having been around to witness the giant strides forward in this field both practically and academically. Therefore, I'd like to start this piece by highlighting a few key points as to why this field has proven so appealing and fulfilling for me. I have met some truly amazing people and witnessed some amazing sport all over the world, but if you really need a good solid career-based reason to become involved in this field, I would confidently say that there is no piece of research that has been done in the field of the Olympic Games or non-disabled sport that cannot be done again with an extra set of interesting issues to throw into the analytical mix. I will return to these issues shortly, but what that means in practical career terms is that the field is wide open for you to make a name for yourself, unlike, say gender and sport where it is far more difficult to carve out a niche for yourself that will get you noticed. There is a growing, but currently still quite small number of researchers who dedicate their time to this field. I have noticed a growing interest particularly amongst students at all levels in carrying out research in this field, particularly for their theses, which bodes well for the future. Interest, however, still lags far behind that taken in the Olympic Games and movement, but as the rather simplistic Boolean search for articles (excluding patents and citations) in Table 28.1 shows there has been a steady increase in the publications with Paralympic Games as their focus. I separated out those that included the words 'Olympic and Paralympic Games' as it is often my experience that with these articles the only real mention of the word 'Paralympic' is in the title, with the article itself focusing largely, and often solely, upon aspects of the Olympic Games. It should also be noted that about 60–70% of articles that appear in these searches with respect to the Paralympic Games originate from the medical or other hard sciences.

I also find that this issue of Olympic and non-disabled sport researchers 'including' the Paralympic Games, but not really taking it that seriously sometimes extends into their use of theory. I am often asked to review journal articles that are clearly written by researchers who have come from an Olympic and non-disabled sport background and who believe that they can simply apply the same theoretical lenses in the Paralympic and disability sport field as they use elsewhere. Although in some cases this might work satisfactorily on one level, it actually

Table 28.1 Results for Google Scholar articles (November 2018)

Date range	*Google Scholar search terms*		
	Olympic Games	*Paralympic Games*	*Olympic and Paralympic Games*
Up to 1988	12,600	8	15
1990–1999	13,800 (1380)	81 (8)	62 (6)
2000–2009	42,700 (4270)	369 (37)	1400 (140)
2010–2018	51,300 (5700)	1800 (200)	7100 (789)
Total	120,400	2258	8577

Note: Numbers in brackets are the average number per year.

means that results are severely lacking in nuance, when in truth the theoretical additions and understanding necessary to achieve this nuanced approach are relatively straight forward to get to grips with and apply.

I am confident that the majority of the key theories used for research in the Olympic and non-disabled sports realm will have been covered in other chapters in this handbook. I will, therefore, constrain myself to introducing those additional theories that will lead to the more nuanced results discussed earlier. These are collectively known as models of disability and can be combined with just about any other theoretical approach to ensure that the 'issue' of disability is included within the analysis of collected data and the explanation of the results. It should be noted that this section is, due to word limitations, necessarily brief. However, the references included in this section should give the reader access to most of the information necessary to gain a good working knowledge of the models themselves and how to apply them.

Normative values

The concept of 'normality' plays an important role in people's views and perceptions of the world around them and the people in it. Most people's concept of normality is historically and culturally located and so a universal concept of normality would appear impossible, as Morris (1993) points out:

> Prejudice is associated with the recognition of difference. In theory 'normal' could be a value-free word to mean merely that which is common, and to be different from normal would not therefore necessarily provoke prejudice. In practice, the word is inherently tied up with ideas about what is right, what is desirable and what belongs.
>
> (*Morris, 1993, p. 101*)

Abberley (1993) argues that the range of disciplines, from medical sociology to social psychology, still retain the notion that disabled people are abnormal, in the sense that their impairment can be explained only in terms of a deviation from a 'standard norm' and that they are the problem for deviating from it. Davis (1997) argues that in order to understand the disabled body, one must return to the concept of the norm, the normal body. He suggests that the majority of writing about people with disabilities has been centred on the disabled person as the object of study, and argues that a focus on the construction of normalcy would be more advantageous. His argument is that the 'problem' is not the person with a disability; the problem is the way that normalcy is constructed to create the 'problem' of the disabled person. It is these two conflicting arguments that form the bases for the medical and social models of disability.

Models of disability

Models of disability form the underpinning building blocks of most of the theoretical approaches taken within the realm of critical disability studies and have been around the best part of forty years. Although a researcher may not directly apply any of these models within their research, understanding these models and their implications for people with disabilities and Paralympic sport are, in my opinion, of fundamental importance no matter what the overarching research approach that is taken. The key arguments for each is briefly laid out next.

Medical model of disability

In brief the medical model of disability posits that any problems that arise as a result of disability are due to the particular physical or intellectual impairment and are, therefore, a problem solely of the individual with the impairment. The impairment is also something that needs to be medically 'cured' in order that the individual fits in with societally accepted norms of function and appearance (Abberley, 1993). The overall result of this is that people with disabilities are perceived by many within non-disabled society as weak, non-contributing members of society who are nothing more than a burden upon the state and the taxpayer (Middleton, 1999).

Social model of disability

In response to the medical model of disability and its impact, disability activists developed a social model of disability, arguing that it is environmental barriers and social attitudes that disable. According to Devine (1997, p. 4), social construction theory "seeks to explain the process by which knowledge is created and assumed as reality". In terms of disability and the use of the social model by disability activists to fight against the dominant perceptions of disability within society, based upon a medical model ethos, Priestley (1998) claims its use has its roots in the work of the Union of Physically Impaired Against Segregation (UPIAS) (1976) and Vic Finkelstein (1980), both in Great Britain. These works "form the core assumptions" for modern-day contributors in this area (Priestley, 1998, p. 80) . Morris (1991) states that this perspective takes the view that if people's attitudes were to change, and there was public policy that legislated that environmental barriers should be removed, then many of the problems associated with disability would disappear. This view is exemplified in the comments of Drake:

> disablement lies in the construction of society, not in the physical condition of the individual. However, this argument is usually rejected precisely because to accept it involves recognising the extent to which we are not merely unfortunate but are directly oppressed by a hostile social environment.
>
> *(Drake, 1996, cited in Imrie, 1997, p. 263)*

Biosocial model of disability

The biosocial model argues that the real position is a combination of the previous two models in that there will always be times when the actual impairment itself will raise issues that changes in perceptions or the built environment cannot overcome. Birkenbach (1990) argues that the social model must recognise that there is a physical state that prevents people with disabilities being afforded equal opportunities and treatment. Their very physical differences mean that society has to react to them and their various needs in a different way from the way it reacts to the same needs of the rest of society. French (1993) rejects the idea that her visual impairment generates disabilities that are wholly socially created. As she comments, her impairment (blindness) disables her from recognising people and makes her "unable to read non-verbal cues or emit them correctly" (French, 1993, p. 17). In response to this Priestley (1998) cites the Northern Officer Group Report of 1996 which states:

> The social model does not deny the existence of impairments and physiological differences . . ., rather, it addresses them without attaching value judgements such as 'normality' and shifts emphasis towards those aspects of our world that can be changed.
>
> *(Northern Officer Group, 1996, cited in Priestley, 1998, p. 85)*

In addition to this, Shakespeare and Watson (1997) feel that this issue of the failure of the social model to acknowledge the role of impairments in producing disability is one that only arises within the area of disability research. They feel that the real issue is the need for a clear and united stance, because "the differences within the movement on the issue of the social model are as nothing compared to the hostility and ignorance with which the social model is greeted in the wider world" (Shakespeare and Watson, 1997, p. 299).

Examples of research that have applied these models, usually using the social model to critique the impact of the medical model of disability include Brittain (2004) (The barriers faced by athletes with disabilities taking part in sport from the grassroots to the elite level) and Huang and Brittain (2006) (The multiplicity and complexity of identity construction for elite disabled athletes within the arena of disability sport).

A theoretical model that has been applied more recently is that of ableism. Ableism has its roots in the ideas of normative values and the models of disability, but is actually more utilitarian in that it allows for the analysis of intersections with other types of normative values such as race, gender and sexuality and the impact that different combinations of bodily identity norms might have upon the way an individual is perceived and treated within a particular society. An introduction to ableism in terms of disability is given next.

Ableism

> Ableism describes prejudicial attitudes and discriminatory behaviours toward persons with a disability. Definitions of ableism hinge on one's understanding of normal ability and the rights and benefits afforded to persons deemed 'normal'.
>
> *(Wolbring, 2012, p. 78)*

Ableism is, therefore, closely associated with the notion of norms and normalcy and the resultant power relationships derived from the imposition of normative values as a mechanism for maintaining the power of one group over another, with those who best fit these construed norms upholding power over those who diverge from them. Kearney, Brittain and Kipnis (2019) claim that:

> While normalcy is existent in the background and is unobtrusive in everyday life for people meeting the established criteria of 'normal', for those perceived to deviate from the 'norm' it often exists in the foreground of their realities and is more prevalent in their perceptions of lived experiences within the social order.
>
> *(p. 7)*

In the context of sport and physical activity for people with disabilities, the prioritisation of non-disabled sport and physical activity and non-disabled bodies within society devalues sport and physical activity for people with disabilities and potentially undermines much of the hard work done by disability activists to gain acceptance for people with disabilities in all walks of life, including as elite athletes. Ableism, therefore, devalues people with disabilities and results in segregation, social isolation and social policies that limit opportunities for full societal participation. The two primary mechanisms through which this occurs are through the ableist attitudes that nearly all people within society are socialised (to varying degrees) into and an inaccessible environment brought about due to the fact that it is generally designed and built with only those who most closely embody normative values in mind.

Internalised ableism

As a result of this almost ubiquitous perception of disability as a pathological issue leading to a digression from a socially expected physical norm, both the non-disabled and People With Disabilities (PWD) within society are strongly encouraged, through numerous sources, to internalise many of the perceptions of disability embedded within an ableist approach to disability. Consequently, it appears to people with disabilities that the causes of many of their problems lie within themselves and their own impairments. This leads to what Reeve (2014) terms 'internal oppression', but is more commonly termed internalised ableism. According to Campbell (2009), therefore, within an ableist perspective the very existence of disability is merely tolerated rather than celebrated as a component of human diversity and that internalised ableism forces people with disabilities to assimilate into ableist norms by assuming an identity other than their own (Campbell, 2008). Campbell (2009) states that internalised ableism operates from a two-pronged approach. The first is dispersal, which leads to a distancing of disabled people from each other that "actively promotes separation between and within groups of the so-called 'stigmatised' peoples" (Campbell, 2009, p. 23) and which Reeve (2014) claims is clearly highlighted by Deal (2003) and Tringo (1970) who ranked different impairments by their degree of perceived social acceptability, which often closely correlates with how far an impairment deviates from socially accepted norms and leads to a hierarchy of disability. In terms of the Paralympic Games this can lead to major differences in the amount and type of media coverage different impairment groups receive. The second approach is emulation, whereby people with disabilities actually adopt and internalise ableist norms. This in turn can reinforce the impact of dispersal by forcing people with disabilities to adhere to normative values and thus distance themselves from people they perceive to deviate from those norms.

Overall ableism is a relatively new theoretical framework in terms of research being carried out with respect to the Paralympic Games. Some authors who have applied it to the Paralympic Games, either directly or indirectly, include Cherney, Lindemann and Hardin (2015) (communication, disability and sport); Brittain and Beacom (2016) (The London 2012 Paralympic Legacy) and Hammond and Jeanes (2018) (Federal Government Involvement in Australian Disability Sport).

Key research outputs focusing upon aspects of the Paralympic Games

I will now turn my attention to the various types of research that have been carried out around the Paralympic Games and some of the key outputs. I have separated these into books and journal articles, although due to my own linguistic disabilities these will be restricted to those published in the English language. The idea with this section is to highlight with examples some of the work currently going on in the field in order to, hopefully, spark new ideas and attract new researchers to this important field of study.

Key books focusing upon aspects of the Paralympic Games

Over the last decade there has been a marked increase in the publication of books focusing upon various aspects of the Paralympic Games, especially by good quality academic publishers such as Routledge, Sage and Palgrave MacMillan. Subject matters include the history of the Games (Bailey, 2008; Brittain, 2014; Goodman, 1986; Scruton, 1998); media and the Paralympic Games (Jackson et al., 2015; Schantz and Gilbert, 2012); legacy and the Paralympic Games (Legg and Gilbert, 2011; Misener et al., 2018); relations to specific Games (Cashman and Darcy, 2008 [Sydney 2000]); the cultural politics of the Paralympic Games (Howe, 2008a); an introductory text to the Paralympic Games (Brittain, 2016); training and coaching the Paralympic athlete (Vanlandewijck and Thompson, 2016, 2011); nutrition and the Paralympic athlete (Broad, 2014) and finally a handbook of Paralympic Studies (Brittain and Beacom, 2018). With the exception of the two historical books by Goodman and Scruton, all of these books have been published in the last ten years. There have been a number of books and handbooks that have also been published with titles including the words 'Olympic and Paralympic Games' (c.f. Dixon and Gibbons, 2014; Girginov, 2014) but almost without exception these books generally include one substantive chapter covering some aspect of the Paralympic Games with rest of the book focusing almost solely upon the Olympic Games. Indeed, Girginov's (2014) *Handbook of the London Olympic and Paralympic Games Volume II* does not even include the word Paralympic in its index, although it does have a limited number of references to disability.

The range of journal articles focusing upon aspects of the Paralympic Games

I will now introduce five of the main areas that social science-based research has been carried out with respect to the Paralympic Games. This is by no means an exhaustive list and, as I have already highlighted, just about any piece of research that has been carried out with respect to the Olympic Games can be done again with a range of extra interesting issues thrown into the analytical mix by applying the theories from the models of disability or ableism previously outlined.

Media and the Paralympic Games

Media coverage of the Paralympic Games is perhaps one of the most common areas of investigation and articles investigating this have adopted a wide range of approaches and focusses including comparing Olympic and Paralympic coverage of a Summer (Chang et al., 2011) and a Winter (Golden, 2003) Games; media coverage of a Paralympic Games within a specific country (Thomas and Smith, 2003 (quantitative and qualitative analysis of British newspaper coverage of the 2000 Sydney Paralympics in terms of text and photographs); qualitative analysis of Czech media coverage of Summer Paralympic Games, 1992–2008 (Tejkalova, 2015); investigating a specific Games (Schell and Duncan, 1999 [Atlanta 1996]); a comparison between countries (Schantz and Gilbert, 2001) or media coverage of an individual Paralympian (Schell and Rodriguez, 2001). There have also been articles investigating how media coverage of the Paralympic Games might impact upon the image of people with disabilities (Howe, 2008b) and how the framing of Paralympic media content might actually negatively impact upon the way people with disabilities are perceived in the wider society (Silva and Howe, 2012). These articles have taken both a quantitative and a qualitative approach employing a range of analytical tools including content analysis and media frames analysis.

Legacy and the Paralympic Games

A more recent focus area for researchers of the Paralympic Games has been that of legacy. With the International Paralympic Committee (IPC) making strong claims regarding how the Paralympic Games and movement can positively impact societal attitudes towards disability and the lives of people with disabilities in general, this has led to increased investigation of these claims. Perhaps the best place to start with this particular issue is with Misener et al. (2013) who carried out a thematic analysis of articles pertaining to Paralympic legacy. Some of the more interesting papers are actually highly critical of the legacy claims made. Purdue and Howe (2015) discuss the power struggles that shape legacy within the Paralympic field. Braye, Dixon and Gibbons (2013) discuss legacy from the perspective of non-sporting disability activists and Braye (2016) tackles the subject from the perspective of retired Paralympians. Brittain and Beacom (2016) compare the views of the British government post-London 2012 with those of disability activists in the UK and highlight how external issues such as competing government policies can impact legacy. Bush et al. (2013) highlight how the Paralympic Games and Paralympic athletes' bodies are sites through which social discourses and processes contribute to the shaping of human relations.

Sports diplomacy, politics and the Paralympic Games

With the perceived increased importance and coverage of the Paralympic Games over the last decade or so, which can in part be attributed to their close links with the Olympic Games and movement, there has been a rise in the number of articles looking at political issues and sports diplomacy in relation to the Paralympic Games and movement. Beacom and Brittain (2016) investigated the issue of the IPC reconciling its role as both a disability advocate and sports regulator, whilst Bundon and Hurd Clarke (2014) investigated the views of athletes with disabilities on strategies for advocacy within the Paralympic movement. Darcy (2003) looked at the politics of disability and access and how they impacted upon the Sydney 2000 Games experience, whereas Novak (2008) looked at how national and international politics impacted upon the participation of Zimbabwe in the Paralympic Games. Brittain (2011) gave a new perspective on the whole apartheid and South Africa debate by looking at how this played out in the Paralympic arena. Finally, Brittain (2006) investigated how the social and economic development within countries participating in the Paralympic Games might impact upon issues such as team size and medal success.

Sports history and the Paralympic Games

There is an abundance of historically based articles related to the Olympic Games, but still relatively few connected to the Paralympic Games. This is partly driven by the fact that source material connected to early Games is relatively scarce and hard to access. However, things are starting to slowly improve with some countries actually starting their own Paralympic history projects, e.g. Australia (Jobling, Naar and Hanley, 2012). Other authors have investigated the impact of joining the Paralympic Games on sport for people with disabilities in their country, e.g. France (Ruffié, Ferez and Lantz, 2014) or looked at an individual Games, e.g. Tokyo 1964 (Frost, 2012). Connected to the difficulties in accessing original source material, Brittain, Ramshaw and Gammon (2013) discuss possible reasons for what they see as the marginalisation of

Paralympic heritage within the wider heritage sector. Other areas that have been investigated include how the Paralympic Games and movement developed in their first sixty years (Legg and Steadward, 2011) and the role the relationship between the IPC and the IOC has played in that development (Legg et al., 2014). Finally there are those who have been highly critical of the way the Paralympic Games and movement have developed (Peers, 2012, 2009) claiming that they have promoted a disabling discourse for people with disabilities in which athletes' voices are often absent or silenced.

Impaired bodies, technology, classification and the Paralympic Games

One final area in which researchers have taken an interest is the intersection of impaired bodies in sport and the use of technology and classification systems to aid both participation and the fair competition. This is an area where issues such as normative values really come to the fore with Howe and Silva (2017) challenging whether the Paralympic Games really are an opportunity to challenge 'normalcy' and Purdue and Howe (2013) questioning what is deemed a legitimate body within the Paralympic Games. Burkett (2010) discusses the use of technology in Paralympic sport and whether this is a kind of performance enhancement or just essential to allow participation. Howe (2008c) claims that the classification system in Paralympic sport, which is designed to ensure fair competition, actually leads to some impaired bodies being celebrated within the movement and others not. Finally Mazzeo, Santamaria and Iavarone (2015) discuss one aspect of what is becoming an increasing issue within the Paralympic movement as it grows in importance – that of cheating, which is often connected to aspects of technology or possible misrepresentation of impairment to gain a more advantageous classification for competition.

Possible areas for future research

As highlighted earlier, there is not really any piece of research that has been carried out regarding the Olympic Games and movement that cannot be done again on the Paralympic Games and movement, with a number of interesting extra issues to add into the analytical mix. This means that the possibilities are currently just about endless. Specific areas of possible interest are the experiences of women with disabilities and athletes with high-support needs (usually those with more severe or multiple impairments) at the Paralympic Games and also how they are portrayed (if indeed they are portrayed) in the media. The level of participation opportunities for athletes with disabilities and their relative success at the Paralympic Games in countries with different levels of development and social inclusion legislation is also another potentially large and fertile area for research.

Conclusion

As academics, we are constantly being told that our research needs to have impact outside of the academic sphere. It is my view that the study of the Paralympic Games and movement is one area where opportunities to have genuine positive societal impacts abounds. On the surface it would appear that the study of the Paralympic Games and movement is a fairly straightforward operation. However, in truth it is a highly complex and yet fascinating field to work in with potential impacts and ramifications far beyond the field of study for, as I hope is clear from the models of disability and ableism section, the issues that manifest themselves in the Paralympic Games and movement actually stem from the wider society and so you cannot understand one without the other.

References

Abberley, P. (1993). Disabled people and 'normality'. In: J. Swain, V. Finkelstein, S. French and M. Oliver, eds., *Disabling barriers – Enabling environments*. Milton Keynes: Open University, pp. 107–115.

Bailey, S. (2008). *Athlete first: A history of the Paralympic movement*. Chichester, UK: John Wiley & Sons Ltd.

Beacom, A. and Brittain, I. (2016). Public diplomacy and the International Paralympic Committee: Reconciling the roles of disability advocate and sports regulator. *Diplomacy and Statecraft*, 27(2), pp. 273–294.

Birkenbach, J. (1990). *Physical disability and social policy*. Toronto: University of Toronto Press.

Braye, S. (2016). 'I'm not an activist': An exploratory investigation into retired British Paralympic athletes' views on the relationship between the Paralympic games and disability equality in the United Kingdom. *Disability and Society*, 31(9), pp. 1288–1300.

Braye, S., Dixon, K. and Gibbons, T. (2013). A mockery of equality': An exploratory investigation into disabled activists' views of the Paralympic games'. *Disability & Society*, 28(7), pp. 984–996.

Brittain, I. (2004). Perceptions of disability and their impact upon involvement in sport for people with disabilities at all levels. *Journal of Sport and Social Issues*, 28(4), pp. 429–452.

Brittain, I. (2006). Paralympic success as a measure of national social and economic development, *International Journal of Eastern Sport and Physical Education*, 4(1), pp. 38–47.

Brittain, I. (2011). South Africa, apartheid and the Paralympic games. *Sport in Society*, 14(9), pp. 1167–1183.

Brittain, I. (2014). *From stoke Mandeville to Sochi: A history of the summer and winter Paralympic games*. Champaign, IL: Common Ground Publishing.

Brittain, I. (2016). *The Paralympic games explained*. 2nd ed. UK: Routledge.

Brittain, I. and Beacom, A. (2016). Leveraging the London 2012 Paralympic Games: What legacy for people with disabilities? *Journal of Sport and Social Issues,* 40(6), pp. 499–521.

Brittain, I. and Beacom, A., eds. (2018). *The Palgrave handbook of Paralympic studies*. UK: Palgrave.

Brittain, I., Ramshaw, G. and Gammon, S.J. (2013). The Marginalisation of Paralympic Heritage. *International Journal of Heritage Studies*, 19(2), pp. 171–185.

Broad, E., ed. (2014). *Sports nutrition for Paralympic athletes*. London: CRC Press.

Bundon, A. and Hurd Clarke, L. (2014). Honey or vinegar? Athletes with disabilities discuss strategies for advocacy within the Paralympic movement. *Journal of Sport and Social Issues*, 39(5), pp. 351–370.

Burkett, B. (2010). Technology in Paralympic sport: Performance enhancement or essential for performance? *British Journal for Sports Medicine*, 44(3), pp. 215–220.

Bush, A., Silk, M., Porter, J. and Howe, P.D. (2013). Disability [sport] and discourse: Stories within the Paralympic legacy. *Reflective Practice*, 14(5), pp. 632–647

Campbell, F.A.K. (2009). *Contours of Ableism: The production of disability and abledness*. London: Palgrave-MacMillan.

Campbell; F.A.K. (2008). Exploring internalized ableism using critical race theory. *Disability and Society*, 23(2), pp. 151–162.

Cashman, R. and Darcy, S., eds. (2008). *Benchmark games: The Sydney 2000 Paralympic games*. Sydney: Walla Walla Press.

Chang, I.Y., Crossman, J., Taylor, J. and Walker, D. (2011). One world, one dream: A qualitative comparison of the newspaper coverage of the 2008 Olympic and Paralympic games. *International Journal of Sport Communication*, 4(10), pp. 26–49.

Cherney, J.L., Lindemann, K. and Hardin, M. (2015). Research in communication, disability, and sport. *Communication and Sport Journal*, 3(1), pp. 8–26.

Darcy, S. (2003). The politics of disability and access: The Sydney 2000 games experience. *Disability and Society*, 18(6), pp. 737–757.

Davis, L.J. (1997). Constructing normalcy: The bell curve, the novel, and the invention of the disabled body in the nineteenth century. In: L.J. Davis, ed., *The disabilities studies reader*. London: Routledge, pp. 9–28.

Deal, M. (2003). Disabled people's attitudes toward other impairment groups: A hierarchy of impairments. *Disability & Society*, 18(7), pp. 897–910.

Devine, M.A. (1997). Inclusive leisure services and research: A consideration of the use of social construction theory. *Journal of Leisurability*, 24(2), pp. 3–11.

Dixon, K. and Gibbons, T., eds. (2014). *The impact of the 2012 Olympic and Paralympic games: Diminishing Contrasts, increasing varieties*. UK: Palgrave.

Drake, R. (1996). Charities, authority and disabled people: A qualitative study. *Disability and Society*, 11, pp. 5–23.

Finkelstein, V. (1980). *Attitudes and disabled people: Issues for discussion, monograph 5*. New York: World Rehabilitation Fund.
French, S. (1993). Disability, impairment, or somewhere in between. In: J. Swain, V. Finkelstein, S. French and M. Oliver, eds., *Disabling barriers – Enabling environments*. Milton Keynes: Open University, pp. 17–25.
Frost, D.J. (2012). Tokyo's other games: The origins and impact of the 1964 Paralympics. *International Journal of the History of Sport*, 29(4), pp. 619–637.
Girginov, V., ed. (2014). *Handbook of the London 2012 Olympic and Paralympic Games*, Vol. 2: Celebrating the Games. London: Routledge.
Golden, A.V. (2003). An analysis of the dissimilar coverage of the 2002 Olympics and Paralympics: Frenzied pack journalism versus the empty press room. *Disability Studies Quarterly*, 23(3/4).
Goodman, S. (1986). *Spirit of stoke Mandeville: The story of Sir Ludwig Guttmann*. London: Collins.
Hammond, A. and Jeanes, R. (2018). Federal government involvement in Australian disability sport, 1981–2015. *The International Journal of the History of Sport*, 35(5), pp. 431–447.
Howe, P.D. (2008a). *The cultural politics of the Paralympic movement: Through an anthropological lens*. London: Routledge.
Howe, P.D. (2008b). From inside the newsroom: Paralympic media and the production of Elite disability. *International Review for the Sociology of Sport*, 43(2), pp. 135–150.
Howe, P.D. (2008c). The tail is wagging the dog: Body culture, classification and the Paralympic movement. *Ethnography*, 9(4), pp. 499–517.
Howe, P.D. and Silva, C.F. (2017). Challenging 'Normalcy': Possibilities and pitfalls of Paralympic bodies. *South African Journal for Research in Sport, Physical Education and Recreation*, 39(1&2), pp. 191–204.
Huang, C.J. and Brittain, I. (2006). Negotiating identities through disability sport: From negative label to positive self-identification. *Sociology of Sport Journal*, 23(4), pp. 352–375.
Imrie, R. (1997). Rethinking the relationships between disability, rehabilitation, and society. *Disability and Rehabilitation*, 19(7), pp. 263–271.
Jackson, D., Hodges, C.E.M., Molesworth, M. and Scullion, R., eds. (2015). *Reframing disability? Media, (Dis)empowerment, and voice in the 2012 Paralympics*. London; Routledge.
Jobling, I.F., Naar, T. and Hanley, M. (2012). The Australian Paralympic oral history project: Remembering, reflecting, recording and promoting disability in sport. *International Journal of Disability, Development and Education*, 59(3), pp. 295–303.
Kearney, S., Brittain, I. and Kipnis, E. (2019). 'Super disabilities' vs 'Disabilities'? Theorizing the role of ableism in (mis)representational mythology of disability in the marketplace. *Consumption, Markets and Culture* (Special Issue on Marketplace Exclusion), 22(5–6), pp. 545–567.
Legg, D., Fay, T., Wolff, E. and Hums, M. (2014). The International Olympic Committee – International Paralympic Committee relationship: Past, present and future. *Journal of Sport and Social Issues*, 39(5), pp. 371–395.
Legg, D. and Gilbert, K. (2011). *Paralympic legacies*. Champaign, IL: Common Ground Publishing.
Legg, D. and Steadward, R. (2011). The Paralympic games and 60 years of change (1948–2008): Unification and restructuring from a disability and medical model to sports-based competition. *Sport in Society*, 14(9), pp. 1099–1115.
Mazzeo, F., Santamaria, S. and Iavarone, A. (2015). 'Boosting' in Paralympic athletes with spinal cord injury: Doping without drugs. *Functional Neurology*, 30(2), pp. 91–98.
Middleton, L. (1999). *Disabled children: Challenging social exclusion*. Oxford: Blackwell Science.
Misener, L., Darcy, S., Legg, D. and Gilbert, K. (2013). Beyond Olympic legacy: Understanding Paralympic legacy through a thematic analysis. *Journal of Sport Management*, 27(4), pp. 329–341.
Misener, L., McPherson, G., McGillivray, D. and Legg, D., eds. (2018). *Leveraging disability sport events: Impacts, promises, and possibilities*. London: Routledge.
Morris, J. (1991). *Pride against prejudice: Transforming attitudes to disability*. London: The Women's Press Ltd.
Morris, J. (1993). Prejudice. In: J. Swain, V. Finkelstein, S. French and M. Oliver, eds., *Disabling barriers – Enabling environments*. Milton Keynes: Open University, pp. 101–106.
Northern Officer Group. (1996). *The disability discrimination act: A policy and practice guide for local government*. Wakefield: Northern Officer Group.
Novak, A. (2008). Politics and the Paralympic games: Disability sport in Rhodesia-Zimbabwe. *Journal of Olympic History*, 16(1), pp. 47–55.
Peers, D. (2009). (Dis)empowering Paralympic histories: Absent athletes and disabling discourses. *Disability and Society*, 24(5), pp. 653–665.

Peers, D. (2012). Patients, athletes, freaks: Paralympism and the reproduction of disability. *Journal of Sport and Social Issues*, 36(3), pp. 295–316.
Priestley, M. (1998). Constructions and creations: Idealism, materialism and disability theory, *Disability and Society*, 13(1), pp. 75–94.
Purdue, D.E.J. and Howe, P.D. (2013). Who's in and who is out? Legitimate bodies within the Paralympic games. *Sociology of Sport Journal*, 30(1), pp. 24–40.
Purdue, D.E.J. and Howe, P.D. (2015). Plotting a Paralympic field: An elite sport competition viewed through Bourdieu's sociological lens. *International Review for the Sociology of Sport*, 50(1), pp. 83–97.
Reeve, D. (2014). Psycho-emotional disableism and internalised oppression. In: J. Swain, S. French, C. Barnes and C. Thomas, eds., *Disabling barriers, enabling environments*. London: Sage, pp. 92–98.
Ruffié, S., Ferez, S. and Lantz, E. (2014). From the institutionalisation of 'All Disabilities' to comprehensive sports integration: France joining the Paralympic movement (1954–2012). *International Journal of the History of Sport*, 31(17), pp. 2245–2265.
Schantz, O.J. and Gilbert, K. (2001). An ideal misconstrued: Newspaper coverage of the Atlanta Paralympic games in France and Germany. *Sociology of Sport Journal*, 18(1), pp. 69–94.
Schantz, O.J. and Gilbert, K., eds. (2012). *Heroes or zeroes? The media's perceptions of Paralympic sport*. Champaign, IL: Common Ground Publishing.
Schell, L.A.B. and Duncan, M.C. (1999). A content analysis of CBS's coverage of the 1996 Paralympic games. *Adapted Physical Activity Quarterly*, 16(1), pp. 27–47.
Schell, L.A.B. and Rodriguez, S. (2001). Subverting bodies/ ambivalent representations: Media analysis of Paralympian, Hope Lewellen. *Sociology of Sport Journal*, 18(1), pp. 127–135.
Scruton, J. (1998). *Stoke Mandeville: Road to the Paralympics*. Aylesbury, UK: The Peterhouse Press.
Shakespeare, T. and Watson, N. (1997). Defending the social model. *Disability and Society*, 12(2), pp. 293–300.
Silva, C. and Howe, D. (2012). The (in)validity of supercrip representation of Paralympian athletes. *Journal of Sport & Social Issues*, 36(2), pp. 174–193.
Tejkalova, A.N. and Strielkowski, W. (2015). Media coverage of summer Paralympic games (1992–2008): A case study of the Czech Republic. *Mediterranean Journal of Social Sciences*, 6(2), pp. 578–582.
Thomas, N. and Smith, A. (2003). Preoccupied with able-bodiedness? An Analysis of the British media coverage of the 2000 Paralympic games. *Adapted Physical Activity Quarterly*, 20(2), pp. 166–181.
Tringo, J.L. (1970). The hierarchy of preference toward disability groups. *Journal of Special Education*, 4(3), pp. 295–306.
Union of Physically Impaired Against Segregation (UPIAS) (1976). *Fundamental principles of disability*. London: UPIAS.
Vanlandewijck, Y.C. and Thompson, W.R., eds. (2011). *The Paralympic athlete*. Chichester, UK: John Wiley & Sons.
Vanlandewijck, Y.C. and Thompson, W.R., eds. (2016). *Training and coaching the Paralympic athlete*. Chichester, UK: John Wiley & Sons.
Wolbring, G. (2012). Expanding ableism: Taking down the Ghettoization of impact of disability studies scholars. *Societies*, 2, pp. 75–83.

29

Olympic and Paralympic Games and human rights

Bruce Kidd

Introduction

As international movements that aspire to contribute to the advancement of humanity and touch on virtually every aspect of the human experience, the modern Olympic Games and the Paralympic Games raise tremendous expectations about human rights. Yet the way that these movements have addressed human rights is at best incomplete. To their credit, they have long served as symbolic beacons for universal values and the inclusion of all peoples in their Games. As much as other institutions, including the United Nations, they have advanced the belief and practice of sport as common to all humanity, regardless of political, social, religious/ideological, gender, ability/disability and economic differences. The International Olympic Committee (IOC) proclaims that "the practice of sports is a human right" (International Olympic Committee, 2016, p. 11) and the International Paralympic Committee (IPC) that "accessibility is a basic human right and a fundamental pillar of social justice" (International Paralympic Committee, 2015, p. 23.) On selected occasions, they have taken unpopular steps to combat discrimination and shore up the principle of universal inclusion. During the long international struggle against apartheid and racism in sports, for example, the IOC became staunch allies of the oppressed black South African majority and their international supporters, marshalling its considerable prestige and organisational monopolies against the sporting representatives of apartheid South Africa. When apartheid was repealed, the IOC was among the first to welcome representatives of a non-racial South Africa to their Games.

On the other hand, both the Olympic and Paralympic movements have had to be pushed into taking action, have interpreted their obligations very narrowly and have only begun to address human rights violations in connection with the hosting of their Games. It is this contradiction that has led the scholar John Hoberman (1986, p. 39) to characterise the Olympic movement as practising 'amoral universalism'.

This chapter sets out the historical relationships of the Olympic and Paralympic sports movements with human rights and places them alongside the articulation and realisation of human rights broadly. These developments were accelerated by the 'rights revolution' begun in the 1960s, when activists began to use the language of human rights, the United Nations greatly expanded the protections, and courts in many countries enforced civil and other rights. Because the IOC and IPC have had different trajectories, I will deal with their histories in turn, with one exception, the issue of their responsibilities for human rights in host cities. Because the Olympic and Paralympic Games are held in the same cities under the auspices of the same organising committees, I will consider human rights in connection with hosting in an integrated discussion in the final section of the chapter.

My perspective is that of a long-time supporter of the Olympic movement who nonetheless believes that much more needs to be done to bring about the protections of human rights to all those who participate in and are affected by Olympic and Paralympic sports. While once the sports movements could justify a hands-off approach on the grounds of non-intervention and the understandable belief that first they had to bring every national community 'into the tent', there is urgent need to replace non-intervention with the idea of a humanitarian responsibility to protect. Moreover, the tent is now full. It's time to raise the threshold. The very legitimacy of international sports is at stake.

The origins of human rights

'Human rights' connotes the idea that there are freedoms, protections and benefits to which all people are entitled by virtue of their being *homo sapiens*, and that governments and all people must respect these rights. Human rights are considered essential not only for life and sustainability but for dignity and respect. They are sometimes divided into various categories, such as political, economic, legal and egalitarian, or civil, social and cultural rights. Human rights are also associated with classes of people, such as workers' rights, women's rights, children's rights, the rights of persons with disabilities, indigenous rights and athletes' rights.

Scholars trace the first significant articulations of human rights to the 17th and 18th centuries Age of Reason in Europe and North America, when philosophers and political thinkers such as John Locke, Thomas Hobbes, Thomas Paine and Jean-Jacques Rousseau advanced the idea of the rights of individuals. They sought to develop political agreements, such as the (English) Bill of Rights (1689), the American Bill of Rights (1791) and the French Declaration of the Rights of Man and Citizen (1789) to protect and give expression to those rights. Inherent in these initiatives was the idea of a common humanity, that people of different backgrounds should enjoy much the same life chances. Such initial efforts radically challenged the previously held and rigidly enforced social hierarchies of the feudal period; however, they nevertheless defined 'humanity' very narrowly. The Bill of Rights did not protect women or the labouring classes, the American Bill of Rights did not extend citizenship to slaves, and the French Declaration entirely ignored women. Yet the very exclusion of such people from what was proclaimed as 'universal' inspired those left out and their allies to fight for their own rights. In France, the Declaration of the Rights of Man and Citizen in 1789 led Olympe des Gouges to proclaim the Declaration of the Rights of Women and Citizen just two years later, and in Britain, Mary Wolstencraft to publish *A Vindication of the Rights of Woman* the following year.

In the 19th century, the worldwide feminist and anti-slavery movements persuaded even more people to accept and fight for the idea of a common humanity and universal protections. One important expression of this was the abolition of the Atlantic slave trade by Britain, France, Sweden, Portugal and the United States in 1807. Another contributing factor was the 'take-off' stage of globalisation during the late 19th and early 20th centuries. International commerce, colonisation, travel and communication, international organisations such as the Red Cross and Boy Scouts, the new international language of Esperanto, global awards like the Nobel Prize, 'world's fairs' and international sporting competitions like the Olympics all raised the expectations of international standards. The first international legal protections emerged from the horrors of World War 1 (WW1), when the international labour and social democratic movements successfully pushed for the creation of the International Labour Organisation, as part of the League of Nations, with a statement of human rights and protections for workers' rights.

A sea change occurred after World War 2 (WW2). The newly created United Nations proclaimed the Universal Declaration of Human Rights in 1948. The Universal Declaration was the last significant achievement of the international coalition (principally the capitalist colonial powers and the Soviet Union) that defeated fascism during the war. It states that 'all human beings are born free and equal in dignity and rights'. Within its 30 articles are both the liberal freedoms prized in capitalist countries (e.g. the freedom of speech, religion, assembly, the press, property and from discrimination, and fair treatment under the law) and the collectivist freedoms valued by socialist countries (e.g. the right to employment and a basic standard of living, including food, clothing, housing and health care, education and leisure (United Nations, 2015).

Beginning in the socially active 1960s, the understanding of human rights has been broadened significantly, as groups that did not feel sufficiently protected by the Universal Declaration campaigned to have their explicit conditions acknowledged and protected in a further series of international conventions and charters. These include:

- International Convention on the Elimination on All Forms of Racial Discrimination (1965);
- Covenant on Economic, Social and Cultural Rights (1966);
- International Charter on Physical Education, Physical Activity and Sport (1978 and 2015);
- International Convention on the Elimination of All Forms of Discrimination Against Women (1979);
- International Convention on the Rights of the Child (1990);
- International Convention on the Rights of Persons with Disabilities (2006);
- United Nations Declaration on the Rights of Indigenous Peoples (2007);

Most of these documents explicitly refer to sports (Kidd and Donnelly, 2000).

The contingency of human rights

Amnesty International (AI, 2018a) argues that human rights are:

> universal – they belong to all of us, everyone in the world;
> inalienable – they cannot be taken away; and
> indivisible and interdependent – governments cannot pick and choose which are respected.

AI (2018b: 12) also counsels that 'none of us can take any of our human rights for granted. . . . The battle for human rights is never decisively won in any place or any point in time.' Human rights are thus political and contingent. Their acceptance requires a complex process of assertion, struggle and negotiation between competing interests in the context of changing social, economic, political and ideological circumstances. While human rights constitute an essential condition for democracy and progress, no advance has come without struggle. The realisation and enforcement of human rights – the extent to which people feel they actually enjoy those rights – depends upon those same social, economic, political and ideological circumstances and the willingness of states and other bodies to step in to protect them when they are violated. During the 'cold war' (1947–1990) between the capitalist and Soviet blocs of states, governments on both sides selectively honoured those aspects of human rights that corresponded to their beliefs and ignored the others, while making ideological propaganda out of the differences. For instance, capitalist governments shamed the Soviet Union and their allies for their denial of individual rights while neglecting the economic and social rights of their own citizens, and vice versa. Not every government has signed the various international undertakings on human rights. The United States has never signed the International Charter on Physical Education, Physical Activity and Sport nor the International Convention on the Rights of the Child. Some countries in the Global South refuse to sign because they allege that the language of human rights constitutes another form of Western domination, the imposition of individual rights over the collective values of traditional society. It took almost ten years and a change in government for Canada to adopt the UN Declaration on the Rights of Indigenous Peoples (Labbé, 2017).

Today, with the rise of authoritarianism, nativist populism and open warfare in many parts of the globe, human rights are almost everywhere under threat. In its 2017–2018 annual survey, Amnesty International (2018b: 14) reports that many governments are 'shamelessly backsliding in their support for human rights', bitterly and often repressively denying the rights of others, especially minorities', immigrants', refugees' and those identifying as Lesbian Gay Bisexual Transgender Queer (LGBTQ), even if they or their predecessors have agreed to the international covenants to recognise and protect such rights. States in every part of the world have denied or restricted their citizens' rights to democratic protest in the name of 'national security', and the major powers are selling more arms to developing countries than ever before. While the United Nations Council on Human Rights monitors compliance, many of the members of that council have deeply flawed records themselves (Calamur, 2018). At the same time, the appalling ravages of poverty, disease and global warming make it even harder for millions to realise the conditions for a life of security, dignity and culture.

On the encouraging side, a 'new era in social activism', represented by 'Me Too', 'Time is Up' and 'Not in My Name', inspired by the promise of human rights, has taken up the cause, calling out demonisation and discrimination, violence and repression and mobilising for progressive policies. Such activism requires tremendous courage and persistence. But it enjoys powerful resonance and support in many countries, and in my view, will ultimately lead to further progressive change.

The long fuse of human rights in sports

Human rights have been implicit in the ideals and moral claims of modern sports right from their 19th-century origins. To be sure, the innovators, organisers and first participants had no interest in universal inclusion – the first sports were developed and played in white, all-male upper-class institutions and preserves as a way of shoring up and affirming masculinity, class, racial and imperial power in Britain, its colonies and the other Western countries. But the ideals of 'fair play', 'a level playing field' and respect for one's opponent they promoted contained the seeds of inclusion. As sports quickly spread – by emigration, emulation, trade and imperialism – such were their popularity and appeal that those excluded sought to create opportunities for themselves, first by creating their own institutions and then by joining with the established organisations. The working classes, women, people of colour, the indigenous and colonised peoples all did this in what constitute the most important and dynamic narratives in the history of modern sports. At each step of this tumultuous, uneven process, those seeking entry into mainstream sports appealed to the claims that sport should be open to all and fairly conducted. Such efforts invariably required concerted struggle, but today people of all genders, classes, racial identities, nationalities, cultures, religions and regions play and watch sports. In societies where those excluded from the democratic franchise made similar arguments, the call for access to sport became harder and harder to resist.

A similar process occurred with the modern Olympic Games, established by Pierre de Coubertin in 1894. Coubertin sought to create international sporting competitions as a way of enhancing intercultural understanding across the nations and, because he was influenced by the 19th-century peace movement, of nurturing a cohort of like-minded men who would serve as a brake on war. To this end, he sought to export sport around the world. While his original Games were permeated with patriarchal, imperial and aristocratic biases and thus restricted to upper-class men from the Western countries, the rapid success of his Games and the logic of peaceful internationalism he preached helped those excluded pursue similar ideas. Between the world wars, a coalition of feminists led by the remarkable Alice Milliat organised what were initially called the Women's Olympics and the socialist parties and the trade unions held Workers' Olympics. In this context, as Chatziefstathiou and Henry (2012) have shown, Coubertin and his colleagues were pressured to allow for the inclusion of women and the working classes.

The Olympics and human rights

Despite the ideology of 'fair play' and the promise of interculturalism, the path to full inclusion and the recognition of human rights in the Olympics has been uneven. While women were officially allowed to compete in the 1928 Olympics in Amsterdam – they had competed as early as 1900 in Paris, but only under the auspices of local organising committees – they were only given a small number of competitive events and shut out of governance altogether. The parity sought by Milliat as a condition of discontinuing the Women's Olympics has still to be realised. After WW2, the IOC treated the representatives of the newly decolonised nations in similar fashion; it gave them access to competition but limited their involvement in governance. The original idea was to appoint one or two new IOC members for every new nation, but once those nations came from Africa, Asia or the Caribbean, the idea was dropped. In 1976, there were 45 National Olympic Committees (NOCs) in Africa, but only seven IOC members from the continent; one of those was a white planter from Kenya, the other an unrepentant white representative of the expelled apartheid South Africa (Keys, 2012). To this day, almost twice as many IOC members come from Europe than any other region.

On the positive side, the IOC has recognised national communities big and small, affirming them with National Olympic Committees (NOCs) and international legitimacy in the Olympic Games, even where those communities have been colonies of imperial states. In 1907, for example, the IOC recognised the Finnish Olympic Committee, even though Finland was a duchy of the Russian Empire. There has been a Puerto Rico Olympic Committee (COPUR) since 1948, even though it remains an unincorporated territory within the United States; in 1980, the COPUR competed in the Moscow Olympics, despite the US-led boycott. Another significant achievement has been the continuation of the Games despite the frequent wars and intractable political conflicts that have plagued modern history. Although some Games have been marred by boycotts, except for the two world wars in the early 20th-century, every Olympic and Winter Olympic Games has been held without fail. These are no mean accomplishments.

The IOC has pursued these outcomes through two cardinal policies, the 'autonomy of sport' and non-intervention in the internal affairs of members and host countries. The latter has been a conscious strategy to realise the overarching priority of intercultural communication and exchange in a diverse, often divided world. It would be impossible to achieve such dialogue, it argues, if it restricted membership or the hosting of Games to those of like-minded views. "To ask the peoples of the world to love each other is merely a form of childishness", Coubertin once wrote. 'To ask them to respect each one another is not in the least utopian, but in order to respect one another it is first necessary to know one another.' For the most part, it has held with this position through more than a century of bitter conflicts, challenges to the recognition of many NOCs, including those from Israel and Palestine, the Soviet Union, the two Germanys, the two Koreas, China and Taiwan, and the boycotts of many Games. The 'low threshold' has ensured an accessible tent, enabling 206 NOCs to be recognised, and the Games to be held on every continent. For much of the 20th century, it also reflected the international consensus around non-intervention in the domestic affairs of nation states.

The IOC has insisted that all host governments recognise duly accredited Olympic participants. The requirement was notably established during the 1936 Olympics in Nazi Germany, when the IOC forced the Nazi organisers to admit all duly IOC-credentialed participants, including Jewish competitors, place token Jews on the German teams, and remove anti-Semitic signs and banners from Garmisch-Partenkirchen, the site of the Winter Olympics, and Berlin, where the Olympic Games took place. These modest conditions did not stop the Nazis' many acts of abuse against their own citizens, nor prevent the saturation of the Games with Nazi propaganda. Yet they created important precedents that stood the IOC in good stead in future Games, particularly during the Cold War when some Western governments sought to exclude athletes and coaches from countries like the German Democratic Republic that they did not formally recognise from participating in Games within their borders. The policy significantly advanced an inclusive internationalism.

The issue that moved the IOC towards an explicit embrace of human rights was apartheid, the repressive system of racial segregation established by the white government of South Africa in 1948. A small white minority enjoyed a high standard of living at the expense of the large black majority. In sport, blacks had always faced discrimination, but prior to apartheid they competed with and against whites in most sports and blacks had represented South Africa in the Olympics. Apartheid prohibited blacks from competing with whites, representing South Africa in international competition, and confined them to inferior facilities and difficult conditions. The South African Olympic Committee (SANOC) held to the government position and refused to allow blacks to enter its trials, let alone send them to the Games, even though some of them were the best athletes in the country. After peaceful efforts to re-integrate South African sport were brutally put down, the black leaders of non-racial sport sought to persuade the international community to cut off all ties with apartheid sport as a strategy to force change. Initially, the IOC's response was lukewarm. Although it suspended the apartheid-supporting National Olympic Committee of South Africa in 1963 and after pressure from the developing countries, the Soviet bloc and the US-based Olympic Project for Human Rights, expelled it in 1970, it did not play an active role in monitoring and enforcing the international moratorium until after the African-led boycott of the 1976 Olympics in Montreal. But then it did, contributing significantly to the legitimisation of the fight against apartheid and its increasing effectiveness.

In 1980, while standing up to the US-led boycott of the Moscow Olympics, IOC members distinguished between the sports boycott of apartheid South Africa, which it supported, and the call to move or cancel the Moscow Games, which it opposed. IOC President Killanin argued that the anti-apartheid campaign was initiated by fellow sportspersons about the human rights of persons within sport, something for which the IOC must accept responsibility, but that it had neither desire nor ability to intervene with the Soviet Union over Afghanistan, the target of the 1980 boycott campaign. These steps took the Olympic movement into a policy field where the growing public concern for human rights jostled uneasily with the traditional culture of non-intervention.

Towards the language of human rights

During the Samaranch years, the IOC assumed further responsibility for the ethical and social conditions of Olympic sport, often in the language of human rights. It admitted more than 50 new NOCs, increased the number of sports and events that women could enter, and elected women to the membership. Through Olympic Solidarity, it steered the largest share of its television revenue into sport development in the Global South, and consolidated links to the United Nations, which was strengthening the recognition of human rights. It established the International Court of Arbitration for Sport to protect athletes from unfair or arbitrary decisions, especially those arising from disputes at Olympic Games, a huge step forward for athletes' rights. It accepted a 'responsible concern' for environmental issues and committed itself to 'sustainable development in sport'. On the other hand, it continued to ignore the actual realisation/enforcement of human rights within Olympic organisations and the countries where Games were held, a policy which increasingly brought it under international scrutiny.

In 1993, when Beijing applied to host the Olympic Games of 2000, Human Rights Watch (HRW), the US Congress and the European Parliament, among other bodies, called upon the IOC not to award the Games to Beijing on the grounds of China's continuing persecution of dissidents. Beijing lost by two votes and it was widely believed that the objections contributed to the unsuccessful result (Riding, 1993). The spotlight only intensified after 2001, when the IOC awarded Beijing the 2008 Games. During the build-up to the Games, neighbourhoods were razed to make way for Olympic facilities, minority workers forcibly removed, pollution increased, critics imprisoned and the international media censored. International criticism mounted, and protests met the international torch relay in many cities across the globe. On the eve of the Games, HRW's Sophie Richardson (HRW, 2008) wrote that 'the Chinese government's hosting has been a catalyst for abuses'. IOC President Jacques Rogge tried to deflect the criticisms, contending that the IOC was 'not a political body' and had no power to enforce compliance with human rights. The IOC, not China, took the brunt of the criticism (Kidd, 2010).

Worldwide protests also took place before and during the 2014 Winter Olympic Games in Sochi, when the Russian government enacted homophobic legislation and stepped up the persecution of LGBTQ persons, while the organising committee trampled workers', indigenous and environmental rights in the construction of facilities. The IOC appeared to be complicit. Although later in the year, as part of his *Olympic Agenda 2020* reforms, President Bach added sexual orientation to Principle 6, the anti-discrimination clause of the *Olympic Charter*, it will take years to repair the damage to the IOC's reputation. A similar story unfolded in Rio. It was a brave decision to award the Games to South America, and there were some heart-warming innovations, especially the recruitment of a Refugee Olympic Team to represent the millions of forcibly displaced people in the world. But the preparations took place against a backdrop of police violence in impoverished communities, the shutdown of popular protests and international demonstrations by ex-patriate Brazilians against the corruption and misplaced priorities of the Games. It was another black eye for the IOC.

The Paralympics and human rights

Competitions for persons with disabilities (PWD) began in the 19C, usually organised by PWD themselves. Sports clubs for the deaf were organised in Berlin in the 1880s; the first international effort, the World Games for the Deaf, took place in Paris in 1924. The Paralympic Games grew out of the wheelchair Stoke Mandeville Games, first organised in 1948, at the time of the nearby London Olympics, by neurologist Dr. Ludwig Guttmann. The 16 competitors were British military veterans suffering from spinal cord injuries. Guttmann soon made his event an annual occasion, invited international competitors (from Holland) in 1952, and tried to connect them with the Olympic movement in 1960, when he held his annual games in Rome one week after the Olympics, calling them the Paralympics. Four hundred athletes from 23 countries took part. The first Winter Paralympic Games were held in Ornskoldsvik, Sweden, in 1976. Amputees and the visually impaired were invited in 1976, athletes with cerebral palsy in 1980 and athletes with other disabilities in 1984 (Legg and Steadward, 2012). The movement seemed indifferent to other issues of inclusion, however, and continued to invite athletes from apartheid South Africa to the Stoke Mandeville Games and the Paralympics until 1985, a policy that cost it considerable international support (Brittain, 2012).

In 1989, at a conference in Arnhem, Holland, four international federations conducting sport for PWD created the International Paralympic Committee (IPC) to provide a single governing body for the Games. In 2018, there were 179 National Paralympic Committees responsible for fielding teams for the Games.

Guttmann, who died in 1980, modelled his Games on the Olympics. The prefix, 'para', comes from the Greek for 'alongside' or 'parallel' and Guttmann dreamed that one day, the Paralympics would achieve the same recognition and status as the Olympics. Under Samaranch, the IOC gradually sought to regularise its relationship to the Paras, providing patronage and financial support in exchange for overall control. The two Games were first held in the same facilities in Seoul in 1988 (and in Albertville in 1992 for the Winter Paralympics) and under the same organising committee in Sydney in 2000. With its growing partnership with the IOC, the IPC gradually shifted the focus from a disability-medical model to one of sport-based competition and the pursuit of athletic excellence. This was fully enunciated in its 'Vision' (2003), which states that the ultimate aim is to "create the conditions for athlete empowerment through self-determination (and to) inspire and excite the world". The Vision anticipated the 2006 International Convention on the Rights of Persons with Disabilities, which shifted the meaning of disability from a medically-defined state requiring charity and social welfare to a right-based condition requiring dignity, full citizenship and access to opportunities, including opportunities for sports, for every person with disabilities (Leclair, 2012).

The IPC focuses its efforts on improving opportunities for PWD and breaking down barriers to participation, a tremendous challenge in a world where more than one billion people, or 15% of the world's population, experience some form of disability. Most PWD reside in the developing countries, where opportunities are severely limited, not just in sports, but in employment, education, rehabilitation and health. Yet where opportunities are available, the benefits are immeasurable (Parnes and Hashemi, 2007). The Paralympic movement faces considerable challenges in enabling women with disabilities to participate – only about 35% of competitors are female – and PWD to serve in leadership positions. Most positions, including the volunteers at Games, are held by the able-bodied, a circumstance that critics contend disempowers PWD and undermines sustainability (Schantz and Gilbert, 2012). The IPC prohibits discrimination on political, religious, economic, disability, racial, gender or sexual orientation grounds but like the IOC, it has no policy nor mechanism to monitor compliance among the IFs and PCs.

Within the movement, the most difficult discussions swirl around its relationship to the IOC. The association with the Olympics has provided significant visibility, organisational expertise and financial support, enabling the Paralympics to become 'the second largest sporting event in the world'. In London in 2008, 2.8 million spectators watched the Games, and Rio claimed a television audience of 4.1 billion in 150 countries and another 1 billion on digital channels. An audience of 2.02 billion watched the 2018 Winter Olympics in PyeongChang on television with a further 251.5 million on digital channels (IPC, 2016). The breath-taking athletic performances powerfully affirm the abilities and accomplishments of PWD and contribute to policy and cultural change within host countries and around the world. On the other hand, critics allege that the IOC's insistence upon separate treatment for the Paralympics, including a refusal to integrate events as the Commonwealth Games has done, relegates sport for PWD to second-class status. Up until 2004, there were wheelchair events on the Olympic programme, but the IOC always presented them as 'demonstration events' in which athletes received different medals; now they are not even held. Advocates also worry that the focus on high performance has reduced competition to the least disabled to the exclusion of the greatest number of PWD and unwittingly provided incentives for cheating and performance-enhancing drugging (Schantz and Gilbert, 2012; Legg and Steadward, 2012; Howe, 2008).

Strengthening compliance with human rights

As the Olympics and Paralympics aspire to model the very best of humanity in a deeply troubled world, they will continue to be expected to contribute to the realisation of human rights. In recent years, the Council of Europe, Human Rights Watch and a coalition of sports bodies calling themselves Mega-Sporting Events Platform for Human Rights (2018) have called upon the IOC and IPC to make human rights, labour standards and anti-corruption measures central to the staging of Olympic and Paralympic Games (Play the Game, 2018). One burning issue at time of writing is the continued administration of sex testing for female athletes by international bodies such as the International Association of Athletics Federations (IAAF) and the Fédération Internationale de Football Association (FIFA). In the most recent version of the long, discriminatory history of such testing, the IAAF has sought to exclude women with naturally high levels of testosterone. No sports body has ever imposed a similar requirement upon male athletes, most of the threatened women come from the Global South and the regulations have little support from scientists or human rights bodies (Karkazis and Carpenter, 2018; Kidd, 2018; Pielke, Tucker and Boye, 2019; and United Nations Human Rights Council, 2019). The Court of Arbitration for Sport (CAS, 2015) struck down the IAAF's first attempt at such a rule, on appeal by the Indian sprinter Dutee Chand. CAS (2019) has upheld the IAAF's revised rule that explicitly targets the brilliant South African runner Caster Semanya, a double Olympic and world champion, and Semanya is challenging this decision in the Swiss Federal Court. Olympic and Paralympic eligibility must be compatible with human rights.

The movements must begin to enforce systematically the rights they espouse in the operations under their auspices. The crisis of 1999 led the IOC to impose new higher standards of personal conduct upon members that reflected the best practices of international governance. The IOC and IPC should now insist upon new higher standards for NOCs, National Paralympic Committees (NPC), International Federations (IFs), Organising Committees (OCOGs) and in the sport-for-development-and-peace opportunities they fund through Olympic Solidarity (Donnelly, 2019). This will require a shift away from the historic policy of non-intervention, but it is urgent. The Olympic tent is now full, so the IOC has much less incentive to maintain a low threshold to ensure a worldwide movement. Given the prestige that the Olympics and Paralympics confer, it is highly unlikely that any NOC, NPC or International Federation will leave. Russia's response to its threatened expulsion from the 2016 Olympics for doping manipulation is a case in point.

Moreover, the international community is moving away from the principle of non-intervention that shaped policy in the IOC's formative years to embrace the ideas of the humanitarian responsibility to protect, human empowerment as a precondition of human security, and the contribution of sport and culture to empowerment. The world is no longer prepared to leave security and human rights completely up to nation states (Welsh, 2002). What is now required is for the IOC and IPC to monitor the realisation of rights among NOCs, NPCs, IFs and OCOGs; negotiate goals and targets for compliance; help organisations develop the appropriate capacities, including the creation of educational programmes and appeal mechanisms; publish report cards, and in extreme cases, take disciplinary action.

Fortunately, the beginnings of such an approach are now underway. Ever since the 2000 Olympics in Sydney, the IOC has monitored environmental or sustainability compliance in conjunction with Games. It has begun to collect participation data from around the world and it has become much more transparent in its own governance and financial transactions. Several bid cities have volunteered equity or human rights goals (e.g. Kidd, 1991; Chicago, 2009). In the bidding for the 2026 Men's World Cup (of football), bid cities were required to provide an analysis of the extent of human rights in the cities where the games will take place and develop a plan to safeguard and strengthen those rights in the build-up and staging of the tournament (e.g. Canada, Mexico and United States Bid, 2018). In 2017, the IOC included reference to human rights with respect to the host city contract for the very first time (Alvad, 2017). In 2018, it announced the creation of a new advisory committee on human rights. A new, Geneva-based Centre for Sport and Human Rights has been created with IOC support. Sceptics fear that there will be much more rhetoric than actual compliance and with many cities in liberal-democratic countries abandoning bids for Olympic and Paralympic Games, the IOC and IPC will not be in a bargaining position to keep the Games going. While the 'new norm' for staging Games requires organising committees beyond 2024 to comply with applicable national and international laws and agreements with respect to facility construction, the environment, health and safety, labour and anti-corruption, the mechanism for ensuring compliance remains unclear.

It will be difficult for the IOC and IPC to retreat from these new directions. It is incumbent upon scholars, sports lovers and activists everywhere to keep their feet to the fire.

References

Alvad, A. (1 March 2017). *IOC includes human rights in Host City contract.* Play the Game.

Amnesty International. (2018a). *International human rights principles.* Available at: https://www.amnesty.ca/our-work/issues/international-human-rights principles?gclid=EAIaIQobChMIy4aanPTl3gIVy16GCh3djQWmEAMYASAAEgJ61fD_BwE [Accessed 21 November 2018].

Amnesty International. (2018b). *Amnesty international report 2017/2018.* The State of the World's Human Rights, p. 12.

Brittain, I. (2012). South Africa, apartheid, and the Paralympic Games. In: J. Leclair, ed., *Disability in the global sporting arena.* Routledge, pp. 97–113.

Calamur, K. (2018). The Human Rights Council is a deeply flawed body. *The Atlantic,* June 20.

Canada, Mexico and United States Bid to Host the 2026 FIFA World Cup. (2018). *Human rights and labor standards,* Section 23, pp. 454–464.

CAS. (2019). *CAS2018/0/5794/5798 Mokgadi Caster Semanya v International Association of Athletics Federations Arbitral Award.*

Chatziefstathiou, D. and Henry, I. (2012). *Discourses of Olympism: From the Sorbonne 1894 to London 2012.* New York: Palgrave Macmillan.

Chicago. (2009). Memorandum of understanding. March.

Court of Arbitration for Sport. (2015). *CAS 2014/a/3759 Dutee Chand v Athletics Federation of India (AFI) & International Association of Athletics Federations (IAAF). Interim Arbitral Award.*

Donnelly, P. (2019). SDP and human rights. In: H. Collison, S. Darnell, R. Giulianotti and D. Howe, eds., *Handbook of Sport for Development and Peace.* Routledge, pp. 141–151.

Hoberman, J. (1986). *The Olympic crisis: Sports, politics and the Olympic order.* New Rochelle, NY: Aristide Caratzas.

Howe, D. (2008). *The cultural politics of the Paralympics movement through an anthropological lens.* Routledge, pp. 65–71.

Human Rights Watch. (2008). *China: Olympics harm key human rights*. Aug. 6.
International Paralympic Committee. (2015). *IPC accessibility guide*. Bonn: IPC.
International Olympic Committee. (2016). *The Olympic charter*. Lausanne: IOC.
IPC. (2016). *Rio 2016 smash all TV viewing records' and 'Record international audiences for PyeongChang 2018*. Bonn: IPC.
Karkazis, K. and Carpenter, M. (2018). Impossible 'Choices': The inherent harms of regulating women's testosterone in sports. *Journal of Bioethical Inquiry*, 15, pp. 579–587. Published August 16.
Keys, B. (2012). The early cold war Olympics 1952–1960: Political, economic and human rights dimensions. In: H. Lenskyj and S. Wagg, eds., *The Palgrave handbook of Olympic studies*. New York: Palgrave Macmillan, pp. 72–87.
Kidd, B. (1991). The Toronto Olympic Commitment: Towards a social contract for the Olympic Games. *Olympika: The International Journal of Olympic Studies*, 1(1), pp. 154–167.
Kidd, B. (2010). Human rights and the Olympic movement after Beijing. *Sport in Society*, 13(5), pp. 901–910.
Kidd, B. (2018). Towards responsible policy-making in international sport: Reforming the medical commissions. *Sport in Society*, 21(5), pp. 773–787.
Kidd, B. and Donnelly, P. (2000). Human rights in sports. *International Review for the Sociology of Sports*, 35(2), pp. 131–148.
Labbé, S. (2017). Why the UN declaration on Indigenous rights has been slow to implement in Canada. *Open Canada*, July 21.
Leclair, J. (2012). Global organisational changes in sport and the shifting meaning of disability. *Disability in the Global Sporting Arena*, pp. 4–25.
Legg, D. and Steadward, R. (2012). The Paralympic games and 60 years of change (1948–2008): Unification and restructuring from a disability and medical model to sport-based competition. In: Leclair, ed., *Disability in the global sporting arena: A sporting change*. Routledge, pp. 31–47.
Mega-Sporting Events Platform for Human Rights. (2018). *Championing human rights in the governance of sports bodies'*.
Parnes, P. and Hashemi, G. (2007). Sport as a means to foster inclusion, health and well-being for persons with disabilities. In: B. Kidd and P. Donnelly, eds., *Literature reviews on sport for development and peace*. Toronto: Sport for Development and Peace International Working Group, pp. 124–157.
Pielke, R., Tucker, R. and Boye, E. (2019). Scientific integrity and the IAAF testosterone regulations. *International Sports Law Journal*, 19, pp. 18–26. Published Feb. 7.
Play the Game. (2018). *Coalition urges the IOC to include labour and human rights*. Play the Game.
Riding, A. (1993). 2000 Olympics go to Sydney in surprise setback for China. *New York Times*. Sept. 23.
Schantz, O. and Gilbert, K. (2012). The Paralympic movement: Empowerment or disempowerment for people with disabilities. In: H. Lenskyj and S. Wagg, eds., *The Palgrave handbook of Olympic studies*. New York: Palgrave Macmillan, p. 360.
United Nations. (2015). *Universal declaration of human rights*. UN.
United Nations Human Rights Council. (2019). Elimination of discrimination of girls and women in sport. March 20.
Welsh, J. (2002). From right to responsibility: Humanitarian intervention and international society. *Global Governance*, 8(4), pp. 503–521.

30

Sport for Development and Peace

Convergence and divergence with the Olympic movement

Simon C. Darnell and Rob Millington

Introduction

When Pierre de Coubertin revived the Olympic movement in 1894, he did so under the belief that sport could and would contribute to peacebuilding, international understanding, and the overall betterment of society (Spaaij, 2012). In the intervening years, the International Olympic Committee (IOC) has sought to position itself as the preeminent international sporting body, in part by continuing to advance Coubertin's vision of the Olympic movement as a positive contributor to social development within an increasingly global civil society. In the early 2010s, two separate but related occurrences converged to solidify the IOC's ambitions in this regard. First, in December 2014, the IOC released its *Olympic Agenda 2020* which provided the "stra tegic roadmap for the future of the Olympic Movement" (IOC, n.d.a, para. 1) and included the goal of further advancing "sport as a unique means for the promotion of peace and development" (IOC, 2014a, p. 6). *Olympic Agenda 2020* notably dovetailed with the United Nations' (UN's) framework for international development, the Sustainable Development Goals (SDGs), which had also positioned sport as an "important enabler of sustainable development" (United Nations, 2015, para. 37). *Olympic Agenda 2020* included a series of recommendations which called for Olympic sport to renew its commitment to sustainable international development. These included: promoting sustainable development in all parts of the Olympic Games, including the bid process (recommendation 2), the hosting of the Games (recommendation 4), and the Olympic movement's daily operations (recommendation 5); continuing to partner with the UN to spread "Olympic values-based education" in school curricula worldwide (recommendation 22); and working to further the reach and impact of its own SDP programme, *Olympism in Action* (recommendation 33) (IOC, 2014a). Such a vision demonstrated the IOC's commitment to, and self-proclaimed leadership within, the burgeoning Sport for Development and Peace (SDP) sector, the loose amalgam of stakeholders that organise sport and physical activity to meet non-sport goals such as gender empowerment, health promotion, and peacebuilding and conflict resolution (Giulianotti, 2011).

The second occurrence took place in May of 2017, when, to the surprise of many, the UN announced the closure of its own Office on Sport for Development and Peace (the UNOSDP) largely in deference to the IOC, and in order to avoid any ongoing duplication between the two organisations with respect to SDP (Wickstrom, 2017). While the IOC and UN have a long-standing relationship, one that has been, at various times, acrimonious and mutually beneficial (Van Luijk, 2018), the passing of leadership and stewardship in SDP from the UN to the IOC reaffirmed the IOC's position within the SDP sector, as well as the broader international development landscape. Taken together, *Olympic Agenda 2020* and the closing of the UNOSDP signalled a new leadership position for the IOC within the field of SDP into the 21st century.

With this context in mind, this chapter explores and discusses various points of convergence and divergence between the conceptualisation and delivery of SDP, particularly in so-called 'developing countries' and the organisation and promotion of the Olympic movement, Olympic Games, and IOC. We argue that while the IOC has long considered the Olympic movement to be a positive force of social development, its most recent activities have also been in the service of establishing its position within the growing and increasingly formalised field of SDP. While such efforts may be laudable, they also highlight, and even expose, some of the negative development implications of Olympic sport, as well as the significant steps still to be taken before the Olympic movement can or should be considered a contributor to sustainable development.

The remainder of the chapter proceeds in four parts. In the next section, we provide a contextual overview of the growth of the SDP sector itself. We then discuss ways in which we see the Olympic movement converging with and diverging from the broader goals of international development and SDP. The Conclusion offers a brief critical appraisal of these tensions, and makes recommendations about what sustainable development in relation to Olympic sport might look like.

The Sport for Development and Peace (SDP) sector

Over the last 30 years, SDP has gained momentum as a highly visible, valued, and viable approach to meeting the goals of international development. SDP emerged more formally in the 1990s, due in part to the entrepreneurial efforts of Olympic athletes like Johann Olav Koss, who founded *Olympic Aid* to raise funds for refugees and humanitarian efforts, before transitioning it into one of the most well-known SDP organisations, *Right to Play* (Coalter, 2010; Kidd, 2008). Since then, SDP has grown into its own recognised sub-field of the field of international development. The SDP sector is comprised of a range of development actors, from corporate to governmental to non-governmental organisations (NGOs), all of who employ sport in pursuit of "development," broadly defined. Indeed, sport is now organised in pursuit of an ever-expansive list of development outcomes, from gender equality, to healthy living, to HIV/AIDS education (cf. Hayhurst, 2013; Giulianotti, 2011).

While such diversity makes SDP difficult to define, the sector does enjoy some common characteristics. For instance, most SDP programmes tend to be concerned with either individual or community development, and operate under the belief or assumption that sport has an almost inherent ability to contribute to social transformation (Coalter, 2010). Others have noted that sport in SDP is often seen as a universal and integrative social practice, praised for its ability to contribute to the social good irrespective of cultural or geographic context (Darnell, 2007), and that most SDP programmes use the global popularity of football as a way to reach marginalised and disenfranchised youth (Schulenkorf, Sherry and Rowe, 2016). Recognising this diversity, here we follow Lyras and Welty Peachey (2011, p. 311) who summarise SDP as "the use of sport to exert a positive influence on public health, socialisation of children, youth and adults, the social inclusion of the disadvantaged, the economic development of regions and states, and on fostering intercultural exchange and conflict resolution."

This growth in size, scale, and popularity of the SDP sector often imparts a sense that sport is a relatively new approach to development. However, as scholars like Kidd (2008) and Donnelly (2011) have noted, SDP has a much longer lineage. Indeed, the history of SDP has roots in the 'rational recreation' movement in Victorian England, the physical education programmes of 19th-century British public schools, and the 'playground movement' in the United States in the early 20th century (Hardy and Ingham, 1983; Millington and Kidd, 2019). In these contexts, sport and physical education offered a means of social and moral education, particularly in imparting ideals of gentlemanliness and industry in young boys, while attempting to stamp out idleness and delinquency. The headmasters of the upper-class, all-male British public schools were instrumental in this regard, providing a structure for the idea that sport could be mobilised as a force of social transformation. These ideas would be taken up by a range of organisations, including the Boy Scouts, Young Men's Christian Association, and the Young Hebrew Association (Kidd, 2011). The notion that sport could promote good health, self-improvement, and respect for authority, as well as invigorating a sense of nationalism, further extended into the realms of militarism and empire building. In this regard, sport was an instrument in many colonial practices, operating as a means of cultural imperialism through 'civilising missions' in the global South. Sports like cricket were seen as a means of training soldiers for such colonial endeavours, while also imparting the British public school values to what were viewed as uncivilised 'Others' (Donnelly et al., 2011; Donnelly, 2011; Kidd, 2011).

This history illustrates that while sport is often connected to the promotion of social good, it has also been connected to imperialism, patriarchy, and social division. As a result, some recent research in the sociology of sport has urged caution when assessing the transformational promises of the SDP sector. A number of scholars have argued that the provision of northern SDP programmes in the global South is reliant upon hegemonic power structures that largely sustain patterns of global underdevelopment (Black, 2010; Darnell, 2007; Hayhurst, Wilson and Frisby, 2011). Such imbalances can, in turn, align with and perpetuate a neoliberal approach to development that places the responsibility for social change on the presumed beneficiaries of SDP interventions, who are arguably the least resourced to enact such change (Levermore, 2008; Hartmann and Kwauk, 2011). In this respect, SDP may fail to contribute to sustainable forms of development because it lacks a commitment to challenging the social and political structures that sustain inequality (Millington, Darnell and Millington, 2018). As a result, Hartmann and Kwauk (2011, p. 289) argue that, at best, SDP should be thought of as an "empty form" that is "like any other tool, technology, or social practice whose meaning, use, and impact is dependent on the ways in which it is employed on how and to what ends it is used."

These histories of sport as a force of social transformation overlap in important ways with the history of the Olympic movement; conversely, the Olympic movement can be considered a precursor of sorts for the contemporary SDP paradigm. For example, the notion of sport as a means to promote social good, or sport as a civilising tool, was well established at the time of Coubertin's efforts to re-instate the Olympic Games (Giulianotti and Armstrong, 2011), and became a hallmark of the Olympic movement. By the latter half of the 20th century, and as the international landscape shifted, the IOC continued to assert a place for sport within international development efforts. Post-World War II, and amidst formal de-colonisation, the IOC aligned itself with the growing support for universal human rights and postcolonial development that were hallmarks of an increasingly globalised world (Roche, 2002; Chatziefstathiou and Henry, 2012). This period saw a shift within the Olympic movement away from a strict focus on the individual character-building focus of sport, and towards broader and more ambitious social and institutional transformations through sport, in ways that were compatible with emerging notions of international development.

The creation of the *Olympic Solidarity* programme is perhaps most illustrative of this. Initiated in the 1960s, *Olympic Solidarity* aimed to provide assistance "for all the National Olympic Committees, particularly those with the greatest needs, through multi-faceted programmes prioritising athlete development, training of coaches and sports administrators, and promoting the Olympic ideals" (IOC, n.d.b). Eventually, the IOC expanded its development portfolio into a range of further initiatives, including *Olympism in Action* (OIA) and the *Olympic Values Education Programme* (OVEP). Even more recently, the IOC has taken notions of Olympic-led development a step further, by supporting the idea that the very hosting of the Olympic Games itself can be a catalyst for international development, particularly for host nations in low- and middle-income countries of the global South, and in the emerging BRICS countries (Brazil, Russia, India, China, and South Africa). Beijing 2008, Sochi 2014, and Rio de Janeiro 2016 all serve as examples of this trend; these Games were positioned as a way to unlock funds for infrastructure development – such as roads, airports, housing, and sport facilities – while offering opportunities for foreign investment and promoting an image of modernity to a global audience (see Black and Van Der Westhuizen, 2004; Millington and Darnell, 2014; Roche, 2002).

In these ways, the Olympic movement has been central to the growth of the SDP sector, and the growth of SDP has, in turn, had a significant impact on the ways that the Olympic movement, and the Olympic Games themselves, are conceptualised, promoted, and organised. What has been less discussed, however, are the impacts of these trends, particularly in the relatively poor countries and regions of the world, and the extent to which the IOC's version of international development aligns with, or diverges from, global trends. We turn to these topics next.

Convergence: international development and the Olympic movement

In this section we explore various points of convergence between the Olympic movement, the SDP sector, and broader trends in international development. Here we draw upon the historical context discussed earlier in order to illustrate how the IOC has positioned itself and the Olympic movement as forces of international development, and in ways that are compatible with the broader SDP sector. Again, *Olympic Agenda 2020* offers perhaps the clearest articulation of this vision. In addressing the 127th session of the IOC in December 2014, IOC President Thomas Bach offered a clear picture of how the 40 recommendations would shape the future of the Olympic movement. Bach remarked:

> If we want to continue to put Olympic Sport at the service of society, which is part of our Olympic Principles, we must engage with this society, we must be in a respectful dialogue with this society. . . . If we want our values of Olympism – the values of excellence, respect, friendship, dialogue, diversity, non-discrimination, tolerance, fair-play, solidarity, development and peace – if we want these values to remain relevant in society, the time for change is now. . . . With a new philosophy in the bidding procedure we are encouraging potential candidate cities to present to us a holistic concept of respect for the environment, feasibility and of development, to leave a lasting legacy.
>
> *(IOC, 2014a, p. 3)*

Bach's comments aligned with the importance ascribed to sustainability (environmental and social) in current development thinking, evidenced in particular by the UN's 2030 Agenda and the SDGs. Bach's comments were also a response to growing criticism regarding the lack of sustainability within the hosting of Olympic Games themselves, as well as the scandals that have surrounded the IOC in recent decades (see Hayes and Karamichas, 2012). To that end, *Olympic Agenda 2020* illustrated a renewed commitment to "put Olympic Sport at the service of society," through a focus on international development. Through *Olympic Agenda 2020*, the IOC promised to work with international organisations such as the UN Environmental Programme (UNEP) and the UN Educational Scientific and Cultural Organisation (UNESCO), while also working to "integrate and implement sustainability measures that encompass economic, social and environmental spheres" (IOC, 2014a, p. 12). It is also committed to expand the IOC's efforts in developing countries through *Olympism in Action*, the *Sport for Hope* programme, and the *Olympic Values Education Programme* (OVEP) (IOC, 2014a), all of which are largely compatible with the goals of the SDP sector and international development.

Indeed, the IOC defines *Olympism in Action* as the implementation of the three Olympic values of excellence, friendship, and respect through six 'fields of activities': development through sport; peace through sport; education through sport; sport at a grassroots level; sport and the environment; and women in sport (IOC, 2009). The goals of the programme, according to the IOC, are to "place sport at the service of the harmonious development of man, with a view to promoting a peaceful society concerned with the preservation of human dignity . . . in the five continents" (IOC, 2007). As a result, *Olympism in Action* has operated in refugee camps where, in partnership with organisations like the UN High Commission for Refugees, sport has been used to address issues of pandemic illness, including HIV/AIDS, while providing health promotion and education opportunities (IOC, 2010). Another component of *Olympism in Action* is the *Olympic Values Education Programme*, which has aimed to implement "Olympic values-based education" in school curricula worldwide, and to further the reach and impact of *Olympism in Action*. In this way, OVEP "integrates sporting values and physical activity into a cultural and educational framework in line with the UN General Assembly Declaration of the Decade of Education for Sustainable Development" (IOC, 2014b, p. 1). OVEP also provides teaching resources created by the IOC, and implemented through the *Olympism in Action* programme, to promote health and help "prevent, or even cure, the diseases of modern civilisation" by using the power of sport as "an educational tool which fosters cognitive development, teaches social behaviour, and helps to integrate communities" (IOC, 2014b, p. 1). Notably, all of these activities are aimed primarily at the world's relatively poor and marginalised, and are largely compatible with the SDP sector and the goals of international development.

Olympism in Action has also been enacted through the IOC's *Sport for Hope* programme, which has led to the construction of Olympic sport centres in Lusaka, Zambia and Port-au-Prince, Haiti. These state-of-the-art facilities are meant to "provide young people and local communities with positive sports and development opportunities" so as to "contribute to a better and more peaceful world through sport" (IOC, 2017a, para. 1). Opened in 2010 and 2014 respectively, the centres in Zambia and Haiti operate as sport academies, complete with facilities for athletics, football, basketball, tennis, handball, volleyball, and hockey, as well as an indoor sports venue, a boxing hall, gym, and a number of educational areas, including classrooms, a library, and internet zone. They also offer access to expert trainers and coaching in a range of Olympic sports. In turn, the centres aim to support social development programming through "sport-based socio-cultural and educational programmes" that target the "most underprivileged, out-of-school local children" with a focus on life skills development. They also have a health mandate, providing health services including hygiene, sports medicine, and health care provided by the Red Cross (IOC, 2017b, para.7).

These efforts within the Olympic movement align with activity in the broader SDP sector that is focused on 'soft' development, such as the provision of social welfare, health, and educational programming. That said, the broader SDP sector also includes efforts towards 'hard' economic and structural development in the global South, such as the building of sports facilities for the world's poorest people. This latter trend has also gained important traction within the Olympic movement in recent years, evidenced by the IOC's efforts to position the hosting of the Games themselves as a catalyst for modernist development, particularly in host cities and nations within low- and middle-income countries, and through the unlocking of (public funds) for development in local infrastructure, the hospitality and tourism industry, transportation, and foreign investment (see Black and Van der Westhuizen, 2004; Cornelissen, 2010). Further, while the IOC and its partners have long been subject to criticism regarding the sustainability of Olympic hosting – particularly with regards to the natural environment – it has begun to position the hosting of the Olympics as a means of achieving sustainable development (see Millington, Darnell and Millington, 2018).

As the most recent of the so-called 'developing countries' to host the Games, Brazil, and Rio de Janeiro 2016, offers a glimpse into such international development discourses as proffered by the IOC. In the lead-up to the Rio 2016 Games, the Olympics were positioned as an opportunity to showcase the city of Rio and the country of Brazil as fully modern, while further stimulating and catalysing Brazilian development into the 21st century (see Darnell and Millington, 2016). Both the IOC and Brazilian Olympic Committee argued that the Games would provide economic stimulus to the country through increased revenues, structural development, and environmental sustainability programmes, while offering opportunities to modernise the four regions of the city in which the Games were to take place, namely Barra, Copacabana, Deodoro, and Maracanã (Millington and Darnell, 2014). After the Games, however, many of these development promises have gone unfulfilled. Specifically, the claims that Rio 2016 would sustain or even improve the natural environment have proved false (Boykoff and Mascarenhas, 2016), the presumed economic benefits of the Games have been undermined by cost overruns (Zimbalist, 2017), and the privileging of consumerism over the needs of citizens (Gaffney, 2018) and the implementation of a far-reaching security apparatus have put real limits on the freedom of Rio's residents (Gaffney, 2018; Barbassa, 2017). There are therefore increasing questions about whether hosting the Olympics is compatible with sustainable development. Thus, while the 'hard' development promises of Olympic hosting, combined with the 'soft' social development programming connected to initiatives like *Olympism in Action*, suggest a convergence between the IOC, the Olympic movement, and the SDP sector, important limitations, and divergences, also exist. In the next section, we discuss these divergences in more detail.

Divergence: development pitfalls in and through the Olympic movement

From the earlier discussion, it is clear the IOC has increasingly sought to position itself as an actor in international development and to align the contemporary Olympic movement with the increasingly institutionalised SDP sector. To do so, the IOC has implemented and supported programmes and policies that converge with the tenets of the SDP sector, particularly through a focus on youth, health, educational and economic outcomes in the global South. That said, there are important ways in which the Olympic movement diverges from SDP. We explore these divergences with the necessary caveat that there is no firm prescription of what does, or does not, constitute SDP activity. Clearly, the activities that fall under the banner of SDP are diverse in form and function, and subject to the parameters set out by its actors and organisation. Our aim here is only to suggest that the approach to development championed by the IOC and seen within the Olympic movement tends to be less than fully democratic, to promote charity over social justice, and to advance a neoliberal vision of change. Recognising, of course, that similar criticisms have been levied against the SDP sector (see Hayhurst, 2013; Nicholls, Giles and Sethna, 2011) as well as the dominant vision of sport-for-development (Hartmann and Kwauk, 2011), we nonetheless suggest that the approach to development within the Olympic movement is in many ways incompatible with the notion of sustainable development through sport.

To illustrate these points, it is helpful to consider the IOC to be an International non-governmental organisation (INGO), which is the kind of organisation that has assumed an increasingly prominent place within global civil society in recent years. Amidst neoliberal globalisation, state and government-led international aid initiatives have been significantly curtailed, leaving a governance gap that has been filled by INGOs. Some INGOs have been praised for their work in international development, particularly for their abilities to build transnational networks, while operating outside the fray of government or corporate influence (Hayhurst, Millington and Darnell, 2015). Yet, the same *ex-officio* status that affords INGOs such flexibility also allows them to escape public accountability and operate with little democratic oversight. Such issues are of particular concern in international development, which is still marked by asymmetrical and postcolonial power relations, and in which aid initiatives can be infused with or compromised by "top-down, Northern, competitive, heterosexual and masculinist traits" (Levermore, 2010, p. 230). With this in mind, there is an ongoing concern that in its promotion of SDP, organisations like the IOC that exist outside of government oversight can largely advance their own interests, while competing with, or even overwhelming, locally driven development organisations and efforts. Such approaches, in turn, have the effect of perpetuating (neo)colonial power dynamics (see Redfield, 2005).

Next, the IOC's promotion of Olympic sport in and through what are commonly thought of as SDP efforts – like the Sport for Hope Centres – may be antithetical to the goals of grassroots humanitarian aid. The issue here is that the IOC's vision of SDP may align more closely with sport development than sport *for* development. As Kidd (2008, p. 371) has argued, sport *for* development, which organises sport in the service of broader social outcomes, is connected to, but is also distinct from, sport development programmes, which are designed "to strengthen the infrastructure of facilities and institutions within which organised sport takes place." A similar distinction has been made by Coalter (2010, p. 298) who differentiates "sport-plus" programmes – "in which sports are adapted and often augmented with parallel programmes in order to maximise their potential to achieve developmental objectives" – from "plus-sport," in which sport is used "to attract young people to programmes of education and training (a widespread approach for HIV/AIDS prevention programmes), with the systematic development of sport rarely a strategic aim" (p. 298). This distinction is crucially important in the relationship between the Olympic movement and SDP because, given the importance of elite sport within the Olympic movement, it is rarely clear if or whether Olympic-led forms of SDP activity lean more towards sport plus or plus sport. Is the Olympic movement's focus on promoting and celebrating elite sporting achievements compatible with the goals of SDP? Currently, there is a strong case to be made that if the social development mandate of the Olympic movement is in actual fact primarily concerned with sport development, then this constitutes a potentially significant divergence from the social and sustainable development goals that are ostensibly hallmarks of the SDP sector.

A further, and related, divergence between the Olympic movement and SDP can be seen in the tension between charity and justice as models of and approaches to development. As we have discussed elsewhere (Darnell and Millington, 2018), social justice and charity can be conflated if and when the popularity of sport is used primarily "to bestow charitable benefits on the poor and marginalised, or to use the 'lessons' of sport to teach people to survive amidst inequality" (p. 2). Here it is useful to recall Hartmann and Kwauk's (2011) differentiation between the dominant and transformative vision of sport for development. The dominant model largely serves to maintain the social and political status quo because, rather than social change, it aims to "resocialise and recalibrate" youth into existing patterns of (global) inequality (Hartmann and Kwauk, 2011, p. 291). By contrast, Hartmann and Kwauk (2011) propose a transformative vision of sport for development, in which individual and/or collective struggles for social justice are privileged. Rather than something to be bestowed, a transformative approach sees development (through sport) as a response to past injustices and a critical engagement with the structures and systems that sustain inequality (Darnell and Millington, 2018). Sport organisations, like the IOC, may proclaim a commitment to a transformative model, based on social justice, but enacting this vision is both rare and difficult.

It is our contention that the IOC's efforts to establish itself as a leader in SDP, combined with the strong focus on sport development within its social programmes, suggest that the contemporary Olympic movement aligns more closely with the dominant vision of sport for development, rather than a transformational one. Further corroborating this position is that the vision of development taken up within the Olympic movement remains a neoliberal one, in which little attention is paid to the power structures that create and maintain unequal development on a global scale. Indeed, some scholars have argued that SDP is nearly tailor-made for neoliberal approaches to international development (see Levermore, 2008) that place the "onus on individuals to be responsible for their welfare, 'healthify' and help the state to cut expenses by participating in these projects" (Hayhurst, 2009, p. 211). For example, *Olympism in Action*, a clearly well-meaning initiative (albeit one that allows the IOC to promote its philanthropic identity, its sports, and its brand) offers little to no engagement with the history or politics of unequal development. In turn, by promoting the development potential of hosting the Games, the Olympic movement continues to advance neoliberal logics of de-regulation, privatisation and accumulation by dispossession, processes that have not only failed to contribute to sustainable development on an international scale, but have had largely deleterious social, economic, and environmental effects (Boykoff, 2014; Gaffney, 2010; Millington, Darnell and Millington, 2018). Thus, despite renewed development rhetoric, we follow Broudehoux (2007, p. 386) in arguing that the cost of the Olympics continue to be "borne by those at the bottom of the economic ladder who endure tax increases, inflation, soaring rents, and an enormous debt that undermines future welfare investments." Such impacts ultimately call into question whether the Olympic movement can or should be considered compatible with the goals of sustainable international development.

Conclusion

In this chapter, we have drawn attention to the history of sport for development, and the ongoing relationship between the IOC, the Olympic movement, and the increasingly institutionalised SDP sector. We have suggested that there are important convergences between the contemporary Olympic movement and the SDP sector, but also significant divergences that call into question whether the Olympic movement and the IOC can or should be considered forces of sustainable development on an international scale.

With this in mind, there are ways that the Olympic movement could move closer to sustainable international development. One is to realise that environmental sustainability – and particularly the threats to humanity posed by climate change – may require acknowledgement that the status quo of building new facilities, in order to host an Olympic Games every two years, is increasingly unviable. Achieving sustainability through Olympic sport may mean scaling back the size and footprint of the Olympic Games in significant ways. Indeed, some changes outlined in *Olympic Agenda 2020* are directed at lowering the cost and size of the Games, and allowing the Games to be held in more than one country, notions that may have environmental benefits while also being attractive to Gulf nations such as Qatar and regional powers like India. These shifts are themselves significant in illustrating that while discourses of modernist development ascribed to the Olympics remain in place, they can be challenged and negotiated.

The other challenge for development within the Olympic movement is how to move beyond the kinds of top-down development that are compatible with neocolonialism and neoliberalism. In other words, is it possible for the Olympic movement to subscribe to a transformative approach to development and, if so, what would this look like? One approach might be to reconceptualise development programmes like *Olympic in Action* and OVEP, and to think of them less as tools for 'educating' people into Olympic thinking and more as lending Olympic support to local sporting forms and local development demands. In this way, the Olympic movement might be less of a leader, but ultimately more of a champion, of sustainable development into the 21st century.

References

Barbassa, J. (2017). Safety for whom? Securing Rio for the Olympics. In: A. Zimbalist, ed., *Rio 2016: Olympic myths, hard realities*. Washington: Brookings Institution Press, pp. 153–178.

Black, D.R. (2010). The ambiguities of development: Implications for 'development through sport'. *Sport in Society,* 13(1), pp. 121–129.

Black, D.R. and Van Der Westhuizen, J. (2004). The allure of global games for 'semi-peripheral' polities and spaces: A research agenda. *Third World Quarterly,* 25(7), pp. 1195–1214.

Boykoff, J. (2014). *Celebration capitalism and the Olympic Games*. London and New York: Routledge, Taylor & Francis Group.

Boykoff, J. and Mascarenhas, G. (2016). The Olympics, sustainability, and greenwashing: The Rio 2016 Summer games. *Capitalism Nature Socialism,* 27(2), pp. 1–11.

Broudehoux, A.M. (2007). Spectacular Beijing: The conspicuous construction of an Olympic metropolis. *Journal of Urban Affairs,* 29(4), pp. 383–399.

Chatziefstathiou, D. and Henry, I. (2012). *Discourses of Olympism: From the Sorbonne 1894 to London 2012*. Basingstoke: Palgrave Macmillan.

Coalter, F. (2010). The politics of sport-for-development: Limited focus programmes and broad gauge problems? *International Review for the Sociology of Sport,* 45(3), pp. 295–314.

Cornelissen, S. (2010). The geopolitics of global aspiration: Sport mega-events and emerging powers. *The International Journal of the History of Sport,* 27(16–18), pp. 3008–3025.

Darnell, S.C. (2007). Playing with race: Right to play and the production of whiteness in 'Development through Sport'. *Sport in Society,* 10(4), pp. 560–579.

Darnell, S.C. and Millington, R. (2016). Modernization, neoliberalism, and sports mega-events: Evolving discourses in Latin America. In: R. Gruneau and J. Horne, eds., *Mega-events and globalization: Capital, cultures and spectacle in a changing world order*. New York: Routledge, pp. 65–80.

Darnell, S.C. and Millington, R. (2018, in press). Social justice, sport, and sociology: A position statement. *Quest,* pp. 1–13.

Donnelly, P. (2011). From war without weapons to sport for development and peace: The Janus-face of sport. *SAIS Review of International Affairs,* 31(1), pp. 65–76.

Donnelly, P., Atkinson, M., Boyle, S. and Szto, C. (2011). Sport for development and peace: A public sociology perspective. *Third World Quarterly,* 32(3), pp. 589–601.

Gaffney, C. (2010). Mega-events and socio-spatial dynamics in Rio de Janeiro, 1919–2016. *Journal of Latin American Geography,* 9(1), pp. 7–29.

Gaffney, C. (2018). Can we blame it on Rio? *Bulletin of Latin American Research,* pp. 1–17.

Giulianotti, R. (2011). The sport, development and peace sector: A model of four social policy domains. *Journal of Social Policy,* 40(4), pp. 757–776.

Giulianotti, R. and Armstrong, G. (2011). Sport, the military and peacemaking: History and possibilities. *Third World Quarterly,* 32(3), pp. 379–394.

Hardy, S. and Ingham, A.G. (1983). Games, structures, and agency: Historians on the American play movement. *Journal of Social History,* 17(2), pp. 285–301.

Hartmann, D. and Kwauk, C. (2011). Sport and development: An overview, critique, and reconstruction. *Journal of Sport & Social Issues,* 35(3), pp. 284–305.

Hayes, G. and Karamichas, J., eds. (2012). *Olympic Games, mega-events and civil societies: Globalization, environment, resistance.* Basingstoke: Palgrave MacMillan.

Hayhurst, L., Millington, R. and Darnell, S.C. (2015). The non-governmental agencies perspective. In: M. Parent and J.L. Chappelet, eds., *Routledge handbook of sports events management: A stakeholder approach.* New York: Routledge, pp. 397–416.

Hayhurst, L.M.C. (2009). The power to shape policy: Charting sport for development and peace policy discourses. *International Journal of Sport Policy and Politics,* 1(2), pp. 203–227.

Hayhurst, L.M.C. (2013). Girls as the 'New' agents of social change? Exploring the 'Girl Effect' through sport, gender and development programs in Uganda. *Sociological Research Online,* 18(2), pp. 1–12.

Hayhurst, L.M.C., Wilson, B. and Frisby, W. (2011). Navigating neoliberal networks: Transnational Internet platforms in sport for development and peace. *International Review for the Sociology of Sport,* 46(3), pp. 315–329.

IOC. (n.d.a). *Olympic Agenda 2020.* Lausanne: IOC.

IOC. (n.d.b). *Olympic solidarity.* Lausanne: IOC.

IOC. (2007). *Teaching values: An Olympic education toolkit.* Lausanne: IOC.

IOC. (2009). *Olympism in action.* Available at: www.olympic.org/olympism-in-action

IOC. (2010). *IOC and UNHRC launch programme for refugees in Namibia.* Lausanne: IOC.

IOC. (2014a). *Olympic Agenda 2020: 20 + 20 recommendations.* Lausanne: IOC.

IOC. (2014b). *Factsheet: Olympic values education program (OVEP).* Lausanne: IOC.

IOC. (2017a). *Sport for hope.* Lausanne: IOC.

IOC. (2017b). *Sport for hope: About the programme.* Lausanne: IOC.

Kidd, B. (2008). A new social movement: Sport for development and peace. *Sport in Society,* 11(4), pp. 370–380.

Kidd, B. (2011). Cautions, questions and opportunities in sport for development and peace. *Third World Quarterly,* 32(3), pp. 603–609.

Levermore, R. (2008). Sport: A new engine of development? *Progress in Development Studies,* 8(2), pp. 183–190.

Levermore, R. (2010). CSR for development through sport: Examining its potential and limitations. *Third World Quarterly,* 31(2), pp. 223–241.

Lyras, A. and Welty Peachey, J. (2011). Integrating sport-for-development theory and praxis. *Sport Management Review,* 14(4), pp. 311–326.

Millington, R. and Darnell, S.C. (2014). Constructing and contesting the Olympics online: The internet, Rio 2016 and the politics of Brazilian development. *International Review for the Sociology of Sport,* 49(2), pp. 190–210.

Millington, R., Darnell, S.C. and Millington, B. (2018). Ecological modernization and the Olympics: The case of golf and Rio's 'Green' games. *Sociology of Sport Journal,* 35(1), pp. 8–16.

Millington, R. and Kidd, B. (2019). Old wine in new bottles: SDP in the trajectory of 'sport for good'. In: S.C. Darnell, R. Giulianotti, D. Howe and H. Collison, eds., *Sport for development and peace handbook.* New York: Routledge.

Nicholls, S., Giles, A.R. and Sethna, C. (2011). Perpetuating the 'lack of evidence' discourse in sport for development: Privileged voices, unheard stories and subjugated knowledge. *International Review for the Sociology of Sport,* 46(3), pp. 249–264.

Redfield, P. (2005). Doctors, borders, and life in crisis. *Cultural Anthropology,* 20(3), pp. 328–361.

Roche, M. (2002). The Olympics and 'global citizenship'. *Citizenship Studies,* 6(2), pp. 165–181.

Schulenkorf, N., Sherry, E. and Rowe, K. (2016). Sport for development: An integrated literature review. *Journal of Sport Management,* 30(1), pp. 22–39.

Spaaij, R. (2012). Olympic rings of peace? The Olympic movement, peacemaking and intercultural understanding. *Sport in Society,* 15(6), pp. 761–774.

United Nations. (2015). Transforming our world: The 2030 agenda for sustainable development. *Resolution adopted by the general assembly.* New York.

van Luijk, N. (2018). The International Olympic Committee: A United Nations permanent observer of post-politics? *International Area Studies Review,* 21(2), pp. 134–149.

Wickstrom, M. (2017). *UN secretary-general closes UNOSDP.* Play the Game.

Zimbalist, A. (2017). The economic legacy of Rio 2016. In: A. Zimbalist, ed., *Rio 2016: Olympic myths, hard realities.* Washington: Brookings Institution Press, pp. 207–238.

31

Home advantage in the Olympic and Paralympic Games

Girish Ramchandani, Darryl Wilson and Chris Gratton

Introduction

The considerable public investment required to host the Olympic and Paralympic Games is often justified in terms of their potential to generate a wide range of benefits for host countries. In 2000, the Olympic Games Global Impact (OGGI) project was launched by the International Olympic Committee (IOC) to improve the evaluation of the overall impacts of the Olympic Games on the host city, its environment and its citizens, as well as to propose a consistent methodology to capture the overall effects of hosting the Games (Gratton and Preuss, 2008). The concept of 'legacy', together with that of 'sustainable sports development', has become an essential part of vocabulary of the IOC and the Organising Committee of the Olympic Games (Girginov and Hills, 2008). Despite the lack of a clearly defined concept, authors generally tend to agree that legacies of major sports events such as the Olympic and Paralympic Games could be positive or negative, tangible or intangible, intended or untended (Mangan, 2008; Gratton and Preuss, 2008; Masterman, 2009), and authors have proposed different perspectives on possible event legacies.

The IOC categorises the proposed benefits associated with hosting the Olympic Games under five broad legacy dimensions. It is worth noting that these legacy dimensions are equally applicable to the Paralympic Games. The five dimensions and their respective sub-dimensions are shown in Figure 31.1.

The sporting legacy dimension in Figure 31.1 consists of two sub-dimensions. First, the sporting venues that are specifically built or refurbished for the Games, which can be used for sport following the conclusion of the Games. For example, permanent venues constructed in connection with the London 2012 Olympic and Paralympic Games such as the Aquatics Centre and the VeloPark have hosted several other major sports events subsequently and are also open for public use. Second, the public interest generated by hosting a major sporting event provides an opportunity to enhance the profile of sport and boost grassroots participation, in order to improve the health and wellbeing of the population. In fact, one of the legacy ambitions of London 2012 was to increase grassroots sporting participation, particularly by young people, and to encourage the whole population to be more physically active (DCMS, 2010). The evidence to support such legacy claims is however mixed. Indeed, a systematic review of

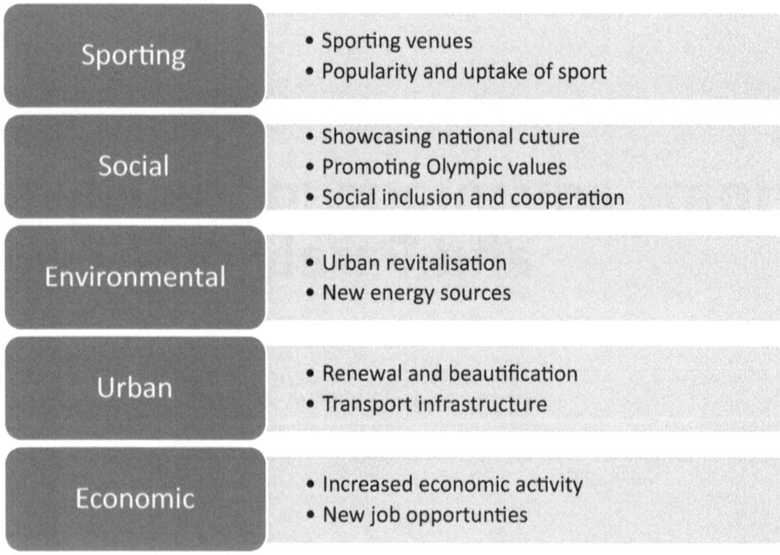

Figure 31.1 Olympic legacy dimensions

Source: Adapted from IOC (2012)

literature by McCartney et al. (2010) found no conclusive evidence of positive health or socio-economic impacts on host populations resulting from major multi-sport events held between 1978 and 2008.

Another type of potential sporting legacy from hosting the Games (not recognised formally by the IOC) relates to elite sport. In this chapter we examine the extent to which nations that are awarded the right to host the Olympic and Paralympic Games benefit from success in elite sport through a quantifiable home advantage or host nation effect. The conceptual framework for home advantage research is first discussed.

Conceptual framework

The most comprehensive and well-researched conceptual model that attempts to explain the home advantage phenomenon was developed by Carron and colleagues. Their model had two iterations. The original framework proposed by Courneya and Carron (1992) incorporated five major components: (1) game location; (2) game location factors; (3) critical psychological states; (4) critical behavioural states; and, (5) performance outcomes. 'Game location' is either home or away depending on where the competition takes place. There are four 'game location factors' that differentially impact on athletes and teams competing at home or away from home, namely (1) the support of the home crowd; (2) familiarity with the home venue; (3) travel fatigue of the away team; and, (4) competition rules in certain sports that may favour the home team. Courneya and Carron (1992) theorised that these four factors contribute to the 'psychological states' of competitors, coaches and officials that in turn contribute to the 'behavioural states' (responses) of these individuals, which ultimately tend to favour home athletes and teams. In short, different types of 'performance outcomes' are potentially influenced by game location, game location factors, critical psychological states and critical behavioural states.

Table 31.1 Home advantage conceptual framework comparison

Component		*Original model*[a]	*Revised model*[b]
Game location	Home	✓	✓
	Away	✓	✓
Game location factors	Crowd	✓	✓
	Learning/Familiarity	✓	✓
	Travel	✓	✓
	Rules	✓	✓
Critical psychological states	Competitors	✓	✓
	Coaches	✓	✓
	Officials	✓	✗
Critical physiological states	Competitors	✗	✓
	Coaches	✗	✓
Critical behavioural states	Competitors	✓	✓
	Coaches	✓	✓
	Officials	✓	✗
Performance outcomes	Primary	✓	✓
	Secondary	✓	✓
	Tertiary	✓	✓

a Courneya and Carron (1992)
b Carron et al. (2005)

Courneya and Carron's (1992) model was subsequently refined by Carron, Loughhead and Bray (2005). A comparison of the original framework and its revised iteration is shown in Table 31.1. There are two key differences between the original and revised models. First, 'officials' were excluded from the latter, not because they do not potentially contribute to home advantage but as, unlike competitors and coaches, they do not have a designated home or visitor status. Second, the revised model incorporated the 'critical physiological states' of competitors and coaches that are associated with game location. The rationale for the inclusion of physiological states in the Carron, Loughhead and Bray's (2005) revised home advantage model was informed by the work of Neave and Wolfson (2003), who proposed that the competitive context of organised sport invokes the natural protective response to territorial intrusion in human beings, combined with the evidence provided by other researchers on the adverse effect of jet lag on athletic performance (Jehue, Street and Huizenga, 1993; Recht, Lew and Schwartz, 1995). In the next section we provide an overview of previous studies that have investigated the home advantage phenomenon in the context of the Olympic and Paralympic Games.

Overview of previous research

Most of the academic literature concerning home advantage in the Olympic and Paralympic Games tends to focus on the Summer Olympic Games. Clarke's (2000) macro-level analysis revealed that 14 of the 17 countries to have hosted the Summer Olympic Games between 1896 and 1996 had won their greatest ever percentage of available medals at home. He also found that host countries typically won a greater percentage of medals at home compared with both their historical away average as well as their average in the Games immediately before and after their home Games. Shibli and Bingham (2008) found that all host nations of the Summer Olympic Games from 1988 to 2004 won more gold medals and improved their medals' table ranking relative to the edition prior to being host. They calculated the average host nation effect to be worth seven gold medals. Subsequently, Shibli, Gratton and Bingham (2012) calculated that all host nations in the Summer Olympic Games between 1988 and 2008 increased the number of sports and disciplines in which they won medals compared with the pre-hosting edition. For sports this average was four and for disciplines the average was five.

Nevill, Balmer and Winter (2012) examined the number of medals won by the 14 countries that had hosted the Summer Olympic Games since the second world war until 2008. Using a logit regression model, they estimated the host nation's odds of winning medals will increase in proportion (ratio) to 1:2.05 relative to its historical away average. The same authors carried out a study to assess the significance of home advantage for different event groups selected from the Summer Olympic Games between 1896 and 1996 (Balmer, Nevill and Williams, 2003). They observed highly significant home advantage in event groups that were either subjectively judged (boxing and gymnastics) or relied on subjective decisions (team games). Similarly, Franchini and Takito (2016) provided evidence for the home advantage effect in five combat sports – boxing, fencing, judo, taekwondo and wrestling – contested during the Summer Olympic Games between 1996 and 2012 for total number of medals, gold and silver medals.

The prevalence of home advantage has also been documented in the Winter Olympic Games. Balmer, Nevill and Williams (2001) found a significant overall home advantage in the Winter Olympic Games during the period 1908–1998 when all events were combined, while controlling for nation strength, changes in the number of medals on offer and the performance of non-host nations. More recently, Pettigrew and Reiche (2016) analysed home advantage in the Summer Olympic Games during 1952–2012 and in the Winter Olympic Games during 1952–2014. Pooling together the Summer and Winter results, they found that Olympic hosts tend to increase their number of gold medals by 4.4 and their total medals by 7.4 relative to their medal count in the previous Olympics four years earlier.

In comparison with the Olympic Games, the academic literature on home advantage in the Paralympic Games is relatively scarce. Wilson and Ramchandani (2017a) were the first to examine home advantage in the Paralympic Games. They found clear evidence of a home advantage effect in the Winter Paralympic Games at an overall country level and in the sports of alpine skiing and cross-country skiing. A subsequent study by the same authors also reported strong evidence of a home advantage effect in the Summer Paralympic Games at an overall country level and specifically in athletics, table tennis and wheelchair fencing (Wilson and Ramchandani, 2017b).

Study design

A shortcoming of previous research is that the findings are often not directly comparable as a result of differing methodologies used by different researchers in terms of how success is defined, how home advantage is calculated and the time span under review. In this chapter, we adopt a consistent approach to the measurement of performance and the calculation of home advantage in the Olympic and Paralympic Games, including both Summer and Winter editions, covering the same time period. Our study includes seven nations that have hosted the Summer Olympic and Paralympic Games and seven nations that have hosted the Winter

Table 31.2 Hosts of the Olympic and Paralympic Games 1992–2018

Summer Games		*Winter Games*	
Year	*Host nation*	*Year*	*Host nation*
1992	Spain (ESP)	1994	Norway (NOR)
1996	United States (USA)	1998	Japan (JPN)
2000	Australia (AUS)	2002	United States (USA)
2004	Greece (GRC)	2006	Italy (ITA)
2008	China (CHN)	2010	Canada (CAN)
2012	Great Britain (GBR)	2014	Russia (RUS)
2016	Brazil (BRA)	2018	South Korea (KOR)

Olympic and Paralympic Games. These host nations are shown in Table 31.2, together with the number of events that were contested in each edition of these competitions in the time frame under consideration. The results of each edition of the Olympic and Paralympic Games in this time frame were sourced from the official websites of the International Olympic Committee (www.olympic.org/olympic-games) and International Paralympic Committee (www.paralympic.org) respectively.

Two key performance indicators (KPIs) were used to measure the level of success achieved by the hosts of the Olympic and Paralympic Games. These were the number of gold medals won and the number of total medals won. For each KPI, home advantage was calculated as the difference between how nations performed at their home Games and how they performed in the Games immediately prior to hosting. For example, Great Britain's performance at home in the 2012 Summer Olympic and Paralympic Games was compared with its own pre-home performance in the 2008 Summer Olympic and Paralympic Games. Once home advantage scores were calculated for each host nation in each competition, a one sample Wilcoxon signed ranked test was used to determine whether there was a genuine difference in nations' performance under host and non-host conditions.

The results of our study are now presented. The results for the Summer Olympic and Paralympic Games are presented first. The results for the Winter Olympic and Paralympic Games are presented thereafter.

Home advantage in the Summer Olympics and Paralympics

Figure 31.2 shows how the last seven Summer Olympic and Paralympic hosts have performed at their home Games compared with their performance in the Games four years prior to being the host nation.

Nations positioned in the top right quadrant of Figure 31.2 improved on both KPIs (gold medals and total medals) at their home edition, whereas the bottom left quadrant features any nations that experienced a decline on both KPIs. Nations located in the bottom right quadrant improved at home in terms of gold medals but won fewer medals in total. Finally, any nations featured in the top left quadrant won more medals at home in total but won fewer gold medals. It can be seen that all seven Summer Olympic hosts increased their number of gold medals won at their home edition and six of them also bettered their total medal count (excluding USA). For the Summer Paralympic Games, a more mixed pattern emerges. Three host nations increased their gold medal and total medal tally at home

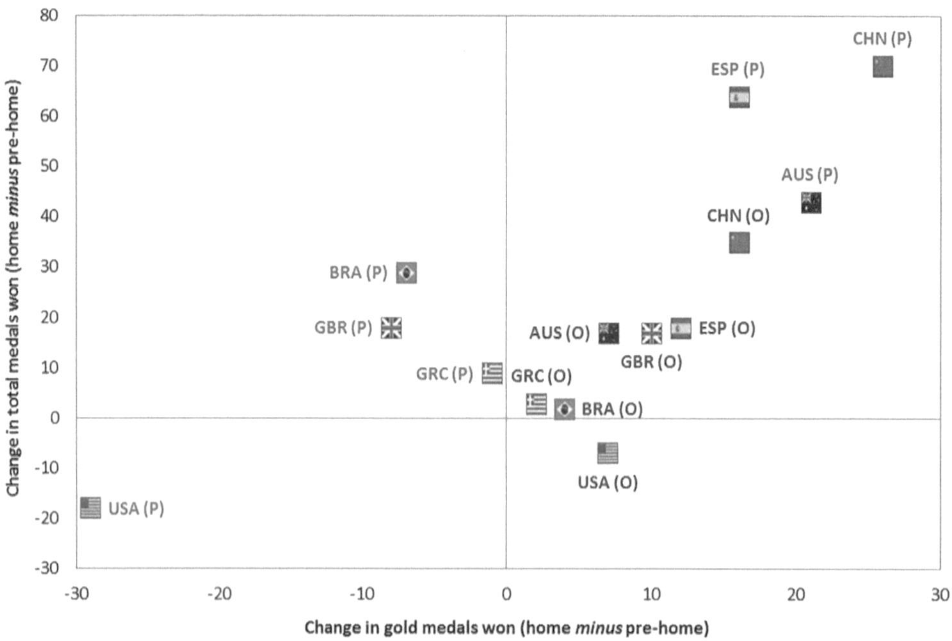

Figure 31.2 Performance in the Summer Olympics (O) and Paralympics (P) by host nation

(Australia, China and Spain), three others improved their total medal count but lost gold medals (Brazil, Great Britain and Greece) whereas for one nation there was a deterioration on both KPIs (USA).

The median number of gold medals gained at home by Summer Olympic hosts in our sample is seven ($p < 0.05$) whereas for total medals the median improvement is 17 ($p < 0.10$). For Summer Paralympic hosts, the median change in gold medals won at home was negative (-1) but this was not statistically significant ($p > 0.10$), whereas for total medals the median change was an improvement of 29 medals ($p < 0.10$).

Home advantage in the Winter Olympics and Paralympics

Figure 31.3 shows how the last seven Winter Olympic and Paralympic hosts have performed at their home Games compared with their performance in the Games four years before being the host nation. All seven Winter Olympic hosts increased their gold medal count at their home edition. Six of these nations also won more medals in total (Italy being the exception in this case). In the Summer Paralympic Games, five hosts improved on both KPIs (China, Japan, Korea, Norway and Russia), one nation improved in terms of total medals but lost gold medals (USA) and one nation lost both gold medals and total medals (Italy).

The median number of gold medals gained at home by Winter Olympic hosts in our sample is four ($p < 0.05$), whereas for total medals the median improvement is six ($p < 0.10$). For Winter Paralympic hosts, the median improvement in gold medals won and total medals won at home is five ($p > 0.10$) and nine ($p < 0.05$) respectively.

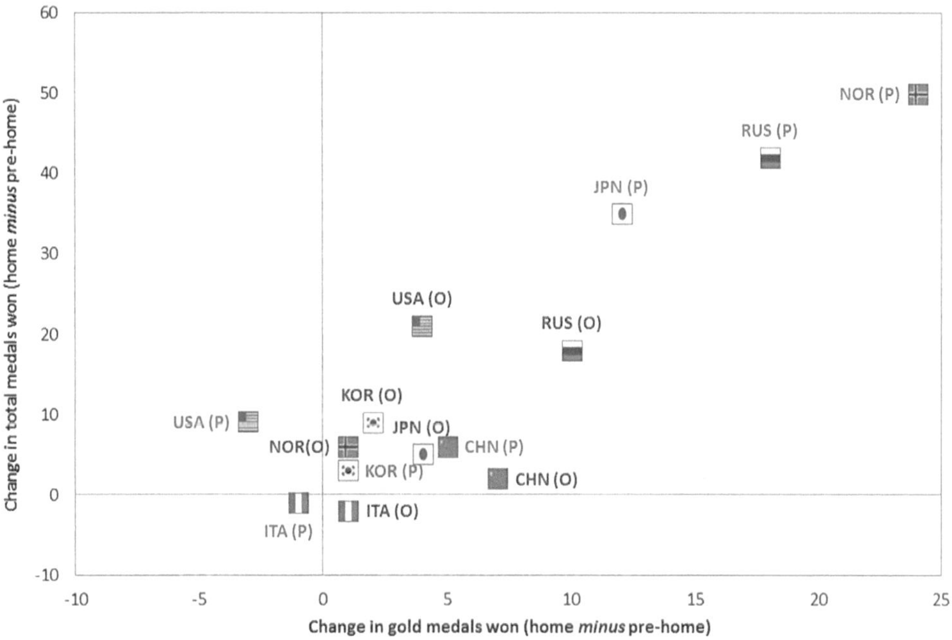

Figure 31.3 Performance in the Winter Olympics (O) and Paralympics (P) by host nation

Conceptual framework revisited

An important question is whether and how nations can influence their performance when hosting the Olympic and Paralympic Games in order to benefit from home advantage. In terms of understanding why a home advantage effect is seen to occur in the Olympic and Paralympic Games, previous research highlights the role of certain game location factors (Carron, Lough head and Bray, 2005; Courneya and Carron, 1992), most notably the influence of the home crowd on officials in certain sports, home athletes' familiarity with local venues and facilities, the detrimental effect of jet lag associated with travelling across time zones on athletes from non-host countries and in some cases competition rules that tend to favour home athletes.

Home advantage in the Olympic Games has been documented as a result of referee bias in sports that require subjective scoring or judgements (Balmer, Nevill and Williams, 2001, 2003; Franchini and Takito, 2016; Nevill, Balmer and Winter, 2012). In their analysis of Great Britain's performance at the 2012 Summer Olympic Games in London, Nevill, Balmer and Winter (2012) reported that crowds appear to have had an important effect on influencing officials to favour the home athletes and hence increase their medal winning capacity. Home competitors' familiarity with local conditions or the venue is also a game location factor sometimes associated with home advantage. For example, Bray and Carron (1993) acknowledged the beneficial effects of familiarity with the venue could contribute to the home advantage in alpine skiing. This observation was supported by Balmer, Nevill and Williams (2001), who noted that the effect of familiarity with local conditions in the Winter Olympic Games was most evident in alpine skiing, where the potential for variation is at its greatest.

Travelling across time zones for competitors from non-host nations can lead to jet lag and affect athletic performance (Reilly, Waterhouse and Edwards, 2005). Moreover, the severity of jet lag and subsequent recovery is a function of the number of time zones crossed (Pace and Carron, 1992). The problems of jet lag can last for over a week if the flight crosses ten time zones or more, and they can reduce performance and the motivation to train effectively (Waterhouse, Reilly and Edwards, 2004). In one previous study of the Winter Olympic Games the number of time zones and direction of travel produced no discernible trends or differences in performance (Balmer, Nevill and Williams, 2001). With respect to rule factors, previous research suggests that home advantage in the Olympic Games is influenced by host nations having the right to contest more medals, field larger teams and compete in a larger range of events than usual, which increases the opportunity to win more medals (Clarke, 2000; Shibli, Gratton and Bingham, 2012).

Beyond these game location factors, there is also evidence that host nations tend to increase their level of investment in elite sport prior to hosting the Olympic and Paralympic Games (Nevill, Balmer and Winter, 2009). To illustrate this point, in the four years leading up to the Beijing 2008 Games, UK Sport (the agency in charge of maximising the performance of athletes representing Great Britain in the Olympic and Paralympic Games) spent £235.1 million to support 27 Summer Olympic sports and this figure increased by 12% to £264.1 million in the four years leading up to the London 2012 Games, when Great Britain was the host nation. The proportionate increase in funding for Summer Paralympic sports in the UK between 2005–2008 (£29.5 million) and 2009–2012 (£49.3 million) was even higher at 67% (UK Sport, 2018). The impact of funding on Olympic and Paralympic performance has also been documented previously in other countries such as China and Australia. For example, Guan and Hong (2016) concluded that the financial support provided by the Chinese government had been the key to the nation's success in the Summer Paralympic Games while Hogan and Norton (2000) found that there was a significant linear relationship between money spent and total Olympic medals won by Australia leading up to its home Games in 2000. The basic point here is that financial support for elite sport is one of the fundamental 'pillars', which can be influenced by policy, through which international sporting success can be produced (De Bosscher et al., 2006). It is therefore entirely plausible that taking a strategic approach to elite sport development by host nations in the build-up to the Olympic and Paralympic Games can contribute to some of the observed home advantage in these competitions.

Conclusion

Home advantage has been shown to exist by separate studies in the Summer Olympic Games (e.g. Balmer, Nevill and Williams, 2003; Clarke, 2000; Franchini and Takito, 2016; Nevill, Balmer and Winter, 2012), the Winter Olympic Games (e.g. Balmer, Nevill and Williams, 2001), the Summer Paralympic Games (Wilson and Ramchandani, 2017b) and the Winter Paralympic Games (Wilson and Ramchandani, 2017a). Because these studies were undertaken in isolation, they focused on different time periods and did not utilise a uniform approach to define performance and measure home advantage in these competitions. Our study uses a standard methodology to test for the occurrence of home advantage in the Olympic and Paralympic Games using two KPIs.

As far as the study of the impacts associated with major international multi-sport competitions is concerned, most of the previous research has involved the Olympic Games, which feature able-bodied athletes. By contrast, there is a paucity of research regarding the impacts associated with hosting the Paralympic Games, which involve athletes with a disability. Indeed, a thematic analysis of Paralympic legacy research by Misener et al. (2013) found that few studies have evaluated the comparative outcomes, legacies and event leverage that the Paralympic

Table 31.3 Average (median) home advantage in the Olympics and Paralympics

Competition	*Season*	*Gold medals*	*Total medals*
		Median HA	*Median HA*
Olympic Games	Summer	7**	17*
Olympic Games	Winter	4**	6**
Paralympic Games	Summer	–1	29*
Paralympic Games	Winter	5	9**

* p < 0.10 ** p < 0.05

Games have generated. Moreover, Gold and Gold (2007) emphasise how the Paralympic Games underline the change from sport as therapeutic competition to that of elite events that carry intrinsic prestige, with growing rivalry over medal tables. It is in this wider academic context that our study makes a novel contribution to the body of knowledge by considering the home advantage phenomenon in the Paralympic Games alongside the Olympic Games.

We conclude by summarising the main findings of our study (see Table 31.3). First, in the case of both Summer and Winter editions of the Olympic Games, there is evidence that host nations experience a statistically significant home advantage effect in terms of gold medals ($p < 0.05$). Second, Summer and Winter hosts of Paralympic Games do not appear to have a significant home advantage (or disadvantage) as far as gold medals are concerned ($p > 0.10$). Third, a statistically significant home advantage effect is evident for total medals in the Winter Olympic and Paralympic Games ($p < 0.05$) as well as in the Summer Olympic and Paralympic Games ($p < 0.10$).

Our study stops short of measuring longer-term performance benefits for host nations as a result of staging the Olympic and Paralympic Games. There is some evidence to suggest that nations who have been awarded the right to host the Olympic Games also tend to improve their performance in the editions that immediately precede and follow their home Games (Nevill, Balmer and Winter, 2009). Heavy investment by host nations in elite sport appears to be an important factor to explain this trend. Home advantage research would benefit from investigating the extent to which any pre-host and post-host effects are also evident in the Paralympic Games. Further research is also required to test whether success in the Olympic and Paralympic Games can act a precursor to wider societal outcomes such as international prestige for the host nation and a feel-good factor among the population.

References

Balmer, N.J., Nevill, A.M. and Williams, M. (2001). Home advantage in the Winter Olympics (1908–1998). *Journal of Sports Sciences*, 19, pp. 129–139.

Balmer, N.J., Nevill, A.M. and Williams, M. (2003). Modelling home advantage in the Summer Olympic Games. *Journal of Sports Sciences*, 21, pp. 469–478.

Bray, S.R. and Carron, A.V. (1993). The home advantage in alpine skiing. *Australian Journal of Science and Medicine in Sport*, 25, pp. 76–81.

Carron, A.V., Loughhead, T.M. and Bray, S.R. (2005). The home advantage in sport competitions: Courneya and Carron's (1992) conceptual framework a decade later. *Journal of Sports Sciences*, 23, pp. 395–407.

Clarke, S.R. (2000). Home advantage in the Olympic Games. In: G. Cohen and T. Langtry, eds., *Proceedings of the fifth Australian conference on mathematics and computers in sport*. June 14–16. Sydney, NSW: University of Technology Sydney, pp. 43–51.

Courneya, K.S. and Carron, A.V. (1992). The home advantage in sport competitions: A literature review. *Journal of Sport and Exercise Psychology*, 14, pp. 13–27.

DCMS. (2010). *Plans for the legacy from the 2012 Olympic and Paralympic games*. London: Department for Culture Media and Sport.

De Bosscher, V., De Knop, P., Van Bottenburg, M. and Shibli, S. (2006). A conceptual framework for analysing sports policy factors leading to international sporting success. *Journal European Sport Management Quarterly*, 6, pp. 185–215.

Franchini, E. and Takito, M.Y. (2016). Home advantage in combat sports during the Olympic Games. *Sport Sciences for Health*, 12, p. 287.

Girginov, V. and Hills, L. (2008). A sustainable sports legacy: Creating a link between the London Olympics and sports participation. *International Journal of the History of Sport*, 25, pp. 2091–2116.

Gold, J. and Gold, M. (2007). Access for all: The rise of the Paralympic games. *The Journal of The Royal Society for the Promotion of Health*, 127, pp. 133–141.

Gratton, C. and Preuss, H. (2008). Maximising Olympic impacts by building up legacies. *The International Journal of the History of Sport*, 25, pp. 1922–1938.

Guan, Z. and Hong, F. (2016). The development of elite disability sport in China: A critical review. *The International Journal of the History of Sport*, 33, pp. 485–510.

Hogan, K. and Norton, K. (2000). The 'price' of Olympic gold. *Journal of Science and Medicine in Sport*, 3, pp. 203–218.

IOC. (2012). *Olympic legacy*. Lausanne: IOC.

Jehue, R., Street, D. and Huizenga, R. (1993). Effect of time zone and game time changes on team performance: National Football League. *Medicine and Science in Sports and Exercise*, 25, pp. 127–131.

Mangan, J. (2008). Prologue: Guarantees of global goodwill: Post-Olympic legacies – Too many limping white elephants? *The International Journal of the History of Sport*, 25, pp. 1869–1883.

Masterman, G. (2009). *Strategic sports event management: An Olympic edition*. Oxford: Butterworth-Heinemann.

McCartney, G., Thomas, S., Thomson, H., Scott, J., Hamilton, V., Hanlon, P. and Bond, L. (2010). The health and socioeconomic impacts of major multi-sport events: Systematic review (1978–2008). *British Medical Journal*, 340, p. 2369.

Misener, L., Darcu, S., Legg, D. and Gilbert, K. (2013). Beyond Olympic legacy: Understanding Paralympic legacy through a thematic analysis. *Journal of Sport Management*, 27, pp. 329–341.

Neave, N. and Wolfson, S. (2003). Testosterone, territoriality, and the 'home advantage'. *Physiology & Behavior*, 78, pp. 269–275.

Nevill, A.M., Balmer, N.J. and Winter, E.M. (2009). Why Great Britain's success in Beijing could have been anticipated and why it should continue beyond 2012. *British Journal of Sports Medicine*, 43, pp. 1108–1110.

Nevill, A.M., Balmer, N.J. and Winter, E.M. (2012). Congratulations to team GB, but why should we be so surprised? Olympic medal count can be predicted using logit regression models that include "home advantage." *British Journal of Sports Medicine*, 46, pp. 958–959.

Pace, A. and Carron, A.V. (1992). Travel and the National Hockey League. *Canadian Journal of Sports Sciences*, 17, pp. 60–64.

Pettigrew, S. and Reiche, D. (2016). Hosting the Olympic Games: An overstated advantage in sports history. *The International Journal of the History of Sport*, 33, pp. 635–647.

Recht, L.D., Lew, R.A. and Schwartz, W.J. (1995). Baseball teams beaten by jet lag. *Nature*, 377, p. 583.

Reilly, T., Waterhouse, J. and Edwards, B. (2005). Jet lag and air travel: Implications for performance. *Clinics in Sports Medicine*, 24, pp. 367–380.

Shibli, S. and Bingham, J. (2008). A forecast of the performance of China in the Beijing Olympic Games 2008 and the underlying performance management issues. *Managing Leisure*, 13, pp. 272–292.

Shibli, S., Gratton, C. and Bingham, J. (2012). A forecast of the performance of Great Britain and Northern Ireland in the London 2012 Olympic Games. *Managing Leisure*, 17, pp. 274–290.

UK Sport. (2018). *Historical funding figures*.

Waterhouse, J., Reilly, T. and Edwards, B. (2004). The stress of travel. *Journal of Sports Sciences*, 22, pp. 946–966.

Wilson, D. and Ramchandani, G. (2017a). Home advantage in the Winter Paralympic games. *Sport Sciences for Health*, pp. 1976–2014.

Wilson, D. and Ramchandani, G. (2017b). An investigation of home advantage in the Summer Paralympic Games. *Sport Sciences for Health*.

32

Debating the future of Olympic and Paralympic legacy

Vassil Girginov

Introduction

The notion of Olympic and Paralympic legacy has undergone a remarkable intellectual and experiential journey. It is reflective of the growing cultural, economic and political appeal of the Olympic and Paralympic Games and the powers of the International Olympic (IOC) and Paralympic (IPC) Committees who own them. The first explicit reference to the Games legacy appears in the 1956 Melbourne Olympics bid's documentation where legacy was envisioned as local sporting infrastructure for the benefit of athletes. Until the late 1990s the notion of legacy was almost absent from the bid cities' candidature files (Gold and Gold, 2009; Leopkey, 2009), and when it received a mention it was afforded only a modest local reference (Girginov and Hills, 2008). However, it needs to be recognised that the absence of legacy from the public discourse prior to the Melbourne Games does not mean that no legacy was created at all. The Games have created significant cultural, social and political capital and have successfully earned their place on the political and economic agenda of governments, media and commercial organisations.

Over the past 20 years (1998–2018) scholars, sport administrators, Olympic promoters and politicians have transformed the notion of legacy from a relatively negligible by-product of the world premier sporting event, to a normative concept promoting institutionalised forms of behaviour and capable of delivering benefits to a wide range of stakeholders. The critical importance of legacy was first institutionally recognised in 2003 with a change in Rule 2 of the Olympic Charter (IOC, 2003). This was followed with three specific recommendations in Agenda 2020, the blueprint for the Olympic movement (IOC, 2014). Finally, the status of legacy, as a key strategic priority for the IOC, was fixed in 2017 in the 'Legacy Strategic Approach. Moving Forward' (IOC, 2017). This document also determines the scope of Olympic legacy which covers seven broad areas including organised sport development; social development through sport; human skills, networks and innovation; culture and creative development; urban development; environment enhancement; and economic value and brand equity (IOC, 2017, p. 17).

Albeit not that explicit, the IPC's approach to legacy has been equally ambitious. The IPC's strategic plan (2015–2018) frames the legacy of the Paralympics as a rational enterprise premised on growth: "By broadening the reach of the Paralympics, growing para-sport events and furthering brand awareness, the Paralympic Movement's transformational legacy will be amplified" (IPC, 2015, p. 14). It further explicitly intertwines legacy with the Paralympic movement's values into a goal-directed project in order to: "Promote the value of the Paralympic Games by maximising legacy and social impact opportunities as well as by harnessing commercial potential" (p. 19). The IPC owes its embrace of the idea of legacy to a large extent to the concerted efforts of the organisers of the 2012 London Olympic and Paralympic Games and the British government who produced the first legacy strategy for disabled people (DCMS, 2009).

The key word in the representation of legacy is 'development' as Games promoters declare their intention to develop different aspects of society and individuals. Therefore, both as a concept and practice, the Games and what is done in their name, represent a normative developmental project, which, as Coubertin (1966) asserted, transcends the mere sporting contest. Two further points in the framing of legacy deserve mention here. The first suggests that the legacy concept is underpinned by a logic of causality. This is an 'if-then' proposition which aims to prove that when staging the Games then a range of positive changes and benefits for individuals, organisations and societies will occur. This logic is rooted in a positivist ontology, which fits nicely with the universalising claims of the Olympic movement. The second point concerns legacy's explicit concern with outcomes that follows closely from point one. This focus is problematic conceptually and practically and as Chalip (2017, p. 28) observed, "the fundamental flaw in the legacy framework is that it is focused on outcomes". As discussed later, a conceptual preoccupation with legacy outcomes has practical implications for politicians and Games organisers because it urges them to clearly identify, plan, manage and evaluate these outcomes.

This chapter extends the debate and practical efforts aimed at conceptualising and operationalising legacy. It submits for debate three questions in the hope that they will challenge the current thinking and help better define this critical issue for the Olympic movement. The 2012 London Olympics marked the first time when a single Organising Committee was responsible for the delivery of both the Olympic and Paralympic Games. This was but one of a series of joint actions of the International Olympic Committee and the International Paralympic Committee designed to ensure a greater consistency and impact of this global event, and the promotion of sport in general. While the legacy visions of the IOC have a longer and richer history and are far more ambitions than those of the IPC, they share the same fundamental concerns and challenges. Therefore, the discussion that follows applies to both Games. The chapter is organised around three key questions including, 'what matters most for the Olympic movement that is worth striving for?'; 'what kind of legacy does the Olympic movement need?'; and 'what is this about legacy we want to know?'

What matters most for the Olympic movement that is worth striving for?

A well-grounded discussion about Olympic and Paralympic legacy ought to proceed not with the event, that is the Olympic or Paralympic Games, but with what they represent. This entails unpacking the notion of the Olympic movement whose philosophy and aspirations the Games epitomise. The Olympic movement emerged at the beginning of the 20th century largely in response to the deplorable moral and physical state of youth and the state of general education, and a belief in the constructive educational role of sport in society, including its ability to promote international understanding and peace. Like other social movements, the Olympic movement, too, embraces the interplay between grievances and beliefs. Thus, the *raison d'être* of social movements is their explicit concern with seeking to remedy or alter some problematic issue (i.e. grievance). The Olympic Charter expresses that "The goal of Olympism is to place sport at the service of the harmonious development of man, with a view to promoting a peaceful society concerned with the preservation of human dignity" (IOC, 2015, p. 13). Recently, this broad goal (i.e. belief) was spelled out into 16 specific actionable areas/activities (IOC, 2010).

Borrowing from Tilly and Wood's (2013) conceptualisation of social movements as including a campaign, performance and display, allows to identify the three main characteristics of the Olympic movement. First, the Olympic and Paralympic movements advocate the need for an organised public effort and makes claims for their authority in promoting ethical sport and educating youth, as well as supporting the development of sport (i.e. a campaign). Second, it ensures the regular celebration of the Olympic Games, and cooperation with public authorities and private organisations in placing sport at the service of harmonious development of man and peace (i.e. performances). Finally, the Olympic and Paralympic movements pledge to take actions to strengthen their unity and to protect the independence of sport (i.e. a concerted display of worthiness, unity, numbers and commitment). These characteristics, and unity in diversity in particular, were reinforced by the movement's strategic document Agenda 2020 (IOC, 2014). Legacy has become the litmus test for the claims of the Olympic movement, whose strategic blueprint, Agenda 2020, boldly states that the IOC "invests more than three million dollars a day – every single day of the year to support world-wide sport. Never before have so many people all around our globe followed the Olympic Games" (IOC, 2014, p. 2).

Social movements make three kind of claims including programme, identity and standing (Tilly and Wood, 2013). The Olympic and Paralympic movements' programme claims concern expressed support for using sport in educating young people, in promoting respect, peace and human excellence in all its forms. Standing claims, on their part, involve strong opposition to any forms of discrimination and exploitation in sport, cheating and violence. Identity claims refer to the standing of the Olympic and Paralympic movements as a unified force based on global solidarity that needs to be considered politically, economically and culturally. Table 32.1 shows examples of the three kinds of Olympic claims and relevant fields of action where a legacy should be left.

A critical point in understanding legacy is the fact that the Olympic movement involves collective making of claims that, if realised, would conflict with someone else's interests. For example, by inspiring people to be more physically active (i.e. programme claims), the Olympic and Paralympic Games often disturb social and natural lifeworld to make way for a new sporting infrastructure. This is often in conflict with the interests of local communities and nature. Furthermore, in combination, claims and action (i.e. campaign) extends beyond any single event and includes three interrelated parties – self-designated claimants, object/s of claim and a target public. It follows that directed action is contingent on identification of causality, blame and responsibility, and has a clear attributional component. Coubertin and his associates and followers framed Olympism as a philosophy of social reform that emphasises the role of sport in world development, international understanding, peaceful co-existence, and social and moral education. Table 32.2 shows the relationship between the main Olympic claims, the claimants,

Table 32.1 Olympic and Paralympic movements' claims and fields of actions

Claims	*Example*	*Field of action*
Programme	Inspire young people	Human development, education, equal opportunity
Identity	Unity of Olympic movement	Sport, education and human development
Standing	Sustainability	Human development and sustainable development

Table 32.2 Examples of Olympic movement's main claims and claim parties

Claim	*Claim parties*		
	Claimants	*Object of claim*	*Target public*
For education	UNESCO	Ministries of Education, NOC	HE Institutions, schools/ colleges
International understanding	UN, EU, IOA	National Governments, NSO	Youth Centres
Equal opportunities	UNESCO, TAFISA, WHO, WUOC, EC, Nike	National Sport for All Associations	Sport clubs Deprived and minorities
Fair and equal competition	WADA, Play the Game, UNEP	NOC, NSO	Sport clubs
Cultural expression	UNESCO, EU, ILO	Culture and Arts Councils	Community groups
Independence of sport	UN, EU	NSO, NOC, Ministries of Sport	Sport organisations
Personal excellence	UNESCO, EU, IF	NSO, Non-profits	Athletes

Source: Girginov (2018, p. 32)

objects of claim and the targeted public. A critical analysis of this relationship is essential for determining how legacies come about and who the main beneficiaries are.

As clear from the table, the implementation of any Olympic and Paralympic claim requires establishing a complex set of relationships and interactions with a range of actors in order to deliver legacy. Thus, the results of Olympic aspirations, as the philosophy that underpins them, have been controversial and contested. It was only logical to encounter the same controversies with Olympic legacies as exemplified by numerous claims and counterclaims (e.g. Brittain, Bocarro and Byers, 2017; Cohen, 2013; DCMS, 2013; Grix, 2014; Holt and Ruta, 2016). The current move to a more strategic approach to legacy taken by the IOC (2017) promises to introduce a more rational planning in the process and eventually greater positive legacies. However, the IOC's (2017) new strategy envisages a single vision of legacy as defined by the local organising committee (OCOG). This is problematic because regardless of the amount of creative wording, by default, any grant legacy vision tends to articulate claims at a high level of abstraction and that are not very meaningful to a number of stakeholders.

Since legacy has become the testing ground for Olympic claims, it ought to move from abstract Humanity claims to the things that matter the most for the Olympic movement – the creation of public value. MacAloon (2008, p. 779) makes this point clear: "Being a movement means *moving* on the things that matter most, or should matter most, not to some abstract Humanity but to real human beings". The main problem of abstract Humanity is that it promotes stateless solutions to the legacy promises. For Rojek (2014),

> Mega events such as the Olympic Games present stateless solutions to particular issues such as injustice, inequality and exclusion because they are hatched outside the parameters of government, do not rely on government sponsorship and appeal to 'the people', not party political congeries.
>
> *(p. 33)*

It is within the powers of all major Olympic stakeholders to deliver meaningful legacies, particularly in the two core domains of sport and education. Increased sport participation figures mean very little if they do not represent real breakthroughs in altering access to sport and education for less privileged or neglected groups. There is a need to revitalise the core purpose of the Olympic movement in a more substantial way and to appreciate that the Games' role is to serve its cause.

What kind of legacy does the Olympic movement need?

What type of legacy should be pursued by the Olympic movement is not just a rhetorical question to be debated at academic conferences but one which carries considerable practical consequences for all stakeholders as well. This is a fundamental issue for the Olympic movement because if it is to deliver on its claims, it needs to be able to introduce meaningful social change at individual, organisational and social levels. As noted, the current preoccupation with legacy outcomes has been rooted in a positivist ontology. It purports that there is a causal relationship between action and outcome, and that by staging the Games certain benefits should occur. A positivist thinking also promotes a highly rational approach to the planning and managing of the Olympics which favours prediction and control, and concepts such as effectiveness, targets and key performance indicators (KPI). It follows that anything that is not quantifiable and measurable would find it difficult to qualify as legacy.

There can be little doubt about the powers of the Olympic and Paralympic Games to stimulate positive changes in society. However, some 20 years of research on legacy has produced a body of evidence that challenges rather than supports the main claims put forward by Games promoters (e.g. Brittain et al., 2018; Brown and Pappous, 2018; Grix, 2017; Weed, 2012, 2013). Table 32.3 summarises the shortcomings of the key Olympic legacy claims. The charge laid over the emphasis on outcomes and neglect for the processes responsible for shaping

Table 32.3 Main charges levied at the legacy of the Olympic Games

Legacy claim	*Charge*
Conceptual	No clearly accepted definition and competing ontologies rooted in positivism;
Political	Prone to contrasting political interpretations and contingent on prevailing political views during the life span of the project; source of democratic deficit – excluding citizens from participation; 'monument complex';
Outcomes	Focus on exogenous not on endogenous outcomes; poorly understood and governed; overemphasis on outcomes and neglect of processes responsible for shaping legacies; contingent on methodology used;
Concert between global and local visions of legacy	Significant dissonance between local, national and global visions of legacy; dissonance between Olympic claims and priorities of national sport policies;
Economic benefits	Hugely overstated and rarely delivered; lack conclusive evidence; front-loaded cost and deferred benefits;
City promotion	No conclusive evidence for Games contribution to city image;
Sport participation	No proven causal relationship between the Games and sport participation; inspirational power of elite sport questionable;
Sustainability	Poor/uneven distribution of benefits; lack of political and financial commitment; limited human ability to predict the future
Management	Huge cost overruns averaging 170% of the stated cost of the Games; focus on deliverable targets, effectiveness, strategy.

Source: Girginov (2018, p. 197)

legacies deserves particular attention. The creation of a Games legacy is a socially constructed process which unfolds over a period of at least nine years – from the inception of the bid idea to delivery (Girginov and Hills, 2008). Therefore, legacy construction has an important temporal dimension that challenges our ability to accurately predict the future. Legacy visions presuppose a good deal of ignorance because we cannot know how they may evolve and what the real cost of realising them over the life span of a Games' project would be. Flyvbjerg and Stewart's (2012) study of the Summer Games from 1960 until London 2012 reported that the average cost overrun of the Olympics is 173% (this is the difference between the bid and the final Games budget). This significant difference between planned and actual expenditures compares very unfavourably with the cost overrun of much more complex and expensive projects such as transport (27–45%) and IT (27%). But Games cost overruns are not just statistical figures. They bear direct impact on legacy ambitions as greater expenditures by host countries on Olympic operational activities mean fewer investments in other areas such as grassroots sports and creating opportunities for people to practice sport.

Shifting the emphasis of legacy from outcomes to processes also entails another substantive difference. The analysis of legacy processes and outcomes represents two very different conceptual and practical propositions. Pawson (2013, p. 27) makes this point plain clear: "process research cannot masquerade as outcome research and qualitative utterances cannot chart quantitative differences". Proper Games outcome research entail very different assumptions, method of investigation and overall project design. Pettigrew's observation drives the point home (1997, p. 338): "the driving assumption behind process thinking is that social reality is not a steady state. It is a dynamic process". Olympic legacy is a social constructive process which unfolds over a sustained period of time, involves multiple stakeholders at international, national and local levels, and the mobilisation and deployment of various resources.

By connecting Olympic legacy outcomes with the processes responsible for them, we get a much better sense of how to proceed in the pursuit of our visions. The interplay between outcomes and processes allows to reveal the power dynamics, structures, discourses and the key actors that shape legacy. Choosing between them is a false proposition because both are equally important and complementary. This conclusion entails moving beyond current Olympic legacy preoccupation with external and tangible aspects such as infrastructure building and job creation and studying subtler but equally important internal aspects such as building capacities at individual and organisational level.

What is this about legacy we want to know?

The previous two sections have made a case about the importance of legacies which had been enshrined in the Olympic Charter (IOC, 2003) and requires candidate cities to develop and implement strategic plans to that end. The idea of legacy has provided the much-needed heuristic device and the link that allows the Olympic movement to objectify its claims and to show their relevance to people, organisations and societies. This link has been codified in a range of causal relationships between sport and personal wellbeing, community and economic development, national pride and other purported benefits and values. However, the Olympic movement claims–Games legacy nexus has proved problematic as event promoters and academics have struggled to provide convincing evidence for the presence of causality.

Given the tensions surrounding the legacy concept, a key question that arises is, if legacy is so important to the Olympic movement, what is this we really need to know about it? The Olympic Games cut across the interest of many stakeholders and involve a significant amount of interactions between a multitude of actors and resources. The legacy of the Games is multifaceted and hence requires different types of knowledge. Habermas's (1981) distinction between technical, practical and emancipatory knowledge is helpful here. The technical knowledge involves those aspects of Olympic legacy concerned with manipulating the environment and the event so that the desired positive benefits occur, and the negative ones are minimised. The practical knowledge, on the other hand, aims at extending our understanding of legacy so that we can achieve consensus between different stakeholders and garner community support needed for their implementation. Finally, emancipatory knowledge circulates at a more abstract level and involves liberating people from the specific constraints imposed on them as a result of framing and imposing legacy visions. But the question of what we want to know about legacy is closely intertwined with the interests of different stakeholders. Habermas's three forms of knowledge correspond to different kinds of interests including technical, practical and emancipatory respectively. Habermas also associates the different forms of knowledge with a specific dominant ontological stance. It is only the technical knowledge that is associated with a positivist science. The other forms of knowledge development require interpretive and critical social science approaches.

Several commentators have revealed the limitations of our legacy knowledge and pointed out the gaps that need to be addressed so a more comprehensive picture of the phenomenon is achieved. An earlier study by Girginov and Hills (2009) took a process-oriented approach to sustainable Olympic sport legacy research and proposed for consideration five key elements including the idea of sustainable sport development legacy; assigning functions to Olympic sports development; collective intentionality; collective rules; and the human capacity to deal with the environment. The authors identified 11 research questions pertinent to different key elements and concerning sustainable sport development legacy. However, in the meantime, the Olympic movement's commitment to sustainable development has grown significantly. The IOC's (2017) legacy strategy identifies 17 key Sustainable Development Goals, as determined by the UN (2017), to which it aims to contribute. These range from tackling poverty, to enhancing the quality of education, climate action and forging partnerships. It follows that we need to enhance considerably our knowledge about the Games' legacies in all three of Habermas's knowledge domains.

Olympic legacy has been the subject of analysis of the first two comprehensive systematic reviews (Scheu and Preuss, 2017; Thomson et al., 2018). Scheu and Preuss studied the legacy of all Summer Games from London 1908 to Rio 2016 and Winter Games from Oslo 1952 to Sochi 2014 and examined 214 articles in their analysis that met the inclusion criteria. The authors noted three main limitations of our knowledge including the lack of longitudinal studies, indicators and methodologies. But the most concerning conclusion was the lack of systematic attempts for establishing causality between Olympic claims and legacy outcomes. Furthermore, Scheu and Preuss also questioned the analytical power of the most preferred conceptual framework for studying legacy, the logic chain based on the theory of change, for being unable to isolate the Olympic effect. These conclusions clearly indicate that conceptual and methodological uncertainties surrounding the legacy concept persist and that more work is needed to determine what we really want to know about legacy.

Thomson et al. (2018) analysed 305 peer-reviewed research articles published between 2000 and 2016. The authors identified 11 different types of legacy and 45 theoretical frameworks employed for studying them. Like Popper's (2005) suggestion that for any body of observation evidence there will always be more than one theory that can account for it, this conclusion suggests that legacy knowledge could be generated from several ontological positions. Thus recognising the equal importance of different ontologies that organise human life is critical for the hugely culturally diverse Olympic movement. An interesting finding of this study points out to the interplay between knowledge and power. While most articles were concerned with legacy outcomes (124/41%), a growing number of studies (54/18%) examined the governance and policy issues that shape the framing and delivery of legacy visions. Legacy claims are premised on the deliberate visions of policy makers and Games promoters to affect the behaviour of others in society, thus they perform an important interpellation function. Legacy visions identify groups and issues in society which are deemed either underdeveloped or unacceptable. The legacy discourse then turns the public gaze towards those groups and issues by exposing them publicly on record while at the same time subjecting to public scrutiny the promises made in this regard by national governments and Games promoters.

It should be noted that despite the multitude of studies and frameworks, so far researchers and Games organisers have failed to answer the fundamental question of how legacies come about. Girginov's (2018) attempt to address this question suggested that the production of Olympic legacy is a four-stage continuing process including 'investing', 'interpelling', 'developing' and 'codifying'. The legacy journey starts not with the Games, but with the *raison d'être* of the Olympic movement. It allows its members to use the accumulated common cultural capital and to invest it into a set of visions which the host city then attempts to implement. Olympic legacy visions are inherently political because they aspire to significantly alter social structures and behaviours. Legacy visions then 'interpell' people and organisations by forging a trusteeship relationship where one party undertakes to change the capacity of another. This relationship could be framed through a range of different forms of engagement designed to both position various parties on the Olympic scene and to reinforce the collective 'can do' mentality. The third step in the legacy making is ensuring participation in interactions stimulated by the Games and getting involved in the resource development process. The final step in the legacy process involves studying, documenting, sharing and remembering legacies so they become cultural capital. Legacies, therefore, have a clear temporal orientation which moves from the past to the present and the future. Legacy visions need to take stock of the past first before they can project a desirable future.

A move away from abstract Humanity requires Games legacy to clearly establish locally meaningful representations of Olympism and to spell out how what has been done in the name of the Olympics contributes to the creation of public value. Critical for achieving advances in each area is the building of individual and organisational capacities in the sport and educational sectors in particular, as the two main pillars of Olympism.

Table 32.4 shows the four stages of the legacy construction process and the pertinent knowledge needed for each of them in the form of some research questions. This is not an exhaustive list of questions, rather it serves to focus the debate on the future of the legacy enterprise. These questions also aim to address the current disbalance between Games' exogenous and endogenous legacies. This is an important task because it reflects much more fundamental issues concerning the tensions between positivist and constructivist ontologies, the role of 'hard' and social sciences in developing legacy knowledge, and eventually who benefits from the Olympic and Paralympic Games.

Conclusion

This chapter set out to further the debate about the future of Olympic and Paralympic legacy. It took the IOC some 100 years to recognise the effects of the Games as the ultimate testament to its claims for human progress and prosperity through sport. Significant advances have been made in the conceptualisation, planning, delivering and measuring of legacies. Nonetheless, critical

Table 32.4 A four-stage process of Olympic and Paralympic Games legacy creation and knowledge needed

Legacy stage	*Knowledge needed/key questions*
Investing	What makes the Games valuable to society that is worth investing?
	Which forms of Olympic capital need to be invested?
Interpelling	How are legacy visions established?
	Who are the main Olympic trustees?
	What legacy claims have been put forward and by whom?
Developing	What is the pre-existing group organisations of different stakeholders?
	How do different stakeholders interact with the Games?
	What are the mechanisms for access to resources for different stakeholders?
	What resources have been exchanged in the process?
Codifying	Who measures legacies and with what instruments?
	How are legacies sustained?
	Who codifies legacy and with what means?

issues remain unresolved and, therefore, scholars and other stakeholders have the responsibility to engage with the subject and to make a positive contribution.

The Olympic and Paralympic movements of the 21st century are different in size, structure and substance from what they used to be in the IOC's formative years of the late 19th century and IPC in the mid 1960s. Their claims are bolder as they encompass areas that had never been associated with sport before. They possess significant material, human and informational resources to support those claims. They also aspire for recognition and partnership with other global movements and organisations. What has been done in the name of the Games and what legacy they leave for groups and societies has become critically important for its future.

In summing up, the answers to the three questions posed by this chapter suggest that what matters most for the Olympic and Paralympic movement and the Games is an explicit concern of legacy studies with issues that matter to real people and are related to equality, access to sport, strengthening the work of sport organisations and preserving the integrity of sport. Regarding the kind of legacy that is needed for the movements, the emphasis ought to be on locally meaningful visions that connect Games outcomes with the underlying processes responsible for their creation. As with the kind of knowledge that needs to be pursued, priority ought to be given to establishing what the Games mean to different communities and how they contribute to the creation of public value.

Olympic and Paralympic legacies do not simply represent a linear causal relationship between visions and outcomes. Since they concern complex human systems and involve multiple interactions and resources, legacies need to be viewed as an emergent combination of attributes, capital, processes, interactions and technologies pertinent to any community of people and organisations. The ultimate purpose of Olympic and Paralympic legacies is the creation of public value. Legacy, therefore, represents both a means and a developmental end in itself.

References

Brittain, I., Bocarro, J. and Byers, T., eds. (2018). *Olympic legacy: Fairy tales or reality*. London: Routledge.

Brown, C. and Pappous, A. (2018). "The Legacy Element . . . It Just Felt More Woolly": Exploring the reasons for the decline in people with disabilities' sport participation in England 5 years After the London 2012 Paralympic games. *Journal of Sport and Social Issues*, 42, pp. 343–368. doi:10.1177 %2F0193723518781237.

Chalip, L. (2017). Trading legacy for leverage. In: I. Brittain, J. Bocarro, T. Byers and K. Swart, eds., *Legacies and mega events. Fact or fairy tales*. London: Routledge, pp. 25–42.

Cohen, P. (2013). *On the wrong side of the track? East London and the post Olympics*. London: Lawrence & Wishart.

Coubertin, P. (1966). *The Olympic idea: Discourses and essays*. Stuttgart, Germany: Olympischer Sport-Verlag.

DCMS. (2009). London 2012: *A legacy for disabled people: Setting new standards, changing perceptions*. London: DCMS.

DCMS/Grant Thornton/Ecorys/Loughborough University. (2013). *Meta-evaluation of the impacts & legacy of the London 2012 Olympic & Paralympic games summary final report*. London: DCMS.

Flyvbjerg, B. and Stewart, A. (2012). Olympic proportions: Cost and cost overrun at the Olympics 1960–2012. In: *Saïd Business School working papers*. Oxford: Oxford University.

Girginov, V. (2018). *Rethinking Olympic legacy*. London: Routledge.

Girginov, V. and Hills, L. (2008). A sustainable sports legacy: Creating a link between the London Olympics and sports participation. *The International Journal of the History of Sport*, 25(14), pp. 2091–2117.

Girginov, V. and Hills, L. (2009). The political process of constructing sustainable London Olympics Sports Development Legacy. *International Journal of Sport Policy*, 1(2), pp. 161–181.

Gold, J. and Gold, M. (2009). Riding the Mexican wave? Deciphering the meaning of Olympic Legacy. The Olympic legacy people, place, enterprise. In: *Proceedings of the first annual conference on Olympic Legacy*, 8 and 9 May 2008. London: University of Greenwich, pp. 9–17.

Grix, J., ed. (2017). *Leveraging sport mega-events legacies*. London: Routledge.

Habermas, J. (1981). *The theory of communicative action – Reason and the rationalisation of society*. Vol. I. Boston, MA: Beacon Press.

Holt, R. and Ruta, D., eds. (2016). *Routledge handbook of sport and legacy*. London: Routledge.

International Olympic Committee (IOC). (2003). *Olympic charter*. Lausanne: IOC.

International Olympic Committee (IOC). (2010). *Olympism in action*. Lausanne: IOC.

International Olympic Committee (IOC). (2014). *Agenda 2020: Recommendations*. Lausanne: IOC.

International Olympic Committee (IOC). (2017). *Legacy strategic approach. Moving forward*. Lausanne: IOC.

International Paralympic Committee (IPC). (2015). *Strategic plan 2015 to 2018*. Bonn: IPC.

Leopkey, B. (2009). *The historical evolution of Olympic Games legacy. Final report to the IOC*. Lausanne: IOC.

MacAloon, J. (2008). 'Legacy' as managerial/magical discourse In contemporary Olympic Affairs. *International Journal of the History of Sport*, 25(4), pp. 2060–2071.

Pawson, R. (2013). *The science of evaluation. A realist manifesto*. London: Sage.

Pettigrew, A. (1997). What is processual analysis? *Scandinavian Journal of Management*, 13(4), pp. 337–348. doi:10.1016/ S0956-5221(97)00020-1.

Popper, K. (2005). *The logic of scientific discovery*. New York: Basic Books; London: Hutchinson.

Rojek, C. (2014). Global event management: A critique. *Leisure Studies*, 33(1), pp. 32–47.

Scheu, A. and Preuss, H. (2017). *The legacy of the Olympic Games from 1896–2016: A systematic review of academic publications*. Working paper Series No. 14. Mainz: Johannes Gutenberg University of Mainz.

Thomson, A., Cuskelly, G., Toohey, K. and Kennelly, M. (2019). Sport event legacy: A systematic qualitative review of literature. *Sport Management Review*, (22)3, pp. 295–321.

Tilly, C. and Wood, L. (2013). *Social movements 1768–2012*. 3rd ed. London: Paradigm Publishers.

United Nations (UN). (2017). *17 goals to transform our world*.

Weed, M. (2012). London 2012 legacy strategy: Ambitions promises and implementation plans. In: V. Girginov, ed., *Handbook of the London 2012 Olympic and Paralympic games: Volume 1*. London: Routledge, pp. 87–98.

Weed, M. (2013). London 2012 legacy strategy. Did it deliver? In: V. Girginov, ed., *Handbook of the London 2012 Olympic and Paralympic games. Volume. 2: Celebrating the games*. London: Routledge, pp. 297–302.

33

Can health-related legacies through physical activity and sport be delivered by the Olympic and Paralympic Games?

Mike Weed

Introduction: rationales for hosting the Games

First and foremost, the Olympic and Paralympic Games are a sport competition. For many people, and for many years, this quadrennial celebration of sport through several weeks of elite competition was rationale enough for the Games, and for prominent cities around the world to come forward to host them. However, as the scale of the Games grew, and the task of hosting became more significant, the notion that there might be rationales and outcomes beyond the simple organisation of a sport competition began to take hold among Games hosts. The 1992 Games in Barcelona were used as a mechanism to accelerate the delivery of an extensive programme of urban regeneration; a key aim for the Sydney Games of 2000 was to position Australia as a centre for business in emerging Asian markets; and the Beijing Games of 2008 were used to help China interact with the global economy, promoting the country as a welcoming place in which to live and visit, and with which to do business (Xu, 2006). Such rationales are necessary because the scale of investment now required to host an Olympic and Paralympic Games means that city or national governments cannot justify investing taxpayers' money on the basis of the sporting competition and spectacle alone. As such, the discourse and debate surrounding the aims and goals for hosting the Olympic and Paralympic Games increasingly focus on their instrumental role in generating immediate and longer-term benefits.

Initially, the benefits that Games hosts suggested were economic, including increased investment, inward tourism flows, urban regeneration and employment. However, as the cost of hosting the Games has grown, along with scepticism about some of the economic legacies, hosts have begun to consider the possibility that a wider range of social and cultural legacy outcomes could be delivered. By the time London was awarded the 2012 Games in 2005, expectations for legacy outcomes had both increased significantly and broadened to encompass a much wider range of socio-economic areas. Partly responsible for this was the International Olympic Committee (IOC), which amended its Olympic Charter in November 2002 to explicitly emphasise the importance of 'promoting a positive legacy from the Olympic Games to the host city and host country' (IOC, 2002), and the bidding process for the 2012 Games was the first conducted under this amended charter. Nevertheless, London itself was also responsible for increasing and broadening legacy expectations, articulating from the outset that the notion of 'legacy', or the imprint left by the Games before, during and after the event, would be the *raison d'être* of the Games. No previous host had been so ambitious or explicit about using the Olympic and Paralympic Games as a catalyst for economic and social good, not only in the host city, but across the country as a whole (Weed, 2010).

A key social legacy that previous Games hosts had flirted with, but that was a clear stated goal of the London 2012 Games from the outset, was that London 2012 would deliver a health-related legacy through increased participation in sport and a healthier and more active population. Consequently, in considering the possibility of health-related legacies through physical activity and sport, the London 2012 Games are an important case study. This is because London 2012 was the first Games to pro-actively set out to achieve such legacies, and as such, it should have been a clear test of the possibility that health-related legacies could be an outcome from an Olympic and Paralympic Games.

Some claims for the impact of the Olympic and Paralympic Games on health have been through an assumed impact on national wellbeing associated with hosting the Games and through a positive impact on wider determinants of health such as improved urban infrastructures, housing and the environment. However, a comprehensive systematic review of evidence for an impact on these factors could locate no evidence for such legacies (McCartney et al., 2010). Furthermore, in terms of demonstrable health legacies from the Games, they are somewhat distal and ephemeral. Hence legacies have tended to focus on increasing physical activity and sport participation, which is demonstrable and measurable, and is widely assumed to have a positive impact on public and population health.

This chapter explores the best evidence for the delivery of health-related legacies through physical activity and sport from Olympic and Paralympic Games. It then examines policy, strategy and outcomes for health-related legacies though physical activity and sport from Games since 2012, focusing particular attention on the London 2012 case. Finally, the chapter discusses whether it is possible to conclude that the delivery of such health-related legacies in practice is possible.

Best evidence for health-related legacies

Governments, event organisers and sport professionals have long suggested that it is self-evident that the Olympic and Paralympic Games inspire others to take part in sport and, by extension, physical activity. The assumption has been that the Games inherently and automatically inspire people and stimulate an increase in demand to participate in sport, or to become more physically active. Consequently, it has been assumed that all that is required to secure an increase in participation is to ensure that there is an adequate supply of sport participation opportunities and sport facilities to provide for what is assumed to be an inevitable increase in demand associated with the Games. These assumptions have also tended to be extended to physical activity, with the same assumed processes of inspiration.

Prior to the London 2012 Olympic and Paralympic cycle, there had been no real attempt to systematically investigate whether evidence from previous Games supported these assumptions. However, two systematic reviews of worldwide evidence, with slightly different remits, conducted in the years before the London 2012 Games, show that while sport mega events can impact upon sport participation, and may have the potential to impact upon physical activity, the potential effects are far more nuanced than governments, event organisers and sport professionals have suggested. In 2010, a systematic review published in the *British Medical Journal* (McCartney et al., 2010) concluded that "the available evidence is not sufficient to confirm or refute expectations about the health or socio-economic benefits for the host population of previous major multi-sport events". Possible impacts on sport participation or physical activity were among the aspects considered as a health benefit of sport mega events by McCartney et al. (2010).

McCartney et al.'s (2010) conclusions would normally invite two possible interpretations: either that no effect on physical activity or sport participation should be expected from the Olympic and Paralympic Games, or that there has been no robust evidence collected that proves or disproves that there is such an effect. However, in this case a third interpretation is suggested. It is certainly true that at the time of McCartney et al.'s (2010) review there was no evidence that sport mega events had resulted in sustained increases in mass participation in sport or in population-level increases in physical activity. But it was also true that no previous Olympic and Paralympic Games had pro-actively and systematically attempted to use the event to raise population levels of physical activity and sport participation. Participation data had merely been examined ex-post to explore whether simply hosting a Games had affected participation levels. Consequently, McCartney et al.'s (2010) review might most usefully be interpreted to mean that there is no evidence for an inherent effect on physical activity or sport participation, in which benefits occur automatically.

The second systematic review, conducted for the UK Department of Health and published in 2009, also showed that there was no evidence for an inherent effect on physical activity or sport participation from sport mega events (Weed et al., 2009). In fact, this review went further in suggesting that there is evidence that inherent effects do not occur. However, focusing initially on sport participation, Weed et al. (2009) also suggested that there is evidence that mechanisms associated with the Olympic and Paralympic Games have had a positive effect on participation where specific initiatives have been put in place to harness such mechanisms to stimulate demand. Furthermore, the evidence suggested that such mechanisms are most effective if initiatives seek to capitalise on anticipation in the run-up to the Games, rather than relying on memory after the event. As such, initiatives to increase sport participation should seek to pro-actively leverage anticipation in the pre-Games period, rather than relying on a memory-driven post-Games effect. However, the initiatives reviewed were largely more local interventions and were therefore not on a large enough scale to affect population level sport participation demand, hence the lack of evidence for an inherent effect among wider national populations that had not been exposed to such initiatives in McCartney et al.'s (2010) review.

Weed et al.'s (2009) review showed that, for sport, there was evidence that a 'demonstration effect', in which people are inspired by elite sport, sports people and sport events to participate themselves, could be harnessed to impact on sport participation demand among two specific groups. First, that an Olympic and Paralympic Games might be harnessed to inspire those that are already participating in sport to participate a little more and, second, that a Games might be harnessed to encourage those that have participated in the past to participate again. For each of these two groups, the effects were largely shown to be leverageable in the pre-Games period, driven by wider anticipation of the Games, rather than after the Games when the presence of the Games in public discourse quickly abates. In addition, and importantly, the evidence also showed that a demonstration effect did not occur in those who do not participate, and never have participated, in sport, and therefore the effect cannot be harnessed to stimulate sport participation demand among lifelong non-participants. This evidence was reinforced in the English context by further analyses of national participation data for England (Weed, 2010), which showed that responsiveness to a demonstration effect was most prevalent among non-sport club members who participated between once a year and twice a week. However, it had little effect on demand among those participating three times a week or more, and had virtually no effect on those who had not participated in sport in the last year.

This evidence for the circumstances in which a demonstration effect might be leveraged also clearly shows that a demonstration effect will not impact upon the physical activity levels of those disinterested in sport. In short, sport cannot be used to inspire and stimulate activity among the least active who do not participate, and never have participated, in sport. In fact, more than this, the review uncovered evidence that seeking to use elite sport, sport people and sport events to inspire physical activity among the least active can have a negative effect. This is through something called a 'competence gap' (Weed et al., 2009), in which the achievements of elite sport people are perceived to be so detached from the lives of the least active, and so far beyond their capabilities, that it reinforces a view that sport and, by extension, physical activity is 'not for me'.

However, looking beyond the demonstration effect and the use of elite sport, sport people and sport events to inspire others, Weed et al.'s (2009) review also offered some interesting emerging evidence in relation to physical activity. The review suggested that a different effect, focusing on celebration rather than sport, could offer some potential to use the Olympic and Paralympic Games to positively impact upon engagement with physical activity.

Weed et al. (2009) found that major events such as London 2012 may, if promoted in the right way, generate a 'festival effect' that may have the potential to be harnessed to promote physical activity among the least active adults. This festival effect derives from the promotion of the 2012 Games as a national festival that is bigger than and beyond sport, but that is also rooted in the lives of local and cultural communities, thus creating a strong desire to participate in some way in an event that is both nationally significant and locally or culturally relevant. Chalip (2006, pp. 110–111) explains:

> The sporting outcomes may matter to some, but there is a sense that something more important – something that transcends the sport – is going on. . . . There is a heightened sense of community among those who are present. This alteration of communal affect has been much studied and documented by anthropologists who study public performances, including sport events. . . . They call the sense of community that is engendered 'communitas'.

Chalip (2006) notes that celebration and camaraderie contribute significantly to the feeling that an event is bigger than and beyond sport, and this aspect of the festival effect is fostered by symbolism and iconography. For example, Kennedy et al.'s (2006) study of the London 2012 bid campaign showed that the symbols and icons of London and Britishness (e.g. the London Eye, Nelson's Column) were combined with athletic acts to create a campaign which was, in and of itself, a spectacle, a form of "affective magnet", where "affect is about our investment in something, a particular experience or practice" (p. 16). Kennedy et al. (2006, p. 19) describe how "[d]esire for 'London 2012' was mapped onto people's existing sites of investment to steer their energy towards the campaign". Such sites of investment were monuments, symbols and icons that transcended sport and helped to engender celebration, camaraderie and communitas (Chalip, 2006).

The key aspect of communitas is that the communality and community spirit that it describes creates a desire, if not an urge, to participate in some way, and that this desire is stronger if the event is perceived to be bigger than and beyond sport. This is the festival effect. However, local (or cultural) relevance remains important. Crompton (2004) and Sparvero and Chalip (2007), in describing the community impacts of sport teams and events, each highlights similar phenomena that they describe respectively as 'psychic income' and 'community self-esteem'. Psychic income and community self-esteem are linked to perceptions that the team or event's value is not in sport, per se, but in what the event or team brings to the community in terms of its own and others' views of its self-worth. This locates the importance of the event or team within community identity, rather than within sport.

Focusing on the celebratory and festival elements of the Games creates a feeling that they transcend sport, and thus has much greater potential to engage those who are not interested in the Games as a sporting competition. However, Weed et al. (2012) note that the goal and challenge for physical activity participation policy and strategy will be to satisfy the desire to participate through providing physical activity opportunities presented as fun community events or programmes, for which the achievement of a 'critical mass' of community engagement may be important. The key to generating a health-related legacy through this process is likely to be to de-emphasise the sporting element of the 2012 Games and promote the festival element.

Clearly, the evidence for demonstration and festival effects suggests a need for a segmented strategy that differentiates sport participation goals, targets and, most importantly, processes, from those for physical activity. In short, the processes necessary to use an Olympic and Paralympic Games to impact upon sport participation are different from those that might harness the Games to impact upon physical activity outside sport. There is also the possibility that promoting elite sport to non-sporty populations in the hope of increasing their physical activity levels will have the opposite effect and thus do more harm than good. This is a particularly important message for sport policy-makers, who often find it difficult to understand that sport does not universally inspire.

In summary, the evidence that an Olympic and Paralympic Games can deliver health-related legacies is focused on the assumed health benefits of sport participation, and the contribution to public health made by increased population levels of physical activity. In terms of the former, and in contrast to the suggestions of governments, event organisers and sport professionals, the evidence shows that there is no inherent effect on sport participation demand from simply hosting an Olympic and Paralympic Games. However, it also shows that sport participation demand among current and lapsed participants in sport has been increased where specific initiatives and strategies have been put in place to harness a demonstration effect from sport mega events to stimulate demand and increase participation in the pre-Games period. The evidence also shows that seeking to use sport-related inspiration to increase physical activity among the non-sporty is not only likely to be ineffective, but to do more harm than good. Thus to achieve health gains through physical activity among the least active, a strategy that is clearly segmented and differentiated from that targeting sport participation is required, in which the festival and celebration elements of the Games are promoted whilst the competitive sport element is de-emphasised.

Testing the evidence for health-related legacies

At a population level, McCartney et al.'s (2010) systematic review shows that there is no evidence that any major multi-sport event prior to the London 2012 Olympic and Paralympic Games had delivered a health-related legacy through physical activity and sport. That is, there is no inherent effect from hosting the Games. But, importantly, no major multi-sport event prior to 2010 had put in place explicit population-wide strategies to deliver health-related legacies through physical activity and sport participation. As such, it is to be expected that there would be no evidence of a population-level outcome as events had not set out to achieve this.

However, the evidence set out suggests that, if effective leveraging investments are put in place, there may be the potential to achieve specific sport participation outcomes through a demonstration effect among specific target groups, namely those who are already participating a little, or those who have participated in the past. This evidence is largely, although not exclusively, derived from more local interventions that were not on a large enough scale to affect population-level sport participation demand. Consequently, the key question is whether the potential identified is scalable to whole populations given appropriate leveraging investments, and whether conclusions about the lack of inherent effects and the inability to attract new people into sport hold if attempts are made to deliver sport participation legacies at a population level.

For physical activity, the evidence suggests the processes are different and focus on a festival effect. The festival effect derives from the promotion of Olympic and Paralympic Games as significant festivals that are nationally significant and locally or culturally relevant. The goal for physical activity participation policy is to satisfy the resulting desire to participate through providing physical activity (rather than sport) opportunities presented as fun community events or programmes. However, when suggested by Weed et al. (2009), the festival effect was an untried and untested process for physical activity promotion among the least active, so key questions include whether it would work in practice, and whether governments and Games hosts would be prepared to de-emphasise the sporting themes of the Games in order to seek to deliver it.

The evidence as set out therefore provides a set of hypotheses that might be tested rather than definitive conclusions that health-related legacies through physical activity and sport can be achieved. Consequently, this section explores how far Olympic and Paralympic Games since 2010 represent a meaningful test of this evidence. First, the Games in 2016 and 2014 are considered, as well as the Commonwealth Games of 2014, before the extended case study of the London 2012 Games is reviewed.

The most recent Olympic and Paralympic Games in Rio in 2016 took place in a context of major political protest, which included a considerable backlash against the hosting of the Games. The political protests surrounded alleged corruption by both the suspended and the acting presidents of Brazil, in the context of a considerable economic downturn. Part of this, however, included *Jogos da Exclusao* (Exclusion Games) and *Calamidadea Ollimpica* (Olympic Calamity) protests that in terms of both scale and longevity went some way beyond the protests that are routinely associated with mega-sport events. In the week before the Games it was reported that nearly two out of three Brazilians believed the Games would bring more harm than good, and that half disapproved of hosting the Games (New York Times, 2016). One of the key suggestions of the available evidence is that for a mega-sport event to deliver increases in physical activity and sport participation, it must take place in a supportive context in which there is a positive engagement with the event and its potential to impact positively on the community, and this was certainly not the case in Rio in 2016. Furthermore, in their analysis of Rio 2016's potential to deliver a health-related legacy through physical activity and sport, Reis, de Sousa-Mast and Gurgel (2014) note that the Rio 2016 bid book (Rio 2016, 2009) highlights a legacy for sport that refers only to developing elite sport participation, and that:

> The health and educational benefits of mass sport/physical activity participation so promoted by the IOC (2008, 2011), particularly through its 'Sport for All' programme, seem to be disregarded.
>
> *(Reis, de Sousa-Mast and Gurgel, 2014, p. 440)*

As such, with an unsupportive context and a lack of leveraging investments for health-related legacies through physical activity and sport, the only test of the evidence that Rio 2016 can provide is for the hypothesis that there are no inherent effects from hosting a mega-sport event.

A similar story to that of Rio 2016 exists for the Winter Olympic and Paralympic Games in Sochi in 2014. A particularly turbulent context was created around the Games by specific legislation passed "against the propaganda of non-traditional sexual orientation to minors" (Muller, 2015, p. 647), which received widespread international coverage and condemnation (Lenskyj, 2014; Van Rheenen, 2014), and Russian intervention, largely seen internationally as aggression, in Ukraine. Furthermore, health-related legacies through physical activity and sport were simply not part of the plans for Sochi 2014, with Games investment being targeted at developing Sochi as "a new world class resort for the new Russia. And the whole world!" (Putin, 2007), with a particular focus on presenting the image of a 'new Russia' as an open, modern and attractive country for tourism, investment and geo-political partnerships (Muller, 2015). As such, with a negative context and no investments seeking to deliver health-related legacies through physical activity and sport, like Rio 2016, Sochi 2014 can only provide a test of the hypothesis that there are no inherent effects from hosting the Games.

Although not an Olympic and Paralympic Games, the XXth Commonwealth Games in Glasgow took place in the same year as the Sochi Winter Games. Glasgow 2014 sought to use the Games to develop health outcomes in the Scottish population, with Games auditors finding that there were clear legacy plans in place, including plans to regenerate rundown areas of the city, and to increase levels of physical activity and sport (Audit Scotland, 2015). Unfortunately, however, Glasgow 2014 appears to have used sport initiatives to target those that did not participate, and never had participated in sport, which resulted in static levels of physical activity in the Scottish population following the Games in both 2015 and 2016 (Scottish Government, 2015, 2016), whilst the first stage of a study examining exercise levels in the most affected communities found residents did less sport after the event than before (Clark and Kearns, 2015). Consequently, Glasgow 2014 appears to provide evidence to support the hypothesis that mega-sport events cannot attract new people into sport.

In summary, therefore, the Games in 2016 and 2014 do not represent particularly good tests of the hypothesis for the ways in which health-related legacies through physical activity and sport might be delivered, suggested by the reviewed evidence. They simply provide further evidence for, and therefore reinforce, the circumstances in which such legacies will not be delivered. Furthermore, as the Olympic and Paralympic Games in 2014 and 2016 did not plan for health-related legacies through physical activity and sport, London 2012, with its clear and pro-active focus on these health-related legacies, would appear to provide the most salient case study.

The London 2012 Olympic and Paralympic Games was the first sport mega-event to explicitly set out to deliver health-related legacies through physical activity and sport, committing to "a goal of seeing two million people more active by 2012 through focused investment in our sporting infrastructure and better support and information for people wanting to be active" (DCMS, 2008, p. 3). The specific detail of this commitment was that it was split in two, with the sport commitment being to get an additional one million people participating in sport three times a week or more over the four years from 2008 to 2012, thus targeting the very groups of people – those already participating between once a year and twice a week – that some of the evidence presented in this chapter (Weed, 2010) had shown to be most responsive to a demonstration effect. This element, therefore, had the potential to be an excellent test of the hypothesis that mega sport events have the potential to get those already playing sport to play a little more, or those that had played in the past to play again.

The second part of the commitment was that a further one million people would be encouraged to increase their physical activity levels to deliver the overall two million target. To achieve this, in 2009 the UK Secretary of State for Health, Andy Burnham, announced a raft of activities seeking to capitalise on the festival effect to use the London 2012 Games to increase physical activity. This suggested that, like the intent for sport, the London 2012 Games would be an excellent test of the festival effect for physical activity, particularly as the announcement followed the delivery to the Department of Health of Weed et al.'s (2009) review setting out the evidence for the effect. Burnham noted in his announcement that "the festival effect – [is] crucial. . . . This, for me, is the effect we need to maximise". Among the initiatives were the development of the Change4Life brand to include Dance4Life and Play4Life, the establishment of a Dance Champions Group, a Walking for Health 2012 campaign, and a national programme of city cycling initiatives. This was the first and, as it turned out, only time that physical activity was differentiated from sport in national legacy policy.

In May 2010, less than a year after Burnham's announcement, a General Election in the UK replaced the previous Labour government with a Coalition government committed to a range of austerity measures to stabilise the economy and the national debt following the global economic downturn. These measures included spending cuts that led to the cancellation of most of the initiatives announced by Burnham in 2009, many before they had begun. This, together with a later acknowledgement (Gibson, 2011) that the physical activity element of the two million target was 'quietly dropped' after the General Election, marked the end of the short-lived differentiated strategy to use the 2012 Games to deliver increased population levels of physical activity. In fact, more than this, it marked the end of any attempt to deliver physical activity outcomes from the Games at all. Thus, from mid-2010 the only health outcomes being sought as part of London 2012 legacy strategy were the assumed health benefits of increased sport participation.

Unfortunately, however, the potential to test the sport participation legacy hypothesis did not fare any better than that for physical activity. Like previous Games before it, and despite a commitment to do so, London 2012 did not invest in measures to stimulate sport participation increases but instead relied on inherent effects. Sport England's strategy (Sport England, 2008) for the four years during which the one million sport participation target would need to be achieved (2008–2012), made little mention of the Olympic and Paralympic Games and set out no initiatives to harness the London 2012 Games to stimulate participation. Similarly, the London 2012 Mass Participation Plan, 'Places People Play' (Sport England, 2010b) contained a £135 million investment that was almost entirely focused on supply; two-thirds for the supply of facilities and the rest for the supply of 'provision capacity', leaders and opportunities. Places People Play contained no strategies to stimulate sport participation increases, only investments to increase supply to cater for the inherent effect on sport participation that it was assumed the Games would bring.

The result, as evidenced by the Active People survey in England, which provided official national statistics, was that despite an encouraging increase of 115,000 people doing sport three times a week in 2008/9, the following year (2009/10) the increase was only 8,000 (Sport England, 2009b, 2010a). The following year, six months after the launch of Places People Play, sport participation figures showed a fall of 4,000 in those doing sport three times a week (Sport England, 2011). Furthermore, post-Games data for England showed that the number of people doing sport at least once a month had increased by an average of 1% per year in the four years since 2007/8, whilst those doing sport at least three times a week had increased by an average of 2.2% per year in the four years since 2007/8 (Sport England, 2012). However, the context for this latter figure is that achieving the participation target of one million people doing more sport would have required an average year-on-year increase of 3%, and that the average increases in the two years prior to the period for which the target had been set (2006/7 and 2007/8) were 4% per year (Sport England, 2009b). Furthermore, in the year following the Games those participating at least once a month actually fell by 1% (Sport England, 2013). By any measure this is not a successful outcome for population-level sport participation and appears to reinforce the evidence discussed in this chapter that there is no inherent impact without effective investment targeting sport participation.

Therefore, despite clear initial goals and targets to develop and deliver health-related legacies through physical activity and sport, London 2012 cancelled the former and relied on inherent effects for the latter. Consequently, while London 2012 had the potential to be an excellent test of the hypothesis that Olympic and Paralympic Games can be used to increase participation among those who are already participating a little, or those who have participated in the past, its reliance on inherent effects meant that, like other Games since, the only hypothesis it provides evidence for is that there are no inherent effects.

Conclusion: are health-related legacies possible?

Two systematic reviews (McCartney et al., 2010; Weed et al., 2009) could not find any evidence that health outcomes other than those related to increased physical activity or sport participation might be deliverable from an Olympic and Paralympic Games. However, evidence from one of these reviews (Weed et al., 2009) suggests that a festival effect and a demonstration effect might have the potential to increase physical activity and sport participation respectively in specific circumstances if carefully leveraged and managed.

London 2012, with its stated goal to achieve health-related legacies through physical activity and sport, should have been a clear test of this evidence. However, potential physical activities legacies were dropped as an aspiration just as bespoke initiatives were due to be implemented, which left the assumed health benefits of increased sport participation as the sole potential contribution of London 2012 to health-related legacies. Unfortunately, like other Games since, London 2012 relied on assumed inherent inspirational effects to deliver a sport participation legacy, and thus served only to reinforce previous evidence that such effects cannot deliver sport participation legacies.

It therefore remains the case that evidence that Olympic and Paralympic Games can deliver a legacy of increased physical activity through a festival effect has not been tested. Furthermore, despite attempts to deliver sport participation legacies, the evidence-based hypothesis that a demonstration effect might encourage those who play a little sport to play a little more, and those that have participated before to do so again, has also not been properly tested. Thus, the failure of Olympic and Paralympic Games to deliver health-related legacies through physical activity and sport is a failure of policy to deliver evidence-based strategies. It is not yet a failure of the potential of the effects themselves. The question of health-related legacies through physical activity and sport therefore remains open.

References

Audit Scotland. (2015). *Commonwealth games 2014. Third report*. Edinburgh: Audit Scotland.

Chalip, L. (2006). Towards social leverage of sport events. *Journal of Sport & Tourism*, 11(2), pp. 109–127.

Clark, J. and Kearns, A. (2015). *The Glasgow 2014 games: Regeneration and physical activity legacy*. Glasgow: University of Glasgow.

Crompton, J. (2004). Beyond economic impact: An alternative rationale for the public subsidy of major league sports facilities. *Journal of Sport Management*, 18(1), pp. 40–58.

Department for Culture, Media and Sport (DCMS). (2008). *Before, during and after: Making the most of the London 2012 games*. London: Department of Culture, Media and Sport.

Gibson, O. (2011). Jeremy Hunt admits London 2012 legacy targets will be scrapped. *The Guardian*, Mar. 29.

International Olympic Committee. (2002). *Olympic charter: In force as from November 2002*. Lausanne: IOC.

International Olympic Committee. (2008). *Report on the 4th world conference on women and sport: Sport as a vehicle for social change*. Lausanne: IOC.

International Olympic Committee. (2011). *Olympic charter*. Lausanne: IOC.

Kennedy, E., Pussard, H. and Thronton, A. (2006). 'Leap for London'? Investigating the affective power of the sport spectacle. *World Leisure Journal*, 48(3), pp. 6–21.
Lenskyj, H. (2014). *Sexual diversity and the Sochi 2014 Olympics: No more rainbows*. London: Palgrave Macmillan.
McCartney, G., Thomas, S., Thomson, H., Scott, J., Hamilton, V., Hanlon, P., et al. (2010). The health and socioeconomic impacts of major multi-sport events: A systematic review. *British Medical Journal*, p. 340.
Muller, M. (2015). After Sochi 2014: Costs and impacts of Russia's Olympic Games. *Eurasian Geography and Economics*, 55(6), pp. 628–655.
New York Times. (2016). Poll finds strong opposition among Brazilians to Rio games. *New York Times*.
Putin, V. (2007). *Speech at the 119th International Olympic Committee Session*. Guatemala (4/7/2007).
Reis, A.C., de Sousa-Mast, F.R. and Gurgel, L.A. (2014). Rio 2016 and the sport participation legacies. *Leisure Studies*, 33(5), pp. 437–453.
Rio 2016. (2009). *Candidature file for Rio de Janeiro to host the 2006 Olympic and Paralympic Games*. Vol 1. Rio de Janeiro: Rio 2016.
Scottish Government. (2015). *Scottish health survey 2014: Main report*. Edinburgh: Scottish Government.
Scottish Government. (2016). *Scottish health survey 2015: Main report*. Edinburgh: Scottish Government.
Sparvero, E. and Chalip, L. (2007). Professional teams as leverageable assets: Strategic creation of community value. *Sport Management Review*, 10(1), pp. 1–30.
Sport England. (2008). *Sport England strategy 2008–2011*. London: Sport England.
Sport England. (2009b). *Active People Survey 3*. London: Sport England.
Sport England. (2010a). *Active People 4*. London: Sport England.
Sport England. (2010b). *Places people play – Delivering a mass participation sporting legacy from the 2012 Olympic and Paralympic Games*. London: Sport England.
Sport England. (2011). *Active people 5, quarter 2 results*. London: Sport England.
Sport England. (2012). *Active people 6*. London: Sport England.
Sport England. (2013). *Active people 7*. London: Sport England.
Van Rheenen, D. (2014). A skunk at the garden party: The Sochi Olympics, state-sponsored homophobia and prospects for human rights through mega sporting events. *Journal of Sport & Tourism*, 19(2), pp. 127–144.
Weed, M. (2010). How will we know if the Olympics and Paralympics benefit health? *British Medical Journal*, p. 340.
Weed, M., Coren, E., Fiore, J., Mansfield, L., Wellard, I., Chatziefstathiou, D. and Dowse, S. (2009). *A systematic review of the evidence base for developing a physical activity and health legacy from the London 2012 Olympic and Paralympic games*. London: Department of Health.
Weed, M., Coren, E., Fiore, J., Mansfield, L., Wellard, I., Chatziefstathiou, D. and Dowse, S. (2012). Developing a physical activity legacy from the London 2012 Olympic and Paralympic games: A policy-led systematic review. *Perspectives in Public Health*, 132(2), pp. 75–80.
Xu, X. (2006). Modernizing China in the Olympic spotlight: China's national identity and the 2008 Beijing Olympiad. *The Sociological Review*, 54(s2), pp. 90–107.

34

Olympic and Paralympic impacts in non-host city regions

Shushu Chen and Dongfeng Liu

Introduction

In Olympic- and Paralympic-related literature, there has already been a significant amount of interest in studying and investigating outcomes, impacts, and legacies of the Olympics, whereby many authors have focused on the Games' economic impacts (Baade and Matheson, 2002; Blake, 2005; Kasimati and Dawson, 2009), socio-cultural impacts (Gibson, Qi and Zhang, 2008; Kavetsos and Szymanski, 2010; Minnaert, 2012), and environmental impacts (Chappelet, 2008; May, 1995). However, studies of the Olympics and Paralympics have traditionally focused either on a host city alone or a host nation as a whole, while neglecting non-host regions within a host nation.

When bidding to host Olympic and Paralympic Games, host nations often claim that the benefits of staging an event can transcend a host city to benefit the entire country (Beijing, 2022 Olympic Winter Games Bid Committee, 2014; British Olympic Committee, 2005). Yet there has been relatively little evaluation of or attention paid to the justifications for investing public money in sporting mega events. It may be argued that, without exploring the Games' effects in the broader context of host nations, the conclusions drawn seem unsystematic and unbalanced.

Such circumstances prompt further reflections on two points: one concerns what evidence exists regarding sporting mega events' (particularly the Olympic and Paralympic Games') impact on non-host regions. Have there been any benefits generated in areas beyond the host city as a result of the events? Another point worth considering is whether nations hosting events have made any real attempt, at the local level, to exploit opportunities whereby potential positive impacts might benefit non-host communities and regions? If so, what lessons could be learned from those cases?

In this chapter, we aim first to provide a general literature review on the topic of impacts in non-host areas, of sporting mega events in general and the Olympic and Paralympic Games in particular. We then present two case studies of non-host areas' – Shanghai's and Leicestershire's – experiences of being part of the Games when their host nations staged the Olympic and Paralympic Games (Beijing 2008 and London 2012 respectively).

Sporting mega events in non-host areas

In the relevant literature, there has been a dearth of material that specifically addresses the Olympics' impacts and legacies for non-host regions, or that explores non-host regions' leveraging experiences of the Games. Only a few pieces of research are relevant here, which are worth highlighting. Bondonio, Guala, and Mela (2008) revealed that, as a result of hosting the Torino 2006 Olympic Games, the competitiveness of the entire northwestern macroeconomic region of Italy within European and international markets has increased. Bondonio and Guala (2011) further compared the impacts of the Turin Winter Games in the host city with the corresponding impacts in other north Italian cities; they concluded that the Games had made a difference to the development of urbanisation and tourism in the host city. Fairley and Kelly (2017) were interested in a non-host city which held pre-Games training camps during the 2018 Gold Coast Commonwealth Games, and they found that strategically planning to leverage pre-Games event training enabled the city to enhance its capabilities and its reputation as an elite training destination.

Much of the current literature on non-host regions/cities pays particular attention to non-host-community residents' perceptions of respective events. For example, a study conducted by Deccio and Baloglu (2002) examined non-host-community residents' reactions to the Salt Lake 2002 Winter Olympic Games. The study revealed that non-host-community residents who expected benefits, economic gains, and increased access to resources as a result of the Olympics tended to feel favourably towards the event; whereas those who were sensitive to environmental concerns did not. These study results seem to contradict those from Karadakis and Kaplanidou's (2012) study, employing a theoretical lens of social exchange theory, which found that residents of both host and non-host areas perceived there to be no potential economic gain from hosting the Olympics.

Another study of non-host-community residents' reactions to the Olympics (Ritchie, Shipway and Cleeve, 2009) indicated that residents from Weymouth and Portland in England supported England's hosting of the London 2012 Olympic Games, although they were also concerned about traffic congestion, parking issues, and potential increases in the cost of living. Additionally, Walton, Longo, and Dawson (2008) attempted a contingent valuation study of the London 2012 Olympic Games as perceived by Bath residents. They found that, in general, non-host residents were willing to subsidise the cost of hosting the event.

Other researchers have focused on the leveraging experiences of non-host communities, beginning with Gardiner and Chalip's (2006) study, where they demonstrated the possibility that a non-host destination – the Hunter Valley region, located two hours by road from Sydney – could benefit from leveraging the 2000 Olympics. Beesley and Chalip's (2011) investigation of Shanghai's case, as a non-host city for the 2008 Beijing Olympics, suggested the failure of such leveraging efforts. As summarised by Gardiner and Chalip (2006), there were two key factors behind the Hunter Valley region's success: one was the implementation of balanced short- and long-term strategies embedded in overall regional development initiatives; the other was the establishment and development of strategic alliances acting as a strong unifying force to drive the leveraging plan forward. These key factors are consistent with findings for Leicestershire (see the next section for a detailed discussion) and for Cheshire in relation to the London 2012 Olympics (Bell and Gallimore, 2015). Looking at the Tokyo 2020 Olympics, more recently, Chien, Kelly, and Gill (2017) also noted the importance of formulating shared objectives so that a strong focus for relevant stakeholders could be provided.

In summary, a review of the existing literature suggests three key points. The first is that research on non-host regions/cities for sporting mega events in general and the Olympics and

Paralympics has been rather limited in terms of its quantity and variety. Particularly, the mentioned studies have not yet treated the impacts and legacies of the *Paralympics* in non-host regions/cities in much detail. This is not surprising given that the research area of the Paralympic impacts and legacies is largely overlooked (Misenser et al., 2013; Weed and Dowse, 2009). In Misener et al.'s (2013) review of the Paralympic legacy research, the reviewed Paralympic legacy studies tend to focus on the host nation/city. To our knowledge, no thorough research of non-host regions' Paralympic legacy has been seriously conducted.

The second point seen in the literature is that research about the impacts of sporting mega-events on non-host areas or non-host regions' *leveraging processes* has limited analytical value. This will continue to be the case unless some theoretical development guides future study in understanding which event impacts and legacies could be generable in non-host areas and how impacts and legacies of sporting mega events could be effectively leveraged and evaluated. The third point is that analysis of the Olympic and Paralympic impact in non-host regions is a highly contextualised research. There is still some scope for fully exploring the contextual features of the non-host regions/cities examined to better understand the reasons behind any success or failure of the leveraging processes.

In the following sections, we turn our attention to two non-host regions/cities: Leicestershire and Shanghai. Some findings from the two cases are published elsewhere (for further reading, please refer to Chen, 2013; Liu, Broom, and Wilson, 2014; Liu and Zhang, 2007); our intention in this chapter is to provide summaries for the two cases, drawing your attention to the leveraging experience and lessons learned from Leicestershire's case and synthesising impacts of Beijing 2008 on Shanghai. The chapter then concludes by highlighting the differences – in terms of regions' priorities for, objectives for, and desired impacts of the Games – between the two cases, deliberately chosen such as to include one with leveraging (Leicestershire) and one without leveraging (Shanghai).

Leicestershire

From the point when London won the bid, in 2005, to host the 2012 Games, there was a corresponding development in policymaking for the London Olympic Games. This development provided a foundation for the creation of a possible Olympic legacy in the UK before, during, and after the Games. A range of relevant documents were published, most notably *Before, During, and After: Making the Most of the London 2012 Games* (DCMS, 2008) and *London 2012 Olympic and Paralympic Games Impacts and Legacy Evaluation Framework* (DCMS, 2009); LOCOG (London Organising Committee of the Olympic Games and Paralympic Games, 2009) published their sustainability plan for the Games, titled *Towards One Planet 2012*.

In order to ensure that the *whole* country was involved in and benefited from the Games, the Nations and Regions Group (NRG) was also set up to work closely with the London Organising Committee of the Olympic and Paralympic Games (LOCOG) and with local government stakeholders. The East Midlands was one of only two regions (the other being the Yorkshire and Humber Region) that did not have any London 2012 Olympic or Paralympic venues. At the regional level, the East Midlands 2012 Delivery Group, as part of the NRG, subsequently formulated policies for championing the East Midlands.

Leicestershire, a sub-region of the East Midlands located approximately 100 miles north of London, also saw London's hosting of the 2012 Olympic and Paralympic Games as a unique opportunity to inspire local people and create a lasting legacy. The Leicestershire Steering Group for the London 2012 Games, consisting of multiple agencies, was subsequently formed; this group had the goal of maximising benefits, arising from London's hosting of the 2012 Games,

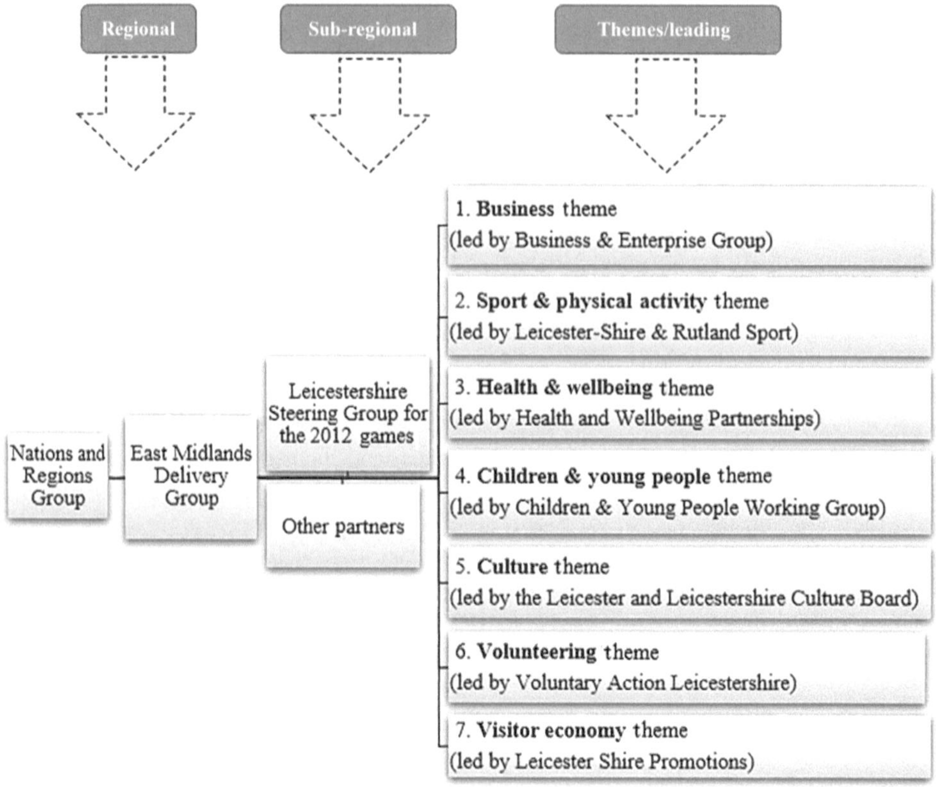

Figure 34.1 London 2012 Games delivery structure

Source: Adapted from Chen and Henry (2016)

for Leicestershire. The key roles of the steering group lay in providing strategic direction and coordinated action for Leicestershire on matters relating to 2012-Games-inspired activities (see Figure 34.1 for the London 2012 Games Delivery Structure manifested through the case of Leicestershire).

In early 2010, £416,000 of funding was received from EMDA (the East Midlands Development Agency) and local authorities, and this money was used to support a three-year legacy programme called Inspire Leicestershire. Inspire Leicestershire – managed by a small team of people with dedicated human and resource capacity – acted as a conduit to the Leicestershire Steering Group and provided support for all 2012-Games-related activities across the sub-region of Leicestershire. The programme was designed to achieve legacy/impacts from London 2012 benefiting Leicestershire in seven areas. The seven visions, representing seven legacy strands identified in Leicestershire, encompass foci including business, sport and physical activity, health and wellbeing, children and young people, culture, volunteering, and visitor economy (Inspire Leicestershire, 2009).

Some English regions other than Leicestershire had planned and delivered London-2012-related activities, to various extents. However, these activities were either administered by an individual manager or supported by a team not specifically created for London 2012. The nature of Inspire Leicestershire's operational structure and the variety of its activities, along with a meticulously planned vision and three-year programme delivery, made the programme distinctive: first of all, its vision and strategy for London 2012 were planned at an early stage, also establishing a small dedicated legacy team with human capacity and resources committed to delivering 2012-related activities; second, key performance indicators were monitored and reported on a quarterly basis to the Leicestershire London 2012 Steering Group, and an external research study was also commissioned for evaluating the programme's overall impacts/legacies for Leicestershire's Games.

The overall achievement of leveraging London-2012-related benefits for Leicestershire was therefore significant in that Leicestershire retained the top position within its region for some key performance indicators concerning various London 2012 programmes/initiatives. For example, Leicestershire won the highest total number of London-2012-related business contracts in the East Midlands region; it had the highest percentage of schools applying to Get Set (a nationwide Olympic and Paralympic education programme); it retained the highest number of participants in the Sportivate programme (a London 2012 legacy programme aimed at increasing sport participation) after the first year of the programme's implementation; and 47 of its local projects were awarded the London 2012 Inspire Mark.

Details of the outcomes of the Inspire Leicestershire programme have been published (refer to Chen, 2013; Chen and Henry, 2016, 2019; Chen and Misener, 2019, for more details). Our focus here is to summarise the lessons learned from this strategic leveraging experience. In the three-year lifespan of the Leicestershire London 2012 Steering Group, several areas in the policy-making process and policy implementation are worth highlighting. Thus, the following discussion aims to identify emerging behaviour patterns for the key agencies within the Leicestershire Steering Group, based on interviews conducted with the key stakeholders.

1 Strategy design and creation of the operational group

An early plan was forged, right after the announcement that London had won its Olympic bid, to have a steering group tasked with maximising the benefits of the London 2012 Olympic Games for Leicestershire. This incorporated a core group of people who were highly motivated, and it actively brought partners together, which attracted buy-in from key regional public agencies at an early stage. A clear vision and fundamental strategies were developed and shared with funding partners. However, for a number of the objectives and remits within the policy structure developed by the steering group, there proved to be difficulty engaging strand leaders because of the lack of consultation and the subsequent absence of consensus on key goals.

With human capacity and resources committed to delivering London-2012-Olympics-related activities, a small dedicated legacy team was established to develop 'home-grown' 2012 campaigns such as My Games, My Legacy. This capacity was unique among the East Midlands sub-regions and, furthermore, among all non-host sub-regions generally. More legacy outcomes were subsequently provided for the Leicester city and for its county.

2 Partnership collaboration

It was recognised by key stakeholders that London 2012 offered great opportunities for partnership collaboration between relevant organisations within the public sector and in other sectors. Stakeholders also indicated that the increase in collaboration helped to establish or to improve relationships between the organisations in question.

During the legacy process, particularly just before the commencement of the 2012 Games, legacy partnership collaboration increased between different strands within the Leicestershire

Steering Group: programmes in some strands were given greater exposure, generating significant success (e.g. the Workplace Challenge, Sportivate, regional Inspire Mark programmes, Cultural Olympiad). In addition, it was a commonly held view among key stakeholders that, through coordinated effort and partnership, the process of maximising London 2012 benefits raised the profile of Leicestershire, the sub-region, and of the nation, creating a positive image of the county. This helped to move sport up the agenda during a period of economic recession.

However, making partnerships work proved to be challenging in several cases. For instance, in the early stages of the legacy process, several of the leaders for the legacy strands expressed confusion as to the role they should play in the development of Leicestershire 2012 legacy activities. Existing capacity and funding resources made it difficult to coordinate the work undertaken on a daily basis with the new London 2012 initiatives.

In addition, tensions and conflicts between Leicestershire's legacy strands and among various bodies (in terms of claiming kudos, for example) resulted in lack of cooperation between key leaders and partners and thus less effective use of local resources, generating fewer benefits from London 2012-related activities. There was also a disparity between Leicester city and Leicestershire county in terms of different engagement and commitment levels.

Nevertheless, the collaboration and teamwork within partnerships increased over time, and the relationships established may subsequently enhance the likelihood of future partnerships being formed and of these partnerships being effective. The experience should help to position partners in such a way as to benefit more effectively from future events.

3 Unpredictable changes in political and economic contexts

After the 2010 general election, changes in government structure at the national and regional levels challenged the delivery of legacy activities, in particular for business activities. In addition, as a result of funding cuts and staff redundancies, key partners had to reassess their priorities; London 2012-related activities moved down their agendas, and this perhaps explains a lack of commitment and support in some legacy strands (e.g. health and wellbeing, and volunteering).

The Leicestershire Steering Group reacted to the aforementioned changes by adjusting strategic priorities. While seven legacy strands were initially identified, strategies and priorities were evolved during the delivery process. As a result, there was an increasing focus on those activities/themes which attracted greater commitment from interested partners and/or which were more likely to generate the most benefits with the given resources. In addition, the overall funding for the Leicestershire 2012 programme was secured before funding cuts happened in the public sector, which minimised the risk of the Inspire Leicestershire initiative being terminated. However, a certain degree of funding uncertainty still existed, which caused significant concerns, particularly about employment, among the operational practitioners.

4 The influence of the Olympic Games

Three factors which emerged from the London 2012 Olympic legacy process were worth noting, as they reflected the fact that policy planning and decision making could be positively/negatively influenced by the nature and development of the event. The first factor was the success of the London 2012 Olympic Games, which positively stimulated the country: the excellent performance of Team GB and Games Makers (the official Olympic and Paralympic Games volunteers) increased people's enthusiasm for the Games, which provided a potential boost for sport and volunteering across the Leicestershire sub-region and the nation. Thus, original impact and legacy targets (particularly those related to intangible effects) could thus be exceeded without any change being made to the nature or the quantity of inputs. The second noteworthy factor which emerged from the London 2012 legacy process related to how, at the beginning of the policy process, sub-regional stakeholders did not know that a series of rules and conditions associated with the Olympic and Paralympic Games would limit opportunities for marketing and promotion activities. For instance, due to the strict London 2012-business-related data and branding protection rules, local Leicestershire businesses could not highlight their success to further encourage more businesses to get involved in advance of the Games. Such specifics of any future event would, therefore, need to be researched early on.

Furthermore, sustaining Leicestershire's legacy leveraged for the Games became an issue due to lack of funding, which directly influenced, for example, the longevity of Inspire Leicestershire; it subsequently became difficult to maintain the talent pool developed during legacy leveraging. Preparing appropriate funding is crucial during the legacy process if there are long-term objectives which need to be achieved.

5 Mechanisms for building and spreading Olympic Games legacy outcomes

During the delivery process, the value of Inspire Leicestershire gradually became clearly evident, especially the programme's contribution to raising Leicestershire's profile, its PR management, its hosting of landmark showcase events, its high quality print and broadcast media coverage, and its facilitation of communication and decision making among partners (such as for the Torch Relay Dress Rehearsal and the celebration event).

Inspire Leicestershire's group of dedicated champions possessed experience of, knowledge of, and commitment to particular areas of work relevant to Leicestershire's legacy themes. These individuals provided critical leadership supporting and encouraging other operational practitioners to deliver London-2012-related activities, and they can be given the credit for such successes as the Get Set programme, for example.

These observations thus allow us to draw some conclusions about lessons learned from the Leicestershire 2012 legacy experience:

Lesson 1: At an early stage of the Leicestershire Steering Group's creation, a reduction in the number of strategic foci would have been likely to decrease conflicts concerning priorities across different legacy strands. Concentrating human resources and funding into fewer foci would therefore be more likely to create tangible outcomes.

Lesson 2: Feedback from some stakeholders on Leicestershire's London 2012 Legacy Strategic Plan document suggested that it was ambiguous, relatively irrelevant to stakeholders' interests, and that it should have been more operational. It perhaps would have been preferable, before the strategic leveraging plan was finalised, to consult key operational leaders in order to identify the key linkages between the nature of the event (in this case, the London 2012 Olympics) and different agencies' policy priorities. Key stakeholders should have been fully engaged throughout the planning, from early on, to make sure that a shared understanding of the potential benefits and actions between the relevant departments and delivery partners could be achieved. Such an approach would have been more likely to result in a detailed strategic document, with relevant operational targets and measurement indicators.

Lesson 3: The life cycle of Inspire Leicestershire spanned a particularly turbulent period in economic, political, and social terms (recession, a change of central government, riots in London). The ability to revisit strategy priorities in such a way as to reflect changing contexts would have been better facilitated if a mixed-scanning approach (Etzioni, 1967) to planning had been adopted, with strategic goals being revisited periodically to be confirmed, amended, or revised as necessary.

Lesson 4: There may be a danger of legacy gains being lost unless the organisations or stakeholders involved continue to leverage the Games' legacy. One means of communication that may be adopted would be web-based information and forum resources promoted through email contact with individuals who have volunteered for or participated in legacy initiatives, for example. Spaces for telling 'stories' of the Games, 'forums for participants', and 'information pages' about future opportunities could be effective.

Lesson 5: Making the most of the London 2012 Olympic Games to benefit Leicestershire required concrete legacy plans for long-term benefits. Improved working relationships between sub-regional and regional partners were established up to 2012. This should be capitalised upon as a basis for future projects. In order to use the unique experience and skills gained from the Olympics to inform the development of Leicestershire local authorities' and key partners' legacy planning for the Games, it is important to set up detailed plans – for example to bid on major showcase event hosting – ensuring more volunteering opportunities to make better use of the volunteering base available.

Lesson 6: Success at maximising the benefits of London hosting the Olympic Games has elevated Leicestershire's potential sporting, cultural, and social prospects. At the national level, in order to sustain the legacy of the Games, the government has been working on attracting over 70 international major sporting events (referred to as the 'Gold Event Series' strategy) to the UK. This means that, to continue the momentum generated at the sub-regional level by the London 2012 Olympics, sporting organisations and local authorities should be prepared and have started planning ahead to maximise benefits (of an economic, sporting, and social nature) from the UK's staging of the upcoming events. In addition, long-term benefits of the Games are worth evaluating to provide an evidence base for policy analysis regarding future events and to act as a benchmark for other regions.

Shanghai

Ever since Deng Xiaoping's economic reform and the implementation of an open-door policy, Beijing and Shanghai have been considered emerging global cities (Yusuf and Wu, 2002). Particularly, Shanghai has been considered the economic and financial capital of mainland China and has hosted sporting major events (e.g. the F1 Grand Prix and the 2002 Tennis Masters Cup) to brand itself as a modern metropolitan city (Liu and Gratton, 2010). The hosting of sporting and cultural *mega events* has been used as a vehicle for Shanghai to increase its international exposure as a city (Liu, 2008) as well as to enhance social and economic development (Lu and Zhang, 2005).

Technically speaking, Shanghai was not strictly a non-host city of the Beijing 2008 Olympics, as it held Olympic Football Group matches. Unlike events such as the FIFA Football World Cup, however, which officially recognise as host cities all those locations where event stadia lie, sporting mega events like the Olympics arguably place media spotlight only on individual host cities themselves (namely, cities which have won an Olympic bid) or on the host countries generally. Cities and regions that are involved with aspects of the Olympics such as the torch relay, pre-Games training camps, and football group matches are still technically considered as non-host regions/cities.

Different to the case study of Leicestershire mentioned earlier, where the legacy planning and leveraging documented here was relatively more systematic, our case study of Shanghai collates only a few sporadic studies conducted by Chinese scholars, because Shanghai did not undertake any serious strategic leveraging or planning for Beijing 2008 (Beesley and Chalip, 2011).

Two general trends are revealed through close examination of the literature encompassing Beijing 2008-related studies carried out in China before and after the Games: the first is that studies have tended to focus more on examining the opportunities, impacts, and effects of the Beijing 2008 Olympics than on how to fully exploit the opportunities at stake or strategically leverage the Games; the second is that most of the pre-existing research has been limited to Beijing, neglecting other Chinese cities' experiences of the Games and the extent to which the Games have impacted those cities. The little research that has examined Beijing 2008's impact on Shanghai can be summarised chronologically in two categories: pre-Games estimates and predictions and post-Games impact studies.

During preparation for the 2008 Olympics, Yi and Liu (2007) predicted that the positive impact of Beijing 2008 on Shanghai would be associated with the aims of boosting tourism and local business development and of enhancing the Olympics' popularity among local citizens. Lu and Zhang (2005) further argued that, although the 2008 Olympics was to be held in Beijing, Shanghai's citizens still experienced something of Olympic spirit and culture (e.g. fair play); this appreciation helped Shanghai's citizens to effectively adapt to the rapid social transformation that Shanghai was experiencing. In addition, according to quantitative research conducted by Fudan University (Li, 2009), 96% of survey respondents (out of 448 Shanghai residents in total) reported that they were interested in watching (via TV or other media platforms) the Beijing 2008 Games.

Using general management and marketing theories, Liu and Zhang (2007) discussed how Shanghai could strategically develop and utilise the resources Beijing 2008 provided. They argued that, given the scale and influence of the event, the Beijing 2008 Olympics would generate 'spillover' effects to other cities in China; however, those effects would not automatically bring benefits, because event benefits need to be strategically leveraged in order to fully explore, operate, and utilise opportunities. Liu and Zhang (2007) considered strategic planning and development, in the context of sporting mega events, to be associated with the development of overall strategies and the building of stakeholder relationships and alliances. They emphasised that maximising the positive impacts of Beijing 2008 on the social, economic, and cultural development of Shanghai required effective coordination and communication between different stakeholders, including the city government, private and public organisations, sports industry, and other sectors. A general model for the formulation of strategies was subsequently proposed. Specifically, to overcome the disadvantages of being an 'away games' location, their model suggested the following six areas for Shanghai City Government to carry out strategic development in: (1) urban image promotion and urban branding; (2) community cohesion; (3) enhancing public health awareness; (4) increasing sport participation rate; (5) promoting the development of relevant industries; and (6) streamlining development targets for future major sporting events hosted in Shanghai (e.g. the 2010 Shanghai World Expo).

Research conducted in the aftermath of the 2008 Beijing Olympics (Xue, Li and Fei, 2009) revealed that, among university students in Shanghai, Beijing 2008 had an impact on awareness of the importance of sport and physical activity participation and on enhancing patriotism and national pride. Examining Shanghai's citizens more broadly (n = 468), Liu, Broom, and Wilson's (2014) study found that Shanghai residents perceived a wide range of legacy impacts for the 2008 Olympics. Specifically, of seven factors ranked in order of significance, the most significant perceived impacts were on 'Identity and culture', 'Psychological income and social capital', 'Networks and cooperation', 'Infrastructure and skills development', 'Sport and health', 'Tourism and economics', and 'Environment'. Shanghai residents considered that Beijing's 2008

Games also helped to promote sports participation and to encourage the construction of sports facilities. Liu, Broom, and Wilson (2014) further suggested that intangible benefits, such as psychological income and emotional benefit, would stand out from and even outweigh the economic benefits in the long run.

In summary, the Shanghai case study is somewhat different from that of Leicestershire. There was limited (if any) leverage planning and delivery taking place in Shanghai before, during, and after the Beijing 2008 Olympics. In the Reports on the Work of the Shanghai Municipal Government of the Year 2008 and the Year 2009 (a type of report summarising the achievement of Shanghai municipal government in the past year, Shanghaigov, 2008b, 2009) and the list of the Key Work of the Shanghai Municipal Government in 2008 (Shanghaigov, 2008a), there was hardly any mention of the 2008 Olympics, apart from stating that Shanghai would 'actively participate in the 2008 Games (mainly by providing Olympic reserve elite athlete talents) . . . and earnestly organise the Olympics football matches in Shanghai and the Olympic torch relay in Shanghai' (Item 21).

Such a deliberate 'neglection' of the leveraging opportunities presented by Beijing hosting the 2008 Olympics seems to stem from the historically competitive relationship between Beijing and Shanghai in matters of social, political, and economic development (Liu, 2008). Shanghai and Beijing are generally considered as two 'neck and neck' municipal cities, in terms of their abilities to host international mega events. After the central government chose to let Beijing bid for the 2008 Olympic and Paralympic Games, Shanghai was 'determined not to be left behind' (Liu and Gratton, 2010, p. 630); and subsequently was prompted to actively seek opportunities to host other influential international mega events. The successful bidding and hosting of the 2010 World Expo can be seen as a demonstration of Shanghai's ability to stage a large and influential mega-event similar to the Olympics. As revealed by Beesley and Chalip (2011), Beijing 2008 'belonged to Beijing, and it was Beijing's chance to showcase China to the world; Shanghai's opportunity to present itself to the world would be realised through the World Expo in 2010' (p. 337). Thus, instead of focusing on exploiting the opportunities presented by Beijing hosting the Olympics, Shanghai focused on what it could learn from another city's hosting of a mega-event so as to then be better able to prepare its own future hosting mission. The hostile competition between Beijing and Shanghai is also discernible in other cases. Anecdotal evidence notes that when Beijing asked Shanghai to host the 2008 Olympic Scientific Congress, Shanghai passed this opportunity and let Guangzhou undertake the event.

Because there were little leveraging efforts made in the case of Shanghai, we could not draw leveraging lessons learned from Shanghai's 2008 experience. However, while the extent to which knowledge transfer has taken place remains unknown, Beijing 2008 essentially served as a learning opportunity for Shanghai in its preparation for and hosting of the 2010 World Expo (Lu and Zhang, 2005; Zhao and Cheng, 2008; Wu and Xu, 2011), including knowledge on specific matters such as cultural development, business development, large-scale visitor reception, and volunteer recruitment management.

Conclusion

This chapter has sought to provide an overview of literature on the impacts of sporting mega-events (particularly the Olympic and Paralympic Games) in non-host regions and to present two non-host cities regarding their experiences during the Games. In Leicestershire's case, the London 2012 Olympic Games impacted on outcomes for Leicestershire. In contrast, the impacts of Beijing 2008 on Shanghai have been rather limited; it seems like more work could have been done by Shanghai, through strategic planning in advance of the Games, to achieve more in terms of leveraging and, subsequently, of successfully generating Beijing 2008 impacts.

Although Leicestershire designed, delivered, and evaluated a better-planned leveraging strategy than Shanghai had done, ambiguity surrounding the leveraging targets and objectives, uncertainty in the economic and political environment, and tensions between different legacy strands were still evidenced in Leicestershire's case; these problems resulted, in part, from the steering group's lack of experience, but they were also a consequence of inadequate support and guidance from the Olympic Organising Committee and national government on how to operate leveraging. A more streamlined, nationwide, and cooperative leveraging system is advocated for future Olympic Games.

We argue that examining the Olympic and Paralympic Games' legacies and impacts means going beyond the usual questions about what the legacies, impacts, and values generated by the Games are. More precisely, it involves studying which regions within host nations benefited from hosting the Olympics and whether any strategic efforts have been made, particularly on the part of areas outside of host cities, to leverage the event's impact such as to maximise the opportunities of becoming an Olympic host nation. Where non-host regions are concerned, many issues still remain unstudied. Attempts to research the scope, objectives, and impacts of the Games in non-host areas are encouraged, not only for the purpose of enhancing the currently limited evidence base but also for the purpose of fully exploring underlying power relations that might exist between stakeholders in host areas and stakeholders in non-host areas.

References

Baade, R. and Matheson, V. (2002). *Bidding for the Olympics: Fool's gold?* Cheltenham: Edward Elgar Publishing Ltd, pp. 127–151.

Beesley, L.G. and Chalip, L. (2011). Seeking (and not seeking) to leverage mega-sport events in non-host destinations: The case of Shanghai and the Beijing Olympics. *Journal of Sport & Tourism*, 16(4), pp. 323–344.

Beijing 2022 Olympic Winter Games Bid Committee. (2014). *Candidature file for the 2022 Winter Olympic Games*. Beijing: The author.

Bell, B. and Gallimore, K. (2015). Embracing the games? Leverage and legacy of London 2012 Olympics at the sub-regional level by means of strategic partnerships. *Leisure Studies*, 34(6), pp. 720–741.

Blake, A. (2005). *The economic impact of the London 2012 Olympics*. Nottingham: Christel DeHaan Tourism and Travel Research Institute, Nottingham University. Available at: www.nottingham.ac.uk/ttri/ [Google Scholar][KD15] .

Bondonio, P. and Guala, C. (2011). Gran Torino? The 2006 Olympic Winter games and the tourism revival of an ancient city. *Journal of Sport & Tourism*, 16(4), pp. 303–321.

Bondonio, P., Guala, C. and Mela, A. (2008). Torino 2006 OWG: Any legacies for the IOC and Olympic territories. *Proceedings: International Symposium for Olympic Research*, 2.

British Olympic Committee. (2005). *London 2012 candidate file [vol. 1]*.

Chappelet, J-L. (2008). Olympic environmental concerns as a legacy of the Winter games. *The International Journal of the History of Sport*, 25(14), pp. 1884–1902.

Chen, S. (2013). *'Our Games Our Legacy' for Leicester and Leicestershire: An empirical study of the London 2012 Games legacy outcomes for a non-hosting region*. An evaluation report for Leicester-Shire & Rutland Sport, EMpowered, Inspire LeicesterShire and Loughborough University. Loughborough: Centre for Olympic Studies and Research, Loughborough University.

Chen, S. and Henry, I. (2019). Schools' engagement with the Get Set London 2012 Olympic education programme: Empirical insights from schools in a non-hosting region. *European Physical Education Review*, 25(1), pp. 254–272.

Chen, S. and Misener, L. (2019). Event leveraging in a nonhost region: Challenges and opportunities. *Journal of Sport Management*, 33(4), p. 275.

Chien, P.M., Kelly, S.J. and Gill, C. (2017). Identifying objectives for mega-event leveraging: A non-host city case. *Marketing Intelligence & Planning*, 0(0), null.

DCMS. (2008). *Before, during and after: Making the most of the London 2012 Games*. London: Department of Culture Media and Sport.
DCMS. (2009). *London 2012 Olympic and Paralympic games impacts and legacy evaluation framework final report*. London: DCMS.
Deccio, C. and Baloglu, S. (2002). Nonhost community resident reactions to the 2002 Winter Olympics: The spillover impacts. *Journal of Travel Research*, 41(1), pp. 46–56.
Etzioni, A. (1967). Mixed-scanning: A 'third' approach to decision-making. *Public Administration Review*, pp. 385–392.
Fairley, S. and Kelly, D. (2017). Developing leveraging strategies for pre-Games training for mega-events in non-host cities. *Marketing Intelligence & Planning*, 35(6), pp. 740–755.
Gardiner, S. and Chalip, L.H. (2006). *Leveraging a mega-event when not the host city: Lessons from pre-Olympic training*. Gold Coast. Queensland: Sustainable Tourism.
Gibson, H.J., Qi, X. and Zhang, J.J. (2008). Destination image and intent to visit China and the 2008 Beijing Olympic Games. *Journal of Sport Management*, 22(4), pp. 427–450.
Inspire Leicestershire. (2009). *Inspire Leicestershire: Leicestershire strategy for the 2012 games*.
Karadakis, K. and Kaplanidou, K. (2012). Legacy perceptions among host and non-host Olympic Games residents: A longitudinal study of the 2010 Vancouver Olympic Games. *European Sport Management Quarterly*, 12(3), pp. 243–264.
Kasimati, E. and Dawson, P. (2009). Assessing the impact of the 2004 Olympic Games on the Greek economy: A small macroeconometric model. *Economic Modelling*, 26(1), pp. 139–146.
Kavetsos, G. and Szymanski, S. (2010). National well-being and international sports events. *Journal of Economic Psychology*, 31(2), pp. 158–171.
Li, S. (2009). *Sample survey and evaluation of Shanghai after the opening ceremony of the Beijing Olympic Games*. Beijing: PeopleNet. Available at: http://media.people.com.cn/GB/22114/49489/147159/8863888.html.
Liu, D. (2008). Co-branding of sports competition and city brands in city marketing. *Journal of Wuhan Sport University*, 42(5), pp. 38–42.
Liu, D., Broom, D. and Wilson, R. (2014). Legacy of the Beijing Olympic Games: A non-host city perspective. *European Sport Management Quarterly*, 14(5), pp. 485–502.
Liu, D. and Gratton, C. (2010). The impact of mega sporting events on live spectators' images of a host city: A case study of the Shanghai F1 Grand Prix. *Tourism Economics*, 16(3), pp. 629–645.
Liu, D. and Zhang, B. (2007). Strategic development and utilization of Beijing Olympics by non-host cities. *Journal of TUS*, 22(1), pp. 42–44.
London Organising Committee of the Olympic Games and Paralympic Games. (2009). *Towards a one planet 2012*.
Lu, X. and Zhang, X. (2005). Beijing Olympic Games and Shanghai. *Journal of Shenyang Physical Education Institute*, 24(5), pp. 26–28.
May, V. (1995). Environmental implications of the 1992 Winter Olympic Games. *Tourism Management*, 16(4), pp. 269–275.
Minnaert, L. (2012). An Olympic legacy for all? The non-infrastructural outcomes of the Olympic Games for socially excluded groups (Atlanta 1996 – Beijing 2008). *Tourism Management*, 33(2), pp. 361–370.
Misener, L., Darcy, S., Legg, D. and Gilbert, K. (2013). Beyond Olympic legacy: Understanding Paralympic legacy through a thematic analysis. *Journal of Sport Management*, 27(4), p. 329.
Ritchie, B.W., Shipway, R. and Cleeve, B. (2009). Resident perceptions of mega-sporting events: A non-host city perspective of the 2012 London Olympic Games. *Journal of Sport & Tourism*, 14(2/3), pp. 143–167.
Shanghaigov. (2008a). *The Key work of the Shanghai Municipal Government in 2008*.
Shanghaigov. (2008b). *Report on the work of the Shanghai Municipal government of the year 2008*.
Shanghaigov. (2009). *Report on the work of the Shanghai Municipal government of the year 2009*.
Walton, H., Longo, A. and Dawson, P. (2008). A contingent valuation of the 2012 London Olympic Games – A regional perspective. *Journal of Sports Economics*, 9(3), pp. 304–317.
Weed, M. and Dowse, S. (2009). A missed opportunity waiting to happen? The social legacy potential of the London 2012 Paralympic games. *Journal of Policy Research in Tourism, Leisure and Events*, 1(2), pp. 170–174.
Wu, B. and Xu, Z. (2011). On the relations between Beijing Olympic culture and Shanghai expo culture. In: *2011 Second International Conference on Education and Sports Education*. Shanghai: 1994–2018 China Academic Journal Electronic Publishing House.

Xue, Y., Li, F. and Fei, H. (2009). *The impact of Beijing Olympic Games on sports consciousness of university students in Shanghai*. Shanghai: The 19th National College Track and Field Research Report.

Yi, X. and Liu, Z. (2007). Research on the impact of 2008 Beijing Olympic Games on Shanghai. In: *The 8th National Sports Science Conference*. Shanghai: 1994–2015 China Academic Journal Electronic Publishing House.

Yusuf, S. and Wu, W. (2002). Pathways to a world city: Shanghai rising in an era of globalisation. *Urban Studies*, 39(7), pp. 1213–1240.

Zhao, W. and Cheng, L. (2008). *The enlightenment of Beijing Olympic Games to Shanghai World Expo*. Shanghai: 1994–2017 China Academic Journal Electronic Publishing House.

35

Legacies beyond the Olympic and Paralympic Games

The case of two Youth Olympic Games

Ran Zhou, Kyriaki Kaplanidou and Dikaia Chatziefstathiou

Introduction

Over the years, the Olympic movement has been progressively growing and evolving to reflect the changing economic, political, and socio-cultural environment (Chatziefstathiou, 2012a). After introducing the Winter Olympic Games in 1924, the International Olympic Committee (IOC) once again expanded its market reach and added the Youth Olympic Games (YOG) into its event portfolio (Hanstad, Parent and Houlihan, 2014). As a new creation in the Olympic movement history, the YOG was proposed in 2007 as a global multi-sporting event which invited youth athletes between 15–18 years old from all around the world to compete, learn, and share (IOC, 2014) and has been considered a best-kept secret for host cities (Judge et al., 2009).

Today, the rising rates of childhood obesity and inactivity have become a worldwide concern. With the prevalence of computer games and television, children seem to be more attracted to a sedentary lifestyle than outdoor activities, resulting in a drastic increase of health-related issues such as overweight, obesity, and low physical fitness among children and adolescents (Judge et al., 2016). To boost engagement in sport and physical activity (PA), the concept of YOG was initiated by the former President of IOC, Jacques Rogge, in an attempt to bring young people back to the play field (IOC, 2014). Although the initial goal of the YOG was to combat obesity and health-related issues, the IOC turned the YOG into more than just a sport competition: "the global vision of the YOG is to educate, engage and inspire young people around the world to participate in sports and adopt the Olympic values" (Lucidarme and Maes, 2010, p. 225). As such, the YOG was promoted as a platform for athletes, as well as all the young talents, to learn and share.

Although the YOG are not of the same scope as the Olympic and Paralympic Games, hosting a mega-event like YOG requires extensive investment and would leave a significant footprint on the host community through its economic, socio-cultural, and environmental impacts (Wong, 2012). As such, the legacies of the YOG need to be taken into consideration, as the YOG serves not only as a platform for athletes to compete and communicate but also a catalyst that may generate lasting benefits for the local population (IOC, 2014). In other words, the impacts of the

YOG may reach beyond participating athletes and have an influence on the host city residents who are parents, coaches, and teachers given their direct relationships with youth and the YOG programmes. However, little of the published work has examined the legacies of the YOG, especially from the residents' perspectives. Moreover, YOG were created as a vehicle to achieve higher sport involvement, as well as an arena to educate people about the Olympic values (Hanstad, Parent and Houlihan, 2014). It is yet to know how sport involvement and Olympic values would affect legacy perceptions given their close relevancy to the YOG agenda.

This chapter provides an overview of the contemporary research with respect to the legacies of YOG. Using the case studies of Lillehammer 2016 YOG and Lausanne 2020 YOG, this chapter discusses residents' perceptions of YOG legacies and their influence on quality of life and event support, a study funded by the Advanced Olympic Research Grant programme of the IOC. It also presents findings with regards to the role of sport involvement and Olympic values in legacy perceptions, quality of life, and event support. From a theoretical standpoint, this chapter sets out to illustrate the effect of individual characteristics (e.g. level of sport involvement and appreciation of Olympic values) on residents' perceptions and behavioural outcomes.

YOG legacies for host community residents

Mega sport events (e.g. Olympic Games and Youth Olympic Games) commonly serve as catalysts for economic, social, and environmental development of the host city and region (Kaplanidou et al., 2013; Wong, 2012). The staging of a mega sport event is associated with vast sums of public spending and capital investment. Thus, when awarded with a mega sport event, the city often expects that the event can bring in significant benefits to justify its large-scale expenses (Kaplanidou and Karadakis, 2010). In other words, the potential to acquire positive legacies from hosting becomes integral to a city's decision to bid for a mega sport event (Leopkey and Parent, 2012).

While the importance of sport event legacy has been recognised, the creation of a precise definition of the term 'legacy' has proven challenging (Kaplanidou et al., 2013). Nevertheless, most researchers seemed to agree on the multi-dimensionality of the legacy concept, which normally encompasses both planned and unplanned, tangible and intangible, positive and negative aspects (Kaplanidou and Karadakis, 2010; Preuss, 2007). We must note however, that a distinction must be made for the use of event impacts and legacies. According to Preuss (2015) and Kaplanidou (2012), there is a temporal element in assessing event impacts and legacies. Oftentimes legacy is regarded as what is left behind by a sport event, hence it focuses on the long-term effect that remains after the conclusion of the event (Stevenson, 2012). On the other hand, impact focuses on the immediate effect that originates prior to or during the event. Event impacts that happen in the preparation stage can initiate potential legacy outcomes if planned correctly (Preuss, 2014). Thus, in this chapter, the term 'event legacies' will be used for post-event outcomes the residents evaluate after the conclusion of the sport event; whilst the term 'event impacts' will be used for pre-event outcomes where the residents evaluate the expected outcomes while they experience the event preparations.

Case studies: Lillehammer 2016 YOG and Lausanne 2020 YOG

The two case studies underpinning this chapter collected both qualitative and quantitative data from the Lillehammer 2016 YOG and Lausanne 2020 YOG using funding from the Olympic Studies Centre Advanced Olympic Research Grant Programme. Impacts may occur before and after a sport event and differences may exist in perceived impacts between events that have taken place in the past and those anticipated to take place in the future (Ma and Kaplanidou, 2017b). Thus, a past and a future event were chosen to provide a more comprehensive analysis of the impacts and legacies, along with their antecedents and behavioural outcomes, perceived by residents of a past host country (i.e. Lillehammer) and a future one (i.e. Lausanne).

The qualitative data were collected in September 2017 from archival material in the IOC Olympic Studies Centre, as well as informal interviews with key stakeholders (e.g. representatives of the IOC, the Norwegian Olympic Committee, the Lausanne 2020 Organising Committee, the Youth Olympic Council in Lausanne, and officials from the 2016 YOG) involved in the 2016 and 2020 YOG legacy planning and management processes. Based on the qualitative data, online questionnaires were created to explore YOG impacts/legacies and related variables (e.g. Olympic values, sport involvement, quality of life, and event support). Questionnaires were administered through emails to residents of the 2016 and 2020 YOG host regions. A total of 171 completed responses (yielding a response rate of 1.07%) were obtained from residents in the city of Lillehammer and Oslo for the 2016 YOG, whereas 307 completed responses (yielding a response rate of 6.14%) were obtained from residents in the city of Lausanne and Geneva for the 2020 YOG. Major findings are summarised in the following sections, in combination with discussions of the related work on mega sport event impacts and legacies, quality of life, event support, and factors that influence these outcomes.

Based on the content of legacies and impacts, the case studies presented in this chapter identified 11 categories of Lillehammer 2016 YOG legacies (i.e. knowledge, tourism, sport development, youth engagement, emotional, environmental, cultural, economic, infrastructure, educational, and negative legacies) and ten categories of Lausanne 2020 YOG impacts (i.e. knowledge, tourism, sport development, youth engagement, emotional, environmental, cultural, economic, infrastructure, and negative impacts). Table 35.1 presents the mean score of each legacy/impact category perceived by the host community residents. In the case of Lillehammer, all legacy categories, except for the negative legacies, received a mean score above the average point (4), suggesting that residents tended to have positive perceptions about the legacies that 2016 YOG brought to the region. The top three ranked categories were cultural (M=5.11), youth engagement (M=5.03), and emotional (M=4.94) legacies, which underlined the salience of intangible legacies – especially those related to socio-cultural and psychological areas. In the case of Lausanne, all impact categories, including the negative impacts (i.e. price inflation, opportunity costs, unneeded facilities, and crimes), received a mean score above the midpoint of 4. This suggested that while a range of benefits were likely to accrue from the 2020 YOG, the event might also impose negative outcomes such as price inflation, high opportunity costs, construction of unneeded infrastructure, and increased crime rate on the residents. Among the positive impacts, residents identified cultural impacts (M=5.44), youth engagement (M=5.38), and sport development (M=5.22) as the most positive changes brought by the Lausanne 2020 YOG. In addition, knowledge ($M_{2016\ YOG}$=4.92, $M_{2020\ YOG}$=5.15) also turned out to be a strongly positive legacy perceived by residents of both Lillehammer and Lausanne.

Although economic impacts and infrastructure legacies seemed to dominate discussions in mega-event studies, our case studies underlined the strength of intangible legacies (such as those associated with social, cultural, and psychological outcomes) in forming positive perceptions among host community residents, which perhaps is tied to the nature of the YOG. Indeed, researchers have suggested that socio-cultural and psychological legacies, albeit less visible, deserved greater attention given their substantial influence on the host community (Chalip, 2006; Minnaert, 2012). For example, relevant literature discusses that intangible legacies related to social and psychological benefits of mega sport events can significantly affect residents' quality

Table 35.1 Residents' mean scores[a] for 2016 YOG legacies and 2020 YOG impacts

Legacies/Impacts	*2016 YOG*	*2020 YOG*
Knowledge	4.92	5.15
Tourism	4.83	5.19
Sport development	4.83	5.22
Youth engagement	5.03	5.38
Emotional	4.94	5.07
Environmental	4.72	4.93
Cultural	5.11	5.44
Economic	4.41	4.95
Infrastructure	4.37	4.94
Educational	4.86	N/A
Negative	3.80	4.34

a Mean scores were based on a 7-point Likert Scale whereby 1=totally disagree and 7=totally agree

of life and their patronage for the success of the event (Kaplanidou et al., 2013; Karadakis and Kaplanidou, 2012).

The creation of intangible legacies was also a central tenet to the hosting of YOG, which was envisioned to leave a lasting impact on sport, cultural, and knowledge development among the new generation (Wong, 2012). In line with the core concept of YOG to promote youth education and knowledge sharing, our interviews with stakeholders highlighted the knowledge benefits accruing from the 2016 and 2020 Games. Specifically, the interviews revealed that YOG created a platform for knowledge diffusion through programmes for athletes, volunteers, and students in the host regions. For athletes, educational activities focusing on sport ethics and anti-doping were launched to promote the spirit of sportsmanship and fair play. Commitments were also made toward helping young athletes develop life skills, experience, and know-how, which would benefit their professional careers in the long run. In terms of volunteering, initiatives were undertaken to improve the competence of young volunteers. For instance, the 2016 Lillehammer YOG offered opportunities to educate 220 young leading volunteers through a two-year programme, leaving a valuable asset to the community of Lillehammer. The legacy initiatives of 2016 and 2020 YOG not only targeted athletes and volunteers, but also involved a wide range of schools where children were engaged in various learning activities (e.g. workshops and school projects) related to the YOG. To achieve the aspiration of creating an enduring knowledge legacy, the university college of Lillehammer established a new undergraduate sport management programme that prepared young talents for leadership roles in sport-related careers.

YOG legacies, quality of life, and event support

The staging of YOG brings about all kinds of positive and negative changes that would inevitably affect residents' life on a daily basis. As main receivers of YOG impacts and legacies, host community residents are involved (either directly or indirectly) in the event planning process and bear the long-term consequences after the end of the event. As a result, residents' quality of life

(QOL) can be influenced through this involvement and interaction process (Kaplanidou et al., 2013). In general, QOL refers to individuals' feeling of contentment with their living environment. It involves perceptions of multiple life domains (e.g. health, security, relationships) and is closely associated with happiness, life satisfaction, and subjective wellbeing (Cummins, 1997; Diener, 2000).

Hosting a mega sport event like the YOG offers host cities the opportunity to strategically plan for positive legacies that can benefit the QOL of residents (Karadakis and Kaplanidou, 2012). Prior research has identified the contribution of intangible legacies, such as those associated with psychological and socio-cultural benefits, to the overall improvement of residents' QOL (Karadakis and Kaplanidou, 2012; Kaplanidou et al., 2013). Compared to other event impacts, it seems that psychological and socio-cultural impacts are more relevant to both personal and community QOL, and they tend to form more positive perceptions among residents that withstand the test of time (Al-Emadi et al., 2017; Karadakis, Kaplanidou and Karlis, 2016). The importance of intangible (e.g. psychological and socio-cultural) legacies for QOL is peculiarly relevant to YOG, given the event targets primarily socio-cultural changes related to sport participation, knowledge development, and education and cultural initiatives undertaken in the host community.

Positive event impacts can enhance residents' QOL and subsequently boost support for the event (Kaplanidou et al., 2013). The support from local residents is critical to the success of sport events because of their involvement and interactions with spectators, visitors, athletes, and other consumers of sport events. The support of residents can turn a sport event into a collective celebration between the hosts and guests, whereas the resistance of residents may result in tensions and conflicts between the local community and event attendees (Prayag et al., 2013). As such, it is important to understand the variables that influence resident support of sport events.

According to the Social Exchange Theory (SET), individuals are more likely to engage in an exchange if they feel such exchange would bring them more benefits than costs (Cropanzano and Mitchell, 2005; Emerson, 1976). In the case of the Olympic Games, SET provides the rationale why people show support for an event when benefits associated with QOL are observed (Kaplanidou, 2012). Here, QOL plays a crucial part in prompting support for the event. Prior research suggested that QOL can function as an exchange platform between event impacts and resident support (Ma and Kaplanidou, 2017a; Kaplanidou, 2017). When residents perceived an event (e.g. YOG) had positive impacts on their QOL (which can be interpreted as benefits from participating in an exchange according to SET), then residents were more likely to show support for this event.

In the cases of 2016 Lillehammer YOG and 2020 Lausanne YOG, we examined the interrelationships between intangible legacy/impact (i.e. knowledge development)[1] of the YOG, personal and community QOL, and event support. For Lillehammer and Oslo residents, the empirical data showed that the knowledge legacy of the 2016 YOG had significant influence on personal QOL and event support. For Lausanne and Geneva residents, knowledge impacts of the 2020 YOG had significant influence on residents' QOL at both the personal and community level, as well as on residents' support for the event. We also found a significant relationship between personal QOL and event support in the case of 2020 Lausanne YOG. This finding underscored the importance of QOL in increasing event support. It demonstrated that the extent to which local residents endorse or oppose the staging of YOG depended on how they perceived the event to influence their personal welfare (Ma and Kaplanidou, 2017b).

Factors influencing legacy perceptions, quality of life, and event support

Sport involvement

As IOC's new initiative targeting the youth market, the YOG was created around the ambition of increasing youth sport involvement to address the growing concern with regards to the escalating drop-off rates in active sport participation and rising youth obesity (Wong, 2011). In such context, promoting sport involvement has been central to the mission and vision of YOG.

The construct of involvement has been applied to understand attitudes and behaviour in sport consumer research (Funk, Ridinger and Moorman, 2004). Involvement with sport and physical activity can create higher levels of knowledge on sport-related topics and change a person's perspectives. Thus, with different levels of sport involvement, residents could view the event impacts differently (Havitz and Howard, 1995; Holt et al., 2009; Kaplanidou and Havitz, 2010; Lau, Milne et al., 2017). Prior research suggested that involvement with sport events through direct experience of spectating created difference in the evaluation of event impacts (Kaplanidou, 2012). Likewise, Karadakis and Kaplanidou (2012) and Karadakis et al. (2016) found that certain legacies were viewed differently before and after the event, with enhanced perceptions towards abstract, non-material, and indirect legacies (e.g. psychological legacies). It seemed that residents' involvement with the event through the hosting experience created socio-psychological benefits for the residents, which could further contribute to their QOL and event support (Kaplanidou et al., 2013). This notion of direct experience and involvement draw our attention to the importance of sport involvement in influencing event impacts, quality of life, and event support. It is, however, quite surprising that no studies exist that examine the role of involvement with sport and physical activity among residents in the formation of event impact perceptions and behavioural outcomes.

Our case studies on YOG host cities (i.e. Lillehammer in 2016 and Lausanne in 2020) explored whether prior involvement with sport and physical activity can create different dispositions toward event outcomes and supportive behaviours. For these two studies, sport involvement is conceptualised as encompassing both psychological and behavioural components. The former includes psychological involvement with sports and psychological involvement in YOG to reflect the context of this research project; whereas the latter includes active behavioural involvement (e.g. participation in physical activity and exercise; Weed et al., 2012) and passive behavioural involvement (e.g. spectating and media consumption; Lee and Trail, 2011). Our empirical data revealed that, despite the absence of a significant influence from psychological involvement with sports, psychological involvement in YOG had a significant positive influence on event legacy (i.e. knowledge) perception in both cases of Lillehammer and Lausanne. In terms of behavioural involvement, the findings showed significant influences of active sport involvement on event legacy perceptions (nine categories) and event support in both Lillehammer's and Lausanne's case. It appeared that residents who engage in sport activities more frequently tended to hold higher perceptions toward the YOG legacies. In the case of Lausanne, we also identified significant influences of active sport involvement on QOL at the community and personal level. Moreover, results from the case studies revealed significant influences of passive sport involvement on all categories of positive event impacts (in Lausanne's case), community and personal QOL (in Lausanne's case), and event support (in both cases).

Olympic values

The heart of the Olympic movement is to promote Olympism and spread Olympic values around the world. The IOC has highlighted excellence, friendship, and respect as the three core components of Olympic values (IOC, 2016). As a new product of the Olympic movement, the YOG has acted as a platform to educate and reinforce the Olympic values among young people on and off the field (Nordhagen and Fauske, 2018). In the recent decades, the extravagant scale and over-commercialisation of the Olympic Games has caused an increased gap between the Olympic ideals and realities. In contrast, the YOG – both smaller in size and having less involvement with sponsors – seems closer to the ideals of Olympism (Nordhagen and Fauske, 2018). With its emphasis on culture and education, the YOG represents an important step of returning to the roots of the Olympics (Hanstad, Parent and Kristiansen, 2013).

Olympism is a philosophy of life with a focus on the educational values inherent in sporting activities. It promotes a world view that governs the overt behaviours and guides people to proceed in life (Chatziefstathiou and Henry, 2009). Chatziefstathiou (2012a, 2012b) has shown how Olympism is a moral paradigm which can be adopted as a pedagogical tool within formal education. It can also be the platform for a moral discourse of people's everyday life (Chatziefstathiou, 2012a) and teach young people about fair play, friendship, respect, and excellence, encouraging them to become active citizens in their communities (Chatziefstathiou, 2012b). Drawing on existing research, it appears that the Olympic values can shape people's beliefs, dispositions, and behaviours, and hence may affect how they view and act towards sport events – for example, how people perceive YOG impacts, their QOL, and their support towards event-related initiatives. Empirical findings from our case studies provided support for some of these propositions. Specifically, we identified significant positive influence of the Olympic values on QOL at both the personal and community level (in the case of 2016 Lillehammer YOG) and residents' support for the YOG (in the case of 2020 Lausanne YOG).

Discussion and conclusion

As one of the world's best-known and most valuable brands, the Olympic brand communicates the essence of the Olympic ideals to people from all over the world. The massive viewership and media coverage of the Olympic Games speak to the universal popularity of the Olympic brand (Hanstad, Parent and Houlihan, 2014). However, in recent years, there were signs showing a declining interest in the Olympic Games, along with a weakening recognition of the Olympic brand, among the younger cohorts. Against this background, the targeting of the youth market became a priority for the IOC (Chatziefstathiou, 2012b). The addition of YOG to the Olympic brand portfolio in 2007 demonstrated IOC's determination to reach out to the younger generation. To capture the interest of a young audience, the YOG introduced creative and innovative event formats such as 3-on-3 basketball, ice hockey skills challenge, BMX, road races, and mixed team competitions (Hanstad, Parent and Houlihan, 2014; Kristiansen, 2015). In addition to the modification of competitive formats, the YOG also used multiple social media platforms such as YouTube, Facebook, and Twitter to engage young fans who were less likely to follow sport news through traditional media (Chatziefstathiou, 2012b).

Although the Olympic Games are held alongside with the Paralympic Games to include athletes with disabilities, currently the YOG only focuses on able-bodied athletes. Notwithstanding, the International Paralympic Committee (IPC) has been discussing the idea of creating the

Youth Paralympic Games (YPC) to showcase para sports. If the host decision was made, an inaugural YPC was envisioned to take place around 2024 (Heng, 2018). Outside of the play field, the YOG encourage a range of social initiatives such as the Young Change Makers+ (YCM+) projects to promote inclusivity and equality for both able-bodied and disabled sport participants (Olympic News, 2018, 2019). Moreover, a unique feature of the YOG is the downplay of competitiveness and the emphasis on culture and education. In line with the vision of YOG which is to inspire young people to take part in sport and live by the Olympic values, the IOC wants the Games to be more than just a sporting competition (Hanstad et al., 2013). The current IOC President Thomas Bach in his New Year's Message for 2018 envisaged the 2018 YOG in Buenos Aires as a sport and cultural festival engaging local communities in a range of activities beyond the actual sport competitions themselves (IOC, 2018). This culture and learning component has been incorporated as part of the Games through the Learn and Share activities (formerly known as the Culture and Education programme) in an effort to create an enduring knowledge legacy for the young people.

The salience of knowledge legacy was underlined in our quantitative and qualitative findings. Our quantitative results identified significant positive effects of knowledge legacy on QOL (at both the community and personal level) and residents' support for YOG; whereas our qualitative findings unveiled substantial knowledge benefits that accrued to athletes, volunteers, and students in the host regions. Today, non-economic benefits play an increasingly important part in the city's decision to host mega sport events. While the potential for a net financial gain from hosting a mega-event seems in question, the non-economic benefits (such as the socio-cultural impacts in relation to broadening sport participation, cultural exchange, and knowledge development) seem to provide better justification for hosting a mega-event (Leng et al., 2014). That is, these socio-cultural impacts seem to relate more to the notion of 'worth it', hence contribute more to residents' support for the event (Kaplanidou et al., 2013). In addition, we identified the influential roles of two factors – sport involvement and Olympic values – in affecting legacy perceptions, QOL, and event support.

A number of practical recommendations can be drawn from these empirical findings. First, it is suggested that host city organising committees should devote more resources to promoting the theme of knowledge legacy of YOG, giving its critical influence on personal and community QOL as well as event support. This includes creating cultural celebration activities and educational programmes (e.g. Learn and Share, volunteer training project), focusing on instilling positive values (e.g. sport ethics, social responsibilities, fairness and equality, friendship and mutual understanding), and improving life skills (e.g. leadership, cooperation, management and communication) of the young people. Second, differentiating marketing strategies for sub-segments of the host population is necessary. According to our findings, residents with higher level of sport involvement tended to be more receptive and supportive of the event; thus, these people should be targeted in the communication of YOG legacies as they are more likely to hold positive perceptions towards the events and get the word out to other people. Finally, proper communication strategies should be in place to spread the Olympic values among youth. With the arrival of digital age, traditional broadcast channels are no longer sufficient in engaging youth around the world. On the other hand, the flourish of new media and social networking sites opens up new opportunities to reach out to younger audiences. Moreover, parents and schools also play a critical part in disseminating the Olympic values and YOG messages to the younger generation. Perhaps, if IOC links its marketing campaign to more school initiatives that bring in parents for educational sessions on YOG and Olympic movement, it will raise more awareness of the Olympic values among children, adolescents, and young adults.

Notes

1 Knowledge was chosen to represent the entire set of event legacies/impacts for two reasons: First, it closely links to the idea of YOG creating knowledge among youth, which locates at the heart of YOG's ambitions. Second, multicollinearity occurred among event legacy/impact variables. As such, knowledge was chosen as the representative legacy/impact type in the regression models, because it had a good factor loading when the entire set of event legacies/impacts were factor analysed to examine whether they all load on one factor.

2 We would like to thank the Olympic Studies Centre of the IOC for the funding opportunity provided by the Advanced Olympic Research Grant to conduct the present study.

References

Al-Emadi, A., Kaplanidou, K., Diop, A., Sagas, M., Le, K.T. and Al-Ali Mustafa, S. (2017). 2022 Qatar world cup: Impact perceptions among Qatar residents. *Journal of Travel Research*, 56(5), pp. 678–694.

Chalip, L. (2006). Towards social leverage of sport events. *Journal of Sport & Tourism*, 11(2), pp. 109–127.

Chatziefstathiou, D. (2012a). Olympic education and beyond: Olympism and value legacies from the Olympic and Paralympic games. *Educational Review*, 64(3), pp. 385–400(16).

Chatziefstathiou, D. (2012b). Active citizens and public policy: The example of the London 2012 Olympic Games. *International Journal of Sport Management, Recreation and Tourism*, 9, pp. 23–33.

Chatziefstathiou, D. and Henry, I.P. (2009). Olympism, governmentality and technologies of power. *Esporte e Sociedade Journal (Sport and Society Journal)*, 12, July–Aug.

Cropanzano, R. and Mitchell, M.S. (2005). Social exchange theory: An interdisciplinary review. *Journal of Management*, 31(6), pp. 874–900.

Cummins, R. (1997). The domain of life satisfaction: An attempt to order chaos. *Social Indicators Research*, 38, pp. 303–328.

Diener, E. (2000). Subjective well-being: The science of happiness and a proposal for a national index. *American Psychologist*, 55(1), pp. 34–43.

Emerson, R.M. (1976). Social exchange theory. *Annual Review of Sociology*, 2(1), pp. 335–362.

Funk, D.C., Ridinger, L.L. and Moorman, A.M. (2004). Exploring origins of involvement: Understanding the relationship between consumer motives and involvement with professional sport teams. *Leisure Sciences*, 26(1), pp. 35–61.

Hanstad, D.V., Parent, M.M. and Houlihan, B., eds. (2014). *The Youth Olympic Games*. Routledge.

Hanstad, D.V., Parent, M.M. and Kristiansen, E. (2013). The Youth Olympic Games: The best of the Olympics or a poor copy?. *European Sport Management Quarterly*, 13(3), pp. 315–338.

Havitz, M.E. and Howard, D.R. (1995). How enduring is enduring involvement? A seasonal examination of three recreational activities. *Journal of Consumer Psychology*, 4(3), pp. 255–276.

Heng, L.S. (2018). *Para sports: Inaugural Youth Paralympic Games at least six years away,* says IPC chief Parsons. Apr. 25.

Holt, N.L., Tamminen, K.A., Black, D.E., Mandigo, J.L. and Fox, K.R. (2009). Youth sport parenting styles and practices. *Journal of Sport and Exercise Psychology*, 31(1), pp. 37–59.

International Olympic Committee. (2014). *Factsheet 1 of 4: The Youth Olympic Games vision and principles*. Lausanne: IOC.

International Olympic Committee. (2016). *Factsheet: Legacies of the games*. Lausanne: IOC.

International Olympic Committee. (2018). *Official website*.

Judge, L.W., Lee, D., Hoover, D.L., Petersen, J.C., Bellar, D.M., Deitz, S., . . . and Holtzclaw, K. (2016). Marketing effectiveness of the Nanjing Youth Olympic Games: Implications for physical activity. *Physical Educator*, 73(3), p. 600.

Judge, L.W., Petersen, J. and Lydum, M. (2009). The best kept secret in sports: The 2010 Youth Olympic Games. *International Review for the Sociology of Sport*, 44(2–3), pp. 173–191.

Kaplanidou, K. (2012). The importance of legacy outcomes for Olympic Games four summer host cities residents' quality of life: 1996–2008. *European Sport Management Quarterly*, 12(4), pp. 397–433.

Kaplanidou, K. (2017). Health-related attitudes and behaviors among Olympic host city residents from Atlanta, Sydney, Athens, and Beijing Olympic Games: Exploring potential legacies. *Event Management*, 21(2), pp. 159–174.

Kaplanidou, K. and Havitz, M.E. (2010). Exploring SI and EI of Olympic sports tourists: Does trip purpose matter? *International Journal of Sports Marketing and Sponsorship*, 11(4), pp. 74–89.

Kaplanidou, K. and Karadakis, K. (2010). Understanding the legacies of a host Olympic city: The case of the 2010 Vancouver Olympic Games. *Sport Marketing Quarterly*, 19(2), p. 110.
Kaplanidou, K., Karadakis, K., Gibson, H., Thapa, B., Walker, M., Geldenhuys, S. and Coetzee, W. (2013). Quality of life, event impacts, and mega-event support among South African residents before and after the 2010 FIFA World Cup. *Journal of Travel Research*, 52(5), pp. 631–645.
Karadakis, K. and Kaplanidou, K. (2012). Legacy perceptions among host and non-host Olympic Games residents: A longitudinal study of the 2010 Vancouver Olympic Games. European *Sport Management Quarterly*, 12(3), pp. 243–264.
Karadakis, K., K. Kaplanidou, et al. (2016). Host and non-host resident awareness and perceptions of legacies for the 2010 Vancouver Winter Olympic Games. *Society and Leisure*, 39(2), pp. 195–209.
Kristiansen, E. (2015). Competing for culture: Young Olympians' narratives from the first winter Youth Olympic Games. *International Journal of Sport and Exercise Psychology*, 13(1), pp. 29–42.
Lau, C.H., Milne, S. and Chui, R.C.F. (2017). Redefining stakeholder relationships in mega events: New Zealand Chinese and the Rugby World Cup. *Journal of Convention & Event Tourism*, 18(2), pp. 75–99.
Lee, D. and Trail, G. (2011). The influence of personal values and goals on cognitive and behavioral involvement in sport. *Journal of Sport Management*, 25(6), pp. 593–605.
Leng, H.K., Kuo, T.Y., Baysa-Pee, G. and Tay, J. (2014). Make me proud! Singapore 2010 Youth Olympic Games and its effect on national pride of young Singaporeans. *International Review for the Sociology of Sport*, 49(6), pp. 745–760.
Leopkey, B. and Parent, M.M. (2012). Olympic Games legacy: From general benefits to sustainable long-term legacy. *The International Journal of the History of Sport*, 29(6), pp. 924–943.
Lucidarme, S. and Maes, M. (2010). Youth Olympic Games: Challenges and impact on the different youth sports policies of the world. In: K. Georgiadis, ed., *17th International seminar on Olympic studies for postgraduate students: Proceedings*. Presented at the 17th International seminar on Olympic Studies for Postgraduate Students: The Olympic Games as a celebration: Evaluation of the Olympic Games of Beijing and the course towards the Olympic Games in Vancouver, Athens, Greece: International Olympic Academy; IOC, pp. 224–240.
Ma, S.C. and Kaplanidou, K. (2017a). Legacy perceptions among host Tour de Taiwan residents: The mediating effect of quality of life. *Leisure Studies*, 36(3), pp. 423–437.
Ma, S.C. and Kaplanidou, K. (2017b). Examining the importance of legacy outcomes of major sport events for host city residents' quality of life. *Applied Research in Quality of Life*, 12(4), pp. 903–923.
Minnaert, L. (2012). An Olympic legacy for all? The non-infrastructural outcomes of the Olympic Games for socially excluded groups (Atlanta 1996–Beijing 2008). *Tourism Management*, 33(2), pp 361–370.
Nordhagen, S.E. and Fauske, H. (2018). The Youth Olympic Games as an arena for Olympic education: An evaluation of the school program, "Dream Day". *Acta Universitatis Carolinae: Kinanthropologica*, 54(2).
Olympic News. (2018). *IOC unveils latest list of young change-maker+ projects*. Aug. 21.
Olympic News. (2019). *Rania Rahardja: Pioneering wheelchair fencing in Singapore through YCM+*. Mar. 1.
Prayag, G., Hosany, S., Nunkoo, R. and Alders, T. (2013). London residents' support for the 2012 Olympic Games: The mediating effect of overall attitude. *Tourism Management*, 36, pp. 629–640.
Preuss, H. (2007). The conceptualisation and measurement of mega sport event legacies. *Journal of Sport & Tourism*, 12(3–4), pp. 207–228.
Preuss, H. (2014). 'Legacy' revisited. In: G. Jonathan, ed., *Leveraging legacies from sports mega-events: Concepts and cases*. Basingstoke: Palgrave, pp. 24–38.
Preuss, H. (2015). A framework for identifying the legacies of a mega sport event. *Leisure Studies*, 34(6), pp. 643–664.
Stevenson, N. (2012). The cultural legacy of the 2012 games. In: *International sports events*. Routledge, pp. 81–95.
Weed, M., Coren, E., Fiore, J., Wellard, I., Mansfield, L., Chatziefstathiou, D. and Dowse, S. (2012). Developing a physical activity legacy from the London 2012 Olympic and Paralympic games: A policy – Led systematic review. *Perspectives in Public Health*, 132(2), pp. 75–80.
Wong, D. (2011). The Youth Olympic Games: Past, present and future. *The International Journal of the History of Sport*, 28(13), pp. 1831–1851.
Wong, D. (2012). No manual available': The creation of a youth Olympic legacy – A case study of Singapore 2010 Youth Olympic Games. *International sports events: Impacts, experiences and identities*. Routledge, pp. 55–68.

36

Arts and culture in the Olympic and Paralympic Games

Beatriz García

Introduction

The notion that the Olympic Games should complement the showcase of elite sport competitions with a programme of arts and cultural activity was central to the vision of Pierre de Coubertin, founder of the modern Olympic movement. It was a notion inspired by Coubertin's interpretation of the Ancient Greek Games tradition, which involved the showcase of human excellence in a variety of forms, from athletics to music and poetry. However, the Olympic cultural programme or 'Cultural Olympiad' has a mixed history and is one of the least visible components within the Olympic Games hosting process. Within the Paralympic Games, the history of cultural and art contributions is much shorter but has rapidly evolved since the year 2000 and become a valuable platform for collaboration between the two Games.

This chapter starts with an overview of the Games cultural programme evolution, from its original presentation in the form of Olympic Art Competitions to its latest incarnation as a four-year Cultural Olympiad and its raise in prominence within the Paralympic Games. The chapter then discusses key trends and challenges, and it ends by touching on the new thinking emerging in the context of the International Olympic Committee's (IOC) Agenda 2020 and the growing cultural and artistic aspirations of the Paralympic movement.

A brief history of art in the Olympic Games

The principle of holding an arts festival in parallel with the celebration of sporting competitions is embedded in the foundations of the Olympic movement. In the Ancient Games, athletes were called to showcase their talents in parallel to philosophers, scholars, poets, musicians, sculptors and high-profile leaders. Pierre de Coubertin defined such gathering of talents as the 'spirit of Olympism', and Olympism was in turn defined as the simultaneous training of the human body and the cultivation of the intellect and spirit, together viewed as manifestations of the harmoniously educated man. On this basis, Coubertin's ambition was to create an environment in modern society where artists and athletes could, again, be mutually inspired. In support of this ambition, the Olympic Charter establishes that "blending sport with culture and education" is the first "fundamental principle" of Olympism (IOC, 2018, p. 11).

In 1906, Coubertin convened a "Consultative Conference on Art, Letters and Sport" in order to discuss how the arts could be integrated into the Modern Olympic Games. As a result of the conference, Coubertin proposed the creation of an arts competition and requested it to be a compulsory part of every Olympic Games celebration from then on (Coubertin, cited in IOC, 1997, p. 92). This competition was called the 'Pentathlon of Muses' and involved the awarding of medals in five classic art categories: sculpture, painting, music, literature and architecture.

From Olympic art competitions to Olympic art exhibitions and festivals (1912–1988)

The first official Olympic Arts Competition did take place at the Stockholm Games in 1912. By 1952, however, the IOC decided to stop this programme. This was due to ongoing operational difficulties transporting artworks across the globe; the complexity of judging artistic entries from increasingly diverse cultural backgrounds; and deep disagreements concerning the principle of 'amateurism' which was a core requisite for participation within the Olympic Games at the time (see García, 2008; Stanton, 2000). Within this first period, the most ambitious Olympic cultural programme took place within the Berlin 1936 Games, an edition which, in line with the propaganda ambitions of the Third Reich, viewed the Olympic Games as a platform to promote the superior qualities of Aryan culture. Organisers invested heavily in the Games' symbolic dimension and facilitated high-quality cultural and artistic productions. The film 'Olympia' by Leni Riefenstahl was a remarkable highlight of the official Games' cultural programme that has influenced film making to this day. Further, the introduction of the Torch Relay, travelling from ancient Olympia in Greece, was a key Berlin cultural programme innovation that has become a cornerstone of the Olympic Games hosting process ever since.

Between Helsinki 1952 and Seoul 1988, arts and culture contributions within the Games took the form of Olympic art exhibitions and festivals. This brought opportunities as well as challenges for the integration of the arts and culture as a core dimension of the Olympic staging process. On the one hand, Games organisers had greater freedom to define the purpose of such programmes and determine who should be presenting what type of work. On the other, eliminating its competitive nature reduced national delegation following. This situation accelerated the trend towards diminishing numbers of Games participants being involved or interested in the cultural programme; and it led to a loss in international focus. The programme was now mainly a platform for local cultural representation and directed according to the specific interests of the host authorities with much less involvement and regulations from Olympic stakeholders and sporting bodies.

After a few editions focused on the presentation of national heritage, the late 1960s and 1970s saw an upsurge in contemporary cultural initiatives and some radical re-thinking about the role and relevance of the arts as a key vehicle to project the Olympic city. Mexico in 1968 presented what remains, to this day, one of the most ambitious and innovative Olympic festivals, spanning throughout one year and acting as a showcase, not only of the best of Mexican heritage and folklore, but also the best Mexican contemporary arts, placing these in the context of leading international artists of the time. Throughout the 1960s and 1970s, other areas where artists and related creative practitioners made major contributions were the design of banners and logos to dress the city and signpost Games venues – what is now termed 'the look of the Games'. The imagery for Tokyo 1964, Mexico 1968 and Munich 1972 are all exemplars of avantgarde visual design rather than standard marketing and branding exercises, and they can be viewed as leading examples of urban cultural policy innovations emerging out of the Games.

Table 36.1 Olympic arts festivals, Summer Games (1952–1988)

Olympiad	*Length*	*Content and themes*
Helsinki 1952	4 weeks	International exhibitions of architecture, painting, graphic arts, sculpture, literature, music
Melbourne 1956	4 weeks	National (Australian) culture
Rome 1960	6 months (*) 3 weeks	National (Italian) culture with an emphasis on history; sporting references in exhibition programme
Tokyo 1964	7 weeks	National (Japanese) high art and traditional culture
Mexico City 1968	1 year	International; high art and indigenous culture; nation-wide celebration of culture Overall title: Cultural Olympiad
Munich 1972	3 months (*) 6 weeks	International; high art and folk culture Overall title: Olympic Summer
Montreal 1976	4 weeks	National: showcase for Canadian provincial culture
Moscow 1980	1 year (*) 5 weeks	National: mass participation, high art and folk culture; national art of the peoples of the USSR
Los Angeles 1984	10 weeks	7 weeks: international festival for domestic consumption 3 weeks: LA and US culture for international Olympic audience
Seoul 1988	7 weeks	Korean high culture and traditional culture for an international audience; international artists and companies; contemporary culture for a domestic audience

Source: Adapted from compilation by Gold and Revill (2007, p. 74) and from official reports of Organising Committees

(*) Length of cultural festival including exhibition runs and pre-Games programme

Table 36.1 is a summary of the key format variations and characteristics of Olympic cultural festivals in this period. As Table 36.1 makes abundantly clear, each Olympic host approached their cultural programming with different priorities and the length of activities varied significantly, from four weeks in Helsinki and Melbourne, to one year in Mexico 1968.

Cultural Olympiads: Barcelona 1992 to London 2012

Another stage in Olympic cultural programming was initiated with the Barcelona 1992 Olympic bid, which proposed that the implementation of a Cultural Olympiad should take place during the four years of the Olympiad – from the end of one Games edition to the start of the next. Barcelona's Cultural Olympiad thus started in 1988, at the end of the Seoul Games, and evolved up to 1992 with a different thematic emphasis for each year. García (2000) notes how this decision stems out of the organisers' vision for the Games as a platform to improve the city's urban landscape and assist in Barcelona's international projection far beyond the Olympic staging period. Indeed, Barcelona 1992 has come to be remembered as the first Games that placed the city at the heart of the Olympic experience.

The four-year format was maintained in subsequent Summer Games editions up to 2012. This was on the initiative of respective host cities rather than an IOC directive, as there has never been a formal requirement to create a four-year cultural programme. This stage in Olympic cultural programme development has also been characterised by two additional phenomena, resulting in large part from the commitment to multi-annual cultural programming. On the one hand, there has been a clearer alignment with local and national cultural policy ambitions than ever before; on the other, the programme has faced growing operational tensions.

The first phenomenon means that priority objectives for the Games have become more clearly aligned with broader cultural, social and economic agendas in the host city. From a cultural point of view, the Games period has been used not only to expand sport audiences but also cultural and arts audiences; furthermore the Games have been used not only to grow sporting facilities, but to advance broader local creative development aspirations (García, 2012). From a social perspective, it is now common for the Games to aspire to improving community inclusion, expanding access to marginal or deprived communities, and strengthening local or national identity (García, 2004). Finally, from an economic perspective, it is now common to present a Cultural Olympiad as a catalyst to advance urban regeneration, reposition the host city and grow cultural tourism (García, 2004). In parallel, new tensions have also emerged, mainly due to the high professionalisation and global mediatisation of the Games (García, 2012). Most notably, the branding tension between 'official' Olympic arts events, sporting competitions and related Games activity has become increasingly apparent and has led on to varied attempts at establishing separate Cultural Olympiad or Olympic Arts Festival brands (García, 2001, 2012).

Rio 2016 was the first Summer Olympic Games edition not to organise a four year Cultural Olympiad since Barcelona in 1988, and this has also been the case in Tokyo 2020. This opens what could become a new stage in Olympic cultural programming, as the focus becomes less about the overall duration and more about the ways in which the cultural programme can shape or project the host city and be part of the 'Olympic experience'. The implications of such change are briefly discussed in the concluding section of this chapter.

Art and culture at the Paralympic Games: Sydney 2000 onwards

Within the Paralympic Games, cultural programming has remained a low priority until the turn of the century. Sydney 2000 was the first Games edition to work towards a high-profile Paralympic Cultural Olympiad and proposed a single team to manage both the official Olympic and Paralympic cultural programme. Further, in the wake of Sydney 2000, a series of agreements between the IOC and the International Paralympic Committee (IPC) resulted in closer synergies between the two Games, including the decision to establish a single organising committee.

In the context of London 2012, the team responsible for the cultural programme committed to expanding organisational synergies into an all-encompassing Games cultural policy narrative, where there was no distinction between Olympic and Paralympic cultural activity. Indeed, the London 2012 Cultural Olympiad incorporated a celebration of long-established UK disability arts organisations as part of its four year national programme and a range of regional cultural programmes placed an emphasis on presenting activity that questioned the notion of 'normality' as a way of bridging the gap between perceptions of 'abled' or 'disabled' bodies, be it in the realm of sports or arts. Further, the Games-time 'London 2012 Festival' spanned over both Olympic and Paralympic fortnights without interruption, thus acting as a symbolic bridge between both events. To maximise visibility, London also created a distinct label and brand for its disability arts programme: 'Unlimited' (see: García and Cox, 2013).

In Rio 2016, there was no capacity to host a four year Cultural Olympiad (see García, 2016) and the Paralympic Games did not incorporate an official art and culture component beyond a collaboration, initiated in 2012 as part of 'Unlimited', between Brazilian and British disabled artists, under the auspices of the British Council. Tokyo 2020 has committed to continuing on the tradition of a joint Olympic and Paralympic cultural programme, although details of programming are yet to be broadly shared with an international audience.

The sharing of a common team and a single programme of activity places the Cultural Olympiad in a significant position to promote greater synergies between Olympic and Paralympic Games in the years to come. This is because all other Games programmes, from the sport competitions to symbolic events such as the torch relay or the ceremonies, follow a different planning and delivery cycle. This could help assert the added value brought by a flexible approach to Games cultural programming.

Main trends, challenges and opportunities for culture at the Games

The dynamic nature of the Cultural Olympiad is manifest in the diversity of formats, objectives and management structures put in place to implement it since it was formally launched over 100 years ago. While the sports competitions and infrastructural dimensions of the Olympic and Paralympic sports programme have become extensively rationalised and standardised, the cultural programme has remained an area open to free interpretation up to this day. This section offers a brief summary of key programming trends over time.

Thematic focus: from sporting heritage to contemporary fusions

The Games' cultural programme has explored a wide range of art forms and thematic emphasis. It started with an exclusive focus on *classic art forms* (fine arts) under a mainly Western (European) canon. Interestingly, during the time it operated as an art competition, rather than just focus on the showcase of old masters and well-known works of art, it effectively encouraged the *production of 'new' artworks* that can be considered a major contribution to the development of Olympic cultural heritage. This is because the art on show had to be inspired by Olympic Games ideals as well as sporting achievement. The founding focus of the Olympic cultural programme thus resulted in the production of a series of distinct artworks, many of which form the permanent art collection at the Olympic Museum in Lausanne.

The move away from competitions into art exhibitions and festivals led to abandoning the production of new 'Olympic' artworks and prioritising instead the showcase of the host's best-known national artists and cultural expressions. The focus continued to be on classic artforms but the remit broadened into national folklore displays. A majority of hosts during this time opted to showcase their national artistic heritage almost exclusively.

By the 1960s, 1970s and 1980s, however, a majority of hosts placed a new *emphasis on contemporary art* and many promoted international art showcases. The most outstanding examples within this period were Mexico 1968, Munich 1972 and Los Angeles 1984, all of which involved world-class artists and invested in new contemporary art commissions to be presented during Games time. Munich and Los Angeles went a step further in their attempts at linking contemporary art trends with the Olympic narrative by introducing the notion of an 'Olympic art poster' series. While the production of Olympic posters was a tradition that had started with the first Modern Games in 1896, renowned artists had never been involved in their production. The point of distinction in Munich, Los Angeles and, subsequently, Sarajevo 1984 and Barcelona 1992, was that world-leading artists of the time were commissioned to produce a visual statement representing Olympic achievement without the need to produce a literal representation of sport.

From 2000 onwards, in line with global cultural policy trends, many Western country hosts expanded into what is commonly termed as *cultural fusion and innovation* as part of their Cultural Olympiad programming. This involved pioneering cross-sector collaborations between the arts, health and technology fields. Vancouver 2010 and London 2012 are two key exemplars in this area. The 'cultural fusion' narrative is, however, mainly a Western construct that contrasts with the approach by most Eastern Games hosts. The latter have continued to prioritise the showcase of traditional arts and their most valued cultural heritage over cross-sectoral collaborations (e.g. Beijing 2008, Sochi 2014), but this is expected to change with Tokyo 2020, which is a Games edition that highlights youth and technology as a top priority within its cultural narrative.

Despite the broadening of topics and format interests, the one area that has remained secondary since the demise of the art competitions has been the exploration of *links between art and sport*. While at every Games edition there are art communities that, on learning about the existence of an Olympic cultural programme, argue in favour of exploring such connection, examples of truly innovative and meaningful collaborations in this domain remain scarce, and most attempts at an art and sport fusion have been unsuccessful from an audience or media-attention point of view. The only exception to this have been the few examples of Olympic art poster series, a tradition recovered by London 2012 after the previous four editions in Munich, Los Angeles, Sarajevo and Barcelona. This tradition is now being led by the newly created IOC dedicated culture team and it is expected that it will feature prominently in all future editions of the Games.

Vision and priority objectives

An analysis of cultural programming choices and priority objectives by Olympic organising committees since Sydney 2000[1] suggests that the vision behind most Cultural Olympiad editions falls within one or several of these four broadly defined typologies:

1 Politics and identity;
2 Economic regeneration;
3 Entertainment, 'look and feel';
4 Cultural and social change.

Next follows a brief commentary over the ways in which these four typologies have materialised.

1 Politics and identity: growing or reigniting national pride

This typology includes Cultural Olympiad programmes that prioritise a local or national target audience and focus on direct live participation opportunities rather than media coverage. The two most dominant approaches are a focus on folklore and popular traditions, or a focus on celebrating classic national cultural icons:

- *Folklore and/or popular traditions:* Cultural Olympiads with this kind of focus tend to be embraced by host communities and perceived as meaningful at grassroots levels; however, such programming is often of little appeal to visitors and the international media. Recent examples include nationwide choral singing and folklore dances presented in the lead to Beijing 2008 and Sochi 2010. In both cases, these showcases were celebrated as an 'unprecedented' attempt at a nationwide cultural programme open to exploring the diversity of Chinese and Russian cultures respectively.

- *Celebration of classic national icons:* This approach can be a source of pride for local communities but, if not carefully curated taking into account community sensitivities, it can be perceived as tokenistic or seen to target international audiences over host citizens. Recent examples include Athens 2004 with its extensive programming of classic Greek theatre in iconic ancient venues, London 2012's programming of an International Shakespeare Festival and Sochi 2014's 'world-class' Russian ballet galas.

2 Economic regeneration: city reimaging and tourism projection

Securing an economic return has become a common priority for Olympic cultural programming since the 1990s, particularly for cities that view the Games as a platform to join the league of so-called 'world cities' or globally successful cities. The main approaches are:

- *Focus on classic and internationally renowned cultural icons:* This tends to be popular with international audiences but it may be viewed as tokenistic or lacking in innovation by local communities if it is not appropriately complemented by traditional or modern cultural expressions. Beyond the examples presented in the previous section, it is worth noting a line of programming in London 2012 which was dedicated to celebrating and pushing forward the tourist appeal of well-known British heritage sites such as Stonehenge, Hadrian Wall, the Tower of London, etc. (see García and Cox, 2013).
- *Projection of modern cultural icons and emerging creative industries:* This is aimed at both local and international audiences and tends to prioritise a 'connoisseur' audience rather than the general public. Cultural programmes with this kind of focus appeal to high-spending cultural tourists and can be very effective in the positioning of host cities as world-class cultural and creative centres. Recent examples include the final Olympic Arts Festival in Sydney 2000, which presented all of its performing arts programme at the iconic Sydney Opera House (García, 2012); as well as the London 2012 Festival, which presented itself as a distinct component of the London Cultural Olympiad, dedicated to celebrating the most excellent and advanced cultural expressions in the UK (García and Cox, 2013).

3 Entertainment, 'look and feel': crowd management, city animation and city dressing

This typology tends to be the least ambitious from a cultural policy and long-term urban strategy point of view but is useful as part of the Games hosting process as it helps address short-term needs regarding crowd control and city dressing to create a festive atmosphere outside the sporting venues. The two main programming formats could be labelled as:

- *Entertainment:* I.e. a focus on open-air activity to entertain and divert the crowds. This was championed by Sydney 2000, which launched the now firmly established tradition of 'Live Sites' as hubs for free activity and entertainment during Games time;
- *Look and feel:* I.e. a focus on visual and graphic design interventions to dress the city as well as sporting venues in a recognisable, unifying look.

In the 1960s and 1970s, there were some excellent examples of Cultural Olympiad integration within what we now understand as the 'look and feel' of the Games. As suggested earlier, Mexico 1968 and Munich 1972 developed cultural iconography components that were, simultaneously: (1) innovative from an aesthetic point of view; (2) unique to the local host; and (3) useful as a Games dressing tool and entertainment aid. However, in the 1980s, 1990s and 2000s, the approach to city and Games venue dressing has shown a lowering of cultural ambition in favour of easily replicable (thus increasingly standardised) formats. This is a trend that may change in the wake of London 2012, where graphic design was once more aligned with place-specific cultural narratives, in particular, the interest in projecting the UK as a world-leading and youth-oriented creative industries centre (see García, 2015; García and Cox, 2013).

4 Cultural and social change: creative innovation and community empowerment

This is the most ambitious of all Cultural Olympiad typologies and the one with greater potential to deliver sustainable and meaningful legacies. It is, however, also the hardest to achieve, as it requires long-term planning to enable adequate linkages between widely diverse stakeholders. If associated with Olympic values and understood as a Games-related opportunity and outcome, it can provide a key platform to add credibility to the Games experience amongst often hard-to-reach communities of interest. The main approaches are as follows:

- *A catalyst for cultural advancements:* This occurs when the Cultural Olympiad acts primarily as a catalyst for artistic and creative innovation, pushing forward a cultural agenda that may have stagnated before the Games were awarded. This has commonly involved dedicated investment on public art during Games time (e.g. Barcelona 1992 'Art in the Street', Sydney 2000 'Sculpture by the Sea', Torino 2006 'Luce di Artista'); the use of unusual spaces to present arts activities for the first time (e.g. London 2012 artistic interventions in remote iconic sites such as Stonehenge); working with new technologies or promoting emerging habits (e.g. Vancouver 2010 'Cultural Olympiad Digital Edition', London 2012 'Pop-up' events, reliant on social media).
- *Social transformation:* This occurs when the programme is used to advance specific or multiple social agendas in line with Olympic and Paralympic Games values such as: empowering youth (e.g. Beijing and Sochi: country-wide youth singing programmes; London2012: youth-oriented programme presenting the work of over 6,000 young or emerging artists), expanding opportunities to engage with or show the work of disabled artists (e.g. Sydney 2000: *Invincible Summer*; London 2012: *Unlimited*), working with marginal communities (Sydney 2000: *Festival of the Dreaming*, led by contemporary Aboriginal artists; London 2012: collaborations with homeless communities and the unemployed).

Delivery formats

Despite the ongoing development of cultural programme objectives and thematic priorities, the underlying challenges in terms of visibility and linkage between artistic programming and other Games activity have remained practically the same throughout one century. As argued by Masterton (1973), García (2012) and Miah and García (2012), these problems have been accentuated by the absence of an international cultural organisation comparable to the international sports federations in its ability to coordinate and support Olympic arts initiatives. Subsequent attempts to address this gap (such as the proposal to establish a permanent Cultural Olympiad foundation in Greece) have lacked sufficient international backing to become viable models. Instead, as is the case with other cultural event networks, transfer of knowledge regarding operational issues has relied on personal connections and informal word-of-mouth rather than being a thoroughly documented and transparent process. As a result, to date, there is no standard model of delivery for the Cultural Olympiad.

As noted previously, up to 1992, the duration of a Cultural Olympiad would vary considerably. Other key variations that affect consistency and easy identification of the programme are its geographical spread and the approach to branding and communications. This is briefly discussed next.

Geographical spread

While most Olympic Games editions have concentrated their cultural programmes in the host city (mainly within central areas or within the Olympic Park and related Olympic venues), with the growth in duration of cultural programming, a parallel ambition has been to involve communities beyond the host city to ensure that the Games are owned at a regional and national level – and, sometimes, internationally. This has brought an additional challenge, as the more disperse the activity, the more difficult it is to ensure that the programme is widely visible and recognised – particularly from the perspective of media coverage (García, 2001).

The first nation-wide cultural programme took place in Mexico 1968, with various attempts at following this trend taking place in the lead to Sydney 2000, Athens 2004, London 2012 and now Tokyo 2020. London established an Olympic first by supporting the creation of 13 regional 'Creative Programmer' posts that coordinated and encouraged Olympic cultural activity in their respective regions, without depending directly on the Olympic Organising Committee for the Olympic Games. This facilitated opportunities for legacy but also made it harder to establish a clear identity and brand. Table 36.2 is a summary table indicating specific focus of cultural programming locations:

Table 36.2 Geographical locations for the Cultural Olympiad

City centre – famous cultural venues:	The most common approach since 1912 and the most popular location of Cultural Olympiad events to this day
City centre – public spaces/ street:	This has grown since the 1960s and is an important area of development as a complement to the so-called Live Sites so that the street entertainment on offer showcases host cultures and/or explores innovative creative practices
Olympic venues/ Olympic Park:	There are few good examples in this area. The scarce presence of cultural programming in Games venues has limited its impact and relevance for Olympic fans. Munich 1972, Montreal 1976 and PyeongChang 2018 presented ambitious artistic programming within the Park, but most editions offer generic entertainment instead, not related to the aspirations of their Cultural Olympiad. London 2012 was the first Games to present a contemporary public art programme within its Olympic Park embodying its vision for innovative, unusual, sustainable and locally representative art.
Host regions/ nationwide/ internationally:	There has been a growing interest in nationwide programming since Barcelona 1992. The most accomplished example to date is London 2012.

Source: Author's elaboration, building on Cultural Olympiad archives (official reports)

Promotional frameworks

To date, the Cultural Olympiad has not been formally included as a clearly distinguished promotional asset within Olympic marketing guidelines. As a result, there have been noticeable variations in the way each edition of the Games refers to this programme. This includes variations in its written denomination (e.g. Cultural Olympiad, Olympic Arts Festival, Olympic Cultural Programme, to name just a few) and marked variations in its visual identity which, at times, presents no resemblance or apparent association with the visual identity of respective Olympic Games editions.

In many cases, the cultural programme has been represented by a visual icon that echoes the main Olympic Games iconography. However, in some instances, the approach has been to create a different brand altogether. This was the case in Barcelona 1992 and Athens 2004. In the latter cases, authors have argued that there were important communication gaps and a lack of promotional synergy with mainstream Olympic activity (García, 2000; Panagiatopoulou, 2016).

Be it as a derivate icon or a distinct brand, the most common challenge for establishing a clear branding association between the cultural programme and the rest of the Games are the commercial restrictions imposed on the use of the Olympic rings. The Olympic rings are the most well-known symbol of the Games and one of the most recognisable brands worldwide. However, Cultural Olympiad activity has rarely been granted access to this asset due to the fact that global Olympic sponsors do not tend to play a part as funders of cultural programming nor agree to be official presenters of artworks during Games time. Instead, most Cultural Olympiad activities are funded by alternative sources which, at times, include competing commercial sponsors.

The London 2012 culture team engaged on extensive Games branding discussions from the moment they were awarded the event. Their objective was to establish a Cultural Olympiad brand that did not conflict with Olympic sponsor interests but allowed cultural contributors to search alternative sources of funding or acknowledge their own long-term sponsors. This resulted in the establishment of an 'Inspired by 2012' mark, a visual icon that was clearly associated with the London 2012 Games but did not include the Olympic rings. This approach was deemed as successful by many British cultural partners and also benefited other types of Games-related programming, such as educational, volunteering and business-oriented initiatives (see García, 2013, 2015; García and Cox, 2013).

It is as yet unclear whether the 'Inspired by' initiative can be replicated in other Games contexts and become an avenue for branding cultural activities without conflicting with Olympic sponsor interests. At the heart of this branding debate lays the question of *who* the Cultural Olympiad is for and what counts as cultural value at the Olympic Games. This is because, for as long as Cultural Olympiad programming is not promoted in association with the Olympic rings, it is unlikely it will be perceived as a core Olympic component and will continue to be excluded from international Games-oriented media coverage. Instead, the trend is to position the Cultural Olympiad as a programme aimed at local and/or national communities competitions and an opportunity for direct engagement and participation, particularly for those not able to access sport competition tickets. This divorces the Cultural Olympiad from other aspects of the Games capable of generating global media spectacle, such as the opening and closing ceremonies. It also divorces the Cultural Olympiad from the original aspiration by Coubertin, which was to ensure it played a central role in the appreciation of the sport competitions.

The future

Since 2014, the IOC has embarked on a comprehensive visioning exercise framed as Agenda 2020 (see IOC, 2014). A commitment within this exercise is to rethink the role of culture in the Olympic Games hosting process and overcome the programme's traditional marginalisation. This is in line with the expanding debate over the need for 'legacy', sustainability and a '360 degree' Olympic management experience (IOC, 2009, p. 27), a term that refers to the IOCs ambition to better integrate all Games programming dimensions and ensure that the sporting competitions are rooted within each of the Olympic cities where they take place.

These aspirations may have important implications for the future of the Cultural Olympiad. First, this approach has impacted on the Candidate City bidding guidelines, discouraging the traditional relegation of 'cultural programming' to a separate chapter in the bid proposal, to make it, instead, a core dimension of the Olympic city and spectators experience that is presented within the introductory sections to the bid. While the effects of such change are still to be seen, this suggests a push for organisers to think more creatively about ways to embed their cultural proposals within the Olympic Games hosting process rather than treat them as a separate programme of activity.

Further, in 2014, the IOC established the Olympic Foundation for Culture and Heritage with staff working on a dedicated cultural strategy and policy framework to guide in the delivery of programming that contributes to the development of a distinct Olympic narrative. This team is looking into options to ensure that Games branding and media relations guidelines are better attuned to the needs of the cultural programme.

Beyond the possibility for clearer and more strategic regulations from an IOC perspective, host cities have also become more effective and strategic in their profiling of culture around the Games hosting process. Be it as a political, economic, social or broader cultural objective, local organisers have become well aware of the importance of contextualising the Games as a global mega-event within a distinct and meaningful cultural programme in order to secure a sustainable legacy. This suggests that the role and relevance of future Cultural Olympiads will keep growing, and the demand for greater clarity and effectiveness in their delivery framework will also expand. Olympic cities may come to prominence through the opportunity to host 16 days of international elite sport competitions, but they tend to be best remembered (and differentiated, from one to the next) by their ability to showcase unique skylines, public spaces and approaches to celebration that are sensitive to their specific heritage and diverse community values, as well as engaged with emerging and globally relevant creative practices.

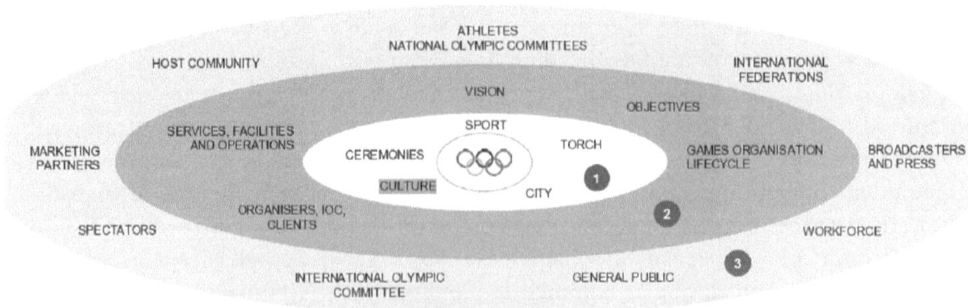

Figure 36.1 Visual representation of 'Olympic experience' components

Source: Adapted from IOC (2008); Author's emphasis

Note

1 Analysis conducted by the author over documentation stored at the Olympic Museum – Olympic Studies Centre relating to every Olympic official cultural programme between Helsinki 1952 and Atlanta 1996, plus Cultural Olympiad materials and observations collated during fieldwork visits to Olympic Summer and Winter host cities from Sydney 2000 to Sochi 2014.

References

García, B. (2000). Comparative analysis of the Olympic cultural program, design and management of Barcelona'92 and Sydney'2000. In: K. Wamsley, S. Martyn, G. MacDonald and R.K. Barney, eds., *5th International symposium for Olympic research*. London: University of Western Ontario, pp. 153–158.

García, B. (2001). Enhancing sports marketing through cultural and arts programmes. Lessons from the Sydney 2000 Olympic Arts Festivals. *Sports Management Review*, 4(2), pp. 193–220.

García, B. (2004). Urban regeneration, arts programming and major events: Glasgow 1990, Sydney 2000 and Barcelona 2004. *International Journal of Cultural Policy*, 10(1), pp. 103–118.

García, B. (2008). One hundred years of cultural programming within the Olympic Games (1912–2012). *International Journal of Cultural Policy*, 14(4), pp. 361–376.

García, B. (2012). *The Olympics games and cultural policy*. Routledge.

García, B. (2013). The London 2012 cultural Olympiad and torch relay. In: V. Girginov, ed., *Handbook of the London 2012 Olympic and Paralympic games. Vol 1: Making the games*. Routledge. pp. 199–214.

García, B. (2015). Placing culture at the heart of the Games. Achievements and challenges within the London 2012 cultural Olympiad. In: G. Poynter, V. Viehoff and Y. Li, eds., *The London Olympics and urban development: The* mega-event ci*ty*. Routledge., pp. 255–270.

García, B. (2016). Why arts need to retake the Olympic stage. *The Conversation* [online].

García, B. and Cox, T. (2013). *London 2012 cultural Olympiad evaluation*. London: Arts Council England.

Gold, M. and Revill, G. (2007). The cultural Olympiads. Reviving the Panegyris. In: J. Gold and M. Gold, eds., *Olympic cities. City agendas, planning and the world's games*. Routledge, pp. 1896–2012.

IOC. (1997). *Memorias Olimpicas, por Pierre de Coubertin*. Lausanne: IOC.

IOC. (2008). *2016 candidature procedure and questionnaire: Games of the XXXI Olympiad*. Lausanne: IOC.

IOC. (2009). *The Olympic movement in society. IOC final report 2005–2008*. Lausanne: IOC.

IOC. (2014). *Olympic Agenda 2020. 20 + 20 recommendations*. Lausanne: IOC.

IOC. (2018). *The Olympic charter*. Lausanne: IOC.

Masterton, D.W. (1973). The contribution of the fine arts to the Olympic Games. In: *Proceedings of the international Olympic academy*. Athens: IOA, pp. 200–213.

Mexico Organising Committee for the Olympic Games. (1969). *The cultural Olympiad. Official Report of the XIX Olympiad*, Vol 4. Mexico: MOCOG.

Miah, A. and García, B. (2012). *The Olympics. The basics*. London: Routledge.

Panagiatopoulou, R. (2016). The cultural Olympiad of the Athens 2004 Olympic Games. In: N. Müller, M. Messing and K. Schormann, eds., *Cultural views of the Olympics*. Kassel: Agon Sportverlag, pp. 133–158.

Stanton, R. (2000). *The forgotten Olympic art competitions. The story of the Olympic art competitions of the 20th century*. Victoria: Trafford.

37

Olympic and Paralympic Games education programmes

Education as engagement from a practitioner's view

Nick Fuller and Heather Barr

Introduction

For many (Chatziefstathiou, 2011; Müller, 2000; Kidd, 1996; Parry, 1998), the advent of the modern Olympic Games cannot be separated from the principles and practice of education. Frustrated by an education system he felt to be failing the young men of France, founder of the modern Olympic movement Pierre De Coubertin looked overseas for inspiration. One place he found it was in the English public school system. De Coubertin was particularly impressed by the central role of competitive sport in the education provided by England's all-male private boarding schools. As recognised by Dikaia Chatziefstathiou, De Coubertin saw this sporting activity not merely as an opportunity to develop boys' physical skills, but as a vital educational tool for building moral and social strength (Chatziefstathiou, 2012). It was on this basis that De Coubertin developed the concept of Olympism.

Today, there is a significant and growing body of academic work which addresses and explores Olympic Education (see, for example, Chatziefstathiou, 2012; Cuplan and Wigmore, 2010; Naul, 2008; Binder, 2005). Notably, there is a much less substantial body of work addressing Paralympic Education. This is despite what I would argue to be a much closer, more crucial link between the Paralympic Games and the principles of social change, personal development, and equality which are central to a twenty-first century understanding of Olympic and Paralympic Education. For the purpose of this chapter, however, we will leave this argument mostly to one side. Instead, we will be exploring what Olympic and Paralympic Education means and looks like today, and how it may begin to look in the future.

Olympic Education is typically understood as:

1 The scholastic study of Olympism;
2 The role of Olympism in formal and informal education and learning;
3 The education programmes developed and delivered by host nations/cities.

In this chapter, we will not be addressing the first of these. As the former Head of Education for the London 2012 Organising Committee (LOCOG), my expertise is as a practitioner. We will therefore focus primarily on the work done by Games' education programmes, and, to a lesser extent, that done by (in)formal learning built on and influenced by the principles of Olympism.

With regards to the latter, Chatziefstathiou has uncovered two key strands of thinking around what this includes; namely, 'Olympism in school physical education' and 'Olympism beyond school' (Chatziefstathiou, 2012). I maintain that, with regards to the former, there are three ways to view Olympic Education:

1 As a critical means by which to engage audiences in host nations and cities;
2 As a means by which to change hearts and minds, and to deliver on a social mission inspired by the Games, though not necessarily *of* the Games; and
3 As a critical pillar of legacy, which is increasingly framed in terms of societal benefits which go above and beyond that of tangible infrastructure projects.

The education programmes and initiatives of the last twenty years all broke new ground in some way: the sheer scale of Beijing 2008; the interesting vocational and Further Education focus of Vancouver 2010, the determined outreach into the least advantaged communities of Rio 2016. For me, two editions stand out in particular as having created the modern Olympic sense of education as an exercise in active engagement: Sydney 2000 and London 2012. Every decision made by every Local Organising Committee (LOC) is subject to the particular social, cultural, political, and economic environments in which these decisions are made. Drawing comparisons is therefore complicated, and declaring 'best practice' or 'most successful' is arguably a doomed endeavour.

And yet, it is important to highlight where Organising Committees have brought fresh thinking to the concept of Olympic Education. Later in this chapter, I will go on to explore how Tokyo 2020 may well be the next to achieve a paradigm shift in the delivery and impact of Paralympic Education. However, for the most part, we will use London 2012 as an example of a Games which placed Olympic and Paralympic Education at the very heart of its organisation. During my time at LOCOG, we were determined to deliver a Games which not only celebrated sporting achievement, but which, in the philosophy of De Coubertin, and in the words of LOCOG Chair Lord Coe, could support young people and 'inspire a generation'.

Sydney 2000: education for engagement

We turn first to the Sydney 2000 Olympic and Paralympic Games. Sydney delivered a comprehensive education programme which truly engaged the host communities. Initiated as part of Sydney's bid in 1992, the 2000 Schools Strategy was largely managed and funded by the New South Wales Department of Education School Sport Unit, primarily for schools in that region. The success of this programme led the Sydney Organising Committee (SOCOG) to establish their own Olympic and Paralympic programmes in 1997. The wide-ranging programmes were supported by programmes in which athletes and mascots were linked to schools, and through which subsidised tickets for the Paralympic Games were available to Australian schools. Susan Crawford, SOCOG National Education Programme Manager from 1997–2001, has highlighted how innovative and cutting edge the Schools Strategy's *Aspire* offer was for its time. *Aspire* was a multi-media schools resource comprising video, posters, a teacher's guidebook and a cutting-edge interactive CD-ROM, with avatars, and produced in conjunction with OBM. Crawford has also drawn attention to the leading edge nature of the Strategy's other programmes, which included:

1 *O-News* – an Olympic student newspaper;
2 *Kids* – an early interactive internet site;
3 *Share the Spirit* – an art programme, part of a range of enhancement programmes across the curriculum.

Helen Brownlee, the New South Wales (NSW) Sport Unit Manager at the time, sees these school programmes as a key strand of SOCOG's strategy "to garner widespread community support". Thus, an early forerunner of London 2012's engagement strategy can be seen in Sydney's approach to education. A direct line can be drawn back from several elements of the London 2012 Get Set programme to the Sydney education offer: a blend of innovative technology and face-to-face interaction; a clear sense of education as a wider engagement tool; an identification of schoolchildren as a sports audience; and an early recognition of the importance of Paralympic education.

Moreover, Sydney followed through with codified legacy programming, particularly in the Olympic arena. The Pierre de Coubertin Awards, Olympic Awareness Week, and a range of Olympic Resources and offers continued to be offered by the Australian Olympic Committee, who invested in an Education Manager to deliver such programmes. By 2018, for example, some 17,600 senior secondary school students had received the Pierre de Coubertin Award, awarded to those who seek to enhance their personal potential through sport.

It is more difficult, however, to assess Sydney's success in legacy and engagement for the Paralympic Games. Sydney 2000 was significant in being the final Paralympic Games to be bid for independently of the Olympic Games. It was, in turn, one of the first editions of the Games to unite the organisation of the Olympics and Paralympics, and, as the International Paralympic Committee (IPC) highlights, the 2000 Paralympics benefited from a number of shared resources with the Olympics. It is certainly true that the Games were successful to a record-breaking level: 1.2 million tickets were sold, and media coverage and spectator numbers were unprecedented and previously unseen. As Simon Darcy notes, it is exactly these metrics – "ticket sales, media coverage, public awareness and spectator engagement" (Darcy, 2016: 53) – which make up "the IPC hope for legacy from Paralympic games". Arguably, then, Sydney 2000 offers a blueprint for successful Paralympic legacy, one built on effective community and school engagement. Darcy, for instance, draws attention to 'the very successful *Reaching the Community* Programme which worked to educate school children about disability and Paralympic sport, encouraging them to engage with and attend the Paralympic Games. The Programme reached around 320,000 children (Horin, 2000; quoted in Darcy, 2016) and has had 360,000 tickets attributed to it (University of East London, 2007). But did it improve attitudes towards the Paralympics and disability? Almost all evidence of this is merely anecdotal: no benchmarking took place to understand the public or young people's perceptions pre-engagement or pre-Games. It is therefore very hard to quantify, finally, Sydney's success in Paralympic Education.

To return to the Olympics, however, it is interesting to note the emphasis of the results quoted when looking at contemporary early research into Sydney's education and engagement programmes. The programmes were *first* seen to heighten awareness and appreciation of the Olympic movement, *then* to foster a sense of national pride, and *then* to inspire a sense of fulfilling one's potential. From this evolving focus emerge three roles of Olympic Education. These map clearly onto the three ways I earlier proposed to view the education programmes of host nations, which in turn, as we will see, are the foundations on which that of London 2012 was built. Sydney's legacy, then, forms a blueprint for how an Organising Committee can use education programmes. It was by building on this and other examples that Get Set was created.

London 2012: mission and vision

Before entering into a discussion of the Get Set programme itself, it is important to pause and address the central role and significance of young people in London's bid to host the 2012 Games. As highlighted in the *London 2012 Olympic Games Official Report*, using "the Games as a catalyst for meaningful social and community change" was central to London's vision for the Games (LOCOG, 2012a: 5). The very start, "this vision provided the foundations" for the London bid (LOCOG, 2012a: 5). An important aspect of enacting this "social and community change" in a sustainable, long-term way was through the promise made in the bid to engage and motivate young people. This "commitment to inspire young people" (LOCOG, 2012b: 5) formed a 'key element' of this vision and London's bid. Get Set, as recognised in the Nielsen's evaluation of the programme was "one of the key ways in which London 2012 delivered on this promise" (LOCOG, 2012b: 5).

In drawing attention to this, I look to highlight how Get Set was absolutely *vision critical* to the delivery of the London 2012 Olympic and Paralympic Games. Of course, LOCOG were bound by requirements set out in the *Host City Contract of Services for the XXX Olympiad 2012* (IOC, 2005). LOCOG committed to "promote the fundamental principles and values of Olympism" through all "social, educational, aesthetic, and moral aspects" (IOC, 2005: 11) of the Games. However, the way in which a Local Organising Committee does so is, ultimately, entirely their prerogative. A strategic programme with the breadth, scale, and legacy of Get Set goes above and beyond the requirements set out in the International Olympic Committee (IOC)'s *Contract*. In fact, in the *Contract* itself, the word 'education' appears only twice; once as previously cited, and once in reference to anti-doping policies (another rich and interesting point of discussion which we will sadly leave aside for this chapter). The decision to place a 'commitment to inspire young people' at the very centre of the London 2012 Olympic and Paralympic Games, and then to keep this promise very directly and specifically through the Get Set programme, went way beyond what the IOC laid out as the host city's responsibility with regards to Olympic and Paralympic Education. As Veal, Toohey, and Frawley (2012: 163) note, the extent to which "the theme of inspiring the youth of the world" was genuinely "influential in the IOC's decision to award the 2012 Games to London" is contestable. However, it is clear that this determination to inspire and engage young people sat at the very heart of the organisation and delivery of London 2012. Olympic and Paralympic Education was inextricable from and vital to this inspiration.

Get Set, official education programme of the London 2012 Olympic and Paralympic Games

Get Set was launched in 2008 and continues as an integrated Olympic and Paralympic Education programme to this day, under the management of the British Olympic Foundation (BOF) and British Paralympic Association (BPA). Get Set is delivered via an online platform and provides flexible, cross-curricular learning resources for young people aged 3–19. The programme is made up of a combination of: always-on educational resources (resources which are consistently available throughout the life of the programme and which represent the core Values); longer-term campaigns and activities, and exclusive, shorter-term campaigns or one-off offers. Underpinning every activity and resource is the teaching of the Olympic Values (friendship, respect, excellence) and Paralympic Values (determination, inspiration, courage, and equality). Get Set sought, and continues to seek, to encourage 'young people to explore what the Values meant to them, and to live the Values in everyday life – at school, at home and in the community' (LOCOG, 2012b). In the run up to the 2012 Games, Get Set delivered new learning content to coincide with every key milestone – such as the Paralympic Handover, the Vancouver Olympic Winter Games, and the Olympic Torch Relay – in order to maintain momentum and ensure that schools felt connected to and part of the London 2012 journey.

But to what extent can we call Get Set a successful Olympic and Paralympic Education programme? I am, clearly, not a disinterested observer of the Get Set phenomenon, but I would maintain that the huge range of campaigns and resources on offer via Get Set, all of which are built on a foundation of the Values, is evidence of what Chatziefstathiou describes as the essence of an Olympic and Paralympic Education programme: "a flexible tool to be used by educators in conjunction with the mega event of the Olympic and Paralympic Games" (Chatziefstathiou, 2011: 185).

Between 2008 and 2012, 85% of all UK schools and colleges registered with Get Set, and the programme also has achieved an all-time reach of 70,392 teacher registrations across 27,586 schools. Within the context of the UK's political and educational landscape, it is a true testament to the success of Get Set – and the value that educators feel it brings to their students – that a voluntary, non-curriculum-essential education programme reached and engaged so many young people in schools and colleges across the UK. It is notable that Get Set achieved national coverage and was not simply used by schools and colleges within the host city. Chen and Henry's (2019) recent study of schools' engagement with Get Set highlights the high levels of engagement with the programme beyond the host city's schools. In addition, a considerable part of its legacy success flows from the national rather than city-wide engagement the programme achieved. It is perhaps even more impressive that, seven years after the London 2012 Games, Get Set remains a relevant and valuable programme, reaching hundreds of thousands of young people every year. The most recent data reveals that three-quarters of teachers registered to Get Set use the website at least once a term and that 80% "would recommend [Get Set] to a colleague" (EdComs, 2019: 7).

Get Set in legacy

The IOC maintains that legacy "is fundamental in the understanding of the mission of Olympism in society" (IOC, 2002; quoted in Girginov, 2012: 1). For Vassil Girginov, "the London 2012 Olympic and Paralympic Games played a key role in further shaping the legacy thinking and set up new standards" (Girginov, 2012: 2), positioning LOCOG's commitment to societal change through the education and inspiration of young people, as "the first full blueprint for Olympic Legacy". Crucially, Girginov (2012: 2) recognises that "Olympic legacies are not given . . . hosting an Olympic Games does not automatically bring social or economic legacy to the host city and country, rather these have to be strategically planned and leveraged". In this way, London 2012 was remarkable, not just in education, but in the assiduous and systemic way it planned for longevity. The huge power of a national network of schools, coupled with the strategic planning and consistent and regular activation of the Get Set programme over many years has, as research continues to highlight, ensured that it successfully delivers 'soft' societal benefits as a legacy of the 2012 Games. For instance, one of Get Set's current programmes, *Travel to Tokyo*, is a values-based, community exercise programme using Olympic and Paralympic athletes and collateral to inspire healthy active communities. *Travel to Tokyo* was recently awarded significant further funding from Sport England (www.sportengland.com), following a successful 17-week pilot, which ensures that it will run through the Tokyo Games and on into 2021. Interestingly, this funding makes explicit an existing and important characteristic of successful Olympic and Paralympic programmes. Namely, that a good programme will harness the huge potential to use children and young people as ambassadors and advocates for the movements to their wider family and community networks. During *Travel to Tokyo's* Merseyside (North West England) pilot, Get Set proved resoundingly its ongoing value and success. The pilot aimed to use the run up to Tokyo 2020 to engage the most inactive families from lower socio-economic groups, encouraging them to be more active together on a regular basis. Around 14,000 children and family members engaged with the programme, which was hugely successful in engaging the most disadvantaged groups: participating schools had an average Pupil Premium of 41% (compared to a national average of 24%). The inclusiveness of the programme is also highlighted in how 84% of all sessions logged were by teams with at least one pupil with a learning disability, and 43% with a physical or sensory disability. Get Set, then, continues to deliver (over a decade since its initial launch) on Lord Coe's promise to use the Olympic and Paralympic Games to engage young people and to "reach people all over the world to connect them with the inspirational power of the Games so that they are inspired to choose sport" (Coe, 2005; quoted in Veal, Toohey and Frawley, 2012: 163). In this regard, Get Set is an exceptional example of where an Olympic and Paralympic Education programme has become a critical pillar of legacy.

Criticism of Get Set

As we have begun to explore, Get Set appears to deliver a vision of Olympism which Pierre De Coubertin would probably recognise himself: one which uses the Games and education in partnership, to inspire young people and their families and communities to engage in physical activity and to live the Values. The levels of understanding of the Olympic and Paralympic Values amongst young people who have engaged with Get Set is a compelling indication of the programme's success (see: EdComs, 2019). However, the usefulness of this kind of evidence in assessing the success of Get Set has rightly been called into question. Chen and Henry, for example, draw attention to the fact that impact is generally "reported via anecdotal evidence that has been led (or funded) by the host nation's government" (Chen and Henry, 2019: 255), arguing that "such evidence is likely subject to bias" and that "there has been little in the way of rigorous investigation of the situation". Such criticism can be well-founded. Annual monitoring and evaluation of some of the Get Set programmes is conducted not by an entirely independent party, but by the research arm of EdComs: the agency of which I am the president, and which is currently responsible for Get Set's delivery. Get Set is supported by a unique – if at times fragile – blend of Olympic, Paralympic, government, commercial, and foundation funding. Indeed, one of its strengths was the inherent flexibility of the programme which facilitated the allocation of discreet packets of public and private funding arranged around LOCOG-funded core resources. The network Get Set has created is highly attractive to many funders, but it could be suggested that it may only remain so if they see evidence that their investment is worthwhile. This must be kept in mind when exploring Get Set's impact, although simply discarding the evidence that the programme is working would also be a brash and unhelpful reaction. The research regularly flags key ways in which the different programmes can be consolidated and improved, and key funders such as the National Lottery, Sport England, and Spirit of 2012 (www.spiritof2012.org.uk) are scrupulous in welcoming learnings about what does not work, as well as what does. However, as the programme reaches its second decade, we should also look for more distanced studies, which either support or challenge the overall view of what legacy success has been achieved.

One challenge levied against Get Set is based on the programme's multi-disciplinary and widely varied nature, which has been viewed by some as a watering-down of a pure, fundamental Values education. It has been argued, for instance, that Get Set merely pays lip service to the Values, without truly educating young people in and engaging them with these Values. Similarly, Get Set fails, it has been argued, to explicitly address the IOC's five Olympic Educational Themes. These were developed "to help young people to understand and practise the principles of Olympism" (IOC, 2016: 84) and 'facilitate the learning of the Olympic Values'. As laid out by the IOC (see IOC, 2016), each theme has a purpose:

1 Joy of effort – 'develop and practise physical, behavioural and intellectual skills by challenging themselves and each other in physical activities, movement, games and sport';
2 Fair play – 'learning fair play behaviour in sport can lead to the development and reinforcement of similar behaviour in one's everyday life';
3 Respect for others – 'accept and respect diversity, and practise personal peaceful behaviour, they promote peace and international understanding';
4 Pursuit of excellence – 'make positive, healthy choices, and strive to become the best that they can be in whatever they do';
5 Balance between body, will and mind – 'physical literacy and learning through movement contribute to the development of both moral and intellectual learning'.

In addition, less specific to Get Set itself, fundamental doubts exist for academics about Olympic education; some have questioned the event's suitability to serve as a platform for promoting education (Kohe and Bowen-Jones, 2016; Lenskyj, 2000; Tomlinson, 2004) given the money-oriented nature of the Olympics (Chen and Henry, 2019).

Money – where it comes from, how it is spent – is consistently a point of controversy around the Olympic and Paralympic Games. In respect of space, I here only lightly touch on the wider debate over Games sponsors, brought recently into the spotlight once more, following Mayor of Paris Anne Hidalgo's rejection of $100m of sponsorship from Total, on the basis that investment from a fossil fuel company "would be at odds with her ambition to make the Games the most environmentally friendly of the modern era" (Sage, 2019). London 2012 and other Olympic Games have consistently been subject to criticism over IOC sponsorship from HFSS (high fat, sugar, and salt) food and drink companies.

There is a difficult negotiation which must take place. On one side, there are the values and vision of a Games' impact and legacy; and on the other, the finitely resourced LOC is tasked with mandatory delivery of tightly defined and key operational elements, while being given an option as to the extent of the delivery of critical legacy pillars, such as education. How can a host nation balance these commitments? Many of London's sponsors invested wholeheartedly and deeply in the vision of inspiring a generation of young people and did so to great effect. In Tokyo 2020, where commercial sponsorship of learning resources is less accepted as common practice, however, we see a new take on how to provide a broader range of resources.

Tokyo 2020: a new model

Tokyo's LOC has created the Yoi Don! programme. In contrast to Get Set, Yoi Don! is not a stand-alone programme of activities. Instead, Yoi Don! provides a platform, a space, within which a variety of approved programmes, delivered by a variety of organisations, are hosted and made available to schools and young people. This platforming approach is an interesting new direction for the education programmes developed and delivered by host nations and cities.

A centralised, robust Values education programme provided by the IPC and IOC, but hosted and adapted by each LOC, if properly supported and promoted to schools, could offer a highly effective – and cost-effective – system of engaging young people in Olympic and Paralympic Education. Indeed, with LOCs under immense pressure and with many competing demands for resource, the hosting and support of a quality-assured, centralised education programme could even offer a way to ensure consistent quality of engagement and impact. It may be that Get Set was the final example of a complete LOC education platform which was built from scratch.

Moreover, the programmes and interventions hosted by Yoi Don! come from specialist governing bodies. For example, the IPC's I'mPOSSIBLE programme and the IOC's Olympic Values Education Programme (OVEP) are key cornerstones of Yoi Don! With their programmes, these bodies bring the very best in expertise, resource, and experience. It is arguably these bodies, not a LOC, who are ideally placed to deliver truly effective education which is integrated with the needs of the Olympic and Paralympic movements. As previously noted, I feel very strongly that much more investment must be put into a study of – and more emphasis placed on the importance of – Paralympic Education. It is a bias which both comes from and led to my appointment as chairperson for the IPC's Education Committee. The Yoi Don! model allows for a specialised, strategic Paralympic Education programme to be integral to a host city's education offer. I'mPOSSIBLE, for instance, is developed by the Agitos Foundation and is the IPC's official Paralympic educational toolkit. It uses the Paralympics and its four Values to raise young people's awareness of an inclusive society. The Japanese edition of I'mPOSSIBLE has been tailored to be easily integrated into the Japanese curriculum and has been distributed free of charge to around 36,000 schools throughout Japan. But the impact of this successful programme does not stop there. The Japanese Ministry of Education, Culture, Sports, Science and Technology has now made a major commitment and approved the inclusion of Paralympic Education in its official curriculum guidelines for all schools. Here we have an example of how Paralympic Education can move beyond a supplement to and engagement tool for the Games, to become an integral part of society.

Conclusion

Today, engagement is a critical component of the work of any LOC. Many host nations have engaged people from beyond the host city – we have already highlighted Sydney as a frontrunner in this – but it was in London 2012 that a systemic approach to uniting an entire nation around the Games was strategised and delivered. Get Set was integral to this. As a result of LOCOG's approach, engagement has become a discipline in and of itself. After London 2012, having seen the effects of a nation unified behind a Games, the IOC laid out a more codified, formal concept of Engagement as part of a Host City's approach. But within this, what does an effective, twenty-first-century Olympic and Paralympic Education programme look like? London 2012 was an exceptional example of a Games where a fully integrated education programme was driven from the very heart of the LOC. Get Set was a crucial element of LOCOG's delivery of a Games to unite and inspire the nation; as such, LOCOG retained responsibility and agency for ensuring the programme successfully reached and engaged young people across the UK. But, of course, the very fact that the core vision aligned so closely with what an education programme could deliver, did mean 'easier' access to the pot of highly finite resources for an education programme – people, money, sponsorship, government support.

Looking forward, Yoi Don! offers a potentially very exciting new way to ensure that engagement and impact are measurable, strategic, and cumulative. Indeed, this model coincides with the IPC's move towards a multi-Game assessment of progress, gathering longitudinal data against consistently articulated and specific outcomes and objectives. I'mPOSSIBLE is an integral part of the IPC's work for awareness, which seeks to increase awareness of the Paralympic movement and its associated values and to foster positive attitudes towards inclusion in society. As I'mPOSSIBLE is now a part of Yoi Don!, the IPC's strategic process for and measurement of engagement, education, and impact is integrated with, not separate to, the delivery of the Tokyo 2020 Games.

Despite a promising new format for delivering education programmes linked to the Games, and the excellent resources increasingly available for translation and localisation from the IOC and IPC, it is crucial that LOCs never lose access to the beating heart of the Olympic and Paralympic Games journey: the opportunity to unite and engage the nation, and the world, around a celebration of effort and excellence. Olympic and Paralympic LOCs have a unique opportunity to activate unique cultural and historic symbols. They can provide access to incredible Olympic and Paralympic collateral, including the Torch, the medals, and the cultural programme, and then build on the inspiration of Games-time opportunities, through schools ticketing programmes. At the heart of it all is the example of Olympic and Paralympic athletes themselves, and an event which captures hearts and minds. This is the aspect of Pierre De Coubertin's nineteenth-century Olympic vision which we should strive to maintain today. As Get Set proved, the Olympic and Paralympic Games can be leveraged to unite, engage, and inspire a nation, and can continue to do so long after the Games themselves have ended. Should we not, then, seek an evolution in Lord Coe's promise to 'inspire a generation'? Instead, we should be looking to education programmes as a vital tool to continue to inspire young people, their families and communities, through the Values and the example of the Olympic and Paralympic movements, and their Games, for generations to come.

References

Binder, D. (2005). Teaching Olympism in schools: Olympic education as a focus on values education. *University lecture on the Olympics, at the Centre d'Estudis Olímpics UAB, International Chair in Olympism (IOC-UAB)*, in Barcelona, Spain.

Chatziefstathiou, D. (2011). Olympism: A learning philosophy for physical education and youth sport. In: K.M. Armour, ed., *Introduction to sport pedagogy for teachers and coaches: Effective learners in physical education and youth sport*. Essex: Pearson, pp. 90–101.

Chatziefstathiou, D. (2012). Olympic education and beyond: Olympism and value legacies from the Olympic and Paralympic games. *Educational Review*, 64(3), Aug. 1, pp. 385–400(16).

Chen, S. and Henry, I. (2019). Schools' engagement with the Get Set London 2012 Olympic education programme: Empirical insights from schools in a non-hosting region. *European Physical Education Review*, 25(1), Feb. 1, pp. 254–272.

Culpan, I. and Wigmore, S. (2010). The delivery of Olympism education with a physical education context drawing on critical pedagogy. *International Journal of Sport and Health Science*, 8, pp. 67–76.

Darcy, S. (2016). Paralympic legacy – Learning from the Sydney 2000 to prepare for Tokyo 2020. *Journal of the Nippon Foundation Paralympic Research*, 4(1), pp. 43–46.

EdComs. (2019). *Get set monitoring and evaluation 2019*. London.

Girginov, V. (2012). Social legacy of the Olympic Games. In: Oxford Brookes University, ed., *Learning legacies*. Oxford: Oxford Brookes University.

International Olympic Committee. (2005). *Host city contract: Games of the XXX Olympiad in 2012*. Lausanne: IOC.

International Olympic Committee. (2016). *The fundamentals of Olympic values education*. 2nd ed. Lausanne: Department of Public Affairs and Social Development through Sport.

Kidd, B. (1996). Taking the rhetoric seriously: Proposals for Olympic education. *Quest*, 48, pp. 82–92.

Kohe, G.Z. and Bowen-Jones, W. (2016). Rhetoric and realities of London 2012 Olympic education and participation 'legacies': Voices from the core and periphery. *Sport, Education and Society*, 21(8), pp. 1213–1229.

Lenskyj, H. (2000). *Inside the Olympic industry: Power, politics, and activism*. Albany: State University of New York Press.

LOCOG. (2012a). *London 2012 Olympic Games official report*. Vol. 1. London.

LOCOG. (2012b). *The get set story: How London 2012 inspired the UK's schools*. London.

Müller, N., ed. (2000). *Pierre de Coubertin 1863–1937 – Olympism: Selected writings*. Lausanne: IOC.

Naul, R. (2008). *Olympic education*. Oxford: Meyer & Meyer.

Parry, J. (1998). Physical education as Olympic education. *European Physical Education Review*, 4(2), pp. 153–167.

Sage, A. (2019). Paris Mayor wrong to reject oil cash for Olympics, says Macron. *The Times*. Published online: https://www.thetimes.co.uk/article/paris-mayor-wrong-to-reject-oil-cash-for-olympics-says-macron-70b56t6q6

Tomlinson, A. (2004). The Disneyfication of the Olympics: Theme parks and freak-shows of the body. In: J. Bale and M.K. Christensen, eds., *Post-Olympism? Questioning sport in the twenty-first century*. Oxford: Berg, pp.147–163.

University of East London. (2007). *A lasting legacy for London? Assessing the legacy of the Olympic Games and Paralympic Games*. London: London East Research Institute.

Veal, A.J., Toohey, K. and Frawley, S. (2012). The sport participation legacy of the Sydney 2000 Olympic Games and other international sporting events hosted in Australia. *Journal of Policy Research in Tourism, Leisure and Events*, 4(2), pp. 155–184.

Index

Note: Page numbers in **bold** indicate tables and page numbers in *italic* indicate figures and boxed text.

Aaker, D.A. 87
Abberley, P. 324
ABC broadcast coverage of Olympics 114
Abeza, G. 85, 88
ableism 326–327
Acosta, J.P. 9
Active People survey (England) 382
Adecco 13, *16*
Ademola, Ade 206
Adidas 164
Adjaye, J. 66, 70–71
Afghanistan National Olympic Committee 270–271, 339
Agenda 2020 (IOC): bidding for Olympic Games and 174, 196; composition of IOC and 212–213; cultural programmes for Olympics/Paralympics and 6, 408, 418; gender issues and 340; good governance and 287; initiation of 183; legacies of Olympic Games and 367; LGBTI+ athletes and 340; New Norm campaign/document and 183, 236; Olympic Channel and 117; Olympic Social Responsibility and 149; organizing Olympic Games and 172; reform of IOC and 212–213, 235–236, 287; Sport for Development and Peace and 345, 348–349; sustainability and 151; synergies with Olympic movement and, maximising 154; themes of 40 recommendations of 235
Ahlfeldt, G. 191
Aján, Tamas 285
Albertville Olympic Games (1992) 76
Alfermann, D. 10
Almeida, A. 105
Altman, D. 56
amateurism issue 47, 82, 142, 204–205, 207–209, 298–299, 409
Amazon Firestick platform 163
ambush marketing 121–122, 130–134
Ammons, D. 38
Amnesty International (AI) 336–337
Amsterdam Olympic Games (1928) 110
Ancient Games 46, 408
Anderson award 23
Anderson, B. 70
Andreff, W. 185–186
Anne, H.R.H. Princess 209
anti-doping regulations *see* World Anti-Doping Agency (WADA)
Antwerp Olympic Games (1920) 205
Aoki, H. 11
Apartheid policy 270–271, 339
Aquilina, D. 11
arbitration for athletes *see* Court of arbitration for Sport (CAS); International Council of Arbitration for Sport (ICAS)
Arnhem Olympic Games (1980) 243
Arnhem Seminar 219, 341
Asian Games (2018) 167
Asian Games (2022) 303
Aspire educational programme 421–422
Association of the International Olympic Winter Sport Federations (AIOWF) 299, 314
Association of National Olympic Committees (ANOC) 267, 314
Association of Paralympic Sports Organizations (APSO) 224
Association of Recognised International Sports Federations (ARISF) 299
Association of Summer Olympic International Federations (ASOIF) 299, 310, 314
associative freedom 251–252; *see also* autonomy of Olympic/sport movement
Athens Olympic Games (2004) 111, 117, 194
Athlete 365 Career+ Outreach Programme 13
Athlete Career Programme (ACP) 13, *13*
Athletes' Association 14
Athletes' Commission (IOC/IPC) 9, 13, 210–211, 222–223, 225, 256
athlete's issues 2–3; *see also specific athlete's name and issue*
athletes' rights *see* Court of arbitration for Sport (CAS)

athletes' sports career model 9–10
Athletics Federation of India 59
Atlanta Paralympic Games (1996) 86
Audi 163
Australian Olympic Committee (AOC) 145–146
Australian Sport Commission 290
autism 38
autonomy of Olympic/sport movement: background information 250–251; challenges to 255–256; classical liberalism and 251–252; constructivist approach to 258–259; Court of Arbitration for Sport and 255–256; defining 'autonomy of sport' and 254–255; external 255–256; freedom of association and 251–252; good governance and 253, 259–260; historical perspective 251–254; ideological foundations 251–252; institutional perspective and 254–255; internal 255–256; negotiated autonomy and 254; overview 4, 251, 260–261; pragmatic autonomy and 254; protecting 256–259, **257**; rational approach to 256–258; responsible autonomy and 250, 253; restraining freedom of association and 252–254; sporting autonomy and 250–251, 254–255; supervised autonomy and 254; World Anti-Doping Agency and 255–256; *see also* political autonomy of NOCs

Bach, Thomas 126–127, 149, 183, 196, 234, 250, 253, 278, 300, 303, 348, 405
Balmer, N.J. 358, 361
Baloglu, S. 386
Banka, Witold 281
Ban Ki-moon 259
Barcelona Olympic Games (1992) 76, 113–114, 142, 173, 375, 410
Baron-Thiene, A. 10
Barr, H. 6
Basic Universal Principles of Good Governance 271, 285, 310
Batuev, M. 302–304
Baumann, A. *13*
Bauman, Patrick 300–301
Bayle, E. 3
BBC broadcast coverage of Olympics 115
Beacom, A. 327, 329
Beckman, E. 37
Beesley, L.G. 386, 394
Begum, Mike 'BrolyLegs' 167–168
Beijing Olympic Broadcasting (BOB) 114
Beijing Olympic Games (2008) 99, 115, 172, 340, 375, 392–394
Berlin Olympic Games (1936) 48, 110, 113, 339, 409
Berlin Wall's fall 210
Berlioux, Monique 208
Bernando, N. 13
bidding for Olympic Games *171*, 172–174, 180, 196
Bill of Rights (English and American) 335
Bingham, J. 358
biosocial model of disability 325–326
Birkenbach, J. 325–326
Bjerke, R. 88
black athletes 339
Blatter, Joseph 212
Blatter, Sepp 317
board renewal of IOC: background information 284–285; context of 285–286; fixed terms and 288–289; good governance and 284; governance within Olympic movement and 286–287; limited terms and 287–292; overview 285, 291–292; rationale of 285–286; strategies 290–291
Bodet, G. 3
Bohonnon, Mac 126
Bondonio, P. 386
books focussing on Paralympic Games 328
Borzov, Valeriy 210
boycott of Olympic Games 77, 155, 270, 339
Brackenridge, C. 58
brain drain 66
brand: consistency 87; equity 87; governance structure 88–89, *89*, 94; policing 134–136; *see also* brand protection; Olympic brand; Paralympic brand
brand protection: ambush marketing and 130–134; background information 130; evolution of 130, 147; International Olympic Committee and 135–136; London Olympic and Paralympic Marks Act 133; Nike and 131; North Face and 131–132; Olympic laws and 130–131; Olympic movement and 130; Olympic rings 130–132; Olympic words/phrases 131; overview 3, 136–137; policing brand 134–136; PyeongChang Olympic Games and 135; Rule 40 135–136, 147; social ambush and 134; Under Armour and 144, 147
brawn drain 66
Braye, S. 94, 329
Bray, S.R. 357, 361
Brazilian Olympic Act 133
Brexit referendum 184
Bridgestone Tire sponsorship of Paralympic Games 102
British Esports Association 162
British Olympic Association (BOA) 27–29, 244, 270
British Olympic Association (BOA) v World Anti-Doping Agency (WADA) 27–29
British Olympic Foundation (BOF) 423
British Paralympic Association (PBA) 36, 423
British Parliamentary Digital, Culture, Media and Sport Committee (DCMS) 36
British Petroleum (BP) sponsorship of Paralympic Games 102–103

Brittain, I. 5, 326–327, 329
broadcast coverage/rights: ABC 114; background information 109–110; BBC 115; countries broadcasting 111, *112*, 113; 8K Super Hi-Vision production and 111; esports 162; in Europe 116; exclusive 111; expansion of coverage in 2000s 114–115; fees 111, 113, 116; future directions 117; historical perspective 110–111; in host nations, developing 113–114; International Olympic Committee and 109, 116, 118; international signal and, first 113; marketing strategy 109–110; NBC 76–77, 103, 114–115; new media and 117; Olympic Broadcast Systems and 114; Olympic Channel and 117; overview 3, 117–118; Paralympic games and 99; Pay per View format and 113; PyeongChang Olympic Games and 100–101, 111, 115, 341; revenues 110, *111*; Sydney Olympic Games (2000) and 76, 111, *112*, 114; television 76–78, 103, 113, 115; 3D 111; value of 115–116; Virtual Reality experiences and 111; Youth Olympic Games and 116
Broom, D. 393–394
Broudehoux, A.M. 352
Brownlee, Helen 42
Brundage, Avery 206–207, 298
Budd, Zola 66
Bundon, A. 329
Burkett, B. 330
Burnham, Andy 381–382
Burn, J. 2
business of Olympics/Paralympics 3; *see also specific issue*
Byon, K. 92–93, 99
Byon, K.K. 99

Camillo Aldao, Ricardo 206
Campbell, F.A.K. 327
Canadian Imperial Bank of Canada (CIBC) 103
Canadian Olympic Committee & Beckie Scott v International Olympic Committee 22
Canadian Olympic Committee (COC) 131–132
Canadian Survey of Disability 105
capital budget 178
Carroll, M. 99
Carron, A.V. 356–357, 361
Carter, James 270
Centre for Sport and Human Rights 343
Cerebral Palsy International Sports and Recreation Association (CP-ISRA) 218, 243
Chalip, L. 366, 378, 386, 394
Chalip, L.H. 386
Chanavat, N. 134
Chand, Dutee 59, 312, 342
changes to IOC *see* reform to IOC
Chappelet, J-L. 192–193, 251–252, 254, 265, 268–269, 285, 301
Chatziefstathiou, D. 5, 404, 420–421
Chen, Nathan 126
Chen, S. 5, 424–425
Cherney, J.L. 327
Cheune, Leonard 60
Chien, P.M. 386
Chiulli, Raffaele 301
citizenship of athletes 66, 70–71; *see also* nationality of athletes
Clarke, S.R. 357
classification/eligibility in sport for people with disabilities *see* disability classification in sport
Clean Venue Policy 123
Clinton, Hillary 55
Club Citoyen Collective Sports programme 13
'Club, The' 210
Coalter, F. 351
Coates, D. 188–189, 191
Coates, John 318
co-branding opportunities 82
Coca-Cola sponsorship 3, 121, 125–126, 131, 165
Code of Ethics (IOC) 56–57, 310
'Code for Sports Governance' 36
Code of Sports-Related Arbitration 315
Coe, Lord Sebastian 177–178, 421, 428
Coke.com/Olympics 126
CokePlay platform 126
Cole, Kenneth 105
CollectifSports Scheme 13
colour casters 162–163
commercialization of Olympics/Paralympics 3, 193–194, *193*, 268, 297–299; *see also specific issue*
Committee of International Olympic Aid (CIOA) 206
common law tradition 24–26
Commonwealth Games Federation (CGF) 40
community capacity building 158n8
compensation for Olympians 142–143
Compliance Review Committee (CRC) 280
composition of IOC: age limits issue and 206, 310; Agenda 2020 and 212–213; background information 203; challenges (1973–1981) and, addressing 207–208; changes to 211–212; commissions and, thematic 207; overview 4, 213; politics and 210; reforms (1981–1999) and, implementing 208–210; role of members and 203; Salt Lake City scandal consequences (1999–2013) and 210–212; self-recruiting process (1894–1921) and 203–205; sporting background 213; stakeholders (1921–1973) and, emerging 205–207; stakeholders and, other influential 210; women 209
conceptual framework of configuration 230
Connick, M. 37
constructivist approach to autonomy of Olympic/sport movement 258–259

Cook, Aaron 65
Corporate Social Responsibility (CSR) 92
corporatisation 230
Cortina d'Ampezzo Olympic Games (1956) 110
cost overruns and organizing Olympic Games 183, *186*, 189, *190*, 194, 196
Cottingham, M. 92–93, 99
Council of Europe 150–151, 253, 312, 342
Council of Europe Charter 151–152, 158n3
Counter Strike GO team 163
Courneya, K.S. 356–357
Court of Arbitration for Sport (CAS): Ad Hoc divisions 25–26, 29; Anti-Doping Division 314; appeals 316; Arbitration Rules 26–27; authority, binding/persuasive 20–21, 23–24; autonomy of Olympic/sport movement and 255–256; awards 22–24, 316; background information 20–21; Chand challenge and 59; civil law and 21–23; common law and 21–23; Court Office 317; decentralized offices of 314; *de facto* system of *stare decisis* and 22–23; *de novo* hearing and 21; dispute-resolution types 314; governance levels in 313, *313*; human rights issues and 342; impact of 309–310; importance of 2, 5, 20; installation of 209; International Olympic Committee and 209, 256–257, 312; legal framework governing 319; nationality of athletes and 68; Ordinary Arbitration Division 314; overview 29–31; Panels 25; Practice of Direction and 20–21; process, review of 26–29; *ratio decidendi* and 22; Russian doping scandal and 278; Semenya case and 60; standard of proof and 24–26; website 314, 318; World Anti-Doping Agency and 278–279; *see also* governance of CAS; *specific case*
Craven, Sir Phillip 41, 92, 220–222, 247, 278
Crawford, Susan 421–422
Crompton, J. 378
Cronin, B. 145
Cuff, Leonard 204
Cultural Olympiad 410–418, **416**
cultural programmes for Olympics/Paralympics: Agenda 2020 and 6, 408, 418; background information 408; challenges 412, 415–416; change, cultural/social 415; contemporary art focus and 412; cultural fusion/innovation theme and 413; Cultural Olympiads (1992–2012) 410–418, **416**; de Coubertin's vision and 408–409; delivery formats 415–416; economic regeneration 414; entertainment 414–415; future directions 418, *418*; geographical spread 416, **416**; historical perspective 408–409; London Olympic Games (2012) and 411, 417; Olympic Art Competitions (1912–1918) 408–410, **410**; opportunities 412; overview 6, 408; politics/identity 413–414; promotional frameworks 417; Rio De Janeiro Olympic Games (2016) and 411; Sydney Olympic Games (2000) and 411, 413–416; thematic emphases 412–413; trends 412; from 2000 onwards 411–412; typologies overview 413–416; vision behind 413
Czempiel, E.-O. 310

Darcy, S. 93
Darcy, Simon 422
Darnell, S.C. 5
Davis, J.A. 125
Davis, L.J. 324
Dawson, P. 386
deaf athletes/deafness 38–40, 85
Deaflympics 39, 50
Deal, M. 327
de Baillet-Latour, Henri 205
Deccio, C. 386
de Coubertin, Pierre 46, 139, 142, 150, 203–205, 252, 338, 338–339, 345, 366–367, 408–409, 417, 420–421, 425, 428
DeFrantz, Anita 209
Delpy, L. 3
Democracy in America (de Tocqueville) 251
democratic procedures and referendums 184–186
Dempsey, Chris 173–174
Deng Xiaoping 392
Denver referendum 173, 186
de Portalès, Hélène 47
Desbordes, M. 134
de Sousa-Mast, F.R. 380
de Tocqueville, Alexis 251–252
Devine, M.A. 325
Digel, H. 192–193
disability classification in sport: autism and 38; background information 34–35; deafness and 38–40; disputes over 35–37; Down Syndrome and 35; elite sport for all and 37–40; evidence-based 36–37; including disabled athletes in Olympics and 41; intellectual impairments and 38; International Paralympics Committee and 34; international sports federations and 37; merging Olympics and Paralympics and, debate over 40–41; multiple impairments 35; opportunities for athletes and 45; overview 2, 42; questioning surrounding 35; robust system of, developing 35–37; separating Olympics and Paralympics 42; technology and impaired bodies 330
Disabled People Movement 94
Discovery Eurosport 116
Dixon, K. 94
Donnelly, P. 347
Dottori, M. 92, 99
Dou, Y. 289
Down Syndrome 35
Dowse, S. 93

Drake, R. 325
Dream Team (United States) 142, 299
dual career of athletes: Athlete 365 Career+ Outreach Programme 13; Athlete Career Programme and 13, *13*; background information 9; benefits of 10–11; Club Citoyen Collective Sports programme 13; CollectifSports Scheme and 13; defining 'dual career' and 9–10; employability gap and, bridging *13*; European Union Guidelines *12*; overview 2, 9, 17; Performance Lifestyle Practitioners and 10; Personal Excellence Advisors and 10; programmes 12–17, *13*, *14*; retirement and 11–12; Scholars Scheme and 15; SNB and 11, 15; TASS Dual Career Accreditation Scheme and 14, *14*, 16; United States Olympic and Paralympic Committee Athlete Career and Education (USOPC ACE) Programme and *16*
Dupree, Tucker *16*
Duty of Care in Sport Review (UK) 9
Duval, A. 68

EA Sport 165
EA Sports FIFA tournament (eCOPA Coca-Cola) 165
East German Democratic Republic (GDR) 269–270
East German women's teams (1970s and 1980s) 46
eCOPA Coca-Cola 165
Edström, Sigfrid 205
educational programmes for Olympics/Paralympics: *Aspire* 421–422; background information 420–421; defining 420; Get Set programme 423–426; I'm POSSIBLE programme 427–428; in Japan 427; London Olympic Games (2012) 421, 423; Olympic Values Education Programme 348–349, 427; overview 6, 427–428; Sydney Olympic/Paralympic Games (2000) 6, 421–423; Tokyo Olympic Games (2020) 426–427; *Travel to Tokyo* programme 424–425; Yoi Don! programme 426–428
Eickman, J. 38
8K Hi-Vision (SHV) production 111
Eland, Ron 66
Electronic Sports League 163, 169
elite sport for all 37–40
Ellis, K. 104
Emery, P.R. 172
Engbersen, G. 67
esports: alignment with Olympic Games and 167–169; arena 169; background information 160–162; broadcast coverage/rights and 162; co-development of game titles between traditional and gaming federations and 165–167; as commercial market 163; data-driven economy and 168; embracing, time for 303; gaming publishers and 165; growth of 167; International Olympic Committee and 160, 165–166; international sports federations and 165–167, 303; monetisation and 168; Olympic movement and 165–167, 303; overview 4, 160–161, 167–169; Paris Olympic Games (2024) and 160; PyeongChang Olympic Games (2018) and 160, 164; Rio de Janeiro Olympic Games discussions and 160; sponsorship 163–164; sports simulators and 168; streaming principles and 162–163; television and 162–163; Tokyo Olympic Games (2020) and 160; traditional sports and 161, 168–169; Youth Olympic Games and 166
European Broadcasting Union (EBU) 116
European Commission 253
European Union (EU) *12*, 253, 271
evolution of IPC: background information 217–218; governance structure *221*, *223*; initial formation (1989–1998) 218–219; overview 4, 218, 226–227; professionalisation (1999–2003) 219–221, *221*, 226; separation of governance and management (2004–2014) 221–224, *223*; streamlining organisational structure (2015–2019) 224–226, **225**
Ewald, Manfred 269–270
external stakeholders 178

Facebook 163
Fairley, S. 386
Fearnley Cup 242
Federal Act on Private International Law (LDIP) (Switzerland) 312, 316–317, 319
Federal Cartel Office (Germany) 135–136, 145
Federal Supervisory Authority for Foundations (Switzerland) 316
Fédération Internationale de Football Association (FIFA) 66, 133, 165–168, 194, 271, 287, 298, 310, 313, 342
Fédération Internationale de Natation (FINA) 295
Fenton, A. 4
Ferrand, A. 3
festival effect of Olympic Games 381–382
FIFA World and eWorld Cups 165, 167
FIFPro 15
financial management in organizing Olympic Games 178
Finkelstein, V. 325
Finlay, C.J. 141–142, 144
Fiss, P.C. 88–89
Flyvbjerg, B. 370
Foreign Corrupt Practices Act (FCPA) 313
Formula E 166
Formula E website 166
Foster, K. 254
François, A. 3

Franchini, E. 358
Frawley, S. 423
Frederick, E. 142, 144
Fredericks, Frankie 213
freedom of association *see* autonomy of Olympic/sport movement
Freitag, M. 185
French Declaration of the Rights of Man and Citizen 335
French, L. 92
French, S. 326
Fuchs, S. 3
Fuller, N. 6
functional areas (FAs) in organizing Olympic Games 171, 179–180
fundraising campaigns by athletes 143
Furlong, John 177
Future Host Commission 174

Galloway, Noah 105
game location factors 356, *357*, 361; *see also* home advantage effect
Games of the New Emerging Forces (GANEFO) 271
Games-time 'London 2012 Festival' 411
gaming publishers 165
Gammon, S.J. 329–330
Garcia, B. 6, 410, 415
Gardiner, S. 386
Gearity, B. 92–93, 99
Geeraert, A. 4, 254, 268, 286–288
gender issues: Agenda 2020 and 340; East German women's teams (1970s and 1980s) and 46; gendered bodies concept and 47–48; International Association of Athletics Federations and 45–46, 49–50; International Olympic Committee and 45–46, 49; overview 51; Paralympic Games and 46; patriarchal views of sports and 47; rules and 45; self-identification and 49–50; sex testing 48, 59–61; trans/intersex athletes 48–50; verification of gender and 48; *see also* LGBTI+ athletes; women's issues
General Assembly of International Sports Federation (GAISF) 154, 161, 207, 299–301
Gérard, S. 3
German Olympic Sports Confederation (DOSB) 135–136, 193
Get Set educational programme 423–426
Gibbons, T. 94
gigantism and Olympic Games 183, 191, 193–194, *193*, 195
Gill, C. 386
Girginov, V. 5, 328, 371–372, 424
Glen-Haig, Mary Alison 209
GoFundMe 143
Gold Coast Commonwealth Games (2018) 386
Gold, J. 363
Gold, M. 363
González, Xavier 37, 99, 222, 247–248
good governance 4, 253, 259–260, 271, 284–285, 287, 310
Goodman, S. 328
Gouttebarge, V. 11
governance of CAS: background information 309–310; dispute-resolution types 314; Federal Act on Private International Law and 312, 316–317, 319; governance concept and 310; 'governance without government' concept and 310; improving, issues to explore for 317–319; International Council of Arbitration for Sport and 313–316, 318; levels of governance within CAS and 313, *313*; metagovernance and 316; models of governance and, practical 310–313, *311*; overview 310, 319; Pérez's model applied to *311*, 313–317, *313*; Swiss law and 312, 316–317, 319; Tribunal Fédéral and 316, 319
governance issues 4–5, 193–194, 211; *see also specific issue and organization*
governance structure of brand 88–89, *89*, 94
Grace, Kate 144
Grady, J. 3, 144–147
Gratton, C. 5, 358
Greenfield, S. 2
Guala, C. 386
Guan, Z. 362
Guinness Beer ad with disabled athletes 103–104
Gundel, Elmar 315
Gurgel, L.A. 380
Guttmann, Allen 210
Guttmann, Dr Ludwig 85–86, 98, 242, 340–341

Habermas, J. 371
Haggman, Pirjo 209
Haizinger, L. 191
Hamburg referendum 188–189, 191, 194
Hammond, A. 327
handicapitalism 42, 105
Hardin, B. 99
Hardin, M. 99, 327
Hargreaves, J.A. 99
Hartmann, D. 351–352
Hatch, M.J. 88
Havelange, João 210
Hawkins, D.G. 254
Haynes, Nico 58–59
health-related legacies: background information 375–376; evidence for 376–379; London Olympic Games (2012) and 375–376, 379, 381–383; overview 5, 376, 383; possibility of 383; rationales for hosting Olympic/Paralympic Games and 375–376; testing evidence for 379–383
Helleland, Linda 280–281
Helm, C. 84–85, 88

Henry, I. 4, 424–425
heteronormativity 55
Heyne, L. 185
Hickey, Patrick 213
Hidalgo, Anne 426
Hilary, G. 288
Hills, L. 371
historical development of International Paralympic Committee (IOC) 4; *see also* evolution of IPC
Hoberman, J. 334
Hodler, Marc 210
home advantage effect: average 363, **363**; background information 355–356; conceptual model comparison 356–357, **357**; key performance indicators and 359; Olympic Games Global Impact project and 355; overview 5, 362–363, **364**; research previously completed 357–358; revisiting conceptual model 361–362; sporting legacy dimension and 355–356, *356*; study design of research 358–359, **359**; in Summer Olympics/Paralympics 357–360, **359**, *360*, 363; in Winter Olympics/Paralympics **359**, 360, *361*, 363
Hong, F. 362
Hooper, Gloria *14*
Horning, D.L. 122–123
Host Broadcasting Organization 114
Host City Contracts (HCC) 152–153, 157, 158n9
Host Contract of Services for the XXX Olympiad 2012 (IOC) 423
host nations: benefits to 385; broadcast coverage/rights in, developing 113–114; in developing countries 350; legacy and 5; overview 5; rationale for 375; urban regeneration and 93; *see also* home advantage effect
Howe, P.D. 4, 92–93, 99, 329–330
Howland, L. 2
Huang, C.J. 326
Huang, S. 288
human resource management in organizing Olympic Games 178
human rights issues: Amnesty International and 336–337; Apartheid policy and 270–271, 339; background information 334–335; Bill of Rights (English and American) and 335; black athletes and 339; Centre for Sport and Human Rights 343; compliance with, strengthening 342–343; contingency of 336–337; Court of Arbitration for Sport and 342; French Declaration of the Rights of Man and Citizen and 335; global activism and 335–336; historical perspective 335–336; Human Rights Watch and 340, 342; international agreements and 336–337; International Olympic Committee and 334, 343; International Paralympic Committee and 334, 343; Jewish athletes and 339; language of 340; LGBIT+ athletes and 2, 54–59, 337, 340; Mega-Sporting Events Platform for Human Rights and 342; new era of activism and 337; Olympic Games and 62, 338–339; overview 334–335; Paralympic Games and 162, 340–342; persons with disabilities 335, 340–342; relationship between IOC and IPC and 341–343; separation of Olympics and Paralympics and 41; in sports 337–338; United Nations Council on Human Rights and 337; United Nations Universal Declaration of Human Rights and 336; women's issues and 338, 341
Human Rights Watch (HRW) 340, 342
Hurd Clarke, L. 329
Hurst, P. 2
Hyper Olympic '84 game 165

IAFF v RFEA & Josephine Onyia 24
Iavarone, A. 330
identity and sports 65; *see also* gender issues; LGBTI+ athletes; nationality of athletes
IHF Handball Challenge game 166
Impact Magazine para-athlete profile 105
implementation mode in organizing Olympic Games *171*, 179–180
I'm POSSIBLE educational programme 427–428
Independent Observer (IO) report 279–280
Independent Person Report (McLaren report) 277–278
India National Olympic Committee 265
Indian Olympic Association (IOA) 265
Ind, N. 88
Indonesia 271
Infront Sports and Media 116
'Inspired by 2012' icon 417
Inspire Leicestershire programme 389
Instant Articles (Facebook) 163
Institute for Management Development (IMD) 286
institutional theory 301–304
Intel 160, 164
intellectual impairments 38
Intelligence Quotient (IQ) 38
internalised ableism 327
internal stakeholders 178–179
International Amateur Athletics Federation (IAAF) 204–205
International Association of Athletics Federations (IAAF) 45, 49–50, 59–60, 165–166, 255, 278, 287, 342
International Basketball Federation (FIBA) 289
International Blind Sports Association (IBSA) 218, 243
International Charter of Physical Education and Sport 253
International Committee of Sport for the Deaf (CISS) 218–219

International Committee of Sports for the Deaf (ICSD) 39–40
International Convention on the Rights of Persons with Disabilities 341
International Coordinating Committee (ICC) 86, 218, 243
International Council of Arbitration for Sport (ICAS) 313–316, 318, 340
International Cycling Union (ICU) 166, 287
International Federation for Para-athletes with Intellectual Impairment (INAS) 35, 38
International Federations (IFs) 34, 275–276
International Federation of Sport Climbing (IFSC) 303–304
International Modern Pentathlon Union (UIPM) 285
international non-governmental organization (INGO) 351; *see also specific name*
International Non-Government Organisation ActionAid 58
International Olympic Committee (IOC): amateurism issue and 298–299; Annual Report (2016) 157; Athletes' Commission 13, 210–211, 256; Athletes' Commission 'All in' Strategy 9; autonomy of 252; Basic Universal Principles of Good Governance and 271, 285, 310; brand protection and 135–136; broadcast coverage/ rights and 109, 116, 118; Code of Ethics 56–57, 310; compensation for Olympians and 142; Court of Arbitration for Sport and 209, 256–257, 312; esports and 160, 165–166; Ethics Commission 212; Executive Board 289, 291, 295, 312; Executive Committee 5; function of 294; gender issues and 45–46, 49; *Host City Contract of Services for XXX Olympiad 2012* and 423; human rights issues and 334, 343; image of 212; international sports federations and 205, 296; International Testing Authority and 280–281; IOC-IPC Agreements and 244–245, 247–248; legacies of Olympic Games and 368; 'Legacy Strategic Approach' and 365; LGBTI+ athletes and 54–56; Marketing Report (2018) 126–127; marketing value of Olympics and 75–76; Members Election Commission 290; mission of 146; National Olympic Committee of India and, suspension of 265; National Olympic Committees and 205, 207; New Norm campaign/document and 172, 174, 179, 236, 300; Nomination Committee 211–212; Olympic Charter and 139; Olympic Foundation for Culture and Heritage 418; Olympic Games Global Impact project and 355; Olympic movement and 345–346; Olympic Summit (2018) 167; organizing Olympic Games and 173, 174, *175*, 180–181, 195; Paralympic brand and 90–91, 180–181; Paralympic Games and 99–100; political autonomy of NOCs and 271–272; political interferences and, cases of 271–272; Reform Commission 211; revenues/revenue model 77–78, 146, 297; Rule 40 and 135–136; social media rules and 140–141; Sport for Development and Peace and 352; sustainability of Olympic Social Responsibility and, 149–150, *152*, 153, 157, 158n7; term limits of board members and 287–290; World Anti-Doping Agency and 277–281; youth market and 404; *see also* Agenda 2020 (IOC); board renewal of IOC; changes to IOC; composition of IOC; reform of (IOC); relationship between IOC and international sports federations; relationship between IOC and IPC
International Paralympic Committee (IPC): Athlete Classification Code 37; Athletes' Commission 9, 222–223, 225; challenges in future 227; disability classification and 34; founding of 87, 241; General Assembly 220; Governing Board 222, 227; Governing Council 287, 290; human rights issues and 334, 343; impact of Olympic movement and 329; IOC-IPC Agreements and 244–245, 247–248; Management Team 222–224, 227; National Olympic Committees and 220; Regional Associations 224–225; role of 84; sports promotion by 90; standing committees 224, **225**; Strategic Planning Congress 220; youth games and 404–405; *see also* evolution of IPC; relationship between IOC and IPC
International Shooting Sport Federation 285
International Skateboarding Federation (ISF) 304
International Sport and Leisure (ISL) 78, 209
International Sports Federation for People with a Mental Handicap (INAS-FID) 86
international sports federations (IFs): criticisms of Olympic Games and 191; disability classification in sport and 37; emergence of 204; esports and 165–167, 303; events created by 298; function of 294; independence of 139; International Olympic Committee and 205, 296; mission of 295; new sports in Olympic movement and 301–304; overview 3; recognition by IOC and, criteria for 295–297; role of 295; *see also* relationship between IOC and international sports federations; *specific name*
International Sports Federations for Persons with an Intellectual Disability (INAS-FID) 218–219
International Sports Organization for the Disabled (ISOD) 86, 218, 220, 224, 243
International Stoke Mandeville Games Federation (ISMGF) 86, 241–243
International Stoke Mandeville Wheelchair Sports Federation (ISMWSF) 218
International Testing Authority (ITA) 280–281

International Weightlifting Federation (IWF) 278, 285
intersex athletes 48–50
Ioannidis, G. 2
IOC-IPC Agreements 244–245, 247–248, 411
Iraq National Olympic Committee 271–272
Isava-Fonseca, Flor 209
ISO certification 153–154
Iuzefovici, Igor 65

Jansen, J. 67
Jeanes, R. 327
Jerdee, C. 105
Jewish athletes 339
Jones, Marion 33n28
Jones, R. 84–85, 88
Jordan, Jerald 39
Jordan-Young, R. 61
journal articles focussing on Paralympic Games 328

Kaplanidou, K. 5, 386, 399, 403
Karadakis, K. 386, 403
Karg, A.J. 91–92
Karkazis, K. 61
Kearney, S. 326
Keller, K.L. 87
Kellison, T.B. 185
Kelly, D. 386
Kelly, S.J. 386
Kennedy, E. 378
Kentish, Robert 205
Kerkhoffs, G.M. 11
key performance indicators (KPIs) 359, 369
Kia Motors sponsorship of Olympic Games 127
Kidd, B. 5, 347, 351
Killanin, Lord 207–208, 270, 298
Kipnis, E. 326
knowledge legacy 405
Koenigstorfer, J. 195
Könecke, T. 188, 191
Koss, Johann Olav 213, 346
Kostakopoulou, D. 68, 70
Kübler-Mabbott, B. 265, 269
Kuwait National Olympic Committee 272
Kwauk, C. 351–352

Ladau, E. 104
Laurell, C. 121
Lausanne Youth Olympic Games (2020) 5, 399–400, 402
Lavallee, D. 10
leadership in organizing Olympic Games 177
Le Clair, J.M. 92
Lee, P.C. 4
legacies of Olympic Games: Agenda 2020 and 367; background information 365–366; of Barcelona Olympic Games (1992) 195; blueprint for 365; claims and fields of actions and 367–368, **367**, **368**; criticism of Olympics and 190–191, *190*, 372; 'development' as key word in 366; dimensions of 355–356, *356*; Get Set educational programme 424–425; host nations and 5; International Olympic Committee and 368; key performance indicators and 359, 369; lack of perceived 194; London Olympics (2012) 390–391; needed for Olympic movement 369–370, **369**; outcomes, connecting to process responsible for 370; overview 372–373; questions involving 370–372; shortcomings of 369, **369**; sporting/sport participation 355–356, *356*, 375, 382; stages of constructing 372, **373**; worthy reasons for Olympic movement and 366–369, **367**, **368**; *see also* health-related legacies; Youth Olympic Games (YOG)
legacy and Paralympic Games 329, 366
'Legacy Strategic Approach' 365
legal issues *see* brand protection; *specific issue*
Legg, D. 40–42, 92, 99
Leicestershire non-host area: background information 387–389; changes in political/economic contexts, unpredictable 390; influence of Olympic Games 390–391; Inspire Leicestershire programme and 389; legacies of Olympic Games outcomes, building and spreading 391–392; lessons learned from 391–392; London 2012 Games delivery structure and 388, *388*; Nations and Regions Group and 387; partnership collaboration 389–390; strategy design/creation of operational group 389
Leininger, A. 185
Lenskyj, H. 57–59
lesbian, gay, bisexual, transgender and intersex athletes *see* LGBTI+ athletes
Les Mills The Trip 168
Letheren, Carol Anne 209
LGBTI+ athletes: Agenda 2020 and 340; background information 53–54; blurring boundaries and 59–61; defining 'LGBTI+' and 54–55; heteronormativity and 55; human rights issues and 2, 54–59, 337, 340; International Olympic Committee and 54–56; overview 2, 61–62; patriarchal view of sports and 58; sex testing and 59–61; therapeutic use exemption and 60; Yogykarta Principles and 55
Lillehammer Games (1994) 76, 80
Lillehammer Youth Olympic Games (2016) 5, 399–402, **401**
Li, M. 10
Lindemann, K. 327
Liu, D. 5, 393–394
Liu, Z. 393
Locke, John 251–252

Logistics FA in organizing Olympic Games 179
Loland, S. 146
London 2012 Mass Participation Plan 382
London 2012 Olympic Games Official Report 423
London Olympic Games (1948) 110–111
London Olympic Games (2012): branding discussions and 417; cultural programmes and 411, 417; educational programmes and 421, 423; health-related legacy and 375–376, 379, 381–383; Host Broadcasting Organization and 114; legacies 390–391; London Olympics association right and 133; project management division and 178; Rule 40 and 140–143; Saudi Arabian athletes at 48; social media and 140; sustainability and 154; YouTube Channel coverage of 117; *see also* Leicestershire non-host area
London Olympic and Paralympic Marks Act (2006) 133
London Olympics association right 133
London Organizing Committee of the Olympic Games (LOCOG) 244, 423
London Paralympic Games (2012) 100–102, 104–105
Longo, A. 386
Loos, A. 196
Los Angeles Olympic Games (1932) 110
Los Angeles Olympic Games (1984) 110–111, 113, 155, 164, 195, 243
Los Angeles Paralympic Games (2028) 104–106
Loughhead, T.M. 357
Lucas, David 100–101
Lynch, Loretta 286
Lyon, Jake 166

MacAloon, J. 259, 368
Maennig, W. 191
Maglione, Julio 287
Manchester Paralympic Games (2002) 40
marketing value of Olympics: background information 75; co-branding opportunities 82; historical perspective 78–79; International Olympics Committee and 75–76; marketing world and, entry into 78, 83; 1988 negotiations and 76; Olympic brand and 79–82; Olympic revenue model and 77–78; overview 3, 82–83; single message and 81–82; successful 79–82; *see also* sponsorship of Olympics/Paralympics
Mason, F. 245
Masters, Oksana 101
Masterton, D.W. 415
Matuzalem (footballer) 319
Mazzeo, F. 330
Mbaye, Keba 309
McCaffrey, Barry 275
McCartney, G. 356, 377, 379
Macdougall, H.K. 91–92
McKeever, Brian 105
McKinnon, Rachel 50
McLaren report (Independent Person Report) 277–278
media innovation companies 165
media and Paralympic Games 327–329
medical model of disability 325
Mega-Sporting Events Platform for Human Rights 342
Meier, H.E. 4, 206
Mela, A. 386
Melbourne Olympic Games (1956) 242
Mercedes Benz 163
Merklinger, Anne 219
metagovernance 316–317
Miah, A. 4, 415
Miesener, L. 329
Miller, C. 104
Milliat, Alice 338
Millington, R. 5
Minoudis, V. 2
Misener, L. 40, 362–363, 387
models of disability 325–326
Molloy, K. 40
Mondello, M.J. 185
Morris, J. 324–325
Mortimer, Joanne 103
Moscow Olympic Games (1980) 77, 155, 270, 339
Moser, J. 185–186
Mrkonjic, M. 254, 268
Müller, C. 185
Munich Olympic Games (2022) 188

Nagano Olympic Games (1998) 234
National Basketball Association (NBA) 209
nationality of athletes: background information 65–66; Budd case and 66; citizenship versus 66; context 66–67; Court of Arbitration for Sports and 68; dual 65; examples of challenges 65–67; future possibilities 70–71; *jus domicili* and 67; *jus matrimonii* and 67; *jus sanguinis* and 67; *jus soli* and 67; *jus talenti* and 66–67; naturalisation and 67; Olympic Games and 67–69; Olympic nationality matrix and 68; overview 2–3, 65–66; Paralympic Games and 67–69; Rule 41 and 68–69; Rule 44 and 68; talent migration and 66–67; transnational citizenship and 66, 70–71
National Olympic Committees (NOCs): Afghanistan 270–271, 339; autonomy of 268–269, 271; establishment of 204; government control of, cases of 269–271; increase in number of 206; independence of 139; India 265; International Olympic Committee and 205, 207; International Paralympic Committee and 220; Iraq 271–272; Kuwait 272; Olympic Channel and 117; Olympic Charter and 140; Olympic paradox and 266;

Olympic Solidarity Plan and 154; organizing Olympic Games and 171; Permanent General Assembly of National Olympic Committees and 207; political role of 266–268; Rule 40 and 136–137, 140; Russian 279; shared social responsibility and 152, 154; social media rules and 140–141; women on boards of 208; *see also* political autonomy of NOCs
National Organising Committee (NOC) 67, 78
National Paralympic Committees (NPCs) 99, 220, 246–247
NBC broadcast coverage of Olympics 76–77, 103, 114–115
NBCOlympics.com 115
Neave, N. 357
Nebiolo, Primo 210
negotiated autonomy 254
Neutron Games 166
Nevill, A.M. 358, 361
new media 117
New Norm campaign/document 172, 174, 179, 183, 229, 236, 238, 300
Nguyen, S.N. 91–92
Nielsen data set 188–189
Nielsen report (2016) 91
Nike and Olympic brand protection 131
NIMBY (not in my backyard) concept 185, 189, 191, *193*, 197n1
Nissan 166
non-governmental organisations (NGOs) 346; *see also specific name*
non-host nations/areas: background information 385; Leicestershire 387–392, *388*; leveraging processes of 387; literature review 387–388; mega-events in, sporting 386–387; overview 5, 385, 394–395; Shanghai 392–394
non-official sponsors of Olympics/Paralympics 144
Nora of Liechtenstein, Princess 209
normative values research 324–325, 330
Northern Officer Group Report (1996) 326
North Face and Olympic brand protection 131–132
Nufer, G. 132, 137

Obinger, H. 185–186
Oiselle sponsorship of Kate Grac 144
Olympic Aid 346
Olympic Arts Competitions 408–410, **410**
Olympic brand: attributes of 81; emergence of 79; essence of Olympic ideals and 404; marketing value of 79–82; Olympic rings, asset of 80–81; single message of 81–82; TOP program and 79; *see also* brand protection
Olympic Broadcast Services (OBS) 77, 99, 114
Olympic Channel 77, 99, 117
Olympic Charter 5–6, 54, 139–140, 143–144, 149, 211, 252, 266, 270, 299, 300, 311, 375, 408
Olympic Congresses 205, 207–209, 271
Olympic Council of Asia (OCA) 303
Olympic Foundation for Culture and Heritage 418
Olympic Games (OG): alignment with esports and 167–169; black athletes and 339; boycott of 77, 155, 270, 339; claims and fields of action 367–368, **367**, **368**; cost overruns 183, *186*, 189, *190*, 194; criticisms of, key 189–192, *190*, 372; environmental damage from 194; festival effect of 381–382; gendered bodies in 47–48; gigantism and 183, 191, 193–194, *193*, 195; human rights issues and 62, 338–339; image of 191; including disabled athletes in 41–42; ISO certification and 153–154; Jewish athletes and 339; LGBTQI+ athletes and 340; merging with Paralympic Games, debate over 40–41, 242; nationality of athletes and 67–69; new sports in 234–235, 301–305; Paralympic Games in same city as 99; perception of 212; programme claims of 367; protests surrounding, political/social 158n4, 267, 380; referendums at 186, **187–188**, 188–189; Refugee Olympic Team and 340; revival of (1896) 150; separating from Paralympic Games 42; sexual politics in 2, 46–47; socio-cultural issues and 48; stakeholders in 178–179, 205–207; women athletes and 338; *see also specific game and issue*
Olympic Games Global Impact (OGGI) project 355
Olympic International Federations (OIFs) 154
Olympic laws 130–131
Olympic movement: Agenda 2020 and synergies with, maximising 152; Agenda 21 for 150; amateurism and 298; brand protection and 130; campaigns for change and 233–236, **237**; change conceptualisation and 230–231; drivers of change and **237**; esports and 166–167; establishment of modern 203; as family 231–233; governance within 286–287; impact of 329; institutional theory and new sports in 301–304; International Council of Arbitration for Sport and 318; International Olympic Committee and 345–346; legacies needed for 369–370, **369**; National Olympic Committees' position in 265–266; new sports and 301–305; organisational parts of 232, *233*; organisations making up 230–231, 237; *raison d'être* of 232; revival of 345; Sport for Development and Peace and 348–352; sports movement and 250; sustainability of 299–301; sustainable development and 371; transformation approach of, suggested 353; as transnational corporation 231–233; worthy reasons for legacies and 366–369, **367**, **368**; *see also* autonomy of Olympic/sport movement; International Olympic Committee (IOC); relationship between IOC and IPC

Olympic Organizing Committees (OCOGs) 75, 78–79, 83, 87, 99, 110, 131, 136, 153, 176–179, 245, 302, 368
Olympic paradox 266
Olympic Programme Commission 301–302
Olympic rings (brand) 80–81, 130–132
Olympics for the Disabled 243
Olympics Education 427; *see also* educational programmes for Olympics/Paralympics
Olympic Social Responsibility (OSR): Agenda 2020 and 149; defining 'shared social responsibility' and 150–151; Host City Contracts and 152–153, 157, 158n9; implementing, challenges of 153–154; need for 150–151; Olympism in making world better and 156–157; overview 3–4, 157; paradoxes associated with 154–155, **156**; relevance of shared social responsibility and 151–153; sustainability and, 149–150, *152*, 153, 157, 158n7
Olympic Solidarity plan/programme 110, 154, 237, 268, 340, 348
Olympic Solidarity Scholarship 143
Olympic spirit 238
Olympic studies 1
Olympic Summits 167, 280
Olympic values 404
Olympic Values Education Programme (OVEP) 348–349, 427
Olympic words/phrases and brand protection 131
Olympism 5–6, 57, 139, 142, 146, 149, 151–153, 156–157, 367, 404, 408, 420
Olympism in Action (OIA) forum (2018) 154, 160–161, 181, 345, 348–350, 352
One City Games model 87, 91
O'Neill, B.A. 267
Oonk, G. 67
operational budget 178
Operations FA in organizing Olympic Games 179
O'Reilly, N. 122–123, 130
organising committees (OCs) 40
Organization for Economic Cooperation and Development (OECD) 312
organizing Olympic Games: Agenda 2020 and 172; background information 171–172; bid committee 172, 176; bidding process *171*, 172–174, 180; bid reasons 172–173; challenges of 192–195, **192**; committee structure 177; Continuous Dialogue Stage 174; cost overruns and 183, *186*, 189, *190*, 194, 196; environmental damage and 194; financial management 178; functional areas 171, 179–180; Future Hosts Commission and 174; human resources management 178; implementation mode *171*, 179–180; International Olympic Committee and 173, 174, *175*, 180–181, 195; leadership role 177; lifecycle of 171, *171*; Logistics FA 179; National Olympic Committee and 171; New Norm campaign/document and 172, 174, 179; Operations FA 179; overview 4, 180–181; planning mode *171*, 176–177; problems associated with bids today 173–174; project management 177–178; pulling out of bid process 173–174, 183, 186; site planning 179; stakeholder management 178–179; success factors in bidding 176; Targeted Dialogue Stage 174; Think and Design phase 176; timeline 171, *171*; venue management 179; work breakdown structure 177; wrap-up mode *171*, 180
Ormond, M. 141
Ornskoldsvik Paralympic Games (1976) 341
Osborn, G. 2
Oslo referendum 188
Oswald Commission 278
Out-of-Home Advertising policy 123

Palowski, Todd 165
Papadimitriou, A. 2
para-athletes 3, 92, 94; *see also specific name*
Paralympic brand: background information 84–85; communication and 92–93; disability community and 93–94; equity of 88; governance structure of 87–90, *89*, 94; historical perspective of Paralympic movement and 85–87; International Coordinating Committee and 243; International Olympic Committee and 90–91, 180–181; media and 92–93; opportunities for athletes and 45; overview 3, 94–95; Paralympic athletes and consistency of 94–95; sponsorship and 91–92, 95; sports programs and 90; strength of 94; *Tae-Geuks* (teardrops) logo 244
Paralympic Education 427; *see also* educational programmes for Olympics/Paralympics
Paralympic Games: books focussing on 328; broadcast coverage/rights and 99; Calgary's 2026 bid for 98; claims and fields of actions 367–368, **367**, **368**; establishment of 46–48; gendered bodies in 47–48; gender issues and 46; historical perspective 98–101; human rights issues and 62, 340–342; International Olympic Committee and 99–100; journal articles focussing on 328; legacy and 329, 366; media and 327–329; merging with Olympic Games, debate over 40–41, 242; nationality of athletes and 67–69; Olympic Games in same city as 99; opportunities for athletes and 45; politics and 329; programme claims of 367; protests surrounding, political/social 380; separating from Olympic Games 42; sexual politics in 2, 46–47; socio-cultural issues and 48; sponsorship 101–106; sports diplomacy

and 329; sports history and 329–330; sports in 45; transportation investment and, extra 247; veterans and 46; *see also* research on Paralympic Games; *specific game and issue*
Paralympic movement 85–87, 92–93, 243; *see also* International Paralympic Committee (IPC); Paralympic Games; relationship between IOC and IPC; research on Paralympic Games
Paralympic Paradox 93
Parent, M.M. 178–179
Paris Agreement (1994) 315–316
Paris Olympic Games (2024) 160, 167
Park, M. 99
Parsons, Andrew 100, 225–226
patriarchal views of sports 47, 58
Pawson, R. 370
Pay per View (PPV) broadcasting format 113
Peachey, Lyras and Welty 346
Pechstein, Claudia 316
People With Disabilities (PWD) 327
Pérez's model *311*, 313–317, *313*
Performance Lifestyle Practitioners 10
Permanent General Assembly of National Olympic Committees (ANOC) 207
Personal Excellence Advisors 10
persons with disabilities (PWD) 103–105, 218, 225, 227, 335, 340–342
Petersen-Wagner, R. 99
Pettigrew, A. 370
Pettigrew, S. 358
Phelps, Michael 144
Piispanen, T. 99
Pinturault, Alexis 125
'Places People Play' 382
planning mode in organizing Olympic Games *171*, 176–177
Platini, Michel 310
play-by-play casters 162–163
political autonomy of NOCs: background information 265; defining 'autonomy' and 268–269; enforcing, present-day 271–272; government control and, cases of 269–271; International Olympic Committee and 271–272; overview 272; political role of 266–268; position of, within Olympic movement 265–266
political governance 4; *see also* autonomy of Olympic/sport movement; board renewal of IOC; political autonomy of NOCs; relationship between IOC and international sport federations; relationship between IOC and IPC
political issues 5–6; *see also specific issue*
politics and Paralympic Games 329
Popper, K. 371
Populous (mega-event company) 169
Porritt, Sir Arthur 206
Pound, Richard ('Dick') 3, 276–277
Practice of Direction (1966) 20–21
pragmatic autonomy 254
Preuß, H. 188, 191
Preuss, H. 185–186, 191, 195, 371, 399
Priestley, M. 325–326
Procter & Gamble sponsorship of Paralympics 101
professionalisation of International Paralympic Committee 219–221, *221*, 226
Professional Players Federation (UK) 11
project management in organizing Olympic Games 177–178
protests surrounding Olympic Games, political/social 158n4, 267, 380–381
Public Television Offices 110
Puerto Rico Olympic Committee (COPUR) 338
Purdue, D. 99
Purdue, D.E.J. 93, 329–330
Purdy, Amy 101, 105, 126
Putin, Vladimir 56
PyeongChang Olympic Games (2018): brand protection and 135; broadcast coverage/rights and 100–101, 111, 115, 341; environmental practices and 194; esports and 160, 164; legacy of sports facilities and 196; new media coverage and 117; Rule 40 and 140; Russian athletes at 155; Russian doping scandal and 279–281, 312; Russian NOC and 279; scholarships 143; sponsorship at 121–122, 124–127
PyeongChang Paralympic Games (2018) 100–101

quality of life (QOL) legacies 401–404

Racketeer Influenced and Corrupt Organization (RICO) Act 313
Radio Television Olimpica (RTO) 114
Ramchandani, G. 5, 358
Ramshaw, G. 329–330
rationalist approach to autonomy of Olympic/sport movement 256–258
Red Cross 349
Reedie, Craig 276
Reeve, D. 327
referendums: background information 183–184; Brexit 184; cause-effect model and 192, *193*; challenges of organizing Olympic Games and 192–195, **192**; criticisms of Olympic Games and, key 189–192, *190*; democratic procedures and 184–186; Denver 173, 186; function of 183–184; Hamburg 188–189, 191, 194; NIMBY and 185, 189, 191, *193*, 197n1; at Olympic Games 186, **187–188**, 188–189; Oslo 188; overview 4, 195–196; participation in 184–185; support for 184; Valais (Switzerland) 213
reform of IOC: Agenda 2020 and 212–213, 235–236, 287; background information 229–230; campaigns for 233–236, **237**; composition of IOC 211–212;

conceptual framework of configuration 230; conceptualising change and 230–231; corporatisation and 230; drivers of change and **237**; modernisation process and, ongoing 237; New Norm campaign/document and 236; Olympic movement as a family and 231–233; Olympic movement as a transnational corporation 231–233, 237; overview 229, 236–238; questions addressed in research 229–230; recommendations 233–236; Salt Lake City Olympic Games bribery scandal and 229, 233
Refugee Olympic Team 340
Refugee Team 143
Reiche, D. 358
Reis, A.C. 380
relationship between IOC and international sports federations: background information 294; changes, recent 299–301; commercialization/professionalization of Olympic Games (1960s–1980s) and 297–299; current environment 295–297; dynamics 301; future research directions 301; historical perspective 297; institutional theory 301–304; list of 296, **296–297**; literature, existing 294; new sports in Olympic movement and 301–305; overview 5, 305; Resource Dependence Theory and 304–305; sustainability of Olympic movement and 299–301
relationship between IOC and IPC: agreements 244–245, 247–248, 411; background information 241–242; early (1948–1999) 242–244; human rights issues and 311–313; IOC-IPC Agreement 244–245; IPC as little brother to IOC 241; IPC's position and 94; One City Games model and 87, 91; overview 4, 241–242, 245–248; rules/regulations in place between 245–247; strengthening of 87; unbalanced 241, 245–247
research on Paralympic Games: ableism 326–327; background information 323–324; biosocial model of disability 325–326; books focussing on, key 328; Boolean search for articles 323, **324**; future 330; internalised ableism 327; journal articles focussing on, range of 328; legacy and Paralympic Games 329; media and Paralympic Games 328–329; medical model of disability 325; models of disability 325; normative values 324–325, 330; outputs focussing upon, key 327–328; overview 5, 330; politics and Paralympic Games 329; social model of disability 325; sports diplomacy 329; sports history and Paralympic Games 329–330; technology and impaired bodies 330
'Resetting Finish Lines' advertising campaign 125
Resource Dependence Theory (RDT) 304–305
responsible autonomy 250, 253
Retired and Transitional Players Report (PFA) 11
retirement and dual career of athletes 11–12
revenue model for Olympics 77–78
Rhodes, R.A.W. 310–311
Richardson, Sophie 340
Richards-Ross, Sanya 142
Right to Play 346
Rights Holding Broadcaster (RHB) 109
Rights Holding Broadcaster (RHB) <or Rights Broadcasting Holder (RBH)> 113–114, 118
Rio de Janeiro Olympic Games (2016): brand protection of rings and 131; broadcast rights and 111; cultural programmes and 411; environmental damage from 194; esports discussions and 160; new media coverage and 117; NIMBY concept and 191; protests surrounding 158n4, 380; Rule 40 and 135, 141, 143–145; Russian doping scandal and 278; sustainable development and 154, 350; women athletes at 47
Rio de Janeiro Paralympic Games (2016) 103–104
Roadmap to Code Compliance (WADA) 279
Robinson, L. 286, 302–304
Rodchenkov Act 313
Rogge, Jacques 211, 268, 398
Rojek, C. 368
Rome Olympic Games (1960) 110
Rosenau, J.N. 310
Rousseau, Paul 298
Rule 40: Australian Olympic Committee and 145–146; background information 139–140; brand protection and 135–136, 147; compensation for Olympians and 142–143; effectiveness of 147; Federal Cartel Office (Germany) and 135–136, 145; International Olympic Committee and 135–136; London Olympic Games (2012) and 140–143; National Olympic Committees and 136–137, 140; overview 3, 146–147; policing 147; PyeongChang Olympic Games (2018) and 140; revision of 145–146; Rio de Janeiro Olympic Games (2016) and 135, 141, 143–145; social media and 140–141; Tokyo Olympic Games (2020) and 145–146
Rule 41 68
Rule 44 68
Russian Anti-Doping Agency (RUSADA) 279
Russian doping scandal 155, 277–281, 312
Russian National Olympic Committee 279

Sahgal, S. 289
Salt Lake City bribery scandal (2002) 155, 210–212, 220, 229, 233, 244, 259, 275, 310–311
Salt Lake City Olympic Games (2002) 76, 91, 386
Samaranch, Juan Antonia 113, 193, 208–211, 271, 298–299, 309

Samsung sponsorship 127, 163
Santamaria, S. 330
Saudi Arabia and Olympic athletes 48
Savulescu, J. 60
Scharroo, Pieter W. 206
Scheu, A. 4, 191, 371
Schiller, T. 184
Schlereth, N.G. 142, 144
Schmid Commission 279
Schmidhauser, Corinne 318
Schmidt, Helmut 270
Schmidt, S.L. 189
Schnitzer, M. 191
scholarships for athletes 143
Scholars Scheme 15
Schrauwen, A. 68, 70
Schreyer, D. 189
Schubert, M. 188, 191
Schulte, Pascal 100
Schultz, M. 88
Scruton, J. 243, 328
Séguin, B. 85, 88, 130
Seippel, O. 65, 188
self-recruiting process of International Olympic Committee 203–205
Semenya, Caster 49, 59–60
Seoul Olympic Games (1988) 76, 244, 299
Seoul Paralympic Organizing Committee (SPOC) 244
sex testing 48, 59–61
sexual politics in Olympics/Paralympics 2, 46–47
Shakespeare, T. 326
Shanerkani, Woidan 48
Shanghai non-host area 392–394
shared social responsibility (SSR) 150–153
Shaw, Chris 173
Shibli, S. 358
Shiffrin, Mikaela 125
Silva, C.F. 92, 330
Simelane, Eudy 58
site planning in organizing Olympic Games 179
SNB (French Basketball Players Association) 11, 15
Sochi Olympic/Paralympic Games (2014) 53–54, 100–101, 117, 135, 194, 265, 278, 313, 340, 380–381
social ambush 134
Social Exchange Theory (SET) 191, 402
social media 117, 126, 140–141
social model of disability 325
social movements 367
socio-cultural issues 5–6, 48; *see also specific issue*
Söderman, S. 121
South Africa 270–271, 339
South African Human Rights Commission 58
South African Olympic Committee (SANOC) 339
Southeast Asian Games (2019) 167
Sparvero, E. 378
Special Olympics International 244
Spiro, P. 68, 70
sponsorship of Olympics/Paralympics: activation process 122–123; ambush marketing and 121–122; background information 98, 120–121; Bridgestone Tire 102; British Petroleum 102–103; challenges 126–127; Clean Venue Policy and 123; Coca-Cola 3, 121, 125–126, 131, 165; current 232; defining 'sponsorship' and 121–122; esports and 163–164; future directions 103–106; historical perspective of Paralympic Games and 98–101; Kia Motors 127; leveraging 120; non-official 144; of Olympians 142–143; Out-of-Home Advertising policy and 123; overview 3, 128; Paralympic brand and 91–92, 95; Procter & Gamble 101; property rights exploitation and 123; at PyeongChang Olympic Games 121–122, 124–126; revenue from 128; Samsung 127, 163; specifications of 123–124; storytelling and 121; three-level system of 122, *122*; TOP and 100; Toyota 99, 101–102; trends 126–127; in United States 100; Visa 3, 121, 124–125, 128; *see also* marketing value of Olympics
SportAccord forum (2016) 154
Sport for Development and Peace (SDP): Agenda 2020 and 345, 348–349; background information 345–346; closure of UN office of 345–346; convergence issues 348–350; divergence issues 350–352; international development and 348–350; International Olympic Committee and 352; Olympic movement and 348–352; Olympic Solidarity programme and 348; Olympic Values Education Programme and 348–349; Olympism in Action and 345, 348–349, 352; overview 5, 346, 352–353; pitfalls of development 350–352; Right to Play and 346; sector 346–348; Sport for Hope programme and 349, 351; summary of 346
Sport England 36, 382, 424
Sportfive marketing agency 116
sport governing bodies (SGBs) 251, 253–260; *see also specific name*
Sport for Hope programme 349, 351
sporting autonomy 250–251, 254–255
sporting disputes 21; *see also* Court of Arbitration for Sport (CAS)
sporting legacy 355–356, *356*, 375, 382 *see* legacies of Olympic Games
sports diplomacy and Paralympic Games 329
sports history and Paralympic Games 329–330
sport as social transformation 346–348
sports simulators 168
stakeholders in Olympic Games 178–179, 205–207
Stambulova, N.B. 10

standard of proof in common law tradition 24–26
Steadward, Dr Robert 'Bob' 211–212, 219–220
Steep 'Road to the Olympics' game 165
Stephanopoulos, Athan 101
stereotypes and Paralympic movement 92–93
Stewart, A. 370
stigmatised peoples 327
Stoke Mandeville Games (1948) 3, 85–86, 98, 242, 340–341
Stoke Mandeville Hospital 218
Storr, R. 2
Strategic Planning Congress 220
Street Fighter game 168
Streicher, T. 189
Strittmatter, A-M. 303
Suarez, D.F. 219
Sum, R.K.W. 10
'supercrip' 92–93
supervised autonomy 254
sustainability of Olympic Games/Olympic movement 299–301
sustainability of Olympic Social Responsibility 149–150, *152*, 153, 157, 158n7
sustainable development 154, 350, 371
Sustainable Development Goals 371
Swiss Civil Code 312–313
Swiss Federal Tribunal 278
Swiss laws and international sports 312, 316–317, 319
Sydney Olympic Games (2000): Arts Festival 414; brand protection of Olympic rings and 131; broadcast coverage/rights and 76, 111, *112*, 114; cultural programmes and 411, 413–416; educational programmes and 6, 421–423; entertainment aspect of 414; environmental practices and, monitoring of 212, 343; professionalisation and 219; rationale for hosting 375; Sydney Paralympic Games (2000) and 341; trans athletes at 62n1
Sydney Organising Committee (SOCOG) 421
Sydney Paralympic Games (2000) 93, 219, 221, 328–329, 341
Symons, C. 2
Symons, J. 56
systemic governance 4; *see also* changes of IOC; composition of IOC; evolution of IPC
Szymanski, S. 251

Tae-Geuks (teardrops) Paralympic logo 244
Takito, M.Y. 358
TASS Dual Career Accreditation Scheme 14, *14*, 16
'Taste the feeling, Together as One!' advertising campaign 125–126
Taylor, Elana Meyers 126
Taylor, T. 286
'Team Visa' 125
technology and impaired bodies 330
television companies 76–78, 103, 113, 115, 162–163
Television and Marketing Services SA (TMS) 109
term limits of IOC board 287–292
testosterone 48, 50, 60
Textbook of Sport for the Disabled (Ludwig Guttmann) 242
Thanou, Katerina 27, 33n28
Thatcher, Margaret 270
therapeutic use exemption (TUE) 60
Thomson, A. 371
Thorpe, H. 302
3D broadcasts 111
Tilly, C. 367
Tokyo Olympic Games (1964) 110–111, 145–146
Tokyo Olympic Games (2020) 100, 145–146, 160, 235, 386, 411–412, 424–428
Tommy Hilfiger clothing line 105
Toohey, K. 423
TOP programme (now Olympic Partners' programme) 78–79, 100, 130, 139–140, 172, 209, 298–299
Toroc environmental management system 153
Torontolympiad 243
Toronto Olympic Games (1976) 243
Torregrosa, M. 11
Tour de France scandal (1998) 275
Toyota sponsorship of Paralympic Games 99, 101–102
trans athletes/policies 48–50, 62n1
transnational citizenship 66, 70–71
Travel to Tokyo educational programme 424–425
Tribunal Fédéral 316, 319
Tringo, J.L. 327
Tripartite Commission 208–210
Triple Cast system 113
Trudeau, Pierre 241
Turin Olympic Games (2006) 113, 117, 386
T v FIG 25
Tweedy, S. 37
XXth Commonwealth Games (Glasgow) 381
Twitch (now owned by Amazon) 163
Tygart, Travis 276–277, 280
Tynedal, J. 92

Under Armour and Olympic brand protection 144, 147
UNESCO Convention on Doping in Sport 312
Union of Physically Impaired Against Segregation (UPIAS) 325
Union of Soviet Republics (USSR) 210, 252, 339
United Kingdom Athletics (UKA) 36
United Kingdom Department of Health 377
United Kingdom National Governing Bodies (NGB) 287
United Kingdom Sport 36, 285
United Nations Convention Against Corruption 312

United Nations Convention on Human Rights for Persons with a Disability 41
United Nations Council on Human Rights 337
United Nations Educational, Scientific and Cultural Organization (UNESCO) 250, 349
United Nations Environmental Programme (UNEP) 349
United Nations General Assembly 253, 259
United Nations Guiding Principles on Business and Human Rights 57, 62
United Nations Human Rights Council (UNHRC) 56
United Nation's International Day of the Persons with Disabilities 105
United Nations Universal Declaration of Human Rights 336
United States Dream Team in basketball 142, 299
United States Olympic Committee (USOC) 79, 100, 142
United States Olympic and Paralympic Committee Athlete Career and Education (USOPC ACE) Programme *16*
University of Nicosia (UNIC) 15
Un-Young, Kim 210, 299
urban regeneration promise of host nations 93
US laws and international sports 313
US Olympic Committee v International Olympic Committee 28

Valais (Switzerland) referendum 213
values of Olympics 75; *see also* marketing value of Olympics; sponsorship
Vancouver Olympic Games (2010) 114, 176
Vatter, A. 185
Veal, A.J. 423
venue management in organizing Olympic Games 179
video game publishers 165
Vikelas, Dimítros 203
Virtual Reality (VR) experiences in broadcast coverage 111
Virtual Regatta game 167
Visa sponsorship of Olympics/Paralympics 3, 121, 124–125, 128
Vizer, Marius 300
Vogue magazine's photoshopping disabilities 103

Wafula-Strike, Anne 36
Wagschal, U. 185–186
Walton, H. 386
Watson, N. 326
Weatherill, S. 254, 259
Weed, M. 5, 93, 377–380, 382
Weitzmann, M. 4, 185–186
Wertheim, P. 288
Wewer, T. 189
Wheaton, B. 302
Wicker, P. 188–189, 191
Williams, M. 358, 361
Wilson, D. 5, 358
Wilson, R. 393–394
Winter, E.M. 358, 361
Wolbring, G. 92
Wolfson, S. 357
women's issues: background information 45–46; composition of International Olympic Committee and 209; de Coubertin's exclusion of 46; with disabilities 341; East German women's teams (1970s and 1980s) and 46; female athletes at Rio De Janeiro Olympic Games 47; gendered bodies concept and 47–48; human rights issues and 338, 341; NOCs board membership 208; overview 2, 50–51; patriarchal views of sports and 47; rules and 45; sexual politics and 2, 46–47; trans/intersex athletes and 48–50; 2016 Rio Games and 47; Women's Olympics 338
Women's Olympics 338
Wood, L. 367
Woodward, K. 2
work breakdown structure (WBS) 177
World Anti-Doping Agency (WADA): autonomy of Olympic/sport movement and 255–256; background information 275–276; British Olympic Association case against 27–29; challenges facing 281–282; Compliance Review Committee and 280; Court of Arbitration for Sport and 278–279; establishment of 275; Foundation Board 276, 280–282; future direction of 281; governance of 276–277; International Federations and 275–276; International Olympic Committee and 277–281; organisational restructuring and 279–281; overview 5, 281–282; purpose of 29; Roadmap to Code Compliance and 279; Russian doping scandal and 155, 277–281, 312
World Conference on Doping in Sport (1999) 275
World Cup (2014) 66
World Cup (2026) bidding 343
World Health Organisation (WHO) 34
World Para Athletics (WPA) 37
World Sailing Federation 167
World Skateboarding Federation 302–303
World Sports Organization for the Disabled 86, 218, 243
World Taekwondo game 166
Worley, Kristen 60–61
wrap-up mode in organizing Olympic Games *171*, 180
Wylleman, P. 10

Yi, X. 393
Yogyakarta Principles 55
Yoi Don! educational programme 426–428

Young Change Makers+ (YCM+) initiative 405
Youth Olympic Games (YOG): Athletes' Commission outreach and 13; background information 398–399; broadcast coverage/rights and 116; esports and 166; factors influencing legacy perceptions 403–404; knowledge legacy and 405; Lausanne (2020) 399–400, 402; legacies for host community residents 399; Lillehammer (2016) 5, 399–402, **401**; market development with 237–238; Olympic values and 404; overview 5, 404–405; quality of life legacies 401–404; recommendations for promoting knowledge legacy 405; social initiatives encouraged by 405; sports involvement and 403
Youth Paralympic Games (YPG) 404–405
YouTube Channel 117

Zhang, E. 289
Zhou, R. 5

